THOMAS M. ACHENBACH, Ph.D., University of Minnesota, is Associate Professor of Psychology in the Department of Psychology and the Child Study Center at Yale University. He has been a National Institute of Health Postdoctoral Fellow at the Yale Child Study Center and a Social Science Research Council Faculty Fellow at Jean Piaget's Centre D'Épistémologie Génétique in Geneva. He has published widely on normal and abnormal child development.

DEVELOPMENTAL PSYCHOPATHOLOGY

THOMAS M. ACHENBACH

YALE UNIVERSITY

THE RONALD PRESS COMPANY · NEW YORK

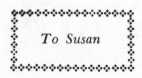

To Susan

Library of Congress Catalog Card Number: 74–75045
PRINTED IN THE UNITED STATES OF AMERICA

Preface

The title of this book, *Developmental Psychopathology,* is intended to emphasize that psychopathology in children is best understood in relation to the changes—progressions, regressions, deviations, successes, and failures —that occur in the course of children's attempts to master the developmental tasks they face. By their very nature, children are designed for change. Nevertheless, the most conspicuous differences between children and adults —those related to the dramatic cognitive, physical, emotional, and social changes that children continually experience—have often been ignored or presented from the perspective of theories about how adult psychopathology results from childhood experiences. A fundamental purpose of this book is to establish the developmental dimension as a primary basis for the study of childhood psychopathology.

A second purpose of the book is to convey what is currently known about psychopathology in children. In presenting theory, research, treatment, and the evaluation of treatment, I have endeavored to be as comprehensive as the state of our knowledge allows. Since "knowledge" is always a function of the knower's assumptions, and since *what* we know depends on *how* we know, it would be misleading simply to present a list of "facts" or to portray childhood psychopathology from a single theoretical perspective. A more accurate picture requires the contrasting of theoretical views and of their preferred methods for obtaining knowledge, as well as integration of the conclusions so far yielded by the various approaches. Insofar as possible, the various treatment approaches and the research on their effectiveness are portrayed in relation to the theories and descriptions of each type of disorder.

Besides presenting our current knowledge about developmental psychopathology, I have felt it important to show how much yet remains to be learned before we will be able to help the majority of troubled children— in a sense, the book is intended to indicate what is *unknown* as well as what is known. As the reader will see, our ignorance is vast, and any commitment to helping children should be a commitment to *testing* our current beliefs and to finding *new* ways of helping, as well as to applying what is already known.

PREFACE

Because I have felt it necessary to present so many aspects of developmental psychopathology from so many perspectives, I am deeply indebted to the many people who have influenced me and who have helped me with this book. I am especially grateful to Robert W. White for his many perceptive—and diplomatic—suggestions and criticisms in the various stages of the manuscript. Others who lent me their expertise in selected areas include David Feldman, Melvin Lewis, T. Kerby Neill, N. Dickon Repucci, Samuel Ritvo, Edwin Rubel, and Edward Zigler. I am also indebted to Miriam Goldberg, who typed and commented on nearly the entire manuscript as well as aiding in other ways; to the many students who read portions of the manuscript; and to Martha Markowitz and Susan Winston, who assisted in the final stages of the work. Research Grant HD03008 from the National Institute of Child Health and Human Development has supported most of my own research discussed in this book. Finally, to my wife Susan I offer my gratitude for assistance on the entire manuscript and for the sacrifices it entailed.

THOMAS M. ACHENBACH

Bethany, Connecticut
February, 1974

Contents

for Neurobiological Development. Some Disorders with Presumed
Organic Etiologies. Psychophysiological Reactions. Some Psychophysiological Reactions of Childhood. Psychopharmacology.

DEVELOPMENTAL PSYCHOPATHOLOGY

1

A Developmental Approach
to Psychopathology
in Children

This is a book about a field that hardly exists yet. Many writings and many workers deal with psychopathology in children, but, to a great extent, the study of psychopathology in children has been simply a downward extension of the study of psychopathology in adults. While most theories of adult psychopathology emphasize pathogenic influences in childhood, these influences have been largely inferred from adult behavior or from the recollections by adults of their childhood experiences. Since it was first recognized that children themselves may be in need of treatment, concepts originating in the study of adult psychopathology have tended to provide the guidelines for the diagnosis and treatment of children. Nearly all training programs in psychiatry, clinical psychology, and social work concentrate on the treatment of adults. Those who wish to obtain training in the treatment of children must typically do so after their basic training with adults. Training in the treatment of child psychopathology often consists of learning the modifications in adult treatment methods that must be made in order to apply them to children.

THE DEVELOPMENTAL DIMENSION IN CHILD PSYCHOPATHOLOGY

This book is based on the view that psychopathology in children differs from adult psychopathology because of the overwhelming significance of developmental processes for all aspects of child behavior, normal or pathological. The work of Piaget and the developmental psycholinguists (e.g.,

3

Brown, 1973; Sinclair-de-Zwart, 1969) dramatically reveals qualitative differences in the way children think at different ages. Even more obvious are the enormous physical changes and changes in social roles that children are continuously experiencing. While developmental processes do not cease at physical maturity, the changes occurring from birth to maturity are of such a quantum nature as to dictate the essential framework within which psychopathology in children must be studied—hence the title *Developmental Psychopathology*. Recognition of the importance of the developmental dimension should prevent us from conceiving of "The Child" as a static hypothetical entity.

A partial case history may help to illustrate the need for a developmental approach to the understanding and treatment of psychopathology in children.

JERRY C., JR.

Jerry was Mr. and Mrs. C's only child. He was born while Mr. C. was away on assignment in his capacity as a foreman for a nationwide construction company. Mrs. C. had been quite ill during pregnancy and the birth was difficult, but Jerry was reported to be in good condition at birth. Jerry's arrival was extremely welcome to his mother, who longed for company during her husband's frequent absences. Mr. C. was less happy about the birth but did favor naming Jerry after himself. Mr. C.'s career had been a sequence of ups and downs in which promotions earned through seniority had been taken away after he disappeared on drunken binges.

Young Jerry was an exceptionally easy baby, usually quiet, placid, and affectionate, and his early development appeared normal. He crawled at eight months and walked at 14 months. His mother devoted a great deal of time to him, absorbing herself completely in caring for him when she became depressed during her husband's absences.

When Jerry had not begun speaking by the age of three, he was taken to a pediatric clinic for a complete medical checkup. Jerry was extremely upset by the medical procedures, but no organic abnormalities were found. An attempt at psychological testing failed because Jerry was too distractible to attend to the tasks. Intelligible speech was completely absent. Speech therapy was tried, but was given up after it appeared to have no effect.

Because Mrs. C. was also concerned about other children's teasing and refusal to play with Jerry, she applied to a child guidance clinic. She was put on the clinic's waiting list, but the family moved away from the area before she was given an appointment.

When Jerry was five, a school official inquired as to why he was not attending kindergarten. Confronted with the need to take action, Mrs. C. brought Jerry to the pediatric clinic of another hospital where she was told that he was retarded, that this was incurable, and that he should be taken to a state institution. Mrs. C. was extremely upset by this suggestion and applied instead to another child guidance clinic. The clinic had a seven-month waiting list, but Mrs. C. persevered.

By the time the C.'s were given an appointment at the clinic, Jerry had begun to speak and appeared able to read a number of words. Interviews with Mrs. C. showed that, while she was very threatened by the possibility of retardation, she had long realized that her son was not normal. He was not a problem at home, but, besides failing to speak, he showed little interest in other children, did not engage in games, and spent much of his time either watching TV or rolled up in a ball under a table in his favorite corner of the living room. Mrs. C. reported that Jerry displayed a phenomenal memory for TV commercials and, as evidence that he was not retarded, he frequently read street signs along familiar routes. However, his mother acknowledged that Jerry's speech was very difficult for anyone but her to understand.

When Jerry was first seen at the child guidance clinic, he was noted to be a solidly built boy, big for his age, with a pale, puffy, expressionless face, and very bright blue eyes. He showed no reluctance to separate from his mother. In the playroom, he walked around looking at various toys and uttering sounds in a sing-song manner. When spoken to, he repeated the sounds of the therapist's voice, but words were almost entirely undistinguishable. However, after several interview sessions, the therapist began to recognize words consistently distorted by the substitution of certain sounds for other sounds. Jerry mechanically read aloud and repeated words he saw printed in the building, such as "Fire Exit." He demonstrated a moderate-sized reading vocabulary by reading words printed by the therapist and words he found on the labels of games and toys.

Jerry soon made up his own abbreviation for the therapist's name, repeated it often at home, and seemed eager to come for his weekly appointments. However, he never engaged in conversation, tending instead to repeat over and over the therapist's name, his own name, TV commercials, the names of places he had visited, etc. His speech was often interrupted with peals of laughter. He also repeated words of the therapist, but scrupulously avoided using the first-person pronouns "I" and "me" and referred to himself only as "Jerry." He avoided looking the therapist in the eye and, though he seemed to like being hugged and tickled, he stood very rigidly and felt like a heavy inanimate object when the therapist lifted him.

Testing on a nonverbal formboard test in which the child is to replace a series of wooden geometric shapes in their proper openings showed exceptional speed, sensory-motor coordination, and dexterity. On a vocabulary test requiring the child merely to point to a picture corresponding to a word spoken by the examiner, Jerry obtained an IQ equivalent of 100, despite so little interest in the task that the examiner had to hold him and continually prod him to attend. When induced to draw a human figure, he drew one that scored slightly below average for his age according to standardized norms.

During therapy sessions, Jerry usually picked out a toy vehicle and lay rolling it on the floor, humming or echoing barely recognizable TV commercials. He occasionally drew maps of places he had visited and named the various streets on the maps. Sometimes he set up simple scenes with dolls in the doll house. Information from Mrs. C. showed that these were usually reenactments of rather routine events at home. Certain deviations from routine, such as the therapist's failure to wear a necktie, upset Jerry so much that he would not accompany the therapist. Jerry kept repeating, "Daddy leave necktie in Florida," a reference to a time when his father mentioned having left a necktie where he had been staying during his last job. Attempts to probe with Jerry his association between the tieless therapist and his father elicited only repetitions of "Daddy leave necktie in Florida." When the therapist donned a tie, Jerry resumed his usual cooperative behavior. Other changes in routine seemed to have no effect.

Since it appeared that at least some of Jerry's intellectual abilities were in the normal range, attempts were made to find a school placement for him. His mother was asked to place him in groups of children whenever possible, such as in Sunday school, in order to see how well he could mix with his agemates. While he seemed happy in these situations, he seemed content to watch the other children and did not interact with them in any way. Since the family could not afford private schooling, the public schools were asked to provide a homebound teacher who visited Jerry's home several times weekly. Arrangements were then made with an especially cooperative kindergarten teacher to have the homebound teacher accompany Jerry to a kindergarten class for an hour a day. Jerry expressed eagerness to go to school and the homebound teacher, who had never been comfortable with Jerry, soon asked to withdraw.

In kindergarten Jerry played by himself and did not partake in group activities, although he did conform to the teacher's instructions and occasionally surprised her with his reading skill and knowledge of maps. After a year of negotiations with the school system, it was possible to have Jerry admitted to a special class for the emotionally disturbed where his social isolation continued, but he did progress somewhat in academic skills.

Meanwhile, Jerry's father quit his job and deserted the family, although he occasionally called from distant places or reappeared unexpectedly, always promising to mend his ways. Mrs. C. attempted to make a new life for herself without her husband, but she now had to depend on public welfare, which barely provided subsistence for her and Jerry. Jerry responded to his father's disappearance by becoming preoccupied with mailboxes and telephones, the sources of the occasional messages from Mr. C. He also talked of Mr. C. and was affectionate toward him whenever he reappeared. Jerry's speech and academic skills continued to improve slowly, but, after several years in the special class, it appeared that he was destined to remain significantly handicapped academically as well as socially. He was especially unable to take responsibilities such as crossing streets alone.

While Jerry's problems are by no means typical of all children needing help, they do illustrate a number of ways in which the study of child psychopathology must differ from adult psychopathology.

Obtaining Treatment

Unlike adults, children almost never initiate treatment for themselves. Jerry would not have been seen for diagnosis or treatment if his mother had not initiated it. He played no part in making the arrangements and was simply taken by his mother to the clinic. It was Mrs. C.'s perseverance during the seven-month wait for an appointment, rather than any subjective discomfort on Jerry's part, that resulted in his eventually being seen. The selection of children for treatment is thus much more a function of parental, rather than children's, discomfort and motivation. Furthermore, the amount of parental initiative has to be considerably higher than that required for obtaining other services for children—Mrs. C's odyssey took her to two hospitals, a speech therapist, contacts with school officials, and the waiting lists of two child guidance clinics before her child received treatment. Had she lived in other areas of the country, she might never have been able to obtain services for Jerry. Once evaluation and treatment ultimately began at the second clinic, she and her husband, whenever he was available, had to accompany Jerry for interviews with a social worker during Jerry's weekly sessions over a period of two years. Parent motivation is thus a primary factor is determining whether treatment will continue even after it has begun.

Most children have no conception of mental health services and many actively resist being taken for treatment. Any preconceptions they have are likely to have been conveyed by their parents. In Jerry's case, his mother had told him that the clinic was a "school," ostensibly to allay his anxiety.

After having been brought to a mental health professional, children do not readily assume the "patient" role that enables workers with adults to begin by asking clients about their problems. Young children are typically reluctant to leave their parents and go with a stranger, especially in the hospitallike environments that characterize many clinics. It may have been significant that Jerry did *not* appear reluctant to separate from his mother despite an unhappy previous experience with medical examinations and his general lack of social experience.

Even if a child is suffering subjective discomfort, he is rarely prepared to tell a strange adult about it and about what he thinks the causes are. Workers with children must adapt themselves to the child's level of communication and must rely heavily upon their own observations of children's behavior and on secondhand information from other observers, such as parents and teachers. Because office contacts may not elicit representative samples of a child's behavior, the child may also have to be observed in a variety of more natural settings.

Effects of Family Functioning

As a consequence of the child's dependence on his family, his behavior is likely to be much more a direct function of their behavior than is true for an adult. No families are without problems. Mrs. C.'s depression, Mr. C.'s erratic behavior, and the threatened, and then actual, breakup of the C.s' marriage were bound to affect Jerry. Were these the causes of Jerry's problems in any direct sense? Certainly, the gratifications and frustrations of his life were intimately tied to those of his parents. Their ways of communicating, interacting, and meeting stress provided the major source of Jerry's knowledge of human behavior. On the other hand, it is likely that Jerry's birth changed the balance of his parents' marital relationship in many ways. When his abnormalities became apparent, it is possible that they elicited such concern from Mrs. C. that she could no longer provide adequately for her husband, who then reacted by displaying progressively more infantile behavior. Any biological vulnerabilities on Jerry's part may thus have been further exacerbated by the reactions he elicited from his parents.

Developmental Level

Another essential difference between the study of child and adult psychopathology is the importance of developmental milestones for children. Mrs. C. was initially motivated to take action only when Jerry failed to speak by the usual time. Although she earlier had been aware of differences between him and other children, the contrast between his lack of speech and the speech of his agemates became so conspicuous that she could no longer deny the need for some sort of action. When no organic reason was found for his lack of speech, it was his failure to achieve another milestone expected for all children, entry into school, that precipitated further action.

While the acquisition of speech is a milestone established by the observed uniformity of children's development, entry into school is a milestone established by societal tradition. Both types of milestones are important in assessing children's development and both are intertwined. Not only are they important in bringing attention to possible abnormalities in the child, but meeting them at close to the "normal" age is very important for the child's further development and adaptation. For example, Jerry's delay in speaking may have resulted merely from slow but not defective maturation in an area of the brain important for speech. He may have begun speaking quite normally at a much later age than the average, simply because of this one unusual characteristic of his biological makeup. However, the fact that he did not speak within the typical age range had broad ramifications for his social and intellectual development. His being ostracized by other children for his lack of speech may have caused him to withdraw from social relationships and to fail to develop the cooperative and competitive skills so necessary for dealing with other people. In addition, his handicap may have elicited further overprotection from his mother, who desperately needed somebody to be close to while her husband was absent and her marriage was deteriorating.

Failure to achieve the developmental milestone of school entry at the usual time produces consequences of its own. Unless the child receives schoollike experiences that enable him to be placed with his agemates, he is likely to be larger and physically more mature than his classmates. This can lead to the child's being ostracized. He may, therefore, develop strategies of coping, such as withdrawal or using physical force, which in the long run are harmful to further adaptation. When Jerry did enter kindergarten, he was already bigger than the other children in the class. He was further distinguished from the other children by his lack of social skills and the special attention of the homebound teacher and the regular teacher.

Just as a child's deviation from developmental norms is an important factor in getting his parents to seek help, evaluation of precisely where he stands with respect to developmental norms and how much he is deviating from them is an essential part of diagnosis. On the basis of Jerry's poor speech, the physician in the second pediatric clinic concluded that Jerry was retarded in all his intellectual functions and would always be so far behind that he should be referred to an institution for the retarded. However, the subsequent evaluation of his perceptual-motor functioning, his understanding of words, and his drawing skills showed that these were all within the normal range for his age. Uniform mental retardation was not, therefore, an appropriate assumption, although it was clear that his social functioning and speech were quite deviant for his age.

With adult clients, the question of mental retardation may sometimes arise, but adults already have a long history of development that can be viewed retrospectively in order to determine when and how they reached the developmental milestones of childhood. This history is usually sufficient to indicate the client's current level of development without further concern for how he is continuing to develop and whether immediate action is needed to help him reach the next developmental milestone.

While it was not clear in Jerry's case *why* his speech and social behavior were so deviant, it was clear that he had the intellectual capabilities for acquiring academic skills and that immediate action was needed in order to insure that he be given instruction. In contrast to adult treatment—which may aim to facilitate self-understanding and to remove discomforting symptoms—treatment of children must focus on helping them reach developmental milestones and to acquire needed skills without which they will be forever handicapped, no matter what the other outcomes of treatment per se.

Diagnosis

Traditional diagnostic practices are oriented toward determining what particular disorder a person has—e.g., schizophrenia, hysterical neurosis, sociopathic personality, chronic brain syndrome, etc. Until very recently, little provision was made for the possibility that children's disorders might differ from adult disorders and that diagnostic practices, therefore, should differ for children and adults. One of the most striking aspects of Jerry's case was his *failure to progress* in certain areas, such as speech and social behavior, rather than a specific set of symptoms corresponding to one of the adult categories. For want of an appropriate diagnosis, Jerry was finally classified in the official diagnostic system as having a "personality trait disturbance." However, this diagnostic classification conveys nothing that would enable other workers to recognize similarities between Jerry and children they might see or to pool experience with cases like his in order to discover what causal factors they may have in common and what treatments seem to be effective for them.

The lack of diagnostic categories appropriate for children's disorders creates severe handicaps for communication and research concerning troubled children. While certain types of child disorders may well be early forms of adult syndromes, most child disorders do not fit easily into the models provided by adult categories. One of the most fundamental prerequisites for progress in the study of developmental psychopathology is the creation of diagnostic classifications designed specifically for child disorders as they really are, rather than as miniature versions of adult disorders.

Goals of Treatment

According to most theories of adult psychopathology, the accumulation of pathogenic influences during childhood is what causes adult disorders. Consequently, it is often assumed that child treatment is simpler and more promising than adult treatment because it can nip the harmful influences in the bud before there is so much to undo. However, the child's dependence on his parents and on such other adults as teachers makes the goals of child treatment in many ways more complex than those of adult treatment. Not only must the child's parents initiate and continue treatment in order for him to benefit, but they must often change their own behavior before there is much hope for change in the child. Thus, the targets of child treatment typically extend to the interlocking behaviors of people other than the child. Moreover, a satisfactory outcome in child treatment may be short-lived because of changes in family circumstances beyond the child's control, such as Mr. C.'s desertion and erratic reappearances. Successful individual treatment of adults may be more durable because adults are usually able to exercise more control over their life situations than are children.

Like the adult treatments from which they originated, many forms of child treatment focus primarily on changing the child through undoing pathogenic influences of the past, although parents are frequently advised to change their behavior as well. While primary focus on the child may be effective in some cases, much more systematic research is needed to assess the actual effects of various approaches in order to determine which ones produce the best long-term results for particular kinds of children.

THEORIES AND CONCEPTS

Largely as legacies from the study of adult psychopathology, there are numerous theoretical viewpoints on psychopathology in children. Practitioners tend to hold a single viewpoint while rejecting the others. As a result, much that has been written is based upon a single theoretical viewpoint rather than upon an integration of what may be valuable from several viewpoints. This has resulted in what might be called a "horizontal" progression within each of the established schools of thought—new writings on child psychopathology tend to be extensions of old concepts and terminology to different areas rather than producing "vertical" progressions whereby old ideas are discarded as new discoveries and syntheses are made. Thus, some current behavior therapists simply advocate broader applications of principles proposed by John B. Watson more than 60 years ago, while some of the psychoanalytic literature does little more than reiterate Freud's hypotheses.

In order to replace horizontal movement with a vertical progression, it must be recognized that many important questions in developmental psychopathology require a convergence of thinking from several points of view and cannot even be meaningfully formulated in a single theoretical language. While practitioners of various approaches may describe Jerry C. in their own languages and prescribe their own favorite treatments for him, the evidence to be reviewed in Chapter 12 demonstrates that no one really knows what causes problems like Jerry's, that there is no known way of preventing them, and that no form of treatment has yet proven very effective.

Important patterns of behavior are always complex and can rarely be specified with complete objectivity. In Jerry's case, for example, how could one best describe what the problem was? His speech? His lack of eye contact? His failure to interact with other children? His absorption in an Oedipal conflict, as revealed in his preoccupation with sexually symbolic mailboxes and telephones? Castration fears symbolized in his reaction to the therapist's lack of a necktie? Even when agreement can be reached about just what the important behavior is, the potential determinants of the behavior must include concepts at many levels of analysis—genes, anatomical structures, physiological processes, cognitive structures, past experience and learning, motives, and the immediate stimulus situation, to name a few possibilities. Thus, not only must we attempt to bring various viewpoints together in order to counteract parochialism, but also the nature of the problem is such as to *require* an ecumenical convergence of thinking.

If the problems of developmental psychopathology require bringing diverse ideas together, how can we choose among them? Can we simply grant each idea equal status and be satisfied with it in the form we find it? Such an approach would carry us little beyond a survey of all the horizontal progressions occurring within the various theoretical camps. The approach to be taken here will emphasize scientific criteria for separating the wheat from the chaff. Details of well-established scientific criteria for the study of behavior will be discussed in Chapter 4, but it will often be necessary to go beyond these in suggesting new ways to formulate and test ideas at the frontiers of our knowledge.

Related to the choice of a scientific approach is a distinction concerning the breadth of what we shall call "scientific." This distinction, made by philosophers of science and discussed further in Chapter 4, is between the *context of discovery* and *the context of confirmation.* Briefly, the context of discovery refers to the initial generation of ideas and hypotheses in whatever subjective, personal, serendipitous, creative, or accidental way in which an individual happens to think. There are no rules nor formulas for this stage of science. However, in order to become usable, the ultimate products of this stage must have some potential for being confirmed by systematic observation of phenomena in the real world. It is to this latter context, the *context of confirmation,* that scientific standards of logic and verifiability apply.

The fact that an idea has not yet fully proven itself in the context of confirmation will not keep us from considering it. However, because many of the ideas in the field have not moved much beyond the earliest stages of the context of discovery, an attempt will be made to emphasize those that seem, at least in principle, to have the potential for being systematically tested, even if a "test" is an indirect one requiring considerable inference from data that only instruments or experts can detect.

STRUCTURE OF THE BOOK

No effort will be made to tempt the reader with the premature closure offered by the comfortable dogmas of any single, all-inclusive viewpoint. One reason for the diversity of the literature in the field is that no single viewpoint can convincingly make sense out of very many of the phenomena. Whenever possible, a theoretical viewpoint will be presented in detail where it is most powerful in explaining significant phenomena. In many cases, disagreement over what *are* the significant phenomena necessitates extended discussion of more than one viewpoint. The most conspicuous instances of this appear in Chapters 8 and 9, and Chapters 10 and 11, where the psychoanalytic and learning theory approaches both offer detailed frameworks for describing and interpreting what may appear to be very similar behavior.

Since a gathering of phenomena under one theoretical umbrella does not seem feasible, we shall, insofar as possible, seek out important questions against which we can test what has been observed and what we think we know. For a variety of reasons, these questions are often hidden beneath the surface of prevailing jargon and tradition. Since this is not a guidebook for day-to-day treatment of children's problems, we can contemplate what might be the best ultimate routes for answering such questions rather than having to come up with partial solutions for immediate application. The selection of what is discussed and the suggested readings following each chapter are intended to provide the reader with leads for pursuing as many different questions as possible.

As preparation for understanding specific types of psychopathology, Chapters 2 through 6 present the historical context from which the study of child psychopathology is emerging, basic issues that often interfere with clear formulation of answerable questions, scientific strategies for studying psychopathology, genetic factors, and crucial aspects of neurobiological development. Chapters 7 through 14 are organized around specific types of psychopathology, while the final three chapters, on classification, diagnosis, and issues in treatment, are designed to serve an integrative function after the reader is familiar with what is presented in the earlier chapters.

SUMMARY

To a great extent, views of child psychopathology have represented downward extrapolations from adult psychopathology. However, it was proposed that the significance of developmental processes makes the study of child psychopathology fundamentally different from the study of adult psychopathology. The manner of obtaining treatment, effects of family functioning, importance of developmental level, diagnostic needs, and goals of treatment all distinguish child psychopathology from adult psychopathology. Hence, the emphasis here on *developmental* psychopathology.

Largely as a result of the influence of theories of adult psychopathology, there has been a "horizontal" progression of concepts within established schools of thought on psychopathology in children, rather than a "vertical" progression of new discoveries and syntheses. Because no one theoretical language appears capable of formulating the diverse phenomena of developmental psychopathology, it is necessary to draw on concepts from many sources. Scientific criteria are needed for evaluating the adequacy of the various concepts. Since the book is not intended as a guide for day-to-day treatment, the focus will be upon finding the best ultimate routes for answering important questions.

2

Historical Context

There are at least two reasons for considering the historical context from which the study of developmental psychopathology is emerging. One is that the field is only now taking on an independent identity. This means that many of the current ideas in the field are best understood in terms of their sources in other fields, especially adult psychopathology. The other reason is that the history of psychopathology manifests some remarkable patterns that are instructive for the future.

EARLY THEORIES OF MENTAL DISORDERS

The history of psychopathology cannot, unfortunately, be portrayed as an uninterrupted march of progress toward better treatment through greater knowledge. It is more accurately portrayed as a series of cycles in which there has been an interplay of social attitudes and theories about mental disorders. From at least the time of Hippocrates (460?–377 B.C.), the ancient Greeks and Romans held organic theories about mental disorders. These mostly dealt with the balance of humoral substances in the body, but also included the belief that hysteria (Greek *hystera* = womb) was caused by wanderings of the womb. Beside somatic treatments such as bloodletting and laxatives to restore balance among the humors, kindness and restful enviroments were prescribed.

During the medieval period, insanity was generally regarded with fear and suspicion as the work of the devil. Treatment ranged from rejection, humiliation, and imprisonment, with all manner of torture, to burning at the stake under the supervision of clerical authorities. Despite a renaissance of Greek physical theories of mental illness, it was not until 1792 that more humane treatment of the mentally ill was actively promoted. Philippe Pinel's unchaining of the inmates when he became head of the Bicêtre Hospital at Paris in 1792 is often credited with beginning the revolution in

14

psychiatric care. However, his action appears to have been very much a product of the reforming spirit of the Enlightenment. Independently in the same year, a group of English Quakers led by William Tuke started a project to build a "retired Habitation" that was to be called a "Retreat" to avoid the stigma of the prevailing terms "asylum" and "madhouse." The Retreat, opened at York, England, in 1796, was designed to provide a family environment, employment, exercise, and the treatment of patients as guests.

That the change in the treatment of the insane was more a product of social attitudes than of new knowledge or theories about mental illness can be observed from the writings of Benjamin Rush (1745–1813). Known as the "father of American psychiatry," Rush belonged to a group in Philadelphia that included Benjamin Franklin and that advocated rational, humanitarian reforms in prisons, the treatment of debtors, education, and medical care for the poor. Improving care for the mentally ill was a natural byproduct of this spirit of reform. However, Rush's medical theory was that "madness" was primarily an arterial disease caused by engorgement of the blood vessels in the brain. In order to relieve this engorgement, he prescribed purges, enemas, and, above all, bloodletting, boasting that he had taken as much as 470 ounces of blood from one patient. He also advocated total deprivation of food, terrifying punishment, and mechanical restraining devices such as a "tranquilizing" chair that he had invented. The wide acceptance of these methods, which may indeed have "calmed" excited patients, is indicated by the fact that his textbook, *Medical Inquiries and Observations upon the Diseases of the Mind* (1812), remained the only systematic American textbook in psychiatry until 1883.

The Rise and Fall of Moral Treatment

Although changes in formal medical thinking did not *instigate* the reforms in handling the mentally ill, the new humane attitudes did crystallize into a formal therapeutic system. This system came to be known as "moral treatment," with "moral" referring to "psychological" as well as having ethical connotations. As Bockoven (1963) describes it, "The moral therapist acted toward his patients as though they were mentally well. He believed that kindness and forebearance were essential in dealing with them. He also believed in firmness and persistence in impressing on patients the idea that a change to more acceptable behavior was expected [p. 76]."

Improvement in the behavior of many patients unchained by Pinel demonstrated that cruel conditions could themselves be responsible for maintaining abnormal behavior. However, this discovery that psychological factors could beneficially affect the insane was not entirely incompatible with the primitive organic theories because organic changes were often attributed to psychological causes such as disappointment, bereavement, etc.

The combination of a spirit of reform, the apparent efficacy of moral treatment, and the compatibility of the new ideas with some aspects of prevailing theory led to a movement in the United States that by 1824 had established several private retreats modeled on the York Retreat in England. Some of these were built with state aid and had provisions for a few paupers, but they were generally middle-class institutions for those who could pay.

Reports of up to 90 per cent cure rates in these institutions gave rise by 1830 to a "cult of curability" (Deutsch, 1949) that replaced the former hopelessness about mental disorders with a boundless optimism. The next significant development was a movement to extend the benefits of moral treatment to the poor through construction of state institutions like the private retreats. In addition to the humane concept of public responsibility for the mentally ill, a weighty argument with state legislatures was that many people could be quickly cured and become taxpayers who would otherwise have to be supported in prisons and poorhouses for life.

The first success of the movement for state hospitals resulted in the opening of the State Lunatic Hospital at Worcester, Massachusetts, in 1833. In 1841 the movement found in a former school teacher, Dorothea Dix (1802–87), a militant crusader who went all over the country exposing the cruelty to which the insane poor were subjected and campaigning for state hospitals. She and her allies were successful in getting numerous legislatures to erect hospitals. By 1844 the hospital movement had grown to the point where the Association of Medical Superintendents of American Institutions for the Insane (now the American Psychiatric Association) was founded. It is significant that the primary concerns of the Association and most of its members were with the general management of their institutions—building plans, heating and ventilating systems, food distribution, etc.—rather than with advancement of theory or research.

The success of the cult of curability had thus led to the creation of a new system of interests vested in the operation of large state hospitals. Had the construction of hospital buildings alone been able to fulfill the expectations generated by the cult of curability, these vested interests would have been all for the best. However, there were three factors, recognized only later, that made it impossible for the new hospital system to fulfill its promise of wholesale cure. The most fundamental factor was that the claims of 90 per cent cure by the early hospitals were invalid. It was not until 1875, well after a new pessimism had set in, that Dr. Pliny Earle published a review of the early hospital statistics which concluded that, among other fallacies, many of the "cures" involved successive releases of the same individual from one or more hospitals. Most deserving of the record for being cured was a woman who had been cured six times in one year and a total of 47 times before she finally died in an insane asylum (Deutsch, 1949)!

The second factor standing in the way of wholesale cure was the failure of the large state hospitals to implement the good features of early retreats that may indeed have optimized their success. The argument that state hospitals would save money by curing the insane poor was translated into the quick erection of cheap buildings by cost-conscious legislatures. Little or no provision was made for the family environment, employment, exercise, and treatment of the patients as guests—the elements that were at the heart of moral treatment.

The third factor that may have worked against cure in the state hospitals was the difference between their patients and those in the private retreats. Patients of the retreats came in small numbers from financially secure backgrounds to which they could return as they improved. By contrast, the clients of the new state hospitals were mostly paupers, often foreign-born, who came straight from prisons, poorhouses, and other degrading circumstances, and who had no secure environment to which to return, should they improve. Even with perfect implementation of moral treatment, it is unlikely that the state hospitals could have promoted healthy self-sufficiency for many of these people.

By the 1860s, the pendulum had again swung back from wild optimism to bleak pessimism about mental illness. The same medical leaders who had been so optimistic in the 1840s were now convinced that most insanity was incurable. State institutions became explicitly custodial.

Like the early swing to a psychological emphasis when humane treatment was introduced, the change in attitude does not appear to have been dictated primarily by advances in medical knowledge or theory. Indeed, advances were occurring in European research on organic pathology in the brain, and Wilhelm Griesinger's textbook (1845) emphasizing organic research was a major step in giving psychiatry a scientific orientation. Likewise, Darwin's *Origin of Species* (1859) and Galton's *Hereditary Genius* (1869) provided ammunition for hereditarian arguments. But, in America, it appears that these scientific contributions tended to provide *rationalizations* for a change in professional attitudes that had already occurred. Until the end of the nineteenth century, American thought about mental disorders continued to be centered upon the state institution providing custodial care in a generally static and pessimistic atmosphere. Certain forces emerged at the beginning of the twentieth century to alter this picture radically. These included psychoanalysis, the mental hygiene movement, and behaviorism, all of which will be discussed later in the chapter.

But what about children up to this point? As stated earlier, the study of psychopathology in children has too often been merely a downward extension of adult psychopathology. Until the twentieth century, even the downward extension of adult psychopathology had hardly been made. A few isolated references to children can be found in nineteenth-century works on adult pathology, and in Europe at least three books were written primarily on mental disturbances in children (cf. Harms, 1967). Yet there were no facilities designed especially for the treatment of children and there appeared to be little concern with disorders unique to childhood that fell short of the extreme kinds of "insanity" observed in adults. To find in the nineteenth century an historical strand that is clearly continuous with our own concern for *developmental* psychopathology, we must turn to the handling of the mentally retarded.

Discovery and Care of the Mentally Retarded

Distinction had often been made between people who had lost their reason (madmen, lunatics) and those who seemed never to have developed reason (fools, idiots). However, the first systematic attention to the retarded, albeit inadvertent, is usually considered to be Jean Itard's attempt to educate the Wild Boy of Aveyron, who was found in a forest in 1799.

Like the movement for humane treatment of the mentally ill, Itard's experiment was as much a product of Enlightenment attitudes of rational humanitarianism as of any theory about retardation *per se*. In fact, Itard only undertook his experiment in training the boy, Victor, because he believed him to be simply an untutored savage who could be civilized through proper instruction. Applying techniques of sensory-motor instruction already in use with the deaf, Itard had moderate success, but after several years he concluded that Victor was fundamentally retarded. Nevertheless, he had demonstrated that even a retardate could be trained to some extent.

Itard's beginning was carried further by Edward Seguin (1812–80) who, first in France and after 1848 in the United States, carried on research into the causes, nature, and treatment of retardation. Seguin believed retardation was curable through "physiological" education that would bring all senses and organs to their peak levels of functioning. The functions to be trained depended upon the individual's specific weaknesses, with perceptual faculties having to be developed before mental training could proceed.

In contrast to earlier periods when retarded individuals were put indiscriminately in mental hospitals or neglected altogether, the early 1840s saw the establishment in Europe of several institutions specially designed for training the retarded. In the United States the first schools for the retarded were begun in 1848. After 1850, the official census distinguished between "feebleminded" and insane persons. As with the mental hospital movement, enthusiasm was quickly generated which resulted in a rapid proliferation of schools. *Unlike* mental hospitals, the earliest state schooling (e.g., in Massachusetts, 1848, and New York, 1851) for the retarded was usually set up for a well-defined *experimental* period.

Another feature that differentiated the beginning of state care for the retarded from the cult of the curability of the insane was the temperate belief that nonexistent intellectual faculties could not be created; the goal of the special schools was merely to develop "dormant faculties" as much as possible.

By 1876, however, when the Association of Medical Officers of American Institutions for Idiots and Feebleminded Persons was founded, the early educational model for treating the retarded and the optimism about making them self-supporting had given way to a custodial model like that for the insane. By the beginning of the twentieth century attitudes toward the retarded had moved beyond pessimism to an outright hostility that lasted until the 1920s. During this "alarmist period" (Deutsch, 1949), the retarded were blamed for most crime and social ills; it was considered essential to segregate them and through compulsory sterilization to keep them from reproducing.

Like the vacillation in attitudes toward the mentally ill, the violent change in attitudes toward the retarded did not result from new knowledge about their affliction. Scientific ideas were influential in that Darwin's *Origin of Species* (1859) and the rediscovery of Mendel's laws of heredity in 1900 provided evidence for the strength of genetic determinants. However, there was little new evidence to demonstrate genetic causation in mental retardation. Instead, the social Darwinism that glorified dominance by the rich and powerful, the eugenics movement for eliminating "bad stock," and the exclusively hereditarian interpretations of family histories, ranging from *The Jukes* (Dugdale, 1877) to *The Kallikak Family* (Goddard, 1912), all represented social attitudes that were unjustifiably generalized to the treatment of the retarded.

DEVELOPMENTS IN THE TWENTIETH CENTURY

The significant developments of the twentieth century must be considered in closer relation to systematic research and theory than those of the nineteenth century. This does not mean that general social attitudes, historical events, fads, and cycles no longer play a role in beliefs about psychopathology. On the contrary, these factors have continued to play a major role in re-creating many of the same trends and countertrends that can be discerned in the nineteenth century. However, the exponential increase in attention to disordered behavior and the rise of a more scientific attitude toward studying this behavior have produced so many influential ideas that recent history must be written in terms of the coexisting traditions spawned by these ideas. The influence these ideas continue to wield makes it especially important to understand their sources and contexts. Perhaps by the eighth decade of the *twenty-first* century it will be possible to characterize the historical significance of the current traditions with the same objectivity we now attribute to our accounts of the nineteenth century.

Oddly enough, the divergent traditions of the twentieth century originated at a time when the study of psychopathology had acquired a classification system that constituted the first systematic and unified framework in its history. Classification had become an important issue only when hospital care spread in the early nineteenth century. There were many attempts at classification, but the need to separate patients who required different kinds of management, e.g., the violent from the depressed, provided a strong incentive for creating classifications that accurately predicted the course of a patient's behavior.

Wilhelm Griesinger's influential textbook (1845) had laid down the dogma that "mental diseases are brain diseases." It was, accordingly, hoped that classification of mental-disease entities could begin with the *description* of symptom syndromes and culminate in the eventual discovery of specific physical causes. The model for the definition of mental disorders was *general paralysis* (later called *paresis,* i.e., "incomplete paralysis"), which had received progressively more precise descriptions between 1798 and the 1840s. What became the defining feature of this disorder was the *combination* of *mental* symptoms, such as forgetfulness and irrationality, with *physical* symptoms of general motor impairment, usually ending in death.

Once adequate descriptions had been made and agreed upon, meaningful theories and research could be formulated to determine the specific cause of the symptoms. Intensive research from the 1840s through the 1870s revealed inflammation in the brains of nearly all patients who died of general paresis. The range of possible causes was gradually narrowed to syphilitic infection. This hypothesis was confirmed experimentally in 1897 by Krafft-Ebing, who showed that paretics did not develop secondary symptoms of syphilis when innoculated with the syphilis virus—because they had already been thoroughly infected. Further confirmation was obtained in 1906 when the Wassermann test revealed syphilis in nearly all paretics. In 1917, infection with malaria, causing a high fever, was found to cure paretics, although malarial treatment was ultimately replaced by penicillin. Systematic description had thus led to the successful identification of a disease entity whose specific cause was ultimately found and could be treated.

The classification system that fully exemplified "descriptive diagnosis" and came to provide the conceptual framework for psychiatry was created by the German psychiatrist Emil Kraepelin (1856–1926). The first edition of his system, published in 1883, was based upon the conviction that all mental disorders, like general paresis, result from brain pathology. Kraepelin's system replaced the previous hodgepodge of idiosyncratic terms and concepts with a comprehensive taxonomy that permitted effective designation of individual disorders in terms that could be more widely understood among professional workers.

By its sixth edition (1899), Kraepelin's system had gained widespread influence and had changed in several respects. In addition to providing descriptions of symptoms presumed to result from brain pathology, he now based his classification partly on psychological processes, studied by means of Wilhelm Wundt's experimental techniques. Also, the course of a disorder from beginning to end was added to symptomatic descriptions and to psychological processes as a defining feature. For example, *dementia praecox* ("insanity of the young," renamed "schizophrenia" by Bleuler,

ed social learning included Karen Horney (1939), Erich Fromm
(47), Harry Stack Sullivan (1953), and Erik Erikson (1950). Among
aining within the orthodox tradition, Anna Freud (1946) elabo-
theory of ego processes and defense mechanisms, and Heinz Hart-
39) and David Rapaport (1951) the theory of ego psychology.

ractice of Psychoanalysis. In addition to the splits resulting from
and theoretical differences, strains arose within the psychoanalytic
over questions of proper qualifications and the exact profes-
tus of psychoanalytic treatment. Some of Freud's early nonmedical
had begun to practice analysis by 1920 and these were followed
who became prominent, including Otto Rank, Anna Freud,
ichorn, Theodor Reik, Ernst Kris, and Robert Waelder. Freud
early believed that psychoanalysis represented a general psychol-
g implications far beyond psychiatry and should not be confined
al practitioners. He maintained that psychoanalytic treatment
medical consultation, but that a broad grounding in anatomy,
y, pathology, biology, embryology, evolution, mythology, the
y of religion, and classical literature was preferable to medical
as preparation for analytic training.

itutes for analytic training were founded, restrictions evolved that
markedly with the informal approach Freud took toward train-
ge oners. During the 1920s, the New York Psychoanalytical So-
ngly condemned all practice by nonmedical analysts, leading to
ble friction with Europeans who had trained many of the non-
nalysts in America. Freud (1926b) strongly defended the principle
edical analysis. Despite later rumors about a change in his posi-
wrote in 1938,". . . . I have never repudiated these views and I
n them even more intensely than before, in the face of the ob-
erican tendency to turn psychoanalysis into a mere housemaid
atry [Jones, 1955, Book 3, p. 301]."

roblem intensified in the late 1930s and early 1940s when numer-
edical analysts fled Nazi persecution to America. Currently, there
rable restriction upon nonmedical analysis within the American
lytic Association, although it varies somewhat among the psycho-
nstitutes and is less pronounced in child psychoanalysis. Several
choanalytic associations and training groups do not restrict non-
nalysis.

yer's "Commonsense Psychiatry"

gh born and trained in Switzerland, Adolf Meyer (1866–1950)
than any other single person to shape American psychiatry in
twentieth century (cf. Lief, 1948). Like Freud, he moved from
nd research based upon organic theories of mental disorder to an
ly psychological perspective. However, his influence was as a

1911) was differentiated from manic-depressive psychosis largely on the
basis of psychological characteristics and the differing courses of the two
disorders. Thus, if a patient recovered, he must have had manic-depressive
psychosis; if he did not recover, he was assumed to have *dementia praecox*.
By 1915, when the fourth volume of his eighth edition appeared, Kraepelin
included a full-fledged category of psychogenic disorders and a category of
personality disorders that he believed to be on the border between illness
and ordinary eccentricity.

Against this newly unified background of terminology for adult psychopathology, five powerful new influences emerged before the first beginnings
of developmental psychopathology can be discerned. These influences
were Freudian psychoanalysis, the "commonsense" psychiatry of Adolf
Meyer, the mental hygiene movement, behaviorism, and the systematic
study of children.

Freudian Psychoanalysis

The progress of neurology as a new medical specialty in the mid-nineteenth century contributed to the tendency to ascribe disordered behavior
to organic pathology. However, by the end of the nineteenth century,
certain discoveries by European neurologists were to lead in a very different direction. These discoveries came about largely through scientific
interest in hypnosis, which had been popularized in the eighteenth century
by Friedrich Anton Mesmer as "mesmerism." It became more respectable
as a scientific topic when the English surgeon James Braid (1795–1860)
published his book, *Neurypnology, or, The Rationale of Nervous Sleep*,
in 1843. While the behavioral phenomena were similar to those induced
by Mesmer, Braid's new medical term, "neurypnology" (soon shortened to
"hypnosis"), his quasi-scientific rationale in terms of nervous sleep, and his
demonstration of the value of hypnosis as an anesthetic laid the foundations
for later work by neurologists.

The subsequent interest of neurologists stemmed from observations of
similarities between hypnotic behavior and the behavior of hysterical patients who had dramatic physical symptoms, such as paralyses and convulsions, with no identifiable organic pathology. Jean Martin Charcot (1825–
93), one of France's foremost neurologists, began using hysterical patients
to demonstrate these similarities at his famous neurological clinic in the
Salpêtrière Hospital, Paris, in 1878. In 1882, he convinced the French
Académie des Sciences, which had thrice previously rejected mesmerism,
that hypnotic phenomena were real and that they were closely related to
hysteria. Another French neurologist, Hippolyte Bernheim (1840–1919),
agreed on the genuineness of the phenomena, but contended that they resulted from normal suggestibility. Although he employed hypnosis to
treat a variety of disorders, he eventually found that the same effects could
be obtained by suggestion in the waking state, a procedure his group began
to call "psychotherapeutics."

Charcot and Bernheim's work with hypnosis led to great interest in the psychological processes that seemed to produce the physical symptoms of hysteria. Charcot's student, Pierre Janet (1859–1947), sought to understand the mixture of bodily and mental symptoms of hysteria in terms of general principles of psychological functioning, thereby bringing together the study of psychology and clinical disorders. Janet proposed that hysterical symptoms occurred when certain *complexes* of ideas became split off or *dissociated* from the rest of the personality. Dissociated complexes concerning the function of a limb could cause the limb to become paralyzed. Other dissociated complexes might activate behavior that the patient could not later remember, as in amnesia. Janet believed that hysterical symptoms might be removed by helping patients to remember the dissociated complexes of ideas, but he assumed that the basic cause of hysteria was a constitutional vulnerability to dissociation.

The most significant figure to arise from the new trend in neurology was Sigmund Freud (1856–1939). He had been trained in Vienna as a physiologist and later as a neurologist. Freud studied with Charcot in 1885–86 and spent a few weeks with Bernheim. Although his first scientific publications culminated in 1891 with a distinguished neurological monograph on aphasia, his theorizing was by the early 1890s almost exclusively in psychological terms.

Freud's older colleague, Josef Breuer (1842–1925), had from 1880 to 1882 hypnotically treated an hysterical patient, "Anna O.," whose recollections of unpleasant thoughts seemed to relieve her physical symptoms. Freud and Breuer collaborated on an article in 1893 that was expanded into a book and published as *Studies in Hysteria* (1895). Regarded as the first important document in psychoanalysis, it contained a theory of the psychological mechanisms of hysteria, case histories, and a chapter on psychotherapy. Unlike Janet, Freud held that dissociation occurred because the dissociated ideas were incompatible with the individual's conscious values and were, therefore, forced out of consciousness by a process he called *repression*.

By 1900 Freud had replaced hypnosis with free association as a tool for revealing unconscious thoughts, had formulated the basic ideas of defense, resistance, and repression, and had become convinced that childhood sexual experiences were important in causing neuroses. Many other elements of psychoanalytic theory were embodied in *The Interpretation of Dreams*, published in 1900. This book was merely ridiculed in official medical circles, but overt hostility met the publication of *Three Essays on the Theory of Sexuality* (1905), wherein Freud asserted that children have sexual desires toward their parents. However, Freud's work gained influence, and in 1909 it received formal academic recognition when he was awarded an honorary doctorate from Clark University.

Specific theoretical developments will be discussed in Chapter 8, but it is important to note here that Freud's ideas continued to change almost

until his death in 1939, by which time psy[...] force in psychological and psychotherape[...] United States and England. Interest in ch[...] 1920, and was promoted by Anna Freud an[...] The psychoanalytic theory of psychosexua[...] received attention far beyond the realm o[...]

The Psychoanalytical Movement. Besi[...] thought, it is instructive to consider brief[...] lytical Movement," as one of Freud's (191[...] first regular meetings for the discussion of[...] home in Vienna in 1902, as the "Psychc[...] 1908 the group became the "Vienna Psych[...] national Psychoanalytical Association wa[...] Gustav Jung, who had met Freud in 190[...] president. Member societies were later fc[...] American cities.

The biography of Freud by Ernest Jor[...] documents the atmosphere that prevailed [...] Having been at first rejected by much of [...] took on some of the characteristics of a s[...] alities and personal conflicts began to pla[...] was at the center, but rivalries among h[...] theoretical issues led to schisms that pro[...] and outside the official psychoanalytic s[...] close to Freud but broke away between [...] Adler, Wilhelm Stekel, and Jung.

In light of these defections, Jones, who[...] since 1908, proposed that "a small group o[...] "as a sort of Old Guard around Freud." [...] quotes Freud as approving the "idea of [...] best and most trustworthy among our me[...] velopment of psychoanalysis and defend t[...] accidents when I am no more." In 1913, [...] of the resulting "Committee," as it was kn[...] which they then had mounted in gold ring[...] in maintaining a theoretical orthodoxy, bu[...] and even two members of the Committee e[...] Rank in 1926 and Sandor Ferenczi in 19[...]

Elaborations of psychoanalytic theory [...] made by some who broke with Freudian[...] mained loyal to it. Among those who [...] known for his theory of the inferiority cc[...] for his theory of the racial unconscious a[...] dreams, and Rank for his theory of the [...] trauma. Neo-Freudians who minimized t[...]

Adolf Me[...]

Althou[...] did more[...] the early[...] training a[...] increasing[...]

emphasiz[...] (1941, 19[...] those rer[...] rated the[...] mann (19[...]

The P[...] personal [...] movemen[...] sional sta[...] adherent[...] by other[...] August A[...] himself c[...] ogy havir[...] to medic[...] required [...] physiolog[...] psycholog[...] education[...]

As inst[...] contrasted[...] ing practit[...] ciety stron[...] considerat[...] medical a[...] of nonme[...] tion, he [...] insist upc[...] vious Am[...] of Psychi[...]

The p[...] ous nonm[...] is conside[...] Psychoan[...] analytic i[...] other psy[...] medical a[...]

teacher, synthesizer, and organizer, not as a proponent of a bold new theory or treatment. Moreover, his work was closely tied to state hospitals and to services for the broad range of disturbed persons rather than being concentrated on a select group who could afford long and expensive treatment.

Shortly after arriving in the United States, Meyer in 1893 was employed in Illinois as one of the first pathologists in a state hospital. His job was to perform autopsies, but he soon found that the lack of adequate life histories and diagnoses made it difficult to draw conclusions from tissue pathology alone. He urged hospital physicians to obtain life histories as they examined patients and to play close attention to patients' mental conditions rather than merely collecting physical facts. His interest in factors preceding mental disturbance also led him to join the Illinois Association for Child Study in1894, with an eye toward getting schools to collect statistics on childhood disorders.

In 1895, he went to Worcester, Massachusetts, State Hospital, still as a pathologist, but now with the opportunity to set up a comprehensive research and training program. His program stressed careful study of patients' needs and symptoms by requiring physicians to make standardized mental and physical examinations with detailed follow-up observations. He also worked closely with the developmental psychologist G. Stanley Hall at Clark University and taught graduate students who were later among the first clinical psychologists. In 1896, he instituted Kraepelin's diagnostic system at Worcester, but modified it according to his belief that the life history and dynamic characteristics of each patient were more important than the classification of disease entities.

In 1902 Meyer became head of the New York State Pathological Institute, which had originally been founded for organic research on the patients of state mental hospitals. He first established basic standards for examinations and record keeping in New York's 13 mental hospitals. With the large amount of standardized data thus made available, he soon discovered that organic causes were rarely revealed in autopsies, except in cases that had been known to be organic before they died. This finding led him to focus primarily upon psychological phenomena and to move away from Kraepelin's "descriptive" psychiatry toward "dynamic" case formulations stressing the complete understanding of each patient's behavior.

To learn more about his patients' prehospital surroundings, Meyer in 1904 began to send his wife to interview patients' relatives in their own homes. Her function soon expanded to include preparing the relatives for the return of the patient after hospitalization and helping to provide follow-up care. She thus created a model for the new profession of psychiatric social worker.

By 1906, Meyer had been favorably impressed by Freud's work and saw in it a kinship to his own version of "dynamic psychiatry." Both emphasized specific experiential history and the dynamic balance of psychological factors within the individual. However, Meyer objected to psychoanalysis' sharp division of mind into conscious and unconscious, its tendency to create a new cult within psychiatry, its contention that symptoms had only symbolic significance, and, later, the popularizations that exploited sex and advocated unrestrained self-indulgence.

As a substitute for descriptive psychiatry's concept of disease entities, Meyer proposed the "reaction type of the psychobiologic unit," the particular way an individual—mind and body—has for adjusting to his life situation. Symptoms, according to this concept, are faulty reactions that an individual may need help in correcting. In order to modify these reactions, the conditions that produced them must be understood and new habits must often be created to replace those that have been disrupted.

Meyer sought to replace the term "insanity" with "forms of unsuccessful adjustment." His view was quite compatible with behavioristic psychology, and, in 1914, now heading the Phipps Clinic of Johns Hopkins University, he started the first course in psychology for medical students, with John B. Watson teaching part of it. Meyer's view also held out great hope for preventive measures that would help people in trouble before their faulty reactions reached symptomatic proportions. Accordingly, Meyer was active in the mental hygiene movement, for which he suggested the name. His drive for standardization and upgrading of psychiatric training contributed to the creation in 1934 of the American Board of Psychiatry and Neurology, whose function is to certify psychiatrists and neurologists. His influence is also evident in the first edition of the American Psychiatric Association's Diagnostic and Statistical Manual (1952), where disorders are listed as "reactions of the psychobiologic unit." Although the 1968 revision of the Manual dropped this terminology, the basic conception is still evident, especially in the childhood disorders. The drug therapies that became widespread in the 1950s are also consistent with Meyer's teaching, at least insofar as they aid in promoting successful overall adjustment rather than being considered panaceas.

The tradition that Meyer established was known by the 1930s as "the American point of view." It had links with the Freudian, mental hygiene, and behavioristic traditions, but was not a systematic amalgam of these. It emphasized behavioral facts, practical understanding of the individual, mind–body unity, and "adjustment." It provided no clear-cut theoretical basis for understanding the psychodynamics of individual patients, but stressed the therapeutic value of sound advice, commonsense counseling, and social service.

The Mental Hygiene Movement

Unlike the traditions stemming from the psychiatric work of Freud and Meyer, the mental hygiene movement stemmed from the excruciating experience of a mentally disturbed layman. Shortly after his older brother developed epileptic seizures, Clifford W. Beers (1876–1943) became obsessed with the idea that he, too, would have epilepsy. In 1900 this obsession reached the point where he was convinced that epilepsy was beginning. Preferring death to the miserable decline he had witnessed in his brother (soon to die of a brain tumor), Beers attempted suicide by jumping from a fourth-story window. Perhaps betraying his ambivalence about suicide, he hung momentarily from the window by his finger tips and dropped feet first, fortunately missing a stone pavement by inches. He was not injured seriously, but was hospitalized and his obsession with epilepsy was replaced by delusions of persecution.

Beers spent the next three years in three mental hospitals that represented a cross section of care—a private profit-making hospital, a private nonprofit hospital, and a state hospital. Little real treatment was offered in any of the hospitals, and he concluded that the doctors simply depended upon improvement in his general physical condition to bring about recovery. Doctors and untrained attendants alike showed little sensitivity and employed threats and punishment to control patients' behavior.

As Beers recovered from his depression and delusions of persecution, he formulated grandiose plans for a worldwide movement to protect the insane. After his release from the last hospital in 1903, he became so excited about his project that he voluntarily returned to one of the hospitals for a month. This time he recovered completely. His plans for a movement to help the insane became more realistic and in 1907 he began writing *A Mind That Found Itself,* an autobiographical book that he hoped would launch the movement in the way *Uncle Tom's Cabin* had stimulated the antislavery movement.

Before publishing the book, he sought the support of leaders in psychology, psychiatry, and other fields. William James donated money to the cause and wrote an introduction to the book. Adolf Meyer lent his support and suggested the name "mental hygiene" for the proposed movement. Published in 1908, the book contained not only a portrayal of Beers's personal saga and an exposé of hospital conditions, but also realistic proposals for needed reforms. It was a humane, witty, and moving document that immediately became popular and is still a joy to read.

The organizational history of the mental hygiene movement began shortly afterward with the founding of the Connecticut Society for Mental Hygiene in Beers's home town of New Haven. In 1909, the National Committee for Mental Hygiene was organized, with Beers as executive secretary, and there was soon a proliferation of subsidiary state and local societies.

The goal of the first society was to "work for the conservation of mental health," by preventing nervous and mental disorders and mental defects, raising standards of care, obtaining and disseminating reliable information, and cooperating with agencies that were in any way related to mental hygiene. The National Committee spent eight years making local, state, and national surveys to obtain factual bases for community programs. In 1917, it helped create the government's system for detecting and treating emotional disturbances among soldiers. The large number of emotional casualties of World War I revealed the need for trained psychiatric social workers, and the National Committee was instrumental in setting up the first training school for them, at Smith College in 1918.

Although social work had existed as a profession in the United States since the 1870s, the concept of mental hygiene now came to provide a quasi-theoretical framework for social workers. This concept replaced the former emphasis on economic and sociological sources of human problems with psychological explanations and the goal of promoting healthy personalities through individual adjustment. However, the mental hygiene societies themselves did not espouse any particular theory, and the Depression of the 1930s brought a renewed emphasis on the effects that general economic factors have on behavior.

Child Guidance. It was the National Committee for Mental Hygiene that first promoted widespread attention to treatment of children's disorders. The earliest clinic for children had been founded in 1896 by Lightner Witmer at the University of Pennsylvania. Coining the term "clinical psychologist," Witmer employed educational methods to help children with school problems. Special legal consideration for juvenile delinquents began with the establishment of a juvenile court in Chicago in 1899, and a clinical approach to delinquency was taken when Dr. William Healey in 1909 founded the Juvenile Psychopathic Institute (now the Institute for Juvenile Research), to work with the Chicago juvenile court. However, it was not until the National Committee's surveys of school children revealed in 1915 how widespread emotional problems were and how meager the facilities, that clinics for children were organized on any scale. Even then, it was only the Committee's own programs and demonstration projects, beginning in 1922, that created a movement for child guidance clinics and for liaisons of mental health workers with courts and schools.

Very much a product of the mental hygiene movement's role in child guidance, the American Orthopsychiatry Association was founded in 1924 as a professional organization of psychiatrists, psychologists, and social workers who did clinical work with children. The term "orthopsychiatry" was coined by analogy with orthopedics to refer to the promotion of "straight-mindedness" through early intervention. The model for the child guidance clinic entailed testing of the child by a psychologist, interviewing of parents by a social worker, and treatment by a psychiatrist, although there are today many variations on this model. The National Committee on Mental Hygiene sponsored the federal legislation that culminated in the establishment of the National Institute of Mental Health in 1949, designed to fund research, training, and community services. In 1950, the committee combined with the National Mental Health Foundation and the Psychiatric Foundation to form the National Association for Mental Health, which continues to play an active role in mental health programs.

Success of the Mental Hygiene Movement. Apart from its invaluable contribution to public attitudes and the creation of services, the significance of the mental hygiene movement is best understood when its sociohistorical context is considered. It, like earlier reform movements, was not a direct product of new advances in knowledge or theory. The term "mental hygiene," with connotations similar to the modern ones, had been used in Germany in the early nineteenth century. An American, William Sweetster, had published in 1843 a book entitled, *Mental Hygiene or an Examination of the Intellect and Passions Designed to Illustrate their Influence on Health and Duration of Life.* Organizations for the protection of the insane had also begun in the nineteenth century, but the first American version, the National Association for the Protection of the Insane and the Prevention of Insanity (1880) died quickly when the Association of Medical Superintendents of American Institutions for the Insane opposed any attempt to investigate and change hospital conditions.

One factor that may have been crucial to Beers's success in founding the mental hygiene movement was a newly prevailing belief in the preventability of disease through public health measures. The control of several organic diseases had led to great enthusiasm for public health movements, as reflected in the founding of the National Tuberculosis Association (1904), the American Child Health Association (1909), and the American Federation for Sex Hygiene (1910). Beers firmly believed that his own breakdown could have been prevented and he made *prevention* a keystone of the mental hygiene movement from its inception.

A second factor in Beers's success may have been the emergence of new forces within psychiatry and psychology that would not by themselves have produced the mental hygiene movement, but that were highly compatible with it. These included the personal influence of Adolf Meyer and his commonsense psychiatry, Freud's emphasis on psychological processes, the rise of behaviorism, and the generally optimistic environmentalism that reached its peak in the 1920s.

Behaviorism carried the strongest conviction about environmental influences, but nearly all shades of thought on child rearing shared the terminology of mental hygiene and emphasized the efficacy of early intervention to promote healthy personality adjustment. Even Arnold Gesell, whose faith in maturation dominated much of child study in the 1930s and 1940s, wrote enthusiastically of the prospects for mental hygiene created by child guidance clinics and the new nursery schools that were infused with the same spirit (Gesell, 1930).

Behaviorism

The behaviorist tradition was formally launched by John B. Watson's manifesto in the 1913 *Psychological Review,* "Psychology as the behaviorist views it." Watson (1878–1958) attacked the dominant schools of academic psychology for their preoccupation with the study of consciousness. He advocated that consciousness be taken for granted and that behavior, the particular means by which organisms adjust themselves to their environment, become the subject matter for psychology.

Watson's conviction that a scientific psychology need deal only with behavior grew out of studies of animal learning where attributing consciousness to animals seemed wholly superfluous. His first public formulation of this viewpoint, in a lecture at Yale in 1908, had received little notice, but by 1913 behavioristic terminology and attitudes elicited a sympathetic reaction in a wide audience. Terms like "habit," "stimulus," and "response" had come into popular vogue after having had a long history in associationistic psychology, and introspectionism, the then dominant school of academic psychology, had reached a point of diminishing returns.

The compatibility between Watson's behaviorism and the new views on mental hygiene was apparent in many ways. His book, *Psychology from the Standpoint of the Behaviorist* (1919), was dedicated to J. McKeen Cattell, who initiated mental testing in America, and to Adolf Meyer. He strongly endorsed Meyer's emphasis on detailed life histories, believed that most problems of the day were due to personality maladjustment, and repeatedly appealed to commonsense, practicality, mental hygiene, and prevention. Watson also approved of psychoanalysis insofar as it promoted freer attitudes about sex and the discussion of personal problems. However, in his textbook, *Behaviorism,* he contended that behavioristic studies of the child were replacing psychoanalysis, which was "based largely upon religion, introspective psychology, and Voodooism [1924, p. 18]."

Acknowledging the importance of general hereditary equipment, Watson nonetheless believed that nearly all important personality characteristics could be shaped for better or worse during infancy and early childhood. He prescribed rigid schedules of parental behavior designed to mold children who would have no unnecessary fears, be independent, require little affection, and fit efficiently into the niches provided by society. Direct forerunners of contemporary behavior therapy were developed in the experimental creation and removal of phobias in young children.

"Habit clinics," sounding very Watsonian but begun by a psychiatrist, D. A. Thom, in 1921, also sought to eliminate undesirable habits of preschoolers. By no means exclusively Watsonian in orientation, they did share the behaviorist view that early bad habits would lead to more serious personality problems in later life, when they would become much harder to treat.

Starting with his Harvard doctoral thesis in 1931, B. F. Skinner carried on the behaviorist fight against "mentalism." He explicitly adopted conditioned responses as the basic units of behavior to be studied, and went further than Watson in rejecting not only mentalism but also the use of physiological explanations to link stimuli and responses. His programmatic research on rats and pigeons was intended to provide general behavioral laws having no reference to what might lie between stimuli and responses.

The principles of his system, outlined in *The Behavior of Organisms* (1938), were soon applied to the creation of a Skinner–boxlike environment for infants ("Baby in a box," 1945) and a fictional portrayal of a scientifically planned cradle-to-grave environment in his novel, *Walden Two* (1948). Skinner regards most current applications of his principles to education and therapy as nothing more than technological extrapolations from his animal work.

Another major contributor to the behaviorist tradition was Clark L. Hull (1884–1952). He also developed principles primarily from animal learning, but was willing to attribute to his subjects many unobservable physiological and, in humans, even mental phenomena. Hull's research on learning was done between 1930 and 1952, with his most important books being *Principles of Behavior* (1943) and *A Behavior System* (1952). His general strategy of creating hypothetical constructs from which testable deductions could be made, the specific construct system he developed, and the interdisciplinary atmosphere he created at Yale's Institute of Human Relations attracted followers from diverse specialties. Through his many prominent students his influence is still apparent in personality, social, clinical, and physiological psychology, as well as in learning theory.

For the historical context of psychopathology, one of the most important events in the Hullian tradition was the attempt by Dollard and Miller in *Personality and Psychotherapy* (1950) to bring together the traditions of psychoanalysis, learning theory, and social science. They accepted many Freudian concepts, but reinterpreted them in terms of Hullian learning theory. It thus appeared that a unified science of behavior, especially of personality and the process of psychotherapeutic behavior change, was emerging.

Despite the popularity of the Dollard and Miller book, no such unified science has emerged. There are numerous reasons why it has not, but, especially in the study of psychopathology in children, it is evident that many of the old traditions remain virtually intact, with none commanding enough convincing knowledge either to sweep the others away or to provide a synthesis that could be accepted by all.

Behavior therapies based upon Watsonian, Skinnerian, and Hullian principles have undergone an enthusiastic revival since about 1958 (see Chapter 10). Joseph Wolpe, Hans Eysenck, Arnold Lazarus, Albert Bandura, Donald Baer, Sidney Bijou, O. Ivar Lovaas, and many others have applied learning theory principles to psychotherapy in new ways. The general framework of learning theory and objective approaches to behavior have also influenced recent developments in diagnosis and in school and community psychology.

Child Study

Like behaviorism, what is here referred to as the "child study" tradition has been concerned mainly with normal functioning, but has often been extended to abnormal behavior. Two facts make the study of normal child behavior a prerequisite for assessing abnormality in children. First, the child is always changing and has not yet reached a stable level of functioning that represents his own typical baseline of behavior. Hence, it is difficult to specify normal expectations for a particular child in order to judge whether some new behavior should be considered "abnormal." The study of representative samples of normal children can yield a picture of the behavior typical for each level of development, thus providing a standard against which to measure the behavior of a particular child. Second, children rarely define their own behavior as abnormal—parents or other adults decide, often against the child's wishes, whether a child will receive special help. Unlike adult treatment, where the client helps to specify the goals, child treatment focuses on restoring development to a course identified as normal from the behavior of children other than the client. For these reasons, the study of normal child behavior is absolutely essential for defining "pathology" in children, as well as for understanding how it may come about and how it may be overcome.

Interest in children *per se* began with theory and philosophical argument long before it led to systematic observation. For example, John Locke (1632–1704) argued that the mind of the newborn is a *tabula rasa,* or blank slate, whose development is determined entirely by experience. Jean Jacques Rousseau (1712–78) maintained that the child is innately good and that his own natural activities, if they are not interfered with, follow an optimal course. Baby biographies were published in 1774 by Johann Heinrich Pestalozzi and in 1787 by Dietreich Tiedemann, but the first one with scientific significance was not published until 1877, when Charles Darwin sought to demonstrate that infant development revealed adaptive mechanisms parallel to those occurring in the evolution of the human species.

G. Stanley Hall (1844–1924), founder of the first psychological journal in America (1887), and the first president of the American Psychological Association (1892), was a chief promoter of psychological child study in the United States. Although his organizing and research activities had many facets, they came to be focused primarily upon "genetic" psychology, so-called not in the sense of "genes," but in the sense of "genesis" or "beginnings." As he and other genetic psychologists (including Piaget) have conceived it, genetic psychology is the study, in an evolutionary framework, of how organisms develop and adapt to their environments. Most of Hall's early research involved giving questionnaires to large numbers of children in order to find out just what they thought and knew at various ages. His monumental book on adolescence (1904) was especially popular because it appealed to the new belief that psychology could produce a scientific system of education.

Many of Hall's students became prominent in the intelligence testing movement that followed publication of the Binet-Simon tests in 1905. These included Lewis Terman, who produced the Stanford-Binet IQ test

(1916), the most popular American version of the Binet. Terman also undertook one of the best-known long-term studies of child development, beginning in 1921 with the identification of 1,000 intellectually gifted children whom he then followed for 35 years (Terman & Oden, 1959). Besides supporting the general stability of the IQ, the study debunked the myth that very bright children become adult misfits. Two other early longitudinal studies that are continuing to yield invaluable data on normal development are the Berkeley Growth Study, begun in 1928 (Bayley, 1968), and the Fels Institute Study, begun in 1929 (Kagan & Moss, 1962).

Research on mental testing reached a peak between 1914 and 1925, while other types of child study showed a sharp rise after 1920 (cf. Goodenough, 1934). Curiously, the belief in a genetically fixed IQ coexisted for many years with the environmentalist belief in the total malleability of personality. Although the environmentalism of the behaviorists continues to be a prominent force, a strong voice gained influence in the 1930s and 1940s for the maturationist view. The voice was that of Arnold Gesell (1880–1961), another of G. Stanley Hall's students. From 1911 until 1948 at the Yale Child Development Clinic and after 1948 at the Gesell Institute, he and his coworkers amassed observational data supporting the belief that development was basically a process of embryological unfolding. In contrast to the tendencies of behaviorism and psychoanalysis to blame all children's problems on parents, Gesell's advice, still influential in newspaper columns written by Louise Ames of the Gesell Institute, emphasized that most child behavior reflects particular stages of development. Thus, the two-and-a-half year-old "acts that [aggravating] way because he is built that way [Gesell & Ilg, 1943, p. 178]."

Since World War II, child study has diversified still further, with research on socialization and personality development becoming popular, followed in the 1960s by new interest in infancy, language acquisition, and cognitive processes. Methodological emphasis has also shifted from the almost exclusive reliance upon observational and correlational approaches to greater sophistication in experimentation, the search for processes and mechanisms that underlie behavior changes, and the direct testing of theoretical propositions.

At another level, the twentieth-century interest in child study can be observed in the popularity of child care manuals and in the government's new roles in relation to children. An early child-care manual, Holt's *The Care and Feeding of Children,* went through thirteen editions between 1894 and 1929. It was explicitly called a "catechism" because it consisted of a long series of mothers' questions and Holt's answers. The most popular current manual, Dr. Spock's *Baby and Child Care,* first appeared in 1945 and has been continually revised since then. It is highly recommended as a readable practical source on the everyday concerns of child rearing.

The United States Government's official role in child care began when President Theodore Roosevelt called the first White House Conference on

Children in 1910. Similar conferences of experts are now called every ten years to make recommendations concerning child welfare. The United States Children's Bureau was founded in 1912 to compile statistics and literature on children. The successive editions of its *Infant Care Bulletin,* first issued in 1914 reflect several cycles of radical changes in child-rearing attitudes since then. Compare, for example, the advice given mothers about masturbation in the 1914 and later editions of *Infant Care:*

1914: Masturbation—This is an injurious practice which must be eradicated as soon as discovered . . . as it easily grows beyond control. . . . If the mother discovers the baby rubbing its thighs together or rocking backward and forward with its legs crossed, she should divert him at once to some other interest. . . . Children are sometimes wrecked for life by habits learned from vicious nurses, and mother can not guard too strictly against this evil. . . . In the case of babies, the treatment consists in mechanical restraints. A thick towel or pad may be used to keep the thighs apart, or at night the hands may have to be restrained by pinning the nightgown sleeves to the bed, or the feet may be tied one to either side of the crib [p. 62].

1929: Frequently at an early age . . . children learn that pleasurable sensations can be aroused by handling or rubbing the genitals, squeezing the thighs tightly, riding on someone's foot, or in other ways accidently discovered. . . . This early period of what may be called sex awareness will pass away unless it is emphasized by unwise treatment on the part of adults. . . .

Punishment and physical restraint are of little value in dealing with this habit, as they tend to fix the baby's attention on what he is doing and may strengthen the habit rather than stop it. . . . The best method of treatment is occupation and diversion. [p. 60].

1963: The baby explores his mouth and ears, and toes and hair with interest, learning about himself and how he feels. In similar fashion, he's going to explore other sensitive areas of his body, too. The baby is not bad when he does so. As he grows, his interests will move beyond his own body to the interesting world about him [p. 31].

Changes in recommended feeding practices have followed a parallel course, from extremely strict four-hour scheduling of all babies to emphasis on the needs of the particular baby, although a trend toward pointing out the benefits of scheduling is beginning to reappear (Spock, 1968). Recommendations on toilet training have shown one of the clearest series of cyclical changes. In the 1914 edition of *Infant Care,* recommendations for bladder training were relatively mild and bowel training was hardly mentioned. By the 1920s, however, the recommendations were for forcing strict regularity on the child's bowel movements, beginning in the first month of life. If the baby did not have bowel movements according to schedule, they were to be induced by inserting a stick of soap into his rectum. Training was to be completed by the age of eight months, at the latest. By the 1940s, the emphasis had shifted to catching the baby when he was ready to be trained and soap sticks were considered to be harmful. By the late 1960s, however, Dr. Spock (1968) expressed the opinion that the main source of training problems was the fear modern mothers had of antagonizing their children, causing them to give up training at the first sign of resistance from the child.

During the early 1960s, the government's role was considerably redefined and enlarged to include more active intervention on behalf of children. This new role was manifest in the founding of the National Institute of Child Health and Human Development (1963) to fund research and services, in greatly expanded federal aid to education, and in the creation of special educational programs for the disadvantaged, such as Headstart and Follow-through. However, during the early 1970s, political changes brought curtailment of many of the initiatives taken in the previous decade.

SUMMARY

The historical context of developmental psychopathology is especially important for two reasons. First, the field's lack of an independent identity means that current ideas must often be understood in terms of their sources in other fields. Second, awareness of certain historical cycles in the study of children and of psychopathology may help us to avoid future pitfalls.

Figure 2.1 presents a rough sketch of the prominent people, events, attitudes, theories, and treatments relating to mental disorders and retardation from the end of the eighteenth century to about 1960. Attitudes and practices fluctuated back and forth during that period, though rarely as a direct result of scientific knowledge. One of the pitfalls repeatedly encountered was the wholesale endorsement of new concepts without adequate testing to determine their most appropriate application. The failure of the new concepts to provide panaceas typically elicited extreme reactions against them, without systematic determination of what was worth keeping.

The study of psychopathology became unified around Kraepelin's "descriptive diagnosis" at the end of the nineteenth century, but five new traditions emerged in the twentieth century—psychoanalysis, Adolf Meyer's commonsense psychiatry, the mental hygiene movement, behaviorism, and systematic child study. Although they have many things in common, these traditions have spawned differing viewpoints that have coexisted rather than having undergone systematic synthesis. Cycles like those noted before 1960 are still occurring, but the current diversity makes it harder to characterize the dominant moods. No approach yet commands enough convincing knowledge to sweep aside the others or to provide a synthesis that could be accepted by all.

SUGGESTED READING

Historical. Deutsch (1949) presents a readable, thorough, and authoritative history of the care and treatment of the mentally ill in America begin-

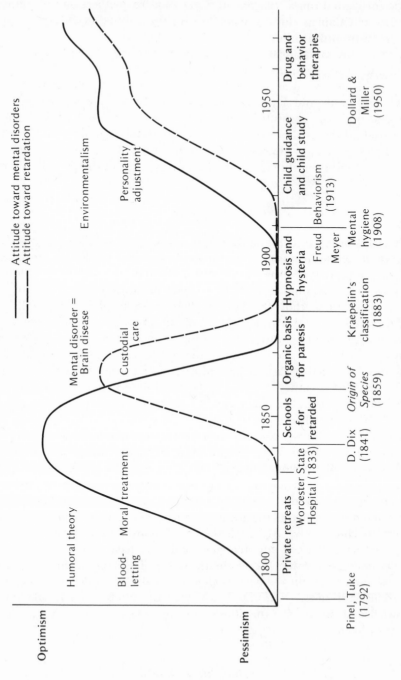

Fig. 2–1. Historical trends in psychopathology.

ning in colonial times. More recent books, by Bockoven (1963, 1972), Dain (1964), and Caplan (1969), admirably document the cyclical characteristics of practices and attitudes toward the mentally ill during the nineteenth century, with implications for the present and future.

Psychoanalysis. Works relating to the theoretical development of psychoanalysis will be discussed further in Chapter 8, but Ernest Jones's (1953) three-volume biography of Freud is highly recommended for its appealing insider's account of the development of psychoanalysis and of Freud himself. An excellent one-volume abridgement by Lionel Trilling and Steven Marcus is available in a Doubleday Anchor paperback, published in 1963.

Mental Hygiene. Clifford Beers's autobiographical *A Mind That Found Itself* (1908) has been reissued many times and is currently being published by Doubleday, with later editions containing updatings of the history of the mental hygiene movement. The book is worth reading not only for its historical significance and its revelations of a disturbed person's experience, but for its intrinsic charm as well.

Behaviorism. Ullmann and Krasner (1969) provide a comprehensive behavioristic treatment of psychopathology that clearly illustrates the conflicts between behavioristic and other views, especially psychoanalytic and medical approaches. In addition to behavioristic techniques for dealing with a large variety of disordered behavior, they present considerable historical context for the development of diverging viewpoints on abnormality.

Child Study. "The Concept of Development" (Stevenson, 1966) contains papers on current concepts of development, including the psychoanalytic, behaviorist, and cognitive concepts, as well as commentaries from various viewpoints. Kessen (1965) provides readings representing important views on children from the eighteenth century through Freud, Watson, Gesell, and Piaget, plus invaluable commentary on the historical trends they represent and where child study stands today. Ginsburg and Opper's *Piaget's Theory of Intellectual Development* (1969) is recommended as a good introduction to what is currently the most comprehensive and compelling approach to the study of normal intellectual development. Wolfenstein (1953) documents the amusing changes in child-rearing advice given in the Children's Bureau's *Infant Care Bulletin* between 1914 and 1951. For those who will soon be parents or want to know what it might be like, see Dr. Spock (1968).

3

Basic Issues in Developmental Psychopathology

Certain basic issues in developmental psychopathology often interfere with the clear formulation of answerable questions. These issues repeatedly recur in various forms in relation to different disorders. The purpose of this chapter is to expose a number of the issues in such a way as to make it easier to understand conflicts between viewpoints and to help in formulating answerable questions that may ultimately lead us to new conceptions.

Some issues result from the separatism characteristic of the traditions discussed in Chapter 2. In many cases, the issues dividing workers in the field are not apparent as explicit theoretical differences. Instead, they result from the implicit assumptions that particular views of man, values, professional training and responsibilities, or the like may help to establish. We will begin with a number of factors that shape people's views of children and their problems. Then we will consider how these views relate to significant conceptual issues in psychopathology and will conclude with the current official system for classifying psychopathology as set forth by the American Psychiatric Association.

ON DOING YOUR OWN THING

Professionals who work with disturbed children include educators, guidance counselors, nurses, police, probation officers, psychiatrists, psychologists, and social workers. Nonprofessionals becoming increasingly important in various roles include psychiatric aides, child-care workers and "house parents" in institutions, foster parents, indigenous neighborhood paraprofessionals, and recreation workers. These groups differ in status, training, responsibilities, social role, and attitudes toward children. The settings in which they work also greatly influence the ages and kinds of children they see, the duration of their contacts with the children, and the kinds of relationships that may be possible with the children and with the other occupational groups.

One can easily imagine a sequence in which a particular child is seen by most or all of these different workers—a teacher may see the child every day in the classroom and may refer him to a school guidance counselor or psychologist; the child may commit a crime and be held by the police; he may be placed under the supervision of a probation officer; he may undergo a court-ordered psychiatric or psychological examination, along with family casework by a social worker; he may receive psychological testing and outpatient psychotherapy at a clinic where a psychiatrist, psychologist, or social worker is the therapist. In some cities, he may have contact with indigenous paraprofessionals working with a clinic, neighborhood organization, or court. If his family situation is very bad, the child may be placed in a state-supported foster home. If his crime is serious enough or he seems badly disturbed, he may be sent to a reform school, state hospital, or residential treatment center. Here he may again be seen by any of the abovementioned professionals, but the workers he has most contact with will probably be nonprofessionals, including house parents, child-care workers, psychiatric aides, and recreation workers. Such a sequence may sound farfetched, but it is surprising how many children are subjected to one like it.

It is obvious that even the most objective, sensitive, and consistent observer would not describe the same child in the same terms if he observed him in all the different possible settings. Each setting and the child's expectations about it influence the child's behavior differently. The child is also influenced by the way he perceives the observer—not just the observer's personal characteristics but his perceived occupational role—as disciplinarian, teacher, cop, parent figure, head shrinker, and the like.

There are thus a large number of factors that would cause the same child to appear quite different to different observers or even to the same observer in different settings. Furthermore because of differences in their training, function, status, and professional ideology, the various professional groups have developed very different ways of looking at children. Even if a child behaved with perfect consistency, different professionals would disagree in their descriptions of him. The result is that the various occupational groups often work in relative isolation from one another or even at crosspurposes when dealing with a particular child. Differences that have crystallized into theoretical models for psychopathology in children will be discussed later, but first there are a number of practical matters that lead to disagreements in perceiving children's problems.

Personality of the Worker

An individual's own childhood—his memory of his childhood experiences as happy, sad, recent, or remote, his relationships with his parents, siblings, and other children—will inevitably influence his reactions to children. These reactions, conscious or not, may lead to the extremes of using the way things were "when I was a kid" as a standard for the way things *ought* to be, or of wanting children to "have all the things I never had." The adult's memories of his childhood also serve as a source for interpreting or empathizing with a child; he may, for example, strongly identify with some children or some kinds of problems, while reacting against others as he did when he was a child.

A person's adult family roles, especially as spouse and parent, also influence his reaction to children. His experience in these roles may cause him to look for or overemphasize factors that have been especially important to him personally. His own children also offer a richer store of knowledge about the hour-by-hour development, fluctuations, joys, and conflicts of children than can be obtained in almost any other way.

Types and Ages of Clients

One's conception of child psychopathology may be greatly influenced by the particular kinds and ages of children he sees. For example, a worker in a clinic for children below the age of five cannot conclude much from what the children tell him, from their peer relationships, or from fluctuations in their academic performance. Instead, he may base his judgments on norms for physical maturation, motor coordination, speech skills, and sensory-motor abilities. If such a worker is inclined to theorize about psychopathology, his thinking is likely to emphasize organic maturation much more than, say, someone dealing with aggressive adolescent delinquents in a residential setting, who is more likely to emphasize factors like impulsivity, ego weakness, and need for structure.

As will be apparent when specific content areas are discussed, contradictory views often arise from the tendency to base broad theoretical generalizations about pathology upon experience with a relatively narrow sample of ages and problems.

Types of Settings

There is wide diversity in the settings that offer services for disturbed children. Apart from the differing theoretical models that they employ, these settings differ greatly in their goals, the conditions under which children come to them, and their relationships to society at large. They also differ in the types of workers they employ, how they are financed, and whether their primary obligations are to parents, government, social agencies, or the children themselves. The latter consideration can be especially important in coloring attitudes toward child psychopathology, e.g., settings that depend upon continuing contact with parents in the course of treating a child are likely to be more aware of ongoing family dynamics than are settings where the parents are minimally involved. The principal types of settings follow.

Child Guidance Clinics. These are the best known and most numerous facilities especially created for helping troubled children. They are typically supported by public funds and have fee scales adjustable to their clients' incomes. In the traditional model, dating from about 1915, parents are interviewed by a psychiatric social worker, diagnostic testing is done by a psychologist, and child psychotherapy is done by a psychiatrist. Members of all three professions do therapy in many clinics, and other procedures, such as parents' groups, conjoint family therapy, and various kinds of children's groups, are becoming widespread.

Children are usually treated on a weekly basis for periods of several weeks to several years. A wide range of problems is seen in these clinics, but the orientation is toward helping with fairly specific and limited problems. Since the child's problem is usually concluded to be a reaction to parental behavior, the parent's contacts with the social worker often become the primary focus of treatment. Consultation with schools about individual children is also carried on by many clinics.

Children below the age of four are seldom seen in these settings, although some guidance clinics do evaluate very young children. Most evaluations of early child development are done in medical hospitals or university medical centers.

Residential Settings. The best residential treatment centers are designed to provide a long-term therapeutic milieu for relatively small numbers of severely disturbed children. They are staffed by child-care workers, teachers, social workers, psychologists, psychiatrists, and recreational workers. Treatment models vary, but most emphasize gradual socialization within a protective environment. Unfortunately, there are few very good centers and the private ones are extremely expensive. Many residential settings for disturbed children are converted orphanages or sections of state mental hospitals that provide little more than custodial care.

Institutions for the severely retarded also run the gamut from strictly custodial to those having active training programs for returning some retarded individuals to society. A recent innovation is the state regional center, designed to help keep the retarded person in his home community by offering sheltered workshops, recreation, day care, and temporary residential care.

Medical Hospitals. Some medical hospitals, especially those connected with universities, have child psychiatric wards. These are generally designed for diagnostic, emergency, and short-term residential treatment purposes. Other medical hospitals house disturbed children in pediatric wards. Hospitals provide a temporary refuge where the extent of a child's problems can be assessed, e.g., following a suicide attempt, a traumatic experience, or a sudden breakdown, but they are almost always characterized by an antiseptic, illness-oriented atmosphere that is frightening to children.

Educational Settings. Probably more children with problems are dealt with in educational settings than in all other settings combined. This is partly because the public schools have to take responsibility for many children who never receive help elsewhere. Most public school systems now have special classes for the retarded and many are introducing special classes for emotionally disturbed and perceptually handicapped children. Many also employ school psychologists, guidance counselors, social workers, and consulting psychiatrists to back up the teachers who are the frontline personnel in dealing with disturbed pupils.

Disturbed children usually have academic difficulties of some sort and academic difficulties can themselves lead to disturbances. In fact, academic problems are the most frequently encountered symptoms in many clinics. Hence, the educational process looms large in any consideration of developmental psychopathology, and the public school system may very well be the best place to handle many problems. Yet, there is a tendency on the part of some school personnel, occasionally reinforced by mental health workers, to use "emotional disturbance" as a label that absolves the school of any further responsibility for a child.

There are also special schools, mostly private though often aided by public funds, that are designed to help children with fairly serious problems. These include schools for children with brain damage, perceptual-motor handicaps, retardation, reading problems, and learning disabilities. Some residential centers for disturbed children are called schools and emphasize educational techniques.

Punitive Settings. Another group of facilities for children with problems is comprised of detention centers and what used to be known as "reform schools," although various euphemisms have now been adopted. They were originally punitive in function and are still largely under the control of police and correctional agencies.

Detention centers are designed for the short-term incarceration of juveniles apprehended by the police. The best among them employ mental health personnel to diagnose problems and to help juvenile courts in making rational dispositions of the children, but many are simply cell blocks in which children are held, sometimes for periods of several months. Juvenile courts are intended to be flexible in deciding what will be most beneficial for the young offender, rather than simply assigning punishments prescribed by law. However, even in the most enlightened juvenile court, options are severely limited by inadequate treatment facilities, lack of knowledge about the efficacy of various dispositions, and the paucity of more moderate alternatives between, say, supervision by an overworked probation officer on the one hand, and incarceration in a state reform school on the other.

Many reform schools employ some mental health workers, but very few are organized around therapeutic or educational goals. Children often leave them prepared more for a life of crime than for continuing their education or for coping constructively with society.

Training and Career Orientation

In addition to the obvious differences between professions and between settings, the training and career orientation of individual workers greatly influence their views of children's problems and the modes of operation which they adopt. One of the most salient factors in this respect is the relative balance between an individual's interests in teaching, research, and practice. Those who are not at all interested in teaching or research are most likely to be found in private practice, to select their caseloads according to personal preferences and economic factors, and to feel relatively little need for fundamental changes in the way things are done. Those who have interests in research and practice may carry on part-time private or clinic practices and have affiliations with universities or public agencies. Those who are strongly interested in teaching and research may carry on some practice or consulting, but have primary appointments in universities or mental health agencies.

Naturally, various combinations of interests and pursuits occur and the same individual may have different combinations at different stages in his career. However, many differences in views arise from how an individual sees the field and his relation to it—whether he accepts things the way they are because he is comfortable with them that way, or whether he is dissatisfied with the current state of affairs and wishes to change things.

In principle, PhD programs in psychology are designed primarily to provide research training, while master's degree programs in psychological testing, school psychology, special education, and social work, as well as medical and psychiatric training, are organized mainly around practice. However, many psychologists prefer practice to research and a nonresearch Doctor of Psychology program has been instituted on a trial basis at the University of Illinois (Peterson, 1969). Conversely, numerous psychiatrists and social workers do undertake research.

MODELS FOR PSYCHOPATHOLOGY IN CHILDREN

Strictly speaking, a theoretical model is an analogy. It may involve using a well worked out theory from one science to represent phenomena that are the subject matter of another science, or it may be a set of concepts developed especially to represent some particular phenomenon. The representation of atomic structure by means of an array of physical particles is a well-known model that has proved very powerful in generating testable hypotheses.

Computer simulations, mathematical models, and schematic portrayals of neural and psychological functions have frequently been used to represent specific psychological phenomena and certain disorders, such as schizophrenia and autism. However, the general "models" that are evident in different views of child psychopathology are seldom capable of consistently linking detectable phenomena with elements of an abstract representation. Rather, the models to be discussed below may be characterized as "frames of reference" in which certain types of concepts, inferences, and technical vocabularies are employed for representing the phenomena of interest.

A particular model is usually implicit in the views of a given worker and some models may be more restricted to particular settings and kinds of disorder than are others. Yet the models are not mutually exclusive and each one may supply useful concepts for the eventual understanding of some aspect of developmental psychopathology.

The Medical Model

This model represents disordered behavior by analogies with physical disease. It played an important role in bringing psychopathology out of the realm of demonology in the eighteenth century and in justifying a scientific approach to disordered behavior in the nineteenth century. It has provided such terms as "pathology," "treatment," "symptom," and "cure," as well as mental "health," "hygiene," and "illness." Official classifications of disorders still reflect Kraepelin's (1883) medical model in which mental disorders were regarded as disease entities with physical causes.

In cases where a physical malfunction causes a disorder, the disease model is probably the appropriate one. However, there is an ongoing debate within the mental health professions as to how far beyond these afflictions the medical analogy should be carried. Since most "mental illness" is observed as disordered or unusual behavior, and few people believe that this behavior is caused exclusively by physical malfunctions, it is often argued that the concepts of "illness," "patient," and "treatment" are misleading when used in this way. Even in cases of mental retardation where organic factors are known to play a role, treatment usually involves educational and psychological methods designed to optimize behavior. Hyperactive children are frequently diagnosed as having "minimal brain damage," but there is rarely any means for confirming this diagnosis organically, and, again, treatment aims to modify the child's behavior, not his brain. There are plausible hypotheses about physical causes for schizophrenia, but here, too, at the present stage of our knowledge, both treatment and research require full attention to behavioral and experiential factors.

In short, the medical model may be perfectly appropriate for some disorders, but too broad an application of it may produce a conviction that all disorders have organic causes, that there is a clear-cut dichotomy between organic and psychological factors, that behavior is important only as a sign of underlying disease processes, and that disordered persons should be regarded as helpless "patients" until they are "cured" by "treatment."

The Psychodynamic Model

Freudian psychoanalysis is the chief contributor to this model, but it is employed in some form by many people who are not psychoanalytically trained. Literally speaking, "dynamic" refers to active physical forces or energy. Freud's original conception was of a quasi-physiological psychic energy that was constantly being redistributed within the person because of arousal, re-routing when deterrents to its release were met, and conversion into other forms when it was repressed. For example, "conversion hysteria" was theorized to involve the conversion of repressed sexual energy (*libido*) into physical energy that influenced some part of the body, e.g., paralyzing a limb. As psychoanalytic theory grew, the concepts of id, ego, and superego were used to designate classes of forces that were likely to come into conflict with one another.

The most concrete representation of the psychodynamic conception would be as a hydraulic system where application of force or blocking of a flow in one part of the system has direct consequences in other parts of the system. While much of the original physiologizing has disappeared, the dynamic conception is very much alive in many beliefs about mental functioning. Psychoanalytic theory still holds that symptoms, slips of the tongue, and dreams are compromises between the partial expression of forbidden impulses and the countervailing defenses. Projective tests, such as the Rorschach and Thematic Apperception Test, studies of motivation—notably McClelland's work on the achievement motive (McClelland, Atkinson, Clark, & Lowell, 1953)—and various kinds of psychotherapy assume that unconscious motives are expressed indirectly. Some extreme forms of the dynamic conception seem to imply that all blocking of impulses is harmful and that psychic health requires direct impulse expression.

The psychodynamic model resembles the medical model in holding that behavioral symptoms are indirect expressions of inferred underlying processes that constitute the real pathology, but it differs from the medical model in emphasizing psychological causes and treatment procedures.

The Behavioral Model

A number of different approaches (discussed in Chapter 10) share a behavioral model for psychopathology. They have in common a set of assumptions, dating from Pavlov, Thorndike, and Watson, about the central importance of overt behavior and the organization of all behavior, normal and pathological, according to a limited number of general principles. They take issue with the medical and psychodynamic models for concentrating on unseen hypothetical entities while minimizing the importance of the troublesome behavior.

Those who employ the behavioral model regard the disordered behavior itself ("symptoms" in the other models), rather than underlying pathology, as the focus of treatment. They do not regard disordered individuals as "patients" who must be cured by treatment, but as people who can take steps to modify behavior that is troublesome to them or to others. Whenever possible, even with children, they enlist the "patient's" aid in devising techniques for overcoming his problems.

Most of the behavioral approaches employ learning principles to explain deviant behavior and to create new ways of adapting to situations that have caused the problems. Many professionals who espouse the behavioral model recognize the importance of biological and social influences, but they contend that these simply contribute to the particular conditions that shape an individual's behavior and that systematic modification of the behavior itself is the only realistic goal.

The Nondirective Model

This might be better termed the "organismic model for man" that has grown out of Carl Rogers's (1951) client-centered nondirective psychotherapy. Virtually all the research and concepts engendered by this view have arisen from the practical application of nondirective therapy. Rogers's basic tenet is that psychotherapy should simply aid a person in becoming what he really, "organismically" is or has the potential to be. The therapist does this by conveying unconditional positive regard for the "client" (as opposed to the "patient" of the medical and dynamic models), and by reflecting the client's own feelings back to him as they are expressed. An important assumption is that the client has within himself the potential for growth that will enable him to reconcile his self-image with the image of how he would ideally like to be.

Virginia Axline (1969) has systematically extended this approach to children. The assumptions are the same as for adults, but, because the verbal medium of self-expression is less meaningful for children, the therapy setting is arranged so that the child's play can serve as his medium of expression. Psychodynamic and behavioral models of functioning are not entirely rejected by nondirective play therapists, but they believe that neither the interpretation of inferred psychodynamics nor the manipulation of behavior benefit the child. Instead, they believe that the therapist must demonstrate complete acceptance of the child as a person and reflect back to him the feelings he reveals. The child is thus encouraged to accept himself and to allow himself to grow toward his own personal identity.

The Sociological Model

Probably the clearest expression of this model for child psychopathology is found in studies of the relation between delinquency and social class characteristics (see Chapter 13). Many of these studies have been undertaken by sociologists, but sociological and social psychological frames of reference are also evident in ideas about family dynamics, family psychotherapy, milieu therapy, community psychology and psychiatry, and work with the disadvantaged.

Insofar as sociological concepts provide a well-defined model, they imply that much behavior considered to be pathological is really quite appropriate for the individual's social circumstances. Thus, juvenile gangs can be regarded as subcultures in themselves. These can be classified and their functions within the larger culture can be analyzed. Within a gang, various social roles can be defined and a member's behavior can be described in terms of the function of his role in relation to the roles of other gang members. Likewise, within a family, one member may be the scapegoat who bears the brunt of family tensions, another member may be the unchallenged leader, etc. This type of model may be quite useful when one is dealing with an entire social unit such as the gang or the family—patterns that are troublesome within the unit or between the unit and other social units can be identified and become targets for intervention.

Of course, groups are made up of individuals, and it is the behavior of individuals that is the basic subject matter of psychopathology. Moreover, there are many cases in which only the individual child can be treated. However, the sheer facts of sociological and subcultural influences and of cultural relativity are too often ignored in evaluating the behavior of a child presented for treatment. Any concept of deviancy must be culturally relative and there may be many problems that can never be ameliorated through treating individuals one by one.

Other Models

Strong adherents of the models just described tend to assimilate all child psychopathology to their particular model. Thus, a person who explicitly or implicitly holds the medical model may think of retardation, neurosis, psychosis, delinquency, and other problems all in terms of sickness, symptoms, treatments, and cures. Someone who believes in the psychodynamic model is likely to think of retardation as ego underdevelopment, of neurosis in terms of unconscious conflicts, of psychosis as failure of early ego individuation, and of delinquency as resulting from superego inadequacies. There are also several approaches, such as the following, that may not offer such general models for pathology, but that are important for their applications in certain contexts. Some looseness may be evident in applying the term "model" to these approaches, but this does not mean that their representations of pathology are less precise than those implied by the more general models.

Educational Models.   These usually take the form of a concentration upon educational techniques to overcome manifest disabilities in reading, perceptual-motor functioning, or learning. Varying degrees of personality support may be offered in the course of teaching children with these problems. Once they exist, no matter how they were caused, these problems can be very damaging to a child's confidence and conception of himself, thus leading to numerous other problems. In some treatment settings, the educational orientation is extended to helping seriously disturbed children master elementary aspects of socialization.

Statistical Models.   Generally speaking, these represent approaches to research, description, and classification rather than conceptions of psychopathology. A characteristic approach is to use statistical methods to find out what kinds of behavior tend to occur together. For example, a list of specific behaviors and self-reports is devised. All of the items on this list that are manifested by a particular child are then scored. When similar lists have been filled out for a large number of children, the intercorrelations of each item with every other item are calculated. It might be found that fire-setting and bed-wetting have a correlation of .80, meaning that most of the children who set fires also wet their beds and vice versa. The intercorrelations are then subjected to other statistical procedures, such as factor analysis, that identify patterns among the correlations. Each pattern is composed of several items, e.g., fire-setting, bed-wetting, poor school work, headaches, and insomnia.

The patterns identified in this way may initially be neutral with respect to theories of psychopathology, but they can be used to classify children in order to find out what produces the patterns and how children with particular patterns can be helped. They may also be used to suggest a theory of psychopathology or to test the predictions that theories make. Statistical approaches are not limited to behavioral items—they can be applied to test scores, reports of psychodynamic inferences, measures of organic functions, biochemical variables, etc., as well as to combinations of all these different types of variables. A major difference between statistical methods for creating groupings and other approaches is that the statistical methods use mathematical criteria for combining observations that are otherwise combined subjectively or according to existing theory.

Developmental Models.   Despite the importance of development for all aspects of child behavior, there is no single clear-cut developmental model for psychopathology in children. Gesell's maturational concept provided a framework for normal development in which pathology was defined as deviations from the norm in rate or pattern. This concept is still crucial for assessing abnormality in children up to about the age of five and for some kinds of developmental retardation beyond that age. Likewise,

Freud's and Erikson's conceptions of psychosexual and psychosocial development portray psychological conflicts typical of various developmental periods. Anna Freud (1965) has offered a "developmental profile" for describing a child in terms of the developmental levels of his psychological functioning, fixations, and conflicts (see Chapter 8). Attempts have been made to reconcile the Freudian ideas of development with Piaget's work (e.g., Wolff, 1960; Gouin-Décarie, 1965), but there has been little extension of Piagetian theory to psychopathology in children. Some statistical approaches (e.g., Achenbach, 1966) have also revealed patterns that invite developmental interpretations, and many attempts at classification have invoked developmental concepts. However, the really important work in bringing concepts of development to bear on psychopathology in children remains to be done.

THE "WHOLE CHILD" ISSUE

The variety of occupations, settings, and models relating to child psychopathology inevitably creates problems of communication. One of the recurring issues in this regard is how to keep sight of the whole child when thinking in terms of pathology, causes, diagnosis, treatment, and research. Adherents of some viewpoints accuse other viewpoints of overemphasizing certain aspects of the child while neglecting his wholeness as a person. It is obvious, however, that anybody who works with children is always confronted with the whole child rather than with a disembodied disease, ego, or response system. On the other hand, anybody who responds to a child, makes judgments and decisions, communicates his reactions, develops hypotheses and theories, or does research is being selective. Consciously or unconsciously, he is abstracting from all there is to be known about the individual.

Viewpoints differ with respect to what they focus on, how narrowly they define what is important, and how clearly they distinguish between observations and inferences. For example, a psychoanalyst may speak as if he has observed an anal fixation in a child, while a behaviorist would maintain that the psychoanalyst has really observed a variety of behavior from which he has made a series of inferences ending in the application of the label "anal fixation."

The problem of what aspects of the child should be given priority is made more difficult by the overlapping nature of traditional categories. The same child could be simultaneously and correctly labeled as brain-damaged, retarded, delinquent, psychotic, and as having neurotic traits and specific behavior problems. This results partly from different concepts of disorders and partly from the different impacts the disorders have on other people. Thus, brain damage refers to a physical defect regardless of its behavioral correlates, retardation is defined by performance on an IQ test, delinquency is behavior prohibited by law, psychosis refers to bizarreness in thinking and behavior, neurotic traits are defined by inferences about psychodynamic conflicts, and behavioral symptoms are behaviors like bed-wetting, thumb-sucking, etc., that are socially disapproved for children of certain ages.

Nomothetic versus Idiographic Approaches

Allport (1937) has argued for a distinction between nomothetic and idiographic methods in the study of personality. The *nomothetic* (Greek *nomos* = law) approach seeks general laws such as those in the natural sciences. The *idiographic* (Greek *idio* = personal, separate) approach seeks laws for portraying the behavior of a particular individual.

According to the idiographic view, even if there are general principles of behavior, the specific influences on an individual are such that he represents a unique outcome of the interaction of all these principles. Since it is impossible to determine the precise nature of all the interactions involved, the best way to predict an individual's behavior is to identify patterns or laws that are peculiar to him. If this does not always make prediction possible, it will at least convey a descriptive understanding of a personality. Thus, after long contact with a child, a clinician begins to recognize certain characteristic responses to particular situations without knowing just how these patterns were established. He may then seek to change the patterns by techniques based on other facts about the child, although he may never have had another child with exactly the same combination of personality and situational factors.

The nomothetic-idiographic distinction has been helpful in focusing two contrasting emphases in the study of psychopathology, but, as Allport suggested, it is a distinction that should have little basis in practice. The engineer assigned to construct a building faces a situation that is as unique because of ground conditions, structural requirements, and techniques at his disposal as is the situation faced by a clinician doing psychotherapy with a particular child. Yet, no matter how unique the building problem, the engineer could not produce a solution that violated general physical laws. Even when the general laws are not fully known, both the engineer and clinician construe the particular situation in terms of their previous experience—in the face of a unique situation they could not help invoking nomothetic principles, whether or not these had been well substantiated.

High regard for individuality is an asset in doing therapy, but it would be difficult to argue either that there are no general principles governing individual cases, or that clinicians can take a *tabula rasa* approach by which they completely dispel past influences upon their judgment of a new client. In fact, no approach to psychopathology completely dispenses with generalized concepts or principles, regardless of how strongly it espouses idiographic values. The psychoanalyst may idiographically portray a child in terms of his ego strength, characteristic defenses, and fixations, while the behaviorist portrays him in terms of habits and reinforcer hierarchies. However, the concepts of ego, defense, fixation, habit, and reinforcer hierarchy are all nomothetic in that their validity and interrelationships are not assumed to be restricted to one individual.

The essential point is that training, diagnosis, treatment, theory, and research are all basically nomothetic enterprises, seeking generalizable knowledge no matter how individualistic the applications may seem. The common quest is for the nomothetic principles that will eventually yield the most powerful techniques for dealing with pathology in *all* individuals.

SUBCULTURAL OR INDIVIDUAL DEVIANCY?

Any assessment of psychopathology requires a standard for normalcy. Unlike adults, children rarely decide for themselves that they want help with their problems. This decision is usually made for them by parents, educators, physicians, and other adults, who apply various standards, some of which may tell more about the adults themselves than about psychopathology in children.

Even after a child has been labeled deviant through referral to a mental health service, the question of what standards he deviates from should continue to be raised. Surprisingly high frequencies of behaviors usually regarded as pathological have been revealed by studies of "normal" children, i.e., children not selected by referral to mental health services (Glidewell, Domke, & Kantor, 1963; Lapouse, 1966; Lapouse & Monk, 1964; Thomas, Chess, & Birch, 1968). Table 3–1 presents the frequencies at various ages of problems found in a longitudinal study (Macfarlane, Allen, & Honzik, 1954). If the parents of a random sample of these children suddenly decided to bring them to guidance clinics, would the clinic personnel diagnose them as normal or would they be accepted for treatment? This is, of course, an empirical question, but it is significant because of the conceptual questions it raises.

There are no explicit and uniform standards for distinguishing healthy from disturbed children in the way that most organic malfunctions can be judged present or absent through physical tests and symptoms. It is, therefore, important to be aware of the kinds of subjective standards applied in labeling behavior pathological and in deciding just what needs to be changed about a child. A major distinction can be made between behavior that nearly everyone, including a child's family and peers, regards as deviant and behavior that deviates from dominant social norms but that is in harmony with the subculture in which the child lives.

Subcultural Deviancy

The subculture to which a child's behavior conforms may be an ethnic, social class, neighborhood, or family group. Precocious sexual behavior,

TABLE 3–1

Percentage[a] of nonclinic children having specific problems.

Problem	Age in years									
	1¾		5		8		11		14	
	Boys	Girls	Boys	Girls	Boys	Girls	Boys	Girls	Boys	Girls
1. Disturbing dreams	16	13	20	29	22	23	26	42	6	4
2. Nocturnal enuresis	75	73	8	10	12	14	15	10	11	0
3. Insufficient appetite	7	10	23	31	16	21	7	13	0	0
4. Masturbation	9	8	8	6	6	2	4	0	0	0
5. Nail-biting	5	3	8	17	16	23	30	40	33	22
6. Thumb-sucking	21	33	5	19	3	12	4	3	0	0
7. Excessive activity	29	17	46	35	38	16	30	16	11	0
8. Speech problems	30	17	18	8	6	12	7	5	0	4
9. Lying	0	0	49	42	41	19	11	0	6	0
10. Stealing	7	3	10	4	9	5	0	0	0	0

[a] Percentages of children in a longitudinal study whose mothers reported that the specific behavior was present in a degree judged by the investigators to represent "problem behavior."

NOTE.—Adapted from Macfarlane, Allen, and Honzik (1954, pp. 66–69). Originally published by the University of California Press; reprinted by permission of the Regents of the University of California.

various kinds of delinquent acts, and academic nonachievement may deviate from middle-class norms, but may be normal for children growing up in subcultures that create pressures and expectations for these kinds of behavior with no incentives for resisting them. If the behavior is damaging to society or the individual, it may be a proper concern for mental-health workers no matter how typical of a subculture it is. Yet, it would be incorrect to attribute it to the same causes or to attempt to change it in the same way in a subculture where it is typical as in one where it is very atypical. In some instances, cultural relativity may dictate that nothing should be done about behavior that is in harmony with the child's own subculture even though it is considered pathological in the dominant culture.

A particular family's highly antisocial or bizarre norms for behavior may create the conditions for some kinds of deviancy that can be regarded as subcultural rather than individual. If evaluated separately, any member of the family might be considered seriously pathological, but it is difficult to separate the deviancy of a child in such a family from the family subculture. The child's behavior may represent a successful adaptation to unusual circumstances. In extreme cases, it would be folly to try to change the child's behavior without removing him from or greatly changing the family. Because even mild behavior problems may reflect family stresses, the child brought for treatment is referred to by some workers as the "symptom" or "messenger" of a disturbed family.

Individual Deviancy

Since almost all child behavior is in part reactive to the family subculture, nearly all deviancy is to some extent subcultural. Yet most children are brought for treatment because their parents acknowledge that something is wrong—even if the parents are contributing to the problem behavior, they do not judge it to be in harmony with their family subculture.

In designating a child's behavior as deviant, there are three general standards for comparison that parents and other adults tend to use. One is an implied comparison of certain *enduring traits* of the child with the way the adult thinks a child *ought* to behave. This is often revealed in complaints that a child has been very fearful "since he was born," that he's *"always* been terribly destructive and now it's reached the point where . . . ," or the like. The parent's standards for the way children ought to behave may be realistic, but the question of just what the parent expects of a child is always relevant. Has the parent's whole perception of the child been formed by the child's behavior early in infancy? Did the parent expect the child to resemble a disliked relative so that these expectations have become a self-fulfilling prophecy? Did the parent have idealized expectations that no child could meet, or does the parent himself behave in such a way that the child cannot react compatibly to him?

A second standard for comparison is the way the child has previously behaved. Thus, a perceived *change* in behavior may be the basis for concern. Obvious questions to be raised include the possibility that the child has reached a new developmental stage or temporarily regressed from one not yet firmly achieved. A parent's awareness of developmental changes may be clouded not only by lack of sophistication, but also by a preference for behavior of a particular stage, e.g., the parent prefers the behavior of late childhood over the behavior of early adolescence. Another question is whether there has been some significant environmental change, e.g., a birth, death, or move, to which the child is reacting. This can work two ways—the environmental change may really have a marked effect on the child, or the parent himself may be so affected that he behaves differently toward the child or exaggerates the child's changes.

A third standard of comparison is the *developmental dimension*. Here the complaint may be that the child is not behaving like other children his age, or that he is not meeting the parent's expectations for that particular age. Although the normal range of behavior patterns at any age is very broad, the developmental standard can be applied fairly precisely to physical growth, to skills like walking and talking, and to intellectual functioning as measured by IQ tests.

Because judgments of individual deviance are largely subjective, they are vulnerable to the distortion of pertinent information. Such distortions by parents have been amply documented by comparing data gathered longitudinally on children's early development with the reports of their parents when the parents were requesting psychiatric evaluation of the children (Chess, Thomas, & Birch, 1966). Despite the fact that the children in this study were only three to seven years old at the time of the psychiatric evaluations, the following major distortions occurred in parental reports:

1. distortion of timing so as to make the sequence of developmental events conform to prevalent theories of causation;
2. denial or minimization of problems, especially of their earlier existence;
3. inability to recall pertinent past behavior;
4. blaming the child for continuing behavior that the mother had earlier encouraged.

A further problem in the assessment of individual deviance is met in cases where a child becomes part of a subculture that is characterized by behavior deviant from both the dominant culture and the subcultural and family standards in which the child was raised. Prominent examples include the hippy, drug, and "street people" subcultures, although youth subcultures that jealously guard their own linguistic idioms, values, and life styles are not a new phenomenon. Such subcultures may perform important functions in the psychosocial development of relatively normal children, but the more bizarre forms often attract children who are already quite deviant. In such cases it may be difficult to assess the individual's personal deviance separately from the subcultural norms that he adopts. A reciprocal relationship may also occur in which the needs of a disturbed child are partially met by a youth subculture that then reinforces ever more deviant and self-destructive behavior.

WHAT IS WRONG?

The question of what is wrong has three foci that are related but that are easily confused with one another. One focus is the *definition* of the disorder: What is the problem, what is troubling the child, how shall we understand it here and now? A second focus is upon the *cause* of the problem: Why does this particular child have this particular problem? How did he get this way and how could it have been prevented? A third focus is upon *treatment:* How can we help this child?

Blurring of the distinctions that exist among definitions, causes, and preferred treatments stems partly from the rudimentary state of our knowledge and partly from the nature of the conceptual models discussed earlier —the models do not confine themselves to one of these foci nor do they clearly distinguish among issues related to definitions, causes, and treatment. Consequently, people who are committed to the medical model's definitions of psychopathology, for example, may prematurely foreclose questions of treatment, although, even if the disease conception of a disorder eventually leads to discovery of its specific cause, the optimal treatment may turn out to be behavioral or psychodynamic. Conversely, a total commitment to the behavioral model for treatment may foreclose definitions and causal hypotheses relating to biological determinants. The purposes of this section are to identify and to separate issues relating to definitions, causes, and treatment that are often implicitly lumped together. These issues will reappear in later chapters when specific disorders and treatments are discussed.

Inferred or Observed Pathology?

All approaches employ some observation and some inference, but they differ markedly in how observations and inferences are used to define their primary subject matter. The medical and psychodynamic models define psychopathology in terms of inferred states, while the behavioral and sociological models tend to define it in terms of observed behavior, and the nondirective model defines it in relation to a particular conception of treatment. These differences cannot help but have an influence on the kinds of causes that will be sought, the kinds of treatment preferred, and the outcomes that will be considered solutions to a child's problems.

One of the recurring arguments around this issue is between the psychodynamic and the behavioral views. Believing behavioral symptoms to be surface manifestations of compromises among intrapsychic forces, the psychodynamicists contend that suppression of symptoms without altering the underlying dynamics is harmful because new symptoms, representing more strained compromises, will be substituted. The behaviorists, by contrast, argue that the "symptomatic" *behavior* is the primary problem and that the problem can be solved by altering the reinforcement contingencies supporting the behavior or by reinforcing new behavior incompatible with it.

Competence versus Performance. Another angle for viewing the inferred versus observed question in developmental psychopathology is suggested by the distinction between competence and performance made in psycholinguistics. Each language is assumed to possess a set of rules (grammar) according to which units (words) of the language are arranged to express a thought. Most informal utterances do not conform fully to these rules—people often speak in partial sentences, interrupt themselves as they change their minds, leave out words that may be inferred from the context, etc. Yet the native speaker of a language can readily recognize arrangements of words that do not make sense because they violate the basic rules of his language. Linguists refer to this implicit understanding of linguistic rules as *competence,* while the overt utterances constitute *performance.*

During the course of linguistic development, the child's overt verbal performance is often out of step with his competence in understanding adult utterances. Thus, the child may demonstrate that he knows the difference between the "truck *pushing* the car" and the "truck *being pushed by* the car" long before his own speech includes a distinction between active and passive forms. On the other hand, a child may correctly imitate a whole phrase that includes an advanced grammatical structure without understanding what it means or being able to apply the structure correctly in other contexts. This would be an example of performance seeming to reflect linguistic competence that does not yet exist.

The distinction between competence and performance is important in assessing intellectual as well as linguistic development. Motivation, distractibility, specific experience, sensory defects, and rapport with the examiner all affect overt performance on tasks designed to test cognitive competence as defined in terms of developmental level. By the same token, odd behavior or defective performance outside the testing situation may be products of many influences and should not automatically be considered to reflect underlying defects in competence.

A child facing a psychiatric interviewer for the first time may appear socially inept and "nonverbal" because of anxiety, but he may manifest considerable competence in these areas under other circumstances. On the basis of their classroom and clinic performance, minority-group children are often labeled nonverbal, while playground observations reveal that they have considerable verbal competence and make good use of it. Likewise, the fact that a child does not learn to read at the usual time may be the result of many factors and does not automatically imply that he has an underlying defect, although piecing together enough information about him may eventually lead to the conclusion that he is indeed one of those rare children whose neurological patterning seems to make reading difficult. Caution should also be exercised in translating observations of "neurotic" behavior into diagnoses of neurosis, of "rigid" behavior into a trait of rigidity, etc.

In short, the distinction between performance and competence is a useful one that should remind us of how complex the determinants of behavior are and should prevent us from prematurely concluding that a particular behavior by itself is *pathognomonic,* i.e., indicative of an underlying pathology or defect.

ETIOLOGY

Organic or Psychological?

A frequent question is whether the *etiology* (cause) of a child's problems is organic or psychological. The etiologies of some disorders are exclusively organic. Among these are gross defects that create bodily malformations, behavioral symptoms, mental retardation, and, often, premature death; an example is a disorder of fat metabolism known as Tay-Sachs disease. Short of this extreme, there are many physical afflictions that influence behavior in varying degrees. These include certain metabolic disorders, endocrine malfunctions, vitamin deficiencies, and brain damage.

Despite the fact that some physical afflictions have relatively direct effects on behavior, the exact form of behavior is seldom determined solely by physical malfunctions. Hence, the question of etiology should almost never be posed in either-or terms. This is especially true for most of the disorders discussed in this book, where no known physical affliction exists, where a physical affliction does not directly account for much of the problem behavior, or where there is no effective way to treat the problem behavior by organic means alone.

Three categories of disorders that create especially tricky problems for sorting out psychological and organic contributions are epilepsy, minimal brain damage, and psychophysiological ("psychosomatic") reactions. All of these will be discussed in more detail in Chapter 6, but their implications for the general issue of etiology are worth noting here.

Epilepsy is defined basically by the fact that a person has seizures attributable to brain dysfunction. Psychological factors also play a role because emotional stresses occasionally help to precipitate seizures. Moreover, the experience of having seizures, the knowledge that one is subject to them, the restrictions placed on certain activities, and the social myths and stigmas attached to epilepsy mean that psychological help and special occupational training are often needed.

Similar problems concerning the interaction between organic and psychological factors are raised by the "minimal brain damage" syndrome, typically defined by the presence of hyperactivity and equivocal signs of neurological dysfunction without firm evidence of brain damage. Many children given this diagnosis may not actually have brain damage, but there is no way of knowing with certainty what aspects of their behavior are due to organic dysfunction and what aspects are due to other factors. In some instances, the contributing organic factors may not involve damage at all, but may result from slow development or from constitutional parameters that are simply at the low end of the normal distribution. In other instances, hyperactive behavior may represent a child's way of handling anxiety at certain ages, there being considerable evidence that this behavior is most frequent in preschool and early school-age children (Achenbach, 1966; American Psychiatric Association, 1968, p. 50).

Understanding pathology in general and helping particular children requires exploration of all possible causal factors, but the brain-damage label too often conveys a sense of hopelessness. Even when warranted, the diagnosis of brain damage should never preclude precise evaluation of a child's psychological functioning and attempts to improve that functioning. Most brain damage does not have an inexorable, uniform, or unmodifiable effect on behavior. On the other hand, failure to diagnose and allow for limitations imposed by organic damage may result in a child being pressured to do things of which he is incapable.

Psychophysiological reactions, popularly known as "psychosomatic," involve physical symptoms that are presumed to be precipitated by psychological stresses. "Psychosomatic" has come to connote imaginary or solely psychological discomforts, and, indeed, certain apparent physical malfunctions, usually classified as hysterical, may have no verifiable organic component. However, psychophysiological reactions are real to the point of being potentially fatal. Among the most dangerous are hypertension (high blood pressure), asthma, ulcerative colitis (inflammation of the large intestine), stomach ulcers, and anorexia nervosa (extreme unwillingness to eat).

Various factors have been hypothesized to cause each specific reaction, but most reactions probably involve an interaction of factors emphasized by several of the hypotheses. This type of interaction has been well documented in adults for ulcers, many of which seem to be caused by a combination of (1) predisposing biological factors such as high stomach acid levels, (2) certain personality dispositions, and (3) precipitating stress (Weiner, Thaler, Reiser, & Mirsky, 1957).

Heredity or Environment?

There is often a correlation among attitudes toward definitions of disorders, conceptions of underlying causes, and beliefs about the ultimate sources of the causes. Thus, those who adhere to the medical model for defining disorders are likely to think in terms of underlying organic causes and hereditary sources for many of these causes. Those who adhere to the psychodynamic or behavioral models are likely to think in terms of psychological causes having environmental sources. However, the correlations among these attitudes tend to be produced more by traditions of training and by conceptual preferences than by logical necessity. True, genetic mechanisms and many diseases directly determine only biochemical processes and not intrapsychic or behavioral phenomena. Yet it seldom makes sense to consider psychopathology solely in terms of biochemical processes. These processes go through many complex stages and are subject to numerous influences before the organism in which they occur manifests their effects behaviorally.

On the other hand, "environmental influences" can never be defined solely as objective environmental events. Environmental events have significance for behavior only as they impinge upon an organism that already exists, has a history, and has its own way of construing and reacting to events. Normal development, for example, can never be explained exclusively as a record of the events that have occurred in the child's presence —bombarding one two-year-old with verbal stimuli may not have the same effect that bombarding another two-year-old will, and certainly will not have the same effect on a one-year-old or an eight-year-old. As Piaget maintains (Piaget & Inhelder, 1969), development always involves a continuing reciprocal relation between organic structures—whose general form is determined by genetically transmitted plans—and the environmental materials with which an organism feeds his structures.

Genotype and Phenotype.　There are various routes by which genetically transmitted codes can affect behavior. Long before a single gene was isolated, hypotheses about the genetic transmission of many physical characteristics were rigorously tested by observing the proportions of offspring having each variant of a trait. Another dimension was added when chromosomes, composed of thousands of genes, could be viewed microscopically. The presence of unusual configurations of chromosomes was then linked to some disorders, such as Down's syndrome (mongolism), that had obvious physical and behavioral manifestations.

Most genetic determinants must still be conceptualized in terms of hypothetical constructs or models that are valuable insofar as they yield testable deductions. The hypothetical genetic composition of an individual is known as his *genotype,* while the observable expression of the genotype is known as the *phenotype.* Genotypes are usually discussed in reference to particular traits rather than with respect to all of the genetically influenced traits an individual possesses.

The study of genetic influences on behavior ("behavior genetics") is inherently more difficult than the study of genetic influences on physical traits because phenotypic behavioral traits are more difficult to define and measure reliably than are physical characteristics. This difficulty is compounded by the fact that phenotypic behavior is influenced by the situation in which it is observed. Nevertheless, behavior genetics has made substantial progress in research on intelligence and personality traits, and genetic hypotheses have been offered to explain various forms of behavioral deviance. An understanding of behavior genetics (discussed further in Chapter 5) is absolutely necessary if the study of psychopathology in children is to advance.

Even when it is recognized that behavior itself cannot be directly inherited, hereditary mechanisms are often thought of in all-or-none terms or in terms of one-to-one relations between a gene and a very specific physical or behavioral trait. Indeed, there are a number of phenotypic traits, especially physical traits, for which the genetic determinants do operate in almost one-to-one fashion, but the vast majority of traits are likely to be influenced by combinations of genetic factors operating together. In some cases, these combinations produce distinctive physical structures, such as the mongoloid features of children having Down's syndrome. What may have greater significance for the broad range of psychopathology, however, is the fact that combinations of genetic and other prenatal influences create general constitutional constellations with which the child meets the world and to which the world reacts.

PROGNOSIS—CURABLE OR INCURABLE?

A *prognosis* is a forecast about the eventual outcome of a disorder. Attitudes toward prognosis are often the product of assumptions about the causes and definitions of disorders rather than being based upon firm evidence from which to judge outcomes. Indeed, obtaining firm evidence about outcomes of psychopathology in children is an arduous enterprise that requires (1) a meaningful way of identifying and classifying disorders, and (2) long-term follow-up of children having a particular disorder but receiving different kinds of treatment. The latter point is especially important because the prognosis is not strictly an attribute of the disorder itself, but depends upon the availability of effective interventions. Many organic illnesses that previously had poor prognoses now have favorable prognoses because new treatments have been discovered.

In psychopathology, the attitudes noted before tend to produce pessimism about disorders believed to have organic causes and relative optimism about those with presumed psychological causes. However, some hereditarily determined organic disorders now have very good prognoses because basic causes have been discovered and effective diagnoses and treatments developed. An example is phenylketonuria (PKU), a severe form of retardation resulting from an inborn error in the metabolism of phenylalanine, a protein present in most foods. The disorder can be diagnosed by urine tests soon after birth and may be prevented from causing retardation if the amount of phenylalanine in the child's diet is drastically reduced.

Problems of precisely identifying and classifying nonorganic disorders and of specifying what constitutes a favorable outcome make prognostication for such disorders more difficult than for many organic disorders. These difficulties may help to explain why there is a lack of conclusive research to determine the optimal kinds of psychological treatment for each disorder.

CLASSIFICATION

Persons or Disorders?

The issue of classification has many facets. Too often classification is regarded as a dry, abstract enterprise for grammarians, librarians, and butterfly collectors that has little relation to understanding the phenomena being classified. Yet, any act of judgment that involves making conceptual distinctions is an act of classification, whether or not it is explicitly recognized as such. Judgments as to what is wrong with a particular child, what the causes are likely to be, whether he can be helped, and what treatment is appropriate all involve classification, no matter what model for psychopathology is employed. Progress in understanding many disorders is hampered by the absence of objective ways of specifying them so they may be consistently identified by different workers. One of the recurring problems in research on and treatment of childhood autism, for example, is the lack of agreement as to which children are autistic—generalizations made by one worker about autism are of no value unless other workers can recognize the kinds of children to whom he is referring.

Various approaches to classification will be detailed in Chapter 15. For now, it is important to note that classifications are valuable insofar as the classes they provide have important correlates and can be applied uniformly by different workers. The kinds of correlates considered to be important depend upon the *function* that the classification is to serve. Clearly, an objective classification of children according to height might be useful in forming basketball teams and might have other correlates such as the children's weights and ages, but classification according to height would not be very helpful in communicating about causes, management, and treatments of their behavioral disorders.

Many of the arguments about how to classify psychopathology result from (1) varying conceptions of what the pathology is, and (2) the different uses people have for classification. Because classifications are justified only by the functions they serve, there can never be a single "correct" classification. For something that involves people in as many different ways as child psychopathology does, a number of different classification systems will no doubt always be necessary. Each of the different systems will deal with only those aspects of the child, his behavior, or the causes of his disorder that are important to the people using the system. Thus, for mentally retarded children, medical personnel need a classification based on the organic causes that they are asked to identify or treat; psychologists may prefer a classification based upon IQ, general etiology (organic versus nonorganic), or patterns of ability; institutional personnel may wish to classify children according to whether they need nursing care, are toilet trained, can feed themselves, are subject to seizures, or are potentially dangerous to other children; school personnel may have to identify children according to the kinds of instruction and educational programs from which they can benefit.

Differences in classificatory needs are evident not only along professional lines, but also in relation to different stages in conceptualizing disorders. Research to identify causes or to develop effective treatment often requires trying out a variety of classificatory principles in order to find groups of children who are homogeneous in some important respect.

The "Whole Child" Issue in Classification

Classifications generally deal with disorders, or attributes of people or their behavior, rather than with whole individuals. Yet, the fact that one is always confronted with whole individuals creates a tendency to identify everything about a person with a disorder he is said to have, as reflected in the use of terms like "the schizophrenic," "the sociopath," "the obsessive-compulsive," etc. As Adolf Meyer put it, the implication is that the disorder " 'has' the patient," rather then that "the person 'has' a certain disorder." (Cf. Kanner, 1957, pp. 726, 727.)

What must be emphasized is that no classification system can possibly take account of *all* the attributes of a human individual—the function of classification systems is simply to provide explicit principles for grouping individuals with respect to *some* of their attributes that are related in important ways to the goals of the classifier, e.g., selecting the people that will benefit most from a certain kind of treatment. Once treatment begins, some practitioners, such as Rogerian psychotherapists, believe they are most effective when they forget a priori principles of classification and react only to what the client presents of himself. However, Rogers (1955) has made explicit provision for identifying elements of personality and therapy that will make possible the prediction of outcomes.

Diagnostic and Statistical Manual of Mental Disorders

The *Diagnostic and Statistical Manual of Mental Disorders* (abbreviated "DSM"), published by the American Psychiatric Association, provides the official categories and nomenclature (system of names) used by clinical and government agencies for tabulating psychopathology. Most medical classification, known as *nosology* (Greek *nosos* = disease), is based upon the physical causes of disorders at whatever level the causes are currently understood. Thus, for example, tumors are now classified mostly by their physical characteristics and locations, although they may someday be classified in terms of specific viruses, genetic anomalies, or whatever causes are discovered.

The DSM generally follows medical principles with regard to disorders having known physical bases. However, behavioral manifestations of these disorders, as well as disorders with no known physical correlates, are also classified. For example, mental retardation is classified according to IQ as borderline (IQ 68–83), mild (IQ 52–67), moderate (IQ 36–51), severe (IQ 20–35), or profound (IQ under 20), but it is also classified according to presumed cause, such as retardation "associated with gross brain disease," "with chromosomal abnormality," "with psychosocial (environmental) deprivation," etc.

The first edition of the DSM (DSM–I, American Psychiatric Association, 1952) contained only the following categories for children's disorders: Schizophrenic reaction, childhood type; adjustment reaction of infancy; adjustment reaction of childhood, with the subcategories of habit disturbance, conduct disturbance, and neurotic traits; and adjustment reaction of adolescence. Although adult diagnoses could also be applied to children, most children seen in psychiatric clinics either were diagnosed as having adjustment reactions or received no diagnosis (Achenbach, 1966; Dreger, Lewis, Rich, Miller, Reid, Overlade, Taffel, & Flemming, 1964; Rosen, Bahn, & Kramer, 1964).

The second edition of the DSM (DSM–II, American Psychiatric Association, 1968) makes more distinctions between child and adult disorders, but large-scale data are not yet available on how the new categories for children's disorders are being put into practice. The major categories and some subcategories of the DSM–II are presented in Table 3–2.

Categories III through X. Unlike Categories I and II, Categories III–X embrace disorders without known physical causes and are organized according to several different principles as follows:

Category III—Among the psychoses, schizophrenia and its subtypes seem to be considered disease entities, the manic-depressive disorders are explicitly called "illnesses," but paranoia can occur as a "state."

Category IV—The neuroses are described in terms of a psychodynamic model: "Anxiety is the chief characteristic of the neuroses. It may be felt and expressed directly, or it may be controlled unconsciously and automatically by conversion, displacement, and various other psychological mechanisms [p. 39]."

Category V—The personality disorders seem to imply person-classification, but they are defined as being "characterized by deeply ingrained maladaptive patterns of behavior that are perceptibly different in quality from psychotic and neurotic symptoms. Generally these are life-long patterns, often recognizable by the time of adolescence or earlier [p. 41]."

Category VI—Psychophysiologic disorders are "characterized by physical symptoms that are caused by emotional factors and involve a single organ system, usually under autonomic nervous system enervation [p. 46]."

Category VII—"Special symptoms" are strictly symptomatic designations, but are defined as if they were manifestations of unnamed underlying pathology: "This category is for the occasional patient whose psychopathology is manifested by a single specific symptom. An example might be anorexia nervosa . . . [p. 47, 48]."

Category VIII—Transient situational disturbances are "more or less transient disorders (including those of psychotic proportions) that occur in individuals without any apparent underlying mental disorders and that represent an acute reaction to overwhelming environmental distress [p. 48]."

Category IX—Behavior disorders of childhood and adolescence include disorders "that are more stable, internalized, and resistant to treatment than transient situational disturbances, but less so than psychoses, neu-

TABLE 3–2

American Psychiatric Association's classification of mental disorders.

I. *Mental retardation* (degrees and causes listed)

II. *Organic brain syndromes* (specific causes listed)

    A. Psychoses associated with organic brain syndromes

    B. Nonpsychotic organic brain syndromes

III. *Psychoses not attributed to physical conditions listed previously*

    A. Schizophrenia

1. Simple	5. Acute episode	9. Childhood
2. Hebephrenic	6. Latent	10. Chronic undifferentiated
3. Catatonic	7. Residual	11. Other
4. Paranoid	8. Schizo-affective	

    B. Major affective disorders

1. Involutional melancholia	4. Manic-depressive illness, circular
2. Manic-depressive illness, manic	5. Other major affective disorder
3. Manic-depressive illness, depressed	

    C. Paranoid states

        1. Paranoia

        2. Involutional paranoid state

        3. Other paranoid state

    D. Other psychoses

        1. Psychotic depressive reaction

IV. *Neuroses*

A. Anxiety	D. Obsessive-compulsive	G. Depersonalization
B. Hysterical	E. Depressive	H. Hypochondriacal
C. Phobic	F. Neurasthenic	I. Other

---

roses, and personality disorders. This intermediate stability is attributed to the greater fluidity of all behavior at this age. Characteristic manifestations include such symptoms as overactivity, inattentiveness, shyness, feeling of rejection, over-aggressiveness, timidity, and delinquency [pp. 49, 50]."

Category X—Conditions without manifest psychiatric disorders and nonspecific conditions are "conditions of individuals who are psychiatrically normal but who nevertheless have severe enough problems to warrant examination by a psychiatrist [p. 51]."

Child or Miniature Adult?

This question is nowhere more crucial than in the definition and classification of psychopathology. Despite the addition in the DSM–II of several new categories specifically for childhood disorders, most diagnostic and classificatory concepts originated with the study of adult disorders. The strong

TABLE 3–2 (Cont.)

V. Personality disorders and certain other nonpsychotic disorders

  A. Personality Disorders

1. Paranoid	5. Obsessive compulsive	9. Passive-aggressive
2. Cyclothymic	6. Hysterical	10. Inadequate
3. Schizoid	7. Asthenic	11. Other
4. Explosive	8. Antisocial	

  B. Sexual deviations (specific deviations listed)
  C. Alcoholism (degrees listed)
  D. Drug dependence (drug groups listed)

VI. Psychophysiologic disorders (specific organ systems listed)

VII. Special symptoms (specific symptoms listed)

VIII. Transient situational disturbances ("adjustment reactions")

A. Infancy	C. Adolescence	E. Late life
B. Childhood	D. Adult Life	

IX. Behavior disorders of childhood and adolescence

A. Hyperkinetic reaction	E. Unsocialized aggressive reaction
B. Withdrawing reaction	F. Group delinquent reaction
C. Overanxious reaction	G. Other reaction
D. Runaway reaction	

X. Conditions without manifest psychiatric disorder and non-specific conditions (specific categories listed)

NOTE.—Adapted from *Diagnostic and Statistical Manual, American Psychiatric Association* (1968).

theoretical emphasis, since Freud, upon the continuity between childhood maladjustment and the occurrence of adult disorders has caused childhood problems to be viewed largely in terms of the adult disorders they are believed to culminate in, rather than being studied in their own right. It is, however, still an open question whether many of the disorders identified in adults can be validly attributed to children.

As will be noted in chapters on specific disorders, the use of the adult terms for childhood disorders may often exaggerate similarities and obscure important differences between disturbed adults and children, even though qualifying terms are used. A prominent example is schizophrenia, a diagnostic category widely used for severely disturbed adults, although by no means without its problems even there. *Schizophrenia, simple type,* is defined in the DSM–II as being "characterized chiefly by a slow and insidious *reduction* of external attachments and interests and by apathy and indifference *leading* to impoverishment of interpersonal relations, mental deterioration, and adjustment on a *lower* level of functioning [p. 33; italics added]." *Schizophrenia, childhood type,* by contrast, is "manifested by autistic, atypical, and withdrawn behavior; *failure to develop* identity separate from the mother's; and general unevenness, gross immaturity and inadequacy in development. These *developmental defects* may result in mental retardation, which should also be diagnosed [p. 35; italics added]." Whether or not it is fully justified, the main basis for the distinction between adult and child schizophrenia is that the adult disorder seems to involve a decline from an attained level of functioning, while the child disorder seems to represent a failure of development.

Empirical evidence on the continuity of a few disorders is available from studies in which children evaluated in clinics were diagnostically appraised again when they were adults. The absence of well-differentiated diagnoses of children has made it impossible to compare children's diagnoses with adult diagnoses in most cases, but descriptions of children's symptomatic behavior have been compared to the diagnoses they received as adults. For example, in one of the most thorough studies of this type Robins (1966) reported: "The shy, withdrawn personality sometimes thought to be predictive of schizophrenia did not predict it. . . . None of the [adult] schizophrenics had been described as a shy or withdrawn child, and only one-sixth as avoiding others or seclusive [p. 258]." On the other hand, Robins found considerable continuity between the presence of antisocial behavior in childhood and the diagnosis of sociopathic personality in adulthood.

SUMMARY

The purpose of this chapter has been to expose a number of issues that often create conflicts among views of psychopathology in children. One set of issues arises from "doing your own thing"—the personalities of different workers, the types and ages of children they deal with, the kinds of settings they work in, and their training and career orientations all influence the way they perceive particular children and the way they view the causes and remedies for pathology in general.

A second set of issues relates to the conceptual models that exist for psychopathology. These include the medical, psychodynamic, behavioral, nondirective, and sociological models, plus approaches that were described in terms of educational, statistical, and developmental models.

A third set of issues revolves around the fact that one is always confronted with a "whole child" in practice, but that selectivity is inevitably exercised in assessing the child's problems, communicating about them, providing treatment, and doing research. Some approaches espouse *idiographic* values, but all approaches basically seek *nomothetic* principles that can guide the understanding of particular individuals.

Several other issues were posed in terms of questions that are frequently raised about the nature of specific problems. One such question was whether behavior that deviates from standards of a dominant culture might actually be quite appropriate for a subculture the child lives in—a social class, ethnic, neighborhood, or family group. If a child's deviance is not clearly subcultural, it is important to judge the standards for the individual deviancy that parents and other adults are using for the child. These standards include the way in which children in general "ought" to behave, the way a particular child has previously behaved, and the way children of a given developmental level usually behave.

A second question, "What's wrong?", pertains to ways in which various approaches define pathology and how these definitions differ in emphasizing inference or observation. Differences in definitions influence the kinds of causes that are sought, the kinds of treatment preferred, and the outcomes that are considered solutions to a child's problems. The distinction between *performance* and *competence* made in psycholinguistics is useful for conceptualizing the relations between observed behavior and inferred characteristics.

The question of *etiology* was raised in two related forms: "Organic or psychological?" and "Heredity or environment?" The point was made that these questions are rarely valid in strictly either-or form since many disorders involve some combination of organic, psychological, hereditary, and environmental factors. A complete understanding of most disorders requires assessing the particular way in which these factors influence the *phenotypic* outcome.

The *prognosis* of a disorder, a judgment of whether it is curable or incurable, does not reflect intrinsic characteristics of the disorder itself, but the state of our knowledge about the disorder. Long-term follow-up studies are required to determine the outcome of disorders under differing conditions, and the development of new treatment methods may produce more favorable prognoses for many disorders.

The final question concerned the fact that all conceptual distinctions involve classification. The value of a particular classification system depends upon how effectively it can be used to group people according to attributes that are related to the goals of the workers using the system. The classification provided by the *Diagnostic and Statistical Manual of Mental Disorders* generally follows a medical model, but a variety of other conceptual principles are also evident in its definitions of disorders having no known physical cause. Viewing childhood problems as forerunners of specific adult disorders may exaggerate the similarities and obscure the differences between child and adult disorders.

SUGGESTED READING

Models for Psychopathology. Ullmann and Krasner (1969) add sociological considerations to a behavioristic approach to produce an updated behavioral formulation they call a "sociopsychological model." They also detail the historical and conceptual development of the medical and psychoanalytic models that contrast with their approach.

The "Whole Person" Issue.   More than perhaps any other view, Carl Rogers's nondirective approach to psychotherapy emphasizes the whole person.   Yet, Rogers has attempted to develop objective methods for assessing the aspects of the client's behavior and beliefs that change during psychotherapy (e.g., Rogers & Dymond, 1954).   In an article entitled "Persons or science?: A philosophical question" (1955), he attempts to contrast and reconcile the subjectivity he advocates in doing therapy with the objectivity needed for science and communication.   Virginia Axline's (1969) extension of nondirective therapy to children reflects the same dual regard for subjective acceptance of the child client as a whole person and for objectivity in the study of the therapeutic process.

Classification.   The scientific and methodological issues related to classification will be discussed in greater detail in Chapter 15, but perusal of the *Diagnostic and Statistical Manual of Mental Disorders* (American Psychiatric Association, 1968) is recommended to provide familiarity with the official vocabulary and categories presently in use.   A report by the Group for the Advancement of Psychiatry (1966) is also recommended for its consideration of the special problems of classifying childhood disorders and its proposal for classification of problems peculiar to children.   Robins's (1966) study, *Deviant Children Grown Up*, focuses primarily upon the relations between antisocial behavior in childhood and adulthood, but also includes good evidence on the relations between other child and adult disorders and a review of earlier studies.

4

Scientific Strategies

The word "science" tends in most people's minds to be associated with the physical sciences. Other disciplines that aspire to qualify as sciences have traditionally attempted to copy the principles that appeared to make the physical sciences so successful.

However, "science" (from Latin *scire* = to know) literally refers to "knowing," or obtaining knowledge. The particular kind of knowledge necessary to deal with psychopathology and the procedures for obtaining such knowledge may be quite different from what is required to put men on the moon, but in both cases the goal is to acquire knowledge that can be applied to reality. While there is a considerable amount of art and guesswork involved in any scientific endeavor, solutions to problems like those presented by psychopathology require knowledge that has moved beyond the personal hunches of a single investigator to the point where it can be communicated to and substantiated by others. The objective of this chapter is to sketch in some of the criteria and strategies for obtaining knowledge about psychopathology in children.

DISCOVERY AND CONFIRMATION

Philosophers of science (Popper, 1961; Reichenbach, 1938) have distinguished two general stages in scientific activity. One stage is called the *context of discovery* wherein ideas are generated in whatever subjective, intuitive, creative, or accidental way in which a person happens to think. Even the most completely formalized sciences have no rules for generating these inspirations and no standards of scientific respectability for the thought processes involved.

The sources of the ideas can include observations of real-world or laboratory phenomena, analogies from other fields, or various thoughts that an individual happens to combine into a guess about the way things might work in the real world. Such ideas may come suddenly, may result from a long period of mental trial-and-error, or may be progressively modified through the systematic gathering of data. The point is that the context of discovery refers to the aspect of science that is *subjective* and that guides the knowledge seeker in his choice of problems, the way he construes them, his speculations on solutions, etc., as contrasted with the systematic procedures required for the verification and communication of knowledge.

The other stage of science is known as the *context of confirmation* or *context of justification*. It is at this stage that the ideas emerging from the context of discovery are formulated in a testable manner and are compared systematically with phenomena in the real world. The particular form that hypotheses take and the procedures for testing them vary among sciences, but a minimum requirement for all ideas making a claim to scientific acceptability is that they have statable consequences that can be compared with some kind of real-world phenomena. The more consistently the stated consequences are corroborated by such phenomena, even if instruments or experts are required to observe them, the more confidence the ideas command.

The distinction between discovery and confirmation does not imply that the two processes are completely separate nor that they always occur in a temporal sequence. In practice there is constant interplay between observation, imagination, exploration, and the generation and testing of hypotheses. Subjectivity in the generation of ideas and objectivity in testing them play complementary roles in the creation of useful knowledge.

Context of Discovery

While all scientific endeavors are subject to the distinction between discovery and confirmation, the distinction is especially pertinent to the study of psychopathology. One reason for this is that the treatment of complex living persons is both a major source of hypotheses and the target for the knowledge acquired. Clinical experience and observations of patients lead to expectations about the kinds of characteristics that tend to occur together and about the causes for these constellations of characteristics. The term *"clinical method"* often refers to the subjective generation of hypotheses in this way, although "clinical method" may also refer to systematic probing or questioning and to procedures for testing hypotheses in the course of treatment.

The process of forming hypotheses through clinical observation and intuition is not qualitatively different from the generation of hypotheses in any branch of science. Special skills or sensitivity may be required for acute observation and effective questioning of patients, but the data obtained are subjectively combined into hypotheses. These hypotheses move into the context of confirmation only when they are stated in testable form and then tested.

Unfortunately, much of the literature on psychopathology fails to distinguish between the essentially subjective process of hypothesis generation and the objective confirmation of hypotheses. Clinical experience may be an important aid in generating hypotheses, but the special requirements for confirming knowledge, discussed below, make it unlikely that clinical experience alone can confirm the hypotheses it generates.

A second reason why the distinction between discovery and confirmation is especially pertinent to psychopathology is that the clinician, like the scientist, is at first presented with a welter of potential observations and the opportunity to develop hypotheses from them. If treatment is to be effective, the clinician, like the scientist, should gradually refine his hypotheses until they have statable consequences that he can compare with new observations of the patient's behavior. Hypotheses that are not borne out should be modified or dropped until the clinician reaches a conception of the problem that is sufficiently consistent with everything he knows about the patient to permit attempts at a solution. Trial-and-error may be involved in finding the correct combination of procedures for helping a particular person and for verifying that improvements are maintained. As with scientific theories, the clinician's formulation of an individual case is useful only when it has statable consequences that can be tested and can guide treatment.

Context of Confirmation

No knowledge is perfectly objective, because knowledge is always a construction of human minds that abstract and synthesize whatever they encounter. However, to be useful for understanding or modifying phenomena in the real world, knowledge must be related as accurately and systematically as possible to those phenomena. Confirmation of ideas about reality requires systematic procedures that vary from science to science. What follows is a discussion of criteria that guide the confirmation of knowledge in the behavioral sciences. Unless ideas evolved in the context of discovery are evaluated according to these criteria, we can never be certain that they are actually "discoveries" rather than just wrong guesses.

Testability. The first step in evaluating hypotheses is to state them in a testable form. If the hypothesis concerns the relationship between two characteristics, it is necessary to decide how the characteristics can be defined or described in a relatively objective manner. Since all characteristics can exist in degrees, even if the "degrees" are just "present versus absent," they are referred to as *variables*, i.e., attributes whose values may vary.

Objectivity as an ideal is best approached when a variable is given an *operational definition,* a definition in terms of a standard procedure or operation that specifies what value the variable has in a certain situation. For example, if a clinician wishes to test his impression that boys who are enuretic have "castrating mothers" (an observation frequently cited in psychoanalytic literature), he must decide what he will accept as a practical definition of enuresis and of "castrating mother."

Defining enuresis operationally is not difficult, but decisions do have to be made about how old a boy must be before his bed-wetting is considered a pathological behavior that may relate to having a castrating mother. The amount or frequency of bed-wetting also needs to be considered in the definition, as does the question of whether direct organic causes play a role.

For a practical test of his hypothesis, the clinician may decide that his definition of enuresis will be restricted to boys over six years old who wet the bed an average of at least twice a week in quantity great enough for an observer, e.g., the father, to notice wet sheets the next morning, and for whom no organic causes such as weak sphincter muscles can be found. The operational definition is thus a certain frequency of reports by the fathers of a particular class of boys. It could have been a physical measurement of the amount of urine emitted in bed, but in this case the fathers' reports may be precise enough and much less troublesome to instrument.

An objective definition of "castrating mother" is somewhat more difficult but not necessarily impossible. Since mothers who operationally fulfill the definition by having castrated their sons are, fortunately, rather rare, it is important to specify behavior or attitudes that justify the label "castrating mother." Having done this, one approach might be to have another clinician interview a group of mothers and decide which ones qualify for the label.

To avoid contaminating the second clinician's judgment, it is essential that he not know which mothers have enuretic sons. More refined versions of this approach might employ two or more clinicians to interview or observe the mothers and to pool their judgments about them. Further refinements would be to observe the mothers outside interview settings, to obtain observations from people who know them, to devise a test for determining whether a mother is castrating, etc. The point is that, before a fair test of any hypothesis can be made, the definitions of the variables it refers to must be specified as objectively as possible in the real world.

Assuming that the variables "enuresis" and "castrating mother" have been satisfactorily defined, the next step is for the clinician to decide whether he thinks there is a *causal* relationship between castrating mothers and enuresis or merely a correlation. Even if most enuretic boys are found to have castrating mothers, while nonenuretic boys do not, this correlation alone does not prove that the mothers' castrating behavior *causes* the enuresis. The causal relationship could conceivably be the opposite—e.g., because a boy is enuretic, his mother becomes castrating—or both enuresis in the boy and castrating behavior by the mother result from a third factor—e.g., they are both reactions to paternal punitiveness.

While the establishment of a consistent correlation between well-defined variables is an important first step in most research on psychopathology, knowledge useful for preventing or treating the pathology usually requires the identification of causal relationships. The ways in which various research techniques can aid in seeking causal relationships are discussed below, but first a few more criteria for guiding the confirmation of knowledge must be introduced.

Reliability. To insure objectivity, the definitions and measurements of variables must be *reliable*. One form of reliability is the degree of agreement between two observers about what value a variable has. In determining which mothers are castrating, *interobserver reliability* would be high if the independent judgments of two clinicians observing mothers at the same time frequently agreed on whether the mother was castrating. If their judgments did not frequently agree, one could not have confidence in their labels of "castrating" and "noncastrating."

Training is often required to obtain high interobserver reliability, but some kinds of complex behavior cannot be reliably judged even by observers with extensive training. Factors such as the observer's influences on the subject's behavior also contribute to unreliability. In these cases it is necessary to find other ways of defining variables or other means for measuring them. One means is to devise a test or an inventory of behavior consisting of a number of items all of which are believed to measure the variable of interest in slightly different ways. The characteristic being measured is defined conceptually as a *trait* and a total score on all the test items becomes the operational definition of the degree to which a person manifests the trait.

The construction of psychological tests has an art and science of its own, but there are two further forms of reliability that are especially pertinent to the use of tests. One is *test-retest reliability*. This is the degree of agreement between the scores a person gets on the same test when it is administered on two different occasions. Because people are always changing and because they are influenced in unpredictable ways by conditions at the moment of testing, it is important to know whether the score obtained on one occasion is likely to represent a persisting characteristic of a person or whether it is the result of momentary conditions. If there is a high correlation between the two scores people obtain when they take the test twice, one can have confidence that the scores are determined more by persisting characteristics of the individuals than by momentary conditions.

Sometimes an assessment of reliability cannot be obtained by retesting because the subjects are influenced by taking the test once, they try to find out answers between testings, etc. In these situations, an *alternate form* of the test is developed to measure exactly the same trait as the original form. Performance on the two forms is then correlated to provide an estimate of test-retest reliability. Although reliability between scores obtained on two occasions is most frequently considered in relation to tests, this form of reliability is just as important for data obtained by other means, such as interviews and observation.

Another kind of reliability is known as *internal consistency* or *split-half reliability*. This is the degree to which all items on a test or behavior inventory are measuring the same trait. Each item is designed to be a miniature test of the trait and the consistency among the items can be determined by correlating people's performance on half the items with their performance on the other half, e.g., performance on the odd-numbered items with performance on the even-numbered items. If internal consistency is low, the total score probably does not measure any unitary trait.

The value of a test is determined by how well it fulfills its intended function. Despite the importance of test-retest reliability and internal consistency, it is important that some tests be sensitive to major changes in people. For example, a test of neuroticism would not be very useful for studying the effects of treatment if it contained only items on which people's responses never change. Test characteristics such as reliability do not inhere in the test itself, but depend upon the responses of people to the items in the test. Effective testing requires continual redefining and balancing of objectives to obtain the best combination of procedures for increasing and objectifying knowledge, whether it is to be used for treating one person or for developing principles that can apply to many people.

Validity. The concept of *validity* is complementary to the concept of reliability. Whereas reliability refers to the agreement of a measurement or judgment with another measurement of the *same* kind, validity refers to the relationship of one measurement to a measurement of a *different* kind. Thus, one cannot appropriately ask, "Is Test X valid?" without specifying the measurement to which Test X is supposed to relate. A test or diagnosis of brain damage, for example, can only be called highly valid when it has been determined by some other method, e.g., autopsy, that brain damage does exist. Since behavioral science deals with many complex variables, validity often depends upon the agreement among several different standards, all of which are acknowledged to be imperfect.

The criteria for validity may also change as new methods are invented. For example, teachers' ratings of children's school performance constituted one criterion against which the Binet-Simon Intelligence Scale was originally validated. The scale was considered valid when scores on it correlated well with teachers' ratings. However, the scores on the test were found to be more reliable and to correlate more often with other kinds of "intelligent" behavior than did the teachers' ratings. Eventually, the intelligence scale and its later revisions became an important part of the criterion against which new intelligence tests were validated. Likewise, in developing a diagnostic method for schizophrenia, a researcher may begin with the pooled judgment of several clinicians as a criterion against which he validates his method, but if the method proves more reliable and more desirable in other respects than the judgments of clinicians, the method itself may become a criterion against which clinical judgments of schizophrenia are validated.

Control Groups. To be certain that a particular relationship exists between two variables, one must have a means for comparing the relationship at different values of the variables. The function of a control group is to permit such a comparison.

A finding that all enuretic boys have castrating mothers does not mean there is a correlation between the two variables unless it is also established that nonenuretic boys have noncastrating mothers. In this case, to establish a correlation between enuresis and castrating behavior by the mother, a minimum standard for comparison would be the mothers of boys who are not enuretic. To insure that any relation between enuresis and castrating behavior was not due to some extraneous third factor, the "control group" of nonenuretic boys and their mothers should be like the enuretic group in as many respects as are feasible. Otherwise, it is possible that all the enuretic boys came from an ethnic group, for example, where mothers are castrating but where enuresis is fully tolerated until age 12, while the control group came from an ethnic group where mothers are noncastrating but where strong incentives exist to cease bed-wetting by age five. On the other hand, if one wished to know simply whether enuresis were more frequent in the former ethnic group than in other groups, one would select a control group from *other* ethnic groups in order to establish a *base-rate* of frequency for enuresis against which the frequency for the first ethnic group could be compared.

Control groups are especially necessary for determining the effectiveness of treatment methods and for sorting out effective from noneffective components of a method. In these situations, where something is done to people, the control group should receive treatment as similar as possible to the treatment of interest except that what is believed to be the effective part of the treatment is omitted. The classical form of this procedure was developed in the testing of drugs. Half the patients receive a new drug while the other half receive a *placebo* (Latin "I shall please"), a drug that the researcher does not expect to be effective. Since the expectations of the researchers can also influence a patient's subsequent behavior, the people administering the drugs and observing the behavior, as well as the patients, are ignorant of ("blind to") who gets the drug and who gets the placebo. This is called a *double-blind* procedure.

Where the use of a control group is impractical or where no individuals are similar enough in important respects to constitute appropriate comparison groups, a person may be used as his *own control*. An example is where a base-rate for a child's symptomatic behavior, e.g., frequency of enuresis, is obtained before treatment and compared to his behavior during treatment. If the symptom subsides, treatment may be temporarily halted to see if the symptom reappears. If it does and can then be removed by reinstituting treatment, the treatment rather than the passage of time or other extraneous factors is probably responsible for the improvement.

THEORIES AND HYPOTHETICAL CONSTRUCTS

To a large extent, theories belong to the context of discovery. Virtually any system of ideas that provides conceptual order for observations of reality can be called a theory. However, a theory only becomes scientifically useful when it leads to testable statements about reality. Pretheoretical "frames of conceptual reference" are sometimes distinguished from relatively well-articulated theories, but a frame of reference is also valuable only insofar as it eventually leads to testable statements.

A theory itself can rarely be completely proved or disproved—it consists mostly of inferences. A deduction from these inferences may be tested and found to be true, but only a specific statement about reality is thereby confirmed. The principles embodied in the theory as a whole command confidence when many findings are consistent with them and few are inconsistent, yet the principles themselves are abstractions that cannot be empirically proved. By the same token, a theory is not disproved by the disconfirmation of specific deductions. It is possible that the deductions were not logically consistent with the theory or that the operations used to test the deductions were inappropriate. In practice, disconfirmation of a few specific statements often leads to further research guided by the original theory but the theory is modified to make it more consistent with the results actually found.

Although the more-or-less formal rules of science apply to objectifying and confirming knowledge, the intellectual life blood of science consists of ideas and theories. As Kuhn (1970) has shown, revolutions in the history of science have generally resulted from the creation of new modes of scientific thinking about a domain of problems rather than from empirical discoveries.

Hypothetical constructs are convenient fictions that are invented, usually as components of theories, to explain observations and to suggest new testable statements about reality. The scientist who introduces a hypothetical construct often believes it represents something real that he will be able to confirm when his methods are sophisticated enough.

The gene was a hypothetical construct that has now been isolated as a "real" entity (Shapiro, MacHattie, Eron, Ihler, Ippen, & Beckwith, 1969), although research in genetics still depends much more upon testable deductions from the well-refined hypothetical construct than on observations of genes themselves. The electron is another construct that has proven so powerful in suggesting testable statements that asking whether it "really" exists is hardly relevant. "Intelligence" and most other psychological traits are constructs that are useful insofar as they suggest testable relations among objectively specified variables. Disease "entities" are also hypothetical constructs that have proven useful, but they should not prevent us from continually trying to reconceptualize behavioral problems in ways that may prove more useful.

In short, theories and constructs are not open to confirmation or disconfirmation in the same way that specific statements about reality are. Theories and constructs are conceptual fictions that are useful insofar as they lead to the objectification of knowledge in the context of confirmation. One can rarely prove or disprove them, but one can choose among them according to their yield of confirmed statements.

CONCEPTS OF CAUSALITY

"What causes X?" is a nearly universal scientific question. However, what qualifies as a cause differs according to how one defines the phenomena of interest, how far back one wishes to go in the causal chain, etc. In the study of psychopathology, the question usually refers to the *etiology* (see Chapter 3) of undesirable behavior. As with all complex phenomena, it is rarely possible to think in terms of simple mechanical, one-to-one relations between antecedent causal factors and specific behavior. It is, therefore, helpful to distinguish the following four concepts of causality.

Necessary Condition

A necessary condition is a factor that must be present for a phenomenon to occur. Without that factor, the phenomenon cannot occur, but the factor may not by itself insure that the phenomenon will occur. In order for a gasoline engine to run, gasoline must be available to the carburetor. The availability of gasoline is, therefore, a necessary condition for the operation of the engine, although it does not insure that the engine will operate—many other conditions such as the presence of oxygen, intact ignition system, etc., are also necessary conditions. Analogously, it has been hypothesized (Meehl, 1962) that a certain genetic factor is a necessary condition for schizophrenia, but that the presence of this factor alone does not guarantee that a person will develop schizophrenia, because other factors such as experience also play a role.

Sufficient Condition

A sufficient condition is a factor whose presence will result in the phenomenon of interest *without* the contribution of any other factors. Thus, if the hypothesized genetic factor in schizophrenia *always* led to schizophrenia, regardless of environment, the genetic factor would be a *sufficient* condition for schizophrenia. However, the conclusion that the genetic factor is a sufficient condition does not mean it is also a necessary condition—perhaps schizophrenia could result from brain damage or poor environment in people without the genetic factor. The genetic factor, brain damage, and poor environment could thus each be a sufficient condition for schizophrenia, but none would be a necessary condition, i.e., a condition without which schizophrenia could not occur.

Necessary and Sufficient Condition

This is a factor which (1) *must* be present for the phenomenon of interest to occur, *and* (2) *inevitably* results in the phenomenon. If schizophrenia can occur *only* in the presence of a certain genetic factor and *inevitably* does occur when that factor is present, then the factor is both a necessary *and* sufficient condition for schizophrenia.

Contributory Causes

These are factors that contribute to a certain phenomenon but are neither necessary nor sufficient to create that phenomenon. If a genetic factor is a necessary but not sufficient condition for schizophrenia, brain damage may be a contributory factor that will bring about schizophrenia in people possessing the genetic factor. However, poor environment may be a separate factor that will also contribute to schizophrenia in people having the genetic factor but no brain damage.

RESEARCH METHODS

Methods for obtaining knowledge about psychopathology can be ordered along several dimensions. No one method is inherently better for all purposes than any other method and most problems are best approached with a combination of methods. Acquisition of knowledge that will be useful in preventing and treating psychopathology requires a convergence of viewpoints upon specific, testable questions. Likewise, defining and answering these questions requires a readiness to adapt methods to specific problems and a convergence of methods rather than the restriction of certain methods to the theoretical orientations that originally engendered them. What follows is a summary of some of the dimensions along which research methods in psychopathology vary and how these methods can complement one another.

Exploratory versus Hypothesis-Testing Research

An idealized model for research prescribes the *testing of hypotheses* that are of the form "If condition X prevails, then result Y will be observed," or "If X increases, then Y will increase." Condition X is regarded as an *independent variable,* one whose value is established at the start. Y is a *dependent variable,* a variable whose value is expected to *depend* upon the value of condition *X*. An example of the first version of the hypothesis would be, "If a boy's mother behaves in a castrating manner (condition *X*), then the boy will be enuretic (result *Y*)." An example of the second version, where the variables are quantified, would be, "The more castrating the behavior of a boy's mother, the more enuretic he will be." The procedure for testing these hypotheses would, as outlined earlier, involve choosing operational measures for the independent and dependent variables and then doing a systematic study to see whether enuresis in boys does vary with the castrating behavior of their mothers.

While the testing of clear-cut hypotheses of the form just described is an important goal of research, it is rarely the only goal. Development of useful theories and constructs requires systematic data-gathering that cannot be confined to hypotheses about relations between two discrete variables. Much research is designed simply to find out what relationships exist among a large number of variables, with no hypothesis more specific than "If relationships can be found among these variables, they will be valuable in formulating more precise research later."

Exploratory research of this type is never completely random because the researcher makes systematic judgments about what is likely to be important, how to define it objectively, how to study it, and how the outcomes might have significance in the long run. Good exploratory research requires as much sophistication about how knowledge can be confirmed as does strict hypothesis testing, but its value lies more in how it can help in building tentative ideas about reality than in finally confirming the testable statements to which these ideas lead.

An example of exploratory research related to the enuresis-castrating mother problem would be where a researcher thinks that mothers' behavior is probably related to enuresis in boys (this can already be considered a general hypothesis) and decides to get as broad a picture as possible of the potentially important differences in the behavior of mothers of enuretic and nonenuretic boys. He then develops interview and observation techniques for rating mothers' behavior on a large number of dimensions, e.g., warm–cold, directive–nondirective, interested–disinterested, castrating–noncastrating, etc., and trains observers to make the ratings. Since the relationship between mothers' behavior and enuresis is in question, the observers should not have their judgments contaminated by knowing which sons are enuretic. It will be noted that the researcher must thus confront many of the same problems as in testing the very specific hypothesis that castrating behavior by mothers is correlated with enuresis in their sons. However, if he had no specific hypothesis to begin with, broad-gauged exploratory research of this nature would be necessary.

In the long run, a broad-gauged exploratory effort might yield more information than the testing of a specific hypothesis. If you were testing only the hypothesis that castrating behavior is related to enuresis and failed to confirm the hypothesis, what would you do next? Well, if it had been just an isolated hypothesis not rigorously deduced from a theory or if you obtained no other information than the fact that the hypothesis was unsupported, the study would have dispelled a wrong impression about reality, but you would be starting from scratch again if you wanted to find out whether maternal behavior is related to enuresis. For this reason, effective research usually combines exploration with hypothesis-testing, either in the same study or in closely related studies. Thus, if you had systematically gathered information about other aspects of mothers' behavior, you might find relationships between mothers' behavior and sons' enuresis that would lead directly to new testable hypothesis or to a constructive revision of any theorizing that had led to the original hypothesis.

In a well-designed study, valuable and often unanticipated information can be gained whether or not a hypothesis is confirmed. Most well-designed studies have both an exploratory value and an hypothesis-testing value. The common thrust in both aspects of research is toward objectifying and systematizing knowledge through controlled observation.

Correlational versus Experimental Research

In a broad sense, all research is *correlational*, i.e., it seeks to identify and confirm correlations among variables. Yet, as illustrated in Fig. 4–1, a *correlation* between two variables does *not* imply that one *causes* the other. A correlation between mothers' castrating behavior and sons' enuresis could occur because both are determined by a third variable, e.g., they are reactions to punitiveness by the father. If this were the case, stopping mothers' castrating behavior would not end enuresis.

Another instance in which causality cannot be correctly inferred from a correlation between two variables is where the two variables may both

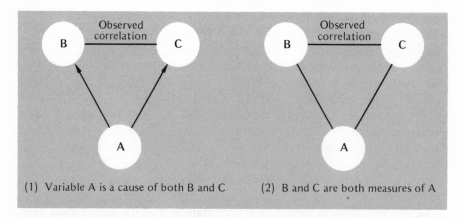

(1) Variable A is a cause of both B and C   (2) B and C are both measures of A

Fig. 4–1. Two situations in which a correlation between variables B and C does not result from a causal relationship between B and C.

be measures of another, more fundamental variable (Fig. 4–1). For example, a finding that children who get the best grades in a special educational program also get the best scores on a standardized achievement test does not prove the program caused the good performance on the achievement test. Good performance in both situations is likely to reflect good intellectual functioning and both variables would correlate highly with a measure of academic potential such as IQ.

A causal relation between the program and performance on the achievement test could only be inferred if it is demonstrated that the correlation between them was not due just to the fact that they both measure intelligence. One statistical technique for doing this is known as *partial correlation* (see McNemar, 1969, for details). This technique is designed to subtract or "partial out" of the correlation between two variables whatever components of their correlation with each other are due to their correlations with another measure. In the present example, an inference of causality could only be made if the correlation between performance in the program and on the achievement test remained high after the correlations they have with a measure of general intelligence were partialed out.

Another way of identifying causal relationships is through *experimental* research. Strictly speaking, experiments involve the *manipulation* of an independent variable in order to see if the value of a dependent variable really does depend upon the independent variable rather than upon some extraneous factor. Thus, to confirm the effect of a tranquilizer on hyperactive behavior, an experimenter can (using a placebo control and double-blind procedure) manipulate or vary the amount of tranquilizer administered (the independent variable) to see if the amount of hyperactivity (the dependent variable) varies accordingly.

For some problems, one cannot directly control the independent variable but can look for *natural experiments* in which all conditions are the same except the value of the independent variable. Unfortunately, in the study of human behavior there are hardly any natural conditions in which only one important variable is known to vary. For example, if one wished to study the early function of a part of the brain, one could search for young children who had suffered damage in that part of the brain to see how their behavior differed from undamaged children. However, whatever caused the damage is likely to have had unknown effects on other parts of the brain, as well as effects on the parents' behavior toward the child and his own view of himself. An attempt to control for these variables might be made by comparing the brain-damaged children not only with undamaged children but also with children who had a different kind of brain damage. Natural experiments in which the role of specific variables can be studied rarely offer the precision of experiments in which variables can be systematically manipulated, although they may be the only means available for studying some kinds of relationships.

There is no inherent contradiction between correlational and experimental approaches to research. Both seek to identify correlations among variables and to move from these correlations to inferences about causality. Well-confirmed correlations are often needed before the parameters of a problem can be sufficiently defined to permit effective experimentation. Findings of a relationship between a dependent variable and an independent variable that has been experimentally manipulated usually provide greater support for causal inferences because the probability that the relationship resulted from extraneous variables is less than in strictly correlational research. However, many important variables cannot be manipulated and experimental manipulation often requires creating unnaturally simplified situations in which other relevant variables are distorted. Since their advantages and disadvantages differ, experimental and correlational methods are best used to supplement one another.

Cross-sectional versus Longitudinal Research

Cross-sectional research involves taking a sample or "cross-section" of a phenomenon at one relatively limited point in time. What can be considered a limited point in time depends upon the phenomenon, but it is usually a period over which the children being studied are not expected to change much under normal circumstances. Thus, the clearest cases of cross-sectional research entail taking a sample of behavior, e.g., by means of a test, interview, or naturalistic observation, over a short period on a particular day. However, much research that entails taking samples of behavior from the same children on two or more occasions is also cross-sectional because the goal is to study variables at a specific point in the child's development rather than as they change over the course of development. Accordingly, giving an IQ test twice in the same week to assess its reliability would be a purely cross-sectional approach. Likewise, a study in which age norms are established for some behavior by sampling the behavior in five-, seven-, and nine-year-olds would be cross-sectional even though the goal might be to portray the behavior at ages five through nine.

By contrast, *longitudinal* research involves studying phenomena in the same individuals over a period during which the individuals are expected to change. The process of change itself and the relations between particular variables at different ages are of primary interest in such studies. Some questions cannot be fully answered without longitudinal research, e.g., questions of the form "Is early behavior X correlated with later behavior Y?" and "Is early event X a necessary and/or sufficient condition for later behavior Y?" There is no way to determine the relations between X and Y without data on the same individuals for both time X and time Y.

Retrospective Approach. If behavior or event X is objective enough and has been recorded objectively when it occurred, it may be possible to study the X–Y relationship *retrospectively* by finding people who show behavior Y and similar people who do not show Y and then checking to see which ones showed or experienced X when they were young. Since the record of past behavior or event X is being compared with current behavior Y at one point in time, the retrospective approach may fulfill the objectives of longitudinal research without requiring the researcher to wait from the occurrence of X until the later occurrence of Y.

Unfortunately, this very tempting strategy brings with it a number of special problems. The most obvious is that important early behavior and events are not objectively and uniformly recorded when they occur unless systematic procedures have been adopted for doing so. Parents' recollections of even such objective facts as the child's age when he first crawled, walked, and talked are notoriously inadequate and subject to distortion (Pyles, Stolz, & McFarlane, 1935; Robins, 1963). Studies have shown that early behavioral characteristics that might relate to later personality or pathology are still less likely to be recorded adequately or remembered by parents, even if such characteristics can be objectively defined (Burton, 1970; Yarrow, Campbell, & Burton, 1970).

A second problem with the retrospective approach to longitudinal goals arises where the Y behavior is pathological and comparisons are made with the early histories of people who do not currently show the Y behavior. If parents are the source of retrospective data, the knowledge that their child is now showing pathological behavior Y may cause them to focus on the pathological aspects of the early history more than do parents of children not currently showing pathology. This *pathological bias* in recalling the earlier life of people considered to be abnormal may sometimes be overcome by utilizing sources of information not influenced by knowledge of current status.

A third problem in retrospective research is that the selection of people currently showing behavior Y and those not showing the behavior may be subject to bias. For instance, suppose you begin with a sample of hospitalized adolescents diagnosed as "schizophrenic" (a summary term for a certain collection of Y behavior). If you find that the second-grade school records (uninfluenced by current status) of 80 per cent of the schizophrenics reported shyness while the records of 20 per cent of hospitalized sociopaths (the non-Y group) reported shyness, can you conclude that shyness is a much more frequent forerunner of schizophrenia than of sociopathy? The correlation may be a useful one, yet the possibility exists that schizophrenics who were not shy in second grade tend not to be hospitalized in adolescence—they may be in reform schools, may die young, or for other reasons may be unrepresented in the hospitalized sample despite the fact that they fit the Y category of "schizophrenia."

Prospective Approach. The best way to overcome these problems is through *prospective* longitudinal research in which children are selected when they are young and information is systematically collected about them as they grow older. Because of the amount of time and effort required to carry out prospective longitudinal studies, an exceptional amount of advance planning and preparatory research, which may be cross-sectional or retrospective, is necessary.

Collection of data as subjects are growing older does not automatically eliminate the problems encountered in retrospective studies. Just as *recent* impressions influence the recall of *previous* observations in a retrospective study, an observer's *first* impressions of a child may influence his *later* observations in a prospective study. Hence, observations at successive time periods should be made independently of one another, e.g., by using different observers at each time period, especially for behavior difficult to score objectively. The observational techniques themselves must also be carefully designed to avoid undue influence upon the child's behavior and development.

Another problem of prospective research is the formation and retention of appropriate samples of children. Since consistent parental cooperation and availability are needed, most long-term prospective studies have employed middle-class children from stable families. Findings on these groups cannot be readily generalized to children from non-middle-class or unstable families. Yet long-term studies can rarely be designed to obtain data on samples that are completely representative of a population. Even if it is practical to begin a study with very large samples of children who are representative of all important socioeconomic, geographic, ethnic, and urban-suburban-rural segments of a population, rates of attrition are likely to vary for the different segments, causing some groups to be underrepresented by the time the study is finished. Broadly representative samples are especially impractical for studing psychopathology because the frequency of most types of pathology is very low in the population at large. No generalizations about forerunners of schizophrenia can be made, for instance, from a sample of 200 children in which only one child eventually becomes schizophrenic.

Because of the difficulty in obtaining broad representativeness and because broadly representative samples yield relatively little information about pathology, samples are often chosen that are deliberately unrepresentative. Thus, to study the antecedents of schizophrenia, a sample of children who have a *high risk* of becoming schizophrenic may be chosen, e.g., the children of schizophrenic parents. Since even among high-risk children many will not become schizophrenic, comparisons can be made between the longitudinally collected information on those who ultimately become schizophrenic and those who do not. Exactly this strategy is being pursued in a longitudinal study of schizophrenia in Denmark, where national medical services make it possible to keep track of even the most unstable families (Mednick, 1970; discussed further in Chapter 12).

Longitudinal studies are sometimes begun under the illusion that everything important there is to know about a child can be recorded and then intercorrelated with later observations to answer all possible questions about development. Unhappily, this expectation is unrealistic because selectivity is unavoidable in the choice of observations and procedures for making them. Moreover, much important information about development can only be obtained by designing special situations for testing well-defined hypotheses, rather than by merely extracting information after-the-fact from observations of the child in natural settings.

Short-term Longitudinal Research. Where well-defined hypotheses about development are to be tested, it is sometimes possible to design a series of longitudinal studies each of which spans a relatively short period of time. These studies are then carried out simultaneously with groups of children of different ages. The results for each group are put together at the end of the study to portray a sequence of development that would have taken much longer to assess if only one age group were used.

A set of simultaneous interlocking longitudinal studies could be used, for example, to determine how thinking develops. One might set up a series of cognitive tasks appropriate for 5- to 7-year-olds, another series for 7- to 9-year-olds, and a third series for 9- to 11-year-olds.

Groups of children who were five, seven, and nine at the start of the study would then be tested over a period of three years. The five-year-olds would finish with the tasks that the seven-year-olds received first, and the seven-year-olds would finish with those the nine-year-olds received first. In this way, one could obtain in three years a picture of the sequence in which cognitive functions develop over a crucial seven years of the life span.

From what was learned about the 7-to-11-year period in the first three years, one could also devise variations and experimental manipulations to use with the youngest group as they aged from 7 to 11 over the next four years. A pathological comparison group, such as retarded children, could also be matched to the normal group for initial level of performance in order to see how their developmental course differed from the normals over a three-year period.

Complex strategies of this sort provide the powerful combinations of exploratory, hypothesis-testing, correlational, experimental, cross-sectional, and longitudinal research that are necessary for advancing the developmental study of psychopathology.

Extensive versus Intensive Research

Most research on psychopathology makes comparisons either among groups or of one group with itself at different times. When differences between groups or within a group over time are found on some variable, these differences are usually assumed to characterize each member of the group as well.

Suppose one group of hyperactive children receives a new drug while a control group of similar hyperactive children receives a placebo in a double-blind procedure. If observers' ratings show significantly greater decreases in hyperactivity for the experimental group, the drug is concluded to reduce hyperactivity and is marketed as a tranquilizer. This is an example of *extensive* research, where the procedures, evaluation of results, conclusions, and consequences are all *extended* over many individuals grouped by the attribute of hyperactivity they have in common.

Nearly all generalizations about behavior depend upon findings on groups of individuals, because no one individual is sufficiently representative to permit findings on his behavior to be generalized to the behavior of others. The number of important ways in which humans vary is so great that generalizations about a particular variable are justified only when findings are based upon a number of people *and* these findings substantially exceed the random variation among the people. The function of most statistical tests is to tell us whether a finding sufficiently exceeds random variation among people to justify the expectation that the finding would appear again if we assessed a group of similar people in a similar way. Thus, a "statistically significant" *probability (p)* value for a difference between two groups (e.g., $p < .05$) indicates that a difference this large could rarely occur by chance (e.g., five times in a hundred) and is, therefore, likely to be real and repeatable.

Although identification of *nomothetic* or general principles (see Chapter 3 on *nomothetic* versus *idiographic* approaches) is a goal of scientific research, the application of these principles to *individuals* is the goal in treating psychopathology. For this reason it is important to look closely at findings of group differences resulting from specific treatments. The finding of a statistically significant decrease in hyperactivity in a group of children receiving a new drug does not mean all children benefited uniformly. Some may have benefited greatly, causing the drop in mean hyperactivity scores for the whole group, while a few failed to benefit or actually became more hyperactive. By examining the scores of individuals, a researcher might be able to spot subgroups who responded to the drug in opposite directions. He can then seek out identifying characteristics for the subgroups showing different reactions and arrive at a more valid picture of the drug's effects according to who receives it.

The purest form of this strategy involves studying variation in one individual under various conditions. This *intensive* approach may be particularly appropriate for finding out what conditions are influencing a child's pathology and/or what treatment is most effective. Thus, a record of fluctuations in a child's behavior may be kept for several weeks. Relations between events in the child's life and changes in his behavior can then be observed and hypotheses formed about the conditions supporting his pathological behavior. These hypotheses can be tested by waiting to see if they predict the child's reactions to new events or by attempting to manipulate the events.

The effects of specific treatments, such as drugs, behavior therapy, or psychotherapy, may be tested by instituting the treatment to see if the pathological behavior decreases, by temporarily halting treatment to see if the pathology returns, and so on, until therapeutic benefits are fully confirmed. Statistical tests can also be used to compare the size of changes in behavior following treatment with random fluctuations before treatment.

While some form of this procedure should be standard practice for assessing the benefits received by a patient, it is rarely implemented except to demonstrate the general efficacy of a treatment method and is too seldom used even for this purpose. Although intensive procedures cannot completely replace extensive methods, wider application of them could change questions like, "Does psychotherapy work?" to more appropriate questions like, "Which combination of procedures benefits this child or category of children most?"

EXPLANATION, PREDICTION, AND CONTROL

Arguments sometimes arise about whether explanation, prediction, or control is the most appropriate general goal of science. Insofar as "science" refers to obtaining knowledge, explanation is probably the most universal goal. However, what constitutes an explanation varies with the subject matter. The ultimate value of most explanations depends upon their usefulness in solving problems.

Many explanations in applied physical science can be evaluated according to whether they yield direct control of important phenomena. Explanations in astronomy, on the other hand, almost never yield procedures for controlling phenomena, but they do yield precise predictions that can be tested against observable movements of the heavenly bodies. Explanations in paleontology yield neither procedures for control nor testable predictions about future events, but, if specific enough, they may be supported or contradicted by new discoveries of fossils.

Since the study of psychopathology is directed toward prevention and treatment, explanations in this field can be evaluated according to their potential for yielding predictions and control. The important predictions and control in psychopathology do not generally concern very specific everyday behavior. Instead, the predictive goals may take forms like the following: "Genotype X is much more likely to result in schizophrenia than is genotype Y." "Early experience X is much more likely to result in schizophrenia than is early experience Y." "Treatment procedures AB are more likely to help a person diagnosed schizophrenic than are procedures CD." "Child A is likely to become more seriously disturbed as he gets older unless treatment T is instituted now." "The parents of child A are not likely to cooperate in treatment X." "Child C's intellectual growth is likely to progress no further."

The goal of controlling behavior takes some of these forms: "In order to prevent schizophrenia in child X, implement procedures Y and Z." In order to help retarded child C use all of his intellectual capacity, provide him with educational procedure X." "To ameliorate child A's depression, provide treatment S."

Clinical versus Statistical Prediction

While methods of control (prevention and treatment) will be discussed in other chapters, procedures for making accurate predictions raise issues that are worth considering here. Meehl (1954) has formulated the prediction problem in terms of clinical and statistical approaches. The *clinical* or *case-study* method of prediction generally involves predicting an individual's behavior from a hypothesis about that individual's psychodynamics and an expectation about the course of environmental events. A clinician who interviews a person, studies his life history, and combines everything he knows about the person and the situation into a guess about the probable outcome is employing clinical prediction.

Statistical or *actuarial* prediction, by contrast, involves combining data according to a predetermined formula in order to obtain the probability of a certain outcome. The kind of data combined may be similar to that considered by the clinician, but the procedure for combining the data into a prediction consists of assigning the person to a class of people for whom the probabilities of various outcomes are known.

A long-used statistical procedure of this type is the table employed by actuaries to set life insurance rates. Insurance companies maintain precise tables of the proportion of people who die at each age each year. Within each age group, the tables are further broken down into other categories that relate to death rates, e.g., sex, occupation, health history. The life insurance premium for a person of a given age, sex, occupation, and health history is then set according to the probability that a person in his category will die within a given period. It is not necessary to know the reasons why particular individuals die—the accuracy with which this year's table portrays the distribution of next year's deaths is the test of the table's predictive power. Prediction from a table is not a precise statement of when a certain client will die, but a statement of the proportion of people showing his characteristics who will die each year.

A similar approach has been applied to the prediction of juvenile delinquency from tables based on such variables as psychological test scores, characteristics of a child's family, ratings of character traits, etc. (Glueck & Glueck, 1959, 1968). The long-term goal in identifying children having a high probability of becoming delinquent is to develop and focus preventive methods upon them. As with all statistical methods of prediction, the predictive accuracy of the Glueck prediction table cannot be known until it has been confirmed or *cross-validated* with a sample of children other than those upon whom the table was developed.

An essential difference between clinical and statistical approaches to prediction, as formulated by Meehl, is that statistical prediction requires precise specification of characteristics that relate to the outcome of interest in a large enough sample of people to permit probability statements about other individuals who share those characteristics. The source of the data may include clinical procedures such as interviews and trait ratings, but the data from these procedures must be specified precisely enough to permit categorizations in actuarial form.

Conversely, clinical prediction may employ data that are precisely categorizable (e.g., marital status) and even quantitative (e.g., IQ, age), but the data are combined and weighted subjectively by the clinician for the particular client. Unlike data from clinical judgments used for statistical prediction, clinical judgments used for clinical prediction do not have to be specified precisely enough for categorization in actuarial form. They can remain intuitions in the clinician's mind as he develops hypotheses from which to make his prediction.

Meehl (1954) surveyed studies that compared the accuracy of clinical and statistical predictions of behavioral outcomes. In virtually all cases, the accuracy of statistical prediction was equal or superior to that of clinical prediction.

Clinical versus "Mechanical" Modes of Data Collection

Another aspect of the prediction problem is that making accurate predictions depends as much on procedures for *obtaining* data about a patient as on procedures for *combining* the data. Data that consist entirely of a clinician's impressions can be distinguished from data that are collected in a more "mechanical" way, e.g., by administering structured psychological tests, by getting answers to specific factual questions, etc.

Since data collected in either the clinical or mechanical mode can be subjected to either clinical or statistical procedures for making predictions, and both kinds of data together can be combined either clinically or statistically, there are at least six separate strategies for prediction:

1. clinical data combined clinically;
2. clinical data combined statistically;
3. mechanical data combined clinically;
4. mechanical data combined statistically;
5. clinical and mechanical data combined clinically;
6. clinical and mechanical data combined statistically.

Thus, Strategy 5 is exemplified by a clinician who derives intuitions from an interview and scores from a test and then combines these clinical and mechanical data mentally to make a prediction. Strategy 6 is exemplified when a clinician's reports of his impressions are fitted into an actuarial table along with test scores to classify a patient and a prediction is made from the typical behavior of other people who have been classified that way. Table 4–1 presents the six separate strategies for making predictions.

Sawyer (1966) reviewed 45 studies in which predictions resulting from the six possible strategies could be compared. The figures in the cells of Table 4–1 are the percentages of studies in which one strategy surpassed the strategy in the cell next to it, plus one half the percentage of studies in which the two adjoining strategies were equal.

Like Meehl, Sawyer found that the statistical methods for combining data produced more accurate predictions than the clinical methods for combining data. The statistical methods were superior whether the data were clinical, mechanical, or both. Thus, in Table 4–1, the strategies designated in the right-hand column (cells 2, 4, and 6) were each superior to the corresponding strategies in the left-hand column (cells 1, 3, and 5). It is also clear from Table 4–1 that the mechanical mode of data collection was superior to the clinical mode whether the data were combined clinically or statistically (cells 3 and 4 versus cells 1 and 2).

TABLE 4–1

Strategies for prediction.[a]

Mode of data collection	Method of data combination	
	Clinical	Statistical
Clinical	1. Intuitive (20%)	2. Trait ratings (43%)
Mechanical	3. Subjective interpretation of scores (38%)	4. Actuarial (63%)
Both clinical and mechanical	5. Mental combination of intuition and scores (26%)	6. Actuarial combination of trait ratings and scores (75%)

[a] Figures in parentheses are the percentages of studies in which a prediction strategy was more accurate than the strategy in the cell next to it, plus one-half the percentage of studies in which the two strategies were equal.

NOTE.—Adapted from Sawyer (1966, p. 192). © 1966 by the American Psychological Association and reproduced by permission.

However, when the interface of each mode of data collection with each method of combining data is compared with every other one, it is evident that the most accurate predictions were made when data came from both clinical *and* mechanical modes, but were combined statistically, i.e., the most accurate predictions occurred in cell 6. It thus appears that the judgments of clinicians can improve the accuracy of prediction over pure mechanical data, but only when they are put into a well-focused form amenable to statistical methods of combination.

It should be noted that none of the studies in Sawyer's review dealt with young children, although 13 dealt with college applicants or students, 10 with military servicemen, and two with delinquents or former delinquents. The lack of studies comparing prediction strategies for young children's behavior reflects the general lack of systematic methodological research on child psychopathology more than any intrinsic difference in the prediction problems for child and adult behavior.

Despite the superiority of statistical methods of prediction, even these are still quite inaccurate, inconsistently used, and applied to relatively narrow problems. Moreover, there are situations for which relevant data cannot be collected on groups large enough to permit statistical predictions about the behavior of new individuals. Consequently, both clinical and statistical approaches to prediction deserve much further research and development. Constant testing of predictions against actual outcomes is the most fundamental requirement for improving both approaches.

SUMMARY

The objective of this chapter was to introduce criteria and strategies for obtaining knowledge about psychopathology in children. Two stages in scientific activity were distinguished: the *context of discovery,* wherein ideas are generated, and the *context of confirmation,* wherein ideas are put in a form subject to testing and then are tested in the real world. A parallel was drawn between the scientist in the context of discovery and the clinician forming impressions of patients. In both cases, the hypotheses generated command confidence insofar as they are confirmed by objective comparison with observable phenomena.

The following criteria guide the confirmation of knowledge: *testability* of hypotheses—best achieved when variables are *operationally defined; reliability* of observations, including *interobserver* reliability, *test-retest* reliability, and *internal consistency; validity* of observations with respect to other kinds of observations of the same variables; and establishment of relationships between variables by observing the variables when they have different values, e.g., through the use of *control groups* or the use of individuals as their *own controls.* Proper use of controls often requires *placebo* and *double-blind* procedures.

While confirmation of statements about reality is a major scientific goal, *theories* provide conceptual order for observations. Theories themselves can rarely be proved or disproved, but choices can be made among them according to their yield of confirmed statements. *Hypothetical constructs* are theoretical fictions that are invented to explain observations and to suggest new testable statements about reality.

Causes of complex phenomena such as psychopathology can seldom be conceived in terms of simple one-to-one relations of mechanical cause and effect. Instead, causes can be thought of in terms of *conditions* that are *necessary, sufficient, necessary and sufficient,* or *contributory* to the occurrence of pathology.

Research methods in psychopathology can be ordered along the following dimensions: *exploratory* versus *hypothesis-testing; correlational* versus *experimental,* according to whether *independent variables* are manipulated; *cross-sectional* versus *longitudinal,* including *retrospective* and *prospective* variants of longitudinal approaches; and *extensive* versus *intensive,* according to whether variation extending across individuals or within single individuals is studied.

Prediction and control (i.e., prevention, treatment) are both goals in the study of psychopathology. Comparisons of *clinical* and *statistical* methods of prediction and clinical and "mechanical" modes of data-gathering have indicated that statistical prediction and mechanical data collection generally produce more accurate predictions than do purely clinical methods. However, no approach is yet very accurate and much further refinement of prediction procedures is needed.

SUGGESTED READING

Scientific Thinking. Thomas Kuhn's short book, *The Structure of Scientific Revolutions* (1962; second edition, 1970) has been acclaimed for its analysis of the way major changes in scientific thinking have historically come about. Kuhn's portrayal of the precedence that theories or conceptual "paradigms" often take over facts is especially pertinent to the study of psychopathology. The need for theory and the risks of overcommitment to theories are both well documented.

Strategies for Developmental Research. Kessen's chapter in the *Handbook of Research Methods in Child Development* (Mussen, 1960) presents a detailed overview of principles and methods of developmental research design. The same volume contains a number of other useful chapters on general methods and specific procedures for studying development. Detailed analyses of concepts of personality structure and development and their implications for research are offered by Emmerich (1968).

Clinical Assessment and Research. The fact that discussions of developmental and clinical research must be sought in separate sources reflects the lack of attention that the systematic study of developmental psychopathology has received. However, three books dealing with issues pertinent to clinical research may suggest to the student ways of synthesizing developmental and clinical approaches. One, *Research Design in Clinical Psychology and Psychiatry* (Chasson, 1967), contains detailed comparisons of extensive and intensive research designs that may also be relevant to cross-sectional versus longitudinal approaches. The second, *The Clinical Study of Social Behavior* (Peterson, 1968), confronts general issues in assessing disordered behavior including examples from child and family pathology. The third, *Introduction to Research in Psychopathology* (Maher, 1970), provides a survey of specific research techniques.

Clinical vesus Statistical Prediction. Meehl (1954) first formulated the issue in the terms that were to become the focus of extended controversy. Gough (1962) reviewed methods, distinctions, and evidence relating to the controversy, while Sawyer (1966) extended the analyses beyond methods for combining data to methods for collecting data. Holt (1970) presents clinicians' arguments against conclusions favoring statistical methods of prediction.

5

Genetic Factors

A dichotomy is too often made between "psychological" and "biological" views of behavioral development. However, the most prominent psychological views of development are all rooted in biological assumptions. Before considering genetic factors in behavior, it is important to recall some biogenetic aspects of the psychoanalytic, learning, and Piagetian theories of psychological development and to consider the relevance of the ethological viewpoint.

VIEWPOINTS ON HUMAN BEHAVIORAL DEVELOPMENT

Psychoanalysis

Freud's concept of an innate, organically based motivational force has been a cornerstone of psychoanalytic theory from its beginning. His original German word for the psychological representation of this force within the person was *Trieb* (drive), but it was widely translated as "instinct." Confusion has arisen because, outside psychoanalysis, the term "instinct" refers to innately determined behavior patterns, while the psychoanalytic term "instinct" refers to motivation rather than to behavior. Among psychoanalysts the term *instinctual drive* is now replacing "instinct" for designating inborn motivational forces (cf. Moore & Fine, 1968).

The two main classes of instinctual drives are the *libidinal* (sexual) and *aggressive* drives. The motives they represent are assumed to be organically based, but psychoanalysis deals with them primarily in terms of *psychic energy*, an hypothetical motivational force in mental functioning considered to be analogous to physical energy. *Psychodynamics* refers to the channeling, directing, and distribution of this energy within the personality.

Although he never detailed the mechanisms, Freud appears to have believed that the sequence of psychosexual development was largely determined by biological rather than cultural factors. Environmental influences were often invoked to explain particular outcomes of each phase, but the biological maturation of the individual, the changes in his instinctual drives, and various constitutional attributes were assumed to determine the nature of the phases.

In current psychoanalytic theory, certain functions of the ego are assumed to follow biological courses of development relatively uninfluenced by the vicissitudes of instinctual drives. These functions thus have *primary autonomy* from the instinctual drives. The autonomous ego functions include perception, motility (walking, use of hands, etc.), intention (planning, anticipation), thinking, and language. Their rate and final level of development are assumed to depend upon specific biogenetic determinants rather than upon the successive rechanneling of instinctual drives (Moore & Fine, 1968).

Learning Theories

There are numerous learning theories, but a general characterization can be made of some of the biological assumptions they have in common. One assumption is that some important behaviors are not shaped solely by environmental influence. These behaviors consist of reflexes that are available at birth or become available through maturation. Just as learning is viewed as a process whereby the individual adapts himself to his particular environment, reflexes are viewed as being inborn adaptive procedures that have evolved in each species through natural selection.

The sucking reflex is of obvious importance for infant survival, but there are also numerous lesser known reflexes that have less obvious survival value or that had survival value at earlier periods in the evolution of the species (see Kessen, Haith, & Salapatek, 1970). Reflexes are especially emphasized in Soviet psychology where the Pavlovian study of learning is known as *reflexology* because it is concerned primarily with the conditioning of reflexive responses.

Learning theories also recognize the existence of innately determined complex behavior patterns (e.g., instincts), but tend to minimize their role in order to focus upon the aspects of behavior believed to be shaped by the environment. Even Watson (1924) acknowledged, for example, that human infants innately fear loud sounds and loss of support, but he maintained that all other fears are built up through learning as a result of the pairing of stimuli with the innately feared stimuli or with painful experiences.

Like psychoanalysis, learning theories assume that motivation stemming from organic needs plays a central role in behavioral development. Hunger, thirst, sex, and various forms of physical discomfort have been commonly postulated as sources of *primary drives*. According to learning-theory views, most early learning consists of acquiring responses that will reduce the intensity of primary drives. Reduction of discomfort by a response *reinforces* the response, i.e., increases the probability that the response will be made again in a similar situation. Recent interest in exploration and other forms of behavior not readily explained by reduction of organic discomfort has led to the postulation of other innate motives such as curiosity (Berlyne, 1960) and competence or "effectance" (White, 1959).

Another biological assumption shared by most learning theories is that the basic laws of learning are similar for many species. Thus, for example, the effects of reinforcement schedules upon eyelid conditioning in rabbits are expected to be generalizable, at least in principle, to other kinds of behavior in rats, pigeons, and humans. This assumption reflects a belief in the continuity from species to species of the biologically based adaptive function of learning.

Piagetian Theory

Piaget's goal has been to understand the nature of human knowledge by identifying the successive procedures children develop for obtaining knowledge. His assumptions and his theoretical strategies reflect his training as a biologist. He maintains that the child's procedures for obtaining knowledge are techniques for adaptation to the environment. He regards well-organized mental procedures (cognitive structures) as functioning like the physical structures of an organism. Just as physical structures have specific functions within the organism, cognitive structures are mental procedures for dealing with specific kinds of information and problems.

A child's grasp of general concepts or principles requires cognitive structures that consist of more than accumulated knowledge of facts. For example, understanding arithmetic requires not only knowledge of a fact like "One plus one equals two," but also an understanding of number that permits deductions like, "Five is one more than four," "Five can be obtained by adding two and three, two and one and two, one and one and one and one and one," etc. The child who has the appropriate cognitive structures for quantity need not be taught all the specific ways in which five can be divided up before he can do arithmetic involving the number five. Likewise, the existence of cognitive structures is evidenced by the child's generalization of a set of procedures to very different concrete objects—he can do arithmetic involving five oranges, sticks, people, pennies, or marks on a paper with equal facility because the cognitive structures can be applied to a wide range of data, rather than being merely the sums of responses to particular stimuli.

Specific Heredity. The means by which cognitive structures develop in the human individual are assumed to be much the same as the means by which physical structures and simple adaptive behavior patterns develop. The genes of each species carry codes or basic plans for the structures that are characteristic of that species. The *specific heredity* of humans, for example, does not include wings, sense organs for detecting infrared light, or fins for swimming, but it does include equipment for walking upright, exercising precise control over vocalization, developing cognitive structures for quantity, etc.

General Heredity.　In addition to genetically based characteristics belonging to a given species, all organisms inherit qualitatively similar modes for adapting to the environment. This *general heredity* can be viewed in terms of two complementary modes for adapting—*assimilation* and *accommodation*. *Assimilation* refers to the tendency of organisms to modify their environments in order to enhance their own functioning. A physiological example is the process of eating, whereby an organism enhances or maintains his functioning by extracting nutriments from food. At the level of intellectual functioning, assimilation is exemplified by the young child at play.　By means of pretense he assimilates objects and situations to his own fantasy—an appealing example of playful assimilation is Piaget's (1951) 16-month-old daughter gleefully pretending that the tail of her toy donkey is a pillow on which she is going to sleep.

Accommodation refers to the tendency of organisms to change themselves in order to adapt to aspects of the environment.　In digestion, the stretching of the stomach as it receives food is an accommodatory process coordinated with the assimilatory processes of extracting nutriment. An elementary behavioral example of accommodation is the infant's progressive modification of his sucking reflex until it is applied directly to the nipple rather than to areas surrounding it.　At a higher level, accommodation is exemplified by the child imitating another person, i.e., making his behavior conform to that of a model in the environment.

While play and imitation are behaviors in which assimilation and accommodation can be seen in relatively pure forms, successful adaptation requires a constant coordination of assimilatory and accommodatory procedures.　Some maladaptive behaviors, such as psychotic thinking, may represent extreme tendencies to assimilate environmental input to the individual's ways of construing it, while excessive conformity may be regarded as a predominance of accommodation.

Factors Contributing to Intellectual Development.　Piaget distinguishes four classes of determinants for human intellectual development. One is the *organic maturation* of the individual, depending largely upon genetically transmitted plans, but also requiring physical nutriment and environmental stimulation.

A second class of determinants can be labeled *experience*. This is the child's observation of and interaction with a variety of environmental situations. Piaget's conception of experience is one of an active partnership in which the child does things to the environment in order to see what will happen. "What happens," i.e., how the environment reacts to what the child does, provides the child with new information about the effects of different kinds of actions.

The third class of developmental determinants can be termed *social interaction and transmission*. This includes the inadvertent and deliberate teaching done by adults and older children, the transmission of information by language and example, and the various guides to concept formation that originate in interpersonal interaction rather than in the child's spontaneous observations of the physical world.

The fourth component of intellectual development is the hardest to describe, but it is the one of greatest interest to Piaget. He believes that knowledge does not consist of photographlike mental reproductions of the environment nor is its form innately determined. Instead, the child *constructs* knowledge by assembling impressions from the environment according to procedures or structures he already possesses. The outcomes of this process are progressively changing as the child faces and creates new situations to which he must apply and adapt his cognitive structures.

This fourth component of development, called *equilibration,* is the process of creating new levels of understanding that take into account new problems of which the child has become aware. It is a self-regulating process whereby the child progressively matches his structures to new input, becomes aware of disparities, modifies his structures, and eventually arrives at a more general understanding. Structures that are flexible and abstract enough to be consistently applicable to many new situations regardless of specific concrete content are said to be *equilibrated*. In other words, these structures are capable of construing many situations according to general principles.

Piaget's concept of the equilibration process has a theoretical status different from his concepts of maturation, experience, and social transmission. The latter three factors constitute necessary but not sufficient conditions for development. Equilibration, by contrast, is the process by which the child brings together what he gains from these other sources in order to create new levels of adaptation for himself. It is a biologically based regulatory process found in some form in all living things.

Animal Ethology

It is clear that all three of the major theories of human behavioral development employ biological assumptions and concepts in important ways. A fourth viewpoint, that of the animal ethologists (cf. Hess, 1970; Lorenz, 1965; Morris, 1967; Tinbergen, 1964), is also becoming ever more relevant to the study of human behavioral development, both normal and abnormal. *Ethology* is the study of the natural unfolding of animal behavior. Ethological studies generally begin with observations of animal behavior in its natural environment, but often move to experimental manipulation of environmental conditions in order to identify precisely the stimuli responsible for eliciting behavior patterns believed to be genetically programmed.

Ethologists have demonstrated intriguing phenomena in numerous species, including imprinting in fowl, fighting and courtship rituals in fish, and social organization in insects. Theoretical extrapolations to human behavior have frequently been made, but, except for important patterns of mutual mother-infant stimulation (Ainsworth 1969; Ainsworth & Bell, 1970; Bowlby, 1969), there is as yet little clear evidence that much complex human behavior can be cast into the models derived from other species. However, ethological methods are beginning to be applied to the study of more complex child behavior, both normal and abnormal (Hutt & Hutt, 1970; McGrew, 1972).

The discovery of innately determined behavior patterns in one species seldom justifies assuming that apparently analogous behavior in other species has similar determinants and functions. Direct extrapolation of animal findings to humans deserves special skepticism. Nevertheless, the inevitable importance of biological functions in human behavior means that ethological viewpoints and research should be applied to humans. Hess (1970) states it as follows:

Fundamentally, it is the ethological *attitude* which is most valuable in the analysis of human behavior, rather than merely the use of particular *terms* used by ethologists. An investigator does not need to be an ethologist or even to have had any direct contact with ethology to make behavior analyses which are congruent with ethological thinking. He merely must approach his subject with a concern for the *complete* context in which observed behaviors occur, including biological bases and adaptive functions [p. 24].

An ethological attitude is helpful in integrating the major psychological views with biological conceptions. Psychoanalysis, learning theory, and Piaget all maintain that behavioral development is part of the process whereby organisms adapt biologically to their environments. They agree in principle that particular strategies of adaptation occur because they are the ones that have proved successful during the course of evolution. However, the plausibility and heuristic value of the specific assumptions made by each psychological view should be evaluated in the light of current knowledge about relations between behavior and biological factors.

Since considerable elaboration and rearticulation of concepts within each of the psychological viewpoints is possible, and since they differ in the aspects of adaptation that they emphasize, none is likely to be disproved by biological evidence. Yet it is important continually to reassess each viewpoint's compatibility with new biological knowledge and to seek ways of synthesizing knowledge about behavior with knowledge about organic factors like those about to be discussed.

MECHANISMS OF GENETIC TRANSMISSION

Knowledge of genetics is playing an ever-expanding role in the study of normal and pathological development. What follows is a brief introduction to concepts that are necessary for understanding general approaches to research on genetic factors as well as some specific disorders for which the genetic mechanisms are well documented.

Chromosomes

The nucleus of every cell in the human body contains tiny threadlike bodies known as *chromosomes* (from Greek *chroma* = color, because they stain selectively within the cell). There are 46 chromosomes in the normal human body cell, arranged into 23 pairs. Chromosomal studies are made by photographing the chromosomes through a microscope, cutting each chromosome out of photographic enlargements, and arranging these into pairs in a standard order according to their lengths and other features of their appearance. This arrangement is known as a *karyotype*. Chromosomal abnormalities in a given individual can be detected by comparing the karyotype made from one of his cells with standardized normal karyotypes of his species. Figure 5–1 portrays a normal human karyotype.

Mitosis. When a typical cell of the body is preparing to reproduce itself to form another body cell, each of its 46 chromosomes doubles and then divides in half, resulting in two groups of 46 chromosomes each. The two groups of 46 chromosomes then migrate to opposite sides of the cell, a wall forms between them and the cell splits, resulting in two new cells, each containing one group of 46 chromosomes identical to the original group of 46. The splitting of the 46 chromosomes to form two new cells each having 46 chromosomes, is known as *mitosis*.

Meiosis. Sex cells or *gametes*—sperm cells in the male and egg (ovum) cells in the female—are not produced in the typical way by the typical kind of body cell. Instead, gametes are produced by special cells located in the gonads and known as *germ cells*. The process by which germ cells produce gametes differs from mitosis in that there is no doubling and splitting of the 46 chromosomes. On the contrary, the members of each of the 23 pairs of chromosomes in the germ cell separate from one another, each set of 23 migrates to the opposite sides of the original cell, a wall forms between them, and two new cells result, each of which has just 23 of the original chromosomes. This process of forming gametes—new sex cells containing just *half* the original number of chromosomes—is called *meiosis*.

Genes

Chromosomes can be readily seen with a microscope, but genes, the actual units of hereditary transmission, are much tinier. Thousands of genes are presumed to be arranged in a linear manner along each chromosome. Until a single gene was isolated through elaborate biochemical procedures (Shapiro et al, 1969), the gene was, strictly speaking, not a "thing" with directly observable properties, but a conceptual fiction or

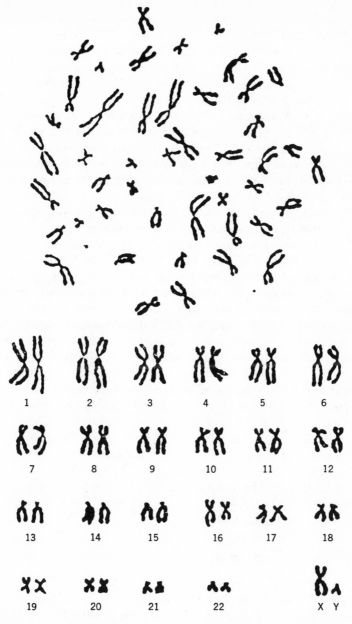

Fig. 5–1. A photomicrograph of the chromosomes in a normal human cell (above) and their arrangement into a standard order known as a *karyotype* (below). Note that the members of the twenty-third pair of chromosomes (lower right-hand corner) differ from one another—since this is the cell of a male, one of these chromosomes is a male (Y) chromosome, while the other (X) chromosome is like that found in the cells of females as well as males. From Penrose (1961).

hypothetical construct that was extremely useful for understanding hereditary transmission. Most genetic theory and research will continue to rely
on well-defined hypothetical properties of genes for a long time to come.
This is true for levels of conceptual analysis pertaining to the physical
locations, movements, activation, and alterations of genes, as well as to
levels of analysis pertaining to the transmission of *phenotypic* traits, the
observable characteristics of the organism.

As deduced by Watson and Crick (1953), a gene is composed of deoxy-
ribonucleic acid (DNA) whose molecule is like two chains coiled around
each other in the shape of a double helix. Structures like the rungs of a
ladder join the two chains in a form resembling a spiral staircase. There
is well-established evidence in some species for the existence of nonchromo-
somal genes composed of DNA but located outside of cell nuclei (Sager,
1965). However, virtually all knowledge of human genetics is based upon
assumptions about genes located on the chromosomes.

When chromosomes are doubling during mitosis, the two chains of the
DNA molecule evidently unwind while portions of each runglike structure
separate. A portion of each rung remains with each of the chains. From
raw materials available in the cell nucleus, a new chain is formed along the
ends of the rungs remaining with each original chain of the DNA molecule.
The result is two new and complete DNA double-helix molecules just like
the original one. Each of the new molecules becomes part of a different
one of the two new chromosomes resulting from mitosis.

The information coded in the DNA molecule must at some point be
transmitted to the location in a cell where it is to set in motion biochemical
chain reactions. This transmission is accomplished in two steps. First, the
information from the DNA molecule is transcribed onto a ribonucleic acid
(RNA) molecule which is molded into a form much like one of the two
helical chains of the DNA molecule. Second, this *messenger RNA* molecule
enters the region of the cell where the genetic information it carries is used
in protein synthesis. The chemical reactions regulated by the messenger
RNA molecules ultimately determine what organs will arise from particular
cells and how these organs will function.

Creation of a New Individual

When a sperm penetrates an ovum at conception, the 23 chromosomes
contained in the sperm's nucleus combine with the 23 chromosomes in the
ovum's nucleus to form 23 pairs. The normal fertilized ovum, known as
a *zygote,* thus has a full complement of 46 chromosomes. Each pair of
chromosomes contains one member from each parent. Miraculous as it
may seem, the members of each pair of chromosomes line up beside each
other in such a way that each gene on each chromosome is next to the
gene on the chromosome from the opposite parent that contains the in-

formation relevant to exactly the same trait. The different variants of genes that control a particular trait and occupy corresponding loci on the paired chromosomes are called *alleles*. For example, one allele, or variant, of the gene for eye color causes blue eyes, while a different allele causes brown eyes. The eye-color allele from the father and that from the mother are located opposite each other in two adjoining chromosomes of the off-spring.

Mendel's Laws

The classical genetic principles formulated by Gregor Mendel in 1866 apply to genetic traits for which there are only two possible alleles and the alleles directly influence the phenotypic traits according to patterns of dominance and recessiveness. If, for example, a child inherits from his mother the allele for blue eyes and he also inherits the blue-eyed allele from his father, he will be *homozygous* for eye color—both alleles are the same, so the *zygote* is *homogeneous* with respect to the genes for eye color. The child will have blue eyes and can pass only an allele for blue eyes to his own offspring.

If the child mates with a person who has alleles only for brown eyes, that person can pass only a brown-eyed allele to their child. Since this child receives the blue allele from one parent and the brown allele from the other, he is *heterozygous* for eye color—the alleles are different, so the *zygote* is *heterogeneous* with respect to his genes for eye color.

According to Mendel's laws, one of the alleles will dominate over the other in the phenotypic expression of the heterozygous genotype for eye color. The dominant allele is generally represented with a capital letter, while the recessive allele is represented with a small letter. Brown (B) happens to be dominant over blue (b). Consequently, the heterozygous (Bb) child of the homozygous blue-eyed parent (bb) and the homozygous brown-eyed parent (BB) will have brown eyes. Yet, since half his chromosomes carry the blue allele and half carry the brown allele, this Bb offspring will pass a chromosome carrying the blue allele to approximately half his own offspring. The phenotypical eye color of these offspring will be determined by whether they receive a blue or brown allele from their other parent, but the offspring who receive the brown allele will have brown eyes, no matter what allele they receive from their other parent.

Figure 5–2 diagrams this sequence of Mendelian genetic transmission. Note that whenever one or both parents are heterozygous for a trait, as frequently occurs, their children are likely to inherit different genotypes for the trait. Moreover, because of the astronomical number of different gene combinations possible from two parents, the probability is virtually zero that two siblings will be exactly the same in all genes unless they come from the same zygote, i.e., are identical twins.

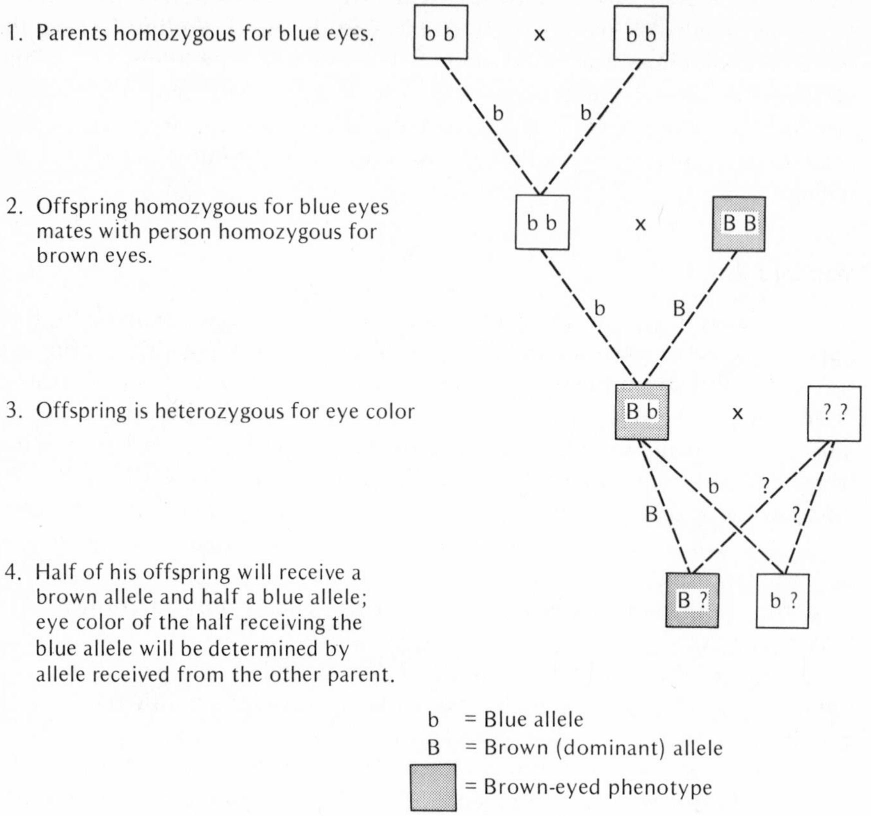

1. Parents homozygous for blue eyes.

2. Offspring homozygous for blue eyes mates with person homozygous for brown eyes.

3. Offspring is heterozygous for eye color

4. Half of his offspring will receive a brown allele and half a blue allele; eye color of the half receiving the blue allele will be determined by allele received from the other parent.

b   = Blue allele
B   = Brown (dominant) allele
☐   = Brown-eyed phenotype

Fig. 5–2. Illustration of Mendelian principles of genetic transmission.

Exceptions to Mendel's Laws

While Mendel's laws have proven enormously powerful in predicting and controlling the heredity of many traits in many species, there are numerous exceptions for which new principles have been proposed. The exceptions to Mendel's laws are especially important for understanding genetic contributions to human disorders since these contributions rarely seem to conform precisely to Mendelian formulas. Because several of the exceptions involve deviations from the principle of dominance–recessiveness, the different alleles of a gene are often designated with an unprimed and primed letter (e.g., A and A') rather than with capital and small letters. This emphasizes the point that neither allele necessarily dominates the other.

Partial Dominance. One kind of exception to Mendelian principles concerns the absence of complete dominance by one allele over another. For some traits, one allele is only *partially dominant* over the other allele.

That is, an individual who inherits both the recessive and dominant alleles (AA') for a trait will be phenotypically more like the dominant (A'A') version of the trait than like the recessive version (AA), but he will not be phenotypically as extreme in that trait as someone who inherits only dominant alleles.

Additivity. Another deviation from the simple dominant-recessive model occurs with alleles that have *additive* effects. In these cases each allele (A and A') contributes a different degree of the phenotypical trait. The strength of a phenotypical trait of a heterozygote (AA') will be halfway between the strength for a homozygote both of whose alleles are of one type (AA) and the strength for a homozygote both of whose alleles are of the opposite type (A'A'). For example, it has been hypothesized that height is influenced by alleles having additive properties. Thus, a person who inherits one tall allele and one short allele will measure halfway between persons who inherit two short alleles (AA) and those who inherit two tall alleles (A'A').

Figure 5–3 portrays the different possible relationships between genotypes and phenotypes that would be expected for classical *dominant* and *recessive* alleles, for *partially dominant* alleles, and for alleles having *additive* effects. Three genotypes are listed on the horizontal axis according to the number of A' alleles present (0, 1, or 2). Phenotypic values are presented on the vertical axis, with 0 representing the value expected for an AA genotype and 2 the value for an A'A' genotype. It can be seen from

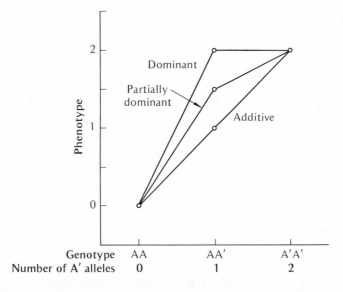

Fig. 5–3. Relationships of phenotype to genotype for alleles having dominant-recessive, partially dominant, and additive characteristics. From McClearn (1970).

the figure that traits for which partial dominance and additivity occur are often manifest in *degrees,* rather than in "either-or" fashion.

Polygenes.   Another major exception to Mendelian principles involves the control of a phenotypical trait by a number of separate genes which together have cumulative effects. Such genes are known as *polygenes,* in contrast to *major genes,* each of which determines a trait by itself. Like the phenomena of partial dominance and additivity, the effect of *polygenic determination* of a trait is to cause the trait to occur in degrees rather than in an either-or fashion. Even a small number of polygenes, each of which has a single dominant and recessive allele, can theoretically create a very wide range of variation in a trait. Traits that vary continuously over a wide range (e.g., height, hair color) are likely to be influenced by polygenes each of whose alleles may have additive effects.

Penetrance.   Penetrance refers to the percentage of cases having a particular genotype in which the genotype is actually manifest as expected. For example, a trait (T) governed by a gene with simple dominant (T) and recessive (t) alleles is *completely penetrant* if it is manifest in 100 per cent of individuals with TT and Tt genotypes. Some traits, however, are known as *partially penetrant* because they are manifest in less than 100 per cent of the TT and Tt individuals. A trait manifest in 90 per cent of the TT and Tt individuals would be called "90 per cent penetrant." Note that partial penetrance differs from partial dominance and additivity because the trait appears *only* in *either* T *or* t forms. The deviation from Mendelian principles involves the lack of perfect predictability of *which* phenotype (T or t) will result from a given genotype, rather than a tendency of the trait to be manifest in degrees, as is the case with partial dominance and additivity.

Expressivity.   *Expressivity* refers to the *degree to which* a trait is manifest in an individual having the genotype for that trait. *Partial expressivity* is the failure of a trait to be completely manifest in all individuals who have the appropriate genotype. Thus, some TT and Tt individuals may manifest a trait in a very mild form or may manifest only some aspects of the trait even though they carry genes that would usually cause complete expression of the trait. The effects of partial expressivity can resemble those of partial dominance and additivity in producing intermediate degrees of a trait. The failure of genes to be completely penetrant or completely expressive may be due to environmental factors or to other genes that moderate or counteract their effects.

Sex Chromosomes and Autosomes

In the human karyotype, the chromosomes designated as the twenty-third pair control the sex of the offspring and a number of other traits. In males, the two sex chromosomes differ markedly from one another (see Fig. 5–1). One member of the pair is the X *chromosome*, which is the same as both members of the twenty-third pair of chromosomes in females. The other member is the Y *chromosome*, which is considerably shorter than the X chromosome.

When gametes are formed by the germ cells of a male, each gamete receives *either* the X chromosome *or* the Y chromosome that was contained in the germ cell. If a male gamete containing the X chromosome fertilizes an ovum, the zygote is XX because the ovum can have received only an X chromosome from the mother. The offspring will be female. On the other hand, if a male gamete containing a Y chromosome fertilizes an ovum, the zygote will be XY and the offspring will be male because the Y chromosome carries the genetic information necessary for development of male sex characteristics. The 44 chromosomes (22 pairs) that are not sex chromosomes are known as *autosomes*.

Sex-linked Genes. Along with the information they carry for sexual development, the genes on the X and Y chromosomes differ from one another in other kinds of information they carry. This explains why some traits are *sex-linked*. For example, color blindness is inherited by boys only through their mothers, even when the mother herself is not color blind. The gene for color vision occurs only on the X chromosome. Women who carry the recessive color-blind allele of the gene on one of their X chromosomes are very likely to have a dominant normal allele for color vision on the other chromosome. This causes them to have phenotypically normal color vision. However, half the woman's gametes will contain X chromosomes having the color-blind allele. If any of these gametes is fertilized by a gamete containing a Y chromosome, the offspring will, of course, be male because of the XY combination. The male will be color-blind because the Y chromosome does not carry a gene for color vision.

On the average, fifty per cent of the sons of a woman who is heterozygous for color-blindness will be color-blind. None of her daughters will be color blind unless her husband is also color-blind, i.e., unless his X chromosomes contain the color-blind allele. If her husband is color-blind, then about half her daughters will be color-blind because they will receive the color-blind allele on the X chromosome they inherit from each parent. Other sex-linked traits transmitted in a similar fashion include hemophilia, baldness, and some forms of muscular dystrophy.

GENETIC CONTRIBUTIONS TO DEVELOPMENT

In order to conceptualize the way in which genetic and other biological factors can contribute to phenotypical development, it is useful to think of them in terms of the schema presented in Fig. 5–4. The bottom category of contributions is designated as *hereditary* and includes only the information directly transmitted by intact genes from the parents. The fact that such genetic information contributes to the formation of a particular phenotypic trait does not mean that environment or other genetic factors have no influence on the trait. It merely means that, insofar as genetic information plays a role, this information is transmitted in a normal way from the germ cells of the parents via their gametes to the chromosomes of their offspring. There the genes become biochemical templates for the development of the offspring. Examples of hereditary disorders include *Tay-Sachs disease* and *phenylketonuria (PKU)*. Both involve defects in metabolism determined by recessive genes and both can result in severe mental retardation.

The next category of contributions to development is designated as *innate*. It includes not only the contributions of normal genetic transmission from the parents, but also genetic effects that result from the mutation and regrouping of genes as they are formed in the germ cells of the parent and transferred to gametes. Mutations can be caused by drugs, disease, radiation, and other factors. Many gene mutations are lethal, but some may cause specific nonlethal traits. Certain mutations may have effects like those of genes transmitted by the usual hereditary mechanisms. An example is a form of mental defect known as *epiloia,* characterized by tumors of the brain and skin, which is transmitted by a rare dominant gene, but which is also believed to be caused in one out of four cases by new mutations (Penrose, 1963).

Beside mutation of genes, chromosomal anomalies are another source of nonhereditary genetic influence. Down's syndrome (mongolism) is one of the best-documented abnormalities resulting from a chromosomal anomaly. The cause is the presence in the female gamete of an extra chromosome similar to the normal twenty-first chromosome. This extra chromosome is produced by a failure, for reasons unknown, of the mother's two twenty-first chromosomes to separate from each other during meiosis. When fertilized by a normal sperm, the female gamete receives another number 21 chromosome, bringing its total to three. This condition is known as *"trisomy 21."* Exactly how the extra chromosomal material causes the mongoloid features, furrowed tongue, and defective intelligence of the offspring is unknown. Forms of extra chromosomal material other than trisomy 21 are also occasionally found in individuals having features similar to Down's syndrome.

The next category of biological contributions to development is designated *congenital* in Fig. 5–4. It includes the effects of conditions that occur between conception and the completion of the birth process. The topmost category in Fig. 5–4 is labeled *constitutional* and comprises any contributions to development that are based in the biological structure of the person, including the effects of disease or injury after birth, as well as hereditary factors, nonhereditary genetic factors, and factors arising from conditions between conception and birth. Nongenetic congenital and constitutional contributions are discussed in later chapters.

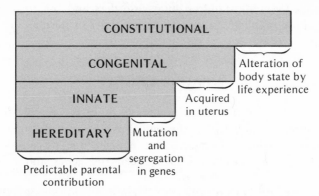

Fig. 5–4. Categories of biological contributions to phenotypical development. From Cattell (1950).

Although their contributions are placed at the bottom of the sequence in Fig. 5–4 and certainly become part of the organism at the very beginning, the effects of genes are not confined to the earliest part of an organism's development. Many genetically influenced phenotypic traits do not appear until long after birth. For example, *Huntington's chorea,* a neural degenerative disease leading to psychotic behavior and death, is caused by a rare dominant allele, but the symptoms do not appear until middle adulthood. Other gene effects, influencing such factors as growth rate, appear to terminate at certain developmental periods.

The Operon Model of Gene Action

The *operon* model (Jacob & Monod, 1961; cf. McClearn, 1970) provides one way of understanding how gene effects may be turned on and off. The model postulates two kinds of genes, *structural genes* and *regulator genes.* A structural gene is a typical gene that produces messenger RNA. Next to the structural gene is an *operator* which is a segment of DNA whose apparent function is to start the transcription of information from the structural gene to the RNA molecule. A regulator gene produces a "repressor" substance that prevents the operator from starting the transcription of information by a particular structural gene to an RNA molecule. The repressor substance may at a certain developmental stage be neutralized by an "inducer" substance, allowing the operator to "turn on" the structural gene. A similar mechanism may turn off genes at certain points in development.

Other mechanisms have also been proposed to account for genetic influences that are evident only at particular periods of development. However, the developmental study of genetic influences is still in a relatively rudimentary state. What is presently most important is that knowledge of genetic mechanisms already provides us with a tremendously rich array of possibilities for understanding some disorders and for creating testable hypotheses about many of the remaining mysteries of normal and abnormal development.

BEHAVIOR GENETICS

"There are no genes *for* behavior or any other phenotypic trait. Genes exert their influence on behavior through their effects at the molecular level of organization. Enzymes, hormones, and neurons may be considered as the sequence of complex path markers between the genes and a behavioral characteristic [Gottesman, 1968, pp. 60–61]."

The basic fact that genetically coded templates do not directly produce behavior creates problems for the study of behavior genetics no different from those in the study of genetic influences on physical characteristics. For physical as well as behavioral characteristics, the long sequence beginning with the transmission of a unit of parental DNA and culminating in the expression of the DNA's code in a phenotypic trait of the offspring is shaped at every step by nongenetic environmental parameters and by the chain reactions set in motion by other units of DNA.

Special Problems of Behavior Genetics

While some problems of behavior genetics are like those in any genetic studies, there are also special problems beyond those encountered in studying genetic influences on physical characteristics. One special problem is the definition of the behavior to be studied. Unlike anatomical characteristics, behavioral traits do not exist as relatively static, potentially visible entities. Instead, they are conceptual categories into which an observer groups his observations and inferences. Terms like "schizophrenia," "intelligence," "aggressiveness," and "extroversion," represent conceptual abstractions that can be systematically used only when they refer to observable behavior.

If one wishes to study genetic contributions to "schizophrenia," for example, specific criteria are needed for deciding who has the phenotypic trait and who does not. In practice, the criterion is often the diagnostic consensus of two or more clinicians who interview each subject and review his test scores and life history data. The assumption is that the clinicians' experience and training enables them to group people consistently into schizophrenic and nonschizophrenic categories, although most studies include an in-between category of subjects for whom the clinicians cannot agree on a diagnosis. Similiarly, studies of genetic contributions to "intelligence" typically employ scores on an IQ test as the criterion for amount of intelligence, while studies of aggressiveness and extroversion may employ personality test scores and observational ratings of behavior.

Reliability and Validity of Assessment.   The study of genetic influences on behavioral characteristics presents the same set of issues that must be confronted in any systematic study of behavior. Among the most fundamental issues are those of the *reliability* and *validity* of assessment, both discussed in detail in Chapter 4.

It would hardly pay to begin the arduous work of seeking genetic influences on phenotypical traits like schizophrenia, intelligence, aggression, or extroversion unless the means for assessing them were reasonably *reliable,* i.e., two separate judgments or measurements of a given person's behavior produce the same conclusion about whether he is schizophrenic, or about how intelligent, aggressive, or extroverted he is.

Likewise, unless means for empirically defining the trait are *valid* with respect to other criteria for the trait, any evidence for hereditary influences will be restricted to the particular measure employed and this measure may not have the same meaning for all workers. For example, if a researcher decides to use crossed eyes as a criterion for schizophrenia, judgments of the trait may be very reliable and it may be possible to demonstrate that hereditary factors influence it. However, unless crossed eyes are also demonstrated to correlate highly with other criteria for schizophrenia, such as delusions, hallucinations, and bizarre behavior, other workers may object that nothing about *their* concepts of "schizophrenia" has been demonstrated.

By the same token, the demonstration of hereditary influence upon scores on a reliable IQ test such as the Stanford-Binet applies only to intelligence defined in terms of that particular test and behavior that correlates highly with it. It says nothing about genetic influences on empirical measures of "intelligence" that do not happen to correlate with the Binet.

Situational Influences.   Besides the special problems of reliability and validity in defining the traits to be studied, behavior genetics must contend with the influence that specific situations have on the expression of behavior. Elaborate techniques may be necessary for observing anatomical structures that are especially tiny or are tightly integrated with other structures, but, once formed, anatomical structures continue to exist as part of the body. Specific behaviors do not have this static quality. They only "exist" under very special conditions. A person who is extroverted or who obtains a high IQ score under some conditions may not display evidence of extroversion or high IQ under other conditions. Experience with a certain set of conditions may also change a person's behavior under those conditions.

While these difficulties by no means preclude the identification of behavioral traits that persist, they do tend to restrict the range of study to behaviors that are conspicuously similar across many situations or that have clear-cut analogs in different situations. Consequently, dramatic forms of mental disorder, plus traits like IQ and extroversion for which successful tests are available, have been the most frequent objects of study in human behavior genetics. Nevertheless, genetic factors are also likely to play a role in behaviors that are more specific to certain situations.

Advantages of Animal Research

Most genetic research is carried out with nonhuman species. Species such as the fruit fly (*Drosophila*), mouse, and rat offer several obvious advantages over humans for genetic research.

One advantage is that an experimenter can control the mating of nonhuman species. By mating brothers with their sisters and repeating this procedure over several generations, he can create *inbred strains,* all members of which have virtually identical heredity. This makes it possible to study environmental effects with "heredity held constant," because any differences among the animals must be due to environmental factors. In addition, members of two inbred strains can be crossbred in order to trace in their offspring the genetic interactions of alleles known to have been different in the two parent strains. Control over mating also permits *selective breeding* of animals in order to find out whether heredity strongly influences a specific trait. A classic study of this type was carried out by Tryon (1940a; 1940b). Rats that performed exceptionally well in a complex maze were bred with one another. Those of their offspring that performed best in the maze were also bred with one another, and so on over several generations. The same was done with rats that performed poorly in the maze. The result was that, by the eighth generation of offspring, there was virtually no overlap in the number of maze errors made by the maze-bright strain and those made by the maze-dull strain, thus demonstrating a strong hereditary component in performance on that particular maze (see Fig. 5-5).

A second obvious advantage of animal research is that an experimenter can control the environment of his subjects. If he has already controlled the heredity of a group of animals, he can subject some to one environment and others to another environment, confident that any phenotypic differences he produces must be due to the environmental variation alone. The reverse strategy is also possible—where genetic control has not been achieved, an experimenter can subject animals to exactly the same environments and assume that phenotypic differences that emerge are due to hereditary factors.

In cases where complete hereditary control is difficult or undesirable, more naturalistic methods resembling those used in human genetic studies may be applied to animals. The principal method of this type is the *pedigree study* in which the distribution of a phenotypic trait is traced among all members of several generations of a family. By determining the relations between proportions of parents and offspring of each sex manifesting the trait, hypotheses can be formed about whether the trait is genetically influenced and what the genetic mechanism is in terms of dominance, penetrance, sex-linkage, etc.

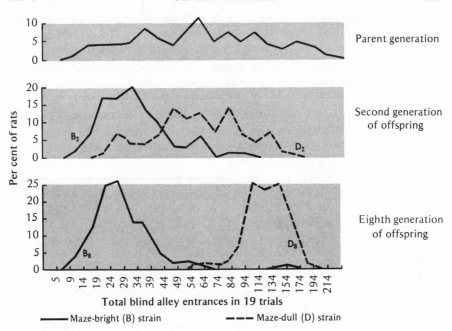

Fig. 5–5. Effects of nine generations of selective breeding on maze performance by rats. From Tryon (1934).

Two further advantages of using nonhuman species make them preferable to humans for pedigree studies as well as for controlled breeding approaches. One of these advantages is the short period between generations—it is possible to produce many generations of animals for a pedigree study during one human generation.

The other advantage stems from the relatively large litter sizes of most animals compared to the human family. On the average, for example, a Mendelian recessive trait (t) should be manifest in one out of four offspring whose parents are both heterozygous (Tt) for the trait (Tt × Tt = TT + Tt + Tt + tt). But even a trait governed by such a simple mechanism may be somewhat difficult to trace in humans because even in families with as many as four children, which is above the average number in Western countries, random deviation from the expected 3:1 ratio is quite probable. As a result, none, one, two, or even four of the offspring may manifest the trait. In larger litters, the underlying genetic mechanism is less likely to be obscured by random deviations from the average proportion of offspring in which it should be manifest.

Limitations of Animal Research

For traits that are very similar in human and nonhuman species, the advantages just discussed dictate that most genetic research will be done with nonhuman species, at least until well-refined hypotheses about the specific genetic mechanisms are developed. This is true of genetic research on resistance and susceptibility to diseases like cancer and on traits like albinism that appear in many species. Unfortunately, most important human behavioral traits and forms of pyschopathology do not seem to have precise analogs in other species. Where apparent behavioral analogs exist in nonhuman species, it has often been possible to demonstrate that they are indeed greatly influenced by genetic factors and to demonstrate interactions between environmental and genetic factors in ways that are strongly suggestive for human behavior.

Once genetic influence on a behavioral trait in a nonhuman species has been confirmed, however, close analysis often reveals factors that greatly limit the applicability of the findings to humans. Tryon's experiment (cited above, 1940a; 1940b), for example, demonstrated strong genetic influences on what appeared to be an important facet of rat "intelligence." Yet, further research has revealed that the superior performance of "bright" rats was restricted to the particular kind of maze that had served as the criterion for the selective breeding. The "dull" rats were equal or superior to the "bright" rats in three out of five other maze tests. There is evidence that distractibility, low food motivation, and fear of the apparatus were the genetically influenced traits that interfered with the "dull" rats' performance in the criterion maze (Searle, 1949). These possibilities suggest that genetic influences on human performance also exist in complex interactions with specific environmental conditions, but they tell us little about exactly what genetic characteristics are likely to influence people's performance on an IQ test, for example.

Genetic influences on other behavioral dimensions in rats, e.g., "emotionality," as measured by defecation in an illuminated open field, have also been demonstrated (Broadhurst, 1958; Hall, 1938). Yet, beyond the suggestion that similar characteristics in humans *can* be genetically influenced, the kind of responses observed and the stimulus conditions appropriate for studying rats tell us little about *how* genetic and environmental factors actually *do* interact to produce whatever we might designate as "emotionality" in humans. Obtaining knowledge about how genetic and environmental influences shape human behavior requires special variations on the genetic research methods possible with animals. These research methods are discussed in the next section.

METHODS IN HUMAN BEHAVIOR GENETICS

Chromosomal Analysis

Since the 1950s, new methods for examining chromosomal material have made possible large-scale and efficient analysis of human chromosomes. Studies have revealed systematic differences between normal chromosomal *karyotypes* (defined on page 100) and those of individuals manifesting certain gross physical and behavioral abnormalities. The existence of an extra twenty-first chromosome ("trisomy 21") in individuals manifesting Down's syndrome has already been discussed.

Like Down's syndrome, *Klinefelter's syndrome* had been identified long before it was discovered that its victims have an extra chromosome. In this syndrome, an extra female chromosome is present in an individual who is otherwise male—he has *sex chromosome trisomy,* XXY. The condition is often not diagnosed until the boy shows incomplete sexual development at puberty. The characteristic physical traits of small testicles, tallness, thinness, long arms and legs, and sterility, are frequently accompanied by low IQ and personality instability (Money, 1970).

Turner's syndrome is a condition in females that is also caused by a sex chromosome abnormality. It usually involves the *absence* of one of the two X chromosomes normally found in females. In certain cases of Turner's syndrome, some cells of the body lack an X chromosome while others have the normal complement of two X chromosomes. Lack of uniformity in the chromosome complement of body cells, such as that found in these cases of Turner's syndrome, is referred to as a *mosaic* condition.

Physical characteristics of girls with Turner's syndrome include short stature, webbed neck, absence of pubertal development, and sterility. Psychological studies show average to superior verbal IQ, deficient spatial abilities, and an "inertia of emotional arousal" (Money & Mittenthal, 1970). The traits may be less pronounced in girls with the mosaic pattern. Since pubertal development can be induced through administration of estrogen, girls with Turner's syndrome marry and can live fairly normal lives if they are helped to cope with the psychological effects of their condition.

A syndrome that was unknown before it was discovered by means of chromosomal analysis (Sandberg, Koepf, Ishihara, & Hauschka, 1961) is the *XYY syndrome* in males. This syndrome is of special interest because its implications for law and the question of free will versus determinism have received widespread publicity in many countries. Perhaps because an extra male chromosome was imagined to double the aggressive "maleness" in an individual, the discovery of XYY karyotypes among inmates of a maximum security prison hospital (Jacobs, Brunton, Melville, Brittain, & Clermont, 1965) led to the assumption that XYY men may be genetically predestined to become criminals. This assumption was used to support arguments that such men should not be held legally responsible for their crimes. Popular preoccupation with the XYY syndrome even led to press reports in 1968 that Richard Speck, murderer of eight nurses in Chicago, was an XYY, although he was not (Engel, 1972). While XYY men have been found who do not display criminal behavior, most research has been designed to identify the karyotype among males who do display criminal or difficult behavior. Studies of XYY males, including some young boys, have revealed the following characteristics: unusual tallness, behavior problems beginning in childhood, below-average range of IQ, excessive daydreaming, social isolation, and unstable occupational history (Owen, 1972).

Large representative samples of infants have revealed a frequency of one XYY karyotype in every 975 male births, considerably lower than the proportion discovered in criminal samples (Hook, 1973). However, until the proportion of XYYs in larger, more representative samples of criminal males can be compared with the infant samples and with representative samples of noncriminal men, the strength of the XYY disposition to criminal behavior cannot be guessed at with confidence. The evidence to date does suggest a statistical relation between the XYY karyotype and behavior, although it by no means indicates that XYY males are inexorably destined to commit crime nor that they account for a large proportion of crime.

Insofar as the extra Y chromosome does influence behavior, it probably does so by creating, at certain developmental periods, a range of behavioral reactions to normal stimuli somewhat different from those in XY males. Environmental histories that lead to normal behavior in XY males may lead to criminal behavior in some XYY males. It is to be hoped, therefore, that the developmental courses of XYY infants will be followed in order to determine what specific environmental inputs lead to criminal and noncriminal outcomes. Knowledge of exactly how environmental conditions interact with XYY genetic factors to produce criminal behavior could suggest preventive measures analogous to the low phenylalanine diet employed to prevent retardation in infants with the genotype for phenylketonuria.

Quantitative Genetics

Despite the importance of chromosomal abnormalities in accounting for some conditions, most genetically influenced pathology is unlikely to involve aberrations in genetic material that are massive enough to be discerned through chromosomal analysis. Studies of representative samples of newborns show that chromosomal abnormalities, some of which have no discernible effects, occur in about one out of every 200 births (Lubs & Ruddle, 1970). This incidence is too small to account for many of the pathological conditions probably influenced by genetic factors. Moreover, the syndromes known to accompany chromosomal abnormalities include distinct physical traits, while many behavioral traits that may be influenced by genetic factors do not appear to be correlated with any obvious physical traits.

Because chromosomal studies, controlled breeding, and pedigree studies cannot tell us much about genetic influences on most important human behavior, statistical techniques have been developed for estimating the relative contributions of heredity to the variability in phenotypic traits. These techniques are especially necessary for studying traits that are influenced by complex polygenic mechanisms.

In order to calculate the relative contributions of heredity and environment for a trait, the trait is coded in a form amenable to quantitative analysis. Traits like IQ, numerically scored personality test performance, height, and weight are obvious candidates for these procedures because they yield continuous distributions of scores rather than being manifest in only one or two qualitatively distinct ways. However, even a trait that appears to be expressed in an all-or-none fashion can be analyzed quantitatively by giving individuals manifesting the trait a score of 1 while individuals without it receive a score of 0.

Heritability.   Once individuals have been scored according to their manifestation of a phenotypic trait, the goal is to calculate the proportion of variation among the phenotypic scores that is due to genetic variation. The total variation in the phenotypic scores is assumed to be the sum of the variation due to genetic factors plus the variation due to environmental factors. Thus, it can be expressed as $V_{phenotypic} = V_{genetic} + V_{environmental}$. The proportion of the phenotypic variation due to genetic variation is generally conceptualized in terms of an estimate of *heritability*. The precise statistical techniques for arriving at an estimate of heritability depend upon the specific problem and assumptions. However, for conceptual purposes,[1] the heritability estimate (H) can be expressed as $H = \dfrac{V_{genetic}}{V_{phenotypic}}$.

Note that estimates of heritability refer to *proportions* of variation among scores rather than to the *absolute* values of any scores. A heritability estimate says nothing about how much an IQ score of 100, for example, could be raised or lowered by a change in environmental conditions. Even with traits yielding high heritability estimates, a given genotype is assumed only to determine a *range* of possible phenotypic reactions to different environments. Thus, the actual score obtained by an individual for a trait will depend upon the degree to which his environment has maximized his genotypic potential for that trait.[2]

Because heritability refers to the proportion of variance in a group of scores that is attributable to heredity, rather than to anything about a single fixed score, it can only be estimated from a group of scores having a variety of values. There is no way to calculate the heritability of the

----

[1] H is often represented as h^2, because h is the symbol for the *correlation* between genotypes and phenotypes for a trait. The correlation between two variables is the square root of the variance that one variable has in common with the other. Thus, if the heritability estimate (written as either H or h^2) is 0.49, the correlation between the genotypes and phenotypes will be $\sqrt{0.49} = 0.70$.

[2] In practice, the variation in scores is operationally defined as statistical *variance*, written as σ^2 ("sigma squared"). Variance is a quantitative index of the degree to which scores are scattered around the mean of their distribution. It is the square of the standard deviation (σ) of the distribution. Accordingly, the quantitative estimate of heritability is the amount of variance due to genetic variance (σ_g^2), divided by the total phenotypic variance (σ_p^2): $H = \dfrac{\sigma_g^2}{\sigma_p^2}$.

score of one individual or of scores that are all identical, because the phenotypic variance in the denominator of the proportion would be zero. The numerator would also be zero, because it is always a portion of the total variance represented by the denominator. If, for example, everyone in a sample has an IQ of 100, no heritability estimate can be calculated for that sample because the variance of the scores is zero—H would equal $\dfrac{\text{zero}}{\text{zero}}$.

One of the most important points about the concept of heritability is that it eliminates the artificial dichotomy between heredity and environment. Since the heritability estimate is based on the assumption that the total phenotypic variance is a sum of both genetic and environmental influences, any change in either genetic or environmental variance will change H. This means that heritability always depends upon the *specific ranges* of *environmental and genetic* factors existing in the population for which it is calculated. Heritability is *never* an *absolute figure* representing the strength of genetic determination for a given trait under all conditions. It is *always relative* to *particular genetic* and *particular environmental* conditions.

Some Illustrations.   To illustrate the complementary roles of heredity and environment in determining the heritability estimate, imagine that 100 unrelated boys are subjected to exactly the same environment. We might find that their IQs at age 10 range only from 99 to 101. At first glance, this would suggest that genetic differences could not be affecting IQ much. However, if we calculate the ratio of genetic variance to phenotypic variance, we would obtain a heritability estimate of 1.00 (100 per cent), indicating that all the variance in IQ is due to genetic factors. This, of course, would be completely accurate because, by making environment identical for these particular subjects, we have prevented the environment from contributing anything to the *variation* among IQ scores. All the phenotypic variation, small as it is, is due to nonenvironmental factors. We might conclude that, as a practical matter, the genetic contributions to variations in IQ under this particular environment are not very *important,* but we could not escape the conclusion that *all* the variation occurring among the IQs is due to genetic factors.

The reverse situation also demonstrates how the heritability estimate is governed by the complementary relation between genetic and environmental influences. If we take 100 boys who all have exactly the same heredity (the equivalent of identical twins, multiplied 50 times), and subject them to 100 different environments, we may also find that their IQs at age 10 range only from 99 to 101. If we calculate the ratio of genetic variance to phenotypic variance, we would find this time that the heritability of IQ was not 1.00, but 0.00. Since the genotypes are identical for all subjects, the only factor contributing to the phenotypic variance must be the environmental differences.

Of course, the pure case of genotypically *different* people experiencing *identical* environments never occurs, and the case of genotypically *identical* people experiencing *different* environments occurs only among identical twins. Nevertheless, the point is that an estimate of heritability for a phenotypic trait is valid only for a population of people having a particular distribution of genotypes and environments—heritability is a statistic for a phenotypic trait *within a particular kind of population,* exposed to *a particular kind of environmental variation.* It does not represent anything intrinsic about the trait independent of population or environment.

The relativistic nature of heritability can lead to some surprising conclusions. For example, if it is assumed that nearly all American middle-class children currently experience environments enriched enough to enable them to realize their full genotypic potentials in IQ, then the heritability of IQ for these children should approach 1.00, because the aspects of environment that influence IQ are uniformly favorable for all the children.

On the other hand, if it is assumed that economically disadvantaged American children are not all experiencing environments conducive to maximizing their genotypic potentials in IQ, the heritability of IQ for these children should be much less than 1.00, because the aspects of environment that influence IQ are far from uniform for them. In a comparison of lower- and middle-class children, Scarr-Salapatek (1971) found exactly the relationships implied by this analysis: The heritability of IQ was considerably higher among middle-class than among lower-class children.

However, if improvements in the lower-class children's environments reach the point where each child is enabled to realize his full genotypic potential in IQ, the heritability of IQ for these children should also approach 1.00. In effect, there may be environmental conditions that constitute *thresholds* that must be surpassed before genetic influences can become fully manifest. Figure 5–6 presents a schematic representation of how environmental thresholds can affect estimates of genetic influence.

In summary, environmental factors influence heritability estimates in at least two important ways. First, certain environmental threshold conditions may have to prevail before genetic influences on the variation in a phenotypic trait become evident at all in a particular population. Second, if the environmental conditions are above the necessary threshold, heritability estimates will generally be highest in groups whose environments are the most uniform.

STRATEGIES FOR OBTAINING HUMAN HERITABILITY ESTIMATES

Since selective breeding, the creation of inbred strains, and pedigree studies have limited applicability to humans, studies of heritability of

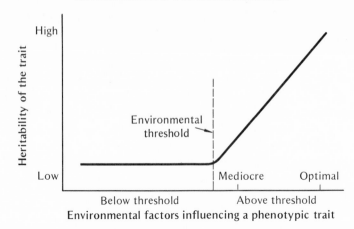

Fig. 5–6. Environmental factors may have to reach a certain threshold before genetic influences on a phenotypic trait can be detected.

human behavioral traits depend upon naturally occurring variations in degrees of genetic similarity.

The most general approach is to study the correlations between scores on a trait for family members differing in degree of genetic similarity. For example, on the average, 50 per cent of the genes of same-sex full siblings are identical because each sibling inherits half the alleles carried by one parent and half the alleles carried by the other parent. Of course, it is theoretically possible for some pairs of siblings to have no genes in common because each sibling received from each parent exactly the *op-posite* set of alleles received by the other sibling. Conversely, some pairs of siblings may theoretically have identical heredity because both members happened to receive exactly the same set of alleles from each parent. However, the probability of either of these extremes occurring is virtually zero. As long as a study of siblings employs large enough samples, pairs of siblings can be assumed to be identical in 50 per cent of their genes, on the average.

The correlations between siblings' scores on a trait can be compared with the correlations between scores of people having less or more genetic similarity. Same-sex half siblings, for instance, are assumed to be identical in 25 percent of their genes, on the average. If the differences between the scores of full siblings who have experienced similar environments are considerably smaller than those for half siblings who have experienced similar environments, the estimate of the heritability of the trait will be high.

Twin Studies

A more refined and widely used way to estimate the heritability of a trait is to compare the degree of similarity between identical (monozygotic or MZ) twins, who have identical genes, with the degree of similarity between same-sex fraternal (dizygotic or DZ) twins, who, like other full siblings, are identical in only 50 per cent of their genes, on the average. A major advantage of this approach is that the environmental histories of both kinds of twins are likely to be more similar than the environmental histories of nontwin full siblings or half siblings. This means that environmental similarities are presumably contributing to phenotypic trait similarities in approximately the same degree for both kinds of twins, while the environmental histories of full siblings and half siblings differ to unknown extents. Methods for assessing blood factors have recently made it possible to determine with great accuracy whether same-sex twins are MZ or DZ. If cotwins do not differ on any of a large number of blood factors, they are assumed to be MZ.

The general rationale for twin studies of heritability is that differences in scores obtained by DZ cotwins result from both genetic and environmental differences between them, while differences in scores obtained by MZ cotwins can be due only to environmental factors, since the twins have exactly the same genes. Thus, the strength of genetic influence on the trait scores can be estimated by subtracting the *differences* in scores obtained by MZ cotwins from the *differences* in scores obtained by DZ cotwins:

$$
\begin{array}{l}
D_{DZ} = \text{Environmental} + \text{genetic influence} \\
\underline{-D_{MZ} = \text{Environmental influence}} \\
\phantom{-D_{MZ}} = \text{strength of genetic influence}
\end{array}
$$

where D_{DZ} represents the differences in scores obtained by dizygotic cotwins and D_{MZ} represents the differences in scores obtained by monozygotic cotwins.

Dichotomous Traits. If a trait is scored dichotomously, the assessment of genetic influences can be made by comparing the per cent of DZ twin pairs in which both members have the trait (are *concordant* for it), with the per cent of MZ twin pairs in which the members are concordant for the trait. [In effect, the amount of *similarity* rather than the amount of *difference* between cotwins is being compared, but the results would be the same as if rates of *discordance* (dissimilarity) between cotwins were used in an analogous formula.]

As an example, Kallmann and Roth (1956) studied concordance rates for schizophrenia in DZ and MZ twin pairs having at least one member who developed schizophrenia in childhood. Both twins eventually became schizophrenic in 22.9 per cent of the DZ pairs and 88.2 per cent of the MZ pairs. This difference in concordance rates was statistically significant ($p < 0.01$) and led the authors to conclude that childhood schizophrenia was definitely influenced by hereditary factors.

The different concordance rates can be used to obtain an estimate of heritability (H) using the formula $H = \dfrac{C_{MZ} - C_{DZ}}{1 - C_{DZ}}$, where C_{MZ} is the per cent of MZ twin pairs concordant for the trait and C_{DZ} is the per cent of DZ twin pairs concordant for the trait. From the Kallmann-Roth data, the heritability estimate for schizophrenia would be:

$$H = \frac{88.2 - 22.9}{1 - 22.9} = \frac{65.3}{77.1} = .85.$$

Traits Scored Quantitatively. For traits amenable to continuous quantitative scoring, heritability estimates are generally derived from ratios comparing the correlation coefficient (r) between scores of MZ cotwins with the correlation between scores of DZ cotwins. [The intraclass correlation rather than the well-known Pearson product-moment correlation is usually employed—see McNemar (1962) for the differences between the two types of correlation.] The general form of heritability estimates based on cotwin correlations is $H = \dfrac{r_{MZ} - r_{DZ}}{1 - r_{DZ}}$, where r_{MZ} is the correlation between scores for MZ twins and r_{DZ} is the correlation between scores for DZ twins. Note that this formula is analogous to the one cited above for estimating heritability from the percentages of MZ and DZ twin pairs concordant for a trait.

As an example of the way in which correlations for MZ and DZ twins are used to calculate heritability, consider Table 5–1. This table contains the average of the correlations found in three studies for the scores obtained by MZ and DZ cotwins on 10 scales of the Minnesota Multiphasic Personality Inventory (MMPI). One of the studies was done with adult twin pairs in Connecticut (Reznikoff & Honeyman, 1967), while two studies were done with adolescent twin pairs, one group in Minnesota (Gottesman, 1963b) and one group in Massachusetts (Gottesman, 1965).

Vandenberg (1967) combined the data of the three studies and calculated the values for heritability (H) shown in the table. For example, on scores for social introversion, the r_{MZ} was .45 and the r_{DZ} was .12. Thus:

$$H = \frac{r_{MZ} - r_{DZ}}{1 - r_{DZ}} = \frac{.45 - .12}{1 - .12} = \frac{.33}{.88} = .37.$$

It must be remembered that the figure .37 does not indicate that social introversion is 37 per cent heredity and 63 per cent environment. The figure .37 means only that 37 per cent of the total *variance* in the scores can be attributed to heredity, because the similarity between MZ cotwins' scores is greater than the similarity between DZ cotwins' scores by an amount that is equal to 37 per cent of the total variance between DZ cotwins' scores.

Since DZ cotwins are not unrelated but have, on the average, 50 per cent identical genes, it might seem reasonable to double the figure .37 in

TABLE 5-1

Values of r_{MZ}, r_{DZ}, and H for MMPI scores based on combined data of three twin studies.

MMPI score	r_{MZ}	r_{DZ}	H
Social introversion	.45	.12	.37**
Depression	.44	.14	.35**
Psychasthenia	.41	.11	.34**
Psychopathic deviate	.48	.27	.28*
Schizophrenia	.44	.24	.27*
Paranoia	.27	.08	.21
Hysteria	.37	.23	.19
Hypochondriasis	.41	.28	.17
Hypomania	.32	.18	.17
Masculinity-feminity	.41	.35	.09
Number of pairs	120	132	

* $p < .05$
** $p < .01$
NOTE.—Data from studies by Gottesman (1963b, 1965), and Reznikoff & Honeyman (1967). Table adapted from Vandenberg (1967, p. 78).

order to provide a more valid estimate of the amount of variance accounted for by genetic relationships in this sample. On the other hand, there is some evidence (Smith, 1965) that the environmental histories of MZ co-twins are more similar than those of DZ cotwins. Scarr (1968) has shown that much of the difference in the environmental histories of DZ twins results indirectly from their genetic dissimilarities, but the greater environmental similarities still might be inflating the correlations of scores found for MZ twins. For these reasons, plus the fact that a heritability estimate is not automatically generalizable to populations differing from the experimental samples in environmental or hereditary variation, the absolute size of the heritability estimate is less important than its statistical significance and its size relative to other scores obtained in the same way.

From Table 5-1, then, we should not conclude that the social introversion score on the MMPI is 37 per cent hereditary, but that, in the samples tested, individual differences in scores for social introversion, depression, psychasthenia, psychopathy, and schizophrenia are likely to have been influenced more by genetic differences than were scores for hypochondriasis, hypomania, or masculinity–femininity. Similarly, our confidence that genetic factors play an important role in, for instance, individual differences in the personality trait of "social introversion"—within the population of American Caucasians sampled—should increase if more studies, using different samples and introversion scores obtained in different ways, also yield statistically significant heritability estimates.

Adoption Studies

Another strategy for estimating the influence of genetic factors on behavioral traits is to study people of known genetic similarity who, because of adoption, have grown up in different environments. Just as twin studies capitalize upon the naturally occurring genetic difference between MZ and DZ twins, adoption studies capitalize upon the environmental differences that can occur when children are raised by foster parents.

Twins Reared Apart. When MZ twins happen to be raised by different parents, their similarities can be compared with the similarities of MZ twins reared together. At least three studies have compared psychological test data on MZ twins reared together with data on substantial numbers of MZ twins reared apart (Burt, 1958; Newman, Freeman, & Holzinger, 1937; Shields, 1962). All three reported intelligence test data that will be discussed in Chapter 7. The latter two studies also reported personality test correlations for MZ twins reared together, MZ twins reared apart, and DZ twins reared together. In both studies, the correlations for MZ twins reared apart were actually *higher* than the correlations for MZ twins reared together and substantially higher than for DZ twins reared together (see Table 5–2).

TABLE 5–2

Correlations for personality test scores of twins reared together and apart.

	Adjustment score [a]	Extroversion [b]	Neuroticism [b]
MZ twins reared together	.56	.42	.38
MZ twins reared apart	.58	.61	.53
DZ twins reared together	.37	−.17	.11

[a] Woodworth-Mathews Personal Data Sheet (Newman, Freeman, & Holzinger, 1937).
[b] Self-Rating Questionnaire (Shields, 1962).

It may seem paradoxical that MZ twins reared apart could be more alike than MZ twins reared together, but it has often been noted that twins living together may influence each other to develop complementary social roles. This would tend to reduce the correlation between the twins in genetically influenced traits below what it might be if the twins were not directly influencing one another.

Nontwin Adoption Studies. Difficult as it is to find identical twins reared apart, it is infinitely more difficult to study traits such as schizophrenia in this manner because, to begin with, only a small percentage of the population manifests the trait. For this reason, other approaches have been developed for studying the effects of heredity on rare traits like schizophrenia in people raised under varying environmental conditions. Rosenthal (1970b) has outlined a number of these approaches as they are being implemented in Denmark where excellent public health services and centralized record-keeping make it possible to keep track of nearly everybody who manifests a serious disorder and to locate members of his family.

One such approach is referred to as the *cross-fostering* research design. It involves studying individuals presumed to have one genotype who are raised by parents of a different genotype. The goal is to see whether the genotype of the child or the environmental influence of the parents is stronger in producing a certain trait. The design is being carried out by locating individuals who had a schizophrenic biological parent but were raised by adoptive parents who show no evidence of schizophrenia. Other individuals are also being located who had nonschizophrenic biological parents, but were raised by a schizophrenic adoptive parent. This cross-fostering design is illustrated in Fig. 5–7(a).

Two further variants of this design are also illustrated in Fig. 5–7. Figure 5–7(b) illustrates a way of testing a "pure" environmental hypothesis. It involves studying children of nonschizophrenic biological parents who are raised by schizophrenic and nonschizophrenic adoptive parents. If the children adopted by schizophrenic parents become schizophrenic, it would indicate that environmental conditions alone can produce schizophrenia.

Figure 5–7(c) illustrates a way of testing the strength of interaction between a hypothesized schizophrenic genotype and the environmental influence created by a schizophrenic parent. Children having schizophrenic biological parents but raised by nonschizophrenic adoptive parents are compared with children having schizophrenic biological parents and raised by schizophrenic adoptive parents. If findings in the other designs demonstrate a strong genetic influence on schizophrenia, the findings of this design could tell us how much the influence of a schizophrenic parent adds to the probability that a child with the presumed schizophrenic genotype will develop schizophrenia.

SOME FINDINGS IN HERITABILITY OF PERSONALITY AND PATHOLOGY

There is a rapidly growing body of literature on the heritability of various human traits. This section will deal with some representative findings on traits other than those, such as IQ and psychosis, that will be discussed at length in later chapters.

Introversion–Extroversion

Introversion–extroversion is a personality dimension that has emerged in numerous studies. Several personality tests provide scores for this dimenion or for dimensions having similar connotations. Nearly all behavior genetic

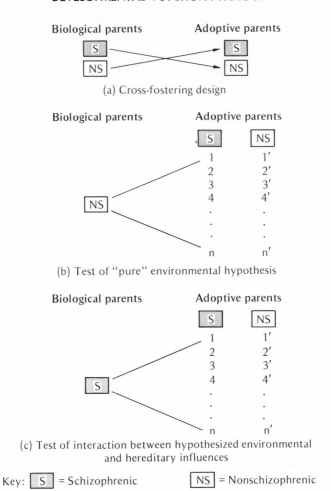

(a) Cross-fostering design

(b) Test of "pure" environmental hypothesis

(c) Test of interaction between hypothesized environmental
and hereditary influences

Key: [S] = Schizophrenic   [NS] = Nonschizophrenic

Fig. 5–7. Three designs for estimating the strength of hereditary and environmental influences on the development of schizophrenia in adopted children. Adapted from Rosenthal (1970b).

studies of introversion–extroversion have reported evidence of hereditary influences on the trait.

In an English study, Eysenck (1956) administered a large number of personality, intelligence, and autonomic measures to MZ and DZ twins aged 11 to 15 years. Factor analysis of all the measures produced three factors that Eysenck interpreted as representing the dimensions of intelligence, introversion–extroversion, and autonomic functioning (e.g., pulse rate, blood pressure). Scores for each twin were calculated from the measures that defined each of the three dimensions and the correlations between MZ and DZ cotwins' scores were used to obtain heritability estimates. As can be seen

TABLE 5–3

**Correlations for MZ and DZ twins
on three factor scores.**

	MZ	DZ	H
Intelligence	.82	.38	.71
Extroversion	.50	—.33	.62
Autonomic	.93	.72	.75

NOTE.—Adapted from Eysenck (1956).

in Table 5–3, the correlations for MZ twins were all significantly higher than those for DZ twins. Although the correlation for MZ twins on extroversion was considerably lower than on intelligence or autonomic functioning, the correlation for DZ twins on extroversion was actually negative, leading to an heritability estimate of .62 for extroversion. This was nearly as high as the estimates for the other two factors.

Eysenck suggested that the negative correlation for DZ twins may have been merely a chance deviation from a true correlation of about zero, but Shields (1962) also reported a negative correlation on extroversion for DZ twins reared together and a lower correlation on extroversion for MZ twins reared together than for MZ twins reared apart (see Table 5–2). The consistency of Shields' findings with those of Eysenck lends credence to the hypothesis that twins living together may influence each other in ways that make them less similar in introversion–extroversion than would otherwise be expected from their genetic similarities. The heritability estimate obtained from Shields' correlations for MZ and DZ twins is .50.

Three twin studies that included MMPI scores for social introversion were mentioned earlier (Gottesman, 1963b, 1965; Reznikoff & Honeyman, 1967). Their combined results yielded a statistically significant heritability estimate of .37 for social introversion. In one of the two MMPI studies involving high-school-age twins, the California Psychological Inventory was also administered (Gottesman, 1965; cf. Gottesman, 1966). This test contains four subscales that had previously been found through factor analysis to define an introversion–extroversion dimension. All four of these subscales yielded significant heritability estimates, with three of them having the highest heritability estimates of any of the 18 subscales on the test.

Vandenberg (1967; Vandenberg, Stafford, & Brown, 1968) also reported a significant heritability estimate for introversion–extroversion scores of twins on the Myers-Briggs Type Indicator, a test based upon Jung's personality typology. None of the other three personality scores on the test showed any evidence of heritability.

Taking a somewhat different approach, Scarr (1969) asked mothers of 6- to 10-year-old MZ and DZ twin girls to fill out an adjective check list describing both daughters. Scarr also had trained observers independently rate the twins on several of the Fels Child Behavior Scales (Richards & Simons, 1941). Based on the mothers' and observers' ratings, heritability estimates for introversion–extroversion were statistically significant and higher than for any other trait.

Although introversion–extroversion scores on a variety of measures in several twin samples have yielded significant heritability estimates, two studies have reported minimal differences between MZ and DZ twins in scores of this type. One study found only slightly higher correlations for MZ twins than for DZ twins (Carter, 1935). However, the personality test used (Bernreuter Personality Inventory) and methods for determining zygosity were probably inferior to those in the more recent studies that have reported significant heritability estimates.

The second study was done in Holland (Wilde, 1964). Correlations between scores on the Amsterdam Biographical Questionnaire were compared for MZ and DZ twins living together with those for twins who had been living apart for at least five years. Ages ranged from 13 to 69 years. Like other studies, differences between the correlation of scores for MZ twins and those for DZ twins living together yielded a significant heritability estimate for introversion–extroversion. However, the correlation of scores for MZ twins reared apart was lower than for DZ twins reared apart. Because most of the twins living apart were adults, this finding does not directly contradict the findings of high heritability for introversion–extroversion among young twins. It does, nevertheless, suggest that the developmental period at which a trait is measured may be an important factor in determining the ratio of genetic to environmental influences on the variance of a trait.

Neuroticism

In a study resembling Eysenck's (1956) previously cited study of introversion–extroversion, Eysenck and Prell (1951) administered a battery of personality tests to MZ and same-sex DZ twins, aged 11 to 14 years. Neuroticism was conceptualized as a trait dimension running from emotional stability and integration at one extreme to instability and lack of integration at the other extreme. The correlation between the neuroticism factor scores of MZ cotwins was .85, compared to .22 for DZ cotwins, for a heritability estimate of .81.

Two studies by Shields have also presented evidence of genetic influence on neuroticism. In the first study (Shields, 1954), the subjects were MZ and same-sex DZ twins, aged 12 to 15 years. Shields' primary data consisted of parents' reports of neurotic behavior in their twins, although relying exclusively on parental memory is risky because parents' perceptions of their children rather than the children's behavior itself is being studied.

The parental reports were used to rate children as (1) neurotic enough to warrant referral to a clinic or other social agency; (2) mildly neurotic;

(3) normal except for slight neurotic traits; (4) well-adjusted. Cotwins received identical ratings in 69 per cent of the MZ pairs and 31 per cent of the DZ pairs. The parental reports were also used to rate cotwins according to whether their specific behavior was (1) completely concordant; (2) essentially concordant; (3) partially concordant; or (4) discordant. Sixty-nine per cent of the MZ pairs but only 12 per cent of the DZ pairs were placed in the first two categories, while 69 per cent of DZ pairs and only 17 per cent of MZ pairs were placed in the completely discordant category.

In his later study, Shields (1962) employed neuroticism scores on a specially devised test (the Self-Rating Questionnaire), thus avoiding the problem of possible biases inherent in parental reports. The correlation of scores was .38 for MZ twins reared together and .11 for same-sex DZ twins, yielding a heritability estimate of .30. As with his findings for extroversion, the correlation of scores for 42 pairs of MZ twins reared apart was actually higher (.53) than that for MZ twins reared together (.38).

Carter's early study (1935) also presented some evidence for hereditary influences on neuroticism, despite the inadequacy of his personality test (Bernreuter) and methods for diagnosing zygosity. He reported correlations of .63 for neuroticism scores of MZ twins and .32 for same-sex DZ twins.

Manic-Depressive Disorders

These disorders are usually considered to begin only in adulthood, but the findings of genetic studies are instructive for the general nature of behavior genetic research into psychopathology. Obtaining reliable and valid diagnostic criteria has been an acute problem in this area. Some studies have lumped together individuals who show only depressive symptoms, those who show only manic symptoms, and those who show a cyclic alternation between both kinds of symptoms, while other studies have separated these three groups on the assumption that they represent three distinct disorders.

In a study of twins who manifested a cyclic alternation of manic and depressive symptoms, Kallmann (1953, 1954) found that both cotwins were affected in 25.5 per cent of 58 same-sex DZ pairs and 100 per cent of 27 MZ pairs. Twenty-three per cent of the nontwin siblings of twins with the disorder were also affected. These results are indicative of high heritability, although the concordance rates might be inflated because the *index cases,* the member of each twin pair with whom the study started, were all mental hospital patients. Kallmann concluded that concordance would probably be lower if less severely disturbed index cases had been included.

Employing family pedigree methods rather than twin comparisons, another team of researchers concluded not only that manic-depressive disorders are heritable, but also that they are governed by one or two dominant genes on the X chromosome (Reich, Clayton, & Winokur, 1969; Winokur, Clayton, & Reich, 1969). Although their work has been criticized for possible unreliability in the diagnosis of the phenotypic disorder (see J. Becker, 1970), they found familial sex distributions of the disorder that were suggestive of genetic transmission via the female chromosome. The X chromosome was further implicated by the finding in two families that red-green color blindness and manic-depressive disorders were highly concordant. Since it is known that (1) the gene for color blindness is located on the short arm of the X chromosome, and (2) genes close together on the same chromosome tend to be transmitted together from parent to offspring, it was concluded that the gene or genes for manic-depressive disorders are located on the short arm of the X chromosome.

Evidence for genetic influences on depression as a personality trait among normal individuals was obtained in the three MMPI twin studies cited earlier (Gottesman, 1963, 1965; Reznikoff & Honeyman, 1967). In both of Gottesman's adolescent samples the heritability for scores on the depression scale of the MMPI was .45, while in Reznikoff and Honeyman's adult sample, the heritability estimate was .38. As Table 5-1 shows, the heritability estimate for the depression score obtained by combining data from all three studies was second in magnitude only to that for social introversion, .35 versus .37.

Infant Behavior

Freedman (1965; Freedman & Keller, 1963) studied the performance of MZ and DZ twins on 22 items of the Bayley Infant Behavior Profile over the first year of life. Each infant was filmed several times. One group of judges scored the behavior of one member of each twin pair while a second group scored the behavior of the other member of each pair, thus eliminating "halo effects" that might result from the similarity in the appearance of cotwins. Any bias due to knowledge of zygosity was also ruled out because zygosity was determined by matching blood factors only after the performance data had been analyzed.

Rather than obtaining heritability estimates from correlations, Freedman compared the magnitude of differences between MZ and DZ cotwins on their average scores for each item of the Bayley Profile. The differences between scores for MZ cotwins were smaller than for DZ cotwins on all 22 items. The 10 items for which the differences between MZ cotwins were significantly smaller than those of DZ cotwins are presented in Table 5-4.

Freedman (1965, 1968, 1971) has argued for an ethological view that emphasizes the evolutionary significance of genetically influenced behavior. He maintains, for example, that social orientation, especially smiling, during the first five months of life, as measured by Bayley Item #1, and fear of strange persons and objects above age five months, as measured by Bayley Item #9, have played an important role in the survival of the species. Like imprinting in fowl, these behaviors serve to maintain a close bond between the infant and his mother. Smiling does this by rewarding the mother for

TABLE 5–4

Bayley Infant Behavior Profile items on which MZ cotwins were significantly more similar than DZ cotwins.

Item no.	Item name
1.	Social orientation: responsiveness to persons.
2.	Object orientation: responsiveness to toys and other objects.
3.	Goal directedness.
4.	Attention span.
6.3	Activity: coordination of hands.
7.	Reactivity: ease with which child is stimulated to response.
9.	Fearfulness: reaction to new or strange people, materials, surroundings.
12.	Sensory areas: preoccupation or interest displayed in: (a) Sights. (d) Sound producing activity. (e) Manipulating, exploring with hands.

NOTE.—Adapted from Freedman (1965).

taking care of the infant, while fear of strangeness does it by causing the infant to avoid separation from his mother. Early members of the species who carried genes resulting in these behaviors survived to reproduce. While fear of strangers may no longer enhance survival, social responses such as smiling still play a large role in determining how a child will be treated. The behavior thus elicited from the mother will in turn shape the child's personality. For example, a child who smiles little is less likely to experience a warm social environment than a child who smiles much. As a consequence, the child who smiles little may grow up expecting less reward from social interactions than children who smile more.

The strength of genetic influence on early smiling in infants was further revealed by Freedman's findings (1964, 1965) that even blind infants smile in response to social stimulation such as cooing and talking by an adult (see Fig. 5–8). Not only is the smiling response innately organized, but it is also accompanied by fixation of the infant's eyes in the direction of the adult's face, even if the infant cannot see the adult because it is blind.

Rutter, Korn, and Birch (1963) have also provided data on the role of genetic factors in infant reaction patterns. They established nine categories for classifying infants' temperamental reactivity:

1. activity level;
2. rhythmicity—regularity of biological functions such as sleeping, waking, eating, appetite, bowel and bladder functions;
3. approach or withdrawal in response to new stimuli including people, places, food, and toys;
4. adaptability to new situations;

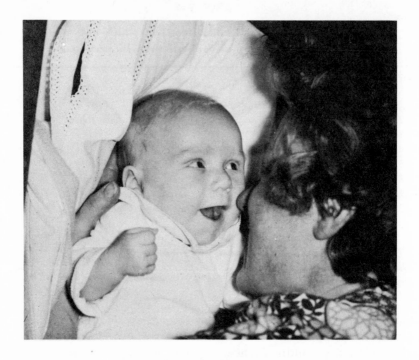

Fig. 5—8. Yvonne, aged 2 months, 20 days, congenitally blind, smiling with eyes toward mother. From Freedman (1965). Reproduced by permission.

5. intensity of reactions;
6. threshold of responsiveness;
7. quality of mood—pleasant, joyful, friendly behavior versus unpleasant, crying, unfriendly behavior;
8. distractibility;
9. attention span and persistence.

For purposes of assessing genetic influences, parents' detailed narrative accounts of the everyday behavior of eight pairs of twins and 26 pairs of siblings were scored according to the nine categories. These accounts were obtained several times during the first, second, and third years of life. As in the Freedman study, zygosity of the twins was not determined until after the data were collected.

Although the samples were too small for heritability estimates, the mean differences in ratings on scales 1 through 7 were all smaller for MZ twins than for DZ twins during the first year of life, suggesting the importance of genetic factors. (Scales 8 and 9 provided insufficient data for analysis.) The differences between DZ cotwins were smaller than between nontwin siblings on four scales and greater on three scales, indicating that DZ twins were hardly more similar than nontwin children having the same degree of genetic overlap, i.e., 50 per cent on the average. All three pairs of MZ twins, including one pair whose members were raised by different families from birth, were more similar across all first-year ratings than were members of a pair of DZ twins whose parents, believing they were MZ, had treated them as similarly as possible. However, after the first year, the greater similarity of MZ cotwins and the equivalent degrees of similarity between DZ twins and nontwin siblings disappeared on several scales. The two scales continuing to show strong evidence of heritability were Scale 1. Activity Level, and Scale 3. Approach–Withdrawal.

CONSTITUTIONAL AND ENVIRONMENTAL INTERACTIONS
IN BEHAVIOR DISORDERS

The longitudinal study in which Rutter, Korn, and Birch (1963) obtained their data provides one of the best available pictures of the complex interactions between constitutional reaction patterns and specific environment. The study is being carried out at the New York University School of Medicine with 136 children (Thomas, Birch, Chess, Hertzig, & Korn, 1963; Thomas, Chess, & Birch, 1968). A primary focus of the study is what the investigators call *temperament,* although they are careful to avoid making it an all-inclusive explanatory concept, as has too often been done with other concepts. They define temperament as "a general term referring to the *how* of behavior . . . the *way* in which an individual behaves . . . the *behavioral style* of the individual child. Temperament is a phenomenologic term used to describe the characteristic tempo, rhythmicity, adaptability, energy expenditure, and focus of attention of a child independently of the content of any specific behavior . . . Like any other characteristic of the organism, its features can undergo a developmental course that will be significantly affected by environmental circumstances [Thomas, Chess, & Birch, 1968, p. 4]."

Employing the nine categories of temperament cited above, quantified ratings of the children's behavior have been made from school observations, teacher interviews, and observations during standard test situations, as well as from frequent parent interviews. While Rutter, Korn, and Birch's findings suggested hereditary influence on some aspects of temperament, the "constitutional" nature of temperament is assumed to include nonhereditary genetic influences, plus accrued influences of the environment beginning at conception.

Of the 136 children in the study, 42 developed significant behavioral disturbances between the ages of two and nine years. It has been possible to document interactions between the children's temperaments and the overt attitudes and behavior of parents, teachers, and peers that led to the appearance of behavioral symptoms. One early temperamental pattern that was overrepresented among children who later developed behavior disturbances was labeled the "difficult child" pattern. It included irregularity in biological functions, withdrawal responses to new stimuli, slow adaptation to environmental changes, frequent expressions of negative mood, and high intensity of reactions. Ten (71 per cent) of the 14 children who manifested this pattern developed clear-cut behavioral symptomatology, although the other 32 children who developed symptoms had different temperamental patterns, including 10 per cent of the children who showed what was called the "easy child" pattern.

No characteristics of the parents of difficult children could be found that initially differentiated them from parents of other children. However, parental reactions differed as the difficult children placed special demands on them:

> A frequent [parental] tendency . . . was to seek explanations based on psychodynamic theories that try to account for a baby's behavior in terms of the mother's attitudes. In these theories, a loving and accepting mother should have a happy and contented child, from which it follows that an unconscious maternal attitude of rejection could be the only explanation for a difficult screaming child. As a result . . . it was not unusual for the mother of a difficult infant who screamed frequently and who made all routines a crisis, to develop self-doubts and feelings of guilt, anxiety, and helplessness . . . .
>
> In attempting to eliminate her infant's frequent periods of loud crying, one mother with such feelings of guilt and helplessness redoubled her efforts to help him—walked him at night, spent long periods of time with him, and responded to his needs as soon as they were expressed. . . . The mother's attempts to quiet the child whenever he cried appeared at first to make the child happy and serene. However, such "happiness" lasted only as long as the mother continued to respond immediately to the child's demands. Once she failed to do so, the child's loud protests and slowness to adapt to demands made upon him made it clear that the mother's previous efforts had not served any constructive purpose. Rather, they had reinforced and perpetuated the child's negative and intense reactions by rewarding them each time they occurred [Thomas, Chess, & Birch, 1968, pp. 79–80].

The study also demonstrated how differences in parental reactions to two children presenting similar patterns determined which child developed behavioral symptoms:

> Both youngsters, one a girl and the other a boy, showed similar irregular sleep patterns, constipation and painful evacuations at times, slow acceptance of new foods, prolonged adjustment periods to new routines, and frequent and loud periods of crying. Adaptation to nursery school in the fourth year was also a problem for both children. Parental attitudes and practices, however, differed greatly. The girl's father was usually angry with her. In speaking of her, he gave the impression of disliking the youngster and was punitive and spent little or no recreational time with her. The mother was more concerned for the child, more understanding, and more permissive, but quite inconsistent. There was only one area in which there was firm but quiet parental consistency, namely, with regard to safety rules. The boy's parents, on the other hand, were unusually tolerant and

consistent. The child's lengthy adjustment periods were accepted calmly; his strident altercations with his younger siblings were dealt with good-humoredly. The parents waited out his negative moods without getting angry. They tended to be very permissive, but set safety limits and consistently pointed out the needs and rights of his peers at play.

By the age of five and a half years . . . the boy's initial difficulties in nursery school had disappeared, he was a constructive member of his class, had a group of friends with whom he exchanged visits, and functioned smoothly in most areas of daily living. The girl, on the other hand, had developed a number of symptoms of increasing severity. These included explosive anger, negativism, fear of the dark, encopresis [bowel incontinence], thumb-sucking, insatiable demands for toys and sweets, poor peer relationships, and protective lying. It is of interest that there was no symptomatology or negativism in the one area where parental practice had been firmly consistent, i.e., safety rules. [pp. 82–83].

SUMMARY

Prominent psychological theories, including those of psychoanalysis, Piaget, and the learning theorists, make strong assumptions about the biological and genetic bases of behavioral development. The viewpoint of animal ethology is also becoming increasingly important for integrating our understanding of biology and behavior.

Much is already known about the general physical process by which transmission of genetic material from parent to offspring occurs. *Chromosomes* can be photomicrographed and arranged into *karyotypes* for study. *Meiosis,* the process by which pairs of chromosomes in the germ cells of a parent divide to form sex cells, can also be observed through a microscope. However, most knowledge about *genes,* the actual molecules of DNA that carry the coded information for development of a new individual, consists of principles inferred from changes in the distribution of phenotypic traits from one generation to the next.

Mendel's laws apply quite accurately to genetically influenced traits for which there are only two possible *alleles* and the alleles influence the phenotypic traits according to patterns of *dominance* and *recessiveness.* However, exceptions to Mendel's laws have required the introduction of additional concepts like *partial dominance, additivity, polygenic determination, penetrance,* and *expressivity.* Some exceptions to Mendel's laws have been accounted for by microscopic discovery of the differences between *female* (X) and male (Y) sex chromosomes.

Biological contributions to development can be thought of in terms of four broad categories, each of which is more inclusive than the one before it: *hereditary, innate, congenital,* and *constitutional.* Disorders that are hereditary include *Tay-Sachs disease,* and *phenylketonuria (PKU). Down's syndrome (mongolism)* and some cases of *epiloia* are innate but not hereditary since they result from nonhereditary genetic aberrations. Because many genetic influences do not appear until long after birth (e.g., *Hunting-ton's chorea*), the *operon model* and other mechanisms have been proposed to explain the triggering of gene effects at specific developmental periods.

Behavior genetics is more complex than the study of genetic influences on physical traits because of the difficulty of defining behavioral traits, of reliably and validly assessing them, and of contending with situational influences on behavior. Nonhuman species offer advantages of convenience and control for studying genetics, but the paucity of precise analogs between human and animal behavior, especially psychopathological behavior, limits the usefulness of animal research for human behavior genetics.

Recent progress in human *chromosomal analysis* has revealed chromosomal anomalies in *Down's syndrome, Klinefelter's syndrome, Turner's syndrome,* and the *XYY syndrome.*

Quantitative genetics employs statistical techniques for obtaining estimates of *heritability*—the ratio of *genetic* to *phenotypic variance* in a phenotypic trait. Heritability estimates refer only to the proportion of variance in a phenotypic trait that is attributable to heredity in a *particular population*. These estimates say nothing about how much the trait can be changed by environment nor about the heritability of the same trait in other populations or environments.

Estimates of the heritability of a human behavioral trait are generally made by comparing the correlation of *monozygotic* (identical) cotwins' scores for the trait with the correlations of *dizygotic* (fraternal) cotwins' scores for the trait. Other techniques include comparing trait correlations for twins reared apart with those for twins reared together and comparing the effects that adoptive parents differing in phenotypic characteristics have on adopted children who are hypothesized to have a certain genotype.

Evidence of heritability has been found for personality traits including introversion–extroversion, neuroticism, manic-depressive disorders, and infant social and temperamental behavior. The ways in which children's constitutional patterns of temperament and parents' child-rearing practices can interact to produce behavior disorders have been documented by means of longitudinal research.

SUGGESTED READING

Animal Ethology. There are several short enjoyable books by animal ethologists that carry broad implications for human behavior. Among them are three by Konrad Lorenz (1952, paperback, 1961; 1965; 1966); one by N. Tinbergen (Second edition 1964, paperback, 1965); and one by Desmond Morris (1967, paperback, 1969). E. Hess's chapter in Mussen (1970) relates current ethological thinking and research directly to human developmental psychology.

Behavior Genetics. Fuller and Thompson (1960) offer the most detailed and complete introduction to research in behavior genetics. A more up-to-date but abbreviated treatment, with special reference to developmental psychology, is provided by McClearn (1970). Anastasi's article, "Heredity, environment, and the question 'how?'" (1958; reprinted in Endler, Boulter, & Osser, 1968) is an important contribution to sorting out implications of various approaches to the heredity–environment problem. Two books edited by Vandenberg (1965; 1968), one edited by Glass (1968), and one edited by Manosevitz, Lindzey, and Thiessen (1969) contain research and theoretical papers on current work in human behavior genetics. Gottesman's (1963b) monograph presents a detailed report of an important human behavior genetic study. Rosenthal's (1970a; 1971) books provide comprehensive summaries of behavior genetic research strategies and findings relating to psychopathology.

Biogenetic Implications of Infant Behavior. Ainsworth (1969) has reviewed the literature on the infant-mother relationship and has contributed original research on infants' exploration, reactions to separation, and attachment to their mothers (e.g., Ainsworth & Bell, 1970). Bowlby (1969) has attempted a theoretical synthesis of the data on infant-mother behavior in terms of an ethologically based behavior control system. Freedman has advocated a synthesis of behavior genetics and ethology in the study of human emotions and personality (1965, 1968, 1971; Freedman, Loring, & Martin, 1967). He has also provided strong evidence for genetic control of early behavior in normal infants (Freedman & Keller, 1963) and for smiling in blind infants (1964).

Interaction of Constitutional and Environmental Factors. The longitudinal study being carried out by several investigators at New York University has provided a wealth of data on constitutional patterns of temperament in infants (Thomas, Birch, Chess, Hertzig, & Korn, 1963) and on how these patterns interact with varying patterns of parental behavior to produce behavior problems (Thomas, Chess, & Birch, 1968). Both books and a summary overview (Thomas, Chess, & Birch, 1970) are recommended for the insight they provide on the dialectical interaction between the behavioral styles of children and their parents and how these interactions shape the child's personality.

6

Neurobiological Development and Dysfunctions

Most pathological behavior is a complex resultant of a child's organic makeup and his experiential history. All aspects of a child's organic makeup can be in some way relevant to understanding his behavior. A child's physical size and attractiveness, for example, influence how people react to him. People's reactions to the child's appearance will, in turn, play an important role in shaping the child's image of himself. A child who looks much younger than other children his age may develop inferiority feelings or may behave immaturely because he comes to perceive himself as consistently falling short of his peers.

Even children who grow at the average rate must contend with the changing expectations that their developing physiques elicit from other people. The onset of puberty and the adolescent growth spurt create especially dramatic changes in appearance that may be difficult for the normal child to reconcile with his previous image of himself. For the child who already has conflicts about himself or for whom puberty and growth are somewhat delayed or accelerated, the psychological effects of the process of physical development may temporarily reach crisis proportions.

Important as the social implications of physical appearance are, this chapter concentrates primarily upon organic development and dysfunctions themselves. The emphasis in earlier chapters on the "developmental dimension" in behavior takes on a much more graphic meaning when we consider organic development. While conceptualizations of behavioral development are generally somewhat abstract, organic development can be readily seen by looking at organisms of different ages. Moreover, the fact that the influence of an environmental event depends upon the state and stage of the organism can be graphically documented for organic development. For example, certain diseases and physical traumas may have devastating effects and may drastically alter the course of development in a young child, but may have little effect if they occur later, while other diseases and traumas show exactly the reverse pattern.

Also especially conspicuous in organic development is the way in which gradual developmental processes bring about a sequence of qualitatively distinct levels of organization and function. From conception onward, each new body cell is a direct product of processes that occurred in the cells already present. Each step along the developmental continuum depends upon the steps just before it and is essential to the steps that follow it. However, the culmination of a number of steps in the formation of a new organ or of a communication network among organs produces a new level of functioning that is in many ways distinct from the preceding level of functioning.

The essential continuity in organic development is obscured somewhat by the practice of counting a person's age from birth. In terms of his developmental history, a person's true age should be reckoned from the moment of conception. The event of birth does not occur at exactly the same developmental age for every human. There is a wide range of variation in age and level of development at birth. Moreover, the *sequence* of organic development followed by those who are born early is about the same as that followed by those who remain *in utero* longer.

Despite the continuity in organic development from the prenatal through the postnatal period, the dramatic change from the intrauterine to the extrauterine environment makes it convenient to separate the prenatal, perinatal, and postnatal periods. Since in this chapter we are concerned with risks to normal development, the environmental change that occurs at birth has special significance for us—many risks existing in the intrauterine environment are absent after birth and vice versa. Furthermore, the child's own behavior has little influence on the risks he encounters before birth, while it greatly influences the risks he encounters after birth. Accordingly, this chapter begins with an account of the normal course of prenatal development and the prenatal risks that can lead to later psychopathology. This is followed by accounts of risks accompanying the birth process and of development from birth through maturity, with its attendant risks. Then come sections on some prominent behavioral categories of organic dysfunction, on psychophysiological reactions, and on psychopharmacology.

PRENATAL DEVELOPMENT

Following conception, the fertilized egg (*zygote*) takes about seven days to drift down the Fallopian tube and implant itself in the wall of the uterus. By the time it is ready for implantation, the *blastocyst,* as it is now called, has grown to the point where it consists of several dozen cells.

After implantation in the uterine wall, the blastocyst develops in such a way that its outer layer forms the placenta while part of its inner layer forms the *embryo*.

The period from two weeks until eight weeks after fertilization is known as the "period of the embryo." During this period, the embryo becomes differentiated into regions such as the head and limbs, and cells become differentiated into specialized tissues such as muscle and nerve. By the eighth week, the child, now about an inch long and known from this point until birth as a *fetus,* is already recognizably human—he has a beating heart, arms, legs, and a nervous system that shows reflex responses to tactile stimuli. Most nerve and muscle cells appear to be present by six months after fertilization. The growth of these tissues during much of the remaining life span consists mainly of developing and enlarging the existing cells rather than adding new cells. The brain grows especially rapidly during the fetal period, and by birth it averages about 25 per cent of its adult weight, which is considerably more than most other organs.

The growth rate of the fetus slows when his size nears the capacity of the maternal uterus, generally at 34 to 36 weeks after fertilization, but growth accelerates again after birth. The degree to which maternal size controls fetal size has been dramatically demonstrated by mating a large stallion with a small Shetland mare and a small Shetland stallion with a large mare. In the first case, the foal was small at birth, while in the second case the foal was very large. However, after a few months, both foals were the same size, and at maturity both were about halfway between their parents in size (cf. Tanner, 1970).

Endocrine Functioning

Beginning with the fetal period, hormones secreted by the endocrine glands play an important role in actualizing the growth plan coded in the genes. Hormones that transfer across the placenta from the mother's blood stream may be the first hormones to influence fetal growth, but by about the eighth week after fertilization the fetal pituitary gland begins secreting growth hormone. By about the thirteenth to eighteenth week, the fetal thyroid gland secretes *thyroxine,* which affects protein synthesis in the brain. If thyroxine production is inadequate, the nerve cells fail to grow normally, resulting in irreversible neurological defects.

The sexual differentiation of the fetus involves hormonal mechanisms that have a significant bearing on later behavioral differences between males and females. During the seventh week after fertilization, action begun by genes located on the Y chromosome of a male fetus causes the as yet undifferentiated gonads to start developing into testes. The Leydig cells of the newly formed testes begin to secrete the male hormone *testosterone* after the ninth week. The testosterone then causes the external genitalia to develop into a penis and scrotum beginning in the tenth week. In the absence of the male hormone, the sex organs take on female form.

Besides affecting genital development, the male hormone apparently influences the structural development of the *hypothalamus,* a part of the brain that later influences emotions and sexual behavior (Money & Ehrhardt, 1972). Animal evidence indicates that the effect of the male hormone on the hypothalamus can occur only within a very short critical period. If enough male hormone does not reach the brain at the appropriate time, the hypothalamus of a male rat, for example, will not differentiate in the usual male manner. Instead, it will develop along female lines, and normal male sexual behavior will not occur in adulthood. Injecting a female rat with male hormone during the critical period will cause her hypothalamus to develop along male lines, preventing the later appearance of female reproductive cycles and sexual behavior (cf. Tanner, 1970).

Although the exact neurological mechanism is not known, Young, Goy, and Phoenix (1964) have shown that prenatally administered sex hormones affect the later behavior of rhesus monkeys. Two genetically female monkeys who received male hormones prior to birth later behaved more like males than like normal females. Compared to normal females, they made many more threatening facial gestures, initiated more play, engaged in more rough-and-tumble play, and withdrew less from the threats and approaches of other monkeys. They also made more frequent attempts at sexually mounting nontreated females and they made pelvic thrusts when mounting.

Experimental manipulation of prenatal sex hormones to determine their effect on postnatal behavior would, of course, be unethical with humans. However, an unanticipated natural experiment occurred as a result of the administration of synthetic hormones to save the pregnancies of women who were prone to have miscarriages. These hormones are related in chemical structure to androgens, the male sex hormones, but they function like the female hormone *progesterone* in protecting pregnancy. Since they resemble both progesterone and androgens, they are known as *progestins.*

It was discovered that daughters born to some women receiving progestins were masculinized to the extent of having an enlarged clitoris, labial fusion, and, in rare cases, a penis with an empty scrotum. Surgery was employed to form female genitals in the cases recognized as female because of their incomplete genital masculinization. No further treatment was needed and the girls' ovaries functioned normally, feminizing the body and inducing menstruation at puberty.

To determine the effects of prenatal androgenization on postnatal behavior, Money and Ehrhardt (1972) interviewed 10 of the girls and their mothers and administered tests of sex-role preferences to the girls when they were between the ages of four and sixteen. Compared to 10 closely matched normal control girls, significantly more of the experimental girls were reported by themselves and their mothers to be tomboys, to participate in vigorous athletics, to prefer boys as playmates and male toys to dolls, to choose utilitarian over feminine clothing, and to give priority to career plans over marriage. However, the androgenized girls did not express dissatisfaction with being girls, did not want to become boys, and did not show any signs of lesbianism. Prenatal androgenization thus appears to influence the postnatal behavior of humans as well as monkeys, although it does not appear to determine sex object choices nor to preclude adoption of a specific sex role identification.

PRENATAL RISKS FOR NEUROBIOLOGICAL DEVELOPMENT

General Condition of the Mother

Malnutrition. Several approaches have been employed in studying the effects of maternal malnutrition upon the developing fetus. The most direct approach has been to study the brains of fetuses whose mothers are known to have been malnourished. This can only be done with precision in nonhuman species where the diets of pregnant animals can be experimentally manipulated and the fetuses can be removed at specified points of development.

A number of studies of rats have shown that maternal malnutrition prevents the fetal brain from growing at its normal rate (Winick, 1969, 1970a, 1970b). Part of the retardation in growth is due to a reduction in the *size* of the brain cells. Yet cell size is also reduced if malnutrition occurs much later in life, and cell size can be increased again if nutrition improves. More crucial is the fact that malnutrition occurring during the fetal period, when most nerve cells are being formed, reduces by about 15 per cent the *number* of cells that are created (Winick, 1970a). No improvement in later nutrition can restore the deficits occurring in cell number. The reduction in brain-cell number occurs not only in the first generation of offspring from malnourished rat mothers, but continues into at least the second generation, even if the first generation was adequately nourished after birth (Zamenhof, van Marthens, & Grauel, 1971). Prenatal malnutrition also retards the formation of *myelin,* a fatty protective covering on nerve fibers that facilitates the transmission of nerve impulses (Benton, Moser, Dodge, & Carr, 1966).

A second approach to studying the effects of prenatal malnutrition has been to compare the condition of human neonates whose mothers were well nourished with the condition of those whose mothers were poorly nourished. Several studies have shown that the general quality of mothers' diets during pregnancy is correlated with the condition of their infants at birth (Burke, Beal, Kirkwood, & Stuart, 1943; Ebbs, Brown, Tisdall, Moyle, & Bell, 1942; Tompkins, 1948). However, a large-scale study of children born to Dutch mothers during a severe famine created by the Nazis in World War II showed that, at age 19, their mean IQs and rates of mental retardation did not differ from those of children born to mothers unaffected by the famine (Stein, Susser, Saenger, & Marolla, 1972). While the children of the malnourished mothers may have suffered in ways not detected in this study, other studies have indicated that the long-term nutritional status of mothers *before* pregnancy is a critical variable (cf. Birch & Gussow, 1970).

Certain specific dietary deficiencies in the mother are known to lead to specific disorders in the child. For example, a vitamin D deficiency can cause the child to be born with rickets (Montagu, 1962), while an iodine deficiency can cause *cretinism,* a syndrome that includes retardation and dwarfing (Lenneberg, 1968). The effects of these specific deficiencies, like those of general malnutrition, are not as reversible when they occur during the fetal or neonatal period as when they occur in more mature organisms.

Maternal Age. The risks of congenital defects, infant mortality, and complications of pregnancy and delivery are generally elevated for mothers below the age of 20 and above 35 (Ferreira, 1970; Hedberg, Holmdahl & Pherson, 1967). Immaturity of the reproductive system may be the source of problems in the younger group, while general processes of aging may be responsible for problems in the older group.

Mongolism (Down's syndrome) is one specific anomaly that is known to be associated with maternal age. Estimates of the incidence of mongoloid births range from about 1 in 1,000 for mothers under 30 to as many as 40 in 1,000 for mothers over 45 (Benda, 1969). Although it is known that most cases of mongolism are due to the failure of the twenty-first pair of chromosomes in the mother's ovum to divide during meiosis, it is not known why the failure to divide is more frequent in the ova of older women (Penrose, 1963).

Maternal Emotions. There are many ways in which the emotional state of the pregnant mother can physically affect the development of her fetus. Strong emotions can cause cortisone, adrenalin, and other hormones to be released into the mother's blood stream. These can, in turn, pass through the placenta and affect the fetus (Thompson, 1957). The mother's emotional state is also likely to affect the mechanical aspects of the birth process itself.

The specific physiological mechanisms by which maternal emotions cause problems for the fetus have not been documented. However, it has been found that pregnant women who scored high on various measures of anxiety later experienced more complications of delivery and had more children with congenital abnormalities than did women who scored low in anxiety (Davids, DeVault, & Talmadge, 1961; Davids & DeVault, 1962). The anxious women did not appear to have any more reason to expect birth complications or abnormalities than the nonanxious women. Besides the general effect of high anxiety, the emotional significance of pregnancy for a particular woman may also result in psychophysiological reactions that affect the well-being of the fetus (Squier & Dunbar, 1946).

Unfortunately, as with many other influences on prenatal development, our most precise evidence is confined to nonhuman species. Thompson (1957), for example, conditioned female rats to fear a shuttlebox by shocking them in it. After the rats became pregnant, they were repeatedly placed in the box without being shocked, but with the door to the previously unshocked side of the box locked, presumably increasing the rats' anxiety. The offspring were raised by foster mother rats who had not undergone the fear conditioning. Compared to control rats also raised by foster mothers, the experimental animals later showed greater emotionality, as indicated by decreased amount and increased latency of activity in an open-field situation and slowness in obtaining food in an alleyway. Hockman (1961) reported similar results and also found among the fearful rats frequent problems such as maternal deaths, abortions, stillbirths, and refusal of the mother to raise her young.

Maternal Illness

A number of infectious diseases can be transmitted from the mother to the fetus, sometimes without the mother herself showing any symptoms. Among these diseases are smallpox, scarlet fever, measles, typhoid fever, anthrax, tuberculosis, and malaria. Syphilis contracted by a fetus in early stages will cause abortion, while a fetus contracting it in later stages will survive to be born with syphilis, often with mental defect resulting. In some cases, the symptoms of the syphilitic infection first appear long after birth when general paresis develops. There is some evidence that mumps contracted prenatally can cause congenital malformations (Penrose, 1963), and conclusive evidence that *rubella* (German measles) in the early months of pregnancy causes defects including deafness, blindness, heart malformation, and mental retardation in the child.

Noninfectious disorders in the mother during pregnancy can also adversely affect the fetus. For example, diabetes in the mother causes the infant to be unusually large and mature-looking at birth, although he is actually quite fragile and immature in his functioning. For women in whom diabetes is not well controlled with insulin, fetal mortality is high as is the risk of neonatal respiratory distress, which is occasionally fatal (Gellis & Hsia, 1959). Fetal and maternal mortality are also high among women having high blood pressure (Montagu, 1962).

Toxemia is a common disorder of pregnancy that involves swelling of the mother's limbs and dysfunctions of the mother's renal and circulatory systems. Its cause is unknown, although its greater frequency in lower- than in middle-class women suggests that nutrition may play a role. Pasamanick and Knobloch (1960a; Pasamanick & Lilienfeld, 1955a) found an elevated incidence of cerebral palsy, epilepsy, retardation, reading disability, motor tics, and hyperactive behavior disorders in children whose mothers had toxemia or unexplained vaginal bleeding during pregnancy. They hypothesized that toxemia and bleeding may cause brain damage through depriving the fetus of oxygen. Moreover, as they point out, any disorder of pregnancy that has severe effects on some offspring may in others cause undetectible damage that plays a·role in the development of later behavior disorders.

Blood-type Incompatibility

If a fetus inherits blood factors that differ in certain respects from those of its mother, reactions in the maternal and fetal blood streams can occur that are damaging to the fetus. The best-known kind of incompatibility occurs when a mother whose blood is negative for the Rh (*Rhesus*) factor carries a fetus who has Rh positive blood because he has received the Rh positive gene from his father. Rh positive blood carries substances called *antigens* that pass through the placenta into the mother's blood. Here they stimulate the production of antibodies that in turn pass through the placenta into the fetal blood stream where they destroy the red blood cells.

The wholesale destruction of the fetal red blood cells (*erythrocytes*) is known as *erythroblastosis*. It causes the child to appear severely jaundiced at birth because of toxic products resulting from the destruction of red blood cells. Many children suffering from erythroblastosis can now be saved by blood transfusions given immediately after birth, but subtle forms of brain damage may still result (Lenneberg, 1968; Penrose, 1963). While Rh incompatibility occurs in about one out of 12 pregnancies, erythroblastosis appears in only about one in 200. First pregnancies are not usually adversely affected by Rh incompatibility because the mother has not yet developed antibodies. In other cases, the fetal antigens may not cross the placenta (Montagu, 1962). However, genetic counseling is advisable in order to ascertain the risk of erythroblastosis when a woman is Rh negative and her husband is Rh positive.

Drugs

Any chemical that crosses the placenta can affect the fetus. Many drugs do cross the placenta and have much more powerful effects on the fetus than on the mother because of the fetus's immature development and because its small size and small blood supply can allow a drug to attain higher concentrations than in the mother.

The drug thalidomide was responsible for one of the most tragic episodes in modern medical history. Thalidomide was present in sedatives prescribed by physicians in Europe and Canada during the early 1960s. A large number of birth defects were noted in the infants of women who had taken thalidomide while pregnant and the drug was eventually found to be the cause. The thalidomide syndrome includes absence or shortening of the leg and arm bones, wide-set eyes, low and occasionally deformed ears, depressed bridge of the nose, and a variety of other anomalies such as malformation of the heart and digestive tract. Extensive psychological study of thalidomide infants has revealed somewhat retarded rates of behavioral development (Gouin-Décarie, 1961).

It has long been known that the heart rate of the fetus increases when his mother smokes tobacco (Sontag & Wallace, 1935). This indicates that at least some of the toxic products entering the mother's blood stream from the smoke also enter the fetal blood stream through the placenta. The exact effects of these products on the fetus are unknown, although it is known that nicotine in mothers' milk produces indications of nicotine poisoning in their nursing infants. Several studies also demonstrate reduced birth weight and elevated prematurity and mortality in babies of smoking mothers (Montagu, 1962).

Recent research on the harmful genetic and fetal effects of other narcotic drugs has not yet produced firm conclusions (Dishotsky, Loughman, Mogar, & Lipscomb, 1971), but morphine and heroin addiction in the mother are known to cause congenital dependency on these drugs in the child (Montagu, 1962). Mescaline and LSD have also been demonstrated to cause very high rates of fetal malformation and death in animals (B. Becker, 1970). LSD has been strongly implicated in the increased rates of abnormalities found in the offspring of human users (Maugh, 1973).

Heavy sedation given the mother prior to delivery causes a depression in the infant's brain waves before and after birth (Hughes, Ehemann, & Brown, 1948) and interferes with his attentiveness during at least the first four days postnatally (Stechler, 1964b). Because of the possibility that heavy sedation may cause asphyxiation leading to permanent brain damage, most physicians now avoid using general anesthesia during labor and delivery.

Irradiation

Radiation is another potential source of damage during the prenatal period. Although radiation probably accounts for very few birth defects under normal conditions (Murphy, 1947), unusual conditions, such as irradiation of the mother's pelvis by an excess of X-rays or by exposure to atomic blasts, are known to affect the fetus. Therapeutic irradiation can produce either abortion or malformation and retardation of the child, but exposures greater than used in ordinary X-ray photography are apparently necessary to cause such harm (Penrose, 1963).

Among pregnant women who were exposed to the Hiroshima and Nagasaki atomic bomb blasts, elevated rates of fetal, neonatal, and infant mortality occurred, as well as retardation and malformation in the infants who survived (Plummer, 1952; Yamazaki, Wright, & Wright, 1954).

THE BIRTH PROCESS

Although many physiological functions are minimally affected by birth, the risks of brain damage during and immediately following birth are greatly elevated by a number of factors. Most of these are related to the potential blocking of the oxygen supply to brain cells. Deprivation of oxygen, called *anoxia,* can quickly damage or kill brain cells. The effects on later behavior and development depend upon the exact location, extent, and timing of the brain damage. Anoxia in the neonate may have its greatest effects on functions very different from those affected by anoxia in the adult.

Cerebral palsy is a general term for a variety of motor defects resulting from early brain damage. Specific effects of brain damage at birth include paralysis of limbs, tremors in the face and fingers, and lack of control over the speech apparatus. Birth damage to the cerebral cortex can cause later retardation in the growth of the bones on the side opposite the brain damage. For example, damage to the left hemisphere of the cortex may cause the right arm to be stunted (Lenneberg, 1968).

One cause of oxygen deprivation during birth is the breaking of blood vessels in the brain because of excessive pressure on the head. The excessive pressure can result from an especially difficult or prolonged passage through the birth canal; from improper positioning of the fetus in the birth canal, as for example, in a *breech delivery,* where the buttocks ("breech") rather than the head emerge first from the mother's vagina, potentially causing excessive pressure against the lower rear part of the head (Penrose, 1963); and sometimes from the use of instruments such as forceps that may be necessary to extract the infant when it does not emerge smoothly.

When blood vessels in the brain rupture, they can no longer carry oxygen to their appointed brain cells. The blood released from the broken vessels may form clots around other cells, thus depriving these cells of oxygen as well. Injuries due to direct pressure can also cause overdevelopment or underdevelopment of myelin on nerves and the formation of scar tissue that interferes with later brain growth and function (Lenneberg, 1968). Prematurely born infants may be especially vulnerable to these effects because (1) their physical structures are more fragile, and (2) the formation of nerve cells may be interfered with before it reaches the point of near-completion found at birth in full-term infants.

Another cause of anoxia is prolonged delay between the time when the infant stops receiving oxygen through the placenta from his mother's blood stream and the time when he begins breathing on his own. An abnormal suspension of breathing is termed *apnea.* While apnea can cause neonatal brain damage, sometimes severe enough to be fatal, the neonate appears capable of enduring longer periods without oxygen than can older people. Rather than being exclusively a cause of damage, the failure to breathe immediately at birth is coming to be viewed as frequently being a symptom of preexisting damage (Tanner, 1970).

Be it primarily a cause or a symptom of brain damage, neonatal anoxia has been demonstrated to correlate with certain deficits in later functioning. A longitudinal study has shown that children who had sustained anoxia *either* postnatally or *both* prenatally *and* postnatally obtained significantly lower IQs than control children at age three, but that the IQ deficit among those who had sustained *only* prenatal anoxia was not statistically significant (Corah, Anthony, Painter, Stern, & Thurston, 1965; Ernhart, Graham, & Thurston, 1960). However, by the age of seven, the differences in IQ between the first two anoxic groups and the control group had also shrunk to statistically insignificant size.

It thus seems evident that early anoxia does not drastically limit later IQ in many cases. On the other hand, significant evidence for a perceptual-motor deficit was found at age seven, but not at age three, while examinations by neurologists revealed significant signs of neural damage at age three but not at age seven for the anoxic children.

The greatest behavioral deficit among the anoxic children at age seven was in social competence, as measured by the Vineland Social Maturity Scale (Doll, 1953). They were especially poor in "self-help" behavior like eating and dressing, in age-appropriate skills, and in general socialization. The anoxic children were also rated by a psychological examiner as being significantly more impulsive and distractible than the control children at age seven.

Precise evidence on the organic and behavioral effects of experimentally induced neonatal anoxia is available from studies of rhesus monkeys. Monkeys born by Caesarean section and then deliberately asphyxiated for 7 to 9 minutes before breathing spontaneously did not show significant behavioral retardation, but autopsies revealed small brain lesions. Monkeys asphyxiated for 15 minutes before being resuscitated lagged significantly behind normal control monkeys in the age at which visual depth perception, certain visually guided behavior, and independent locomotion developed, but, once these functions had appeared, they took on normal form. However, learning and memory deficits have been reported to occur in older monkeys experimentally asphyxiated at birth (Sechzer, Faro, Barker, Barsky, Gutierrez, & Windle, 1971). It thus seems well-established that some effects of severe neonatal anoxia, when it is not merely a symptom of preexisting damage, may disappear with development, while other effects persist or are not even manifest until later stages of development. This may be because certain damaged areas of the brain only begin to be fully utilized at advanced developmental stages.

Early Birth and Low Birth Weight

Until recently, the term *premature* was used to designate babies who were born before the usual 40-week gestational period or who weighed less than 2,500 grams (five and one-half pounds) at birth. However, many babies under 2,500 grams, especially those between 2,000 and 2,500 grams, have been in the uterus a full 40 weeks, are healthy, and are small simply because the mother is small (Tanner, 1970). Similarly, many babies who are born after less than 40 weeks of gestation are of normal size and health. Tanner (1970) advocates substituting the more specific terms *low birth weight* for infants under 2,000 grams and *short gestation period* for infants born early. He maintains that infants who have had a gestation period of the normal duration but who are still below 2,000 grams at birth often have some defect that has interfered with development and that may not be overcome through later development.

Several studies have shown elevated frequencies of later behavioral and neurological abnormalities in children of very low birth weight (Caputo & Mandell, 1970; Drillen & Ellis, 1964; Braine, Heimer, Wortis, & Freedman, 1966). The correlation between degree of subnormality in birth weight and incidence of neurological abnormality has been demonstrated in a longitudinal study by Harper, Fischer, and Rider (1959). They gave neurological examinations and standardized tests (Gesell, Stanford-Binet) to groups of children who at birth had weighed, respectively, less than 1,501 grams, from 1,501 to 2,000 grams, from 2,001 to 2,500 grams, and more than 2,500 grams. Figure 6–1 portrays the percentage of children at each birth weight who showed signs of neurological abnormality at the age of 40 weeks and again at three to five years.

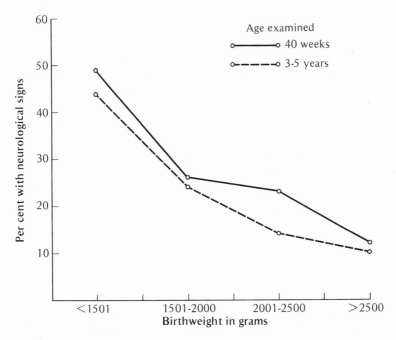

Fig. 6–1. Per cent of children at various birthweights with later signs of neurological abnormalities. Data from Harper, Fischer, and Rider (1959).

Note that the percentage of children with apparent abnormalities is four times as great in the under-1,501 gram group as in the over-2,500 gram group. However, many of these children had only minimal or questionable signs of damage and there was a general tendency for the signs to become milder between the earlier and later examinations.

Short gestation period by itself, aside from its correlation with various complications, does not seem to affect the development of later functions such as walking if the onset of the function is calculated from the date of conception rather than the date of birth. Douglas (1956) compared the age of walking in short-gestation, low-birth-weight infants with that for matched normal control infants. Although the short-gestation children walked at later ages, calculated from birth, the groups were approximately equal when age was calculated from conception.

POSTNATAL DEVELOPMENT

Brain Growth and Development

In terms of percentage of its adult weight, the brain is one of the most advanced organs of the body at birth and throughout childhood. The brain at birth averages about 25 per cent of its adult weight, at six months 50 per cent, at two and one-half years, 75 per cent, and at five years 90 per cent.

The rates of growth are not uniform for all parts of the brain. At birth, the *midbrain, pons,* and *medulla—brain stem* structures responsible for basic reflex activities like breathing—are, in terms of the final percentage of brain volume they will account for, the most advanced in size. The *forebrain,* or *cerebrum* which includes the *cerebral cortex* and *thalamus* and is needed for higher mental processes and voluntary movements, is the next most advanced in size. The *cerebellum*—influential in coordinating complex motor activity—is the least advanced in size, although it rapidly catches up by the age of one. Figure 6–2 presents a schematic representation of the three major regions of the brain—the brain stem, cerebrum, and cerebellum.

While initial growth in the size of the brain is probably a necessary condition for some aspects of further development, neither weight nor size are sufficient criteria for the maturity of the brain or any of its components. In fact, even *nanocephalic* ("bird-headed") *dwarfs,* who at adulthood average 30 inches in height and have brains the size of a neonate's, develop speech and some other higher mental functions (Lenneberg, 1967).

There is believed to be little formation of new nerve cells after birth, even to replace cells that are destroyed. Instead, normal postnatal brain development consists mostly of increases in what Tanner (1970) calls the *connectivity* among nerve cells. By connectivity is meant the physical interconnectedness that makes it possible for one cell to influence another. The increasing efficiency, extensiveness, and complexity of this connectivity

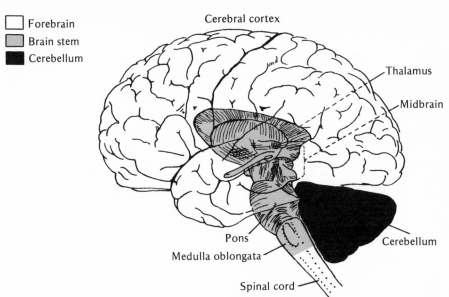

Fig. 6–2. Side view of three major regions of the human brain. The *brain stem* (including *midbrain, pons,* and *medulla*), the *thalamus,* and the *cerebellum* are normally hidden beneath the *cerebral cortex.* Adapted from Penfield and Roberts (1959). © 1959 by Princeton University Press and reprinted by permission of the publisher.

among brain cells and structures appears to underlie much of behavioral development.

It is especially in the cerebral cortex that changes which may underlie behavioral development continue long after birth. Neural cells grow in size and their *dendrites* and *axons*—the fibers that carry impulses *toward* and *away from* the cells, respectively—grow in length, forming connections with other nerves and various parts of the body. The axons also acquire coverings of myelin, the fatty insulating substance that facilitates the conduction of nerve impulses.

As described by Anokhin (1964), myelin forms on fibers carrying impulses to specific cortical areas at the same time as it forms on fibers carrying impulses away from these areas. In other words, functional units of the nervous system rather than specific geographical areas, such as the cerebral cortex, become myelinated together.

The order of myelination is quite regular in normal human brains. The axons of many nerves involved in reflex behavior are myelinated by the time of birth. Others that play a role in vision, complex motor coordination, and voluntary action myelinate rapidly during the first year. Still others, located in the frontal cortex and apparently involved in symbolic thought

and learning from individual experience, continue to myelinate into maturity and old age (Yakolev & Lecours, 1967).

In addition to nerve cells, the brain contains many *glial cells,* also known
as *neuroglia.* These are cells of the supporting tissue that continues to form
around nerve cells after birth. By maturity, glial cells constitute about 90
per cent of the cells in the brain (Tanner, 1970). Figure 6–3 illustrates typical nerve and glial cells.

Because of the large variety of developmental changes in the cortex that
may be correlated with behavioral development, a number of criteria are
used for determining the maturity of parts of the cortex. These include
the size of nerve cell bodies, which increases; the length of dendrites and
axons, which increases; the density of neurons, i.e., the number of nerve
cells per unit volume of cortex, which decreases as the nerve cell bodies and
their dendrites and axons grow; and the degree of myelination, which increases (Tanner, 1970).

According to these criteria of maturity, the cortex is very immature at
birth. Much of the reflexive behavior occurring during the first month of
life may not involve cortical control, since this behavior occurs even in
infants born without cortex (Jung & Hassler, 1960). Orienting responses to

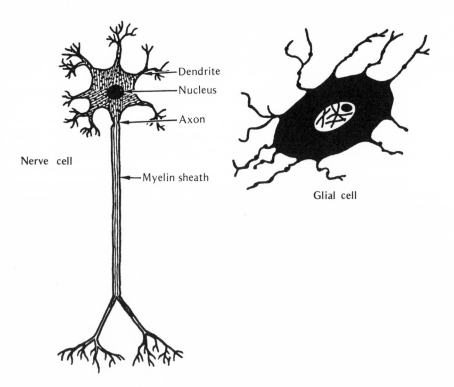

Fig. 6–3. A nerve cell and a glial cell typical of those found in the brain and
other parts of the nervous system. Adapted from Scott (1969).

stimulation also occur in infants without cortex, but the fact that such infants fail to habituate to stimuli suggests that the cortex does have inhibitory functions very early in life (Brackbill, 1971).

EEG Evidence.   Much of the research on the functional development of the human brain has involved the study of variations in electrical potential ("brain waves") produced by the electrochemical activity of the brain.   These variations are believed to originate from current flowing through the thousands of nerve cells in the cerebral cortex (Eichorn, 1970).   They can be recorded from electrodes placed on the scalp.   The recording is traced out on graph paper by a polygraph and is called an *electroencephalogram* (EEG).

In normal adults, the EEG pattern is characterized by readily identifiable rhythms during waking and light sleep.   These rhythms are replaced by slow, irregular pulsations during unconsciousness and deep sleep.   Although the infant EEG does show some differences correlated with sleep and wakefulness beginning at the eighth fetal month, both the sleeping and waking EEGs are diffuse and irregular until at least a month after birth.   This corroborates the evidence of brain and behavior studies that the newborn is "precorticate," i.e., functions that will be based in the cortex and will account for the rhythmic patterns in adult waking EEGs are at a very minimal level.

There are significant changes in the waking EEG at the ages of about 2 years, 6 years, and 11 years, which happen to be the ages at which Piaget has identified major advances in intellectual development (Corbin & Bickford, 1955; Gibbs & Knott, 1949).   Other aspects of the progressive organization and maturation of the brain are also consistent with the stagelike nature of mental development hypothesized by Piaget and others (Tanner, 1970).

Cerebral Dominance

The cerebrum of mammals is divided into two nearly symmetrical halves, the *cerebral* hemispheres.   One of the best-documented and most significant features of human brain development is the phenomenon of *cerebral dominance*.   Cerebral dominance refers to the fact that, in adults, one hemisphere appears to dominate in certain functions.   *Lateralization of function* is another expression for the fact that certain functions depend more upon one side of the brain than on the other side.

Hand preference and speech are the two behavioral manifestations that have long been associated with cerebral dominance.   Because the motor neurons connected to one side of the body are controlled by the cerebral hemisphere on the *opposite* side, it has often been assumed that the left cerebral hemisphere is dominant in people who are predominately right-handed, while the right hemisphere is dominant in people who are left-handed.   Since areas of the brain controlling speech were known to be typically located in the left hemisphere of right-handers, it was believed that the speech centers of left-handers were in the right hemisphere.   However, much recent evidence from the effects on speech of brain lesions and operations indicates that handedness is a very inaccurate guide to the localization of speech functions. The left hemisphere appears to be responsible for speech functions in many left-handers as well as right-handers, although right cerebral dominance and *incomplete lateralization* of speech function—where both hemispheres play a role—seem to be more frequent in left- than in right-handers (Hecaen & deAjuriaguerra, 1964; Penfield & Roberts, 1959; Zangwill, 1960).

The small correlation found between handedness and location of speech functions may be accidental or may be due to the fact that early damage to the left hemisphere causes the right hemisphere to take over speech functions as well as preventing other functions from developing in the left hemisphere (Penfield & Roberts, 1959).

Recent anatomical studies indicate that parts of *Wernicke's area*—an area of the cortex considered responsible for recognition of patterns of spoken language—are larger in the left hemisphere than in the right hemisphere of most brains, and that these differences in size exist at birth (Geschwind, 1970; Geschwind & Levitsky, 1968). This further suggests that the left hemisphere is the "normal" seat of speech functions in humans and that localization in the right hemisphere is usually due to "abnormal" circumstances.

Development of Lateralization. Despite the fact that the left cerebral hemisphere seems to be the "normal" seat of speech functions, there is considerable evidence that the two hemispheres do not begin to function differently until after the age of one and that they do not become irrevocably specialized until much later. The two cortical areas primarily responsible for speech, *Broca's area* and *Wernicke's area,* appear to mature in both hemispheres about the age of seventeen to twenty months (Peiper, 1963). The physical development of these areas at this time correlates well with observations that children all over the world begin systematically to use and understand language at approximately this period (Lenneberg, 1967).

Broca's area is involved in the production of speech, while Wernicke's area is involved in the recognition of the patterns of spoken language (Geschwind, 1970). The division of speech functions between these two areas means that, when one area matures ahead of the other, speech performance and speech comprehension may be at very different levels. Lenneberg (1962) has described an extreme case of a boy who, by the age of eight, was still unable to speak words, although extensive testing showed that he comprehended language well. An organic defect was assumed to have prevented the acquisition of the motor skill necessary for spoken language, but this did not prevent development of language comprehension.

Evidence for the development of lateralization of speech functions comes from the study of children who have had one cerebral hemisphere removed surgically. Known as *hemispherectomy,* this operation is performed when severe damage in one hemisphere causes persistent seizures and *hemiplegia*—paralysis of one side of the body, always the side opposite the damaged hemisphere. The evidence indicates that both hemispheres participate in speech development before the usual lateralization to the left hemisphere is completed (Basser, 1962). In at least one reported case, damage occurring to the right hemisphere as late as age five interfered temporarily with speech development, indicating that the speech function had not yet been completely relegated to the left hemisphere. In some children, however, early malfunction of one hemisphere may cause speech to be lateralized in the other hemisphere right from the beginning. Early symmetrical damage to *both* hemispheres, by contrast, can cause delays in lateralization and speech development (Dreifuss, 1963).

Psychological testing reveals that, after hemispherectomy, performance improves if the damage was sustained before the age of one, while it often declines if the damage was sustained after age one (McFie, 1961). Apparently, where the damage occurs before age one, the intact hemisphere can function better when hemispherectomy ends interference from the damaged hemisphere. Where the damage occurs after age one, the defective hemisphere may continue to be responsible for some functions that are lost when it is removed. This suggests that, until about the age of one, the two hemispheres may be *equipotential* for most intellectual functions, i.e., each is capable of acquiring these functions. However, from one until about the age of five, each hemisphere becomes increasingly specialized and less able to take over functions that have been assumed by the other hemisphere. If this is the case, one-sided damage occurring after lateralization has taken place cannot be so readily overcome by the undamaged hemisphere as before lateralization.

Endocrine Functioning

As mentioned earlier, hormones secreted by the endocrine glands begin during the fetal period to play an essential role in translating genetically coded information into the growth of the child. Because of the complexity of the endocrine system, only some highlights of endocrine functioning as it pertains to development and pathology will be presented here.

The *pituitary gland,* located below the brain, is known as the "master gland" of the endocrine system. It is so called because it secretes a number of hormones that are carried by the blood stream to other glands. The pituitary hormones then stimulate these glands to produce their own secretions. The activity of the pituitary influences growth and development in a number of ways. For example, it produces hormones that stimulate the production of *thyroxine* by the *thyroid* gland, *cortisone* and *adrenal androgens* by the *adrenal* gland, *testosterone* by the *Leydig cells* of the male *testes,* and *estrogens* by the female *ovaries,* all of which are necessary for normal growth. The pituitary also produces a growth hormone of its own. Figure 6–4 portrays the locations in the body of the endocrine glands.

Just as pituitary hormones regulate the activities of other glands, the

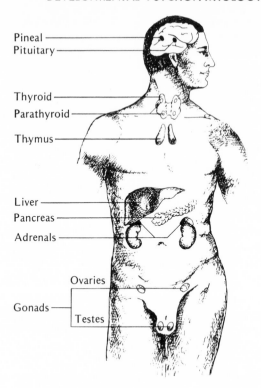

Fig. 6–4.   The endocrine glands of the body.   Adapted from Maher (1966).

pituitary itself is stimulated to release these hormones by releaser substances originating in nearby areas of the brain.   The releaser substances are thought to be switched on and off in response to certain specific stimuli, such as a change in the level of the relevant hormone present in the blood, as sensed by specialized sensor cells near the cells producing the releasers.   There is thus a complex feedback circuit consisting of a sensor, releaser, pituitary hormone, and hormone secreted by a gland in response to the pituitary hormone, which in turn influences the sensor again.

Normal development requires different quantities of various hormones at different stages.   For example, the secretion of testosterone by the Leydig cells in the testes of a male fetus must begin about 10 weeks after conception if the differentiation of the male genitals is to occur.   However, the secretion of testosterone drops to negligible levels from birth until puberty, when it increases again in order to stimulate the development of adult sexual characteristics.

The normal changes in levels of hormone production are believed to occur because nerve impulses from various parts of the brain alter the thresholds of the sensors in the feedback circuit (Tanner, 1970).   Thus, from birth to adolescence, the threshold of the sensor for testosterone in males is set so that production of testosterone is discontinued at levels much lower than those reached prior to birth or at puberty. Similarly, the threshold for thyroid hormone appears to drop during the first two years and then to increase again at adolescence. The many normal changes occurring in endocrine functions at adolescence cause conspicuous changes in physique and behavior, and confront most teenagers with significant problems in psychosocial adjustment.

Abnormal biochemical influences, dietary deficiencies, and disease can disrupt the endocrine system at various points. For example, brain lesions and specific genetic defects can cause premature increases in sex hormone output, resulting in early puberty. An extreme instance has been reported of a girl who reached menarche at the age of three and one-half years (Gesell, 1940). Accidental ingestion by children of sex hormones has shown that male and female sex organs will mature in direct response to hormonal stimulation long before normal puberty, with no other physiological preparation necessary (Tanner, 1970).

Lack of pituitary hormones due to malfunction of the pituitary or deficiencies in the releasers that stimulate it can cause pituitary dwarfism. Moreover, there is now evidence that extreme emotional deprivation can in some cases cause a central nervous system disturbance that in turn causes a pituitary dysfunction. The pituitary dysfunction reduces production of growth hormone and results in severe growth retardation *(psychosocial dwarfism)*, as well as behavioral disturbance (Money, Wolff, and Annecillo, 1972; Powell, Brasel, Raiti, & Blizzard, 1967).

Endocrine Reactions to Stress. In addition to their role in helping to actualize the genetic growth plan, the endocrine glands play a major role in helping the organism to cope with various threats to its well-being. An especially important component of the body's physiological defense involves the interplay of the pituitary and adrenal glands, and is known as the *pituitary-adrenal axis.* When the body meets stress, such as a local injury, the pituitary secretes a hormone that stimulates the adrenal glands to secrete *corticoids.* Corticoids are substances that serve as part of an "alarm reaction" throughout the body. The alarm reaction precedes the efforts of tissues in the affected area to resist effects of the injury. Certain byproducts of the corticoids can be measured in the blood and urine in order to study the strength of physiological reactions to various kinds of stress.

Experimentally induced psychological stressors such as a simulated plane crash and arousing movies have been shown to influence the level of the corticoid byproducts in the same manner as do physical stressors (Berkun, Bialek, Kern, & Hagi, 1962; Handlon, 1962). As will be discussed later in this chapter, individual differences in the intensity and configuration of physiological reactions to stress are likely to be important factors in the development of psychophysiological ("psychosomatic") disorders such as ulcers, asthma, skin eruptions, etc. Besides constitutional determinants of these reactions, prior experience may play a role in shaping them. For example, it has been found that periodic removal of infant rats from their nest promotes faster physical development and increases physiological responsiveness to stress such as shock and extreme cold in adulthood, as indicated by corticoid byproducts and behavioral measures. However, the same animals are relatively unresponsive to nonthreatening environmental changes (Levine & Mullins, 1968).

Effects of Sex Hormones on Behavior. In addition to influencing the prenatal development of sex organs and the hypothalamus, and instigating the development of adult sexual characteristics at puberty, sex hormones appear to play a role in cognitive functioning. Broverman and his colleagues have hypothesized that sex hormones influence activation and inhibition in the functioning of the central nervous system (Broverman, Clarkson, Klaiber & Vogel, 1972). The sex hormones are believed to do this by affecting the production and effectiveness of *neurotransmitters*— chemical substances that help to transmit nerve impulses across *synapses,* the points at which nerve endings meet one another. Both estrogens and androgens are hypothesized to affect neurotransmitters in such a way as to speed up transmission of neural impulses, but estrogens appear to be more effective than androgens in doing this. Greater neural activation facilitates what Broverman calls *automatization* behavior, speedy, accurate performance of overlearned repetitive tasks. However, high neural activation may interfere with functioning on tasks that require delay or inhibition of familiar responses, reversal of usual habits, or problem-solving. Apparently as a result of the superior activating effects of estrogen, females are faster than males on tasks like naming colors, crossing out letters and numbers, reading, writing, typing, and simple calculations. Conversely, males are superior on tasks like mirror tracing, maze performance, and counting backwards, all of which require inhibiting quick habitual responses.

As evidence for the activating effects of estrogens, EEG patterns indicative of high activation have been shown to occur prior to ovulation and to disappear following ovulation, when another hormone, *progesterone,* inhibits the effects of estrogens. Furthermore, women taking estrogen medication as treatment for disrupted menstruation show activated EEG patterns like those of normal women prior to ovulation, while when taking progesterone in addition to estrogen they show less activated EEG patterns, like those of normal women after ovulation (Vogel, Broverman, & Klaiber, 1971).

Androgen level has been demonstrated to be directly related to automatization in males. Adolescent males whose cognitive style was characterized by "strong automatization"—i.e., they performed better at tasks facilitated by automatization than at tasks requiring conceptual restructuring —have been found to have physical characteristics known to result from high androgen levels, such as large biceps and chests, and extensive body hair. Measures of androgen byproducts in the urine were also found to correlate significantly with the automatization cognitive style (Broverman,

Broverman, Vogel, Palmer, & Klaiber, 1964; Klaiber, Broverman, & Kobayashi, 1967). In another study, adolescent boys who were deficient in androgen showed increases in automatization ability after they were treated with
androgens (Stenn, Klaiber, Vogel, & Broverman, 1972). EEG patterns and
automatization behavior are also influenced by androgens administered to
normal adult males (Klaiber, Broverman, Vogel, Abraham, and Cone,
1971).

In addition to the influence of sex hormones on the normal range of
cognitive and behavioral differences, there is now evidence that some reading problems and hyperactive behavior in children above the age of 10
are related to poor automatization ability which, in turn, results from low
sex hormone production (Broverman et al, 1972). However, the Broverman et al hypotheses have not gone unchallenged, as Parlee (1972) has
objected to the lumping together of various abilities and neurological
characteristics along the dimensions of automatization versus perceptual
restructuring. Furthermore, Dawson (1972) has provided evidence that
differences in the socialization of males and females interact with hormonal
differences in determining cognitive styles and abilities.

POSTNATAL RISKS FOR NEUROBIOLOGICAL DEVELOPMENT

Lack of Environmental Stimulation

There has been much controversy about the role of environmental stimulation in human development. Unfortunately, "stimulation" has many
different connotations, few of which have been objectively specified. No
humans exist in environments totally devoid of sensory stimulation. Excessive uniformity of sensory stimulation, as produced in sensory deprivation experiments, is known to cause discomfort for most adults, but no
physiological harm, at least over the relatively short periods of several days
studied so far (Solomon, Kubzansky, Leiderman, Mendelson, Trumbull, &
Wexler, 1961).

Animal Evidence. More extreme sensory deprivation than is permissible
with humans has been experimentally produced in animals. In order to
study the role of visual stimulation in neural development, Wiesel and
Hubel (1963) sewed shut one eyelid of newborn kittens. At three months of
age, many of the nerve cells fed by the deprived eye were found to be
markedly shrunken as compared to nerve cells fed by the normal eye. Sewing the eyelids of two-month-old, visually experienced kittens for a period
of three months produced similar, but less severe, changes in the nerve cells.
No changes were produced in the nerve cells of an adult cat whose eyelid
was sewn shut for three months. A translucent contact lens placed over one
eye of newborn kittens—admitting light but no patterning—had some detrimental effect on the development of nerve cells, but less than did sewing
the eyelids. Thus, to develop normally, nerve cells fed by sensory receptors

apparently require input from those receptors, with patterned input being better than unpatterned.

Rosenzweig, Krech, Bennett, and Diamond (1968) have done extensive studies of the effects of environmental stimulation on rats' brains. Rats chosen from the same litters—thereby roughly equated for genetic factors —were raised under one of three conditions:

1. Environmental Complexity and Training (ECT), where they lived together in a large cage provided with "toys," were given daily experience exploring an open-field apparatus, and were trained on a variety of mazes;
2. Social Condition (SC), where they lived a normal colony life;
3. Isolated Condition (IC), where they lived in individual cages, unable to see or touch other animals.

The brains of rats raised in the enriched ECT condition were found to be significantly heavier than those of rats in the less stimulating IC condition. *Acetylcholinesterase,* the enzyme that metabolizes the synaptic neurotransmitter *acetylcholine,* was also present in significantly greater amounts in the brains of the ECT rats.

As for behavioral measures, ECT and IC rats did not differ on simple discrimination-learning problems, but the ECT rats were significantly superior on complex problems. The SC rats, raised in normal laboratory-rat environments, tended to be intermediate between the ECT and IC rats on all measures, both behavioral and physical, indicating that stimulation had a positive effect over the normal environment, while isolation had a negative effect. The environmental effects were found in adult as well as juvenile rats and disappeared when stimulation ceased, although Levine's work, cited earlier (Levine & Mullins, 1968), has shown that early stimulation has lasting effects on later *endocrine* functioning in rats.

Human Evidence.   Since it is clear that extreme variations in early stimulation *can* influence the neurobiological development of *nonhuman* species, the important question is whether the variations actually experienced by *human* children *do* significantly influence their neurobiological development.   Aside from the previously cited evidence that, in some cases, extreme *emotional* deprivation interferes with pituitary functioning (Powell et al., 1967), there is no direct proof that the kinds of sensory restriction experienced by some human children do interfere with neurobiological development.

However, there is evidence demonstrating physical, intellectual, and emotional retardation in infants raised in institutions where there happens to be little stimulation. Provence and Lipton (1962) have poignantly described the daily routine of infants living in an orphanage which was until recently quite typical in this country. The children lay all day in their cribs, were fed from bottles propped beside them, and were handled only for routine washing and changing. The monotony of the environment was very close to that created in a sensory deprivation experiment, and the infant's limited ability to create stimulation for himself may have made the experience even more sensorially depriving than that of the typical adult in the deprivation experiment.

In reviewing the literature on the effects of institutionalization, Casler (1961, 1968) has concluded that the sensory deprivation found in many institutions significantly interferes with neurobiological development in children just as it does in animals. Another view of the effects of institutionalization is that it breaks or prevents the formation of attachment to a primary mothering figure (Bowlby, 1969). These two views are not necessarily mutually exclusive—the traditional institutional setting deprives a child of both sensory stimulation and the opportunity for attachment. Moreover, a responsive mothering person is one of the best of all possible sources of well-patterned sensory stimulation closely tuned to variations in the child's receptiveness.

Despite the frequently found retardation of institutionalized children on measures of infant development, it is not certain that the effects of early institutionalization cannot be overcome later. For example, Dennis and Najarian (1957) reported that foundlings in an extremely depriving institution were significantly retarded on infant tests, but were normal on nonverbal intelligence tests administered between the ages of four and one-half and six years. It is possible that the early effects of sensory and maternal deprivation on performance are at least partially overcome when the child can move around on his own. Sayegh and Dennis (1965) also found that extra experience in sitting and manipulating objects for an hour each day for 15 days markedly improved performance of foundlings on infant tests, but the gains ceased when the supplementary experience ended.

Even in the absence of conclusive evidence for persisting biological effects of institutional sensory deprivation on young humans, it is likely that many aspects of development related to socialization, motivation, and specific learning are critically and perhaps irrevocably influenced by extreme sensory deprivation in early life.

Malnutrition

The problem of malnutrition in childhood is nearly overwhelming on a world-wide scale. Graham (1967) estimates that well over 50 per cent of the inhabitants of the world have survived varying degrees of malnutrition in early life. To make matters worse, cultural changes are causing breast feeding to be abandoned in many underdeveloped countries before adequate dietary substitutes are available (Mönckeberg, 1968). While malnutrition at any time in life may be physically harmful, malnutrition during the fetal period and early infancy appears to have the most severe and irreversible effects on brain development because, as detailed earlier, nearly all nerve cells are formed by the age of about 6 months.

Compared to adequately nourished infants who died of other causes, the brains of infants who died of malnutrition before the age of two have been found to contain markedly fewer cells, especially in the cerebrum and cerebellum, but also in the brain stem (Winick, Rosso, & Waterlow, 1970). Studies of children who were malnourished during their first year, but who received improved nutrition later, reveal persisting deficits in head circumference (Graham, 1967; Stoch & Smythe, 1963, 1968), which has been shown to be a good indicator of brain growth (Winick & Rosso, 1969). Long-lasting deficits in infant test and IQ test performance have also been found in impoverished children subjected to early malnutrition, even after improved nutrition had eliminated the obvious physical effects (Brockman & Riccuitti, 1971; Cravioto & Robles, 1965; Mönckeberg, 1968).

In one of the longest follow-up studies of malnourished children, Stock and Smythe (1963, 1968) compared malnourished South African children with a matched group of South African children whose nourishment was more adequate, although still not optimal. The children were between the ages of 10 months and 3 years when they were first tested and were 11 years old at the final testing. Living conditions of the malnourished group were considerably worse than those of the control group, although IQs and head circumferences of the parents did not differ significantly between the groups and living conditions of the malnourished group improved over the course of the study. Physical measurements, including height, weight, head circumference, and maturity of EEG patterns all remained significantly lower in the malnourished children than in the controls. Likewise, significant deficits of 15 to 20 points were found in Gesell tests of development and several different IQ tests. The malnourished children were also significantly slower in their rate of school progress. Unfortunately, as is often the case, the effects of poor environment and family conditions cannot be separated from the effects of malnutrition on the behavioral measures.

Of greater certainty is the fact that specific vitamin deficiencies cause diseases including rickets, beriberi, scurvy, and pellagra, all of which can produce damage to the growing brain (Ford, 1960).

Brain Lesions

Brain lesions can result from many causes and have many different effects. Impacts sustained in automobile accidents, falls, and direct blows can injure brain tissue just as they injure the tissue of any other organ. Some diseases may be accompanied by *encephalitis*—inflammation of brain tissue—or *meningitis*—inflammation of the *meninges,* the membranes enveloping the brain and spinal cord. These can leave temporary or permanent damage. Among such diseases are measles, mumps, "lethargic" or "epidemic" encephalitis ("sleeping sickness"), various bacterial and viral infections, scarlet fever, and tuberculosis of the nervous system (Ford, 1960). Certain other relatively rare afflictions, known as *degenerative diseases,* cause progressive deterioration of specific parts of the nervous system.

Neoplasms (tumors) and cysts can destroy brain tissue or interfere with its functioning by creating direct pressure against it, as can *hydrocephalus* —an excess of cerebrospinal fluid in the head, usually caused by injury or disease. Although more frequent in old age than in childhood, hemorrhaging of weakened blood vessels can deprive brain cells of oxygen. The immature brain may also be damaged by ingestion of poisons, including household substances such as cleaning fluids and insecticides, drugs commonly found in medicine cabinets, alcohol, narcotics, and by inhalation of carbon monoxide. Lead poisoning due to eating lead-based paint from furniture and walls has occurred in epidemic proportions in city slums and can result in brain damage to the point of mental retardation and death. Certain allergic reactions can also produce damage in the growing brain (Ford, 1960).

The Effects of Brain Damage.   Although it is well-documented that all of the above can cause brain damage, many factors such as the age and general health of the child and the specific circumstances of the insult to the brain influence the nature and effects of the damage. This fact, plus the fact that precise documentation of the physical effect is possible only in cases where death and autopsy occur soon after the insult, mean that most information on the effects of brain damage is highly inferential. As will be discussed in the next section on disorders resulting from presumed organic dysfunction, most studies of the effects of brain damage are done with groups that are heterogeneous with respect to the location and type of damage—because direct evidence of the location and type of damage is difficult to obtain prior to autopsy.

Despite the inevitable heterogeneity of the children studied, Teuber and Rudel (1962) have succeeded in demonstrating some general relations between age and the effect of brain damage on certain psychological functions. Three perceptual tasks revealed three different patterns of relations between behavior and age in cerebral-palsied children who had suffered brain damage before the age of one. In one task, the child was placed in a chair that could be tilted at various angles to the left and right. A device that emitted audible clicks was then moved in an arc over the child's head where he could not see it. The child was asked to report when the sound was right above the middle of his head. Five-year-old children—both normal and brain-damaged—were very accurate in locating the sound, even when they were sharply tilted to one side. However, older normal children made large constant errors in locating the sound, due to attempts to compensate for the tilt of the chair. These constant errors peaked in adolescence and remained large among normal adults. Older brain-damaged children, by contrast, made *small* constant errors of over-compensation, so that, by the age of 11, brain-damaged children were considerably *more* accurate than normal children—because, like younger children, they were not influenced by the tilting of their bodies.

In a second task, the sound source was gradually moved from a position on the child's left or right toward a position directly over his head. The child was to report when the sound reached the point directly over his head. Unlike the influence of body tilt on position judgments, the starting position of the sound—to the left or right—had the greatest influence on five-year-old children, causing their judgments of center to be displaced toward the starting position. This "starting position effect" decreased as children got older, but brain-damaged children were more affected by starting position at all ages than were normal children.

In a third task, the child was blindfolded and the chair was tilted to the left or right. It was then brought slowly toward the vertical until the child said he felt upright. Five-year-old children reported feeling upright when they were still tilted markedly to the starting side, while older children made progressively smaller self-righting errors. Brain-damaged children made larger errors than normal children at early ages, but the size of their errors decreased more with age than those of normal children, so that, by the age of 12, brain-damaged and normal children performed similarly. Figure 6–5 summarizes the contrasting relations between age and the effects of brain damage on these three different tasks.

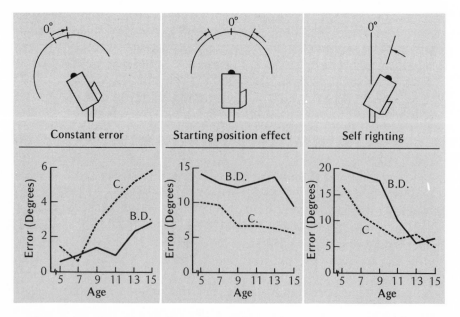

Fig. 6–5. Contrasting effects of early brain damage on perceptual functioning at various ages. B.D. signifies brain-damaged group; C. signifies control group. From Teuber and Rudel (1962).

The important point illustrated by these findings is that the effects of brain injury depend greatly upon the *age* of the child. Some aspects of functioning, such as those involved in the starting position effect, may be influenced at all ages. For other aspects of functioning, such as those involved in the self-righting effect, the child can "grow out of" the abnormality. For still others, such as those involved in producing the constant error, the child may "grow into" the abnormality. Some kinds of damage may also be more detrimental if they occur early than if they occur later because they interfere with acquisition of basic skills. For example, damage causing deafness very early in life will prevent a child from acquiring language, while the same damage occurring after language is acquired will not cause language to be lost. Conversely, some forms of damage are more handicapping when they occur late than when they occur early. As discussed previously, the right hemisphere appears capable of taking over speech functions when the left hemisphere is damaged early in life, but not later. It is thus essential to avoid the error of stereotyping "the brain-damaged child" without considering his age, the role of specific functions that may be impaired, and the possibility that impairments may be compensated for either by further development or by special education.

SOME DISORDERS WITH PRESUMED ORGANIC ETIOLOGIES

While some symptoms can be readily traced to specific organic dysfunctions, many individuals are classified as "organic" or "brain-damaged" because of a combination of behavioral symptoms, neurological "signs" (e.g., defects in motor reflexes), and organic and psychological test patterns, without the exact nature of any organic dysfunction ever being determined. As pointed out earlier, this is inevitable because it is usually impossible to examine directly the brains of individuals who do not die soon after their brains are damaged. However, the result is that most diagnosis and treatment in those cases revolves around diagnostic categories that are broadly descriptive and that may include individuals with very different and largely unknown etiologies for their symptoms. The following sections deal with the most widely used of these descriptive categories.

Brain Damage and "The Brain-Damaged Child"

The Strauss et al Studies.　During the 1930s and 1940s, Alfred E. Strauss, Heinz Werner, Laura Lehtinen, and their colleagues carried out extensive studies designed to develop methods for diagnosing and educating brain-damaged children (cf. Strauss & Lehtinen, 1947). Their primary strategy was to find variables on which brain damage might interfere with performance in distinctive ways. For example, the patterns in Set I of the "Tactual-Motor Test" shown in Fig. 6–6 consisted of raised rubber thumbtacks placed among rows of flat thumbtacks. The patterns in Set II were

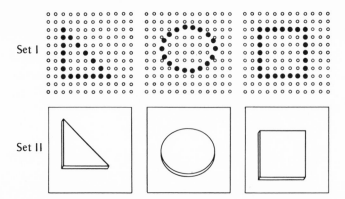

Fig. 6–6. Tactual-Motor Test used by Werner and Strauss to identify brain-damaged children. From Strauss and Lehtinen (1947). © 1947 by Grune & Stratton and reprinted by permission.

carved in relief on smooth wooden backgrounds. Children were asked to feel the patterns with their fingers without being able to see them. Brain-damaged children were expected (and found) to have difficulty in drawing the Set I patterns because the backgrounds had distracted them from perceiving the patterns separately, while they were expected to have no difficulty in drawing the Set II patterns because the smooth backgrounds were not distracting.

Groups of normal children, retarded children assumed to have no brain damage, and retarded children believed to be brain-damaged were tested on the perceptual tasks as well as on various cognitive tasks. They were also rated on personality and behavioral scales. Those characteristics on which the brain-damaged children scored differently from the other two groups were then used for diagnosing brain damage in children in whom damage was suspected but not confirmed by other methods.

Largely from this body of pioneering research, there evolved a standard picture of "the brain-damaged child." The picture included hyperactivity, impulsivity, distractibility, short attention span, emotional lability, poor perceptual performance, and clumsiness, although most of these symptoms have been observed to disappear during late childhood. Where the suspicion of brain damage rests largely upon this *hyperkinetic behavior syndrome,* the terms *Strauss syndrome, diffuse brain damage, brain injury, minimal brain damage, minimal brain dysfunction,* and *minimal cerebral dysfunction* have been frequently applied. The term *perceptual-motor handicap* has also become almost a synonym for unconfirmed brain damage.

The Concept of "The Brain-damaged Child." The popularity achieved by the diagnosis of brain damage in children is illustrated by a survey of 99 consecutive admissions to a child guidance clinic (Lezak & Dixon, 1964).

Of the 99 children, 37 were diagnosed as having some organic condition. Thirty-one of them were called "brain-injured," while six received other organic diagnoses, primarily of convulsive disorders. Ten of the "brain-injured" children took EEGs, and five of these were abnormal. All the children had neurological examinations, but abnormalities were detected in only three. The diagnoses thus rested largely upon behavioral observations. However, as Birch (1964) points out:

. . . the *fact* of brain damage in children and the *concept* "the brain-damaged child" are quite different matters. As a *fact,* brain damage refers to any anatomic or physiologic alteration of a pathologic kind present in the nerve tissues of the brain . . . The *concept* "the brain-damaged child" . . . has been used to designate a certain pattern or set of patterns of behavioral disturbance . . . .

One major obstacle to knowledge has been the tendency to consider the problem of the "minimally brain-damaged child" as a problem in the singular. The essential inadequacy of the term "brain damage" for purposes of classification derives from the contradiction between its singular form and the plurality of content which it seeks to embrace [pp. 4–6].

Supporting Birch's objections to blaming certain behavior patterns exclusively on "brain damage," an extensive study of preschool children known to have brain damage demonstrated that the hyperkinetic behavior syndrome was not a consistent sign of brain damage (Ernhart, Graham, Eichman, Marshall, & Thurston, 1963). Parents' ratings of hyperactivity, aggressiveness, emotionality, and demandingness were not significantly different for brain-damaged and normal children, although the brain-damaged children were rated as being significantly more *inactive,* infantile, negativistic, and compulsive. In general, personality ratings by parents and psychological examiners both showed relatively small differences between brain-damaged and normal children. Cognitive and perceptual-motor measures revealed deficits among the brain-damaged children, but these deficits did not follow the patterns reported for brain-damaged adults and often attributed to brain-damaged children. Rather than being concentrated mainly in areas involving perceptual functioning, the deficits were fairly uniform for all areas measured, including vocabulary.

Problems in Diagnosing Brain Damage. If the hyperkinetic behavior syndrome and particular patterns of psychological test performance are not inexorable products of brain damage, how can we study brain damage and its consequences in the many ambiguous cases where it is suspected but cannot be confirmed by a history of known injury or by surgical procedures? The EEG, neurological examinations, and developmental histories suggestive of physical injury are the most frequently used diagnostic indices of brain damage. Neurological examinations consist of tests of motor reflexes including knee jerk and Babinski, tests of sensory acuity, and tests of visual fields and pupillary reflexes. A distinction is made between *hard* *signs* of neurological damage—such as paralysis, anesthesia (lack of sensation in part of the body), and major reflex changes—and *soft signs* like poor fine-motor coordination, impaired visual-motor coordination, poor balance, clumsiness, and *strabismus* (incoordination of the eyeballs). Hard signs are usually present when damage is severe enough to be apparent in other ways, while only soft signs are present in the children under discussion here.

Unfortunately, numerous studies have shown low correlations among the various psychological, behavioral, EEG, neurological, and developmental indices of brain damage (e.g., Paine, Werry, & Quay, 1968; Schulman, Kaspar, & Throne, 1965; Stevens & Milstein, 1970; Wikler, Dixon, & Parker, 1970; Werry, 1972b). Systematic comparisons between children having the hyperkinetic behavior syndrome and control groups comprised of healthy children and children with other types of problems have also revealed high frequencies of abnormal EEGs and other signs of brain damage in the *nonhyperkinetic* groups (Capute, Niedermeyer, & Richardson, 1968; Graffagnino, Boelhouwer, & Reznikoff, 1968; Stevens, Sachdev, & Milstein, 1968).

Another approach to diagnosis of minimal brain damage has been to observe the effects of amphetamine drugs on the child's symptoms. Amphetamines are widely used in the treatment of hyperkinetic behavior because, contrary to their effects on adults, they seem to suppress children's activity. Wender (1971), among others, has maintained that, if amphetamines successfully suppress a child's·hyperkinesis, the etiology of the hyperkinesis is probably organic. This general strategy of diagnosis will be discussed further in the section on psychopharmacology. However, it has certainly not resolved the main issues involved in relating behavioral problems to unconfirmed organic dysfunction in children.

There is no question that organic dysfunction may create certain handicaps, but the field currently suffers from a lack of agreement about the extent of such handicaps and how to define, classify, diagnose, and treat them. It appears that one of the prerequisites for progress is, as Birch points out (see p. 167), a readiness to stop considering brain damage as a problem in the singular and to start studying it in pluralistic terms, that is, to take seriously the possible differences in the source, extent, and location of the damage, and the age, specific behavioral deviations, and psychological history and environment of the child as crucial determinants of each child's problem and treatability.

Unless we can obtain a better understanding of the relations between brain function and behavior, some children whose problems really are *not* affected by organic dysfunction will continue to be treated as if they are organically defective—with the pessimistic connotations often unjustly accompanying such diagnoses—while others whose problems really *are* affected by organic dysfunction will continue to be treated as if only their parents and their own psychodynamics are to blame.

Central Processing Dysfunctions

Another category of disorders based upon presumed organic dysfunctions involves specific problems in acquiring skills normally developed during childhood. These disorders are often grouped under the heading of central processing dysfunctions. Reading and speech problems have received by far the most attention and will be discussed below, but general learning disabilities, inability to write (*agraphia*), difficulties with quantitative skills, and various problems in integrating input from different sense modalities have also been regarded as central processing dysfunctions (Chalfant & Scheffelin, 1969). As with the "brain-damaged child" syndrome, most research and theory concerns the numerous cases in whom no organic dysfunction can be directly confirmed.

Reading Problems. In many children, poor reading performance is attributed primarily to emotional problems, poor education, low motivation, and/or general environmental disadvantages. These factors certainly can interfere with the acquisition of reading, and they will be discussed in later chapters. However, there are children whose reading problems do not seem to be due primarily to these factors. Such children are often diagnosed as having *specific developmental dyslexia,* defined as: "A disorder manifested by difficulty in learning to read despite conventional instruction, adequate intelligence, and sociocultural opportunity. It is dependent upon fundamental cognitive disabilities that are frequently of constitutional origin [Research Group on Developmental Dyslexia of the World Federation of Neurology, quoted by Critchley, 1970, p. 11]."

Numerous theories have been proposed to account for specific developmental dyslexia, although most emphasize a basic, possibly hereditary, inability to integrate and coordinate information from written representations of words and to relate it to the sounds of spoken words. The condition was previously known as *word blindness,* implying that the child was simply "blind" to meanings carried by written words. Critchley (1970) argues for the existence of developmental dyslexia as a distinct syndrome on the basis of the following observations:

1. its persistence into adulthood;
2. peculiar errors made in reading and spelling;
3. the elevated frequency of the disorder in some families;
4. the greater incidence among males (although nearly all disorders are more frequent among males);
5. the absence of signs of serious brain damage or perceptual defects;
6. the absence of significant psychological origins;
7. the continued failure to read despite conventional instruction;
8. the presence of normal intelligence.

As with many other disorders, no operational criteria for identifying children with the problem have been uniformly applied. It is thus difficult to draw conclusions from conflicting evidence reported by various authors, because it is hard to tell whether they all studied children with the same type of problem. Be that as it may, an extensive study in Sweden has confirmed an above-average incidence of reading problems in families of children with specific difficulties in acquiring reading (Hallgren, 1950). The excellent Swedish health and educational systems made it possible to obtain information complete enough to derive and support a genetic model for the inheritance of dyslexia, although lack of an operational definition of the syndrome and of checks on the reliability of diagnosis prevent the data from decisively confirming the genetic hypothesis. The genetic model implies that approximately 10 per cent of the Swedish population have the genotype for dyslexia. Other estimates for the prevalence of dyslexia have ranged from 5 per cent to 25 per cent (cf. Critchley, 1970). While not necessarily supporting a genetic hypothesis, several studies have indicated that slow perceptual-motor maturation is involved in developmental dyslexia (De-Hirsch, Jansky, & Langford, 1966; Satz, Rardin, & Ross, 1971).

Despite the evidence that developmental dyslexia is a genuine and probably organically based handicap, a long-term follow-up study of boys who were dyslexic showed that they achieved adult occupational and educational status equal to a control group of boys who had good early reading skills (Rawson, 1968). Because the boys came from very advantaged backgrounds and received individualized reading instruction, the findings do not mean that all dyslexics will overcome their handicap, but it does indicate that serious reading problems *can* be overcome under optimal conditions.

Speech Problems. One general class of speech problems involves poor articulation of words (*dysarthria*). While some of these problems might reflect central processing dysfunctions, most are due to defects in, injuries to, or immaturity in the motor apparatus for producing speech sounds.

A second class of speech problems involves an inability to understand or produce speech. When the inability is virtually complete, it is referred to as *aphasia;* in less serious degrees, as *dysphasia*. Inability to understand speech is known as *receptive* or *sensory aphasia* (or dysphasia), while inability to produce speech is known as *expressive* or *motor aphasia* (or dysphasia).

Brain damage occurring after speech develops can cause temporary or permanent aphasia (or dysphasia) of the receptive and/or expressive type. The prognosis for recovery from aphasia due to damage in the speech centers of one hemisphere is much better among young children than among adults because of the readiness with which the other hemisphere of the child's brain seems able to take over speech functions.

Beside aphasia resulting from damage after speech develops, there is a class of speech disorders known as *congenital* or *developmental aphasia* in which the child fails to develop speech spontaneously at the normal age. The boy described by Lenneberg (1962) who, by the age of eight, could not speak at all but could understand language demonstrates the existence of congenital motor aphasia without receptive aphasia. However, it is unlikely that congenital receptive aphasia could exist without also preventing the development of speech.

Like developmental dyslexia, congenital aphasia is assumed to have organic causes, but they are rarely known. No particular organic signs are uniformly present in most cases of aphasia. Goldstein, Landau, and Kleffner (1960) found somewhat more defects in motor functions among aphasic children than among a control group of deaf children, but there were virtually no differences in the percentage of children in each group with minor neurological signs or with abnormal skull X-rays or EEGs. Thirty-two per cent of the aphasic children had no detectable neurological abnormalities at all.

The problem of diagnostic heterogeneity is further illustrated in a study by DiCarlo (1960), who reassessed 67 children previously diagnosed as having congenital aphasia. He found that the speech problems were due to generally retarded mental development in 28 of the children, to emotional disturbance in 20 cases, and to defective hearing in 15 cases. He concluded that only four of the 67 children had the characteristics of congenital aphasia, with their primary problem being an organic dysfunction of the speech centers of the brain.

The Epilepsies

Epileptic disorders, also known as convulsive disorders, exist in many forms and have a variety of etiologies. What they have in common are temporary interruptions of normal consciousness or activity due to excessive discharges of electrical energy in nerve cell bodies (gray matter) of the brain. Wilder Penfield, one of the foremost authorities on the neurological features of epilepsy, describes the genesis of an epileptic attack thusly:

As long as the gray matter is normal, the energy of the nerve cells is employed only in the coordinated functional mechanisms of the brain. But if some area is injured by disease or pressure or lack of oxygen, the gray matter, although it may continue to function, may do so with abnormal additions of its own. There seems to be a defect in the regulating mechanisms which normally limit excessive discharge. Thus, sometimes months or years after injury, an abnormal area "ripens" slowly into a self-discharging electrochemical unit. This is called an *epileptic focus*.

In such an area or focus, excess electrical energy is formed and so, from time to time, unruly mass-discharges may be released. Such an explosive discharge produces an *epileptic fit*. The fit is large or small, depending upon the extent and intensity of discharge and the position of the gray matter involved. Consequently, the subject may suddenly make aimless movements over which he has no control, or he may have strange sensations or little dreams or memories. From one point of view these seizures are experiments carried out by disease upon the brain. As each attack unfolds, it may demonstrate to the watchful observer the position of the abnormality and also the functional uses of the area involved [Penfield & Roberts, 1959, p. 6].[1]

1 Wilder Penfield and Lamar Roberts, *Speech and Brain Mechanisms* (Princeton, N.J.: University Press, 1959). © 1959 by Princeton University Press and reprinted by permission of the publisher.

Types of Epileptic Attacks

There are a number of different patterns of epileptic attacks. A given individual may manifest one or more of the following types of attacks or various mixtures of these types.

Grand mal epilepsy. This is the best-known type of attack. It often begins with an *aura,* a warning period during which feelings of tension, depression, excitement, or elation may occur. The aura is followed by a brief *tonic* phase in which there is rigid contraction of the muscles, causing the body to stiffen. Then comes the *clonic* phase in which the body jerks rapidly, the tongue is often bitten, and the mouth foams. When the spasms subside, the individual usually falls into deep sleep. Unconsciousness seems complete during the attack and there are no memories of it, although confusion and a headache are often present upon recovery.

Petit Mal Epilepsy. The petit mal attack is most common in childhood (Scott, 1969). It consists merely of a brief lapse of consciousness, often evidenced by a fluttering of the eyelids, with no warning or recovery period. It is sometimes accompanied by slight jerking of the arms and legs, throwing the person off balance and causing him to fall.

Jacksonian Epilepsy. Named after the great British neurologist, J. Hughlings Jackson, this type of attack differs from the grand and petit mal attacks in that the person remains conscious during it. It consists of a tingling or involuntary movement in a particular region, e.g., one finger, which then spreads to larger and larger areas, often leaving the affected muscles weak for hours or days afterward.

Psychomotor Epilepsy. This represents one of the most problematic types of epilepsy because, while there is an interruption of consciousness, a sequence of well-organized activity may occur before the attack ends. Thus, it is possible that during an attack an individual may commit a crime or do something that is quite out of character. Because it is difficult to determine objectively whether a psychomotor attack has occurred at a particular time, psychomotor epilepsy has often been invoked as a legal defense in criminal cases.

Diagnosis and Treatment of Epilepsy

Unlike the "brain-damaged-child" syndrome and some of the central processing dysfunctions, persisting epileptic attacks can be confidently attributed to organic malfunction. However, the exact nature of the malfunction and the mechanism by which it produces the various epileptic phenomena are often unknown. Epilepsy for which a specific cause can be isolated is called *symptomatic epilepsy.* An epileptogenic focus in the brain can often be verified by means of the EEG, as illustrated by the EEG wave patterns in Fig. 6–7.

Type of EEG wave	Form and frequency	Conditions of occurrence
Alpha	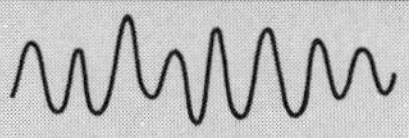 8-14 cycles/sec.	Normal activity seen at back of the head.
Beta	 above 14 cycles/sec.	Normal activity. Marked increase with anticonvulsant medicines
Theta	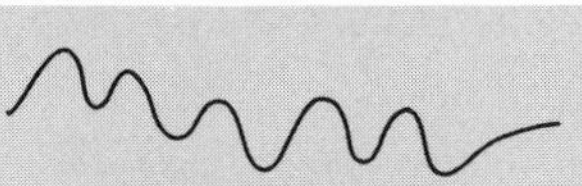 4-7 cycles/sec.	Occurs in drowsiness and many diseases.
Delta	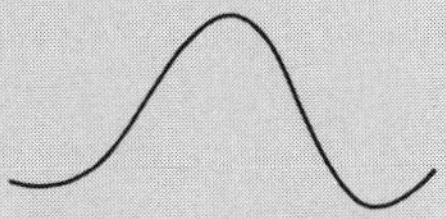 below 4 cycles/sec	Occurs in deep sleep, also in many disorders including brain tumors.
Spikes	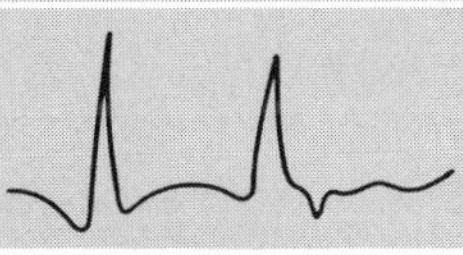	Occurs in patients with epilepsy.
Spike and Wave	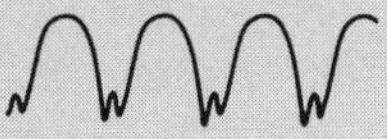	Occurs mainly in children with 'petit mal' attacks.

Fig. 6–7. Some different types of normal and abnormal EEG activity. Adapted from Scott (1969).

Causes of symptomatic epilepsy include head injuries at birth or later, tumors, diseases of the blood vessels in the brain, encephalitis, meningitis, and various congenital and degenerative diseases. Diseases of other parts of the body can also cause oxygen deprivation and toxic states that create epileptogenic lesions in the brain; so can poisons such as alcohol, lead, and ergot.

In addition to symptomatic epilepsy, there are cases in which a person experiences one or more seizures but no abnormalities can be found with the EEG, skull X-rays, or other tests. When no cause can be found, the disorder is called *idiopathic, genuine,* or *essential epilepsy.* Until recently, it was assumed that idiopathic epilepsy was a distinct type resulting from a general organic, probably hereditary, dysfunction in the brain, rather than from a specific lesion. Consistent with this view, several studies have demonstrated elevated frequencies of epilepsy and abnormal EEGs in the families of epileptics (cf. Goldensohn, 1965). However, it is now argued that most epilepsies should be regarded as resulting from specific lesions even if these have not been found (Gastaut, 1969). The elevated frequencies of epilepsy and EEG abnormalities in some families may be due not to specific genetic dispositions to epilepsy but to genetically low resistance to epileptic seizures once damage has occurred (Metrakos & Metrakos, 1970), or to genetic dispositions to prenatal and perinatal abnormalities which in turn cause brain damage that can result in epilepsy (Pasamanick & Lilienfeld, 1955b).

Once a disorder has been diagnosed as epilepsy, preventing seizures is a major goal. Not only do seizures and fear of seizures create a considerable handicap for the sufferer, but they may also create further brain damage due to anoxia, because oxygen consumption in the brain increases up to 50 per cent during a seizure (Scott, 1969). Fortunately, the seizures of most epileptics can now be partially or completely prevented by regular ingestion of anticonvulsant medication. Even when seizures are controlled, however, the epileptic must contend with the knowledge that he may have further seizures, with restrictions on activities like driving, with occasional side effects of the medication, and sometimes with other effects of the brain damage that is responsible for the seizures. For these reasons, psychotherapeutic and special educational measures are often required to help the epileptic adapt and avoid psychological stress that may precipitate an attack. There is good evidence that intensive psychotherapy with epileptic children can reduce the frequency of attacks to below what is achieved with medication alone (Gottschalk, 1953, 1956).

PSYCHOPHYSIOLOGICAL REACTIONS

A distinction is sometimes made between *psychosomatic* and *somatopsychological* disorders. According to this distinction, disorders that produce physical symptoms but have important psychological determinants are called psychosomatic, while disorders that originate with physical dysfunctions but have psychological effects are called somatopsychological. In either situation, however, a vicious circle can develop whereby physical symptoms increase psychological stress which in turn leads to new or intensified physical effects.

The term *psychophysiological* is replacing "psychosomatic" for designating the first type of disorder, because "psychosomatic" refers to a general approach in medicine that emphasizes taking account of both the physical and the psychological aspects of a patient's condition, no matter what the etiology. "Psychosomatic" has also come to connote imaginary or solely psychological discomforts. Certain apparently physical malfunctions, usually classified as hysterical, may indeed have no verifiable organic component, but psychophysiological reactions involve real physical symptoms that in some cases can be fatal. Among the most dangerous psychophysiological reactions are asthma, *hypertension* (high blood pressure), *ulcerative colitis* (inflammation of the large intestine), stomach ulcers, and *anorexia nervosa* (extreme unwillingness to eat). Others that can become severe handicaps include rheumatoid arthritis, vomiting, nausea, skin eruptions, migraine headaches, diarrhea, constipation, pains, muscle cramps, menstrual irregularities, and allergies. Complete physical examination and continuing medical care are necessary in many of these disorders.

General Hypotheses about Psychophysiological Reactions

Various ways of understanding psychophysiological reactions have been proposed. One early hypothesis was that heredity, previous illness or other factors create a somatic weakness at some location in the body and that this weak link later becomes the site of physical reactions to stress. An early psychoanalytic hypothesis was that a psychophysiological symptom symbolizes a particular psychological conflict. For example, it has been argued that stomach ulcers symbolize internalized aggression against the mother (Garma, 1950). Still another hypothesis was that pathogenic maternal behavior creates stresses to which the child responds somatically (Garner & Wenar, 1959).

Recent work has attempted to take account of a broader range of factors potentially related to psychophysiological reactions. Studies have shown that, on the basis of interview data, experienced observers from whom all medical cues are withheld can rather accurately guess what psychophysiological disorders patients have (Alexander, French, & Pollock, 1968; Graham, Lundy, Benjamin, Kabler, Lewis, Kunish, & Graham, 1962; Ring, 1957). These findings suggest that there are some consistent relations between personality and psychophysiological disorders, after the disorders have developed. However, such relations could be at least partially determined by the effects of the disorders once they are present.

Physiological Reaction Patterns. Another approach has been to study physiological reactions to stress by individuals who do not already have physical symptoms. Lacey, Bateman, and Van Lehn (1953) tested the hypothesis that there are individual differences in the patterns of physiological reactions to stress and that these are consistent despite differences in stress. They measured galvanic skin response (GSR), heart rate, and variability of heart rate in college students who experienced four different types of stress: fast-paced mental arithmetic, hyperventilation (very rapid breathing), being prodded to rapidly produce words beginning with a particular letter, and having a foot immersed in ice water. Subjects differed markedly in the physiological measures showing the greatest reactions. Moreover, in a given subject, the measure that showed the greatest reaction for one stress usually showed the greatest reaction for the other stresses as well, suggesting that particular psychophysiological symptoms may result from the general pattern of an individual's autonomic functioning, regardless of the stresses he experiences.

Evidence for a direct relation between specific psychophysiological symptoms and individual patterns of stress reaction was obtained by Malmo and Shagass (1949). They subjected mental patients to a standardized painful stimulus while heart rate, respiration, and electrical potential in the muscles of the neck were being recorded. They found that patients who had previously complained of cardiovascular symptoms showed significantly greater changes in heart rate and breathing than did patients without these complaints. Likewise, patients who had previously complained of head and neck aches showed significantly more increases in neck muscle potential than did other patients. Few of the patients were reporting somatic symptoms at the time of the experiment, but it appears that the site of a previous symptom in a given patient tended to be the focus of the patient's physiological reaction to stress.

Specificity of Emotion. A further step in studying physiological reaction patterns was taken by Ax (1953), who added several physiological measures to those used by Lacey et al (1953) and employed stress situations designed to evoke two very strong but distinct emotions, fear and anger. Like Lacey et al, Ax found that individual subjects had characteristic patterns of physiological responses that were evident during both types of stress. However, he also found that fear and anger influenced the patterns of physiological responses in different ways that were consistent for nearly all the subjects. Thus, both the individual's preexisting pattern of functioning and the type of emotion appeared to affect physiological reactions to stress.

Graham and his colleagues have studied physiological reactions to specific emotional attitudes induced by hypnosis. First they interviewed patients already suffering from psychophysiological symptoms in order to obtain statements of what each patient felt was happening to him and what he wanted to do about it at the time the symptom occurred (Grace & Graham, 1952). Then they used hypnosis to suggest to normal subjects the stress situation and feelings reported by patients with a particular disorder. Physiological measurements were employed to determine whether a specific feeling did indeed produce reactions characteristic of a particular disorder.

As an example, hypnotized subjects were induced to imagine that a "Dr. X" was about to burn their hand with a match. In certain experimental sessions each subject was further told that he would feel very mistreated but would feel unable to do anything about it, the experience reported by sufferers of *urticaria* (hives). During other sessions, the subject was also told he would feel mistreated, but now he would want to hit and strangle Dr. X, the experience reported by people with *Raynaud's disease* (cold, oxygen-deprived hands). It was found that the skin temperature of the subjects' "unburned" hand went up when they were given the "hives attitude," as it does in actual hives, while the temperature of their "unburned" hand went down when they had the "Raynaud's disease attitude," as it does in Raynaud's disease (Graham, Stern, & Winokur, 1958).

Conditioning. There is mounting evidence that some physiological responses can be conditioned. For example, it has been demonstrated that human heart rate can be controlled through operant conditioning (Ascough & Sipprelle, 1968; Lang, Sroufe, & Hastings, 1967). If physiological responses can be conditioned, it is possible that some psychophysiological reactions are learned—certain neutral stimuli that are paired with stimuli that naturally elicit physiological responses later elicit the physiological responses by themselves.

Such a mechanism has been demonstrated for the development of asthma by guinea pigs (Ottenberg, Stein, Lewis, & Hamilton, 1958). The guinea pigs were first made allergic to egg white by injecting them with large amounts of it. A solution of egg white was then sprayed into a previously neutral experimental box while the animals were in it. Some of the animals later had asthmatic attacks whenever they were placed in the box even though no egg white was present. After 13 consecutive daily trials in the box without egg white, however, the asthmatic attacks ceased in all the animals, demonstrating extinction of the learned response. The fact that some of the animals never did "learn" the asthmatic responses and that rates of extinction varied considerably suggests that individual constitutional differences also played a role.

SOME PSYCHOPHYSIOLOGICAL REACTIONS OF CHILDHOOD

Many types of psychophysiological reactions are characteristic only of particular age groups. Hypertension, for example, tends to be most frequent in adults while anorexia nervosa is most frequent in adolescents. Three categories of disorder that have received considerable study in children and adolescents are discussed below. However, it should be noted that many of the other types of psychophysiological reactions also occur in childhood. Moreover, some childhood psychopathology may be an early version of what in adulthood is manifest as a psychophysiological reaction. Evidence for this possibility was obtained in a longitudinal study by Stewart (1962). She found that adults who developed severe psychophysiological reactions, especially stomach ulcers and hypertension, had shown greater depressive tendencies on personality inventories administered during adolescence than had adults who were either symptom-free or behaviorally maladjusted.

Anorexia Nervosa

This term literally signifies a severe loss of appetite for emotional ("nervous") reasons. Until the 1968 edition of the American Psychiatric Association's *Diagnostic and Statistical Manual,* it was officially classified as a psychophysiological reaction. The 1968 edition of the *Diagnostic and Statistical Manual* (American Psychiatric Association, 1968) classifies it as a "special symptom reaction," along with other "feeding disturbances" such as overeating. Despite this reclassification, anorexia nervosa is mentioned here because much of the literature on it treats it, like obesity, as a psychosomatic or psychophysiological disorder.

The changing terminology reflects conflicts about just how such disorders should be best understood and treated. Because anorexia frequently comes to professional attention only when it is so severe as to be life-threatening, much of the literature has originated in medical settings where severe anorexics are confined while receiving special feeding. However, studies that go beyond analysis of a single case history have shown a large variety of personality patterns, precipitating events, and outcomes among individuals with anorexia nervosa (Bliss & Branch, 1960; Blitzer, Rollins, & Blackwell, 1961; Lesser, Ashenden, Debuskey, & Eisenberg, 1960).

The studies are in agreement that the term "anorexia" is a misnomer because in many cases the individual has not lost his appetite, but fears or avoids eating despite being hungry, or reluctantly takes food only to regurgitate it later. The findings of these studies have led to the conclusion that anorexia nervosa is primarily a symptom that may have different significance in different individuals, rather than being a unitary disease entity.

Anorexia nervosa is much more frequent in females than in males. It seldom occurs before the age of 10, although a syndrome involving refusal or vomiting of food and known as *infantile rumination* occurs during the first two years of life. Since many anorexics are pubescent girls, the avoidance of food has often been interpreted as an attempt to prevent adolescent physical development because of a fear of sex. Children described in the studies cited above also reported fears of becoming fat, but seemed totally unconcerned about their emaciated appearances.

Treatment has traditionally consisted of hospitalization with psychotherapy and tube feeding when necessary to prevent starvation. However, behavioral procedures have been used to lessen specific conscious fears associated with food and to provide positive reinforcement for eating (Bachrach, Erwin, & Mohr, 1965; Hallsten, 1965; Lang, 1965). The success of these methods in helping anorexics regain normal eating habits appears to support the conception of anorexia nervosa as a specific symptom that needs to be dealt with directly in its own right, no matter what the presumed psychodynamic etiology.

Asthma

Physiologically speaking, asthma involves a contraction of the muscles of the bronchial tubes which carry air into the lungs from the windpipe. This contraction restricts air passing in and out of the lungs, causing suffocation in extreme cases. It can occur as a reflex response to local irritation of the bronchial tubes or as a result of direct innervation from the hypothalamus during emotional states.

Many asthmatic attacks are caused by infections such as pneumonia and whooping cough, or by exceptional sensitivity of the bronchial tissue to *allergens,* substances that produce allergic reactions. Other attacks may be caused by combinations of allergic, infective, and emotional factors or by emotional factors alone. In a study designed to distinguish children whose asthma is due primarily to infective or allergic factors from those whose asthma is due primarily to psychological factors, Rees (1964) concluded that allergens alone were responsible for asthma in only 5 per cent of the cases. Infective factors alone were responsible in 21 per cent of the cases and psychological factors alone in another 21 per cent. In the remaining 53 per cent of the cases, asthma was attributed to various combinations of allergic, infective, and psychological factors.

In another study, Bernstein and Purcell (1963) found that some children quickly lost their asthmatic symptoms after being hospitalized away from home while other children showed no improvement and required continuous steroid drug treatment. An intermediate group showed improvement but continued to require occasional medication. Those children who showed rapid improvement had, before admission, been reported to show more neurotic symptoms and their parents to have more negative attitudes toward them than was true for the children who did not improve. When asked to list what brought on their attacks, significantly more of the former group listed negative emotions while more of the latter group listed organic precipitants (Purcell, 1963). It thus appears that psychological factors played a much greater role in the asthma of the former group than in that of the latter group.

Further evidence for the existence of distinct subgroups among asthmatic children has been obtained by using an index of somatic predisposition to allergy called the Allergic Potential Scale (APS; Bloch, Jennings, Harvey, & Simpson, 1964). The APS consists of quantitative scores for the incidence of allergies in a child's family, a blood count during an allergic episode, skin test reactivity to allergens, total number of allergies, and the ease of diagnosing specific allergens.

Asthmatic children scoring low on the APS, i.e., those assumed to have low somatic predispositions to asthma, were found to display significantly more psychopathology on a number of measures than were children scoring high on the APS. Similarly, the mothers, their marital interactions, and their relations with their asthmatic child showed significantly more pathology in the low-scoring group than in the high-scoring group. It thus seems clear that generalizations about children with asthma must be constrained by the degree of somatic versus psychological influence on the particular child's symptoms.

Unfortunately, most generalizations in the literature regarding psychological correlates of asthma have failed to distinguish between degrees of somatic and psychological influence. This tendency has resulted in many clichés about "the asthmatic child" and his family that are contradictory or that fail to find support in systematic studies (e.g., Dubo, McLean, Ching, Wright, Kauffman, & Sheldon, 1961; Fitzelle, 1959; Margolis, 1961; Rawls, Rawls, & Harrison, 1971).

Gastrointestinal Ulceration

Considerable study has been made of three different types of gastro-intestinal ulceration—*peptic ulcers,* which are lesions in the lining of the stomach; *duodenal ulcers,* which are lesions in the lining of the *duodenum,* the topmost section of the small intestine; and *ulcerative colitis,* lesions in the *colon* (large intestine).

Peptic and Duodenal Ulcers. Although these ulcers are popularly as-sociated with the hard-driving executive, they occur in children as well. Research on the relations between personality, stress, and physiological mechanisms reveals that the conditions for ulcer formation involve con-siderably more than a simple relation between personality and the symp-tom.

Stomach acid secretion normally begins when food is consumed and ends when it has been digested. However, excess stomach acid can eat away the linings of the stomach or duodenum, eventually forming ulcers. Although many studies have demonstrated that people with ulcers have high stomach acid levels, the most compelling evidence on the etiological role of stomach acid comes from longitudinal studies in which people without ulcers but differing in stomach acid levels were studied in order to determine who eventually developed ulcers.

In a massive study of 4,460 adults and 1,600 children between several months and 16 years of age (Mirsky, 1958), blood tests were used to ascer-tain individual levels of *pepsinogen,* a substance produced by the stomach glands that is converted into the digestive enzyme *pepsin* and is highly correlated with stomach acidity. Subjects with the highest and lowest levels of blood pepsinogen were then studied over several years. A number of those with high pepsinogen levels developed ulcers while *nobody* with low pepsinogen levels did. Ten per cent of the children with high pepsinogen developed ulcers between the ages of 4 and 14 years. Many of those who developed ulcers showed increases in pepsinogen above their usual high levels just before the appearance of ulcer symptoms. Three times as many men as women had high pepsinogen levels, corresponding to the three-to-one sex ratio generally observed among ulcer patients. It thus appears that high pepsinogen levels, probably genetically determined because they are present from infancy, plus exacerbation of these high levels, are part of the physiological predisposition to ulcers.

In another study by Mirsky and his colleagues (Weiner, Thaler, Reiser, & Mirsky, 1957), the interactions between high pepsinogen levels, personality predispositions, and situational stress were demonstrated in the production of ulcers. Pepsinogen levels were determined by blood tests in 2,073 draftees. Sixty-three men with the highest pepsinogen levels and 57 with the lowest levels were administered gastrointestinal X-rays, psychological tests, and interviews by researchers blind regarding the pepsinogen group to which each man belonged. Gastrointestinal X-rays were readministered after 8 to 16 weeks of basic training.

At the first examination, three men were found to have healed duodenal ulcers, while one had an active ulcer. All were in the high pepsinogen group. Five more men developed active ulcers during basic training. All these were also in the high pepsinogen group.

The psychological tests were used to identify men likely to develop ulcers because of their presumed fear of expressing hostility and need to please in order to avoid alienating others. Of the 10 men predicted to be the *most* ulcer prone, nine had high pepsinogen levels and seven had ulcers. Hence, the factors of (1) high pepsinogen level, (2) certain personality characteristics, and (3) the precipitating stress of basic training seemed to contribute jointly to the formation of ulcers.

A post hoc analysis of psychological test factors correlating significantly with high pepsinogen secretion revealed evidence of persistent conflicts about oral dependency among the high pepsinogen men. These characteristics are consistent with the personality patterns reported by Alexander (1950) for ulcer sufferers. However, Mirsky (1958) has suggested that, rather than being the *result* of psychodynamic conflicts, excessive gastric secretion may *cause* conflicts around oral dependency. Since it can be present from birth, high gastric secretion may prevent an infant from responding to feeding with the normal degree of physiological relaxation. In such cases:

. . . even the mother with an excellent integrative capacity, i.e., "a strong ego," and without any hostile rejecting attitudes, will be only partially successful in her efforts to provide that physiologic satiation which permits the infant to pass successfully through the purely biologic and into the psychologic phases of dependency. The child's insatiableness may induce frustration in the mother whose need to gratify the infant stems from her own unconscious wishes to be loved and cared for. Hostile and rejecting attitudes may develop in the mother in reaction to the unsatiated and thereby "rejecting" infant. As a result, infantile passive, oral-dependent wishes will persist [Mirsky, 1958, p. 299].

Even if problems about oral dependency do in fact characterize ulcer sufferers, this does not mean that exceptional increases in gastric secretion must result only from exacerbation of these particular problems. It may be that gastric secretion occurs as a response to other kinds of emotional stress as well, although oral dependency may influence what kinds of environmental events are construed as being stressful. Wolf & Wolff (1947), for example, directly observed the stomach activity of a patient who had a *gastric fistula* (a surgical opening in his stomach). They found increases in gastric secretion in response not only to emotions involving dependency but to a variety of other strong emotions as well.

In a study designed to determine whether oral dependency feelings were crucial in gastric secretion, Mahl and Karpe (1953) measured the amount of hydrochloric acid secreted by the stomaches of two patients during psychoanalytic therapy hours. They also scored transcripts of the hours according to the degrees of anxiety, hostility, and oral dependency experienced by the patient. They found that hydrochloric acid secretion was high during hours when the patients were judged to be experiencing high anxiety, but there was no consistent relation between oral dependency and acid secretion.

Kehoe and Ironside (1962) studied the relations between gastric secretion and five hypnotically induced emotional states. Their results further contradicted the oral dependency hypothesis in that gastric secretion was highest during anger and lowest during hopelessness and helplessness. Animal experiments have also demonstrated ulcer production during experimentally induced stress that was not necessarily related to oral dependency (e.g., Porter, Brady, Conrad, Mason, Galambos, & Rioch, 1958).

Ulcerative Colitis.   Despite numerous studies, the physiological mechanisms involved in ulcerative colitis are not as well understood as those in peptic and duodenal ulcers. Stomach acid is unlikely to be involved because of the distance of the colon from the stomach. Severe diarrhea or constipation often accompany ulcerative colitis, but these are evidently not essential causative factors since it has been reported that rectal bleeding, rather than diarrhea or constipation, is the first symptom in about 68 per cent of the cases (Engel, 1954; Fullerton, Kollar, & Caldwell, 1962). Typically, ulceration and bleeding periodically become exacerbated, often necessitating hospitalization. In some cases, severely ulcerated segments of the colon are surgically removed.

A number of personality characteristics have been attributed to both adult and child sufferers, but a somatic predisposition has also been generally assumed. A study of children hospitalized with ulcerative colitis revealed neither a specific psychological causal factor nor much evidence for a familial somatic disposition to colitis (Finch & Hess, 1962). Fathers of all the children were reported to be passive and ineffectual, while mothers were aggressive and dominating. The children were reported to have "primitive fantasies involving the . . . sexual and digestive organs . . . and repeated concern that the body was somehow faulty or defective [p. 822]." However, passive, ineffectual fathers and aggressive dominating mothers may well characterize many children without ulcerative colitis, and concern about digestive organs and a defective body is not surprising in children hospitalized because of severe gastrointestinal pathology. In fact, a controlled *comparison* of ulcerative colitis patients with patients having other gastrointestinal illnesses showed no differences in psychopathology (Feldman, Cantor, Soll, & Bachrach, 1967).

PSYCHOPHARMACOLOGY

Psychopharmacology refers to the study of drug effects on behavior and on psychological states and processes such as mood, anxiety, and cognition. Drugs that have such effects are known as *psychoactive* or *psychotropic,* and their use for therapeutic purposes is known as *chemotherapy* or *pharmacotherapy.* Another term coming into use is *behavioral pharmacology,* which refers to the study of functional relations between behavior and drugs in order to describe the mechanisms by which drugs alter behavior (Thompson, Pickens, & Meisch, 1970). "Psychopharmacology" is the more general term and better characterizes most current approaches to drugs in relation to psychopathology. Later chapters will deal with some uses of drugs as therapy for specific disorders and with drug abuse by children and adolescents.

Until the recent rise of illegal drug use, professionals in the field of psychopathology were primarily interested in drugs for their potential therapeutic value. Various sedatives have long been used with epileptics and psychiatric patients, and *Benzedrine,* an *amphetamine* drug, was used to treat hyperactive children as early as 1937 (Bradley, 1937).

In the early 1950s tranquilizing drugs brought a veritable revolution in the care of chronic psychiatric patients. Because the tranquilizers seemed to suppress excitement and violent behavior, they made it possible to do away with mechanical methods for restraining patients and to release or transfer many chronic patients to less restrictive settings. The success of tranquilizing drugs in reducing the troublesome behavior of excited patients was accompanied by the success of antidepressant drugs in stimulating some depressed patients. Tranquilizers and antidepressants soon gained popularity for outpatient prescription by practitioners in a variety of medical specialities. This was followed by freely available and heavily advertised nonprescription versions of these drugs which are now widely used by the public.

The possibility that drug advertising and medical prescription of psychoactive drugs have contributed to the rise in drug abuse has aroused considerable controversy. For example, Lennard et al (1970) cite a number of drug advertising practices designed to convince physicians that certain drugs will easily alleviate the personal and emotional problems of patients, including children. In one advertisement they cite (*Journal of the American College Health Association,* 1970), the tranquilizer *Librium* is portrayed as relieving anxiety aroused in a college student when, among other things, "Exposure to new friends and other influences may force her to reevaluate herself and her goals," and "Her newly stimulated intellectual curiosity may make her more sensitive to and apprehensive about unstable national and world conditions." In another typical advertisement (*American Journal of Diseases of Children,* 1969), a tearful little girl appears with the caption "School, the dark, separation, dental visits, 'monsters,'" and a message recommending that the physician prescribe *Vistaril* when such anxieties get out of hand.

Lennard et al criticize the tendency manifest in such advertising to re-label normal personal problems of growth and change as medical-psychiatric problems to be solved simply by taking drugs. Little evidence is usually provided that such medications really do have the benefits implied. Moreover, whether a medication can relieve symptoms or not, the physician who prescribes it is in effect promoting drug-taking as a technique for solving everyday problems.

The contemporary trend of increasing prescription of psychoactive drugs seems to be contributing to the recruitment of more and more persons into a way of life in which the regulation of personal and interpersonal processes is accomplished through the ingestion of drugs. Thus, when a physician prescribes a drug for the control or solution (or both) of personal problems of living, he does more than merely relieve the discomfort caused by the problem. He simultaneously communicates a model for an acceptable and useful way of dealing with personal and interpersonal problems [Lennard et al, 1970, p. 439].[2]

The degree to which psychoactive drug prescription *has* spread or *should* spread to the treatment of childhood behavioral problems is also a controversial topic. One prominent child psychiatrist who has conducted systematic research on drugs, with both positive and negative outcomes, states:

Among the welter of conflicting contentions [about drug effects], the drug house copywriter wanders freely, citing selected references which favor his product and apparently augment its sales. Yet, if the pitch sells, does not a good part of the fault lie with us, the physicians, who are so readily persuaded by so little scholarship?

The remarkably high rate at which drugs are prescribed for the treatment of behavior disorders in children, despite the paucity of evidence to substantiate their efficacy, draws attention immediately to certain features of these disorders and their treatment. Such heavy use implies that complaints about disturbing behavior must be quite common in medical practice. Alternative modes of treatment must be either unfamiliar to physicians, or unsatisfactory in their experience, or considered too burdensome to undertake [Eisenberg, 1968, p. 625].[3]

Another prominent child psychiatrist who is an expert on drug therapy for children stated in the same year:

. . . there is still a curious reluctance to use drugs in the out-patient psychiatric treatment of children, both in private practice and in many child guidance clinics.

2 H. L. Lennard et al, "Hazards Implicit in Prescribing Psychoactive Drugs," *Science,* 1970, **169** (438–41). © 1970 by the American Association for the Advancement of Science and reprinted by permission.

3 L. Eisenberg, "Psychopharmacology in Childhood: A Critique," in E. Miller (Ed.), *Foundations of Child Psychiatry* (New York: Pergamon Press, 1968). © 1968 by Pergamon Press and reprinted by permission.

Fears have been raised that drugs will dull perception, stifle learning and destroy the psychotherapeutic relationship [Fish, 1968, p. 60].[4]

While statistics are lacking on the actual quantities of psychoactive drugs prescribed for children, the difference in views as to whether the rate is "remarkably high" (Eisenberg, 1968) or "there is still a curious reluctance" (Fish, 1968) may stem partly from different evaluations of how often drugs *should* be used. Eisenberg implies that they may already be used too indiscriminately, while Fish implies that irrational fears are preventing them from being used as widely as they should be.

The question of whether a drug is used appropriately should, of course, be answered according to factual knowledge of the short-term and long-term effects of the drug upon a specific type of disorder in a particular child. Lack of sufficient knowledge of this sort is partially responsible for controversies over whether drugs are too widely or too cautiously used.

Many drugs that generated enthusiastic clinical impressions were later found to be ineffective with patients in other settings or to have harmful side effects. Although the objective study of drug effects employing *placebo controls* and *double-blind* experimental procedures (see Chapter 4, for details) is a minimum prerequisite for knowledge as to whether the drug is beneficial, advertising and clinical claims for drugs are too seldom based upon unequivocal positive results from studies of this type. Even when positive results are obtained in such studies, normal scientific precautions regarding the generalizability of the findings to other patient groups and to symptoms not specifically evaluated in the studies should not be ignored. Such precautions are especially important in the application of drug findings to children because their biological immaturity, as well as other developmental considerations, may greatly influence how a given drug affects them (cf. Minde & Weiss, 1970). A prominent instance, which is still not well understood but which appears to have happy consequences, is the paradoxical finding that amphetamines seem to have tranquilizing effects on some hyperactive children, although amphetamines produce in adults exactly the *opposite* effect, i.e., stimulation.

Mechanisms of Drug Action

The biochemical details of how various drugs may create the effects they do are beyond the scope of this text. However, one general hypothesis concerning the presumed psychotherapeutic effects of certain drugs is that the drugs overcome defects in the chemical neurotransmitters that facilitate transmission of impulses across neural synapses. The drugs might do this by affecting the production of the neurotransmitters or by inhibiting the

4 Barbara Fish, "Drug Therapy in Children's Psychiatric Disorders," *Clinical Psychopharmacology: Modern Problems in Pharmacopsychiatry*, 1968, 1 (60–72). © 1968 by S. Karger, Basel and New York, and reprinted by permission.

production of substances that interfere with the normal work of the neuro-transmitters.

The effects of many drugs may depend in part on the patient's interpretation of the physiological changes he perceives. Thus, a drug may be beneficial for an individual if the conditions under which he takes it, his expectations, and the physiological changes he perceives are all appropriate for him. Experiments by Schachter and his colleagues (Schachter, 1966; Valins, 1970), for example, have shown that physiological symptoms of excitement induced by the drug *epinephrine* can produce very different emotional states depending upon the immediate psychological and social context in which the drug effects are experienced. The emotional effect of the drug is, therefore, a complex product of physiological and cognitive factors.

Drugs are likely to differ greatly in the ways in which they achieve their effects. However, it is often assumed that disorders that improve with drug therapy must have resulted exclusively from organic defects. As mentioned earlier, Wender (1971) has incorporated this assumption into his strategy for diagnosing minimal cerebral dysfunction. He maintains that if a child's hyperactivity is alleviated by amphetamine drugs, this constitutes evidence that the hyperactivity was due to cerebral dysfunction. Unfortunately, this hypothesis can only be verified either by a much more precise understanding than we have of how amphetamines decrease hyperactivity in children, or by independent evidence for the existence of brain damage in the hyperactive children who are helped by amphetamines, coupled with evidence for the absence of brain damage in the hyperactive children who are not helped by amphetamines.

Some Psychoactive Drugs Used to Treat Children

Major Tranquilizers.   These are drugs that are known or are believed to have powerful tranquilizing effects that go beyond sedation. The most potent tranquilizers are the *phenothiazines*. Of these, *chlorpromazine* is the best studied and most widely used. It decreases aggressive and destructive behavior in young autistic and schizophrenic children (Eisenberg, 1968). There is also evidence that it reduces hyperactivity and distractibility in nonpsychotic hyperactive children (Weiss, Werry, Minde, Douglas, & Sykes, 1968; Werry, Weiss, Douglas, & Martin, 1966). However, it does not appear to improve learning by these children (Freibergs, Douglas, & Weiss, 1968). Side effects include jaundice, sleepiness, and skin sensitivity.

Sedatives and Minor Tranquilizers.   These are less potent than the major tranquilizers and appear mainly to induce drowsiness. *Phenobarbital* is a long-used and inexpensive sedative, but it has the paradoxical effect of exciting hyperactive children, just as amphetamine stimulants paradoxically reduce hyperactivity in some children (Conners, 1972). *Diphenylmethane* derivations and *propanediol* derivatives are minor tranquilizers with effects apparently similar to phenobarbital (Eisenberg, 1968).

Stimulants. *Dextroamphetamine* and *methylphenidate* are examples of stimulants having the paradoxical effect of reducing hyperactivity and are used primarily for treating overactive and distractible children. Side effects include loss of appetite and insomnia. Addiction may occur in adolescents, with psychosis resulting from very large doses (Eisenberg, 1968).

Antidepressants. These are seldom used with children because children are rarely diagnosed as being depressed. However, Frommer (1967) maintains that many children with symptoms such as pains, headaches, insomnia, fears, mood disturbances, social maladjustment, and school failure, are actually depressed and should be treated accordingly. She reported improvement in significantly more of such children aged 9 to 15 treated with a combination of an antidepressant (*phenelzine,* trade named *Nardil*) and a tranquilizer (*chlordiazepoxide,* trade named *Librium*) than in those treated with a combination of a sedative and a placebo. Another antidepressant, *impramine,* has been used to control enuresis, but with conflicting results in different studies (Eisenberg, 1968).

SUMMARY

By the beginning of the *fetal* period, at the eighth week after conception, the child has achieved recognizably human form, with a nervous system that shows reflex responses to tactile stimuli. Most nerve cells are present by six months after conception, and nearly all have been formed by birth. Later growth in the brain consists mainly of enlargement of the nerve cell bodies, lengthening of their *dendrites* and *axons*—the fibers carrying impulses toward and away from the cell bodies—and the development of the *glial* cells of the supporting tissue.

Hormones begin to play a role in actualizing the genetic growth plan during the fetal period: the *pituitary gland* begins secreting *growth hormone* by about the eighth week; *testosterone* secreted in the ninth week by the testes of a male fetus instigates development of male genitalia and male characteristics of the *hypothalamus* in the brain; *thyroxine* from the *thyroid gland* aids protein synthesis in the brain after about the thirteenth week.

Risks during prenatal development include *maternal malnutrition,* factors associated with *maternal age* and *maternal emotions, maternal illness, blood-type incompatibility, drugs,* and *irradiation.*

The birth process can cause neurological damage either through direct pressure on the child's head or through *anoxia. Apnea* (failure to breathe) immediately after birth is also a cause of potentially damaging anoxia.

Elevated frequencies of behavioral and neurological abnormalities have been observed in children of exceptionally low birth weight and/or born much earlier than the normal 40-weeks gestation period. Low birth weight or short gestation may be symptoms of other problems or may increase vulnerability to other risks.

At birth, the brain is closer to its adult weight than most other organs, and it grows very rapidly during childhood. Much of postnatal brain development consists of increases in *connectivity*—the physical interconnectedness—among nerve cells. The *cerebral cortex* is very immature at birth and early reflexive behavior is controlled primarily by the *brain stem*.

Between the ages of about one and five, many functions become relegated to one or the other of the two *cerebral hemispheres*. This process of *lateralization of function* is especially marked for speech functions, which usually become localized in the left hemisphere.

Hormones play important roles in regulating development throughout the life cycle. They are also important components of the body's reactions to stress, and they influence behavioral tempo. The *pituitary gland* is the *master gland* of the endocrine system because it produces hormones that stimulate other glands to produce their own hormones. The pituitary and other glands are part of a complex feedback circuit in which "sensor" cells, reacting to the level of hormones in the blood, stimulate the production of "releaser" substances that induce the pituitary to produce its hormones. These, in turn, stimulate hormone production by other glands. Abnormal biochemical influences, dietary deficiencies, diseases, and extreme emotional deprivation can disrupt the endocrine system at various points.

Male and female hormones (*androgens* and *estrogens*) play a major role in the development of adult sexual characteristics at puberty. They also appear to influence cognitive and behavioral functioning, especially in relation to activation and *automatization* behavior.

Postnatal risks for neurobiological development include malnutrition and brain lesions caused by injury, disease, asphyxiation, and poisoning. Extreme sensory deprivation has been shown to interfere with neurobiological development in animals and might have similar effects in humans. The effects of brain damage on a child's functioning depend greatly upon the child's age, general health, and other factors.

Certain disorders with presumed organic etiologies are classified according to broad descriptive categories. These include the *brain-damaged child syndrome,* where the assumption of brain damage rests upon the child's hyperkinetic behavior, perceptual-motor deficits, and/or "soft" neurological signs; *central processing dysfunctions,* such as *developmental dyslexia* and *aphasia;* and the *epilepsies.*

Numerous hypotheses have been proposed to account for *psychophysiological reactions.* Physiological predispositions, personality characteristics, and precipitating stress are all likely to play roles in many of them and are well-documented for *peptic* and *duodenal ulcers.*

Psychoactive drugs such as *tranquilizers, stimulants,* and *antidepressants* are now used to treat psychopathology in children, although there is considerable controversy about their value. Many drugs used with adults have different and even opposite effects on children.

SUGGESTED READING

Neurobiological Development. Tanner (1970) presents an authoritative overview of physical development from conception through maturity. His sections on the endocrinology of growth, development of the brain, organization of the growth process, and interaction of heredity and environment are especially pertinent to developmental psychopathology. In the same volume, Eichorn (1970) presents a review of relationships between the EEG and development. Other useful readings are the chapter on prenatal development in Mussen, Conger, and Kagan (1969), which contains exquisite *Life* magazine photographs of the fetus *in utero,* and a paper by Lenneberg (1968) on relations between age and the outcome of central nervous system disease in children.

Brain Function. Gazzaniga's (1967) brief summary of his research on "split-brain" patients (people who have undergone severing of the connections between their cerebral hemispheres) is highly informative with respect to the lateralization of functions in the cerebral hemisphere of the brain. A more detailed summary and analysis is provided in his book entitled *The Bisected Brain* (1970). *Speech and Brain Mechanisms,* by Penfield and Roberts (1959), is a short classic by two of the world's foremost neurologists. Based largely upon neurosurgical evidence from human patients, the book covers such topics as functional organization of the human brain, the recording of consciousness, cerebral dominance, mapping of the speech area, and the learning of languages, all in relatively nontechnical language. Lenneberg's (1967) book, *Biological Foundations of Language,* offers massive evidence for the biological basis of language development and some of its relations to thought.

Malnutrition. Birch and Gussow (1970) extensively survey the literature on the relations between malnutrition, health, and children's learning. They also document the degree to which social class is related to all three variables and the consequences for the disadvantaged children at the bottom of the social class ladder.

Sex Hormones. Evidence for the roles of sex hormones in cognitive functioning and some theoretical conclusions are summarized in a *Psychological Review* article by Broverman, Klaiber, Kobayashi, and Vogel (1968). The implications of this work for learning disabilities in children are presented by Broverman, Clarkson, Klaiber, and Vogel (1972). Contrasting views have been presented by Dawson (1972) and Parlee (1972), while Money and Ehrhardt (1972) survey developmental aspects of the physical differences between the sexes.

Brain Damage. Birch (1964) has edited one of the most useful collections of papers on the biological, behavioral, and social aspects of brain damage in children, which includes his own critique of the "brain-damaged child" concept. Wender (1971) presents arguments for the use of amphetamines in diagnosing and treating "minimal brain dysfunction," although Twitchell's (1971) critical review of Wender's book should also be read.

Epilepsy. A helpful survey of phenomena, terminology, mythology, theory, and treatment related to epilepsy is contained in Scott's (1969) book, *About Epilepsy,* while an overview of epilepsy in children is provided by Livingston (1972).

Psychopharmacology. Amid the current proliferation of drugs, claims, and controversy, Eisenberg (1971) offers a reasoned appraisal of psychopharmacological approaches to child psychopathology. For possible hazards in prescribing psychoactive drugs, see Lennard, Epstein, Bernstein, and Ransom (1970).

7

Intellectual Development
and Retardation

KEVIN

His neonatal course was difficult, with poor feeding and frequent vomiting. During the first two months of life, he sweated excessively and had . . . propulsive vomiting after each feeding. There were repeated respiratory infections during the first months of life; one episode at four months of age was sufficiently severe to require brief hospitalization . . . Kevin did not sit without support until eleven months of age, and did not stand without support until the age of twenty-one months. The parents and pediatrician were concerned with his slow development by the time the child was six months of age. A Gesell evaluation at that time indicated that he had motor and adaptive backwardness. On examination at age twenty-one months, he was found to have . . . behavorial organization appropriate for a child fifteen months of age . . . . Single syllables were not repeated until the child was over two years of age; single words were not used until after he was three . . . and short phrases only appeared between the fourth and fifth years.

Neurological examination at three years eight months indicated a marked disturbance in gait. . . . Swallowing was noted to be poor and drooling excessive.

The first formal psychometric evaluation was carried out when Kevin was four years three months of age. At testing, he was . . . friendly, cheerful, cooperative within limits, but readily distractible and restless. Testing was incomplete because he tired quickly. However, a basal age on the Stanford-Binet of two years six months was established, with some successes occurring at the four-year level. Intelligence testing was repeated at five years one month . . . . A mental age of three years eight months, with an I.Q. score of 72 was recorded.

Kevin, despite his mildly subnormal intelligence, occasional hyperactivity, and prominent motor and speech disorders, was not an excessively difficult child to manage. Although he was moderately active and irregular as an infant, he characteristically tended to approach new situations and to express a positive mood.

191

An early easy distractibility, coupled with a high level of persistence in the first year, came to be replaced after the second year by moderate distractibility but continued high levels of persistence. Perhaps most significantly, from the early months of life onward he was a child whose responses were characterized by a low level of intensity. Thus, even abnormal behaviors were mildly expressed.

From the sixth month of life onward, when they first became convinced of abnormality in his development, his parents accepted the fact that his difficulties in learning and his developmental delays derived from primary neurologic damage. Within this framework they have been highly accepting and very fond of the boy. Demands have usually been appropriate to the level of his intellectual and physical capacities, and efforts at training have been both consistent and patient. Social contact with other children was encouraged and planned for, and the child was placed in a normal nursery school for children one year his junior. Since the age of six he has been in a special school for brain-injured children. Within his limitations, his course in school has shown good social functioning with peers and teachers. Learning has been slow, but progresses. His overall behavior has not presented major problems other than those involving the modifications of management necessary because of his intellectual and physical limitations. At no time has he been considered to present any significant degree of behavioral disturbance [Thomas, Chess & Birch, 1968, pp. 128–30].[1]

CARL W.

When . . . Carl's father talked about his 10 children, he was not hesitant about singling out one of them as "no good." That child was Carl. Today Carl has similarly rejective feelings about his parents for he does not view them as making any contribution to his life except for providing the basic essentials until he quit school in the third grade. In Carl's eyes he is a self-made man, and he owes all that he is to himself. He taught himself what he needed to know about work, personal appearance, and life in general; he thinks so little of the guidance of his parents that he can no longer remember what his father's occupation was.

Similarly he thinks so little of the contribution of the schools that he can no longer utilize anything that he was taught in the schools or even remember how he felt about them. School for Carl was one frustrating experience after another, for he could not or did not want to learn anything offered by the school. When the expectations became too demanding in the third grade he simply quit attending with no regrets at the time or now . . . .

He says . . . "I quit school while I was in the third grade and grabbed the first train out of here and I've been on my own ever since." Being on his own has meant a succession of jobs in . . . unskilled labor connected with farming, construction, and mining. . . .

In describing himself as a self-made man, Carl says. "I ain't never asked no one for nothin'." He sees no contradiction between his denial of any outside influences or help in his life and his total support today by welfare agencies. . . . Carl continued the pattern characteristic of his parents who relied on welfare support for more than half of their subsistence. Carl claims his right to such support because, "I hurt my back in the mines and two years ago I fell off of a ladder and since

---

[1] A. Thomas, S. Chess, and H. G. Birch, *Temperament and Behavior Disorders in Children* (New York: New York University Press, 1968). © 1968 by New York University Press and reprinted by permission.

then I can't do nothin'. We're getting $254 a month from the government and my lawyers are fighting for the $4000 I got coming from compensation."

Carl is presently living with his second wife in a rented home. They have five children and "Two hundred fifty dollars a month don't go far with these five kids of mine [Carl's childhood IQ was 54 on the Stanford-Binet test; Baller, Charles, & Miller, 1967, pp. 284–85)]."

ROCKY F.

Rocky . . . seemed almost completely incapable of reading while he spent eight years in the [special class] and showed only slightly more aptitude in other school subjects. With his fists, however, he displayed a resourcefulness that soon brought him to the attention of boxing promoters not only locally but regionally. An older brother . . . became the manager for a boxing career that established Rocky as one of the very great fighters of his generation.

Earnings as a professional boxer enabled Rocky not only to surround himself with many physical comforts—even luxuries—but to invest in enterprises that became more than adequate replacements monetarily and otherwise for the benefits which were realized from boxing. Doubtless the business acumen of the older brother had much to do with these successes. Rocky and his attractive, musically quite talented wife own a home presently valued above $40,000. He has provided generously for the physical comforts of his parents and for other relatives, and he enjoys the close friendship . . . of a number of socially influential persons who for the most part shared vicariously in his triumphs as a boxer and have remained loyal to him [Rocky's childhood IQ was 66 on the Stanford-Binet; Baller, Charles, Miller, 1967. pp. 281–82]."

In most states, the IQ scores of the three individuals just described made them automatically eligible for placement in public school special classes for the retarded. Kevin's IQ score was in the range generally labeled "borderline retarded" (IQs 68–83 on the Stanford-Binet test), while Rocky and Carl's scores were in the "mildly retarded" range (IQs 52–67). Over 30 million other Americans would obtain IQ scores in the borderline and mildly retarded ranges, while about 230,000 would score in the "moderately retarded" range (IQs 36–51), 170,000 would score in the "severely retarded" range (IQs 20–35), and 110,000 would score in the "profoundly retarded" range (IQs 0–19; Heber, 1961; figures extrapolated from Dingman & Tarjan, 1960, Silverstein, 1973). Between two and six million Americans are officially classified as retarded and 200,000 of these reside in institutions (Tarjan, Wright, Eyman, & Keeran, 1973).

It is evident from the sheer magnitude of these figures as well as from the case histories that the differences among people obtaining low IQ scores are probably greater than their similarities. They comprise an extremely heterogeneous group in terms of the reasons for their low IQ scores, the implications of these scores, their special problems and needs, and the degree of happiness and fulfillment they attain during their lifetimes.

Another important fact is revealed by the numerical distribution of IQ scores below the arbitrary lower limits of the "normal" range. This is that the vast majority of people who score below the normal range are not really very far below that range in terms of their potentials for attaining adult social and occupational competence in western society. Only a tiny percentage are so handicapped as to be candidates for life-long care by other people. Most of the rest are potentially capable of attaining a wide variety of occupational and social roles.

As is well known, that target of so much controversy, the IQ score, is by no means a perfect predictor of attainments outside the testing situation. However, to the extent that IQ scores are valid indices of adult occupational capabilities, people scoring in the upper 40s can be trained as stock clerks, rug weavers, painter's helpers, domestic workers, and operators of many machines. Those scoring in the mid-50s are capable of shoe repairing, operating movie projectors and some printing presses, working as short-order cooks, making pottery, and doing assembly work in factories. Those with IQs in the low 60s are capable of being variety store sales clerks, painters, and wood finishers, among other things (Rotter, 1971).

Until the advent of compulsory schooling, little special notice was taken of most of the people who today would be classified as retarded. Those who met the traditional "village idiot" stereotype no doubt included psychotic, delinquent, diseased, brain-damaged, and epileptic individuals whose oddities may or may not have included consistently low levels of intellectual functioning. As outlined in Chapter 2, the first systematic attempts to distinguish the retarded from the insane and to provide special education for the retarded came early in the nineteenth century. The first educational attempts were, however, directed primarily toward those who were severely deficient and/or who had clearly recognizable physical abnormalities that were believed to be correlated with very low intelligence.

It was primarily the institution of compulsory schooling that caused uniform standards of intellectual performance to be applied to large segments of the population. Since schooling was organized according to an age-graded sequence, failure to meet certain performance criteria at the same age as other children caused a child to be stigmatized, usually by being required to repeat grades. Consequently, many children, who in previous generations would not have been singled out, were now identified as being below the norm in intellectual performance. In effect, it was a change in social institutions, rather than any change in the distribution of "intelligence," that increased the proportion of the population classified as being subnormal in intelligence.

One consequence of the discovery that many children fell behind their age mates in school performance was the establishment of public school special classes for these children. Most western countries, including the United States, had special classes by 1900 (Kanner, 1964). A second consequence was that screening procedures were sought for identifying children whose low ability would prevent them from benefitting from regular schooling. The best known of these procedures originated with Alfred Binet and

Theodore Simon, who first published a series of intelligence test items in 1905.

THE MEASUREMENT OF INTELLIGENCE

Attempts to define and measure intelligence systematically did not begin with Binet and Simon. Francis Galton, a cousin of Darwin, devised in the 1880s numerous tests of sensory and motor functions. They included tests of sensory acuity, reaction time, and the number of taps a person could make in 30 seconds.

Galton firmly believed such tests to be valid measures of intellectual ability, which he maintained was both hereditary and unitary. His student, J. McKeen Cattell, coined the term "mental test" in 1890 and was largely responsible for originating testing in the United States. Unfortunately for the assumption that the sensory-motor tests measured a unitary faculty of intelligence, little correlation was found among individuals' scores on the various tests (Sharp, 1898), or between the tests and either teachers' ratings of intelligence (Bolton, 1891) or academic grades (Wissler, 1901).

Development of the Binet-Simon Scale

In contrast to Galton and Cattell, Binet and Simon were not motivated by a desire to demonstrate either the unitary or the hereditary nature of intelligence. The purpose that led to the construction of their famous intelligence scale was a purely practical one. Their efforts are worth recounting in detail because their objectives, their techniques, and their final product played a large role in establishing the general format retained by many intelligence tests today.

After most other western countries had instituted special classes for children who performed poorly in regular classes, the French Minister of Public Instruction in 1904 appointed a commission to formulate plans for educating such children in France. Binet, who had already been experimenting with intelligence tests for 15 years, and Simon took over the task of devising objective procedures for determining which children should be assigned to special classes because they were intellectually incapable of profiting from regular instruction. As Binet and Simon described the situation, the commission:

. . . decided that no child suspected of retardation should be eliminated from the ordinary school and admitted into a special class, without first being subjected to a pedagogical and medical examination from which it could be certified that because of the state of his intelligence, he was unable to profit, in an average measure, from the instruction given in the ordinary schools.

But how the examination of each child should be made, what methods should be followed, what observations taken, what questions asked, what tests devised, how the child should be compared with normal children, the Commission felt under no obligation to decide . . . .

It has seemed to us extremely useful to furnish a guide for future Commissions' examination . . . . It must be made impossible for those who belong to the Commission to fall into the habit of making haphazard decisions according to impressions which are subjective, and consequently uncontrolled. Such impressions are sometimes good, sometimes bad, and have at all times too much the nature of the arbitrary, of caprice, of indifference. Such a condition is quite unfortunate because the interests of the child demand a more careful method. To be a member of a special class can never be a mark of distinction, and such as do not merit it, must be spared the record . . . we are convinced . . . that the precision and exactness of science should be introduced into our practice whenever possible, and in the great majority of cases it is possible [Binet & Simon, 1905b, pp. 9–10].

The last paragraph of this quotation contains a message that Binet and Simon were to repeat often and that they believed to have wide applicability in the study and treatment not only of mental retardation, but of all conditions regarded as psychopathological. They maintained that the effectiveness of education and treatment could never be judged without standardized objective methods for assessing the individual before and after education or treatment.

It is not by means of prior reasonings, of vague considerations, of oratorical displays, that these questions can be solved; but by minute investigation, entering into the details of fact, and considering the effects of the treatment for each particular child. There is but one means of knowing if a child, who has passed six years in a hospital or a special class, has profited from that stay, and to what degree he has profited; and that is to compare his [initial diagnosis] with his [final diagnosis], and by that means ascertain if he shows a special amelioration of his condition beyond that which might be credited simply to the considerations of growth. But experience has shown how imprudent it would be to place confidence in this comparison, when the two [diagnoses] come from different doctors, who do not judge in exactly the same way, or who use different words to characterize the mental status of patients [Binet and Simon, 1905b, p. 12].

Note that Binet and Simon are pointing to the problems of *reliability* and *validity* that arise in the assessment of all variables (discussed in Chapter 4). They regarded the lack of reliable and valid diagnostic procedures in all areas of psychopathology as preventing adequate studies of epidemiology, etiology, treatment, and prognosis.

In their efforts to devise procedures for identifying children who were intellectually retarded, Binet and Simon were committed neither to a theory of the determinants of intelligence, nor to a belief in its immutability. They were pragmatists who sought only a reliable and valid measure of the child's *current* intellectual functioning.

Our purpose is to be able to measure the intellectual capacity of a child who is brought to us in order to know whether he is normal or retarded. We should, therefore, study his condition at the time and that only. We have nothing to do either with his past history or with his future; consequently we shall neglect his etiology, and we shall make no attempt to distinguish between acquired and congenital idiocy . . . . As to that which concerns his future, we shall exercise the same abstinence; we do not attempt to establish or prepare a prognosis and we leave unanswered the question of whether this retardation is curable, or even improvable. We shall limit ourselves to ascertaining the truth in regard to his present mental state [Binet & Simon, 1905a, p. 37].

Since the Galton-Cattell sensory-motor tests had clearly failed to predict academic performance, Binet and Simon sought tests that would tap processes more like those actually used in school. They assumed that judgment and reasoning were the basic processes of higher intellectual functioning and they attempted to devise tests that measured these processes in action. Because they wished to distinguish children whose thinking was below normal for their ages from those whose poor school performance was due to factors like inadequate cultural and educational backgrounds, poor school attendance, low motivation, distractibility, and emotional instability, they sought test items that required neither specific previous education nor high motivation. In order to minimize the influence of specific previous knowledge, they included items that were as heterogeneous and as diverse as possible and that did not require academic skills such as reading and writing.

Binet and Simon argued that proper evaluation of a child suspected of subnormal intellectual functioning should not be limited to intelligence testing but should include a complete medical and pedagogical (school achievement) examination. The medical examination was to determine whether organic conditions might be responsible for poor performance on the intelligence test, while the pedagogical examination rather than the intelligence test was to determine the child's current level of academic knowledge.

In selecting items for their tests, Binet and Simon gave each item to a number of normal children at several age levels. An item remained a candidate for the final form of the test only if the percentage of children passing it increased sharply with age. The assumption was that the intelligence scale should measure intellectual *development* rather than any static quality of functioning. If an item was passed by a majority of normal children at a certain chronological age, by fewer children below that age, and by rapidly increasing percentages of children at each year above it, then the item was considered to be representative of the "mental age" (MA) corresponding to that chronological age. Thus, an item that was passed by increasing percentages of children at ages 6 through 10, with 8 years being the first age at which a majority passed it, was designated as being representative of the MA of a normal 8-year-old.

A related principle of the Binet-Simon approach was that a child's intellectual performance was not to be evaluated in terms of any *absolute* level of ability, but only in terms *relative* to the performance of other children his age. Hence, the average performance of, say, 8-year-olds was the norm against which the performance of individual 8-year-olds would be judged. Although their norms were based upon small samples of children who were not representative of the entire population, Binet and Simon were well aware of the potential relationships between test performance and such factors as socioeconomic status (SES). The children whose performance actually provided the norms happened to be from lower-class neighborhoods of Paris. Later research has shown that the average test performance of upper SES children generally exceeds the average performance of lower SES children. If Binet and Simon had employed more upper SES children, the level of performance considered typical for a particular age might have been different.

By 1908, Binet and Simon had assembled their best tests into a complete scale of intelligence. Shortly before Binet's death in 1911, they published a revision of the scale that simplified administration and scoring procedures. The scale consisted of five items at nearly every age level from three to fifteen years, plus five at an "adult" level. Certain items that appeared on the early scales still appear in some form on the most recent American revision (Terman & Merrill, 1960). These include short-term memory for digits; naming common objects; copying a square; putting together the two halves of a bisected rectangular card; finding parts missing from familiar figures; solving complex logical problems; and defining abstract words.

When a child passed all items at a certain year level (called his *basal* level), he was then given items at the succeeding levels until he reached a level where he failed all the items (called his *ceiling* level). His MA was calculated as the sum of his basal MA, plus one-fifth of a year of MA for each item passed above his basal level.

The same procedure has been retained on the current revision of the Binet, except that, because there are 6 items at most levels, each item counts one-sixth of a year (2 months of MA). Thus, on the current revision, if a child passed all 6 tests at the 6-year level (his basal level), 4 at the 7-year level, 3 at the 8-year level, and none at the 9-year level (his ceiling level), his mental age would be calculated as follows:

Year Level	Number of Tests Passed	MA Credits
VI	6 (basal age)	6 years
VII	4	8 months
VIII	3	6 months
IX	0 (ceiling age)	+ 0

$$\text{MA} = 7 \text{ yrs.} \quad 2 \text{ months}$$

Binet and Simon considered a child to be retarded enough to need special education if his MA were more than 2 years below his chronological age (CA).

What about criteria for validity and reliability? Just as the resources and techniques available at the time limited the size and representativeness of the samples of children on whom the norms were based, these factors also limited research on validity and reliability. However, from the samples of several hundred children who were available for study, Binet and Simon (1908) were able to derive the following types of evidence for the scale's validity:

1. Children who were independently judged by teachers as being very bright all did well on the test.
2. Children who were three or more years behind in their scholastic performance all obtained MAs on the test below their CAs.
3. Most children performing normally in school obtained MAs corresponding to their CAs.
4. Children could rarely pass items located above their ceiling levels, i.e., the levels at which they had failed all items.

Some degree of test-retest reliability was established by analyzing the performance of a few children given the tests about two weeks apart. It was found that the number of changes in items passed and failed was relatively small.

Summary of the Binet-Simon Approach

The Binet-Simon approach laid down the following ideals for intelligence testing:

1. The purpose of the test was to provide a relatively objective procedure for determining whether a child's intellectual functioning was sufficiently below average to warrant special education or treatment.
2. Scores obtained on the test were considered to be merely estimates of *current* functioning that carried no implications about the reasons for that level of functioning (e.g., heredity, disease, environment), or about the immutability of that level of functioning.
3. The test was to measure thinking-in-action in as many different ways as possible so that it would not be unduly influenced by specific skills or information.
4. The test was to be only one part of a thorough evaluation that should include a medical examination to identify possible organic reasons for poor performance and a pedagogical examination to determine a child's level of academic achievement.
5. The test was intended to measure a child's current intellectual *development,* rather than anything considered to be a permanent quality or a "state" of intelligence.
6. Levels of intellectual development were defined by what normal children at each chronological age could typically do, rather than by reference to a theoretical scale of development.
7. The validity of the test was to be initially determined (a) by external criteria such as correlations of test scores with teachers' ratings, school performance, and the CAs of normal children; and, (b) by internal criteria such as the ordering of successes and failures on the items of the test.

8. The reliability of the test was to be judged by determining whether children's performance on the test changed markedly between two administrations of it a short time apart.

Subsequent Developments in Testing

Within a very few years the Binet-Simon Scale made a worldwide impression. Henry Goddard, an American psychologist who was director of one of the first centers for psychological research on retardation, translated the scale and began using it in 1908 with retarded children at the Vineland, New Jersey, Training School. Despite initial skepticism, he found to his surprise that children's performance on the scale corresponded well with what was known about their behavior outside the test situation. Another American, F. Kuhlmann (1912), showed that the average of several teachers' ratings of retarded children's abilities correlated well with Binet MAs, although the teachers' ratings agreed poorly with one another.

Goddard proposed that adult retardates be classified according to the MAs they obtained on the scale, with those whose MAs fell below 2 years being labeled "idiots," those with MAs of 3 to 7 years being labeled "imbeciles," and those with MAs of 7 to 12 years being labeled "morons." His terminology was widely adopted and remained in use for many years.

Goddard also published a condensed translation and revision of the Binet-Simon Scale for use with American children. By 1916, he reported that he had distributed 22,000 copies and 88,000 record blanks and that versions of the scale were being used in Canada, England, Australia, New Zealand, South Africa, Germany, Switzerland, Italy, Russia, China, Japan, and Turkey (Goddard, 1916). Such a response to what was an admittedly crude attempt at objectively classifying children's abilities was symptomatic of the new interest in the measurement of intelligence for purposes of education, care, and treatment.

The intense interest in measuring intelligence also had another source. This was the heredity-environment controversy that had been raging since Darwin's *Origin of Species* (1859) and Galton's *Hereditary Genius* (1869). Although Binet and Simon considered their efforts to be neutral with respect to this controversy, many hereditarians seized upon the Binet-Simon Scale as a means of objectively measuring innate capacities and of demonstrating the degree to which heredity dominated over environment in the determination of intelligence.

Not the least of these hereditarians was Henry Goddard, who, beside being known for his work in intelligence testing, was an active leader of the eugenics movement to sterilize the retarded and who became famous for his book, *The Kallikak Family: A Study in the Heredity of Feeble-mindedness* (1912). In this book, Goddard traced two lines of descendants from a revolutionary War soldier, Martin Kallikak. One line began when Kallikak during the war fathered a child by a feeble-minded tavern girl. The other began with the children Kallikak fathered by the respectable girl he married after he returned home. The fact that many of the descendants of the first union were feeble-minded, delinquent, poor, and alcoholic, while most of those from the second union were of good reputation was interpreted as evidence for the almost exclusively hereditary determination of intelligence. Goddard gave little weight to the obvious differences in the environments in which members of each line were raised.

The 1916 Stanford-Binet

The practice of using the absolute differences between a child's MA and CA as an index of retardation meant that a child of 16 with an MA of 12 years was considered to be as handicapped as a child of 8 with an MA of 4 years. Since the latter child is likely to be more handicapped for his age than the former child, Lewis Terman, in his 1916 Stanford revision of the Binet-Simon Scale, adopted a *ratio* of MA/CA as an index of ability. This *intelligence quotient* (IQ), multiplied by 100 to avoid decimals, meant that a 16-year-old with an MA of 12 years would have an $IQ = MA/CA = 12/16 \times 100 = 75$. An 8-year-old with an MA of 6 years would be considered to have a similar degree of handicap for his age, because $IQ = MA/CA = 6/8 \times 100 = 75$.

As the Stanford-Binet became the most widely used test and the standard against which most new tests were evaluated, the IQ, as an index of presumed *rate* of intellectual development, became both a household word and the focus of the controversy over the inheritance of intelligence. Emphasizing the IQ score, and thus treating intelligence test performance as a measure of *rate of development,* also constituted a subtle but significant shift away from the position of Binet and Simon that test performance should be regarded only as an index of *current* intellectual functioning, rather than as a long-term prognosticator.

If one knows only that an 8-year-old performs like a typical 6-year-old on a test, one is much more likely to think about the child's actual current functioning than if one is told, "He has an IQ of 75," which implies to most people a permanent inferiority of considerable degree. Indeed, the author has encountered professional mental-health workers who, when told that a 16-year-old "has an IQ of 75," consider the youth to be too retarded for psychotherapy or counseling. Other workers object strenuously that the test must be wrong because they know the youth can read, write, and tell time. Yet, if the workers in either case had stopped to consider that the IQ of 75 indicated only that the youth's intellectual performance is like that of most 12-year-olds (i.e., MA 12), it is unlikely that such misinterpretations would occur, since average 12-year-olds can benefit from therapy and are capable of reading, writing, telling time, and much more.

By the same token, the variety of occupations previously cited as being possible for adults obtaining IQ scores in the "retarded" range is not at all surprising when one considers the MAs represented by those IQs. According to 1972 norms for the Stanford-Binet (Terman & Merrill, 1973), the average adult has an MA of 17 years. A person 18 years or older who obtains a "moderately retarded" IQ in the upper 40s has an MA of about 8 years. There are numerous occupations that require no more than the mental capabilities of an 8-year-old if proper training is provided.

To return now to the 1916 Stanford-Binet, Terman started with many new potential test items, and he obtained norms based upon 1,000 children selected to be roughly representative of native-born children. He found the IQ scores in his standardization sample to be symmetrically distributed around the mean of approximately 100 in a form close to that of a normal curve (Terman, Lyman, Ordahl, Ordahl, Galbreath, & Talbert, 1917). He also reported that test-retest reliabilities of IQ scores were very high over periods up to four years. This apparent stability of the IQ score and its similar distribution at various ages were interpreted as supporting the hereditarian hypothesis that Terman, like Goddard, held.

Terman also proposed that the "IQ test," as it was now known, be used to identify very bright children in order to place them in special classes appropriate to their abilities. He began a longitudinal study in which he traced the lives of more than a thousand of these children for approximately 35 years (Terman & Oden, 1959). Their superior achievement throughout school and adulthood provided another type of validation for the IQ score as a measure of intellectual ability. The adult social success of these children also effectively rebutted the prevailing myth that exceptionally high intelligence, or "genius," was typically associated with social maladjustment, or "madness."

Intelligence tests gained further status when group and individual forms proved effective in the screening and placing of over a million soldiers during the First World War (Yoakum & Yerkes, 1920). By 1920, the use of IQ tests in various forms had become widespread in education and industry. Many states soon passed laws that made the IQ one criterion for special class and institutional placement. Thus, if a child had an IQ below a certain point (usually 70, 75, or 80), he was eligible for special education or care, although most laws neither required nor guaranteed that these be provided.

Despite the prevailing environmentalistic attitudes regarding child rearing and personality development, there was a strong and almost universal presumption in favor of a hereditary basis for the IQ score, providing it was obtained under the appropriate standard testing conditions and there were no obvious negative influences such as emotional instability. The intelligence test had thus taken on a significance much different from that intended by Binet and Simon, and one certainly unjustified by any conclusive scientific evidence.

The 1937 Revision of the Stanford-Binet.   One innovation of the 1937 revision was that two alternative forms of the test (Form L and Form M) were provided, both similar in the types of items but differing in specific content (Terman & Merrill, 1937). In effect, this made it possible to administer the test twice without the child's prior knowledge of specific content influencing the two scores to the same extent and without his second test score being influenced by learning from the first test. The reliability of the IQ score could now be determined by correlating scores on the two forms rather than by merely correlating scores on the same test given twice. In fact, the correlations between IQ scores on the two forms given a few days apart were found to be in the .90s for children in nearly all age and IQ groups (McNemar, 1942).

Beside introducing alternate forms, Terman and Merrill employed much more thorough standardization procedures than had been used before. Their norms were based on 3,184 subjects, including a minimum of 100 boys and 100 girls at each CA between 2 and 14, plus 50 of each sex at each age from 15 to 18. The subjects were drawn from 11 states in such a way as to make their distribution as similar as possible to that of the whole native-born American population in terms of geographical region, socio-economic status, and urban versus rural environment, although it was limited by the fact that only whites were used.

Because the finding that the 1916 Stanford-Binet IQ scores were nearly normally distributed (Terman et al, 1917) had led to the assumption that the *true* distribution of IQs was normal, final item selection and scoring were designed to produce IQ distributions as nearly normal as possible. The scoring of the new test was thus intended to preserve the distribution *assumed* to characterize intellectual abilities, no matter what the "true" distribution might be.

The 1960 Revision of the Stanford-Binet. The 1960 Stanford-Binet combined what had been found to be the best items from the 1937 Forms L and M into a single scale called Form L–M. Performance by 4,498 white subjects was used as a basis for updating the content of items, for selecting items that correlated highest with total score, and for revising the scoring. The major innovation in the 1960 revision was that IQ scores were no longer calculated simply as a ratio of MA to CA. Instead, each IQ was defined as a fixed number of standard deviation units from the mean of the normal distribution of scores obtained for each age level. This practice had begun on adult tests where MA had little meaning because typical adult performance had not been found to increase much beyond the age of about 20.

Scoring was arranged so that the mean total score in the standardization sample for a given age was defined as an IQ of 100 for that age. One standard deviation from the mean was set equal to 16 IQ points. Thus, a child scoring one standard deviation below the mean for his age receives an IQ of 84, while a child scoring one standard deviation above the mean for his age receives an IQ of 116. Figure 7–1 depicts the theoretical distribution of scores on which the 1960 Binet IQs are based. It has been found that the percentage of children with very low IQs is greater than predicted by the curve. This is a significant point for theories of cultural-familial retardation to be discussed later in the chapter.

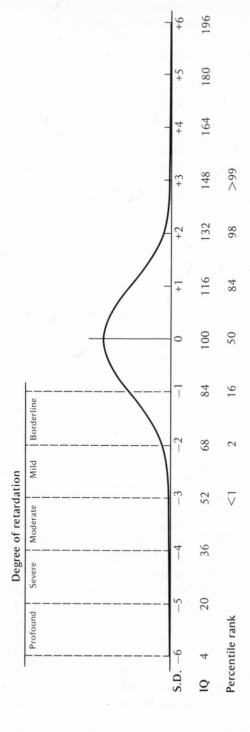

Fig. 7–1. Theoretical distribution of scores on which 1960 Stanford-Binet IQs are based, together with standard deviations, IQ scores, percentile ranks, and degrees of retardation. From Pinneau (1961). The percentage of people with very low scores has been found to be greater than predicted by this curve (see Fig. 7–5).

As indicated in the figure, the cut-off points for the various degrees of retardation outlined at the beginning of the chapter are in terms of standard deviation units below the mean. For example, "borderline retardation" includes scores between one and two standard deviations below the mean (IQs 68–83). It is obvious from the figure that the exact cut-off points for these categories are totally arbitrary.

The purpose of scoring IQs in terms of deviation units was to insure that a specific IQ always represented the same distance above or below average at any age. Because MA scores were not perfectly normally distributed at every age, the IQs yielded by the MA/CA ratio had means differing from 100 at some ages, and some IQs represented larger deviations from the average score for one age than for another. This is reflected in the fact that, for example, an eight-year-old who achieves an MA of eight does not obtain a deviation IQ of 100 but of 98 on the 1960 Binet. New norms were obtained in 1971 and 1972 by testing a national sample of 2,100 children, including nonwhites (Terman & Merrill, 1973). Although the items were the same as in the 1960 revision, average performance at some ages had improved to such an extent that considerable disparity now exists between deviation IQs and IQs calculated from the MA/CA ratio.

The Wechsler Tests

Although the Stanford-Binet is still probably the most widely used test for judging mental retardation (Silverstein, 1963), the tests developed by David Wechsler are also widely used for individual evaluations of intellectual functioning. The original Wechsler test, the Wechsler-Bellevue ("W-B"), was first published in 1939, primarily for use with adults. This test, its later revision—the Wechsler Adult Intelligence Scale ("WAIS"; 1955)—and its two downward extensions for children—the Wechsler Intelligence Scale for Children ("WISC"; 1949) and the Wechsler Pre-school and Primary Scale of Intelligence ("WPPSI"; 1967)—were standardized on several thousand people chosen to be representative of the American population. Only whites were employed for the W-B and WISC, but nonwhites were included for the WAIS and WPPSI. The Wechsler tests differ in two major ways from the Binet tests.

First, the Wechsler tests do not yield an MA score. This is largely because it was found that average performance was highest for adults between the ages of 20 and 25 and that performance was lower among adults above these ages. The concept of MA as a score that normally increases with CA was thus untenable for adults. IQs were, therefore, defined simply in terms of deviation units from the mean of scores obtained by the standardization sample of people of a given age, the procedure adopted in the 1960 revision of the Binet. Fifteen IQ points are credited for every standard deviation away from the mean. Accordingly, a person one standard deviation below the mean in performance for his age obtains an IQ of 85, while a person one standard deviation above the mean obtains an IQ of 115.

The fact that the Binet and Wechsler tests differ in the relations they assign between standard deviation units and IQ scores illustrates again the arbitrary nature of any particular IQ score. Most people obtain somewhat different IQs on the two tests. For example, a person three standard deviations below the mean on the Binet (where each standard deviation equals 16 IQ points), obtains an IQ of 52, while if he is three standard deviations below the mean on the Wechsler tests, he obtains an IQ of 55.

The second major difference between the Wechsler and Binet tests is that, instead of containing several different items at each of a series of age levels, the Wechsler tests contain subtests, each of which has a group of items of a particular type. When a person is tested, he receives each subtest, beginning with its easiest items and ending when he has failed a certain number in succession. Several of the subtests are considered to tap primarily verbal ability and their scores together yield a *Verbal IQ*. On the Wechsler Intelligence Scale for Children (WISC), the verbal subtests are: 1. *General Information* (questions of factual knowledge); 2. *General Comprehension* (questions of common sense); 3. *Arithmetic;* 4. *Similarities* (questions of how two things are alike); 5. *Vocabulary;* 6. *Digit Span* (short-term memory for several series of digits), an optional test. The other subtests are considered to tap primarily nonverbal ability and their scores together yield a *Performance IQ*. The performance subtests are: 1. *Picture Completion* (finding missing parts of common figures); 2. *Picture Arrangement* (putting several pictures together to reconstruct cut-up figures or stories); 3. *Block Design* (arranging colored blocks to match designs portrayed in pictures); 4. *Object Assembly* (putting together puzzlelike pieces to reconstruct objects); 5. *Coding* (quickly and accurately copying symbols); 6. *Mazes* (tracing pathways through mazes printed on paper), an optional test. Scores on all the verbal and performance subtests together yield a *Full Scale IQ*.

Other Types of Intelligence Tests

Although the Wechsler and Binet tests are the most frequently used tests for judging intellectual subnormality, there are numerous other tests for measuring children's intellectual performance. Some of these will be discussed in Chapter 16. Two categories of tests that happen to be frequently considered in conjunction with the Wechsler and Binet tests are *infant development tests* and *group IQ tests*.

The infant tests employ a series of standardized sensory-motor tasks to determine whether an infant is progressing at the rate typical of the infants in a standardization sample. These tests generally yield a *developmental quotient* (DQ) that is similar in conception to the IQ. However, longitudinal studies have shown little correlation between infant DQs and later IQs (Bayley, 1970; McCall, Hogarty, & Hurlburt, 1972). This is not surprising since IQ tests require symbol manipulation and other complex behavior which simply does not exist at the ages for which the infant tests are designed.

Group IQ tests are paper-and-pencil tests that can be administered to groups by minimally trained examiners. They are intended to be screening devices for identifying individuals whose exceptionally low performance suggests that they should be evaluated further by individual testing. Although the IQs yielded by these tests may be rough indices of a child's current functioning, their scores are often interpreted in an excessively literal manner by school personnel and others.

VALIDITY OF IQ TESTS

The value of any psychological test lies in its accuracy in identifying characteristics of an individual that are predictive of his behavior outside the test situation. Intelligence tests are worthless if they fail to correlate with important extratest behavior. Using a test to aid in making decisions about individuals and in evaluating the effects of particular experiences, education, or treatment is justified only if it has been shown that performance on the test indeed predicts the behavior of people like those under consideration. What evidence is there, then, that intelligence test scores reliably predict academic performance?

Children in Regular Classes

Much of the evidence is in the form of correlations between IQ test scores and academic performance by children who are close enough to the normal range of school performance to be in regular classes. The correlations of IQ test scores with achievement test scores and grade average typically range from the high .40s to the high .70s (e.g., Achenbach, 1970b; Bond, 1940; Stevenson, Hale, Klein, and Miller, 1968).

Since any correlation between two variables is not an inherent characteristic of the variables, but depends upon the people for whom the variables are measured, it is important to compare the correlations obtained for different groups. Accordingly, Tulkin and Newbrough (1968) compared the correlations between group IQ scores (Lorge-Thorndike) and achievement test scores for several hundred black and white fifth- and sixth-graders in Maryland. The mean correlation bewteen verbal IQ and achievement test scores was .78 for blacks and .75 for whites. When broken down by social class, the correlations were .81 for both black and white upper-class children, .62 for lower-class blacks, and .64 for lower-class whites (Tulkin, 1968). Social class differences thus appeared to influence the predictive power of the IQ scores more than did racial differences in this sample.

The long-term predictive power of group IQ tests for academic performance was studied by Embree (1948). He compared the childhood IQ scores of people who had all attended the same high school between 1921 and 1945 and who later entered college. The mean childhood IQ of all who began college was 118; of those who obtained bachelor's degrees, 123; of those who obtained advanced degrees, 126; of those who graduated with honors, 133; and of those who were Phi Beta Kappa, 137. This suggests a considerable degree of long-term validity for IQ scores obtained by children all of whom had the opportunity and motivation to begin college.

For a broader range of children, including those who did and did not attend college, Ball (1938) found a correlation of .71 between group IQ test scores obtained in 1918, while the children were in grades two through ten, and their occupational levels in 1937. He also found a correlation of .57 between the 1923 IQ scores of a similar group of children and their 1937 occupational levels. This lower correlation was presumably because fewer members of the 1923 group had yet attained their maximal occupational levels.

Children Classified as Retarded

The validity of IQ tests for predicting the approximate academic performance of school-age children seems fairly well established. The IQ score, however, is virtually never the sole criterion for classifying a child as "retarded." A child who is doing well in school is unlikely to become a candidate for special classes, no matter what his IQ score. Children who are doing poorly over a long period and who consistently obtain low group test scores are usually retested on an individual test before decisions about special class placement are made. After placement in a special class, periodic retesting and evaluation are supposed to be done to insure that the child remains appropriately placed.

Once a child has been classified as being in need of special education, his IQ on an individual test is used to aid in determining what sort of special class he should attend. The usual division, especially for public school special classes, is between children with IQs of 20 to 50 (referred to as "trainable") and those above 50 referred to as "educable"). Surveys have shown that between 74 and 89 per cent of the children classified as retarded score in the educable range (Farber, 1968; Birch, Richardson, Baird, Horobin & Illsley, 1970).

Classes for trainable children provide training in social skills, self-care, and safety rules, with academic instruction being limited to reading of a few important words, simple arithmetic, and important factual knowledge. Classes for educable children offer most of the usual academic subjects, but at a slower pace and with lower goals than classes for children in the normal IQ range. Studies of the relations between IQ scores and achievement by children in the educable range have generally reported correlations in the same range as found for normal children, i.e., from the upper .40s to the upper .70s (e.g. Cochran & Pedrini, 1969; Kimbrell, 1966; Mueller, 1969).

Social Competence

Since social competence is often a more important goal of education for low IQ people than is academic achievement, it is also important to consider the relations between intelligence test scores and measures of social competence. The best-known measure of social competence is the Vineland Social Maturity Scale (Doll, 1953). This is a series of practical behavioral items (e.g., dresses self, bathes self, cares for self at toilet) arranged in levels according to the ages at which children normally attain them, much as test items are arranged on the Binet. All the items a child can do are scored, the total score yielding a Social Age (SA). This is useful in judging the level of care a child is likely to need.

Social competence measured in this way has been found to correlate with intelligence test scores to about the same degree as academic performance does. In one study of retarded children, the Binet MA correlated .72 with Vineland Social Age (Saslow, 1961), while in another study Binet IQ correlated .69 with scores on the Cain-Levin Social Competency Scale (Goldschmid & Domino, 1965).

The correlations obtained between intelligence test scores and academic performance and childhood social competence are large enough to justify their use as aids to prediction, but the scores are by no means so infallible as to become the only basis for decisions about children's education. Many factors that may influence school performance, such as imagination, artistic and other specific abilities, motivation, and personality are simply not measured by standard intelligence tests.

Moreover, although occupations requiring much abstract thinking are successfully attained only by those whose academic performance is above certain levels, there are many other occupations for which performance of this type is less relevant (Super & Crites, 1962). It is evident, therefore, that for low IQ children whose academic performance may be consistently poor, our responsibility should not end with assignment of the child to a diluted form of the usual academic curriculum, but should include provision of genuine educational opportunities and occupational training that may, when necessary, last as long as the graduate training offered to people who happen to have higher IQs. Table 7–1 summarizes the typical behavioral competence of people in the retarded IQ ranges when they are at ages 0–5, 6–20, and over 21.

LONG-TERM STABILITY AND CHANGE IN IQ SCORES

The question of whether children's IQ scores remain stable over the course of development has frequently been confused with the nature-nurture question. Evidence for stability in IQ scores has been used to argue that intellectual ability is genetically controlled, while evidence for changes

TABLE 7–1

General behavioral competency expected of people with low IQs
at various ages. This table integrates chronological age,
degree of retardation, and level of intellectual,
vocational, and social functioning.

Degree of Mental Retardation	Preschool Age 0–5 Maturation and Development	School Age 6–20 Training and Education	Adult 21 and Over Social and Vocational Adequacy
Profound (IQ 0–19)	Gross retardation; minimal capacity for functioning in sensorimotor areas; needs nursing care	Some motor development present; may respond to minimal or limited training in self-help	Some motor and speech development; may achieve very limited self-care; needs nursing care
Severe (IQ 20–35)	Poor motor development; speech minimal; generally unable to profit from training in self-help; little or no communication skills	Can talk or learn to communicate; can be trained in elemental health habits; profits from systematic habit training	May contribute partially to self-maintenance under complete supervision; can develop self-protection skills to a minimal useful level in controlled environment
Moderate (IQ 36–51)	Can talk or learn to communicate; poor social awareness; fair motor development; profits from training in self-help; can be managed with moderate supervision	Can profit from training in social and occupational skills; unlikely to progress beyond 2nd grade level in academic subjects; may learn to travel alone in familiar places	May achieve self-maintenance in unskilled or semiskilled work under sheltered conditions; needs supervision and guidance when under mild social or economic stress
Mild (IQ 52–67)	Can develop social and communication skills; minimal retardation in sensorimotor areas; often not distinguished from normal until later age	Can learn academic skills up to approximately 6th grade level by late teens; can be guided toward social conformity	Can usually achieve social and vocational skills adequate to minimum self-support but may need guidance and assistance when under unusual social or economic stress

NOTE.—Adapted from *Mental Retardation Activities of the U. S. Department of Health, Education, and Welfare*, p. 2. United States Government Printing Office, Washington, 1963. From Millon (1969).

in IQ scores has been used to argue that ability is environmentally determined.

In reality, neither great stability nor instability in IQ scores automatically supports either of these positions. Aside from the fact that not everybody would agree that an IQ test is an adequate measure of intellectual ability, it should be noted that there are many other traits for which stability across ages would be a very misleading guide as to the degree of heritability. For example, hair color is highly heritable but undergoes many changes during a lifetime, while one's preferred language is not at all heritable but rarely changes.

Empirical Studies

Several longitudinal studies have shown significant correlations between scores obtained in early childhood and those obtained by the same individuals in adolescence and adulthood. Figure 7–2 summarizes the findings of four of the most thorough of these studies.

It can be seen from the figure that, in the one study where they were reported, infant development tests had negligible (actually, *negative*) correlations with IQ test performance at age 18. However, the correlations of test scores at age three with later scores were moderately high in all four studies. By age nine, the correlations were quite substantial.

Although the age of final testing ranged from 12 years in the Fels Research Institute study (Sontag, Baker, & Nelson, 1958), to approximately 30 years in the Bradway and Thompson study (1962), the differences in correlations are not simply a function of the number of years between testing, of the amount of practice subjects had with a given test, or of the overlap in items that may occur when the same test is given at different ages. As an illustration, the highest correlation between scores at age 3 and scores at a later age, a correlation of .59, was reported by Bradway and Thompson even though their interval between testings was by far the greatest (approximately 27 years) and there had been only one other administration of the criterion test (Stanford-Binet) in the intervening years (at approximately age 12). Furthermore, Bradway and Thompson found an even larger correlation (.64) between the Binet at age 3 and the WAIS, which had not previously been administered, at age 30.

While the studies indicate that most children's test performance retains approximately the same position relative to that of other children over the years, especially after age 6, they do not show that the exact IQ score remains constant. As was discussed earlier, differences in scoring systems make a person likely to obtain different scores on different tests. For example, the average score by one group of subjects in the Bradway and Thompson study at age 30 was 124 on the Binet and 110 on the WAIS. When these same subjects were retested at approximately age 42, their average scores were 130 on the Binet and 118 on the WAIS (Kangas & Bradway, 1971).

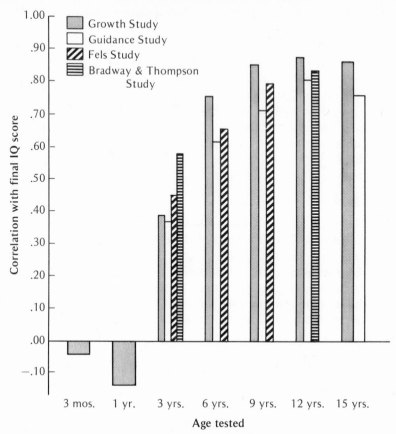

Fig. 7–2. Correlations between early and later test scores from four longitudinal studies. 1. Berkeley Growth Study (Bayley, 1949): Correlations of Wechsler Bellevue at age 18 with California Infant and Preschool Tests below age 6, Stanford-Binets at ages 6 to 12, and Terman-McNemar Group Test at age 15. 2. Berkeley-Guidance Study (Honzik, MacFarlane, & Allen, 1948): Correlations of Wechsler-Bellevue at age 18 with California Preschool Test at age 3 and Stanford-Binets at ages 6 to 15. 3. Fels Institute Study (Sontag, Baker, & Nelson, 1958): Correlations of Stanford-Binet at age 12 with Stanford-Binets at ages 3 to 9. 4. Bradway and Thompson (1962) Study: Correlations of Stanford-Binet at approximately age 30 with Stanford-Binets at approximately ages 3 (actual average age = 4.0) and 12 (actual average age = 13.6).

Despite the fact that the correlation between IQs at 30 and 42 was .77 for the Binet and .73 for the WAIS, IQs on both tests had increased. The rise in mean IQs indicated that performance continued to improve during adulthood, while the test norms are based upon cross-sectional samples in which the older adults did not perform better than the younger adults. However, the mean scores in the longitudinal samples changed less during childhood than during adulthood, perhaps because cross-sectional standardization was more appropriate for the narrower age range of childhood.

Nevertheless, the IQ scores of some children in all the studies changed markedly over the course of testing, with 42 per cent changing more than 10 points and 22 per cent more than 15 points between ages 3 and 12 in the Bradway-Thompson study (Bradway, Thompson, & Cravens, 1958), and 9 per cent changing 30 or more points between ages 6 and 18 in the Berkeley Guidance Study (Jones, 1954). Figure 7–3 illustrates some typical patterns of variability in the Binet IQ scores obtained by six children in the Fels study. Note that there are few sudden changes of large magnitude. Most large changes in IQ represented culminations of gradual, long-term trends.

ORGANIC PATHOLOGICAL CONDITIONS KNOWN TO RESULT IN RETARDATION

There are many conditions in which pathological deviations from organic normality are assumed to result in mental retardation as it is reflected in consistently low IQ scores and poor social competence.

Many of these conditions have in common only the symptom of mental retardation, just as many organic abnormalities have in common only growth retardation as a symptom. While the causes of the symptom of mental retardation may be as diverse as the causes of growth retardation, some of the problems of socialization and education created by the symptom may be similar for children in whom the causes are different. Both the heterogeneity in etiologies and the possible similarities in needs should thus be kept in mind when considering mentally retarded people.

Conditions Known to Result from Genetic Anomalies

Down's Syndrome and Other Chromosomal Abnormalities. Several syndromes known to result from chromosomal abnormalities were detailed in Chapter 5. One of the best known of those accompanied by retardation is *Down's syndrome (mongolism)*, which occurs in about two out of every 1,000 live births (Benda, 1969). This syndrome was described in 1866 by an Englishman, Langdon Down, who believed that children manifesting it were evolutionary throwbacks to the Mongol race. However, after the invention in the 1950s of methods for studying human chromosomes, children with Down's syndrome were found to have one more than the normal complement of 46 chromosomes (Lejeune, Gautier, & Turpin, 1959). The extra chromosome has been traced to the failure of the twenty-first pair of the mother's chromosomes to separate during meiosis. When these two chromosomes join with the single twenty-first chromosome contributed by the father, the result is three number twenty-one chromosomes in the child instead of the normal two. For this reason, Down's syndrome is now designated as *trisomy 21*.

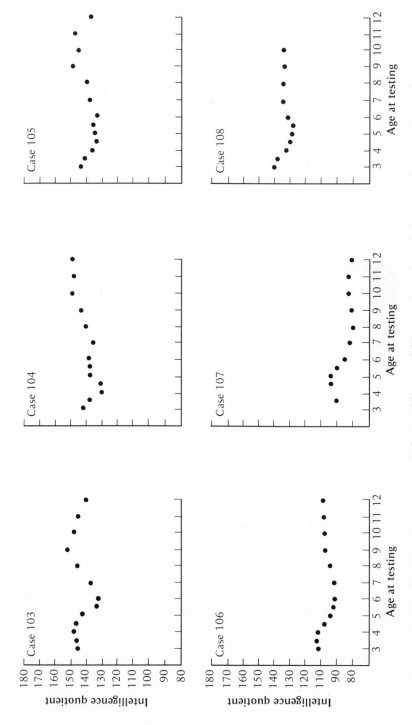

Fig. 7–3. Stanford-Binet IQ test scores obtained by six children in the Fels study between the ages of 3 and 12. From Sontag, Baker, and Nelson (1958). © 1958 by the Society for Research in Child Development and reprinted by permission.

By mechanisms not yet understood, the presence of the extra chromosomal material causes the child to have a somewhat small skull, large fissured tongue protruding from a small mouth, almond-shaped eyes with sloping eyebrows, flat nasal bridge, short crooked fifth finger, and broad, square hands with a *simian* ("monkeylike") crease running straight across the palm.

A fairly wide range of IQs has been found, with a few as high as the borderline retarded range. The test-retest reliability of Binet IQs over a one-year period has been reported to be .88 for mongoloids, about the same as for normals (Share, Koch, Webb, & Graliker, 1964). However, several studies have shown that the mental age of mongoloids advances steadily until it reaches a plateau, usually at approximately the mental age of three and one-half to five years (Cornwell & Birch, 1969; Ross, 1962; Zeaman & House, 1962). When their MAs level off, the IQs of mongoloid children naturally begin to drop—not because their ability decreases, but because, as their CAs continue to increase, the gap between their performance and that of older normative groups on the IQ test steadily widens.

Among the other syndromes known to involve chromosomal abnormalities and to be accompanied by retardation is *Klinefelter's syndrome,* in which a male receives an extra female chromosome (i.e., XXY, known as *sex chromosome trisomy*). The condition includes small testicles, tallness, thinness, long arms and legs, and failure to mature sexually.

A third syndrome is the *Cri-du-Chat* ("cat's cry") syndrome in which portions of one chromosome are missing. The child has a weak, catlike cry, plus some mongoloid features, though with eyes slanting opposite to those of mongoloids.

Phenylketonuria and Other Single Gene Conditions. Phenylketonuria (PKU) occurs in about one out of 10,000 live births (Carter, 1970). Unlike the gross chromosomal abnormalities in Down's, Klinefelter's, and Cri-du-Chat syndromes, the basis for PKU is a recessive gene transmitted by typical Mendelian mechanisms. If a child receives the gene from both parents, neither of whom may be phenylketonuric because they are not homozygous for the gene, he will lack certain liver enzymes necessary for converting the amino acid phenylalanine into another essential amino acid, tyrosine. Tyrosine is normally converted into other chemicals important to physical development.

The failure to metabolize phenylalanine, which is found in many foods, causes it to accumulate and to be converted to phenylpyruvic acid and other abnormal metabolites. These cause severe retardation in mental development, a light coloring due to lack of skin and hair pigmentation, a musty body odor, hyperactivity, seizures, and dry skin. Experiments with monkeys who were fed large amounts of phenylalanine in infancy show that severe disturbances in social behavior are also direct effects (Chamove, Waisman, & Harlow, 1970). There is evidence that phenylpyruvic acid reaching the fetus from the blood of a PKU mother can cause brain damage and retardation, even though the offspring itself does not have the genotype for PKU (Levy, 1969).

Phenylpyruvic acid can be detected in an infant's urine by chemical tests that are now routinely made in many states. Although some individuals who have high phenylpyruvic acid levels do not develop the symptoms of PKU, infants found to have high phenylpyruvic acid levels are usually put on a special low-phenylalanine diet.

A number of variables affect the success of dietary treatment. One is the age at which the low phenylalanine diet is begun, with age three months appearing to be about the end of the critical period during which instituting the diet can prevent mental retardation. Berry (1969) reports that the later IQs of children whose dietary treatment began by three months ranged from 102 to 118, while the IQs of their older PKU siblings who received special diets only after age one ranged from 55 to 83. Among still older phenylketonurics, the special diet did not improve intellectual functioning, although it did improve their behavior somewhat.

A second variable affecting the success of dietary treatment is whether an appropriate level of phenylalanine and protein can be determined and maintained. While too much phenylalanine results in PKU, too little can result in malnutrition that also interferes with development. Maintenance of an appropriate diet requires close supervision by the child's family and medical personnel. It is not known exactly how long such a diet must be maintained to avoid the neurological damage that might occur if phenylalanine intake reached normal levels. Unfortunately, the need to maintain such rigid dietary control and the parents' and child's concerns about it can create secondary problems in personality and social development.

Several other syndromes of mental retardation result from genetically transmitted defects in metabolic mechanisms that cause neurological damage through harmful excesses or shortages of certain chemicals in the body. Among these are *Tay-Sachs disease, gargoylism, Niemann-Pick disease,* and *galactosemia.* The latter is due to the absence of the enzyme required to metabolize galactose, a carbohydrate found in milk. Like PKU, the symptoms of galactosemia can often be prevented if an appropriate diet low in galactose but containing adequate substitutes is instituted early enough (Donnell, Bergren, & Koch, 1969).

Cretinism (hypothyroidism) is another disorder that may result from a genetically based enzyme defect. This defect prevents proper synthesis of the thyroid gland's hormone, thyroxine. Cretinism can also result, however, from a variety of other factors that deprive the body of thyroxine—these include congenital absence of the thyroid gland, damage to the thyroid, and iodine deficiencies in the mother's diet during pregnancy or in the child's diet after birth. Conspicuous bodily features include dwarfism, thick skin and lips, coarse, heavy features, and a protruding tongue. The cretin approximates the traditional stereotype of the retarded person and, until the mid-nineteenth century, "cretin" was a generic term for the retarded. Treatment with thyroid extract, first tried in 1891, can bring marked improvement.

Other genetically transmitted conditions include those where a specific bodily malformation restricts brain development. An example is *microcephaly* ("small headedness"), where the cranium is exceptionally small while the face is close to normal size. Microcephaly is transmitted by a single recessive gene (Heber, 1961), but may also result from various prenatal and perinatal diseases and traumas.

Conditions Known to Result from Nongenetic Organic Abnormalities

Many prenatal, perinatal, and postnatal factors that can damage the nervous system were discussed in Chapter 6. The degree of initial damage, recovery, and final handicap depends to a large extent on the developmental stage the nervous system has reached when it is afflicted. For example, *rubella* (German measles) contracted by the mother during the first three months of pregnancy often causes severe defects in the fetus, while the same disease contracted later in the fetal period or after birth does not cause damage. Other diseases that can cause damage at various periods include syphilis, scarlet fever, tuberculosis of the nervous system, degenerative diseases of the nerves, and, rarely, measles and mumps.

Brain injury can also be caused by X-rays and by certain drugs administered to the mother during pregnancy, by mechanical pressure on the child's head during birth, by deprivation of oxygen due to delays in breathing at birth, by poisons such as lead and carbon monoxide, and by intracranial tumors and cysts. Some early brain infections, tumors, and injuries can cause cerebrospinal fluid to accumulate in the head, a condition known as *hydrocephalus,* which results in the child's head being abnormally enlarged. There is also considerable evidence that malnutrition of the mother during pregnancy and of the child during infancy can result in retardation by preventing normal brain development (cf. Birch & Gussow, 1970). Incompatibility between the blood type of a mother and her fetus is another potential cause of early brain damage that was described at length in Chapter 6.

A large variety of motor disorders resulting from nonprogressive abnormalities of the brain and often accompanied by low IQ are lumped together under the generic term *cerebral palsy,* or, in England, *spasticity*. These abnormalities may have diverse etiologies, but cerebral palsied children are considered together as a group because their problems may necessitate similar types of treatment, education, and rehabilitation. Since the neurological disorders leading to cerebral palsy are diverse, there is no reason why there should be uniformity in the IQs of cerebral palsied children. Several studies have reported that, while the majority of cerebral palsied children have subnormal IQs, a substantial minority are of average or superior IQ. Despite the possible effect of motor problems upon IQ test performance, these studies have also reported that the classification of cerebral palsied children's performance by means of standard 1Q tests is generally quite reliable, with the test-retest correlations being as high as for normal children (Klapper & Birch, 1967; Schonell, 1956; Taylor, 1959).

NONORGANIC PATHOLOGICAL CONDITIONS ASSUMED TO RESULT IN RETARDATION

The vast majority, probably 75 per cent, of people judged retarded on the basis of low IQ scores and poor social competence are physically normal by current medical standards (Stein & Susser, 1960b; Zigler, 1967). They do not have any identifiable organic pathology known to play a causative role in retardation. The poor intellectual performance of these people may indeed result from organic conditions that have not yet been identified, but current diagnostic classifications provide categories for retardation that is assumed not to result from organic pathology.

Mental Retardation Associated with Environmental Deprivation

Retardation classified in this way is attributed to "deprivation at an early age of opportunity for learning experiences which are essential for adequate functioning in our culture" (Heber, 1961, p. 40).[2] Two such cases were reported by Freedman (1969) as follows:

These youngsters are the middle children of a sibship of four. Their parents are intellectually within the normal range . . . . There is no known history of mental deficiency in either of their very large and extended families. The older sibling has been able to maintain himself at expected grade· level in a regular school setting . . . . It seems that during her second and third pregnancies the mother developed the conviction that her offspring would be born defective. In the light of this foreordained conclusion, she elected both to keep them isolated from birth on and to devote a minimum of her time to them . . . .

The little girl was confined to a room she shared with her older brother. He had a bed, but she slept on a straw pallet on the floor, He came and went as he pleased, but she remained totally confined to the room. The little boy, by contrast was confined by himself to a room eight by ten feet in size. Aside from a crib and potty, this room was bare of furniture . . . . The only window was covered by burlap sacking.

The following is a description of their behavior when they were found and of its evolution over the next thirty months.

Ann, at age 6, was unable to feed herself or to talk meaningfully although she did repeat some words and sentences in echolalic [echolike] fashion. She displayed

[2] The definitions employed here correspond to those employed in the Second Edition of the American Association on Mental Deficiency's *Manual on Terminology* (cf. Heber, 1961). A new revision appeared in 1973, but has not yet come into wide use (Grossman, 1973).

no affective reaction either to her mother or to the strangers who came to investigate . . . she ranked below the third percentile in physical development. She was incontinent of urine and feces and indifferent to the overtures of the [hospital] staff. Much of her time she spent sitting up in bed rocking. She was however, able to stand and walk without assistance. During the . . . 8 weeks hospitalization she is said to have become continent, learned to feed herself, learned to call some objects by name and at times seemed to display affectional responses to members of the staff. She was returned to her family for another nine months before the slowly moving legal process eventuated in placement in a foster home.

The description from the foster mother indicates that the gains made during her hospitalization were short-lived. Although she was able to pass objects from hand-to-hand and to her mouth, this nearly seven-year-old child could neither handle eating utensils nor feed herself by hand. (At home her only food is said to have been moderately thick gruel served in a nursing bottle). She was described as extremely obedient, and it was noted that when told to she would sit for hours in one position. She exhibited no interest either in her environment or in her body . . . .

Ann has progressed from an echolalic, repetitious and meaningless use of a few words to a considerable vocabulary. She now uses some abstract concepts. However, she continues to articulate poorly. She was in foster care a year before she began to use the first person pronoun. Six months later, differentiation of herself from the environment was still incomplete . . . .

The younger sibling, Albert, was isolated *in toto*. Like Ann, he was fed exclusively by bottle . . . . We have reason to believe that his mother only entered the room to feed and diaper him. In his later years we know that it was her wont to place him on the potty where he would, on command, sit for long hours. However, he never learned the intended connection between the potty and excretion.

When he was hospitalized at age four . . . he was well below the third percentile in both weight and height. He walked with a peculiar waddling gait, and he was incapable of even the most elementary use of his hands. Neither the manipulation of objects nor hand-to-mouth activity were present; he was unable to masticate, was incontinent of urine and feces and totally devoid of articulate speech. The only vocalizations recorded were grunting sounds and at times screams.

During the hospitalization locomotion improved, and he became able to hold his cup and clutch toys. He was never observed to play with objects or people. [Freedman, 1969, pp. 247–51].

In light of their very retarded physical development, the dietary regime of the children cannot be completely ruled out as a contributory factor. However, severe emotional deprivation, as suffered by these children, has been implicated as a cause of pituitary dysfunctions which reduce the production of growth hormones, thereby resulting in severe growth retardation without malnutrition (see Chapter 6; Lenneberg, 1968; Powell et al, 1967). Moreover, Ann and Albert's growth rates did not accelerate after twenty months of ample diet, suggesting that diet alone was not responsible for their conditions.

Four Binet tests given to Ann at ages seven and eight yielded IQs of

30, 39, 46, and 40. Three tests given to Albert at ages five and six yielded IQs of 36, 42, and 38. Both children continued to show little interest in people and objects long after placement in foster homes.

In a case reported by Mason (1942), a girl, Isabelle, was born illegitimately to a woman who was deaf and aphasic due to early brain injury, who was totally uneducated, and who could communicate only by idiosyncratic gestures. From the time her pregnancy was discovered, the mother and, subsequently, Isabelle, were kept in a locked room behind drawn shades. When Isabelle was six and one-half, the mother escaped with her.

Isabelle was found to be extremely malnourished and was suffering from rickets that made her legs so bowed that the soles of her shoes came nearly together. Shortly afterward, she attained an MA of 19 months on the Binet and a social age of 39 months on the Vineland Social Maturity Scale (cf. Davis, 1947). Mason, a speech therapist, recounts Isabelle's speech progress as follows:

11–16–38: Admittance to Children's Hospital, Columbus, Ohio.

11–17–38: Cried almost continuously; would not partake of food except milk and crackers; showed either recoil, disinterest, or fear of everyone with whom she came in contact.

11–20–38: My second visit, Isabelle showed interest in the watch, ring and doll which I brought her. Partook of some food when seated at a small table.

11–25–38: First vocalization. Attempt to say the words "ball" and "car" and "bye" (good-bye).

11–26–38: Repeated the words "baby" and "dirty" in imitation of words spoken to her in the form of play. "Baby" was the most distinct articulation to date.

11–30–38: Said "flower," "one," "two." Jabbered succession of nonsense syllables in imitation of my rather lengthy explanation to Jane that she should not appropriate Isabelle's toys.

12–03–38: Isabelle began to associate the word with its object; does not associate individuals with their names, but recognizes her own name when spoken.

12–08–38: Said: "watch, ring, blue, car, ball, lady, bell, bow-wow, hot, cold, warm, one, two, three, red, dirty, pretty, baby."

1–13–39: Distinguished yellow from the other colors and said "yellow" voluntarily.

2–08–39: Says the following sentences voluntarily: "That's my baby; I love my baby; open your eyes; close your eyes; I don't know; I don't want; that's funny; 'top it— 'at's mine [when another child attempted to take one of her toys]."

2–11–39: She now associates people with names.

3–02–39: Isabelle said, "Say please," when I asked her to hand me something. Later said, "I'm sorry," when she accidentally hurt another child's finger.

3–04–39: Isabelle said, "I love you, Miss Mason."

3–09–39: Identified printed form of the words, blue and yellow, and matched the word with the color.

3–10–39: Isabelle matched the printed forms of cow, sheep, dog, and cat with corresponding pictures.

3–13–39: Isabelle pointed to pictures in her book, saying: "This is a boy; this is a baby, etc." Said, "I'm sleepy."

4–01–39: Isabelle goes about humming nursery rhymes, "Here we go round the mulberry bush," and "Baa, baa, black sheep [Mason, 1942, pp. 301–2]."

After a year and a half of education, Isabelle had learned between 1,500 and 2,000 words, could count to a hundred, identify coins, and do arithmetic involving numbers up to 10. By the age of eight and one-half she was described as being intellectually normal and as having made an excellent adjustment, being an imaginative, affectionate, and loving child.

The contrast between the remarkable development of Isabelle and the unhappy outcomes in most other cases of this sort seems attributable, at least in part, to the factor of social contact. Even though Isabelle's physical environment was severely restricted and her mother could provide no experience with language, she was able to learn rapidly and to adjust well once the opportunities became available, evidently because of her interactions with her mother. However, the interpretation is by no means unambiguous, because the influence of variations in constitutional equipment and of Isabelle's education program cannot be judged with certainty.

Mental Retardation Associated with Emotional Disturbance

The classification system of the American Association on Mental Deficiency (AAMD; Heber, 1961) provides two closely related categories that are lumped together for present purposes. One is retardation associated with "a period of prolonged emotional disturbance," while the other is retardation associated with "psychotic or major personality disorders such as autism or childhood schizophrenia, where there is no reasonable evidence of cerebral pathology [Heber, 1961, p. 40]."

Poor IQ test performance is found in many children who have behavioral and emotional disorders of psychotic proportions. In fact, as will be discussed further in Chapter 12, one basic problem in studying the etiologies of severe disorders such as autism is to form a coherent picture of the most characteristic symptoms, including cognitive, behavioral, and emotional, in order to determine the chicken-and-egg sequence among them.

Case studies of less severely disturbed children demonstrate that their emotional problems can also play a role in their general level of intellectual functioning, as illustrated in a case report by Lowell (1941):

Danny R . . . was found to be such a misfit in Kindergarten that after a few weeks he was offered for a Binet test. . . .

The first Binet showed such mental immaturity [IQ = 82] that the child was excluded from Kindergarten for a year. The next year Danny moved into another school district . . . . He had seemed so "queer" that the teacher asked for a Binet. This time he tested normal [IQ = 98], so he was placed in the first grade in September in spite of his lack of social adjustment. The mother was called in and only then was light thrown on his peculiarities. The teachers had complained that the boy seemed to live in a little world of his own. . . . He wasn't interested in group activities and was noticeably poor in his motor coordination. He had a worried look on his face most of the time and watched the clock with undue anxiety.

The mother explained that while Danny was still a baby his father had developed encephalitis. In order for the mother to work they moved to the grandparents' home, where Danny could receive care. Unfortunately, Danny's grandfather was a high-strung, nervous old gentleman who was much annoyed by the child's noise, and expostulated so violently at times that Danny became "petrified" with fear. As a result, he sat on a chair for hours at a time, scarcely breathing, lest it disturb "grandpa". . . . It wasn't until several years had passed that the mother realized her boy was not developing normal habits and interests, and when he was excluded from Kindergarten she decided she must take him away from the grandparents' home. They moved into a different neighborhood and the boy once more entered Kindergarten.

The next few years were a period of educational, social, and emotional growth for the starved child. It is not surprising that the child amazed his teachers with his achievement, for a new world had opened up before him. He became an inveterate reader and could solve arithmetic problems far beyond his grade level. Physically frail, he has been under a doctor's care much of the time, and because of his fear complex, he was also treated by a psychiatrist. He made friends with boys in spite of lack of physical prowess. Recently because of his excellent school work, he was given a fourth Binet [the third had yielded an IQ of 111] and found to have an IQ [132 at age 11] sufficiently high to warrant placement in [an advanced class], where he is now enjoying competition with minds as keen as his own [Lowell, 1941, pp. 353–55].[3]

A case in which a steady decline in IQ, as measured by annual testing, may have resulted from an unhealthy relationship to the parents was reported by Honzik, MacFarlane, and Allen (1948) in the Berkeley Guidance Study:

Case 764 is an example of a gradual lowering of IQ from 133 [at age 2] to 77 [at age 18]. . . . She is an only child born when the mother was 44, the father 37. The estimated IQ of the mother is 65 to 70 The father is a skilled mechanic. The parents went to school until age 14.

Obesity began in late preschool years and increased steadily until [a diet was instituted] at age 14. . . . Weight was normal at 17. There were, however, no IQ variations in relation to these physical changes. She was always overindulged by the mother, who lived to feed her and keep her young and who was always complaining that her daughter never gave her enough affection [Honzik et al, 1948, pp. 313–14].

[3] F. E. Lowell, "A Study of the Validity of IQs in Retest," *Journal of Applied Psychology*, 1941, **25**, (353–55). © 1941 by the American Psychological Association and reprinted by permission.

On the other hand, another case from the same study indicated that continuing stress may be accompanied by a rise in IQ:

"Case 553 is a boy whose mental test scores increased from a preschool sigma score of — 2 [two standard deviations below the mean] to later sigma scores of + 2.4 [standard deviations above the mean] in spite of a bad physical history. He is small-statured, thin, with very poor musculature, and presents a history of early ear infections and chronic bronchitis from infancy, headaches (early glasses), stomach pains (appendectomy); he has had three operations and three serious accidents. Only one 6-month period in his life has been free of illness. In spite of a frail frame, . . . an early strained family situation, and relatively low mental test scores in his early preschool years, his tested ability steadily increased until 9, from which time he has maintained high and fairly stable scores. His mother is a normal-school [teachers' college] graduate; his father completed high school. His greatest security lies in his intellectual interests and achievements, but he has made good social adjustments and an amazingly good adjustment to his handicaps [Honzik, 1948, p. 314].

Case studies by themselves cannot decisively confirm whether emotional problems are a significant causative factor in many of the cases of poor intellectual functioning where organic abnormalities are not discovered. One comparison of the IQs of nonpsychotic children being treated for emotional disturbances with the IQs of their "normal" (untreated) siblings showed no significant differences, although the disturbed children's IQs were slightly lower on the average (97.6 vs. 99.7; Wolf, 1965). However, children with IQs in the retarded range and those in slow learning classes were excluded from the study. There is also a possibility that the untreated siblings, coming as they did from families in which there was a disturbed child, may have had problems that interfered with their intellectual functioning, thus causing their IQs to be lowered as well. Hence, while it is virtually certain that emotional problems *can* interfere with intellectual functioning as measured by an IQ test, it cannot be concluded with certainty whether such problems *do* in fact lower intellectual performance to the retarded range in very many cases.

The term "pseudoretardation" has sometimes been used in reference to poor intellectual performance attributed to emotional factors. However, if attention is kept on the child's actual level of performance—rather than on irrevocable classification as "retarded" or "nonretarded"—there is little need to compound the conceptual ambiguities further with terms like pseudoretardation. Evaluation of any child should always include consideration of the role emotional and environmental stresses may be playing in his current functioning and of the possibilities for improvement.

CULTURAL-FAMILIAL RETARDATION

Of that 75 per cent of people judged retarded without identifiable organic abnormalities, most have IQs above 50 and are diagnosed as *cul-*

tural-familial retarded. The *Manual* of the American Association on Mental Deficiency (Heber, 1961) defines this diagnostic category as follows:

> In addition to absence of reasonable indication of cerebral pathology, classification in this category requires that there be evidence of retardation in intellectual functioning in at least one of the parents and in one or more siblings where there are [siblings]. . . .
>
> There is no intent in this category to specify either the independent action of, or the relationship between, genetic and cultural factors in the etiology of cultural-familial mental retardation. The exact role of genetic factors cannot be specified since the nature and mode of transmission of genetic aspects of intelligence is not yet understood. Similarly, there is no clear understanding of the specific manner in which environmental factors operate to modify intellectual functioning [Heber, 1961, p. 40].

Both the term "cultural-familial" and the definition reflect one of the major dilemmas this type of retardation presents. The dilemma is whether the etiology should be attributed primarily to the cultural aspects of the environment the child grows up in or to genetic factors transmitted to the child from his parents. The fact that there should be evidence of retardation in other members of a child's family to warrant fully this diagnosis can be justified by an assumption of either a primarily cultural or a primarily genetic etiology. The American Association on Mental Deficiency's definition is explicitly ambiguous in that it regards neither the posssible genetic basis nor the possible environmental basis as being well enough understood to justify a choice between them or a synthesis of them.

The significance of "cultural-familial" retardation extends far beyond the usual scope of child psychopathology. This is not only because of the large number of people who may be so classified, but because recent attention to the school problems of poor children has engendered a host of concepts and controversies rooted in the same ambiguities as the definitions of cultural-familial retardation. Since the problems of poor children are often summarized in terms of below average IQs, poor school performance, and low social competence, and since neither their problems nor their backgrounds show marked qualitative changes at any particular cut-off point on the IQ or social competence continuum, many of the hypotheses invoked to explain their problems are similar to those regarding cultural-familial retardation.

As one of the first popular euphemisms applied to these children during the 1960s, "culturally deprived" reflected the cultural deprivation hypothesis of the etiology of cultural-familial retardation. The term implied that poor children's school problems resulted from their being deprived of "culture." With the recognition that poor and minority groups do, like all other human social groups, have cultures—though they may differ from those of wealthier people—the term cultural deprivation was replaced by a variety of others, including just plain "deprived," "economically deprived," "environmentally handicapped," "disadvantaged," etc.

Arthur Jensen's (1969) interpretations of the evidence for the heritability of IQ test scores brought back into play the "familial" hypothesis as an explanation for poor children's lack of school success, and the nature-nurture debate was reactivated in much the same popular form it had retained for seventy years before being abandoned in the early forties to specialists in mental retardation.

Epidemiology of Cultural-Familial Retardation

Before attempting to clarify the relations between possible "cultural" and "familial" factors in poor school and IQ test performance, it is important to determine whether the empirical distribution of retardation suggests that a category based upon either or both of these hypotheses is worth taking seriously. One way to do this is through epidemiological studies that examine the distribution of retardation attributable to various causes.

One of the most thorough studies of the prevalence of mental retardation and its various possible etiologies was carried out in Aberdeen, Scotland, by Birch et al, (1970). Aberdeen was selected as an almost ideal site because detailed medical, social, and familial data had been collected on nearly all births for over a decade; medical services were available irrespective of economic status; uniform health and educational records were maintained for all children; public school and health services were provided for virtually all retarded children regardless of social class; the population was ethnically homogeneous and relatively stable with low rates of in- and out-migration; and all children received uniform ability testing at the age of seven.

The customary Aberdeen procedure was such that all seven-year-old children who obtained a group test IQ below 75 were given individual IQ tests by a school psychologist. The psychologist's findings and recommendations were then used together with a review of each child's medical and social history, general social competence, school achievement, and reports from teachers and other school personnel in making a decision about special education. Parents could appeal any decision to higher school and government authorities.

All children between the ages of 8 and 10 who had been classified as retarded by the school system were included in the study by Birch et al. Selection of a well-defined age group is important because at young ages only children who are obviously far below average and have organic syndromes are usually identified as retarded, while at later school ages many who have shown poor school performance for a long time and who have IQs not very far below average (e.g., 70–75) may also be classified as retarded. At still later ages, when school performance and IQ are no longer important criteria, some of those who were classified in school as retarded make social adaptations that do not result in their continuing to be identified as retarded. As an illustration, a typical study reported that, in Syracuse, New York, 0.45 per cent of children up to age five, 3.94 per cent of children aged five to nine, 7.76 per cent of children aged 10 to 14, and 4.49 percent of adolescents aged 15 to 19 were identified as retarded (New York State Department of Mental Hygiené, 1955).

Birch et al found that 28 per cent of the retarded children had IQs less than 50 and evidence of organic conditions assumed to be responsible for their retardation. Forty-six per cent had IQs of 50 or more and no evidence of organic etiology, while 24 per cent had IQs of 50 or more with evidence of organic etiology.

The authors analyzed the rates of each type and level of retardation within five socioeconomic (SES) groupings: Classes I–IIIa included all nonmanual workers from clerks through professionals, while Class IIIb included skilled independent manual workers, Class IIIc other skilled workers, Class IV semiskilled workers, and Class V unskilled workers.

The rate of cases with IQs below 50 and organic etiologies was virtually identical in all social classes. However, the rate of cases with IQs of 60 or more, whether or not they had signs of organic etiology, increased sharply from 0 in Classes I–IIIa to about 3 per cent in Class V (see Fig. 7–4).

It is conceivable that the total absence in Classes I–IIIa of cases having

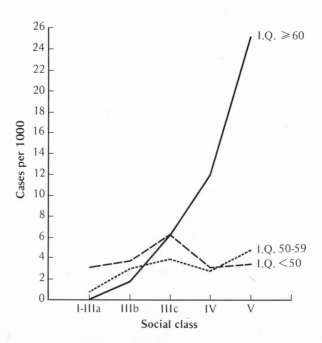

Fig. 7–4. The prevalence of different levels of IQ in mentally subnormal children from different social classes. From Birch et al (1970). © 1970 by The Williams and Wilkins Company and reprinted by permission.

IQs of 60 or more resulted from a bias among school officials against considering upper-class children retarded unless they had very low IQs. To check this, Birch et al analyzed the SES distribution of children who at age 7 had obtained test scores below 75 but who had not subsequently been classified as retarded. They found the same sharp increase in the percentage of such children from Classes I–IIIa to Class V as among the children who had been classified retarded. The addition of these children did not change the gradient portrayed in Fig. 7–4. Other studies of the relations between SES, degree of retardation, and etiology of retardation have reported similar findings (e.g., Halperin, 1945; Kushlick, 1966; Stein & Susser, 1960a, 1960b, 1963).

Compared with Class IV and V children who had higher IQs, those classified as retarded came significantly more frequently from families having more than four children, poorer housing (though nearly all lived in public housing), more people per room, and more mothers with low-status premarital occupations. The average IQ of the children in these families was 77 and more than one-half of the siblings of the retarded children had IQs below 75. It is clear that most of the children classified as retarded without signs of organic etiology did indeed fit the diagnostic criteria for cultural-familial retardation.

Cultural-familial Retardation as the Low End of the Normal Distribution of IQ

A view held by many researchers is that cultural-familial retardation simply represents the low end of the normal distribution of IQ, rather than being attributable to pathological factors different from the determinants of IQ at higher levels in the distribution. According to this view, the *excess* of low IQ persons over what would be predicted from the normal curve comprises people whose retardation is due to pathological factors such as those described in previous sections. This excess is especially pronounced below IQ 50 where the normal curve predicts that there should be extremely few people and where most of the people appear to be victims of specific pathological factors that have interfered with their intellectual development. The remainder of people with IQs in the retarded range, the cultural-familial retarded, most of whom have IQs above 50, are assumed to be simply the unfortunate recipients of the lower portion of the nonpathological influences which create IQ differences among people higher in the distribution as well.

Figure 7–5a portrays the distribution of IQs theoretically expected from the normal curve on which IQ scores are based, while Figure 7–5b portrays the approximate form of the distribution actually found in most studies (e.g., Dingman & Tarjan, 1960; Penrose, 1963).

If the above view is valid, then a full understanding of cultural-familial retardation requires not the identification of a specific etiological defect,

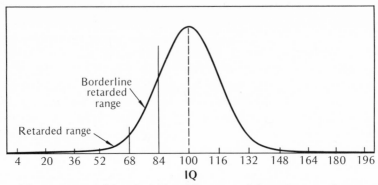

(a) Distribution of Stanford-Binet IQs expected from the normal curve.

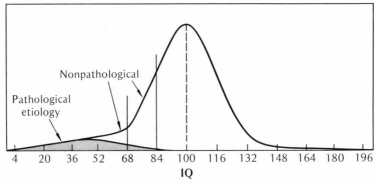

(b) Approximate distribution of IQs actually found, with individuals having signs of pathological etiology separated from those not having signs of pathological etiology.

Fig. 7–5. Comparison of the theoretical distribution of Stanford-Binet IQs with the approximate form of the distribution actually found. **Based on Dingman and Tarjan (1960); Penrose (1963); and Zigler (1967).**

but an understanding of the factors, genetic and/or environmental that work together to determine the IQs of biologically normal people at all points along the distribution.

Genetically Oriented Hypotheses. These hypotheses assume that, in biologically normal people, IQ test performance is to some extent polygenically determined—i.e., it is influenced by several genetic factors (polygenes) that operate together to produce a broad range of genotypes that are phenotypically reflected in the normal distribution of IQ scores. (If the genetic concepts and terminology are unfamiliar, see Chapter 5 for a review.)

Most polygenic hypotheses postulate at least five genes, but, to illustrate these hypotheses in simple form, suppose that two genes, A and B, influence IQ. Assume that one allele of each gene (call it +; e.g., A+B+) en-hances IQ test performance, while the other does not (call this one °; e.g., A°, B°). Finally, suppose the effects of the two alleles (+ and °) of each gene are not dominance versus recessiveness, but that the two alleles are additive—that is, a person having one A° allele and one A+ allele is inter-mediate in IQ between a person having two A° alleles and a person having two A+ alleles, everything else being equal. These suppositions of polygenes having alleles which function additively happen to be strongly supported for many human physical characteristics, such as height, which are measurable on a continuous scale and which are roughly normally distributed.

If a person is homozygous for the IQ-enhancing alleles, his genotype is A+A+B+B+ and his IQ should be very high. If a person is homozy-gous for nonenhancing alleles, his genotype is A°A°B°B°, and his IQ should be very low.

When two people having these different homozygous genotypes mate, each of their offspring receives an A+ allele and a B+ allele from the par-ent who is homozygous for + alleles. Each offspring also receives an A° allele and a B° allele from the parent who is homozygous for ° alleles. Consequently, the genotypes of all the offspring have one A+ allele, one A° allele, one B+ allele, and one B° allele. Because the alleles of both the A and B genes are assumed to have equal effects in enhancing IQ, the off-spring should have IQs intermediate between those of the A°A°B°B° parent and the A+A+B+B+ parent.

When the heterozygous offspring mate, each can contribute any one of four possible combinations of alleles to each of his own children: A°B°; A°B+; A+B°; or A+B+. Since A°B+ has the same effect as A+B° on pheno-typic IQ, the parent would contribute an intermediately IQ-enhancing combination to one-half of his offspring, a nonenhancing combination (A°B°) to one-quarter of his offspring, and a highly enhancing combination (A+B+) to the other one-quarter. If his mate also has the heterozygous genotype with one A+, one A°, one B+, and one B° allele, the mate can also contribute any of these four possible combinations to their child. Thus, the child could end up with any one of the following 16 combina-tions, falling into five categories of genotype for IQ, according to the num-ber of + alleles present:

		A+A+B°B°		
		A+A°B+B°		
	A+A°B°B°	A°A+B+B°	A+A+B+B°	
	A°A+B°B°	A+A°B°B+	A+A+B°B+	
	A°A°B+B°	A°A+B°B+	A+A°B+B+	
A°A°B°B°	A°A°B°B+	A°A°B+B+	A°A+B+B+	A+A+B+B+
0	**1**	**2**	**3**	**4**

The phenotypic IQs assumed to occur for each of these five categories would be:

0. very low IQ because there are no + alleles;
1. low because there is only one + allele;
2. average because there are two + alleles and two ° alleles;
3. high because there are three + alleles;
4. very high because all four alleles are +.

Notice that even though there are only five possible categories of genotype resulting from the two genes, the distribution of IQ represented by these genotypes is roughly normal in shape. If the heterozygous parents, each having one A+, one A°, one B+, and one B° allele, produced 16 children, the most likely distribution of the children's genotypes would be that represented above—one child would have each of the possible combinations of the alleles of the A and B genes. In terms of IQ, one child would be very low, four would be low, six would be average, four would be high, and one would be very high.

Since the distribution of phenotypic IQs is, in fact, continuous rather than being composed of five distinct steps, nobody contends that such a simple model by itself explains IQ differences. However, if it is assumed that experience, motivation, and other characteristics of the individual, plus inconsistencies in IQ tests, influence the phenotypic expression of these genotypes in the IQ score, then a continuous distribution of IQs could easily result from the five categories of genotype produced by two genes. Most children without organic syndromes who have IQs from about 50 to 70 might be assumed to have Genotype 0, those with IQs 71 to 90, Genotype 1, those with IQs 91 to 110, Genotype 2, those with IQs of 111 to 130, Genotype 3, and those with IQs above 130, Genotype 4.

Each of the phenotypic IQ ranges would thus be assumed to represent a possible *reaction range* for each of the five categories of genotype, the exact phenotypic IQ for a given genotype depending upon nongenetic factors. If this were the case, the possible phenotypic reaction range for each genotype would be likely to overlap with that of the next higher and next lower genotypes, so that, for example, a person with Genotype 1 might attain an IQ over 90 under ideal environmental conditions or below 71 under very poor environmental conditions.

If one adopts the extreme hereditarian hypothesis that nongenetic factors (other than unreliability in IQ tests) play no role at all in IQ differences, it would still take only 12 different genes to account for the continuous distribution of IQs (Gottesman, 1963a). Such an hypothesis assumes that there are as many different genotypes for IQ as there are "true" phenotypic IQs, and that each genotype, being the sole determinant of IQ, has no reaction range.

The Nongenetic Hypothesis. The view that people who meet the diagnostic criteria for cultural-familial retardation are essentially normal individuals whose ability happens to be at the low end of the normal distribution does not demand an assumption that genotypic differences are responsible for differences in phenotypic IQ. If one adopts the extreme environmental hypothesis that, except for rare abnormal genetic conditions like those responsible for mongolism and PKU, there is only one human genotype for IQ, then all phenotypic differences in IQ are attributable to nongenetic factors that determine where within that genotype's reaction range an individual's phenotypic IQ will fall. If random nongenetic factors cause the differences in phenotypic IQ, it is likely that the distribution of phenotypic IQs they produce would be as continuous and as close to the normal one as if genetic factors were responsible for IQ differences. Individuals at the low end would be those who had encountered only non-IQ-enhancing influences, while those at the top end had encountered only IQ-enhancing influences. Thus, the fact that the distribution of IQ scores may be continuous and normal says nothing about the degree of genetic or environmental influence on them.

Relations Between Phenotypic IQs and Genotypes under Various Hypotheses. Figure 7–6 portrays the relations between phenotypic IQs and genotypes hypothesized by:

1. an extreme hereditarian hypothesis that assumes *no* phenotypic reaction range for each of the possible genotypes;

2. one of the many possible interactionist hypotheses, this one assuming only two genetic factors with large enough phenotypic reaction ranges for the five possible genotypes to account for a continuous distribution;

3. an extreme environmentalist hypothesis that assumes only one genotype with a large enough reaction range to account for a continuous distribution.

The extreme hereditarian hypothesis would be tenable only if IQ tests were perfectly reliable, i.e., they yielded exactly the same score for an individual on each testing. Since most people's scores change from one testing to the next, the hypothesis that each phenotypic IQ represents a different genotype for IQ seems untenable.

If the extreme hereditarian hypothesis seems untenable as an explanation for cultural-familial retardation, the important question to be asked is whether the evidence points to the existence of one human genotype with a reaction range spanning the distribution of IQs from roughly 50 to its upper limits, or to the existence of more than one genotype having either narrow or broad reaction ranges. Consideration of this question requires, first, a brief summary of the evidence on the *heritability* of IQ—the proportion of variance in IQ scores that is attributable to genetic differences. If there were no evidence that genetic differences are correlated with phenotypic differences in IQ under any naturally occurring conditions, then even the moderate interactionist hypothesis portrayed in Fig. 7–6b could be rejected

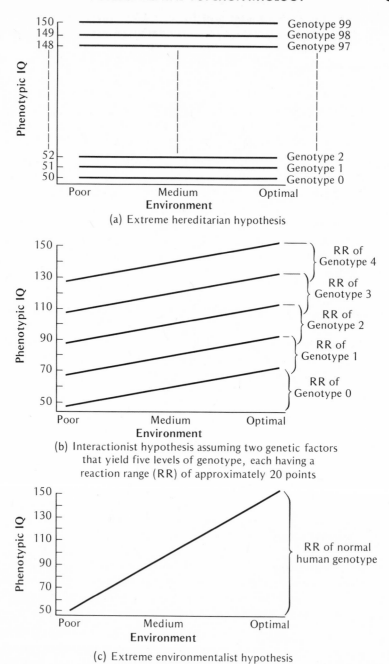

Fig. 7–6. Relations between phenotypic IQ and genotype according to (a) an extreme hereditarian hypothesis, (b) an interactionist hypothesis, and (c) an extreme environmentalist hypothesis.

and only the extreme environmentalist hypothesis portrayed in Fig. 7–6c would be tenable.

Evidence on the Heritability of IQ

Recall from Chapter 5 that the heritability (represented as H or h^2) of a trait in a specific group is defined as the proportion of the total *phenotypic variance* (represented as V_p) of the trait in that group that can be attributed to *genetic variance* (represented as V_g). For conceptual purposes, this relation can be represented:

$$H = \frac{V \text{ genetic}}{V \text{ phenotypic}}$$

where V phenotypic is assumed to be a resultant of all genetic and environmental components. Accordingly, if *every* difference in the phenotypic IQs of members of a specific group is attributable to genetic differences among the group members, H will equal 1.00.

Heritability Estimates from Twin Studies. The most direct evidence regarding genetic influences on IQ comes from studies in which the correlations between the IQs of identical twins are compared with the correlations between the IQs of same-sex fraternal twins. These comparisons are of interest because identical twins are the products of a single fertilized egg (*zygote*) that has divided, giving each half the same complement of genes. Fraternal twins are the products of two eggs that have been fertilized by two different sperm. Thus, identical twins, referred to as *monozygotic* (MZ), have identical heredity. Fraternal twins, referred to as *dizygotic* (DZ), have, on the average, only 50 per cent of their genes in common, the same as any other two siblings.

Because both members of a twin pair are born at the same time, it is assumed that the size of environmental differences between MZ and DZ pair members reared together are small and roughly similar. The primary reasons, therefore, that DZ co-twins should differ more than MZ co-twins on a trait like IQ would be genetic ones.

The usual formula for estimating heritability from twin data is:

$$H = \frac{r_{\text{MZ}} - r_{\text{DZ}}}{1 - r_{\text{DZ}}}$$

where r_{MZ} is the correlation between scores of MZ cotwins and r_{DZ} is the correlation between scores of DZ cotwins (see Chapter 5 for details). Table 7–2 summarizes the findings of 17 studies in which heritability estimates for intelligence test scores could be derived from the differences between correlations of MZ and DZ cotwins' scores. These studies were done in six countries over a period of 40 years. They differed in the ages of twins studied, the intelligence tests used, and their techniques for diagnosing the zygosity of the twins.

TABLE 7-2

Correlations between intelligence test scores of MZ and DZ twins, and heritabilities found in a number of twin studies.

	Year	Author	r_{MZ}	r_{DZ}	H
Germany	1930	Von Verschuer	not reported		.62
U. S. A.	1932	Day	.92	.61	.80
England	1933	Stocks & Karn	.84	.65	.54
U. S. A.	1937	Newman, Freeman, & Holzinger [a]	.90	.62	.74
Germany	1939	Gottschaldt [b]	not reported		.82
Sweden	1952	Wictorin [a]	.89	.72	.61
Sweden	1953	Husen	.90	.70	.67
England	1954	Blewett	.76	.44	.57
U. S. A.	1953	Thurstone, Thurstone, & Strandskov [c]	not reported		.65
England	1958	Burt	.97	.55	.93
France	1960	Zazzo	.90	.60	.75
U. S. A.	1962	Vandenberg [c]	.74	.56	.41
U. S. A.	1965	Nichols	.87	.63	.65
England	1966	Huntley	.83	.66	.50
Finland	1966	Partanen, Bruun, & Markkanen [d]	.69	.42	.51
U. S. A.	1968	Schoenfeldt	.80	.48	.62
U. S. A.	1970	Owen & Sines	.93	.68	.74

[a] Average of 2 tests.

[b] Average of 39 tests, recalculated from graph of twin differences.

[c] Average of 6 tests, recalculated from twin differences.

[d] Average of 8 tests.

NOTE.—Adapted from S. G. Vandenberg, "What do we know about the inheritance of intelligence and how do we know it?" In R. Cancro (Ed.), *Intelligence: Genetic and environmental influences.* New York: Grune & Stratton (1971), p. 197. © 1971 by Grune & Stratton and reproduced by permission.

The range of heritability estimates was from .41 to .93, the median being .65. This indicates that genotypic differences were related to phenotypic differences in all the populations studied, although the degree of heritability for the different test scores in the different populations varied considerably. As was stressed in Chapter 5, the fact that a heritability estimate is a *ratio* of presumed genetic variance to the resultant of genetic *and environmental variance* means it is only valid for groups having the same kind of genetic *and environmental variability* as the twin samples tested. Thus, none of the studies by itself, nor any combination of them, can be used to estimate the *true* heritability of IQ, because there is no "true" heritability of the trait independent of particular environmental differences. At most, the figures in Table 7–2 convey estimates of the heritability of intelligence test scores in 17 subpopulations of a population that might be defined as twentieth-century northern European and American whites living in a rather broad range of environments.

MZ Twins Reared Apart. Another approach to determining whether genotypic differences are related to differences in phenotypic IQ is to compare the correlations between the IQs of MZ twins reared apart (i.e., identical heredity, but different environments) with the correlations for MZ twins reared together (identical heredity and similar environments) and DZ twins reared together (50 per cent identical heredity and similar environments). The findings of four studies of MZ twins reared apart are summarized in Table 7–3.

TABLE 7–3

Correlations of intelligence test scores of MZ twins reared apart.

Country	Year	Author	Pairs	r_{MZ}
U. S. A.	1937	Newman et al	19	.67
England	1962	Shields	38	.78
Denmark	1965	Juel-Nielsen	12	.68
England	1966	Burt	53	.88
		Combined	122	.82

NOTE.—Recalculated and combined by Jensen (1970).

Note that all four correlations in Table 7–3 for *MZ* twins reared *apart* exceed all but two of the 14 correlations in Table 7–2 for *DZ* twins reared *together*. The two correlations based on the largest numbers of MZ twins reared apart exceed all the correlations for DZ twins reared together, as does the correlation based on all 122 MZ twins reared apart (Table 7–3). The correlation of .82 for all the MZ twins reared apart is not far below the median correlation of .89 for MZ twins reared together, but is considerably above the median correlation of .62 for DZ twins reared together.

Filial Regression. A third type of evidence for genetic influences on IQ differences is one that appears paradoxical at first glance. This is the finding that parents with IQs toward the extremes of the distribution have children with IQs that average closer to the mean of the distribution than the parents' IQs are. Thus, low IQ men with low occupational status have children whose IQs average *higher* than theirs, while high IQ men with high occupational status have children whose IQs average *lower* than theirs. Figure 7–7 illustrates this tendency of the mean IQs of children of fathers classified by IQ and occupational standing to *regress* toward the mean of the entire population, as it was found in a study by Burt (1961).

The same tendency was found in Terman's longitudinal study of gifted children whose mean IQ was 151. When these children grew up, most achieved upper socioeconomic status. When they became parents, the mean IQ of their children was only 133 (Terman & Oden, 1959).

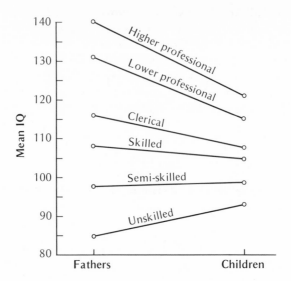

Fig. 7–7. Relations between the mean IQs of English fathers at various occupational levels and the mean IQs of their children. After Burt (1961).

In both the Burt and Terman studies, the IQs of the children of parents at each IQ level were roughly normally distributed around their respective means. Thus, for example, in Burt's study, unskilled men having mean IQs of 85 produced children whose mean IQs were 93 and there were about as many children at each level above and below 93 as would be expected from a normal distribution having 93 as its mean. Likewise for the children of professional men having mean IQs of 140—the children's IQs were symmetrically distributed around a mean of 121. In Terman's study, the IQs of the offspring were distributed all the way from the retarded range to the 190s, though with only 2 per cent under 100 (compared to 50 per cent in the general population) and over 32 per cent above 140 (compared to 1 per cent in the general population). Hence, even though the mean IQs of the children are closer to the overall mean than the IQs of parents having extreme IQs, low IQ parents produce considerably more low IQ children than do high IQ parents and vice versa.

It is difficult to see how any theory that attributes differences in IQ solely to differences in socioeconomic advantages could account for the finding that people of the lowest socioeconomic status (SES) have children averaging substantially higher in IQ than they do, while those from the highest SES have children with IQs averaging substantially lower than their own. However, these findings are highly compatible with the models for polygenic influence on IQ, even with the oversimplified model using only two genes, A and B.

To illustrate, suppose we start with a man having the lowest genotype for IQ, A^{o}A^{o}B^{o}B^o. It is impossible for him to marry anyone with a lower genotype, because there are no lower genotypes. If mating were entirely random with respect to genotype for IQ, the very low genotype man would be at least 15 times as likely to marry a woman having a higher genotype than to marry a woman having a genotype like his own, simply because there are 15 times as many kinds of higher genotype (recall the distribution of genotypes on p. 229).

Since, in Western countries, the phenotypic IQs of spouses have been found to correlate approximately .50 with each other (e.g., Conrad & Jones, 1940), it is unlikely that the man with the very low genotype would marry anyone with a genotype at the very high end of the scale (A+A+B+B+). However, there are still 14 times as many kinds of genotype ranging from low to high as there are A^{o}A^{o}B^{o}B^o genotypes, and 10 times as many in the low to average range as in the very low range.

If the man with the very low genotype marries a woman with the next higher genotype than his own, one having a single + allele rather than no such allele (e.g., A+A^{o}B^{o}B^o), then she can contribute each of the following four combinations to their offspring: A+B^o; A^{o}B^o; A+B^o; A^{o}B^o, because either of her A alleles (A+ or A^o) can be transmitted with either of her B^o alleles. Since the man with the A^{o}A^{o}B^{o}B^o genotype can contribute only ^{o} alleles, half their children will have genotypes like his wife's, with one + gene (A+A^{o}B^{o}B^o) and half will have genotypes like his, with no + genes. The result is that, if environmental conditions remain constant, the mean IQ of his children will be halfway between his and his wife's IQs.

If, as is statistically quite probable, he married a woman with an average genotype having two + alleles, the average IQ of his children would be still higher because:

1. if she had an A+A+B^{o}B^o or A^{o}A^{o}B+B+ genotype, she would contribute one + allele to each of their children; or

2. if she had an A+A^{o}B+B^o, A^{o}A+B+B^o, A+A^{o}B^{o}B+, or A^{o}A+B^{o}B+ genotype, she would contribute two + alleles to half their children and none to the other half.

The reasoning from the genetic model would be the same if we began with a man having the highest genotype (A+A+B+B+). The conclusion would be that his children are more likely to have lower genotypes than one like his.

The fact that low IQ people do indeed tend to marry people with higher IQs has been demonstrated by Dinger (1961), while the opposite trend for high IQ people was demonstrated in the Terman study (Terman & Oden, 1959).

While the filial regression phenomena may appear to suggest that each generation must be more homogeneous for IQ than the last, this is not the case, because people with genotypes in the intermediate range continue to produce children having genotypes at the extremes. Recall the two-gene example on page 230 in which, for every 16 children produced by people with average genotypes, there is likely to be one child with the lowest possible genotype, four with the second lowest genotypes, six with average genotypes, four with the second highest genotypes, and one with the highest possible genotype.

Evidence for Polygenic Influences in Cultural-Familial Retardation

The evidence from the twin studies and the regression of filial IQs indicates a significant genetic component in the rank ordering of phenotypic IQs among northern European and American whites living in a moderately broad range of environments. It suggests that there is more than one genotype for IQ in this population, and that the extreme environmentalistic model positing a single genotype, as in Fig. 7–6(c), is inadequate. Since the extreme hereditarian model positing a different genotype for every IQ phenotype, as in Fig. 7–6(a), also seemed untenable, only a model including more than one genotype, each having a phenotypic reaction range, as in Fig. 7–6(b), seems plausible.

Several important questions remain regarding the cause of cultural-familial retardation per se. The first question is whether it is likely that IQs as low as the retarded range can reflect nonpathological polygenic mechanisms or whether some other explanation must be found.

Although most of the twin and regression studies cited above included some individuals whose IQs and other characteristics qualified them as cultural-familial retarded, the most direct approach to assessing the role of nonpathological polygenic transmission in retardation has been through family studies. One of the largest and most thorough began with the collection of detailed data on the families of 549 individuals admitted between 1911 and 1918 to an institution for the retarded in Minnesota (Reed & Reed, 1965). The Kuhlmann revision of the Binet was given at that time to all applicants for admission and to some members of their families.

A follow-up study of all 82,217 locatable descendants of the grandparents of the original patients was begun in 1949. Family pedigree charts were constructed and all people for whom sufficient data were available were classified either as retarded (IQs below 70 and/or other strong indications of retardation) or as not retarded.

The group included many having average and high IQs as well as those with IQs below 70. It was found that the mean IQs of children having at least one parent with an extreme IQ regressed toward the overall mean, just as did those reported by Burt (1961) and Terman & Oden (1959). Thus, the IQs of children having one retarded and one nonretarded parent were symmetrically distributed around a mean closer to the population mean than were the IQs of the retarded parents. Furthermore, as evidence for a poly-genic model which assumes that many retardates are not homozygous for non-IQ-enhancing alleles, children with two retarded parents had mean IQs of 74, somewhat above the upper cut-off point of 69 employed for classifying the parents as retarded, and the IQs of these children extended up into the average and above-average ranges.

Table 7–4 presents the distribution of IQs among children of two re-tarded parents and of one retarded and one nonretarded parent. Not all the retardates who reproduced met the criteria for cultural-familial retarda-tion, but separate analysis of a subgroup of 50 families (18,730 members) who clearly did meet these criteria showed patterns similar to those in Table 7–4. The evidence for polygenic influences on the IQs of the cultural-familial retarded is thus consistent with that for polygenic influences on IQs higher in the distribution.

TABLE 7–4

IQ range of tested children of retarded parents.

Type of parents	IQ range of children						Total	Average IQ	Per cent retarded
	0–49	50–69	70–89	90–110	111–130	131+			
Retardate × retardate	6	29	36	17	1	0	89	74	39.4
Male retardate × normal	0	12	41	75	24	1	153	95	7.8
Female retardate × normal	6	15	32	43	10	1	107	87	19.6

NOTE.—Adapted from Reed & Reed (1965).

THE ROLES OF ENVIRONMENT

Even though polygenic mechanisms appear to influence the *rank order-ing* of IQs in the general population and in the nonpathologically retarded, none of the evidence yet cited speaks directly to the determination of phenotypic IQ *levels* or of adaptive behavior that may be possible for peo-ple assumed to have a minimum number of IQ-enhancing genes. Evidence is available on two important questions raised by the failure of the genetic model alone to deal with the problems of phenotypic levels of IQ and adap-tive behavior.

One question is whether the reaction ranges of genotypes for IQ are large enough so that providing good environments for people presumed to have low genotypes can substantially raise their levels of functioning above what would be expected in poor environments.

The second question is, in what specific ways do the typical experiences of the cultural-familial retarded shape their personalities and behavior?

Environment as a Crucial Determinant of IQ Level

The Skeels Study. One of the most dramatic demonstrations that environmental differences can cause major differences in IQ level and adaptive functioning was begun by Skeels (1966) in the mid-1930s. Skeels noticed that two one-year-old girls, transferred from an Iowa orphanage to an institution for the retarded because they appeared severely retarded, improved markedly after the transfer. Repeated testing in their new environment showed that their behavioral and intellectual development reached and remained within the normal range. The children happened to be the only preschoolers in wards with mildly retarded women who had quickly "adopted" them and taken a warm maternal interest in them. Their experience contrasted sharply with that of children in the orphanage, where busy nurses had little time for individual attention and where sensory stimulation was at an absolute minimum.

Skeels was able to arrange for the transfer of 10 more orphanage children to similar wards in the institution for the retarded. These children, together with the original two girls' and a third previously transferred to another institution for the retarded, comprised an *experimental* group of 13. All the children had been considered unsuitable for adoption because of apparent retardation. Testing just before transfer, when the children averaged 19 months in age, showed mean developmental and intelligence quotients of 64, although negligible correlations of infant tests with later IQ make this figure of doubtful significance (e.g., Bayley, 1949). Each child remained in the institution for the retarded until it was felt he had gained maximum benefit. Eleven were then adopted, one remained in the institution because of continued low functioning, and one was returned to the orphanage.

A *contrast* group of 12 children who had remained in the orphanage until at least age four was later selected for comparison. Their mean DQs and IQs were 87 at the first testing (mean age 17 months).

The family backgrounds of the children were very poor, with ten in each group being illegitimate. Mean IQ of the five mothers tested in the experimental group was 70, while a sixth was known to be retarded. Mean IQ of the nine mothers tested in the contrast group was 63.

At the second testing of each group of children, the mean IQ of the experimental group was 92, after an average stay of 19 months in the institution for the retarded. The mean IQ of the contrast children was 61 after an average of 31 months in the orphanage beyond the first testing. At the third testing, when the experimental children averaged six years in age, their mean IQ was 96, while the contrast children, averaging seven years in age, had a mean IQ of 66.

It seems evident that contrasting early life experiences produced major differences in the IQs of the experimental and contrast children. What is far more important, the "real-life" correlates of IQ bore out the apparent differences in the children's functioning. When followed up at ages between 25 and 35 years, the average education attained by the 13 experimental children was grade 12 and all were self-supporting. All had been married, although one was divorced. IQs of their children ranged from 86 to 125, with a mean of 104. Of the 11 who had held jobs (two of the married women had not), nine had worked at skilled levels or higher. Their average income was above the average for the state as a whole.

By comparison, the average education attained by the contrast group was fourth grade. Four of them still resided in state institutions, a fifth had died in an institution for the retarded, six were unskilled, and one, perhaps because of his good fortune in being placed in a school for the deaf at age 8, was a skilled typesetter. Only the typesetter and one other had married, the latter being subsequently divorced. The only children were four belonging to the typesetter, their IQs ranging from 103 to 119, and one belonging to the divorced man, his IQ being 66.

At first glance, the dramatic results of the Skeels study appear to contradict the evidence for polygenic influence on IQ. The IQs and other characteristics of most of the mothers of both the experimental and contrast children, as well as the characteristics of the putative fathers, strongly suggest genetic backgrounds like those of the cultural-familial retarded. Yet the difference between the environments of the experimental group and the contrast group, whose environment was not atypical for orphanages, resulted in a large IQ difference by early school age and differences in later life achievements as great as would be predicted from this IQ difference.

The Skodak-Skeels Study.   Data from another study of orphans carried out by Skodak and Skeels (1949) demonstrate how the environmental and genetic pieces of the puzzle may fit together. The subjects of the study were 100 Iowan children who had been adopted before the age of six months during the 1930s and who were available for individual IQ testing at three intervals thereafter.

As in the Skeels study, the mean IQ of the 63 biological mothers who could be tested was considerably below that attained by their children raised in adoptive homes. The mean IQ of the mothers was 86, with 11 being under 70. The mean IQ of their children, tested at an average age of 14, was 106, with only 1 below 70.

Despite the 20-point difference in mean IQ level, the *correlations* of the children's IQs with the IQs and education of their *biological* parents were much *higher* than with the education of their *adoptive* parents. (IQs were not obtained for the biological fathers or adoptive parents, but education has been repeatedly found to correlate highly with IQ.) Figure 7–8(a) presents the correlation of the children's IQs with the IQs and education of their biological mothers and the education of their adoptive mothers, while Fig. 7–8(b) presents the correlations of the children's IQs with the

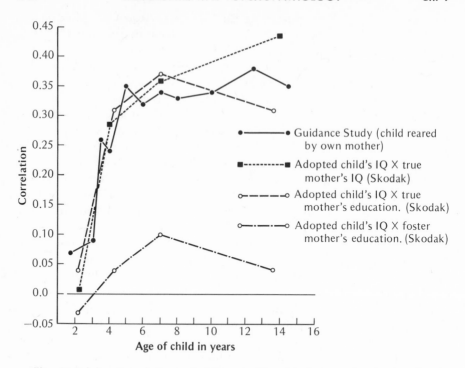

Fig. 7–8 (a). Correlations of children's IQs with their mothers' education in the Berkeley Guidance Study and with biological mothers' IQ and education and foster mothers' education in the Skodak-Skeels (1949) study. After Honzik (1957). © 1957 by the Society for Research in Child Development and reprinted by permission.

education of their biological fathers and adoptive fathers. Corresponding correlations of children's IQs with their biological parents' education are presented from the Berkeley Guidance Study (Honzik, 1957), in which all the children were raised by their biological parents.

Notice that the correlations of children's IQs with their biological mothers' IQs and with the education of both biological parents rose along nearly identical paths whether the children were raised by their biological parents or by adoptive parents. The highest correlation of the adopted children's IQs with their adoptive parents' education was about .10, this being with adoptive mothers' education when the children were 7 years old. The correlations at the final testing were only .02 with adoptive mothers' education and .00 with adoptive fathers' education, compared to .44 with biological mothers' IQ, .32 with biological mothers' education, and .42 with biological fathers' education. Two earlier studies also reported substantially higher correlations of children's IQs with the abilities of their biological parents than with those of their adoptive parents (Burks, 1928; Leahy, 1935). The correlations of adopted children's IQs with biological mothers' IQs

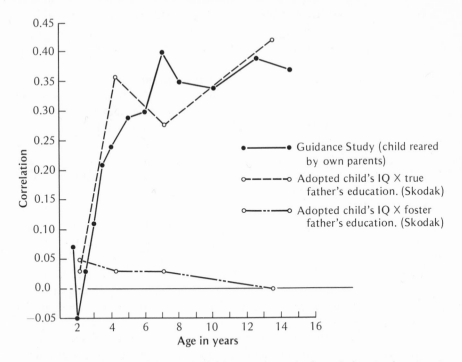

Fig. 7–8 (b). Correlations of children's IQs with their fathers' education in the Berkeley Guidance Study and with biological and foster fathers' education in the Skodak-Skeels (1949) stuly. After Honzik (1957). © 1957 by the Society for Research in Child Development and reprinted by permission.

and fathers' education were not far below the median of .50 found for correlations between biological parent and child IQs in 13 studies of children raised by their biological parents (Jarvik & Erlenmeyer-Kimling, 1967).

The Role of SES. Averaging the IQs of Skodak-Skeels children over all ages having at least 15 scores in each SES shows that children adopted into upper SES homes obtained IQs less than two points higher than children adopted into lower SES homes—despite a detectable bias toward placement of children of better educated mothers in upper SES homes. This finding is important in its own right because it suggests that the correlations typically found between children's IQs and their biological parents' social class are due more to the correlated genotypic characteristics of the children and their parents than to the effects of SES on the child, except perhaps at the lowest extremes (cf. Burt, 1961; Conway, 1958).

Conclusions. The adoption studies have been criticized on a number of grounds. Some of the criticisms have been answered by Skeels (1940), but some justify reservations about the size of the purported environmental effects. One such criticism is that the biological mothers' IQs may have been underestimated because they were tested in the stressful period following surrender of their babies. However, the educational histories of the mothers suggest that their IQ scores would not have been much higher under ideal testing conditions.

A second criticism is that regression effects could partially account for the increases in children's scores above their mothers'. Recall from Fig. 7–7 that fathers with mean IQs of 85 had children whose mean IQs were 93 and fathers with mean IQs of 131 had children with mean IQs of 115 (Burt, 1961). Accordingly, eight points of the difference between the mean IQs of the adopted children (106) and their biological mothers (86) in the Skodak-Skeels study and 16 points in the Skeels study (96 versus 70) could have been due to regression effects alone.

It is unlikely that regression effects could account for the fact that the experimental group's IQs rose beyond those of the contrast group in the Skeels study. However, the higher initial IQs of mothers in the experimental group than in the contrast group (70 versus 63), plus certain characteristics of the contrast group that made them unadoptable and that also could have pathologically affected IQ (e.g., one was brain-damaged at birth, two had evidence of congenital syphilis), might account for some of the ultimate IQ differences.

Bearing in mind the reservations about the size of postnatal environmental effects on the IQs, the picture that emerges reveals the hypothesized interaction between (1) genetic mechanisms determining the rank ordering of IQs within a set of environmental conditions, and (2) environmental conditions determining the actual levels of the IQs. The differences between the mean child and maternal IQs—20 points in the Skodak-Skeels study (minus about 10 points for regression and underestimation of maternal IQs), and 26 points in the Skeels study (minus about 18 points for regression and underestimation of maternal IQs)—plus the difference between the experimental and contrast groups in the Skeels study—30 points (minus perhaps 8 points for the initially lower maternal IQs and possibly worse physical conditions of the contrast children)—demonstrate that childrearing conditions considered to be normal in western society produce IQs between 8 and 22 points higher than substandard conditions.

Yet, once the "normal" level of childrearing conditions is reached, it appears that genotypic differences outweigh differences due to parent education, occupation, or income in determining the phenotypic differences that appear. Together the evidence for environmental effects on IQ and the correlations between the IQs of adopted children and their biological mothers support the polygenic model evolved from the studies of heritability cited above, especially since all the adopted children were from the same general population of American whites of northern European ancestry on whom the model was based (cf. Skeels, 1966; Skodak & Skeels, 1949).

If the foregoing analysis is correct, then the term "cultural-familial retardation" need no longer be considered an ambiguous cop-out, although a term like "environmental-genetic retardation" might be more literally correct. Many people in this category probably have lower genotypes for IQ than do most people with higher phenotypic IQs, but postnatal environmental factors also play a role in preventing them from maximizing their genetic potentials. A major practical implication of these conclusions is that providing children of low IQ parents with improved home environments from infancy onward can bring many of them above the retarded and borderline ranges of IQ. More importantly, it is likely to help them develop adaptive behavior within the range required for self-sufficiency in western society.

The Role of Environment in Shaping Personality and Behavior

A growing body of research indicates that much of the seemingly maladaptive behavior of the retarded is due not to intrinsic properties of slow intellectual development, but to the particular experiences encountered by many children with slow intellectual development. This research deals primarily with those retarded children, mainly the cultural-familial retarded, whose slow intellectual development is not attributable to known pathological etiologies. The research is based on the assumption that, in nonpathological retardation, the course of cognitive development differs from normal development primarily in its rate and final level rather than in its qualitative nature.

Comparability of MA-matched Normals and Retardates. Since a "level" or "stage" of cognitive development is a hypothetical construct rather than a directly observable entity, tests are employed as operational indices of the hypothesized course of development. If MA on the Stanford-Binet is used as an index of cognitive development, the cognitive level of a ten-year-old who has an MA of 6 and an IQ of 60 without pathological etiology is assumed to be similar to that of a six-year-old having an MA of 6 and an IQ of 100.

Another approach to measuring cognitive development is to use experimental tasks specifically designed to identify hypothesized stages. Piaget and his collaborators have presented the most comprehensive theory of cognitive development and have devised numerous experimental tasks for identifying the stages that their theory postulates.

For many years it was argued that the cognitive levels of a retarded and a normal child who achieved the same MA on a test were not really similar because they had probably passed different items that merely happened to sum to the same MA score. However, recent studies have shown that retardates whose low IQs are without known pathological cause differ little from MA-matched normals in the patterns of Binet items they pass and fail (Achenbach, 1970a, 1971a). MA-matched normals and nonpathological retardates have also been found to differ little on versions of Piagetian tasks requiring a minimum of motivation and academic skills (Achenbach, 1969,

1973; Gruen & Vore, 1972). It therefore appears that the general cognitive competence represented by the Binet MAs of nonpathologically retarded children is roughly similar to that represented by similar MAs in normal children. If the cognitive competence of nonpathologically retarded children is indeed similar to that of MA-matched normals, then these retardates should be able to do as well as MA-matched normals in learning and problem-solving situations.

Behavioral Differences Between MA-matched Normals and Retardates. The repeated finding in early studies that retardates failed to perform as well as MA-matched normals led to the postulation of various defects in retardates to account for the apparent differences between their thinking and that of normals having the same MA. An example was the postulation of an intrinsic *rigidity* in retardates' thinking. This was supported by the observation that (institutionalized) retardates, much more than MA-matched (noninstitutionalized) normals, continued doing a monotonous repetitive experimental task even when given the opportunity to switch to something else (Kounin, 1941a, 1941b). Viewing traits like rigidity as intrinsic characteristics of the "retarded mind" helped create stereotypes such as that of "The Retardate" as a being whose rigidity prevented him from learning, who innately liked boring, repetitive tasks, and who had a wonderful sense of rhythm.

More recent research has revealed that much of the behavior thought to stem from intrinsic differences between people with low IQs and those with higher IQs can be traced to specific experiences that may differentiate most retardates from most normals.

In the case of rigidity, Zigler and his coworkers (cf. Zigler, 1971) found that the amount of social deprivation retarded children had experienced prior to institutionalization was correlated with the amount of rigid, perseverative behavior they displayed on tasks like those used by Kounin. This suggested that peculiarities of the child's history—rather than his retardation per se—increased perseverative behavior over that displayed by noninstitutionalized MA-matched normals. Other observations led to the hypothesis that socially deprived institutionalized children's perseveration on monotonous, repetitive tasks was being reinforced by the supportive attention provided by the experimenter. Such attention was believed to be especially reinforcing because the children typically received so little attention from adults.

This hypothesis was tested by giving the same tasks under the same conditions to *noninstitutionalized retarded* children and *institutionalized normal* children (generally orphans). If the perseverative behavior were solely a product of the cognitive rigidity supposedly inherent in retardation, then the noninstitutionalized retarded children should be as perseverative as the institutionalized retarded children, while the institutionalized children of normal IQ should not be any more perseverative than other children of normal IQ. On the other hand, if the perseverative behavior of the insti-

tutionalized retarded resulted from their desire for supportive adult attention, rather than from intrinsic cognitive rigidity, then other socially
deprived children, such as institutionalized normals, should be perseverative
in similar situations. By contrast, nondeprived children, including retardates living at home, should not be perseverative.

It was found that institutionalized children of normal IQ showed the
same kind of behavioral perseveration as institutionalized retarded children, while noninstitutionalized retarded children did not. The history
of social deprivation, leading to high motivation for supportive adult attention, rather than inherent cognitive rigidity, thus appeared to account for
the perseverative behavior of institutionalized retarded children.

Numerous other studies have since demonstrated the influence of social
reinforcement on the behavior of institutionalized children, both retarded
and nonretarded. When these factors are taken into account and properly
controlled for, institutionalized retarded children can perform as effectively
as noninstitutionalized retarded and normal children similar in MA.

Other experiential variables have been shown to account for many of
the ways in which the behavior of nonpathologically retarded children is
inadequate compared to that of normals of equivalent mental age. Two
of the most prominent are summarized below.

History of Failure and Low Expectancy of Success. As a child grows up
he is repeatedly compared to other children of his age. By his second or
third year, he is not only aware of the comparative judgments others are
making, but he is constantly making such comparisons himself. From an
awareness of the gross difference between his own capabilities and those
of older people, a child moves to an awareness of more subtle differences
between his own capabilities and those of the primary reference group that
society, especially the school, defines for him. This reference group usually
consists of normal children of his own age.

While many pathologically retarded children may be spared comparison
with normals because their physical stigmata mark them from the beginning
as abnormal, most nonpathologically retarded and some pathologically
retarded children accumulate a history of repeated failure to achieve the
norms set by their age-mates before they are identified as retarded and
placed in special educational settings. This history of failure makes them
fearful of applying their intellectual resources, even to learning and problem-solving of which they may be capable. Much of their behavior is directed toward avoiding situations where they may fail again, rather than
being directed toward the acquisition of new skills which their age-mates,
reinforced by previous success, are willing to attempt.

Numerous experimental studies have demonstrated that, compared to
MA-matched normals, the retarded expect little success, set low goals for
themselves, and ultimately settle for minimal levels of success on tasks
where their cognitive competence indicates that they can do much better
(e.g., MacMillan, 1969). This is especially true for retarded children who

feel that they are competing with normals (Rosen, Diggory, & Werlinsky, 1966; Schwarz & Jens, 1969). Even experimentally contrived failure experiences produce heightened expectations of failure and reliance on failure-avoiding behavior in retardates (Ollendick, Balla, & Zigler, 1971).

Outer-directedness and Cue-dependency. Another aspect of children's behavioral development is that, as they grow older, they typically become less and less reliant on cues from other people. In infancy, imitation is an essential, universal, and probably genetically based human strategy for acquiring new behavior. Much of the new behavior is reinforced by the success it brings in attaining the immediate goals of the child, such as opening doors and cookie jars, providing new means of communicating desires, etc.

During early childhood—by the mental age of about one and one-half or two, according to Piaget (1951)—the intellectual development of the child makes it possible for him to begin constructing mental representations of problem situations and possible solutions to them. He may do this using pictorial mental images, words, or kinesthetic representations. Whichever medium of mental representation he employs, the important point is that his behavior can now be guided by *mental* trial-and-error rather than by exclusive reliance on *external* cues such as the behavior of other people.

While powerful, the child's thinking during this period is still essentially empirical rather than logical, because—again according to Piaget—it lacks the framework of logical principles that do not normally develop until about the MA of five to seven years. Thus, the prelogical child is dominated by associations among the salient surface characteristics of things and situations rather than being able to derive abstract principles that go beyond surface characteristics.

After the MA of about seven, the child—now referred to by Piaget as being *concrete operational*—is capable of employing mental operations based upon abstract principles. This new capability is manifest in the child's ability to construct classifications of objects and to understand that, regardless of appearance, quantities do not change as long as nothing is added or taken away ("conservation").

By the MA of about 11, the child becomes capable of what Piaget calls *formal operational* thinking. This is abstract logical thinking which no longer depends upon concrete representations, such as quantities and objects, but which can deal with hypothetical constructs such as those used in science, political theory, law, theology, etc.

The new intellectual capabilities appearing in the course of cognitive development make possible many new strategies for problem-solving beyond the early strategies of imitation and associative learning, although the early ones remain available. For example, a normal adult unfamiliar with the procedures followed at a formal state banquet may carefully imitate others rather than trying to deduce exclusively by logic which of the many utensils should be used for each course of the dinner.

As most children grow up, the standards which others and they themselves set for their performance rise in such a way as to require progressively more advanced thinking. If the child generally feels he is succeeding in meeting the standards set for him, he is likely to retain confidence in his thinking and to use the progressively more advanced strategies as he becomes capable of them.

By contrast, the child whose cognitive capabilities lag behind those of his age mates meets failure rather than success when he relies on his own thinking. He therefore continues to rely on the more primitive strategies of imitation and associative learning whenever possible, even in situations where use of his own thinking would be advantageous.

Zigler (1971) has described as *outer-directed* the tendency to approach problem-solving by relying excessively on cues from other people. He and his colleagues have experimentally demonstrated that retarded children are more *outer-directed* than normals of the same MA and that failure experiences can increase the outer-directedness of both normal and retarded children (Sanders, Zigler, & Butterfield, 1968; Turnure & Zigler, 1964).

It has also been demonstrated that retardates provided with an obvious mechanical cue in a problem situation rely much longer on the cue than do MA-matched normals, even though retardates not given the cue solve the problem as quickly as MA-matched normals (Achenbach & Zigler, 1968). However, retarded children having a teacher who had deliberately maximized their success experiences and reinforced them for independent thinking were found to be no more dependent on mechanical cues than were MA-matched normals. This indicates that the dependency on external cues, which prevents many retarded children from using their cognitive capabilities, can be modified through appropriate educational intervention. The fact that a strategy of reliance on superficial cues, to the detriment of effective thinking, is not confined to the retarded, has been demonstrated by the finding of such strategies in some normal children as well (Achenbach, 1970b, 1971a).

CARE AND EDUCATION OF THE RETARDED

Except for the very small percentage of individuals in whom intellectual handicaps can be prevented or ameliorated through medical, dietary, or psychotherapeutic measures, proper care and education are the essential prerequisites for helping the retarded maximize their potentials. Simply bringing all institutional environments up to fully humane standards could improve the behavior of many of the severely retarded, even without well-planned educational, recreational, and social programs. Just how bad some of these environments are and what the purely political and bureaucratic obstacles are to improvement have been movingly documented in Blatt and Kaplan's (1966) book, *Christmas in Purgatory,* and Blatt's (1970) *Exodus from Pandemonium.*

In addition to the creation of humane living conditions, the replacement of large custodial institutions by a variety of social and educational services suited to the individual needs of the retarded and their families can further enhance the functioning of many retarded people, as well as reducing the number who become institutionalized. While severity of mental and physical disability is a factor in the institutionalization of some children, behavior problems and lack of family and community resources for supervision lead to the institutionalization of many who are not severely disabled (cf. Eyman, O'Connor, Tarjan, & Justice, 1972).

One alternative model to the traditional institution is the system of state regional centers begun in Connecticut in 1961. Each regional center is a relatively small unit that serves a clearly delineated local population area. It provides more-or-less permanent accommodations for a few residents who cannot remain in their own or foster homes. More importantly, it provides temporary accommodations whenever necessary for retardates who can live with their families or in foster homes most of the time, day services for some who return home at night, accommodations for some who work or study in the community during the day, counseling and referral services for families, sheltered workshops, and educational and recreational programs for residents and nonresidents. It also originates and coordinates other services and living arrangements, such as group homes and half-way houses.

Public School Programs

The public school is the first and, in many cases, the only source of education for most borderline, mildly, and moderately retarded children, who together comprise more than 90 per cent of the retarded population. Public school special classes are typically divided into those for children who, for educational purposes, are classified as *trainable* (IQs about 20 to 50), and those for children classified as *educable* (IQs about 50 to 75 or 80). While the merits of special class versus regular class placement for retarded children have been long debated, in practice not much more than one-third of the retarded in the United States actually receive special education in any form (based on 1963 figures; Mackie, 1965).

Trainable Children. Classes for trainable children are oriented toward simple self-help skills, safety rules, social adjustment, and rudimentary academic accomplishments such as counting and recognizing a few words important even in the protected lives that the trainable must lead.

The few published studies of public school classes for the trainable reveal little measurable academic benefit, but are generally inconclusive because of a lack of well-defined curricula, goals, and measuring instruments, and because the retardation of these children is due to a wide variety of pathological causes that make for very different educational prognoses (Kirk, 1964). One apparent benefit from such classes is that parents are helped to obtain more realistic conceptions of their children's limitations. If the regional center system or analogous models are widely implemented, an important function of classes for the trainable could be to provide preliminary preparation for the occupational and other programs that the child can attend when he reaches adolescence.

Educable Children. In terms of their intellectual levels, these are the children for whom the highest goals can be set, but to whom the most imagination, resourcefulness, and understanding must be dedicated if they are to be helped significantly.

Gunzberg (1968) found that half of the mildly retarded 16- to 25-year-olds reached a reading level of at least 7 years 9 months, while 10 per cent reached the relatively adequate level of 11 years 2 months. More than half could tell time adequately and deal with small amounts of money for bus fares and lunches. Forty per cent could fill out employment application forms.

Of the borderline retarded, half reached a reading level of at least 9 years 3 months, while 10 per cent reached a level of 12 years 4 months. Nearly all could tell time adequately, while about three quarters could deal with small amounts of money and fill out employment application forms.

There have been several long-term follow-up studies of children classified as educable retarded during their school years. The one spanning the longest period began with a follow-up in 1935 of 206 adults who had childhood IQs of less than 70 and had been in public school special classes between 1916 and about 1930 (Baller, 1936). Groups who had childhood IQs of 75 to 85 and 100 to 120 were matched to the retarded for sex, nationality of descent, and age. A final follow-up was done by Baller, Charles, & Miller (1967) when the average age of the retarded subjects was 56.

Although there was considerable attrition, especially due to an extremely high accidental death rate among the retarded, 119 remained for comparison with the other groups. Only 8 of the retarded had been institutionalized, most of them having severe physical handicaps. Forty-eight per cent of the retarded, compared to 84 per cent of the borderline group and 90 per cent of the average group, were married and living with their spouses. Considerably more of the retarded than the other groups had been divorced or never married.

Sixty-five per cent of the retarded were entirely self-supporting, compared to 94 percent of the borderline and 96 per cent of the average groups. The kinds of occupations in the two lower groups did not differ much, although 72 per cent in the retarded, compared to 50 per cent in the borderline and less than 1 per cent in the average group were semiskilled or unskilled laborers.

The two lower groups were similar in the percentage (approximately 8 per cent) who had criminal convictions, while there were none in the average group. Participation in social, recreational, and political activities was minimal for the low IQ group, higher for the borderline group, and highest for the average group.

A noteworthy finding was that, among the 15 retarded individuals retested, IQs increased from a mean childhood Binet IQ of 60 to a mean WAIS IQ of 75 at age 45 and 82 at age 56. Part of the initial increase was due to high scores on the performance scale of the WAIS, the Binet being a more verbal test. However, much of the increase is probably due to the fact that mental development continued beyond the age that the test builders had assumed it would cease. Increases of IQ in adulthood were also found among the 18 borderline subjects retested, from a mean IQ of 81 in the 1920s to 89 in the early 1960s. Increases have likewise been found in longitudinal studies of adults in the normal IQ range (Bayley, 1966; Kangas & Bradway, 1971). The mental competence represented by an adolescent IQ score should thus not be considered the limit a person will reach.

Other follow-up studies of children classified as educable retarded have supported the finding that a large percentage, usually between 50 per cent and 80 per cent, become at least marginally self-supporting adults, though they are considerably less self-sufficient than people with IQs in the average range or even in the borderline range who have grown up in roughly similar socioeconomic conditions (e.g., Bobroff, 1956; Dinger, 1961; Kennedy, 1966; Peterson & Smith, 1960; Skaarbrevik, 1971).

Close analysis, however, shows that, beside being in the bottom SES and being socially isolated, low IQ people have an extremely insecure existence and are rated by employers as performing worse than other people from the same SES in the same jobs. In addition, it appears that more of their children are academically retarded than are children with similar IQs and SES but higher IQ parents (Edgerton, 1967; Kennedy, 1966). Moreover, ridicule by fellow workers, lack of awareness and responsibility about normal job expectations, such as punctuality, and unrealistic salary expectations present significant obstacles to job stability in low IQ people (Peckham, 1951).

A long-range problem is the progressive decrease in the unskilled jobs traditionally filled by the retarded—from about 59 per cent of the labor force in 1900 to 24 per cent in 1965 and 22 per cent projected for 1975 (Goldstein, 1964). This fact makes it imperative that the care and education of the educable retarded no longer be left to the haphazard measures that have typically prevailed.

Improving Education for the Retarded

While the foregoing portrays the situation as it typically is today, this situation is far from ideal. What follows is a brief summary of some findings on specific attempts at improvements in education, broadly defined.

Special Classes. Possibilities for improving conditions for noninstitutionalized retarded children are increasing as more states require local school systems to provide special education for the retarded. Yet, simply creating a class defined as "special" because its members have low IQs is not sufficient to insure educational benefits. In fact, most studies have shown that low IQ children in regular classes do as well or better academically then low IQ children in special classes, although some evidence was found that children in special classes are better adjusted socially (Fitzgibbon, 1967; Guskin & Spicker, 1968; Kirk, 1964; Quay, 1963). The findings are generally inconclusive, however, because, where children in the two types of class were compared within a school system, those in special classes were usually the ones who had initially done poorly and/or had behavior problems in regular classes. In studies where the regular class children were from school systems having no special classes, it is likely that troublesome low IQ children were simply kept out of school rather than attending regular classes.

Goldstein (1967) attempted to control for these factors by randomly assigning 6-year-old children with IQs under 85 to special or regular classes in school systems not previously having special classes. The new special classes were taught by well-trained teachers who used a carefully constructed curriculum guide.

After four years, there was little difference in the academic performance of the two groups, although special class children performed better on measures of productive thinking and they showed less attempt to avoid difficult questions on an orally administered questionnaire. On the other hand, the special class children interacted less with neighborhood peers than did the regular class low IQ children.

Post hoc analyses showed that children with IQs of 80 and below did better academically in special classes while those with IQs above 80 did better in regular classes. Since IQs of 75 or 80 are the usual upper cut-off points for special class placement, the results suggest that early special class placement can be beneficial. They leave open the question of whether the more typical procedure of assigning to special classes only children who have already failed in regular classes for a few years is beneficial.

Two studies have indicated, however, that the typical form of special class placement may be better than regular class placement for retarded children's self-acceptance and for their acceptance by others. In one study, the self-concepts of 7- to 15-year-olds improved steadily from the time they were told they would be placed in special classes until a year after placement when their self-concept scores dropped slightly (Towne, Joiner, & Schurr, 1967; cf. Guskin & Spicker, 1968). The improvement was apparently due to a change in the reference group with whom the children compared themselves, from normal to other low IQ children.

In the second study, normal boys rated educable retardates in a special class of their progressive elementary school significantly higher on a scale of social acceptance then they rated retardates integrated into their own ungraded classes (Goodman, Gottlieb, & Harrison, 1972). Girls did not differentiate between the segregated and integrated retardates, but, like the boys, they rated all the retardates significantly lower than children of normal IQ. It was suggested that the behavior problems of many retardates are easier for other children to accept when the retardates have been clearly labeled as handicapped.

Behavior Modification Approaches. The small differences in academic performance found between retardates in regular and special classes does not mean they are doing well in either setting. This fact, together with the apparent social disadvantages of regular classes for many retardates, suggests that educational programs should be maximally focused upon providing retarded children with the kinds of training that will directly help them to advance to postschool situations most advantageous to them as individuals, rather than hoping that watered-down regular school programs will eventually make them into normal, albeit somewhat watered-down, adults.

Considerable work has recently been done in the application of behavioral principles (detailed in Chapter 10) to the education of the retarded (cf. Meyerson, Kerr & Michael, 1967; Thompson & Grabowski, 1972; Ullmann & Krasner, 1969). This ranges from the training of self-care and language and the elimination of self-destructive behavior in severely retarded people, to the teaching of specific academic knowledge and skills, such as the alphabet, word recognition, counting, and telling time, social skills, and occupational skills in less severely retarded people.

In many cases a primary function of behavior modification techniques is to decrease disruptive behavior so that teaching of constructive behavior can begin. Various approaches are possible, from immediate food reward for single responses to programmed instruction and teaching machines in classrooms (cf. Malpass, 1967). Because aspects of many behavior modification techniques can be easily taught, it has also been possible to create *therapeutic pyramids* in which a professional person trains nonprofessional assistants who then supervise retarded assistants in the application of behavioral principles to the training of younger or more severely retarded individuals (Whalen & Henker, 1969, 1971). Beside being a relatively inexpensive way to help a large number of retardates, therapeutic pyramids offer the possibilities (1) of greatly enhancing the self-esteem and functioning of the retarded assistants by giving them meaningful work, and (2) of creating self-perpetuating improvement in the behavior of retarded populations.

Implications for the Future

As Gardner (1969) has pointed out, the methodology of behavior modification research still leaves much to be desired, especially with respect to the evaluation of the permanence of behavior changes. However, the following assumptions, gleaned mostly from research in behavior modification, seem to be valuable guides to future work with the retarded:

1. Within their biological limits, all people are capable of acquiring new behavior.
2. Current behavior is largely the result of past and present environmental contingencies.
3. Constructive changes in a child's behavior depend upon changes in the environmental contingencies that shape and support it—such change can often be brought about by changes in the behavior of people around him, be they institutional personnel, family members, teachers, or other retardates.
4. Planned implementation of behavioral change requires precise specification of behavioral goals that are within the capabilities of the child to reach and of the environment to support—the kind of self-sufficiency expected of physically normal children with average IQs is not an appropriate goal for most pathologically retarded children and may not be appropriate for many nonpathologically retarded children, at least not at the same ages as for children with higher IQs.
5. Long-term maintenance of improved behavior may require maintenance of environmental conditions designed to support it—a retarded child who has learned to utilize his full capabilities is likely to require continued reinforcement that is not typically provided by a world geared to people with higher IQs.

Some of the most important work left to be done in aiding the retarded lies in implementing the practical implications of principles such as the ones just enumerated. These include drastic changes in the institutional environments of the severely retarded and in special education programs for less severely retarded children; much improved family counseling and support services to aid families of the retarded in accepting and adapting to their children and helping them to maximize their potentials; and replacement of monolithic institutions with long-term, community-based planning, educational, vocational, counseling, and support services providing a range of living and working opportunities tailored to the needs of each individual.

SUMMARY

People classified as retarded because of their low IQs and poor social competence constitute an extremely heterogeneous group. Like growth retardation, intellectual retardation has many different causes, occurs in many different degrees, and has many different consequences.

Mental retardation was first recognized as a social problem in the nineteenth century, beginning with the "discovery" of the severely retarded and followed by "discovery" of the mildly retarded when compulsory schooling imposed uniform, age-graded standards for intellectual performance.

The Binet-Simon tests of 1905 to 1911 were the first to be widely accepted as practical methods for identifying subnormal scholastic aptitude in a relatively objective way. Although the original tests entailed no assumptions about the determinants of scholastic aptitude or its immutability, the evidence that IQ scores predicted achievement well, were roughly normally distributed, and tended to be stable over several years was cited by hereditarians as proof that "intelligence" was genetically fixed.

Because IQ scores correlate moderately well with social competence and academic achievement, degrees of retardation are currently labeled according to several somewhat arbitrary IQ ranges on the Stanford-Binet test: *Borderline* retardation, IQs 68–83; *mild,* IQs 52–67; *moderate,* IQs 36–51; *severe,* IQs 20–35; *profound,* IQs below 20.

Nearly all of the very small percentage of retarded people whose IQs are in the profound and severe ranges have definite organic pathology. They account for most of the institutionalized retarded. Organic conditions known to produce retardation include chromosomal anomalies such as *Down's syndrome (mongolism),* single gene conditions such as *phenylketonuria (PKU),* and diseases and brain damage resulting from a variety of other causes. Some of these conditions can be effectively treated through medical and dietary measures.

There is evidence that other pathological conditions such as extreme environmental isolation and emotional disturbance can also produce mental retardation.

The vast majority of retarded people have IQs above 50 and no known pathological etiologies. Those having close relatives who are similarly retarded are classified as *cultural-familial* retarded on the assumption that "cultural deprivation" and/or familial genetic factors have limited their intellectual development. Three models for understanding the possible interplay between environmental and genetic factors in the determination of IQ are: (1) the *extreme hereditarian* model of *polygenic* determination, which hypothesizes a different genotype for every phenotypic IQ; (2) an *interactionist* model of *polygenic* determination, which hypothesizes a phenotypic *reaction range* for each of several genotypes for IQ; (3) an *extreme environmentalist* model, which hypothesizes a single nonpathological genotype, with all phenotypic differences being attributed to environmental differences.

Evidence from studies of the *heritability* of IQ—based upon correlations between IQs of MZ and DZ twins reared together, IQs of MZ twins reared apart, *filial regression* of IQs, and the relations of adopted children's IQs to those of their biological and foster parents—was interpreted as supporting the interactionist model for the determination of IQs above 50 in the absence of pathological etiology.

Environmental influences on the level of phenotypic IQ within a genotypic reaction range and on the personalities and behavior of the retarded were documented. Evidence was presented that behavior once considered to result from inherent characteristics of the retarded, such as *rigidity*, is really due to specific aspects of retardates' experiential history, such as *social deprivation*. Similar findings indicated that retardates' *low expectancy of success, outer-directedness*, and *cue-dependency* are due to their repeated experiences of failure in attaining the standards appropriate for normals of similar chronological age.

Long-term follow-ups of mildly retarded people have shown that about 50 per cent to 80 per cent become self-supporting, though marginally so and with little social participation.

Changes were proposed in models of care, from isolated monolithic custodial institutions and haphazard public school education, to community-based units offering a wide variety of services to retardates and their families, public school classes designed to prepare retardates realistically for their postschool situations, and the application of behavioral principles to the improvement of adaptive behavior.

SUGGESTED READING

General text. *Psychological Problems in Mental Deficiency,* by Sarason and Doris (1969), goes far beyond the usual textbook in that it conveys the social and historical context and mythology that have caused and are still causing the retarded so much humiliation and unnecessary suffering.

Epidemiology of retardation. The epidemiological study by Birch et al (1970) is an in-depth study of all the children classified as retarded in a community presenting nearly ideal conditions for such research. The nature of the community made it especially valuable for identification and study of the nonpathologically retarded without the usual confounding factors of linguistic, cultural, or racial differences or differential access to medical, educational, and housing services.

Intelligence and experience. Hunt's (1961) book of this title provides an intensive analytic review of evidence on the nature-nurture issue and the belief in predetermined development. It is written from the point of view of an environmentalist who nonetheless takes concepts of cognitive structure seriously. Despite their methodological imperfections, the key studies by Skodak and Skeels (1949) and Skeels (1966) on the relations between IQ and environment and between the IQs of foster children and their biological and foster parents are important milestones in the nature-nurture controversy, as is Honzik's (1957) reanalysis of their and other data.

Institutionalism. In case there are any doubts that snake-pit conditions still exist in our institutions for the retarded and that there are tremendous political, bureaucratic, and attitudinal obstacles to improving them, Blatt and Kaplan's (1966) *Christmas in Purgatory,* and Blatt's (1970) *Exodus from Pandemonium* should dispel all such doubts. The task-oriented book by Thompson and Grabowski (1972), *Behavior Modification of the Mentally Retarded,* portrays similar conditions, plus the advantages and limitations of behavioral techniques for bringing improvement within the walls of the institution itself by changing administrative, staff, and patient behavior.

Personality and Motivational Factors in the Behavior of the Retarded. The growing body of research on the relation of retarded cognitive development to personality and motivational determinants of behavior has been summarized by Zigler (1971). His arguments for maintaining a theoretical distinction between retardation due to specific defects and that characterized by general slow development presumably due to nonpathological polygenic mechanisms is presented in *Science* (1967). Two attacks on Zigler's distinction between "defect" and "developmental" theories of retardation, together with his response, were published in the *American Journal of Mental Deficiency* (Ellis, 1969; Milgram, 1969; Zigler, 1969).

8

The Psychoanalytic Theory
of Psychoneurotic
Disorders

Psychoanalytic theory is by no means the only conceptual framework applicable to the disorders referred to here as "psychoneurotic." In fact, one of the fundamental issues in the study of psychopathology today concerns the choice of a theoretical model or frame of reference for portraying, understanding, and treating disorders referred to in the psychoanalytic tradition as psychoneurotic. Chapter 3 dealt at length with the problem of competing viewpoints and models in the study of child psychopathology.

At the risk of perpetuating the rivalry between the psychoanalytic model and the learning theory models to be taken up in Chapter 10, I have chosen to devote separate chapters to them and their ways of portraying and treating domains of disorders that overlap considerably. I see three reasons for separating the psychoanalytic model for "psychoneurotic" disorders and the behavioral models for "behavior" disorders, even though the same child may be considered by some to have a psychoneurotic disorder and by others to have a behavior disorder:

1. Despite prodigious efforts (e.g., Dollard & Miller, 1950; Marks & Gelder, 1966) to bring together the theoretical concepts of psychoanalytic and learning approaches, many child treatment and research centers, as well as many individual practitioners, adhere almost exclusively to one of the approaches and have little sympathy with the other approach.
2. Much that has been written on child disorders adheres more or less exclusively to one point of view or the other. Both these bodies of literature contain informative observations on the nature and course

of normal as well as pathological behavior in children, and there is as yet no basis either for completely rejecting one body of literature as too full of falsehood to be worth considering, or for completely reinterpreting the data from one body in the theoretical language of the other.

3. Both approaches offer general models of functioning that purport to be applicable outside the domains typically encompassed by the concepts of psychoneurosis and behavior disorders. Other areas that are dealt with in this book and to which both approaches claim applicability are psychotic disorders (Chapter 12), juvenile delinquency (Chapter 13), classification (Chapter 15), and diagnosis (Chapter 16).

FREUD'S INITIAL THEORY OF NEUROSIS

Sigmund Freud's theory is not the only psychoanalytic theory, but it is the one to which all others trace their roots. With later elaboration by Anna Freud and others, it also constitutes the dominant psychoanalytic theory of childhood neurosis. (See Bryt, 1972, for a review of non-Freudian psychoanalytic approaches to child problems.)

There were two major stages in the development of Freud's theory of neurosis. Since the second stage brought a fundamental change in the original theory more than two-thirds of the way through Freud's psychoanalytic career, both stages must be considered in order to understand many of the fundamental tenets that have become part of psychoanalytic doctrine.

Charcot and Janet

After doing research in physiology, Freud in the 1880s became interested in the physical symptoms of *hysteria.* These include a variety of disruptions in organ functions, such as paralyses, anesthesias (losses of feeling), and blindness.

In 1885 and 1886, Freud studied with Jean-Martin Charcot, a famous Parisian neurologist who had been studying hysteria since the late 1870s. Charcot found that many hysterical symptoms did not follow the known principles of anatomy and that they had no identifiable organic etiology. He also found that hysterical symptoms could be induced and removed through hypnotic suggestion.

After observing the effects of hypnosis, Charcot's pupil, Pierre Janet, began studying the mental states of hysterical patients. He found that hysterical patients often had curious amnesias for certain memories. In extreme cases, called *hysterical fugues,* a person would suddenly leave home and take up a completely new role in life, with apparently complete amnesia for his previous life, until he "awoke," oblivious to the period of amnesia.

Believing that this "splitting of consciousness" was the crucial characteristic of hysteria, Janet hypothesized that particular groups of thoughts *(complexes)* were separated or *dissociated* from one another as a result of an innate weakness in a person's capacity for psychological synthesis.

Josef Breuer

A Viennese colleague of Freud's, Josef Breuer, reached a different conclusion when he discovered that hysterical symptoms could be permanently removed if, during a hypnotic state, a patient remembered the situation in which the symptom began and freely expressed the emotion accompanying the symptom's formation. Breuer also found that the patient's recall of the pathogenic situation often explained the specific symptoms. For example, during a hypnotic trance, Anna O., a girl suffering from a hysterical disturbance of vision, remembered that, while she was caring for her mortally ill father, he had asked what time it was. She had strained to see her watch through her tears so that she could reply quickly without betraying her anxiety. Remembering the situation and expressing her previously suppressed feelings were followed by disappearance of her visual symptoms.

Breuer gave the name *hypnoid state* to the period of intense but unexpressed emotion when symptoms were formed. He regarded the suppression of emotion during such a state, rather than an innate defect in psychological synthesis, to be the cause of the splitting off or dissociation of complexes of ideas from consciousness. He called the therapeutic release of suppressed emotion *abreaction* or *catharsis*.

Breuer's theory that the psychological hypnoid state was primary, with the splitting of consciousness being a byproduct, represented a significant advance, because it accounted for the specific symptoms of a patient and it offered what appeared to be a permanent cure for the symptoms through the abreaction of suppressed emotion. It also represented the birth of the psychodynamic model, embodying conflicts between impulses striving toward expression and mental forces opposing the impulses, which Freud was to develop into psychoanalytic theory.

Studies in Hysteria

Breuer and Freud collaborated on what is generally regarded as the first publication in the psychoanalytic literature, *Studies in Hysteria* (1893–95). This was a series of case reports on hysterical women, including Anna O., plus Breuer and Freud's hypotheses about the mechanisms of hysteria. Freud hypothesized that ideas that are unacceptable because they are incompatible with most of the ideas constituting a person's ego are forced out of consciousness by a process he called *repression*. The *affective* (emotional) excitation associated with such unacceptable ideas is also forced out of consciousness. However, the excitation remains active and can be *converted* into a somatic form that results in the innervation of the organs that manifest the hysterical symptoms. The form of hysteria characterized by bodily dysfunctions thus came to be designated as *conversion hysteria*.

Freud found that some patients could not be hypnotized, while some who could be hypnotized could not recover their repressed memories. However, by urging a patient to relax and to say whatever came to mind—the psychoanalytic technique that became known as *free association*—Freud found that he could piece together fragmentary hints of the repressed complex of unconscious ideas. The patient's resistance to becoming aware of the repressed ideas could be circumvented when the analyst's interpretations gradually helped the patient see the unconscious meanings of his own words. The symptoms could be relieved when the patient gained enough insight to make the repressed ideas and affect conscious.

Types of Neurosis

In a publication of 1894, Freud distinguished between *psychoneuroses,* which he thought resulted from defensive repression of unacceptable ideas, and other kinds of neuroses, which he called *actual neuroses.* Freud believed that actual neuroses were manifestations of the physiological pressures of sexual tension resulting from the blocking of orgasm, as in *coitus interruptus.* While the concept of the actual neurosis has never gained much acceptance, it remained an important contrast to the concept of *psycho*neurosis in Freud's writings.

Among the psychoneuroses, Freud distinguished *traumatic* or *retention* neuroses from the *defense* psychoneuroses which are the main focus of psychoanalytic theory. He considered traumatic or retention neurosis to involve a retention of affective excitation which had been aroused by traumatic stimuli but which had not been released at the appropriate time. Freud believed that these neuroses could be cured through abreaction.

Defense Psychoneuroses. It is Freud's theory of the defense psychoneuroses that forms the cornerstone of psychoanalytic theory. In the initial version of the theory, the term "defense" was virtually synonymous with "repression." In conversion hysteria, according to the theory, repression forced both the unacceptable idea and its affective excitation out of consciousness, but the affective excitation was converted into somatic excitation which, in turn, caused the innervation of bodily organs.

In broadening his theory of defense psychoneurosis to other conditions, Freud hypothesized that the capacity for conversion of affective excitation into somatic innervation was unique to people with a predisposition to hysteria, whether or not these people actually developed clinical symptoms. By contrast, observations of obsessional and phobic patients led him to conclude that, lacking the capacity for conversion, they could not exclude from the "psychical sphere" the affect attached to unacceptable ideas. Instead, repression acted to blot out the *connection* between the unacceptable idea and the affect attached to it. Obsessional and phobic patients, unlike hysterical patients, acknowledged remembering an unacceptable idea, but claimed that they had either not thought about it much or that they had managed to keep from thinking about it. The unacceptable idea thus remained accessible to consciousness in a weak, unemotional form, but the affect accompanying the unacceptable idea became attached to other, more acceptable ideas, causing the person to become obsessionally preoccupied with them. When anxiety was the affect that had been separated by repression from the original idea, its attachment to a new idea caused the person to become phobic toward whatever was represented by that new idea.

Hysterical, obsessional, and phobic symptoms were thus all assumed to result from unconscious conflict between the ego and ideas unacceptable to it, but the consequences of repression differed, partly because of pre-existing characteristics of the patient. Freud also hypothesized that hallucinatory psychoses could be explained by the same principles. In psychoses, repression of the unacceptable idea was so complete that every aspect of reality associated with the idea was systematically distorted or forced out of consciousness.

Libido Theory

Fundamental to Freud's conceptual model was his hypothetical construct of a quantity of affective excitation that could be converted into other forms, displaced, discharged, and attached to new ideas:

I should like . . . to dwell . . . on the working hypothesis which I have made use of in this exposition of the neuropsychoses of defense. I refer to the concept that in mental functions something is to be distinguished—a quota of affect or sum of excitation—which possesses all the characteristics of a quantity . . . which is capable of increase, diminution, displacement, and discharge, and which is spread over the memory traces of ideas somewhat as an electric charge is spread over the surface of a body.

This hypothesis . . . can be applied in the same sense as physicists apply the hypothesis of a flow of electric fluid. It is provisionally justified by its utility in co-ordinating and explaining a great variety of psychical states [Freud, 1894].

In every patient he analyzed, Freud found that the unacceptable ideas eliciting repression seemed to be sexual in nature. He also found that free association invariably elicited childhood memories of sexual seduction and that the formation of symptoms in adulthood seemed to occur in situations that reelicited the emotions first aroused during the childhood sexual experiences. However, upon further investigation of the childhood seductions, Freud found that many of them could not actually have taken place. He concluded that they were fantasies motivated by the patient's own sexual desires during childhood.

Following this conclusion, radical for his time, Freud attempted to reconstruct from his patient's free associations the developmental course of the psychological aspects of childhood sexuality. In his *Three Essays on the Theory of Sexuality* (1905), he laid out hypotheses that formed the conceptual framework of the psychoanalytic theory of *psychosexual development*, much as it remains today.

First, Freud proposed that the hypothetical quantity of affective excitation described above had its biological source in the sex *Trieb* (the German word for *drive*, often misleadingly translated as "instinct" or "instinctual drive"). His concept of the sex drive extended well beyond traditional notions of genital sexual desires, however, and included forms of pleasure obtainable through nongenital bodily stimulation.

Second, he gave the name *libido* to the hypothetical quantity of excitation or energy arising from the sex drive. He employed the term *object* to refer to the person toward whom a libidinal impulse was directed, and he called the investment of libido in the mental representation of an object *cathexis*.

Third, having assumed a permanent biological source for libido, Freud proposed that all the observed phenomena and inferred processes of neurotic and psychotic disorders should be expressed in terms of the distribution of libido. He later proposed that aggressive impulses came from a second instinctual drive, "the death instinct," but this has not received much theoretical elaboration.

Libidinal Phases. Freud hypothesized that the primary focus of libidinal arousal progressed in phases from one sensitive body area (erogenous zone) to another over the course of early biological maturation. According to this hypothesis, the first phase, lasting until about age 18 months and designated as the *oral phase*, was characterized by preoccupation with the mouth, the stimulation obtained through it, and the activities carried out with it.

During the second phase, designated as the *anal phase* and lasting from age 18 months to three years, stimulation and activities of the anal area were the focus of libidinal arousal.

During the third phase, designated as the *phallic phase* and lasting from about age three to five years, the penis of the boy and the clitoris of the girl became the foci of libidinal arousal. Like the mythical Greek King Oedipus who killed his father and married his mother, the boy was hypothesized to seek the exclusion of his father in order to seduce his mother, while the girl sought the reverse. However, fear of punishment by the same-sex parent—castration in the boy and the feeling by the girl that she had already been castrated—forced the child to repress his Oedipal wishes.

Repression was portrayed as holding the libidinal impulses in check and diverting them to constructive activities of learning and socialization during the *latency* period, from about age five to puberty. The process of diverting libido into constructive activity was referred to as *sublimation*.

At puberty, the upsurge of libido accompanying sexual maturation was hypothesized to cause a renewal of the struggle between the ego and libidinal impulses. Several outcomes of this struggle were possible: (1) discharge of libido through genital relations with a member of the opposite sex; (2) fixation at or regression to infantile modes of libidinal discharge, considered to be perversions in adults; or (3) psychoneurosis, in which repression prevents libidinal discharge and forces it into substitute channels that produce psychoneurotic symptoms. Psychoneurotic symptoms were thus considered to be *substitute* manifestations of impulses that were libidinally motivated.

Symptom Formation

According to the early psychodynamic model, repression is a necessary precondition for psychoneurotic symptoms, but it does not by itself determine the form those symptoms will take. Instead, symptoms are formed as compromises with or substitutions for repressed impulses that threaten to break through the barrier of repression. Factors such as the exact nature of the repressed impulses, the presence or absence of ability for conversion, constitutional differences in drive strength, and specific experiences that have influenced libidinal organization during psychosexual development all influence the form symptomatic compromises or substitutions take when the ego is threatened by the *return of the repressed*. To use Freud's terminology, the final form symptoms take is *overdetermined,* i.e., determined by multiple factors.

Anxiety

During the first 20 years of psychoanalysis, Freud and his coworkers were primarily occupied with demonstrating the existence of repressed motives and the basis of adult neurosis in childhood sexuality, and with the development of psychoanalytic organizations and treatment procedures. However, Freud gradually turned his attention to a problem that was to become central in later conceptions of neurosis. This was the problem of *anxiety*. Freud distinguished *psychoneurotic anxiety* from *realistic anxiety,* which is a response to objective danger, and from *anxiety arising somatically* from the blockage of libidinal discharge in actual neuroses. He also described three forms of psychoneurotic anxiety:

1. free-floating anxiety that was ready to attach itself to any one of a large number of situations the patient thought of;
2. anxiety attached to a specific phobic object or situation;
3. a state of anxious apprehension that did not seem to become attached to any particular idea (Freud, 1917).

Freud's general hypothesis as to the source of psychoneurotic anxiety was that repressed instinctual drives that threatened to break through repression were converted into the affect of anxiety (Freud, 1915). Thus, like the anxiety he observed in the actual neuroses, psychoneurotic anxiety was considered to be a toxic endproduct of blocked libido.

Personality Structure

A change in Freud's thinking about psychoneurotic anxiety accompanied his proposal (1923) that mental functioning could be viewed in terms of three distinct structural entities:

1. the *id,* which embodies the instinctual impulses, aggressive as well as sexual;
2. the *ego,* the coherent executive organization of mental processes which is the seat of consciousness and perception, which controls voluntary activity, and from which proceed repressions against id impulses unacceptable to it;
3. the *superego,* or *ego ideal,* a precipitate in the ego which is formed when the child resolves his Oedipus complex by incorporating the moral standards and prohibitions he associates with his same-sex parent.

Because he believed that guilt was produced by the ego's failure to meet the standards imposed by the superego, Freud now saw in the conflict between ego and superego another possible source of anxiety. He interpreted the excessive guilt found in many neurotics as indicating that neurotic anxiety was supplemented by the fears of castration, conscience, and death embodied in the superego.

Summary of Freud's First Theory of Neurosis

The main points of Freud's theory of psychoneurosis prior to the major revision he made in 1926 can be summarized as follows:

1. *Defense psychoneuroses* resulted from conflict between the ego and impulses that were unacceptable to it.
2. The ego defended against unacceptable impulses by *repression.*
3. In *hysterical* neuroses, the affective excitation attached to the unacceptable impulses was *converted* to somatic innervation that produced bodily symptoms such as paralyses, anesthesias, and other dysfunctions; in *obsessional* and *phobic* neuroses, repression separated the affective excitation from the unacceptable impulse, but the affective excitation remained in the psychical sphere and became attached to other ideas.
4. The quantity of affective excitation embodied in id impulses was given the name of *libido* and was hypothesized to have its biological source in the sex drive.
5. Observed phenomena and inferred processes of the neuroses and psychoses were to be explained in terms of the distribution of libido.

6. The libido was hypothesized to go through *oral, anal,* and *phallic* phases, followed by relatively successful repression during the *latency* period and a renewed upsurge at puberty.

7. The outcome of the struggle between the ego and the increased libidinal impulses at puberty determined whether an adult's libido would be discharged through mature genital sexuality, would regress to or remain fixated at earlier stages of expression (i.e., would be perverted), or would be blocked by excessive repression, resulting in neurotic symptoms.

8. Symptoms were seen as *overdetermined substitutions for* or *compromises with* repressed libidinal impulses.

9. Undischarged libido was transformed into *neurotic anxiety.*

10. The id-ego-superego theory of personality structure implied that excessive guilt observed in neurotics might be due to the augmentation of neurotic anxiety by fears of castration, conscience, or death embodied in the superego.

FREUD'S REVISED THEORY OF NEUROSIS

Anxiety

With the publication of *Inhibition, Symptoms, and Anxiety* (1926a), Freud made a number of changes in his theory that put together many of the old elements in new ways. He now hypothesized that anxiety states were reproductions of the physiological and psychological responses every human being has experienced during the trauma of birth, when sudden separation from the intrauterine environment, mechanical pressure of the birth process, deprivation of oxygen, and change of temperature elicit emergency physiological reactions such as rapid respiration and heartbeat, as well as, presumably, an overwhelming sense of helplessness. Just as objective danger situations can continue throughout life to elicit these reactions in proportion to the degree of trauma threatened, so, Freud hypothesized, can situations and instinctual impulses that are not actually dangerous, but that are associated with situations that seemed dangerous in childhood.

Typical danger situations of childhood that can threaten to reach traumatic proportions and that can continue to be sources of anxiety included: (1) separation from the mother, resulting in potentially traumatic overwhelming of the immature ego when biological needs are not satisfied; (2) upsurges of libidinal drives that might overwhelm the adaptive mechanisms of the immature ego; and (3) the threats of castration or withdrawal of love as punishment for the expression of libidinal impulses.

Signal anxiety. Now viewing psychoneurotic anxiety as a response of the ego to threatened re-creation of dangers faced in childhood, Freud reversed his earlier theory of the relations between repression and anxiety. Rather than considering anxiety to be a toxic *endproduct* of repression, he now hypothesized that anxiety aroused by stimuli associated with childhood dangers *instigated* repression by goading the ego into defending against the potentially dangerous impulse or situation before it could become traumatic. The relatively small degree of anticipatory anxiety that instigated defensive action was called *signal anxiety,* because it served as an advance signal of impending danger.

Defense

A second innovation in Freud's theory was that he now broadened the concept of defense to include techniques other than repression that the ego could use to avoid traumatic anxiety. He had previously mentioned many of these techniques but had heretofore regarded them as secondary devices for helping to prevent the return to consciousness of impulses that had been repressed. Defense mechanisms besides repression included *reaction forma-tion*—replacement in consciousness of a threatening impulse with its opposite; *undoing*—ritualistic reversal or undoing of acts or events that elicited anxiety; and *isolation*—preventing an anxiety-arousing situation from leading to further anxiety-arousing thoughts or events by interposing after it a period in which nothing must happen. (Isolation later came to refer also to the repression or isolation of affect connected with a threatening thought.)

Symptom Formation

If anxiety were indeed the stimulus that elicited the ego's defensive efforts, rather than being the endproduct of repressed libido, then a new conception of psychoneurotic symptoms was implied. Instead of being compromises with or substitutes for libidinal impulses, symptoms were now viewed as contrivances of the ego for avoiding the danger situation signaled by the signal anxiety when initial defensive measures failed to eliminate the anxiety. Symptoms thus functioned to help the ego avoid or reduce anxiety, rather than solely as substitute or compromise techniques for discharging libido. However, symptoms were still considered to be overdetermined by the nature of the threatened danger, the strength and nature of the impulses associated with it, constitutional factors, the individual's previous experience in warding off the danger, and current reality.

The Case of "Little Hans." The contrast between Freud's initial and later theories of neurosis and symptom formation is nicely illustrated by his own reinterpretation of cases that he had previously reported. One was the famous case of "Little Hans," whose horse phobia and its treatment by his father under Freud's direction had been detailed by Freud in a lengthy report of 1909. The case was of great significance because it revealed Freud's hypothesized Oedipal dynamics at work in a child rather than through reconstructions by adults during analytic treatment. It showed the child's concern with sexual matters, his concern about the absence of a penis in females, his fear of castration as a retaliation for masturbating and for having sexual desires toward his mother, and his fear and hostility toward his father. Since the parents took part in the treatment, family dynamics and many details of the child's experience were also more directly revealed than was possible when only reports by the patient were available.

Long before the outbreak of the horse phobia, Hans's parents had recorded their observations of the child's behavior and these were made available to Freud. When he was two, Hans showed a lively interest in his "widdler," his word for penis. He asked his mother if she had one and, upon seeing a cow being milked, he exclaimed, "Oh, look! There's milk coming out of its widdler!" (Freud, 1909, p. 7). When Hans was three and a half, his mother, finding him fondling his penis, threatened that she would have "Dr. A." cut it off. Freud interpreted this event as being the source of Hans's castration complex.

Hans's curiosity about widdlers remained unquenched and he excitedly exclaimed about the sizes of widdlers on various animals he observed. When asked by his mother why he was so intent on seeing her undress, he replied that he wanted to see her widdler, which he thought must be as big as a horse's since she was so big. When Hans observed his baby sister being bathed, he remarked, ". . . her widdler's still quite small. When she grows up it'll get bigger alright." Three months later, he said in a pitying voice, "She *has* got a tiny little widdler," and made a similar observation with respect to a doll he undressed.

Hans became very affectionate toward other children, hugging them and begging to sleep with a particular 14-year-old girl. He also seemed to fall completely in love with an eight-year-old girl, blushed in her presence, and talked about kissing her and sleeping with her.

Hans sometimes fretted about what would happen if his mother went away and he had no mother to "coax with" (caress). On these occasions, his mother had often taken him into her bed. When Hans was four and three-quarters, he had a nightmare from which he woke up crying and said to his mother: "When I was asleep I thought you were gone and I had no mummy to coax with."

Some days later, Hans came into his mother's bed, saying, "Do you know what Aunt M. said? She said: 'He *has* got a dear little thingummy [penis],'" which is what his visiting aunt had indeed remarked when she saw him being bathed four weeks previously. Two days later, on his daily walk with his nursemaid, he began to cry to be taken home so he could coax with his mother. The next day, his mother took him out herself to see why he now resisted his walk. This time, after much uneasiness, he expressed the fear that a horse would bite him. At bedtime he again wanted to coax with his mother. He then cried about the prospect of having to go out the next day and later expressed the fear that a horse would come into his room. These symptoms continued and intensified.

Freud's original interpretation was as follows:

The disorder set in with thoughts that were at the same time fearful and tender, and then followed an anxiety dream on the subject of losing his mother and so not being able to coax with her anymore. His affection for his mother must therefore have become enormously intensified. . . . It was this increased affection for his mother which turned suddenly into anxiety. . . . Han's anxiety, which thus corresponded to a repressed erotic longing, was like every infantile anxiety without an object to begin with; it was still anxiety and not yet fear. The child cannot tell (at first) what he is afraid of. . . .

. . . the states into which he fell . . . before going to sleep . . . were characterized by anxiety mixed with tenderness. These states show that at the beginning of his illness there was as yet no phobia whatever present, whether of streets or of walking or even of horses. If there had been, his evening states would be inexplicable; for who bothers at bedtime about streets and walking? On the other hand it becomes quite clear why he was so fearful in the evening, if we suppose that at bedtime [a time when he had previously admitted to fondling his penis] he was overwhelmed by an intensification of his libido—for its object was his mother, and its aim may perhaps have been to sleep with her. . . .

His anxiety . . . corresponded to repressed longing. But it was not the same thing as the longing. . . . Longing can be completely transformed into satisfaction if it is presented with the object longed for . . . anxiety remains even when longing can be satisfied. . . . It can no longer be completely retransformed into libido; there is something that keeps the libido back under repression. This was shown . . . on the occasion of his next walk when his mother went with him. He was with his mother, and yet he still suffered from the anxiety—that is to say, from an unsatisfied longing for her. . . . But his anxiety had stood the test; and the next thing for it to do was to find an object. It was on this walk that he first expressed a fear that a horse would bite him. Where did the material for this phobia come from? Probably from the complexes . . . which had contributed to the repression and were keeping under repression his libidinal feelings towards his mother [Freud, 1909].

Much of the rest of the case history is taken up with unraveling the details of how horses came to be selected as the phobic objects that helped the child justify his anxiety. The choice of horses was shown to be overdetermined by Hans's initial interest in their large widdlers; his association of his mother's size with a horse's size and his inference that her penis should therefore be as large as a horse's; his having been distressed by seeing a horse fall and by seeing a friend who played horsie falling in a similar fashion; his father having been the first to play horsie with him; his association of his father's black mustache with the muzzles worn by horses; and warnings about being bitten by a particular white horse, warnings that happened to have been phrased in the same way as his mother's warnings not to touch his penis.

Hans's reactions to the interpretations made to him by his father at Freud's suggestion and, on one occasion, by Freud himself, appeared to confirm that he had indeed projected onto horses the anxiety aroused by his repressed libidinal impulses toward his mother and by the repressed fear and hostility toward his beloved father which accompanied these impulses. In his discussion at the end of the case history, Freud summarized his theory of what he then called "anxiety hysteria" (now more often known as *phobic neurosis*):

An anxiety hysteria tends to develop more and more into a phobia. In the end the patient may have got rid of all his anxiety, but only at the price of subjecting himself to all kinds of inhibitions and restrictions. From the outset in anxiety hysteria the mind is constantly at work in the direction of once more psychically binding the anxiety which has become liberated; but this work can neither bring about a retransformation of the anxiety into libido, nor can it establish any contact with the complexes which were the source of libido. Nothing is left for it but to cut off access to every possible occasion that might lead to the development of anxiety, by erecting mental barriers in the nature of precautions, inhibitions, or prohibitions; and it is these defensive structures that appear to us in the form of phobias and that constitute to our eyes the essence of the disease [Freud, 1909].

The phobic symptom as a compromise which provided Hans with a justification for his anxiety while it simultaneously helped hold the repressed impulses in check and permitted some libidinal gratification was analyzed thusly:

. . . the essence of Hans's illness was entirely dependent upon the nature of the instinctual components that had to be repulsed. The content of his phobia was such as to impose a very great measure of restriction upon his freedom of movement, and that was its purpose. It was therefore a powerful reaction against the obscure impulses to movement which were especially directed against his mother. For Hans horses had always typified pleasure in movement . . . but since this pleasure in movement included the impulse to copulate, the neurosis imposed a restriction on it and exalted the horse into an emblem of terror. Thus it would seem as though all that the repressed instincts got from the neurosis was the honour of providing pretexts for the appearance of anxiety in consciousness. But however clear may have been the victory in Hans's phobia of the forces that were opposed to sexuality, nevertheless, since such an illness is in its very nature a compromise, this cannot have been all that the repressed instincts obtained. After all, Hans's phobia of horses was an obstacle to his going into the street, and could serve as a means of allowing him to stay at home with his beloved mother. In this way, therefore, his affection for his mother triumphantly achieved its aim. In consequence of his phobia, the lover clung to the object of his love—though to be sure, steps had been taken to make him innocuous [Freud, 1909].[1]

1 Quotations from Freud excerpted from Chapter IV, "The Defence Neuro-Psychoses," in Vol. I of *Collected Papers of Sigmund Freud*, edited by Ernest Jones, M.D., translation under the supervision of Joan Riviere, and from Chapter II, "Analysis of a Phobia in a Five-year-old Boy," in Vol. III of *Collected Papers of Sigmund Freud*, edited by Ernest Jones, M.D., translation by Alix and James Strachey. Published by Basic Books, Inc., by arrangement with The Hogarth Press, Ltd., and the Institute of Psycho-Analysis, London, and reprinted by permission.

Revised Interpretation. In his 1926 reinterpretation of the process of symptom formation, Freud rejected his earlier contention that Hans's anxiety had arisen from the process of repression or from the libido of the repressed impulses. Instead, he maintained that fear of castration was the source of Hans's anxiety and this was what motivated his ego to repress both sexual impulses toward his mother and aggressive impulses against his father. Since thinking of the beloved father as a source of danger and a target of aggression were both unacceptable, a symbolic substitute in the form of horses was created when repression alone had failed to eliminate the anxiety-arousing impulses. The choice of horses as the phobic objects was over-determined by many of the factors detailed in the 1909 report, although Freud maintained that children's animal phobias were generally symbolic of castration fears.

Freud identified two advantages achieved through the substitution of a fear of being bitten by a horse for the fear of being castrated by the father:

1. Fearing horses rather than his father avoided the conflict between Hans's love for his father and the fear and hostility toward his father which resulted from his libidinal impulses toward his mother.
2. Thinking of horses as the source of his anxiety made it possible for Hans to avoid further anxiety simply by avoiding horses.

In effect, according to Freud, what Hans perceived as an objective external danger of castration was replaced by the objective external danger of being bitten by a horse.

Summary of Freud's Second Theory of Neurosis

Freud's second theory of anxiety and neurotic symptom formation held that:

1. The physiological and psychological characteristics of anxiety were miniature reproductions of the reactions experienced during the birth trauma.
2. Potentially traumatic danger situations, such as separation from the mother and threats of castration during childhood, produced anxiety reactions similar to the reaction experienced during the birth trauma.
3. Libidinal impulses and other stimuli previously associated with childhood danger situations triggered a small amount of *signal anxiety* in the ego; the discomfort caused by the signal anxiety prodded the ego to employ defensive mechanisms, e.g., *repression, reaction formation, undoing,* and *isolation,* against the threatening stimuli, lest they lead to the previously experienced danger situations.
4. Psychoneurotic symptoms were overdetermined devices created by the ego for avoiding further increases in anxiety when initial defensive measures against the anxiety-arousing stimulus failed.

THE EGO AND THE MECHANISMS OF DEFENSE

In a book bearing the above title, Anna Freud (1936) elaborated considerably upon her father's conceptions of the ego and its defensive functions. Much of the book was based upon psychoanalytic work with children, which she had been among the first to begin on a formal basis in the 1920s. Besides emphasizing clinical observations and analysis of children as a basis for theory, the book was innovative in making the ego rather than unconscious id impulses the focus of interest. Miss Freud maintained that many analysts had previously reserved the term "psychoanalysis" exclusively for the study of repressed instinctual impulses, affects, and infantile fantasies, and that analysts had been too unconcerned with problems of the patient's adjustment to current reality. Her own focus on the ego as both the medium through which other aspects of personality were revealed and the agency that mediated the demands of id, superego, and reality was characteristic of a new trend in psychoanalytic theory that became known as *ego psychology*.

Emphasis on the ego, however, did not mean abandoning the analytic goal of identifying and interpreting unconscious mental activity. On the contrary, the task of the analyst was enlarged to include bringing into consciousness the unconscious activities of the ego. These unconscious activities were viewed as being primarily defensive operations taken to avoid anxiety. They could be exposed to the analyst through the kinds of resistance the ego put up to prevent unconscious id impulses from becoming conscious. In the adult, interruptions in a train of free associations were taken to signify that anxiety-arousing ideas were nearing consciousness. The way in which the patient avoided approaching these ideas could show what defense mechanisms he characteristically used to deal with dangerous impulses. Exposure of these defense mechanisms allowed the analyst to deduce the particular way in which the patient's ego had formed his neurotic symptoms.

Interpretation to the patient of his techniques for avoiding anxiety-arousing thoughts could lead him to insight into his defense mechanisms as well as to eventual insight into the unconscious impulses he was defending against, his superego prohibitions, and the explanations for his neurotic symptoms.

With child patients, the technique of free association was not feasible in its pure form, but id impulses were hypothesized to be more clearly revealed in children than in adults by dreams, day-dreams, play, and drawings. In the absence of free association, means other than interruptions of free association were sought for identifying defensive operations in the egos of child patients. A means proposed by Melanie Klein (1932), another early child analyst, was the observation of interruptions and inhibitions in the child's use of toys provided in the therapy room. These interruptions and inhibitions were assumed to have the same meanings as interruptions in the free associations of adults occurring when anxiety-arousing ideas approached consciousness.

Another means for identifying the ego's characteristic defensive operations, a means favored by Miss Freud, was to note unusual reactions by the child to events that were normally expected to have particular emotional consequences. For example, if a child reacted with excessive tenderness where jealousy was to be expected, it was inferred that the ego had intervened and the ego's techniques for avoiding an anxiety-arousing affect could be identified and brought to consciousness through interpretation.

In keeping with her attention to analysis of the ego and its defensive operations, Miss Freud enumerated the various defense mechanisms that were by then becoming part of analytic theory. These included the four mentioned by her father in 1926, i.e.. *repression, reaction-formation, isolation,* and *undoing.* To these four she added:

> *denial*—of unpleasant facts;
>
> *displacement*—of an affect onto an object or person other than the appropriate one;
>
> *identification with the aggressor*—becoming like the person, especially a parent, who threatens one;
>
> *intellectualization*—binding of instinctual drives in intellectual activities;
>
> *introjection*—incorporating the demands of another person, especially a parent, as if they were one's own so that one reacts against forbidden impulses according to the other's demands, whether or not he is present;
>
> *projection*—attributing one's own forbidden impulses to an external object or person;
>
> *regression*—to earlier modes of functioning;
>
> *reversal*—of one's impulse into the reaction that should be felt if the impulse were directed from outside against oneself;
>
> *sublimation*—channeling instinctual drives into culturally valued activities;
>
> *turning against the self*—re-directing against the self aggressive impulses that were originally aimed at others.

As an illustration of how several defense mechanisms are generally employed together, Miss Freud returned to the horse phobia of Little Hans:

Here we have a clinical example of simultaneous defensive processes directed respectively inwards and outwards. We are told that the little boy's neurosis was based on impulses quite normally associated with the Oedipus complex. He loved his mother and out of jealousy adopted an aggressive attitude toward his father which, secondarily, came into conflict with his tender affection for him. These aggressive impulses roused his castration-anxiety—which he experienced as objective anxiety—and so the various mechanisms of defense were set in motion. The methods employed by his neurosis were *displacement*—from his father to the anxiety-animal —and *reversal* of his own threat to his father, that is to say, its transformation into anxiety lest he himself should be threatened by his father. Finally, to complete the distortion of the real picture, there was *regression* to the oral level: the idea of being bitten. The mechanisms employed fulfilled perfectly their purpose of warding off the instinctual impulses; the prohibited libidinal love for his mother and the dangerous aggressiveness towards his father vanished from consciousness. His castration-anxiety in relation to his father was bound in the symptom of a fear of horses but, in accordance with the mechanism of phobia, anxiety-attacks were avoided by means of a neurotic inhibition—Little Hans gave up going out of doors [A. Freud, 1936, pp. 75–76].[2]

Later Developments in Ego Psychology

The most notable attempts to extend orthodox psychoanalytic theory have been in the area of ego psychology. While proposals in this area have not changed the basic psychodynamic theory of neurosis, they have aimed at broadening psychoanalytic theory into a general psychology that might provide better guidelines for understanding individual development and for modifying the goals and techniques of treatment. Only the proposals that have had the most direct bearing on analytic thinking about children's development are dealt with here.

Freud originally maintained that the ego developed solely out of the conflict between the id's demands for immediate satisfaction and the organism's need to adapt to reality in order to survive. For example, he hypothesized that thinking, one of the most important ego functions, originated when the hungry infant hallucinated his mother's breast to temporarily satisfy id demands for food when none was available. In the course of successive conflicts between id demands and reality constraints, the hallucinatory process became more highly developed and more independent of immediate conflict to the point where it provided a basis for symbolic representation of future possibilities. Thinking became rational when the child learned to use words to represent reality mentally. Other ego functions such as memory, perception, and motility were hypothesized to develop analogously out of conflicts between the child's id demands and reality constraints that made techniques for delay, substitution, and circumvention of id demands advantageous for adaptation.

Ego Psychology and the Problem of Adaptation

Until about the time of Freud's death in 1939, psychoanalysis concentrated on the various manifestations of the id's power in its conflicts with the ego. The id–ego struggle was repeatedly illustrated in examples derived from free association, slips of the tongue, dream analysis, and symptom formation. However, the shift of focus to the ego made in Anna Freud's (1936) book, *The Ego and the Mechanisms of Defense,* was followed up by Heinz

---

[2] Anna Freud, *The Ego and the Mechanisms of Defense,* translation by Cecil Baines. ⓒ 1946 by International Universities Press and reprinted by permission.

Hartmann in his book, *Ego Psychology and the Problem of Adaptation* (1939), and in a series of articles (Hartmann, 1950a, 1950b, 1964).

Since psychoanalytic evidence from free association, slips of the tongue, dream analysis, and symptom formation dealt with conditions in which the ego is not functioning at its strongest, and since ego functioning does not usually reveal conflict, Hartmann suggested looking beyond conflictual situations in order to understand the structure and origins of the ego. He singled out two questions in particular:

1. Does the ego originate solely from the conflict between id demands and the child's need to adapt to reality?
2. What is the source of the energy that enables the ego to maintain all of the complex functions attributed to it?

Origins of Ego Functions

Ego Functions Having Primary Autonomy. Hartmann proposed that many of the ego's functions ordinarily develop and operate independently of id-reality conflicts. He chose the term *conflict-free sphere of the ego* for the collection of functions which at any moment might be operating relatively independently of conflicts. Among the ego functions that are normally conflict-free he included perception, intention, thinking, language, recall, motor development, grasping, crawling, walking, and many maturational and learning processes. He maintained that, rather than being an outgrowth of conflict, the potential for developing these functions is present from the beginning of life. Moreover, a number of them, such as perception, memory, and associative learning, are *prerequisites* for, rather than byproducts of, the ego's relationships to instinctual drives and love objects. Accordingly, Hartmann hypothesized that rudimentary forms of these ego functions are, like the id drives, part of the heredity of the individual that has been shaped through evolution to enhance adaptation to the "average expectable environment." He referred to ego functions that do not arise out of conflict as having *primary autonomy*.

Ego Functions Having Secondary Autonomy. Besides ego functions having primary autonomy, Hartmann acknowledged that there are also ego functions that arise, as Freud had maintained, out of the organism's way of adapting to conflicts between id demands and reality constraints. These functions are mainly the defensive operations. However, according to Hartmann, these defensive operations can become general adaptive mechanisms in their own right and can function in the absence of the conflicts out of which they arose. For example, a child who handled his jealousy over a new sibling by becoming very loving (reaction formation) might continue to be loving because of the positive responses it earned from others. Functions that arise from conflict but become autonomous and eventually join the conflict-free sphere of the ego were said to have *secondary autonomy*.

Thus equipped with an array of conflict-free functions, some being auto-nomous from the beginning and some gaining autonomy after originating in conflict, the ego came to be considered an important subject of study in its own right, independent of its immediate conflicts with id impulses. An implication of this position is that progress in psychoanalytic ego theory will require attention to the ways in which man's repertoire of behavior is nor-mally put together over the course of development. As Hartmann (1950b) acknowledged, this brings the focus of psychoanalytic theory closer to the subject matter of developmental psychology and requires methods other than the traditional methods of psychoanalysis.

The Ego's Sources of Energy

Because psychoanalysis retained its dynamic model, which portrays be-havior as being motivated by the energy of the instinctual drives, the in-creasing complexity and autonomy ascribed to the ego raised the question of how its activities are energized. Freud's original theory was that the mental apparatus is powered by libido.

Since attributing all motives to instinctual impulses was incompatible with his later concept of the ego as the source of defensive operations *against* instinctual impulses, Freud proposed that some libido became temporarily *neutralized,* i.e., became free of its erotic aims and available for other pur-poses. This neutralized libidinal energy was hypothesized to power the ego's activities.

There are suggestions by both Freud and Hartmann that, since ego activi-ties may be pleasurable in their own right, the ego might also have some independent energy of its own (cf. Hartmann, 1964). However, Hartmann (Hartmann, Kris, & Loewenstein, 1949) extended Freud's original concept of neutralized libido only to contend that the ego's energy was derived from the aggressive as well as the sexual drive and that such energy could be permanently rather than just temporarily neutralized.

Because some of the autonomous ego functions were portrayed as oper-ating from the first days of life and because the notions of neutraliza-tion of energy were becoming increasingly incompatible with modern physio-logical concepts, other theorists have proposed that the ego be regarded as having its own instinctual energy from the beginning. These proposals have included an *instinct-to-master* (Hendrick, 1943), an *urge-to-motility* (Mittelmann, 1954), and an *effectance motive* or motive to achieve compe-tence (White, 1963).

A somewhat different direction was taken by David Rapaport. Until his premature death in 1960, Rapaport attempted to extend psychoanalytic ego psychology by treating various cognitive functions as if they were inde-pendent of drive states altogether and by constructing a psychoanalytic theory of learning (Rapaport, 1967, posthumous).

ERIK ERIKSON'S THEORY OF PSYCHOSOCIAL DEVELOPMENT

One of the best-known contemporary contributors to psychoanalytic thinking is Erik H. Erikson. His book, *Childhood and Society* (1950; second edition 1963), has become a staple in college courses on child development and abnormal psychology, as well as being widely read in professional circles. In many respects, Erikson's work can be considered an extension of ego psychology because he focuses upon the developing ego, its conflicts, and its sense of identity.

Stages of Psychosocial Development

On the basis of observations made in diverse cultural settings, Erikson has hypothesized a series of developmental stages that represent the typical ways in which the child's unfolding biological needs and capacities engage him in patterns of interaction with the adults around him. He specifies the origins of these patterns of interaction in terms of three components:

> *zones* of the child's body, corresponding roughly to the erogenous zones of Freud's psychosexual theory;
> *modes* of action the child employs;
> *modalities* of social interaction which the child learns as outgrowths of the interpersonal exchanges occurring around his various modes of action.

Erikson summarizes his hypothetical sequence of zone-mode-modality development in terms of the ways in which various modes of action, centered in particular zones, become prototypes for social modalities.

Oral-Sensory Stage I—Getting. The zone of greatest initial importance is what Erikson calls the *oral-sensory zone.* This includes the facial apertures and the upper nutritional organs. The first general mode of approach for the infant is *incorporation,* because the infant's greatest needs are to incorporate input from the world. Food from the mother is the most obvious input the infant incorporates, but Erikson stresses that the skin and sense organs also hunger for proper stimulation. For this reason, he refers to the first stage as the *oral-sensory stage,* rather than just the "oral stage," as Freud called it.

When all goes well with the child and his mother's relation to him as provider, the incorporative mode remains dominant during this stage and the child learns the basic social modality that Erikson designates as *getting,* i.e., being successful in receiving what is given to him and in getting other people to give him what he needs. When all does not go well, because of the mother's failures at providing or the child's failures at receiving—for physiological or temperamental reasons—other modes may inappropriately dominate. For example, the *eliminative mode,* normally dominant at a later stage, may prematurely dominate in a child who repeatedly thrusts out food after intake. Such an occurrence interferes with the child's learning the social modality of getting and this may obstruct later personality development.

Oral-Sensory Stage II—Taking.   The second stage hypothesized by Erikson is a continuation of the oral-sensory stage and incorporation remains the dominant mode.   However, the incorporative activities are now biting and sensory-motor activity directed at grasping and discerning specific stimuli.   Erikson refers to the social modality arising from the *active incorporative* mode as *taking*.   He believes that progress through this stage normally involves some trauma for the child, including the pain of teething, conflict with his mother over weaning, and the likelihood that his mother will devote less attention to him.

Anal-Urethral-Muscular Stage.   Erikson hypothesizes a third stage of development focused in the *anal-urethral zone*.   Two conflicting modes of action, *retention* and *elimination,* become crucial during this stage.   Children in all societies are likely to experience this stage in some form when maturation brings well-formed stools, the musculature for sphincter control, and general muscle development that gives the child power over his environment through holding on and pushing away.   Because of these developments, Erikson calls this the *anal-urethral-muscular stage,* in contrast to the Freudian term "anal stage."

Western society, with its demands for strict control over when and where feces and urine are voided, makes more of an issue over these functions than do most other societies.   Erikson calls the social modalities developed from the retention and elimination modes *holding on* and *letting go*.   He maintains that the social and individual forces determining the relative balance between the two social modalities during this stage will influence the relative dominance of the two in later life as well.

Locomotor and Infantile Genital Stage.   In the fourth stage hypothesized by Erikson, the *genital zone* becomes especially interesting and sensitive to children of both sexes. Sexual curiosity, erotic genital sensations, and the Oedipus complex all become factors in behavior.   However, because the child's freedom of locomotion also increases markedly, Erikson refers to the stage as the *locomotor and infantile genital stage,* rather than as the "phallic stage" referred to by Freud.   Erikson maintains that the dominant mode of action is usually *intrusive,* as suggested "in ambulatory exuberance, in aggressive mentality, and in sexual fantasies and activities" (Erikson, 1963, p. 88).

It is in this stage that the experience of girls and boys is said to diverge decisively:

Girls often undergo a sobering change at this stage, because they observe sooner or later that although their locomotor, mental, and social intrusiveness is as vigorous as that of the boys', thus permitting them to become perfectly good tomboys, they lack one item, the penis, and, with it, important prerogatives in most cultures and classes. While the boy has this visible, erectable, and comprehensible organ to which he can attach dreams of adult bigness, the girl's clitoris only poorly sustains dreams of sexual equality, and she does not even have breasts as analogously tangible tokens of her future. The idea of her eventual *inception* of the intruding phallus is as yet too frightening, and her maternal drives are relegated to play fantasy or baby tending. On the other hand, where mothers dominate households the boy can develop a sense of inadequacy because he learns at this stage that while he can do well outside in play and work, he will never boss the house, his mother, or his older sisters. His mother and sisters may, in fact, get even with him for their doubts in themselves by making him feel that a boy is really a somewhat repulsive creature [Erikson, 1968, pp. 117–18].[3]

The social modality of the locomotor and infantile genital stage is what Erikson calls *making,* in the sense of "being on the make." For both sexes, this involves "head-on attack, enjoyment of competition, insistence on goal, pleasure of conquest [Erikson, 1963, p. 90]." In the boy, the emphasis is on "making" by phallic-intrusive means. In the girl, by contrast, it changes to "making" by teasing, provoking, or snaring through making herself attractive and endearing. This represents a partial reversion to the incorporative modes originally developed in oral and sensory areas. The girl is likely to become more dependent and demanding and is permitted to do so except in cultures that cultivate intrusive and locomotor behavior in girls.

Rudimentary Genital Stage. Erikson calls his fifth hypothetical stage the *rudimentary genital stage.* Here the normally dominant mode is *generativity* for both sexes, with male generativity being primarily *intrusive* and female being *inclusive,* both being oriented toward an eventual coming together in procreation. Although Erikson does not designate it as a "modality," *genital mutuality* is the normal social pattern to be developed in this stage. Erikson maintains that all adult neurotics are handicapped in their sexual lives by traces of pregenital modes of incorporation, retention, elimination or intrusion which, rather than genital mutuality, dominate in their orientations toward sex.

Nuclear Conflicts During Development

In addition to the sequence of psychosocial stages in terms of zones, modes, and modalities, Erikson has proposed that there is a typical sequence of nuclear psychological conflicts or crises that humans face in the course of their development. The conflicts of childhood and early adulthood are closely related to the stages of psychosocial development. As with the progression of psychosocial stages, the exact resolution of each dominant conflict influences the form the next conflict will take and its possible resolutions.

---

[3] Erik H. Erikson, *Childhood and Society,* 2nd ed., rev. (New York: Norton, 1963). © 1950, 1963 by W. W. Norton & Co. and reprinted by permission.

It also influences the long process of the ego's formation of an identity for itself. Erikson's stress on interaction between the individual and society is illustrated in the assumptions that he says underlie his charting of such a sequence:

(1) that the human personality in principle develops according to steps prede- termined in the growing person's readiness to be driven toward, to be aware of, and to interact with, a widening social radius; and (2) that society, in principle, tends to be so constituted as to meet and invite this succession of potentialities for interaction and attempts to safeguard and to encourage the proper rate and the proper sequence of their unfolding [Erikson, 1963, p. 270].

Basic Trust Versus Mistrust.   The first nuclear conflict faced by the child is whether he will develop a sense of *basic trust or basic mistrust.* Smooth, loving, and mutually regulated interactions with his mother pro- duce comfortable satisfactions of basic needs which, in turn, lead the child to a sense of basic trust in his mother and the world she represents to him. As this trust develops, he can afford to let his mother out of his sight with- out undue anxiety because he forms an inner conviction that she will return. Failure to achieve basic trust results in a basic mistrust of the world and the people in it, and a lack of the earliest foundations of ego identity. These foundations are hypothesized to depend upon the formation of inner repre- sentations of predictable people and things in the real world.

Autonomy Versus Shame and Doubt.   The second nuclear conflict is associated with the muscular-anal stage and concerns the child's develop- ment of a sense of autonomy as he succeeds in meeting standards set for him by his parents and himself, especially in matters of toilet training. The child's failure to meet these standards because they are excessively high, because parental criticism is too harsh, or for other reasons can produce a fundamental sense of shame about himself and doubt about the value of what he does.

Initiative Versus Guilt.   The third nuclear conflict is associated with the locomotor-genital stage. It involves the child's development of initiative based upon confidence in his autonomy, capacities, and goals. The danger is that the child's aggressive initiatives will result in fear of real or fantasied consequences that can lead to guilt over his goals and the damaging effects his powers might have. This is especially true when the specific character- istics of a child's Oedipal situation lead to an excessively intense castration complex.

Industry Versus Inferiority.   This is the name Erikson has given to the nuclear conflict associated with the latency period. During this period, chil- dren in all cultures receive some form of systematic instruction. The child's ability to make use of this instruction is crucial in developing skills neces- sary for progress toward mature adult roles. Failure to develop culturally

TABLE 8–1

A summary of Anna Freud's Diagnostic Profile.

I. *Assessments of Development*

A. Drive Development

1. Libido

a. Phase development—Has child proceeded to age-adequate stage (oral, anal, etc.)? Is appropriate phase dominant? Regressed from his highest level to an earlier one?

b. Libido distribution—Is self cathected as well as object world? Is narcissism sufficient to insure self-esteem without overestimation of the self and undue independence of others?

c. Object libido—Have level and quality of object relations proceeded according to age? Regressed from his highest level to an earlier one? Do object relations correspond to the level of phase development?

2. Aggression

a. Are aggressive expressions present?

b. Does type of aggressive expression correspond to level of libido development?

c. Are the expressions directed toward object world or self?

B. Ego and Superego Development

1. Defects of ego apparatus serving perception, memory, etc.?

2. Status of ego functions (memory, reality testing, etc.)?

3. Are defenses directed against individual drives or against drive activity and instinctual pleasure in general? Are defenses age-adequate, too primitive, or too precocious? Is defense balanced, i.e., does ego have many important defenses available, or is it restricted to single ones? Is defense effective, especially in dealing with anxiety? Does it result in equilibrium, or disequilibrium, lability, or deadlock? Is defense against drives dependent on object world or on child's superego?

4. Any interference of defense activity with ego achievements?

II. *Regressions and Fixation Points*

Since it is assumed that all infantile neuroses are initiated by libido regressions to early fixation points, the location of these trouble spots in child's history is vital. These are betrayed by:

A. Forms of behavior which allow conclusions as to the repressed id processes; e.g., obsessional character where cleanliness, orderliness, punctuality, hoarding, doubt, etc. betray difficulty with impulses of anal-sadistic phase.

B. Fantasy activity revealed in personality tests and psychoanalysis.

---

valued skills can lead to a lasting sense of inferiority that will interfere with further development, often keeping the child fixated at the levels of infantile conflicts.

Identity Versus Role Confusion. At puberty, childhood ends and the nuclear conflict is one of *identity versus role confusion*. Formation of an ego identity at this point requires more than a summation of each of the identities formed by the outcomes of the previous conflicts. It also involves the ego's ability to integrate previous identities with the upsurge in libidinal demands at puberty, with basic aptitudes, and with the social-role oppor-

TABLE 8–1 (Cont.)

C. Symptoms having known relations to surface and depth determinants, such as symptoms of obsessional neurosis, but not symptoms, such as lying, stealing, and bed-wetting, which have a variety of causes.

III. *Dynamic and Structural Assessments (Conflicts)*

Behavior is governed by conflicts of internal with external forces or of internal forces with each other. Conflicts should be classified as:

A. External conflicts between id-ego agencies and object world (arousing fear).

B. Internalized conflicts between ego-superego and id after ego agencies have taken over in representing to the id the demands of the object world (arousing guilt).

C. Internal conflicts between incompatible drive representations, such as activity vs. passivity, masculinity vs. feminity, etc.

IV. *General Characteristics of the Child*

A. Level of frustration tolerance.

B. Degree of sublimation potential.

C. Overall attitude toward anxiety, e.g., whether child tends to actively master danger situations.

D. Relative strength of progressive devel-opmental forces vs. regressive tendencies in child's personality.

V. *Diagnosis*

Based on the foregoing assessments, the clinician must decide among diagnostic categorizations such as the following:

A. In spite of current behavior disturbance, personality growth is within the wide range of "normality."

B. Symptoms are of a transitory nature and can be classed as byproducts of de-velopmental strain.

C. There is a permanent drive regression to fixation points which leads to neurotic conflicts.

D. There is drive regression plus ego and superego regressions which lead to in-fantilisms, borderline psychotic, delinquent, or psychotic disturbances.

E. There are primary organic deficiencies or early deprivations which distort develop-ment and produce retarded, defective, and nontypical personalities.

F. There are destructive processes at work of organic, toxic, or psychic origin which have caused or are about to cause a dis-ruption of mental growth.

NOTE.—Adapted from A. Freud (1965, pp. 65–66). © 1965 by International Universities Press and reproduced by permission.

tunities that are available. Role confusion, sometimes reflected in doubts as to one's sexual identity and in delinquent and psychotic episodes, results if the adolescent fails to develop a sense of ego identity that gives him confidence in the continuity of his personal "sameness," as perceived by both himself and others.

Conflicts in Adulthood. The final three conflicts, *intimacy versus isolation, generativity versus stagnation,* and *ego integrity versus despair,* are hypothesized to be typical of adult development, although the outcomes of the child and adolescent conflicts are assumed to influence their forms and resolutions.

ANNA FREUD'S "DEVELOPMENTAL PROFILE"

As a continuing leader in the application of psychoanalytic treatment to children, Anna Freud has proposed adaptations of psychoanalytic theory for the conditions under which children are treated. Criticizing the use of adult diagnostic categories for children, Miss Freud advocates that the diagnosis of children's disorders be based upon the developmental sequence hypothesized by psychoanalytic theory. She maintains that pure description of a child's symptoms is useless and that analytic therapists should assess the child in terms of factors like his drive, ego, and superego development; the degree of stability of the borders between his id, ego, and superego; his degree of progress from primitive, id-dominated *(primary process)* thinking to rational, ego-dominated *(secondary process)* thinking; and his progress from seeking immediate gratification (the *pleasure principle*) to delaying immediate gratification in the interests of adaptation (the *reality principle*).

Developmental Profile

As a model for analytic diagnosis, Miss Freud offers a *developmental profile* which provides a basis for comparing a child's development to the normal developmental sequence. Table 8–1 presents the diagnostic profile in abbreviated form.

In effect, the developmental profile summarizes what Miss Freud considers to be the current state of analytic thinking as it applies to the diagnostic description of child psychopathology. Visible in the profile are the outlines of the psychoanalytic theories of the instinctual drives, including the sexual and the aggressive drive; the id-ego-superego personality structure; the ego's defenses and other functions; the basis of neurosis in libidinal regression and fixation; and the role of dynamic conflict in behavior.

The adaptation of these theories to child psychopathology is accompanied in Section IV of the profile by a sketch of the individual characteristics of the child patient that have bearing on his prognosis for improvement. It is accompanied in Section V by diagnostic categories that may be employed in deciding whether and how the child should be treated.

While the developmental profile provides a summary of the current state of Freudian psychoanalytic theory with respect to child analysis, there has been little published research on how a child's standing on each variable (e.g., libido distribution) is to be objectively determined, how the assessments of the child on all the variables taken together are to be synthesized, and how valid such a synthesis might be as an index of prognosis and a guide to the most appropriate treatment. Most publications on the profile present only an illustration of how it was filled out for a particular patient or how it might look for a particular type of patient (e.g., Heinicke, 1965; Laufer, 1965; Michaels & Stiver, 1965).

SUMMARY

Most *psychodynamically* oriented workers define *psychoneurosis* in terms of Freudian theory. Other theoretical viewpoints, such as those derived from learning theory, portray many of the same disorders in different terms.

In his earliest theory, Freud maintained that psychoneuroses resulted from *conflicts* between the *ego* and *id* impulses that the ego sought to *repress* because they were unacceptable to it. In *hysterical* neurosis, the repressed excitation behind unacceptable impulses was *converted* into somatic innervation that produced bodily symptoms. In *obsessional* and *phobic* neuroses, repression separated the excitation from the mental representations of the unacceptable impulses, but the excitation became attached to other ideas.

The sex drive was hypothesized to be the somatic source of the excitation behind repressed impulses. Freud sought to explain mental functioning in terms of the dynamics of *libido,* a hypothetical quantity of sexual energy. Freud later postulated an aggressive drive as another source of psychic energy. Libidinal arousal was hypothesized to be focused successively in the *oral, anal,* and *phallic* regions during early *psychosexual* development. *Neurotic conflicts* were considered to be based on *fixations* and *regressions* to conflicts associated with these foci. *Neurotic symptoms* were portrayed as *overdetermined* compromise expressions of, or substitutes for, repressed libidinal impulses. Libido blocked by repression was believed to be *transformed* into neurotic anxiety.

In 1926, Freud reversed the role attributed to neurotic anxiety. Rather than being a *toxic endproduct* of repressed libido, he now regarded anxiety as being aroused in the ego by libidinal impulses associated with traumatic situations in childhood. Resurgence of a dangerous libidinal impulse initially triggered a small amount of anxiety that served as a *signal* to the ego that a danger associated in childhood with the impulse might recur unless defensive measures were taken. The concept of defense was broadened to include *defense mechanisms* other than repression which the ego could employ to avoid increases in anxiety. Symptoms were now regarded as creations of the ego for avoiding or reducing anxiety, rather than solely as substitute or compromise expressions of libido.

Elaborating on her father's revised theory of the ego, Anna Freud maintained that the goal of analysis must not be merely to bring repressed id impulses into consciousness, but to provide insight into the unconscious defensive activities of the ego. She enumerated many defense mechanisms beside those mentioned by her father and was among the first to apply formal psychoanalysis to children.

In extending *ego psychology,* Heinz Hartmann maintained that some ego functions have *primary autonomy* in that conflict is not required for their development, while other ego functions arise out of conflict as defense mechanisms, but may then achieve *secondary autonomy* and function in the absence of conflict. Hartmann also theorized that the ego was powered by instinctual energy that had become freed *(neutralized)* from its original sexual and aggressive aims.

In his portrayal of *psychosocial development,* Erik Erikson has focused on the ways in which the child's biological development engages him in interactions with adults around him. Basic components of these interactions are the child's *bodily zones,* the *modes of action* focused in the bodily zones, and the *social modalities* that arise from the modes of action. Erikson has postulated five developmental stages characterized by different modes of action and social modalities:

1. the *oral-sensory* stage, when the mode is *incorporation* and the social modality is *getting;*
2. a *second part* of the *oral-sensory* stage, when the mode is *active incorporation* and the modality is *taking;*
3. the *anal-urethral-muscular* stage, when the modes are *retention* and *elimination* and the modalities are *holding on* and *letting go;*
4. the *locomotor and infantile genital* stage, when the mode is *intrusive* and the modality is *making;*
5. the *rudimentary genital* stage, in which the mode is generativity—*intrusive* in the male and *inclusive* in the female. *Genital mutuality* is the normal outcome of this stage.

Erikson also describes eight nuclear conflicts associated with the course of psychosocial development: *Basic trust versus mistrust; autonomy versus shame and doubt; initiative versus guilt; industry versus inferiority; identity versus role confusion; intimacy versus isolation; generativity versus stagnation;* and *ego integrity versus despair.*

Anna Freud has proposed a *developmental profile* for describing a child with respect to libidinal and aggressive drive development, ego and super-ego development, regression and fixation points, and conflicts. Although the developmental profile represents a summary of orthodox psychoanalytic clinical theory as applied to children, there has been little published research on how a child's standing on each variable is to be assessed and on how effective the profile is as a guide to prognosis and treatment.

SUGGESTED READING

Development of Sigmund Freud's Thinking. Among the most central works in the development of Freud's theory of neurosis are *Studies in Hysteria* (with Breuer, 1893–1895); *The Neuro-psychoses of Defense* (1894); *The Interpretation of Dreams* (1900), especially Chapter 7, which contains the most complete version of Freud's early model of the mind; *Three Essays on the Theory of Sex* (1905); and the presentation of his revised theory of neurosis in *Inhibition, Symptoms, and Anxiety* (1926a). Freud's *General Introduction to Psychoanalysis* (1916) and *New Introductory Lectures on Psychoanalysis* (1933) provide especially readable overviews of his thinking. The case of "Little Hans," published as *Analysis of a Phobia in a Five-year-old Boy* (1909), is also important for its portrayal of the psychodynamics of symptom formation in an Oedipal child. For another view of the case, Wolpe and Rachman's (1960) textual critique of Freud's report should be read with the original. The best English translation of Freud's works is the *Standard Edition of the Complete Psychological Works of Sigmund Freud* (1953–1966). Ernest Jones' three-volume biography, *The Life and Work of Sigmund Freud,* is an "official" biography by one who was close to Freud from the early days of organized psychoanalysis and who had the cooperation of many others close to Freud. It is a fascinating book and should be read by anyone wishing to understand the development of psychoanalysis. An excellent one-volume abridgment is available in paperback (1963).

Anna Freud.   Because of her own contributions as well as her paternity, Anna Freud continues to be a central figure in analytic thinking, especially as it is applied to children. Her book, *The Ego and the Mechanisms of Defense* (1936), is a cornerstone of psychoanalytic ego psychology. Her later book, *Normality and Pathology in Childhood* (1965), is probably the most prominent book in the contemporary psychoanalytic literature as it applies to children. A short recent book, entitled *Difficulties in the Path of Psychoanalysis: A Confrontation of Past with Present Viewpoints* (1969), presents her view that the popular influence won by psychoanalysis creates certain threats to its survival.

General Works on Psychoanalysis.   Holzman (1970) gives a concise and authoritative summary of psychoanalytic theories as applied to psychopathology, including the development of Freudian theories and later additions to them. The American Psychoanalytic Association has issued *A Glossary of Psychoanalytic Terms and Concepts* (Moore & Fine, 1968) which provides authoritative definitions of terms.

Psychoanalytic Theory of Neurosis.   George Mahl (1971) offers a comprehensive psychoanalytic view of neurotic functioning that draws heavily on evidence, concepts, and vocabulary outside psychoanalysis. Much of Mahl's presentation is based upon what has been the most ambitious attempt to operationalize psychoanalytic concepts and to synthesize them with research findings. This was the book *Personality and Psychotherapy* by Dollard and Miller (1950), which attempted to bring together in a common data and conceptual language the traditions of psychoanalysis, behaviorism, and cultural anthropology.

Psychosocial Development.   The most widely read extension of analytic theory since Freud's death has been Erik Erikson's portrayal of psychosocial development. While their concepts are untested—and perhaps untestable—and their direct influence on psychoanalytic practice is questionable, Erikson's *Childhood and Society* (second edition, 1963) and *Identity, Youth, and Crisis* (1968) are worth reading because they have contributed much to contemporary thinking about children's social development and because Erikson's observations bring out important dimensions of development not adequately handled by other theoretical viewpoints.

9

Clinical Application of the Psychoanalytic Approach

Orthodox psychoanalysis of children, like that of adults, requires four to five treatment sessions per week for a period often exceeding three years. Because of the length and cost of treatment and the fact that most analysts do not complete their training in adult analysis until they are nearly 40 (Lewin & Ross, 1960), with additional years required for training in child analysis, only a tiny proportion of children judged neurotic will ever be offered analysis. Further restricting the application of child analysis are the assumptions that a weak ego and excessively delinquent behavior make analysis unfeasible and that the prelatency and adolescent periods are usually unsuitable because of the rapid personality changes taking place.

Anna Freud (1968) also cites individual factors that may make analysis inappropriate for a particular child. Such factors include intense developmental crises, illness, the acquisition of a physical handicap, and the death of a parent. Other factors making analysis inappropriate are environmental interferences with development, such as environmental deprivation or disturbed parent behavior.

Once these factors have been ruled out, Miss Freud contends, the best remaining candidates for child analysis are those whose development is being jeopardized by classic neuroses based upon the Oedipus complex. In these neuroses, the obstacles to personality growth are assumed to be: Internalized conflicts between the id, ego, and superego; unsuitable defenses against drives; anxiety; fixations of libido on earlier stages; regression; and repression of aggression.

In accord with her view that neuroses arising from intrapsychic conflicts are the most appropriate targets for child analysis, Miss Freud specifies the goals of child analysis in terms of altering the balance of forces within the personality to bring about greater harmony among them. In adult analysis, these goals are to be attained primarily through: The interpretation of ego resistances and id content; the offering of the analyst as an object onto which the patient *transfers* his feelings about his own parents and from whom the patient obtains help in reworking these feelings; and the bringing of unconscious thoughts into consciousness.

In child analysis, however, the patient's immature ego, his inability to use introspection and free association, and his tendency to deal with conflict through action rather than through thought, often cause other elements of the analytic relationship to play a larger role than is the case with adults. These elements include verbalization and clarification of unrepressed thoughts; direct suggestion by the analyst; corrective emotional experience resulting from the child's relationship with the analyst as an understanding adult; and manipulation of the child's environment through the analyst's advice to parents. Nevertheless, Miss Freud (1965) warns that allowing these elements to predominate can undermine the goal of relieving internal conflicts through bringing them into consciousness. She contends that reducing a child's symptoms without relieving his internal conflicts results in *symptom substitution,* i.e., the creation by the conflicts of new and more intractable symptoms.

PSYCHOANALYTICALLY ORIENTED PSYCHOTHERAPY

In contrast to full-scale analysis, most psychoanalytically oriented child therapy is carried out on a once- or twice-weekly basis for less than three years by psychiatrists, psychologists, and social workers who have not been formally trained as psychoanalysts. It also differs from orthodox psychoanalysis in that it deals with wider ranges of ages and problems than those recommended for analysis. Moreover, it differs from orthodox analysis in often being dominated by verbalization and clarification of preconscious thoughts, direct suggestion by the therapist, corrective emotional experience, reassurance, and advice to parents, i.e., by the elements that Anna Freud would minimize in full-scale analysis.

Despite the fact that analytically oriented child therapy is much more common than full-scale child analysis, little has been pubished on the theory and practice of this therapy as a separate enterprise. Most publications portray it as a watered-down form of analysis that aims at symptom relief through solving immediate preconscious conflicts rather than at relieving the central unconscious conflicts. Brody (1964) is one of the few to give analytically oriented child therapy a positive statement of aims distinct from those of full-scale analysis. Among the aims she cites are:

1. to increase the capacity for reality testing;
2. to strengthen object relations;
3. to loosen fixations.

However, the basic theoretical language and frame of reference, as well as the observations and techniques on which analytically oriented therapy draws, continue to be those of the psychoanalytic literature.

TYPES OF NEUROSIS

Seven categories for childhood neurotic disorders have been presented in the classification system proposed by the Group for the Advancement of Psychiatry (1966). Beside phobic and obsessive-compulsive neuroses, these categories include a subdivision of hysteria into "conversion type" and "dissociative type," plus "anxiety" neurosis, "depressive" neurosis, and "other" neuroses, such as traumatic neuroses. Most children considered to be neurotic show mixtures of symptoms from various categories. However, only the three types of neurosis—phobic, obsessive-compulsive, and hysterical— dealt with in most of the analytic literature are detailed below.

Phobic Neuroses

Phobic neuroses (previously called "anxiety hysterias") provide an especially good focal point for our later consideration of differences between analytic theory and treatment on the one hand, and learning theory and behavioral treatment on the other. This is true because phobic symptoms can be objectively identified, they are relatively common, there are fairly clearly stated theories of phobic symptom formation from both viewpoints, and there are large literatures on the treatment of phobias by both approaches.

The definition of phobias contained in the American Psychoanalytic Association's *Glossary of Psychoanalytic Terms and Concepts* (Moore & Fine, 1968) states:

In phobias the various *ego* defenses against dangerous *instinctual drives* operate in such a way that the inner danger seems to become an outer one. Unacceptable inner strivings of a sexual or aggressive nature have been repressed because of the irrational, unconscious fear of castration by the father. When these impulses threaten to emerge into *consciousness,* intense castration anxiety results in their *projection* and *displacement* onto an outside object or situation. For example, the hatred and fear of a loved father may be shifted finally to some animal. The advantages are evident: the elimination of conscious awareness of the hatred and fear of the father permits continued closeness to him, while the animal, to which the fear is referred, can be avoided. Though unresolved conflicts of the *oedipus complex* contribute in a major way to phobias, preoedipal problems provide a significant basis for their development [p. 73].

Note that the essence of the phobia is not considered to be the fear of the external object itself, but an unconscious internal conflict that generates fear. The fear is in turn *displaced* onto stimuli in the outside world that have a symbolic significance for the child. Consequently, the goal of treatment is to relieve the unconscious conflict rather than to remove the fear of the external phobic object. Removing the fear of the phobic object without relieving the unconscious conflict is believed to result in the substitution of new phobias or other symptoms for the original phobia. Most of the psychoanalytic literature stresses that a psychoneurotic phobia is only one part of a larger symptom picture that includes excessive dependency and avoidance defenses as well as fears other than the main phobia (cf. Andrews, 1966; Kessler, 1972).

Analysis of a Phobic Child. The case of Frankie, a boy analyzed by Berta Bornstein (1949), has become a classic in the psychoanalytic literature. Three facts make it especially revealing of the contemporary state of psychoanalytic theory and treatment. One is that Bornstein, a prominent figure in child analysis, considered it worthy of a 45-page report because of the discrepancy between the apparent simplicity of the phobic symptom and the complicated ego structure she detected behind it.

The second fact is that the particular phobic symptom for which Frankie was brought to treatment—fear of going to school *(school phobia)*—is a common one about which much has been written from the psychoanalytic viewpoint. However, a major point of contention is whether school phobia should be considered primarily a fear of school or a manifestation of anxiety about separation from the mother (cf. Andrews, 1966; Berecz, 1968; Frick, 1964; Sperling, 1967).

The third fact that makes the case of Frankie especially illuminating is that, in his early twenties, Frankie experienced school phobic symptoms and again underwent psychoanalysis with a prominent analyst who reported the relations he observed between Frankie's problems as a child and as an adult. This analyst's report provides an unusual opportunity to observe the long-term outcome of personality patterns hypothesized to have been significant in early childhood and to observe the bearing child analysis may have had on them.

Because the convictions psychoanalysts hold about their theoretical concepts and methods of treatment are closely intertwined with the behavior of patients during analytic sessions and the responses of patients to interpretations, Bornstein's report is reproduced at length, although still greatly abbreviated from its original form.

Frankie, a 5½-year-old boy of superior intelligence who was eager to learn, was brought into analysis because of a severe school phobia. . . . He became panic-stricken if his mother or nurse were out of sight. . . . His phobic symptom had existed for more than 2 years. . . .

His sister Mary was born when Frankie was 3 years and 3 months old. Upon the mother's return from the hospital he displayed marked anxiety. He grew more ill-tempered toward his mother and his coolness toward her increased to such an extent that she became disturbed and made conscious efforts to win the child's affection. Despite her strong urge to devote herself to her little daughter, she left the baby in the care of a second nurse while she and Frankie's nurse were at the boy's disposal. . . .

When she occasionally wanted to leave him, he became violent, panic-stricken, and clung to her desperately. But immediately after, when left alone with the nurse, his outburst subsided, and the tyrannical child became curiously submissive.

The mother had suffered considerably from Frankie's rejections. In his clinging attitude she began to see a sign of the child's love, and she was so deeply impressed by his fear and his need of her protection that she succumbed to his phobic arrangements.

The child's anxiety reached its first peak when he was brought to nursery school at the age of 3 years and 9 months. . . . He went to school for only 2 days. Each time, he had to be taken home because of his wild attacks of fear and screaming, and nothing could make him return to school. A second attempt to send him to a different school was made when he was 4½. Although the mother not only accompanied him to school, but actually stayed in the classroom with him, his anxiety did not subside. . . .

The analyst suggested that treatment be postponed until after a period of preparation for analysis in which the school was to co-operate with the analyst. This pre-analytic phase was designed to create a conflict in the child between his symptom and reality. To be sure, Frankie was already suffering from an internal conflict as shown by his phobia. However, as long as his phobic demands were met, he was insulated against anxiety . . . and in this state there was no reason for him to want to overcome his phobia. By our preanalytic scheme we hoped to produce in him insight into his need for help, without which no psychoanalytic treatment can make any progress. Thus, as soon as the child showed signs of a firm positive attachment to the school, his teacher was to inform him that his mother could no longer be permitted to be present. When the child protested that he could not remain alone, he was to be told that there was a person. the analyst, who might be able to help him stay at school, and to withstand the pain of his mother's absence. . . . Frankie, conscious of his conflict and his desire for help, was brought to the analyst, who now could act as a mediator between him and the school. . . .

His dramatic play during his first session led straight into his conflicts, just as in adult analysis the first dream often leads into the core of the patient's neurosis. . . .

Frankie started his first session by building a hospital which was separated into a "lady department," a "baby department," and a "men's department." In the lobby, a lonely boy of 4 was seated all by himself, on a chair placed in an elevated position. The child's father was upstairs visiting "a lady" who, he informed us, when questioned, "is sick or maybe she's got a baby, maybe—I don't know, never mind." He made the point that newborn babies and mothers were separated in this hospital. Casting himself in the roles of a doctor and a nurse, he attended to the babies in a loving way, fed and cleaned them. However, toward the end of the play, a fire broke out. All the babies were burnt to death and the boy in the lobby was also in danger. He wanted to run home, but remembered that nobody would be there. Subsequently he joined the fire department, but it was not quite clear as to whether the firemen had started the fire or put it out. Frankie announced: "Ladies, the babies are dead; maybe we can save you!" Actually only those lady patients who had no babies were rescued by him. The one whom he several times—by a slip of the tongue—had addressed as "Mommy," however, was killed in the fire. . . .

This game, which was repeated in the analysis for many weeks, betrayed the intensity of the boy's fury against his mother and sister. He could not forgive his mother for her unfaithfulness. He took her going to the hospital as a desertion of him and a sign of her lack of love. She must suffer the same tortures which he had suffered when she left him. He said, as it were: "I don't love you either; I hate you, I don't need you, you may die in the hospital. If you hadn't had a baby I would love you."

Frankie, who so thoroughly punished his mother by the withdrawal of his love, naturally lived in continual fear of retaliation. He could not stay at home or go out without his mother because he needed the presence of just that person against whom his aggressive impulses were directed. The presence of the ambivalently loved person prevents the phobic from being overwhelmed by his forbidden impulses and assures him that his aggressive intentions have not come true. . . .

In order to bring about an *ego change,* we chose for interpretation from the different themes revealed in the child's play that element in which the patient represented his ego. It was evident to us that he himself was the lonely 4-year-old boy in the hospital game, although feelings of sadness and loneliness had not been mentioned by him in his play. On the contrary, in his game he demonstrated only the *defense* against loneliness and sadness. . . . .

We must remember that at the time of the analysis Frankie himself did not know anything of his sadness. . . . He had replaced it by his aggressive and tyrannical demands to which he later reacted with his phobic symptoms. Both aggression and anxiety were the end-product of an initial sadness and without recapturing that initial affect so that the patient was aware of it, no real ego change could be brought about. . . .

In order to introduce this emotion into the child's consciousness without arousing undue resistance, the loneliness of the little boy in his game became the subject of our analytic work for several weeks. The analyst expressed sympathy for the lonely child who is barred from his mother's sickroom and who is too little to understand why his father is admitted. Frankie responded to the analyst's sympathy with growing sadness, which could be discerned only from his facial expression. The analyst's sympathy made it possible for him to tolerate this affect.

Once he had been able to face his sadness, Frankie showed relatively little resistance when his specific situation was examined. We asked whether by any chance he was a child who had been left alone while his mother was in the hospital. . . . He turned to his mother with the question: "Was I alone, Mommy?" and before she could answer, he told about his father and his nurse's presence, adding that his nurse would "never, never leave him alone."

. . . ample material referring to abandonment corroborated the appropriateness of selecting his sadness as the first content of our interpretation. To him, being sent to school was an aggravating repetition of former separations: it happened just after his sister's nurse had left and his own nurse and mother had to share in the care of the baby. Thus, he lost not only his mother but also his nurse "who would never, never leave me alone." *This repetition of the traumatic experience of being abandoned* brought about the climax of his anxiety. . . .

By continually connecting his recent experiences and emotions to their genetic counterparts, his sadness and jealousy, the pathological tie to his nurse was loosened. . . . Only now his own jealousy appeared in its proper place, openly directed against his little sister. . . .

Once the hostility toward his mother was diminished, his relationship to her seemed greatly improved, and his repressed love came to the fore. With this resolution the manifest school phobia subsided. He was able both to stay in school and to attend his analytic sessions without his mother's presence. . . .

Although Frankie's conquest of his aggressiveness toward his mother now made it possible for him to re-experience and to express his normal positive oedipal conflicts, he did so only in the analytic session. At home, the child's reaction to the father seemed to be emotionally neutral. He was, for instance, apparently unaffected by his father's frequent arrivals at and departures from home during war time. . . . Only in his dramatic play and fantasy material did he reveal his hostility toward men. Innumerable play episodes also betrayed Frankie's interest in procreation and his urge to know "what was going on" between his parents. . . .

In the most frequent of his play dramatizations, a father was absent and a mother was alone. Then an apparently friendly man, a butcher, a policeman, or a vegetable man (each impersonated by Frankie), came to dinner. The "friendly" visit always ended with an attack on the mother who was killed. The ending was always the same: the visitors were taken by the police and sentenced to death by the judge, both of whom were again personified by Frankie.

It was our next task to connect these fantasies with his actual experiences. This was achieved by confronting him with a paradox: his lack of emotion about his own father's coming and going, and the excitement the child showed in his play when visitors arrived. The mother had reported that prior to the outbreak of his neurosis, Frankie had shown signs of irritability toward visitors, especially toward his grandfather. . . .

In the course of discussing his irritation toward visitors, Frankie admitted that there was actually no reason for him to assume that visitors would attack his mother. Nevertheless, he felt that he had to guard her against threatening dangers, especially if she were out of his sight. "She might run away," he said. "She might be run over, or her car might break, or men might kill her in the subway." We finally understood that he was afraid that all of these dangers would lead to a second hospitalization, just as when his mother had had her baby.

The circle was closed. The danger which threatened the mother from relations with men would result in what was the gravest danger to him: the arrival of a new baby. He had to guard against a repetition of this traumatic experience. . . .

With the process of internalization of his conflicts the actually threatening nurse was replaced by imaginary objects, mainly wolves, who stood guard under his bed and kept him from getting up and investigating what might be happening in the parental bedroom. . . .

. . . His configuration of the wolves contained as elements the punitive and protective parent figures as well as his own impulses The wolves punish his intentions and prevent their fulfillment Their symbolic role as superego was strikingly confirmed in a drawing which Frankie called the WOLVES' STATUE. It showed an oversized wolf (in human form) with outstretched arms, floating above Frankie in his bed, under which a number of smaller-sized wolves (also in human form) were engaged in mysterious activities, obviously of a sexual nature. . . . Frankie said: "It shows what the wolves hope for, what they will look like some day."

The dread of wolves which had haunted the child for weeks finally led to the analysis of his castration fear. In his stories and in his play, the mother's attackers who previously had been punished by death, now were punished by almost undisguised castration. In his pictures he endowed God with monstrously elongated arms and legs, only to cut off these limbs with scissors. Immediately after such operation he tried to undo this symbolic act of castration by drawing innumerable new arms and legs. Frankie derived reassurance from the idea that destruction is not necessarily irrevocable and consequently dared to express the thoughts of castration without any symbolic disguise. Mother's attackers were imprisoned and he, as a doctor, subjected the prisoners to operations which usually threw him into a state of exaltation . . . he exclaimed: "Those criminals, they have to be operated on. Off with their wee-wees. It has to come off!"

The material obtained from his play actions, in which men violently attack women, was interpreted to him in terms of his fantasies about intercourse. The treatment made it possible for him to re-enter the oedipal phase, and the father then acquired that emotional importance in the child's reality which was due him in terms of the oedipal relationship. . . .

When Frankie's nurse had left the household, his father had seemed to him to take over many of her functions in laying down rules and regulations for Frankie and his mother. Frankie sought passive sexual gratifications from his father such as soft patting on his buttocks that he had previously induced the nurse to do for him. The father acquiesced until he recognized Frankie's seductive manner and became more reserved toward Frankie. Frankie fantasied that the only way to get the passive gratification he wanted was to be a woman, but his castration fears compelled him into masculine activities. Yet his passive cravings remained and now aroused anxiety that was manifested in fears of being kidnapped.

The essential feature of these new kidnapping fantasies was that they contained on open reference to genital or anal gratifications and that the *factor of passive locomotion was dominant*. As long as these fantasies were of moderate intensity, carrying two toy revolvers sufficed as a magic gesture to ward off anxiety. But whenever his repressed passive desires increased in intensity, the fantasy of being kidnapped lost its playful features, and he went into attacks of violent panic in which he was unable to distinguish between the world of fantasy and reality.

To avoid such states of panic which the intensity of his passive desires repeatedly brought about, Frankie was forced to evolve an entirely new attitude. He began to ignore reality. Signs of passivity were eradicated and were replaced by feelings of omnipotence. He gave his parents nonsensical orders and was greatly annoyed if they were not carried out; he struck his sister and parents for not obeying unspoken orders. His world was divided into two camps: rulers and slaves—and he belonged to the world of rulers and supermen, who were characterized by incredible cruelty. . . .

The analyst suggested that he was identifying himself with his tough radio heroes and criminals in order to ward off his passive desires. This interpretation had a negative therapeutic result. He reacted to it by strengthening this particular defense. His demands became even more fantastic, and from time to time his behavior resembled that of a megalomaniacal patient. He claimed that he was actually a king. . . . The fantasies of omnipotence were extensive; he called the exalted role he played in the universe, King Boo-Boo.

His dictatorial behavior at home and his fantastic ignoring of reality took on such proportions that it became questionable whether he could remain in his usual environment. This acute situation threatened the continuation of his treatment. . . .

It was necessary that he be told that his behavior had actually one aim: to be sent away. This would be the realization of the one thing he had dreaded most: to be separated from his parents. We should like to amplify on the session which followed, and which brought about the decisive change in Frankie's attitude.

The analyst found him in the waiting room, the paper basket on his head, hilariously throwing books and blocks at his mother. . . . When alone with him, she asked him what he *really* thought the effect of his actions would be. She conceded that he acted as if he were a great king and as if he expected complete submission from his environment. But she expressed her doubts that he himself really believed in the truth of these ideas. She called to his attention the fact that his behavior would not have the desired effect and that no matter what he did, nobody would accept him as a superman or as King Boo-Boo. Frankie replied quickly: "Oh, they will find out some day, and they will do what I want!"

Referring to several incidents during the analytic sessions in which he had acted out his King Boo-Boo ideas, she told him that even her positive relationship to him was influenced by his "actions." "Even before you enter my office, I can't help thinking: 'For goodness sake, what will Frankie try to do today; what is he going to break and to destroy today?'" He interrupted quickly: "Oh, you shouldn't care. You get paid for that, even more than it costs."

He was then asked whether he knew what had brought about this change in his behavior; after all, there had been a time when he had cared quite a bit for people, and when he had wanted to be with his mother all the time. Frankie replied triumphantly: "So that's fine; now I am cured of my fears, and I don't want to be with Mommy."

The analyst did not agree with him as to his being cured. She thought that he was still very much afraid, just as scared as he was at the time when he did not want to come to his session because he believed the analyst was a kidnapper. Only now he tried to hide his fear even from himself . . . now she was seriously worried about his behavior. Therefore, she must show him that his King Boo-Boo behavior would end in something of which she had always thought he was terribly afraid. . . .

The analyst told him she was compelled to assume that he wanted to create a situation where his being sent away was the only possible outcome. . . .

The child listened calmly, although this was quite unusual in this period of unmanageable wildness. Eventually he asked seriously: "Where can you send me? My parents promised they would never send me to a camp or to a boarding school if I didn't want to go there. And you yourself told me that children cannot go to jail. . . ."

Thereupon the analyst told him about hospitals which specialized in treating children whose sickness led them to behave in unacceptable ways. He interrupted: "But I'm not sick; I have no temperature." The analyst stated that people who seriously believed that the world was divided into camps "of an almighty king and the rest slaves" are seriously ill, even without a temperature and belong in special hospitals. . . . Suddenly realizing that the analyst referred to mental illness, he became quite frightened and asked, "Do you think I'm crazy? Do you think I belong in a crazy house?"

Without waiting for an answer, he wanted to know in detail how those hospitals were run, how children were kept there, whether they were visited by their parents, what kind of toys they had, whether they were permitted to have knives and blocks and whether they were analyzed there. Our answers obviously disappointed him; they did not fit into his picture of exciting fights between attendants and patients and between kidnappers and the kidnapped.

The psychodynamics of this analytic session brought about a decisive therapeutic gain which may be explained as follows:

1) The beginning of the analytic session permitted Frankie to re-experience and to act out the full grandeur of his world of fantasy. He had an opportunity to demonstrate his narcissistic omnipotence, his disdain for reality and his belief in the inferiority and weakness of the analyst.

2) The next analytic step was a thrust into his unconscious, and a demonstration that his unconscious aim was to enforce a separation from home. This was a contradiction of his omnipotence which even the almighty King Boo-Boo could not overlook.

3) He readily picked up the suggestion about enforcing a separation and revealed his unconscious desire by the great interest he showed in the place to which he would be sent. By asking one question after another, he began to consider the reality of what would happen if his unconscious desires were really fulfilled. . . . The ego discovered that fulfillment of these unconscious desires was drab and monotonous if carried out in reality. . . .

Only then did Frankie start to doubt the wisdom of carrying his King Boo-Boo fantasies into reality. . . .

The following months during which the child was able to work through the conflict about his passivity were a period of consolidation during which he was preparing himself for the termination of his analysis.

The prospect of ending the analysis revived for him the pain of separation from his mother at the time his sister was born. This prompted us to use these last months for further working through his relationship to his mother. During the weeks of our analytic interpretation of his early oral frustrations, his anger against her was reactivated and he demonstrated an unusually strong oral envy and aggression. Whenever he suspected that his mother preferred his sister to him, whenever she did anything for the little girl, he either gave vent to his fury against his mother and sister, as in earlier periods, or became depressed. . . .

Toward the end of the analysis, Frankie recognized that his megalomaniacal behavior and fantasies were defenses against suffering and death, as well as against passive strivings. Facing the demand that he give up fantasies of King Boo-Boo's immortality, he resorted again to phobic mechanisms, but restricted them to more realistic proportions. Bornstein reviewed the long path to this achievement as follows:

When Frankie entered his analysis, he was completely enslaved by his symptoms. His preoccupation with his mother and with the need for assurance that he could obtain gratification without endangering his existence, resulted in a constriction of his ego. He had not accepted any external ideals and there were hardly any indications of internal prohibitions. These are the signs of a severe lag in the formation of a superego.

During his oedipal phase, his fears were displaced from real objects such as his mother, his nurse, and his father, to imaginary objects and situations. . . .

Considering what had caused the lag in superego formation, we must refer to two factors. One is that his environment did not provide him with a clear-cut frame of reference as to objects of identification. For example, his mother acted like a child in relation to the nurse, and it was the nurse who exercised authority. Yet he sensed that the nurse took a secondary position whenever his father made his sporadic . . . appearances during wartime. . . . The second and more important factor was that this nurse combined her prohibitions with libidinal gratifications. . . . [I]nstead of forming the basis of a superego, these sexualized prohibitions laid the foundation for a masochistic perversion. . . .

Once he could give up acting out his King Boo-Boo fantasies, he could transfer his omnipotence to others who represented his ego-ideals. He could accept his father as a strong and enviable figure without becoming passively dependent on him. . . .

. . . [In the second-to-last session] We could observe that the derivatives of his initial fears were firmly embedded in an adequate relationship to reality without eliciting fear, although the contents of his past conflicts were present to his mind.

A prognosis in child analysis is not easy. We are by no means sure that we have forestalled a later recurrence of Frankie's neurosis. But . . . when he could face danger without resorting to pathological anxiety or belief in magic and omnipotence—then we knew that the secondary process had won a victory over the primary process. And this we thought, was the utmost a boy of 8½ can achieve—even with the help of child analysis.[1]

Frankie's Second Analysis.   When Frankie was in his early twenties and beginning an especially competitive period in his education, he experienced symptoms which led him to seek analysis again. A summary of the analysis was later published (Ritvo, 1966). The quotations below are from an unpublished report.

. . . Although his anxiety was fairly well controlled with the aid of the obsessive and compulsive character traits which he developed, he did suffer several attacks of neurotic anxiety during adolescence and in the several years immediately preceding his return to analysis. These outbreaks were accompanied by obsessional symptom formation, and a compulsion to touch things three times and to speak his words in groups of three syllables. If he did not do this the "sanction" would be a poor grade on an examination. The formation of symptoms coincided with the intensification of the old passive feminine strivings which had required pathological defenses in childhood. In early adolescence they were stirred by homosexual play with peers and in later adolescence by the covert homosexual advances of an older man. Although the patient succeeded in warding off these temptations, it was at the cost of the outbreak of anxiety and symptoms. . . .

How did this young man . . . appear to the world he lived in outside the analy-

[1] Berta Bornstein, "Analysis of a Phobic Child," *Psychoanalytic Study of the Child,* 1949, 3–4 (181–226). © 1949 by International Universities Press and reprinted by permission.

sis? His fellow students would probably not be aware of his acute discomfiture and self-consciousness in ordinary social situations which were related to his easily feeling slighted, rebuffed or rejected and to his constant competitive comparison with his fellows. . . . His professors would have found him sometimes active in discussions, sometimes detached, not realizing that this depended on whether he thought the professor had a high regard for him or whether he thought he was out of favor and held in low esteem. He elected courses largely on the basis of whether he thought the professor would like him or would be antagonistic and inclined to attack, punish or harm him. Girls he dated probably found him serious most of the time though capable of a light-hearted playfulness. However, if a girl he had been dating was not in at midnight or two o'clock in the morning to answer his telephone call he could immediately become the Frankie of old who had been so vengeful with his mother when she returned from the hospital after the birth of his sister. He became willful and arbitrary, easily aroused to a petulant and angry jealousy and demanding that his intellectual superiority be recognized. . . . With sister . . . he talked about psychoanalysis. She expressed confidence and encouragement while he expressed doubt and skepticism. With his mother, the old angry, demanding, vengeful attitudes were no longer present in the overt relationship between them, though they were still very much alive in a variety of displaced forms.

With his wife . . . he was patient and attentive, and admiring of her endowments and attainments. What may have appeared to the outside as simple devotion could be seen in the transference as a repetition of the situation in childhood when he took revenge on his mother (analyst) by refusing her care and attention and turned to his nurse (wife) instead. In a similar fashion he was solicitous of his wife's jealousy of his exclusive relationship with me in the analysis and warned me repeatedly that he might have to leave me and rebuff my ministrations as he had his mother's, if his wife suffered because of her jealousy. Besides this repetition from childhood, the relationship with his wife also reversed the childhood situation and enabled him to control actively what he had formerly experienced passively. . . . The passive libidinal strivings towards the object which had been so intense in childhood and had been gratified in the toileting experiences with his nurse, remained in his deep-rooted preference for passive manipulation rather than exercising the active role in intercourse, a preference which was reflected in a periodic disturbance of his potency.

When he returned to analysis, the immediate conflict situation was the brilliant conclusion of one phase of his preparation for a career and the decision to start on another more definitive phase. . . . The intense competitiveness of the school situation, the pending irrevocable commitment to a career with its measurement of achievement which might be less than he considered ideal and might tarnish his hitherto bright record, all contributed to the outbreak of anxiety with the feeling of being trapped and wanting to get out. . . .

It was the same anxious feeling of being trapped which at the age of five had made it difficult for him to remain in school and had led to his entering analysis. Thus, after a gap of more than 15 years one of the immediate reasons for returning to analysis was his difficulty in remaining in school without the help of analysis, certainly a striking demonstration of the tendency of unconscious mental phenomena to repeat themselves quite faithfully.

Equally disturbing at the time of his return were his obsessive doubts about the functioning of his mind. These doubts had an unmistakable similarity to his earlier concern about masturbation and the intactness of his genital. . . .

In the two exacerbations during adolescence the anxiety and doubts about his mind had become so severe that he could not read or listen to the radio because he had to keep going back over a word to test his retention. He now feared the symptoms would return with the intensity they had in adolescence. . . .

The same conflicts for which he sought a solution by the formation of phobic symptoms as a child in the phallic-oedipal phase he later tried to cope with by the obsessive doubting about his mind. The fear of erections, the masturbation conflict, the death wishes of the oedipal conflict, the danger of castration were all included in the manifold forms of the preoccupation with the functioning of his mind. . . .

So much did he value knowledge and intellectual understanding as a means of mastering his neurotic fears that he wanted to have a complete record of both analyses so that he could study it and have available at all times an armamentarium of knowledge to apply as needed. . . .

As an adult there were many references in dreams to his unconscious wish for anal and oral homosexual gratifications. . . . One acceptable derivative form of gratification assumed by his oral and anal impulses was enjoying the steady and sure supply of money from his father and anticipating the prospect of eventually having his father's assets as his own. He hungrily desired the respect of his father and other men, but feared there was nothing behind his facade of intelligence and ability for his father and other men to respect. He felt that if he got poor grades, which meant a low evaluation, he would "slip back into a sea of defecation." He linked his revulsion of dirtiness and defecation with a fear of being poor. In early adolescence when he had to defend himself against the homosexual temptations offered by his peers he could not eat in the home of his poor friend because he felt the food was cheap and "defecation-covered". . . . By contrast, the intellectual activities which he idealized were thought of as a type of . . . sterilization. It was a way of keeping things clean and not dirtying them with mushy, soft, fecal emotions. . . .

. . . Whereas the [childhood] fears had placed the focus on what the forces in the outside world might do to him, the doubts [in adulthood] shifted the focus to what he had in him to cope with the dangers outside. The world now required more of him and he *had to* cope with it. His more highly developed reality-testing capacities could no longer permit his unreasonable fears nor his magic omnipotence (King Boo-Boo) to persist. At the same time his advancing capacity for abstract and logical thinking enabled him to erect a system of thought operations and obsessive doubting, so that the neurotic conflict continued in a form which could not be objectively tested and therefore could pass the scrutiny of the more mature ego. . . .

After two-and-one-half years, Frankie broke off the second analysis because he was leaving the vicinity. The analyst considered him to be much improved, but did not regard the analysis as complete. Frankie's professional work was highly successful and his marriage remained stable, yet he still had strong feelings around competition with his sister and was preoccupied with thoughts of dying. Six years later he again entered analysis with another analyst, but no report of this analysis is available. Nevertheless, the reports by Bornstein and Ritvo provide what may be a unique record of psychoanalytic data obtained at two very different stages in an individual's life. They illustrate the process of analysis, the kinds of observations employed by analysts, the interpretations made from these observations, and the analytic theory of phobic neuroses in children. The questions of the validity of such interpretations and the efficacy of the treatment will be taken up later in the chapter.

Obsessive-Compulsive Neuroses

The definition of obsessive-compulsive neuroses presented in the *Glossary of Psychoanalytic Terms and Concepts* (Moore & Fine, 1968) states:

> . . . A type of psychoneurosis . . . characterized by obsessional thoughts and compulsive acts. In addition, rumination, doubting and irrational fears are often present. All of these are accompanied by morbid anxiety when the intruding thoughts or repetitive acts are prohibited or otherwise interfered with.
>
> The clinical picture of obsessional neurosis results from both a libidinal regression to the *anal-sadistic phase,* (usually because of severe conflict during the *oedipal phase*) and the ego's defensive activities which . . . include the mechanisms of *isolation, reaction formation,* and *undoing.* Other major characteristics underlying the symptomatology are *ambivalence,* a regression to magical thinking, and indications of rigid and destructive *superego* functioning. The *conflicts* usually involved in this neurosis are closer to those of the prephallic phase of *psycho-sexual development* than to those of the phallic-oedipal period [p. 65].

Notice that the latter definition stresses the hypothesis that the clinical symptoms result from libidinal regression to the anal-sadistic phase. The notion that obsessive and compulsive defenses are based in the anal phase is widespread in psychoanalytic literature. This has given rise to the concept of the *anal* or *compulsive character,* a personality type characterized by orderliness, obstinacy, and parsimony for whom anal functions have an exaggerated significance. The obsessive-compulsive neurosis is not equated with the compulsive personality, however, because the anal fixations ascribed to the neurosis are, like those in other neuroses, hypothesized to be *re-aroused* by *regression* which has resulted from unconscious conflict, rather than merely being persistent character traits (Sandler & Joffe, 1965). The child diagnosed as suffering from an obsessive-compulsive neurosis may thus be considered a candidate for analysis while the child who has developed a compulsive personality structure may not. In fact, despite their excessive concern for cleanliness, orderliness, and conformity, children with compulsive personalities often perform well and exhibit a lively pseudomaturity, although severe stress may cause their obsessive-compulsive defenses to become temporarily exaggerated. Cass (1967) summarizes the psychoanalytic view of the triggering of an obsessive-compulsive neurosis as follows:

The "choice" of regression as a defense in the obsessive-compulsive is thought to depend upon one or more of the following factors: (1) the outcome of the original anal-sadistic stage; (2) the strength of the phallic drives and of the threat opposed to their expression; (3) the strength of the ego. The attraction backward to the anal-sadistic stage may be due to constitutional factors, to unusual anal gratifications, to phallic frustrations which drive the child to seek earlier gratifications, or to the association of anal gratification with security gratification—for example, with approval for accepting the training procedures . . .

From the point of the regression on, the neurotic conflict takes on the characteristics of the anal stage and the predominant defenses are those typical of this stage. However, the residuals of the original phallic conflict are very often apparent in the symptoms of the compulsive disorder and the conflict per se often comes to light after the anal-sadistic conflicts are worked through in therapy.

Very often, in obsessional children, the content of the obsession is clearly phallic in meaning while its structure and mode of representation are clearly anal. For example, the phallic conflict may be preserved in a cathexis for cars, keys, or rockets while the repetitiousness, controllingness, stubborn retention, and sadistic use of these obsessions bear the stamp of the anality to which the child has regressed. Moreover, the excitement which a child displays over his obsessive object or compulsive ritual is often likened to that which is normally invested in the oedipal object. The obsession has become the "only love" of his life and the one area where constructive energy and curiosity are evidenced.

. . . symptom formation originates as a defense against instinctual oedipal demands . . . there is, because of the regression, the defense against anal-sadistic strivings as well. The conflict is waged between these strivings and the newly formed superego. The more fully developed the child's superego is, the more the threat becomes one of danger from within, that is, the loss of self-respect and the fear of annihilation. . . .

The compulsive act or compulsive thought (obsession) is both a substitute for the warded-off impulse and a stand against it. It has both the symbolic meaning of defense and of gratification. In some symptoms, the instinctual aspect is more prominent; in other symptoms, or, at other times within the same type of symptom, the defensive, anti-instinctual aspect is more prominent; still other compulsive symptoms clearly represent the struggle between instinct and defense [pp. 97–99].[2]

In his report of his reanalysis of Frankie, Ritvo emphasized that Frankie's phobic defenses were replaced by obsessive-compulsive defenses as he grew older. The association of phobias with obsessions and compulsions is a common theme in the psychoanalytic literature, and Achenbach (1966) empirically found through factor analysis of child symptoms a syndrome in which phobias, obsessions, and compulsions were the most prominent symptoms.

Despite the frequent reference to obsessive-compulsive defenses throughout the psychoanalytic literature, there are few detailed reports of analytic treatment of children considered to be suffering from obsessive-compulsive

[2] L. Cass, "Psychotherapy with the Obsessive—Compulsive Child," in *The Practice of Psychotherapy with Children*, G. Newton and S. Levine (Eds.). (Homewood, Ill.: The Dorsey Press, 1967), pp. 97–99. © 1967 by The Dorsey Press and reprinted by permission.

neuroses. Because of the paucity of information he found in the literature, Judd (1965) surveyed the clinic records of 405 disturbed children under age 12 to determine how many were obsessive-compulsive. He found 34 (8.4 per cent) who had these symptoms. Elimination of cases in which the obsessive-compulsive symptoms were not the most prominent evidence of pathology or were not severe left only 5 cases (1.2 per cent) out of the 405. Twenty-five of the 29 eliminated were diagnosed schizophrenic, while the other four were diagnosed brain-damaged, corroborating a frequently reported association of obsessive-compulsive symptomatology with disorders that receive these diagnoses. In samples of 300 disturbed boys and 300 disturbed girls, none of whom had evidence of organic etiology, Achenbach (1966) found 14 boys (4.7 per cent) and 12 girls (4 per cent) who manifested the "obsessions, compulsions, and phobias" syndrome derived empirically by factor analysis.

While the percentage of children manifesting obsessive-compulsive syndromes is generally found to be small, and the percentage having what psychoanalytic theory regards as obsessive-compulsive neurosis is likely to be still smaller, Judd found that the percentage having obsessive-compulsive neuroses in an adult patient sample was exactly the same, 1.2 per cent (21 out of 1,624), as he found in his child sample. In both the Judd and Achenbach studies, as in most other reports, the obsessive-compulsive children were found to average considerably higher in IQ than other patient groups.

Despert (1955) has argued that many children showing severe obsessive-compulsive symptoms but ultimately diagnosed psychotic (usually schizophrenic) should really be diagnosed as having obsessive-compulsive neuroses because these children are still testing reality, are aware of the strangeness of their behavior, and are protected by their defenses from a complete break with reality. The fact that Despert's conception of obsessive-compulsive neurosis may overlap other workers' conceptions of psychosis could explain why she reports that 17 per cent (68 out of 401) of child patients in her files were obsessive-compulsive neurotics. The large disparity between this figure and the 1.2 per cent reported by Judd is at least partly symptomatic of the lack of objective diagnostic criteria for discriminating among various categories of psychopathology. The issue of the unreliability of diagnostic classification will be taken up at length in Chapter 15.

The following case illustrates obsessive-compulsive symptoms in a boy diagnosed neurotic by Despert and schizophrenic by two other practitioners. Despert reports that the course of therapy bore out her diagnosis, but she acknowledges that a break from reality might have taken place without therapy.

A. S. came to treatment . . . at the age of 9⅓ years, was treated for 2½ years and has made a fairly good adjustment, his progress being followed through his mother's therapist. Diagnosis: *severe obsessive-compulsive neurosis,* although two psychologic tests done at one-year intervals by two independent psychologists formulated a diagnosis of *schizophrenia.* . . .

Complaint, as formulated by the mother at the time of referral, was that "his imagination makes up talks. At school he is said to be a genius, yet his accomplishments fall short of his intelligence. He laughs, giggles. He masturbates extensively, stays in the bathroom a long time, says he does magical things there. He has many compulsions, must square things. Has obsessive thoughts regarding his parents' death."

The father, in his mid-forties, is . . . a passive, ineffectual individual, a poor provider—a schizoid person who "went through several crises, one religious." He is tense and moody.

The mother, in her late thirties, . . . has a severe cleanliness compulsion and, for instance, would sterilize the nursing bottles many times in succession, in the belief that at some point she might have contaminated her hands. As a result of her "germ" phobia, she kept the child from human contacts for several years. She suffered a depression lasting five or six weeks after the birth of the child. She is overanxious and, for instance, said: "It's an abnormal thing with me that I must know every minute where he is."

When seen, the patient was overactive, excitable. He spoke under great pressure, with some incoherence. This was, however, due in large extent to the rush of ideas, and clarification could be obtained. There was a wealth of fantasies regarding his phobias, some of which were expressed in bizarre manner; for instance, he related his nightmares about bugs: "I found some kind of seeds, buried them, a plant grew and some big giant bugs came out at the ends." . . . his bug phobia and his obsession regarding bugs were such that "I was almost a bug myself." There were similar fantasies about a crocodile in his cellar. Once he had actually pushed his parents on the street, then fantasied them "lying still, dead on the street." However vivid were these fantasies, he knew them to be fantasies; while he was troubled by them, he felt that he got lost in these fantasies because of his intense anxiety. He was much troubled by his constant indecision . . . owing to obsessive thoughts he had about himself, his parents and his friends. "How can I make a decision? I'm never sure. . . ." Many compulsive acts and prayers were carried out in a partly conscious attempt to relieve his guilt: guilt regarding masturbation, guilt regarding death wishes toward the parents [Despert, 1955, pp. 245–46]." [3]

Although the boy described by Despert had serious problems by any criteria, an important question is whether the psychoanalytic concept of neurosis is the only possible explanation for his obsessive-compulsive symptoms. The severe stress created by his parents' behavior would have meant trouble for any child. The fact that his mother not only engaged in obsessive-compulsive behavior but imposed it on her child was likely to influence his behavior directly without the necessity for regression to the anal-sadistic phase, as emphasized by the psychoanalytic definition. On the other hand, the fact that both parents were severely disturbed suggests the possibility of a genetic influence such as has been identified for some of the severe disorders to be described in Chapter 12. Thus, the interpretation of obsessive-compulsive symptoms in terms of the psychoanalytic model may provide

[3] J. L. Despert, "Differential Diagnosis Between Obsessive-compulsive Neurosis and Schizophrenia in Children," in *Psychopathology of Childhood*, P. H. Hoch and J. Zubin (Eds.). (New York: Grune & Stratton, 1955), pp. 240–53. © 1955 by Grune & Stratton and reprinted by permission.

plausible leads as to the meaning of certain behavior for the child without necessarily telling us the etiology of the child's problems or how he may be helped.

Hysterical Neuroses

The psychoanalytic definition of hysterical neuroses contained in the *Glossary of Psychoanalytic Terms and Concepts* (Moore & Fine, 1968) portrays both conversion symptoms and dissociative states as manifestations of the same type of underlying neurosis.. The *Glossary* states that hysterical neuroses are:

. . . characterized clinically by 1) conversion symptoms and 2) an apparent affective indifference to the disturbance. . . . Occasionally, either separately or together with the foregoing, there are episodic states or major "hysterical spells," characterized by the *dissociation* of mental functions (e.g., double or multiple personalities, fugue states, somnambulism, major *amnesias,* etc.).

Conversion symptoms are physical manifestations not caused by or related to anatomical or physiological pathology. Among these are symptoms derived from motor, sensory or visceral reactions—anesthesias, pains, paralyses, tremors, deafness, blindness, vomiting, hiccoughing, etc. However, hysterical patients are often convinced their symptoms are due to objective physical disease, although their affective reactions are inappropriate to such conviction.

These syndromes are unique in every individual, and analysis demonstrates that they are historically determined by specific repressed experiences in the individual's past. They represent an expression in "body language" of specific unconscious *fantasies,* developing as a compromise in the conflict between an instinctual wish which has given rise to *anxiety* and the defense against that wish. . . .

Hysterical symptoms occur when there is difficulty at the level of resolution of the *oedipal conflict.* Here the wish for the incestuous love object represents the chief danger. The major defenses used are *repression* and *regression,* leading to dissociated bodily and affective symptomatology that acts as a distorted substitute and compromise for the original infantile sexual gratification. The choice of *symptom* (including affected organ or body zone) is predominantly based on the content of the unconscious fantasy and the ability of the organ to symbolize the unconscious forces involved. These symptoms are thus, par excellence, an example of the "return of the repressed," both the instinctual wish and the defense against it are re-enacted in the symptom . . . [p. 49].

As with the distinction between obsessive-compulsive neurosis and compulsive personality, a distinction is made between hysterical *neurosis* and hysterical *character* or *personality.* The distinction is based on the assumption that symptoms of hysterical neurosis result from a regression to certain conflicts and defenses, while hysterical personality involves a relatively permanent manner of functioning that may or may not lead to symptom formation, depending upon the stresses encountered.

Hysterical personalities are reported to occur much more frequently among females than among males. They are regarded as being overdramatic, flamboyant, suggestible, coy, seductive, and manipulative in a passive-aggressive way. Despite a veneer of social poise, they are likely to be overly dependent on their environments for establishment of their own identities. Although they appear to invite heterosexual relations, they evidence strong repression of sexual impulses and difficulties in the establishment of sexual relationships (cf. Group for the Advancement of Psychiatry, 1966).

Since the days of Charcot and Freud, there appears to have been a sharp decline in the incidence of dramatic hysterical symptoms among adults. This decline may be attributable to the dissemination of the idea that mental stresses can produce unusual physical symptoms, thus undermining the effectiveness of the more dramatic and bizarre symptoms as unconscious solutions to neurotic conflicts. Changes in social mores may also have played a role in lessening the intensity of conflicts over the expression of sexual impulses. However, dramatic hysterical symptoms are still reported in children from unsophisticated backgrounds (Dawes, 1953; Proctor, 1958, 1967; Starr, 1953) and a substantial number of child patients manifesting less dramatic symptoms are diagnosed hysteric (Proctor, 1967; Robins & O'Neal, 1953), as are many adult female patients (Purtell, Robins, & Cohen, 1951).

In a survey of 191 cases seen at the child psychiatry unit of the University of North Carolina Hospital, Proctor (1958) found 25 (13 per cent) that he regarded as meeting psychoanalytic criteria for conversion or dissociation hysteria. Many of the children exhibited the kinds of dramatic symptoms that are said to be rare today. These included uncontrollable pelvic thrusts, grotesque giant steps, a dissociative state in which a 12-year-old boy ran up and down the ward clutching his testicles while screaming in terror, and another in which a child hid under a bed in terror of his hallucination of a headless man.

As with extreme obsessive-compulsive symptoms, the problems of differentiating between neurosis and psychosis arose, but Proctor maintained that the diagnosis of hysteria was firmly established in all 25 cases. He attributed the high incidence of dramatic hysterical symptoms to the unsophisticated "bible-belt" backgrounds from which many of the children came. In many of their homes, the children were caught in fierce conflicts between repressive religious mores and the impulses aroused by seductive and irresponsible adult behavior.

In a survey of two New England hospitals, Purtell et al (1951) found that 12.9 per cent of the women psychiatric patients were diagnosed hysteric, while there were no male hysterics. Unlike the North Carolina children, most of the women reported pain as the chief symptom and did not exhibit classical hysterical organ dysfunctions. Ninety-eight per cent of the women also had sexual symptoms such as frigidity and disgust or indifference toward sex. Although their mean age was only 36, they had averaged 6.4 hospitalizations for various physical symptoms, compared to 3.2 hospitalizations for a control group of women with chronic medical illness and 1.2 for healthy control subjects.

A number of male hysterics were found in military hospitals where symptoms brought the prospect of pensions, discharge, or relief from duty. Unlike the women, the men generally did not have sexual symptoms. They reported a small number of focal physical complaints rather than the large number of vague complaints characteristic of the women, who averaged 23 symptoms each.

Robins and O'Neal (1953) undertook a follow-up study of children who had exhibited hysterical symptoms when hospitalized in a St. Louis children's hospital. They found that 8.3 per cent of the child psychiatric patients showed hysterical symptoms. Upon follow-up of 37 of these patients, at an average period of nine years after hospitalization, five (all female) were diagnosed as having clear-cut hysterical neuroses, 10 had anxiety neuroses, four had other psychiatric or physical afflictions, 12 had symptoms that could not be adequately diagnosed, and six were considered to be completely well. From the patients' life-history data, Robins and O'Neal concluded that the onset of hysteria was unusual before the age of nine and rare before the age of five and that boys who were diagnosed hysteric in childhood did not appear to be hysterics in later life.

The onset of dramatic hysterical symptoms has often been reported to be quite sudden. Such hysterias were, of course, the chief subject of Freud's early work and they are still considered to be among the best candidates for psychoanalytic treatment. Well-timed interpretation of the repressed impulses and defenses is regarded as being very effective in removing dramatic symptoms, although hypnosis, reduction of anxiety through tranquilizers, and environmental manipulations are also acknowledged by analytically oriented practitioners to be capable of relieving symptoms (Proctor, 1967). The disappearance of dramatic hysterical symptoms is often as sudden as their onset, although, in the studies cited above, vague and undramatic hysterical symptoms usually showed no signs of disappearing after many years (Purtell et al, 1951; Robins & O'Neal, 1953).

The following is a typical case in which psychoanalytic interpretive techniques are applied:

Over a two-week period prior to her hospital admission, a robust and vigorously active 14-year-old adolescent had been subject to epileptic-like seizures. Ward observations of these "spells" demonstrated many atypical phenomena not in keeping with a . . . cerebral disorder. During this same period of time she became disinterested in food, complaining of nausea.

Heralding her seizures she experienced a pervading fear of death. She would simultaneously complain of . . . a throbbing sensation involving the whole skin surface [beneath the waist] with a noticeable exception of the genital area. During the course of her seizure the motor phenomena would often be goal-directed; she would involve the attendant, who was close by for protective purposes, in a combative struggle and exclaim "I will break your horns off, you bull."

During her lucid intervals when visited on the ward, she would make an unsuccessfully awkward attempt to cover herself with bed sheets on the approach of the examiner. Quite invariably these attempts at modesty would instead result in a consistent display of parts of her body including the genital region. This sequence represented a clear demonstration of her ambivalent attitudes toward the male—alternately self-protecting and inviting.

The parents described their daughter as a fearless, undaunted, and challenging tom-boy who had "not known fear" until her current illness. She had always been highly contemptuous and disparaging of boys, refusing to associate with them. At the same time her crude and rough demeanor reflected a masculine identification; this largely stemmed from an outspoken envy, the basis of which she listed in outlining their numerous advantages within her subcultural group.

Highly volatile fuel was added to the fire by her parents who were unusually frank in informing their daughter of their deep disappointment when they learned of her sex at birth. Repeated jokes which revolved around the preferential status of boys kept her burning envy stoked.

Psychodynamic Impression: Within the three weeks preceding the onset of her illness, three events seemed psychologically significant in determining her current emotional upheaval:

a. Onset of menarche which served as a reality confirmation of her no longer deniable femininity.
b. She was being given classes on sex instruction within her parochial school wherein the disastrous consequences of sexuality were underlined.
c. Within the neighborhood a rape-murder incident had been highly publicized and was repetitiously discussed by the mother with a good deal of detail.

Her spell was a dramatization of a sexual assault including the struggle with the assailant. The triple series of events accentuated her feminine role and the dangers inherent therein. Thus her heretofore masculine identification . . . ceased to be able to serve its defensive purposes. The projection of her own destructive and damaging intents (stemming largely from envy of men) onto the male heightened his dangerous qualities for the girl [Starr, 1953, p. 225].

RESEARCH RELATED TO PSYCHOANALYTIC VIEWS OF "NEUROTIC" DISORDERS

In Chapter 4, a distinction was made between two stages in scientific activity. One stage is called the *context of discovery* wherein ideas are generated in whatever subjective, intuitive, creative, or accidental way an individual happens to think. The other stage of scientific endeavor is known as the *context of confirmation*. It is at this stage that the ideas emerging from the context of discovery are formulated in a manner that is generalizable, that is clearly communicable to others, and that makes the validity of the ideas testable. When the presentation of the ideas has reached this stage, their implications can be compared with real-world phenomena through experimentation or other forms of systematic observation. The more consistently the implications of the ideas are objectively corroborated through observation, the more confidence the ideas command.

Two important criteria for evaluating the objectivity of observations used to confirm ideas are: (1) Their *reliability*—the degree of agreement in the independent judgments of two or more people making the observations; and, (2) their *validity*—the degree to which the observations are shown to relate to other kinds of observations also directed at identifying the variables or relationships in question. (See Chapter 4 for further details of these criteria.) The purpose of testing ideas in the most objective possible manner is not simply to confirm or disconfirm them but to provide a basis for revising them in ways that will make them more useful, e.g., in preventing and treating psychopathology.

Despite the vastness of psychoanalytic literature, the ambitiousness of psychoanalytic theorizing, and the impact psychoanalytic views have had on contemporary thought, the analytic literature reports few attempts to move basic ideas out of the context of discovery and into the context of confirmation. The psychoanalyst Colby (1958) writes:

. . . we need to make systematic observations of specific phenomena rather than try haphazardly to range over the entirety of complex individual case histories. Most of all, we need systematic experiments designed to ask and answer specific questions.

The lack of controlled experiment in which essential variables are manipulated or held constant constitutes the greatest weakness of psychoanalysis as a science. We cannot advance through thought only, or through waiting to observe nature's experiments. We must actively try to test out which hypotheses fit the empirical facts. For one reason or another . . . psychoanalysts shy away from testing hypotheses. They seem to believe that if a plausible hypothesis can be formulated, it deserves to be considered an explanatory law or principle. They seldom take the next step of testing out which among many plausible hypotheses can be confirmed or disconfirmed.

Finally, besides systematic observations and systematic experiments, we need a careful, logical re-evaluation of our theory construction. . . there exist many logical contradictions and incorrect deductions which should be weeded out [pp. 9–10].

Possible Reasons for the Failure to Test Psychoanalytic Hypotheses

The failure of analysts to test their ideas more systematically may be partly due to the fact that, once Freud's persuasive writings gained a fair hearing, the truth of his most basic discoveries seemed evident to so many professional workers that further research to verify them appeared superfluous. Among the basic assumptions now shared by nearly all professional mental health workers are:

1. the deterministic nature of psychological functioning, e.g., the assumption that all thoughts and behavior are determined by antecedent events, although there is disagreement about the mechanisms of causation;

2. the existence of unconscious mental processes and motives, although

not all workers give as much weight as Freud to the "dynamic" unconscious composed of repressed impulses;
3. the reality of childhood sexuality—prepubertal children have intense
sexual curiosity and fantasies, become aroused sexually, and direct
sexual desires toward people around them, including their opposite-
sex parent.

A second reason for the failure to move analytic ideas into the context
of confirmation may have been Freud's unique role in the development of
analytic thought. He was the originator of the basic concepts, inventor of
the treatment, leader of the "psychoanalytic movement," and chief revision-
ist of the theory throughout his lifetime. While many others have written
on psychoanalysis, he remains the authority to whose writings all others make
reference. Nearly every article in the psychoanalytic literature quotes him
and most attempts at innovation are based upon exegesis of his writings
to show that the proposed innovation is consistent with what Freud said or
with what he might have said if he had written more about a particular
topic. Whatever the reason for this need to refer everything back to the
writings of a long-dead pioneer of the context of discovery, it is hard to deny
that it exists. In addressing newly graduated analysts, Colby (1958) says:

> It is easy enough to tell young analysts to carry out systematic observation, ex-
> periment, and theory reconstruction. Why wouldn't they do so anyway without
> this tiresome exhortation? In part, because they are afraid. Unfortunately in psy-
> choanalysis there exists an unfavorable atmosphere for change. Physicists are ex-
> hilarated by experiments leading to new data and overjoyed when hitherto accepted
> laws are proved inadequate. . . . But practitioners in psychoanalysis do not always
> welcome such efforts, and they can make it hard for the young psychoanalyst inter-
> ested in them. They consider ability in psychoanalysis to be proportionate to fa-
> miliarity with Freud's writings and skill to consist of adroitness in moving the same
> old conceptual furniture to new positions in the same old conceptual house. An
> idea is measured in terms of whether Freud thought of it (legitimate) or whether
> he didn't (unwarranted). Priority in psychoanalysis is often not a matter of who
> thought of what first but who knows when Freud thought of it first [pp. 10–11].

A third reason for the failure to move psychoanalysis into the context of
confirmation may stem from Freud's own attitude toward research, the influence this had on the analysts he trained, and the continuing transmission
of this influence through the training programs, societies, and journals organized by his followers. Freud (1940) insisted that the teachings of psychoanalysis could only be judged by those who had repeated its "incalculable
number of observations . . . upon himself or upon others [p. 9]." While
specialized training may be necessary before a person can evaluate teachings
in many specialized fields, there has been a tendency in the analytic literature to treat analytic training as not only a necessary qualification, but as a
qualification *sufficient* to guarantee the validity of a person's psychoanalytic
observations and hypotheses. Thus, the fact that a person has been trained

as an analyst often seems to exempt him from having to translate his personal hunches into testable form, to distinguish clearly between his observations and his inferences from them, and to provide evidence for the reliability and validity of data he uses to support his hunches.

Riess (1972), a psychoanalytically oriented psychologist, points out that even fewer attempts have been made to move the ideas and methods of child analysis into the context of confirmation than have been made with adult analysis. However, he defends the lack of research on the following grounds:

Research requires an attitude which in some respects is antagonistic to a fundamental assumption of all analytic therapy, namely, that the therapist maintain an interested, empathic, but nonjudgmental stance vis-a-vis his patient. The therapist-analyst is constantly searching, but his interests are not in re-searching with his patient, for he is convinced that no situation can be replicated on the same subject and that no two subjects can be adequately matched. Thus the sacred elements of "control" and "repeatability" seem to be beyond the realm of possibility.

. . . the analyst resists the intrusion of experimentally introduced variables into the treatment process because of concern for the relationship with the patient and for the goal of treatment, which is the increased efficiency of the patient [pp. 1178–79].

There is no doubt that, according to the tenets of psychoanalytic practice, the analyst must assume an attitude of watchful waiting for connections to appear among the associations of his patient and must attend also to the associations evoked in himself as an intuitive guide to treatment. This process is akin to the search or discovery processes in other fields. However, the value such processes may have in treatment of patients does not logically preclude attempts to move the hypotheses thus generated into the context of confirmation where the wheat is to be separated from the chaff for the ultimate purpose of more effectively bringing about "the increased efficiency" of patients.

As for controlled follow-up studies to determine whether psychoanalysis is more beneficial than other treatments or no treatment, Riess (1972) objects that such studies present an almost unsolvable problem—that of differentiating changes due to maturation from those due to therapy. The rigorous study of the effects of treatment is indeed difficult and this issue will be taken up at length in Chapter 17. However, the problem of change due to extratherapeutic factors such as maturation is no different for evaluating the effectiveness of psychoanalysis than it is for evaluating the effectiveness of any other treatment, be it behavioral or organic. Control groups, who receive no treatment or other treatments, were invented precisely for the purpose of comparing changes in them with changes in individuals undergoing the treatment of interest.

Despite the paucity of studies in which psychoanalysts have attempted to move their ideas from the context of discovery into the context of confirmation, considerable research has been inspired by psychoanalytic theory and practice in one way or another. For our consideration of childhood psychopathology, two primary questions must be asked of this research:

1. Are what psychoanalytic theory defines as "neurotic" disorders *caused* in the way the theory implies?
2. Does psychoanalytic treatment *ameliorate* or *cure* such disorders?

These two questions are, in principal, separate issues because it is possible that the theory of how neuroses are caused is correct, but that the treatment is ineffective in undoing the causes. Conversely, it is possible that the theory is incorrect, but that the treatment is beneficial for reasons other than those implied by the theory.

RESEARCH ON PSYCHOANALYTIC VIEWS OF THE CAUSES OF NEUROSIS

Levels of Psychoanalytic Doctrine

Because terms and concepts representing various conceptual levels are freely intermingled in the psychoanalytic literature, Waelder (1962), a prominent exponent of the scientific aspects of psychoanalysis, has distinguished several levels of discourse relating to analytic doctrine. A prerequisite for evaluating research on analysis is the sorting out of propositions that belong to different levels such as those distinguished by Waelder.

According to Waelder, the most fundamental level is the *level of observation,* comprising the firsthand observational data that the analyst obtains from his patient. Such data consist of things the patient says and does and how he says and does them.

Waelder's second level is the *level of clinical interpretation.* This refers to the analyst's interpretations of the connections among his observations, i.e., his impressions and hypotheses about the particular meanings underlying the patient's behavior.

Waelder's third level, the *level of clinical generalizations,* refers to "statements regarding a particular type, e.g., a sex, an age group, a psychopathological symptom, a mental or emotional disease, a character type, the impact of a particular family constellation, or of any particular experience, and the like [p. 620]." Such generalizations abound in the psychoanalytic literature and many have become commonplaces of clinical lore. An example is the generalization that the typical mother of an enuretic boy has "depreciatory attitudes toward males that make her demand that her son be both ineffective and rebellious [Pierce, 1967, p. 1381]."

The fourth level distinguished by Waelder is the *level of clinical theory,* comprised of "theoretical concepts which are either implicit in the [clinical] interpretations or to which the interpretations may lead, such as repression, defense, return of the repressed, regression, etc. [p. 620]."

Two further levels of discourse, considered by Waelder to be relatively abstract and unimportant for the clinical concepts, are the *level of metapsychology,* including such concepts as cathexis, psychic energy, etc., and the *level of Freud's philosophy.* Ideas at the level of Freud's philosophy are, of course, not relevant to research on the origins of neurosis. Ideas at the level of metapsychology are of some relevance because so much of clinical theory and interpretation invokes them as explanatory constructs. For example, the psychosexual stages are defined in terms of the distribution of psychic energy and neuroses are said to involve regressions and fixations in the distribution of this energy. However, psychic energy has not been equated with any kind of biochemical energy (Rapaport, 1959). It seems destined to retain the metaphorical significance given it by Freud, and there have not been serious attempts to test its existence, to define its properties objectively, or to measure it. The same is true for concepts like cathexis, id, ego, and superego, although measures of "ego strength," as a general synonym for strength of personality, have been included on objectively scored personality tests such as the Minnesota Multiphasic Personality Inventory (cf. Dahlstrom & Welsh, 1960).

Since the levels of Freud's philosophy and of metapsychology do not offer researchable issues regarding the origin of neuroses, the following sections deal only with research related to the other four levels distinguished by Waelder.

Level of Observation.   Although observations of behavioral events during analytic treatment, such as the words and play of the patient, form the primary data base upon which psychoanalytic thinking is built, there has been little attempt to record accurately these behavioral events so that they may be reassessed by others or by the therapist himself. Few therapists even make extensive written notes during treatment sessions. This is understandable in light of the interference note-taking may create with the therapist-patient relationship and with the therapist's thinking. However, one of the keystones of the analytic view of psychological functioning is that human perception and memory are extremely vulnerable to distortion by unconscious and preconscious influences. Coupled with the limitations of memory and cognition, these factors make it unlikely that a therapist can retain a completely accurate mental record of the patient's behavior and of his own during each treatment session. While Freud emphasized how amazing the analyst's memory can become for behavior related to "significant" themes in a patient's associations, it is hard to imagine that much important behavior is not lost or distorted in the analyst's memory. Thus, better empirical evaluation is needed for many of the reported observations used to support psychoanalytic interpretations, generalizations, and theory.

Some attempts have been made to record patient and analyst behavior on tape and film for research purposes. Haggard, Hiken, and Isaacs (1965) made a detailed study of the effects of sound filming on both the patient and therapist. They secured the cooperation of three analysts and adult patients who agreed to the filming of their sessions. Extensive notes by an analyst on another case were used to provide a rough control against which to compare the therapy process in the other three cases. The therapists in the three "experimental" cases also reported their own observations and reactions in considerable detail.

On the basis of their data and a review of other studies, Haggard et al drew two major conclusions. One was that the research conditions did not disrupt the essential processes of therapy such as the verbalization of free associations, the patient's transference onto the analyst of his feelings toward his parents, the working-through of intimate emotional conflicts, and the personal growth of the patient. A second conclusion was that the therapists appeared to be more disturbed by the research context than were the patients, but experience with being observed eventually reduced most therapists' anxiety about it. Haggard et al also reported an unpublished study by H. Bolgar in which comparisons of tapes with therapists' summaries of sessions that had just ended showed numerous omissions and reorganizations of the material by the therapists, including reversals of therapist-patient sequences.

Level of Clinical Interpretation. The problem of moving from the actual behavior of the patient to the analyst's interpretations is more complex than that of obtaining an accurate record of behavior. Accurate observation is a necessary condition for correct interpretation, but the way in which the analyst mentally codes and remembers observations is inextricably intertwined with his interpretations.

The seriousness of this problem is illustrated by Wolpe and Rachman's (1960) textual analysis of the case of "Little Hans," to which Freud (1909) devoted a 145-page report because he believed it so clearly supported his theory of the Oedipus complex and neurotic symptom formation. Like any case report, this one was likely to have selectively emphasized observations that supported the author's theory. The data provided Freud by Hans's father were also likely to have shown such a bias because Hans's parents were described by Freud as being "among my closest adherents."

Despite the likelihood that observations were selected to fit the theory, Wolpe and Rachman point out numerous instances in which the report itself reveals that behavior and ideas that Freud or Hans's father attributed to Hans actually originated with them, with little evidence being reported to show that they might have been spontaneous in Hans. In one instance, immediately after Hans developed his phobia, Freud told Hans's father "that he should tell the boy that all this nonsense about horses was a piece of nonsense and nothing more. The truth was, his father was to say, that he [Hans] was very fond of his mother and wanted to be taken into her bed. The reason he was afraid of horses now was that he had taken so much interest in their widdlers [Freud, 1909, p. 28]."

A second instance concerns Freud's contention that, for Hans, a biting white horse symbolized a widdler. Hans's father had repeatedly told him horses don't bite, but Hans told of hearing a friend's father warn her away from a particular white horse lest it bite. Hans's father replied, "I say, it strikes me it isn't a horse you mean, but a widdler, that one mustn't put one's hand to." Hans: "But a widdler doesn't bite." Father: "Perhaps it does, though." Hans then "went on eagerly to try to prove . . . that it really was a white horse [he was afraid of]." The next day, Hans replied to a remark of his father by saying that his phobia was "so bad because I still put my hand to my widdler every night [Freud, 1909, p. 30]." In a third instance, when Hans expressed a fear of large animals at the zoo, his father had said to him: "Do you know why you're afraid of big animals? Big animals have big widdlers and you're really afraid of big widdlers [Freud, 1909, p. 33]." Hans denied this.

While we can never know exactly what the sequence of Hans's behavior really was nor whether Freud's interpretations were indeed correct, more recent studies have shown that analysts are unlikely to agree in their interpretations of patients' behavior. Seitz (1966) reports that he and several other analysts spent three years in independently interpreting detailed sequences of observations noted by other analysts in the course of treatment. Seitz and his colleagues met frequently to compare their interpretations and to create guidelines for improving the reliability of their judgments. Although no quantitative measures of reliability were reported, Seitz concluded that the results, in terms of consensus of interpretation, were "strongly negative."

In a study that did report reliability measures, two analysts who had graduated from the same training institute made ratings of the transcripts of the Haggard et al (1965) recordings of adult patients' reactions during five-minute periods following important interpretations and noninterpretive interventions by the therapists (Garduk & Haggard, 1972). The ratings were made on 4-point scales for variables considered important in psychoanalysis. Table 9–1 presents the categories in which the analyst judges rated the patient reactions and the correlations between the two judges' ratings. As can be seen from the table, the degree of agreement between the two judges for such key variables as anxiety and blocking-of-associations was not above the level expected by chance, and correlations between the judges' ratings did not exceed .52 for any of the categories.

Table 9–1 also portrays reliabilities of ratings of adult patient behavior during entire tape-recorded therapy sessions, as reported by Auerbach & Luborsky (1968). The correlations between the ratings of two experienced analytically trained clinicians ranged from .26 to .70, with a median of

TABLE 9–1

Reliability of psychoanalysts' ratings of patient functioning during therapy.

Garduk & Haggard Study (1972)		Auerbach & Luborsky Study (1968)	
Variable	Reliability of ratings[a]	Variable	Reliability of ratings[b]
1. Anxiety	.11	1. Anxiety	.54
2. Depression	.32	2. Depression	.52
3. Anger, hostility, aggression	.52	3. Hostility to others	.70
		4. Hostility to therapist	.47
4. Defensive and oppositional associations (denial, repudiation, doubt, hostility to therapist; tries to distort, change subject)	.46	5. Quality of experiencing	.42
		6. Warmth to therapist	.46
		7. Guilt and shame	.46
		8. Empathy to therapist	.30
		9. Dependency	.42
5. Presence of affect	.28	10. Activity	.55
6. Pleasant affect	.21	11. Receptiveness	.26
7. Surprise	.30	12. Impact on patient	.47
8. Ego dysfunctioning (disruption, confusion, inability to function)	.04		
9. Symptomatology (alterations or aggravation in symptoms)	.13		
10. Communication of conscious material (factual, objective information)	.35		
11. Communication of deeper-level material	.23		
12. Blocking of associations	.13		
13. Understanding and insight	.37		
14. Transference-related material	.52		

[a] Correlations between 2 analysts' ratings of 120 5-minute segments of treatment following significant interpretations and noninterpretive interventions. Correlations above .18 are $p < .05$.

[b] Correlations between 2 analysts' ratings of 60 treatment sessions. Correlations above .25 are $p < .05$.

.46. However, on 9 of the 12 variables, correlations between the ratings of one clinician and a clinically untrained rater were higher than the correlations between the ratings made by the two clinicians. This indicates that analytic training did not necessarily enhance reliability of judgment.

That somewhat higher reliabilities were obtained in this study than in the Garduk & Haggard (1972) study may be due to the fact that tapes of whole sessions rather than written transcripts of segments were rated.

Despite the low reliabilities in judgments, Luborsky (1970) has put the recorded interview data to imaginative use in studying the contexts in which expressions of neurotic symptoms occur during therapy. His technique is to choose symptomatic expressions (e.g., momentary forgetting, reports of stomach pain and headache) that occurred during a taped session and then to have raters independently score various themes in segments of the sessions immediately preceding and following the symptom expression. Comparisons of the themes detected shortly before and after symptomatic expressions have revealed the recurrence of a particular theme for a given patient just before his symptom appears. For example, one patient repeatedly showed momentary forgetting of what he intended to say whenever he was approaching expression of a wish for warmth or sexual contact with a woman. Luborsky hopes to be able to demonstrate by his technique that symptom formation occurs whenever unconscious anxiety-arousing thoughts near consciousness.

Level of Clinical Generalizations.   Most of the literature relating to psychoanalysis does not explicitly separate clinical generalizations from the other levels identified by Waelder. It is often hard to determine whether a clinical generalization has arisen primarily from clinical theory or from an analyst's impression that a particular clinical observation or interpretation is widely generalizable.

In a study that aimed explicitly at testing clinical generalizations, Achenbach and Lewis (1971) searched the psychodynamic child literature for reasonably clear generalizations about boys having either enuresis or encopresis (bowel incontinence). Eleven generalizations were found for encopresis and 13 for enuresis. These were reformulated as declarative sentences the evidence for which could be judged in individual cases. An example for encopresis is: "The parents infantilize the boy"; for enuresis: "The mother emasculates her son."

The files of a psychoanalytically oriented child clinic and training center were then searched for records of boys who had been treated for either enuresis or encopresis without evidence for organic etiology. Records of boys having learning disorders but neither of the other two symptoms were also located to provide a comparison group. From each group of records, boys were selected who could be matched to a boy in each of the other two groups for race, socioeconomic status, age, IQ, and number of clinical interviews. Eighteen triads of cases were thus created in which all three members were similar on the matching variables but differed in whether they had enuresis, encopresis, or learning disability. The case histories averaged 37 single-spaced typed pages in length and were based on an average of 38 interviews with the child, plus more than that with his parents.

In order to test the validity of the clinical generalizations, a child psychoanalyst read all the case histories and rated the evidence in each case for each of the 24 statements derived from the clinical generalizations. To prevent the analyst's judgment from being contaminated by knowledge of which symptom was present in a case, the records he read were copies of the histories in which all references to any of the three symptoms had been obliterated.

Of the 24 clinical generalizations, the analyst's ratings showed statistically significant ($p < .05$) support for two. At least one such significant finding could have arisen by chance since 24 comparisons were made (.05 × 24 = 1.2), although other evidence indicated that the support for these two generalizations was unlikely to be an artifact of chance. The nonsignificant differences between the symptom groups on the other 22 statements favored 9 of the clinical generalizations and contradicted 13.

An attempt was made to determine whether invalidity in the observations and interpretations reported in the case records or in the analyst's interpretations of them might have accounted for the absence of support for the clinical generalizations. This was done by comparing the analyst's ratings on the 24 statements in two groups of the cases that had been separated according to a criterion other than the single symptoms of enuresis, encopresis, and learning disability. The two groups were separated on the basis of differences in the *patterns* of symptoms they showed, as identified by factor analysis of symptoms recorded from their records by a clinically untrained research assistant. The analyst's ratings significantly differentiated these two groups on 8 of the 24 statements.

The fact that the analyst's ratings significantly differentiated cases on as many as 8 statements out of 24 indicates that lack of support for the clinical generalizations did not result from sheer randomness in the analyst's ratings, due either to the inadequacy of the records or of his judgments. Instead, it suggests that the clinical generalizations did not apply to the single symptoms of enuresis and encopresis in the way they had been stated in the literature.

Several studies have been made of clinical generalizations about antecedents or correlates of behavior assumed to involve oral conflicts. Sewell and Mussen (1952) interviewed mothers of five- and six-year-olds to determine whether their children had been breast or bottle fed, demand or schedule fed, and gradually or abruptly weaned, all considered by analysts to be important variables in the establishment of oral conflicts. Assessments of the children's behavior were obtained from three sources: The mothers' reports on several "oral" symptoms—stuttering, nail-biting, slowness in acquiring speech, bashfulness about talking, finger-sucking, eating difficulties; the children's scores on a personality test administered by a trained clinician; and teachers' ratings of the children on various traits. No statistically significant support was found for relations between infant feeding procedures and behavior or adjustment at ages five and six.

Studies of correlates of "oral" pathology are exemplified by two that have reported relations between measures of "oral" personality test responses and certain types of pathology in adults. In one study, Wolowitz (1964) found that alcoholics preferred soft, sweet, liquid foods suggestive of oral passivity more than did normal control subjects, who preferred sour, spicy, crunchy foods suggestive of oral sadism. In the other study, Weiss and Masling (1970) found that the Rorschach (inkblot test) responses of alcoholics, stutterers, and patients suffering from ulcers or obesity were significantly higher than those of control subjects on an index of oral imagery. However, three other "oral" groups—heavy drinkers, asthmatics, and thumb-suckers (the only group comprised mainly of children)—were not significantly higher than controls in oral imagery on the Rorschach.

Unfortunately, the verification of correlates of pathology does not by itself indicate that the pathology *resulted* from particular conflicts or particular stages of psychosexual development. It indicates only that, once a person has a particular form of pathology, he also differs from other people with respect to the verified correlates. Verification of correlates may aid in the further refinement and testing of causal hypotheses, but correlations of this nature do not imply causation.

Studies of antecedents and correlates of "anal" traits have paralleled those for oral traits. Hetherington and Brackbill (1963) attempted to determine whether obstinacy, parsimony, and orderliness, the three traits used by analytic writers to define the "anal" or "compulsive" personality, correlated with one another in five-year-old children and whether toilet training factors had influenced the traits. They gave the children 10 experimental tasks designed to measure the traits, but the trait measures did not show the predicted correlations.

The children's parents were also given lengthy questionnaires to determine their toilet training practices and their own degrees of obstinacy, orderliness, and parsimony. No support was found for the analytic hypothesis that too early, too late, or too severe toilet training leads to obstinacy, parsimony, or orderliness in children. Instead, the children's scores on these traits correlated with their parents' scores on them, suggesting that the traits had been influenced by the children's identifications with or learning from their parents.

Level of Clinical Theory.   As with the level of clinical interpretation, little research at the level of clinical theory has been directed at determining which assertions are consistently supported by observation. Instead, there is an assortment of studies some of which happen to cluster around particular theoretical concepts. Few of the studies deal with children, although most analytic concepts are assumed to apply equally to children and adults.

In reviewing studies which he considered to bear on psychoanalytic theory, Sears (1944) presented evidence related to five categories of concepts: Fixation and regression; aggression; substitution; projection; and repression. Much of the evidence was gleaned from studies of learning in which human or animal behavior was interpreted in Freudian terms. For example, frequency of reinforcement, strength of drive at the time of learning, and amount of reward were taken as rough indices of the degree of fixation a pattern of behavior was likely to have acquired. Some evidence was found that subjects "regressed" to earlier, strongly "fixated" behavior when later-learned behavior was frustrated. Freud's assertion that frustration could goad an animal or person to aggression was also supported to some extent by laboratory-type studies (cf. Dollard, Doob, Miller, Mowrer, & Sears, 1939).

Under the heading of "substitution," Sears reported a number of findings suggesting that subjects' motivation to carry out certain activities could be reduced through substitute activities when the original ones were blocked. However, he concluded that there was no evidence for the *sublimation* of libidinal impulses in activity having a "higher" cultural value. For example, in a study of 40 "brilliant, healthy, esthetically refined" young bachelors whose characters and achievements were suggestive of sublimation, it was found that none of the men had foresaken sex and that they all habitually obtained direct genital gratification through autoerotic or heterosexual activity (Taylor, 1933).

Studies of the influence of motivation on the perception of ambiguous stimuli were interpreted by Sears as providing evidence for projection. Hunger, for example, was found to increase the number of food responses by subjects guessing what the missing parts of incomplete stimuli might be. In a study in which college students rated themselves and their fraternity brothers on various traits, Sears (1936) found that students who were rated very high on a trait, but who rated themselves low on the trait, tended to rate others exceptionally high on that trait. However, the "defensive" nature of this projection may be questionable because it was found for desirable traits like generosity as well as for undesirable traits.

In an experimental study of projection, eight-year-olds were given a preferred and a nonpreferred toy and were then asked to give one to a friend to play with (Wright, 1940). They were later asked which toy the friend would have given away. As compared to control children who had not been required to give up a toy, fewer children who had just experienced the conflict situation considered their friends generous enough to give away the preferred toy.

Repression, the fifth concept reviewed by Sears, has continued to be tested more than the other concepts. As of Sears's writing, the chief research evidence for repression was the finding in several studies that people have more difficulty in remembering unpleasant than pleasant experiences, whether the experiences had been induced experimentally or had occurred prior to the study.

Before going on to more recent studies, however, the reaction of a prominent analyst to the studies reviewed by Sears should be noted:

Many of these laboratory charades are pedestrian and limited demonstrations of things which have been proved over and over again in real life. . . . Experimental facilities should not be wasted on issues which are already clearly proved, and to which human bias alone continues to blind us. The experimentalist should rather take up where the naturalist leaves off. He may ask the naturalist to guide him on a field trip, so that he can satisfy himself concerning the observations which the naturalist has made and has brought to him for investigation. It is not his duty or responsibility, however, to prove in the laboratory the existence of data which the naturalist reports to him. Much controversy about the empirical data of analysis has arisen because people have refused to look at facts which are clearly observable in the analytic situation [Kubie, 1952, pp. 64–65].

Few would argue as to the enormous differences between the typical analytic hour and the "laboratory charades" reviewed by Sears. The relevance of most of the studies to the analytic situation is indeed far from clear. But, in view of the lack of evidence for the reliability and validity of analytic observations, interpretations, and generalizations, Kubie might be asked just what the clearly observable *facts* in the analytic situation are that people have refused to look at? And how can these facts be more effectively conceptualized so that they can be agreed upon by analysts and be better utilized for treatment and prevention?

The fact that people's free associations, dreams, and slips of the tongue are not random but are correlated with other aspects of their behavior is no longer in dispute. Nor is the existence of unconscious influences or childhood sexuality. Yet, beyond these basic assumptions, which are shared by most mental-health workers, it is not clear what observations of the "naturalist" (i.e., analyst) referred to by Kubie have been so precisely formulated and so firmly verified that more objective research—experimental or otherwise—is not needed before they can be used with confidence. In the absence of more systematic attempts by analysts to move their ideas about the nature and causation of neuroses into the context of confirmation, it is also difficult to lay down guidelines for research by others that will not be rejected by analysts as "laboratory charades" or as unwarranted intrusions by "experimentalists" into realms reserved for "naturalists."

Interactive Designs

A general experimental design for testing Freudian personality concepts has been proposed and utilized by Sarnoff (1971). He calls the design an *interactive design* because it focuses upon the interaction between individuals' standing on particular traits and their reactions under varying conditions.

In a simple version of the design, Sarnoff and Corwin (1959) tested the hypothesis that castration anxiety is manifested in fear of death and that increases in sexual arousal will produce increases in fear of death by castration-anxious men. Projective test responses were used to identify two groups of college men differing in castration anxiety. The men were also given a questionnaire which included items designed to measure fear of death. Several weeks later, half the castration-anxious men and half the nonanxious men were shown photos of nude women. The other half of the men in each group were shown nonarousing pictures of clothed women. Finally, all the men were given the fear-of-death measure again.

The prediction was that there would be an *interaction* between a man's initial standing on castration anxiety and the experimental condition (arousing or nonarousing) in producing changes in fear of death. Men who were high on castration anxiety were expected to show greater increases in fear of death than were low-anxious men in the arousing condition, but no differences in change of fear were expected in the nonarousing condition. The results confirmed the predictions and were interpreted as supporting the Freudian theory of the relations between castration anxiety, fear of death, and sexual arousal.

The general advantage of this type of experimental design for testing Freudian concepts is that it focuses not just upon predicted correlates of personality characteristics, but upon the way in which personality characteristics are related to people's reactions under *varying* conditions.

Are Neurotic Disorders Caused in the Manner Implied by Psychoanalysis?

Taken together, the research cited so far does not add up to much of an answer to the question of whether neurotic disorders are *caused* in the way that psychoanalytic theory implies. Some of the principles of mental functioning, such as repression, that are invoked in the explanations of neurosis have been supported by research, others have not, and many others have not been tested. No attempt appears to have been made at formulating the *necessary* and *sufficient* conditions for the production of what analytic theory defines as a neurosis, much less at testing such a formulation.

Perhaps the closest attempts at experimentally studying the causes of neurosis have involved the creation of conflicts in animals by rewarding them for learning complex patterns of behavior and then making the consequences of the learned behavior painful, e.g., with electric shock. Symptoms such as compulsions, generalized fearfulness, phobias, and psychophysiological reactions have been thus produced in animals. However, Masserman (1943, 1950, 1963), a leader in this research who happens to be a trained psychoanalyst, interprets the results as failing to support the Freudian conception of neurosis. He explains the "neurotic" symptoms in terms of conflicts between conditioned patterns of behavior that arise from incompatible needs (e.g., the need to get food and to escape pain), and he has demonstrated the removal of the neurotic symptoms by modifying the incompatible behavior patterns, mainly through conditioning.

An approach that may come somewhat closer to documenting the natural history of neuroses in humans is the study of childhood experiences in large groups of neurotic and nonneurotic people. However, in a review of 40 years of studies, Frank (1965) concluded that no factors were found in the parent-child interactions of neurotics that were unique to them or that could distinguish them from other pathological groups or from nonpathological controls. A complementary finding was that most people selected for study because of their good mental health had experienced traumas and parental discord, tension, illness, and repressiveness in degrees usually associated with the background of psychiatric patients (Renaud & Estess, 1961; Schofield & Balian, 1959).

It may be possible to blame the lack of causal evidence on the crudeness of our current concepts and techniques for studying the precise interactions of parents and children. Accordingly, only by devising better methods for looking at those interactions are we likely to move closer to accurate natural histories and more valid concepts of how neuroses actually come about. In their longitudinal study of relations between children's temperamental characteristics, their parents' behavior, and the development of disorders, Thomas et al (1968) have attempted to do just this. One of their key conclusions has to do with the central role attributed to anxiety in producing neurotic symptoms in children:

. . . in the young child, anxiety has not been evident as an initial factor preceding and determining symptom development. Where anxiety has evolved in the course of the development of a child's behavior disorder, it has been a secondary phenomenon, a consequence rather than a cause of symptom development and expression. Similarly, the removal of symptoms by a successful parent-guidance procedure has had positive consequences for the child's functioning, and has not resulted in the appearance of overt anxiety or of new substitutive symptoms.

We have found it unnecessary to invoke concepts regarding presumed states of intrapsychic conflict or the operation of psychodynamic mechanisms of a purposive ideational character to explain the origins of behavioral disturbances in young children. In each case of an excessively stressful and maladaptive interaction between the child and his environment, a parsimonious formulation in terms of objective and overtly evident characteristics of the child, patterns of parental functioning, and other specific environmental influences has been sufficient to account for the genesis of the problem behavior. However, intrapsychic conflict and psychodynamic defenses, as well as anxiety, have been evident in some older children as later developments in the child's response to the unfavorable and sometimes threatening consequences of an initial maladaptation.

It is, of course, true that once anxiety, intrapsychic conflict, and psychodynamic defense mechanisms appear, they add new dimensions to the dynamics of the child's functioning and contribute to his interactions. When this happens, they may substantially influence the subsequent course of the behavior problem. The painfulness of severe anxiety when it is overt makes it a striking symptom which may dominate our perceptions of the clinical picture. The elaborate psychological techniques utilized to minimize or to avoid distress may also contribute dramatically to the elaboration of pathological patterns of behavior and thought. It is, therefore, not surprising that in retrospective studies that begin when the child already presents with an elaborated psychological disturbance, the prominent phenomena of anxiety and psychodynamic defenses dominate clinical thinking, and come to be labeled as primary, rather than as secondary, influences in the genesis of behavior disturbance [pp. 188–89].[4]

The conclusions of Thomas et al do not deny the basic assumptions of psychological determinism, unconscious influences, childhood sexuality, or the meaningfulness of free associations and other analytic data such as dream reports. However, they do suggest that factors considered by analysts to *cause* children's neuroses may in fact be *effects* or may have other nonetiological significance.

RESEARCH ON THE EFFECTIVENESS OF PSYCHOANALYTIC TREATMENT

The general problem of evaluating treatment of psychopathology is an extremely complex one that will be taken up at length in Chapter 17. However, since each of the major viewpoints on the various disorders is closely linked to a method of treatment, it is important to consider evidence for the efficacy of these treatments in direct relation to their theoretical bases. Very few studies of the efficacy of psychoanalysis have been published. None has systematically compared the effects of analysis with the effects of a different treatment or of no treatment in substantial numbers of patients who were shown to be initially well-matched to the analytic patients.

Effects of Child Psychoanalysis

What appears to be the only study of the effects of child psychoanalysis also appears to be the only study that compared analysis with another treatment in patients matched to the analytic patients, although there were only four patients in each group (Heinicke, 1965, 1969). In this study, four latency age boys with learning disorders received four-times weekly psychoanalysis while four others received psychoanalytically oriented therapy once a week. Therapy lasted from one and one-half to two and one-half years. Mothers of the boys were seen once a week and fathers were seen whenever it was deemed appropriate. Unfortunately, details of the boys' initial stand-

---

[4] A. Thomas, S. Chess, and H. G. Birch, *Temperament and Behavior Disorders in Children.* (New York: New York University Press, 1968). © 1968 by New York University and reprinted by permission.

ing on the matching variables were not reported. By the end of treatment, ratings on 3 out of 45 clinical dimensions significantly favored the boys receiving analysis, although 2 significant differences would be expected by chance alone in 45 comparisons.

When ratings were again made one and two years after treatment, the number of significant differences increased to 6 out of the 45 dimensions. What the differences were and whether they favored the analytically treated boys were not reported. Standardized achievement tests indicated slower improvement in reading and spelling by the analyzed boys during treatment, but faster improvement by them after treatment, although the lack of information on initial and final scores makes it impossible to determine whether they started off and ended up ahead of or behind the other boys.

Effects of Adult Psychoanalysis

More attention has been paid to evaluating the efficacy of adult analysis. However, the studies are even less adequate than the one study of child patients. In what appears to be the most complete study, Knight (1941) summarized the results in previous samples and added to them cases from the Menninger Clinic with which he was associated. Since the available reports on analysis had not used uniform methods or criteria for evaluating improvement, Knight selected cases that could be identified by general diagnostic grouping and could be roughly assigned to the overall categories of "apparently cured," "much improved," "improved," and "no change or worse." Five hundred thirty-four cases of neurosis were reported, of which 151 were discarded because they had not stayed in treatment at least 6 months. Of the remaining patients, 242 (63.2 per cent) were judged to be cured or much improved.

Although he provided no information on diagnosis, Feldman (1968) obtained a similar figure (64 per cent) for the proportion of cases judged to have been " 'good' or 'very good' analytic experiences for student analysts, and . . . the patients improved significantly" in the clinic of the Southern California Psychoanalytic Institute. His figure was based upon 99 out of all the 120 cases accepted for treatment over an approximately 13-year period. The 99 cases averaged between 300 and 400 treatment sessions. The 21 cases omitted were excluded for reasons generally unrelated to outcome.

In another study, a committee of the American Psychoanalytic Association sent questionnaires to association members in order to obtain their judgments of results in cases they had treated (Brody, 1962; Masserman, 1963). Of 595 neurotic patients upon whom data were obtained, 306 were reported to have been "completely analyzed." Of these 306, judgments were obtained on 210, of whom 60 per cent were regarded as being cured or greatly improved.

Other data have been reported from what appears to have been a later stage of the study reported by Brody and Masserman (Hamburg, Bibring,

Fisher, Stanton, Wallerstein, Weinstock, & Haggard, 1967). However, portions of the data were lost and outcome questionnaires were eventually submitted on only 3,000 of the original 10,000 patients for whom initial descriptive forms had been submitted by their analysts. Some of the patients had undergone analytically oriented therapy, some analysis, and some both treatments at different times. Because of the many problems pointed out by the authors in the design of the questionnaires, in obtaining adequate responses from analysts, and in forming diagnostic classifications, the statistics on outcome cannot be regarded with much confidence. About the only result worth noting here is the large disparity between the percentage of cases in which symptoms were reported to be cured (27 per cent) and the percentage reported to be "improved in total functioning" (97 per cent), although the degrees of improvement in total functioning were not specified. Symptom cure thus appeared to have little influence on the analysts' judgments of improvement.

Comparison with Effects of Other Traditional Treatments

The figures on the effects of psychoanalysis with adult neurotics are presented in Table 9–2, along with figures from studies of neurotics who underwent other types of traditional outpatient treatment, including visits to general practitioners and nonintensive outpatient psychotherapy, plus figures on neurotics who applied for but did not receive treatment. None of the studies is completely satisfactory from a methodological point of view. In both studies of psychoanalysis, many cases were omitted for having dropped out or having been incompletely analyzed, the patient's analyst was apparently the sole judge of outcome, there is no information on follow-up status, and the patient's own view of his treatment is not reported. However, many of the other studies share similar problems. Only results from the better studies have been included in the table, but the figures might be regarded at best as upper bounds for improvement by neurotics receiving the various treatments in their typical form.

As methodology in research on the effects of psychotherapy has become more sophisticated, it has focused increasingly on variables such as the interaction between therapists having certain personality types and patients having certain problems. However, the findings of these more sophisticated studies have not basically altered the picture conveyed in Table 9–2—the evidence still indicates that approximately two-thirds of adult neurotics will be judged cured or much improved under a wide variety of conditions. Moreover, a survey of studies of neurotic children treated by various methods has produced similar figures—the average rate of improvement calculated from 3 studies was 61 per cent (Levitt, 1963).

A crucial question to be asked of all the figures on treatment is: "What percentage of the patients would have improved without treatment?" The Denker (1946) study (Table 9–2) has often been cited as a baseline for im-

TABLE 9–2

Results of treatment in psychoneurosis.

Type of treatment	Number of patients	Approximate length of treatment	Per cent cured or much improved
Adult—Psychoanalysis			
Brody, 1962	210[a]	3–4 yrs.	60.0
Knight, 1941	383[b]	6 mos.–several yrs.	63.2
Adult—General practitioner			
Denker, 1946	500	1 yr.	44.6
		1–2 yrs.	27.0
		2–3 yrs.	9.6
		3–4 yrs.	5.2
		4–5 yrs.	3.6
		Total	90.0
Adult—Clinic waiting list (no treatment)			
Barron & Leary, 1955	23	7 mos.	55.0
Wallace & Whyte, 1959	44	2–7 yrs.	65.3
Adult—Outpatient clinic psycho- therapy			
Barron & Leary, 1955	127	8 mos.	66.0
Carmichael & Masserman, 1939	70	1 day–18 mos.	55.7
Luff & Garrod, 1935	355	7 mos.	59.1
Neustatter, 1935	33	21 sessions	63.6
Adult—Private psychiatric practice (includes some inpatients)			
Yaskin, 1936	100	2 wks.–4½ yrs.	67.7
Child—Outpatient psychotherapy			
Levitt, 1963	230	5–19 sessions	61.0

[a] Original sample was 595, but 289 were omitted because incompletely analyzed and 96 because they could not be located for follow-up.

[b] Original sample was 534, but 157 were excluded because they broke off treatment after less than 6 months.

provement of neurosis among adults without psychotherapy (e.g., Eysenck, 1965). Denker's cases represented 500 consecutive claims for disability insurance payments because of neurosis so incapacitating as to prevent the claimant from earning money. An insurance investigator and a physician verified the incapacitating nature of the neurosis at approximately three-month intervals.

Most of the claimants were clerical workers, executives, teachers, and professionals, the occupational classes from which most analytic patients are drawn. They were treated by general practitioners with "sedatives, tonics, suggestion, and reassurance," and none received more than "super-ficial" psychotherapy (Denker, 1946, p. 2164). Within two years, 71.6 per cent were considered sufficiently recovered to end their disability payments. After five years, the number had reached 90 per cent.

Denker's criterion of improvement has been justly criticized for its super-ficiality (cf. Meltzoff & Kornreich, 1970), but, in the absence of clear specifica-tion of criteria for improvement and of evidence of reliability and validity of judgments in the psychoanalytic studies, Denker's findings cannot be lightly dismissed. Moreover, Denker's percentage of improvement was based on the entire group of 500 who had been initially diagnosed neurotic. In Brody's report on psychoanalysis of neurotics, only 306 (51.4 per cent) of the original 595 patients were considered to have been completely analyzed. Only 210 (68 per cent) of these 306 were reported upon. Even if it is as-sumed that the 96 completely analyzed patients who were not reported upon had improved at the same 60 per cent rate as the 210 who were reported upon, the proportion improved from the initial group of 595 treated is 184/595 or 30.9 per cent. Similarly, in Knight's (1941) study, if all 534 neu-rotic patients who began analysis are taken as the base on which improve-ment is calculated, then the 242 judged to be improved represents only 45.3 per cent.

While the efficacy of a treatment should not be judged by its results with inappropriate patients or with those who do not complete treatment, the problem of determining *who* is appropriate for analysis remains a major one. The figures of 30.9 per cent and 45.3 per cent improvement derived from the Brody and Knight studies, respectively, are based upon neurotic patients all of whom seemed appropriate enough to be accepted for analysis. Further evidence of the selection problem was revealed in a study of 100 people re-ferred by analysts to an analytic institute. These people were interviewed and evaluated by a panel of senior analysts for supervised treatment by an-alysts in training at the institute (Knapp, Levin, McCarter, Wermer, & Zetzel, 1960; Zetzel, 1965). Although only one-third of the patients initially referred to the institute were considered suitable for analysis, one-third of those accepted were also found within a year to be unsuitable because of character disorders, borderline psychoses, and long-standing pathology that had not been evident during evaluation.

To return now to the initial question of whether psychoanalysis can cure or ameliorate neuroses, the existing data provide no objective evidence for its efficacy. The data indicate that it is not superior to traditional methods that are cheaper and less time-consuming and that it may be inferior to such methods if judged by the percentage improved among all patients who begin treatment. The only direct test of the efficacy of child analysis showed no clear evidence for the superiority of analysis over once-weekly therapy (Heinicke, 1969). However, there is also no evidence that other traditional forms of treatment for neuroses produce more improvement than would occur without treatment.

SUMMARY

Child psychoanalysis is considered appropriate for only a tiny proportion of disturbed children, primarily those who have classic neurotic conflicts, are between the ages of about six and puberty, and have adequate home situations. The goal of child analysis is to relieve unconscious conflicts by making them conscious and reworking the feelings connected with them. The child's play is regarded as a partial replacement for the technique of free association so crucial in adult analysis. Treatments other than analysis are believed by some analysts to carry the risk of *symptom substitution.*

There have been few published reports of attempts by analysts to move their ideas from the *context of discovery* to the *context of confirmation.* Unconscious psychological influences, childhood sexuality, and psychological determinism are acknowledged by nearly all mental-health workers and systematic evidence exists for some other analytic hypotheses. Other hypotheses have been contradicted by research findings, while most have never been adequately formulated for testing. Controlled studies show low reliability for analysts' judgments of patient functioning during analytic treatment.

Evidence is lacking for the analytic theory of how child neuroses are caused. Recent research suggests that the analytic theory of etiology is inaccurate in that anxiety may often follow rather than precede the development of symptoms in young children. There are very few studies of the effectiveness of analytic treatment with neurotic children or adults. No studies show it to be more effective than less time-consuming traditional methods.

SUGGESTED READING

Psychoanalytic Treatment.   Pearson (1968) presents criteria for selecting cases, ways of dealing with parents, details of treatment settings and procedures, and other matters related to the practice of child analysis, at least as it is carried on by members of one American analytic institute. Colby's (1958) short book, *The Skeptical Psychoanalyst,* is recommended as an aid in the self-analysis of anyone who is considering analysis as a profession.

Psychoanalytic Guide for Parents.   Selma Fraiberg's book, *The Magic Years: Understanding and Handling the Problems of Early Childhood* (1959), is an entertaining psychoanalytically oriented guide to behavior often observed up to the age of six. Unlike some books written from the psychoanalytic viewpoint, it is well informed as to aspects of development other than the psychosexual, especially the cognitive aspect that may account for much of the delightful magic displayed in children's thinking during the "magic years."

10

Behavioral Theories
and Methods

Behavior modification is becoming a generic term for attempts to change undesirable or inadequate behavior in a systematic manner, usually through the manipulation of environmental consequences of the behavior. *Behavior therapy* is a somewhat narrower term for efforts directed at modifying behavior considered to be pathological. The term "behavior modification" will generally be employed here because all behavior therapists would agree that they seek to modify behavior, while some who seek to modify behavior shun the term "therapy" because it implies that the problem behavior is caused by illness. Referring to a person whose behavior is to be changed as a "patient" is also shunned by some, with "client" being the preferred term.

It bears repeating that the presentation of psychoanalytic theory and behavioral theories in separate chapters risks perpetuating the rivalry between two major models for psychopathology. In practice, however, many publications, practitioners, and treatment and training centers view psychopathology more or less exclusively in terms of one model or the other. The fact is that a fair presentation of the field of psychopathology in its current state can ignore neither, and the gulf between them remains wide in both theory and practice.

Since much of the thrust of behavior modification is directed against alleged inadequacies of the psychodynamic model, and since the latter has been heretofore dominant, behavior modifiers have done more to compare and contrast the behavioral and dynamic models than have psychoanalysts. These efforts provide us with more of a basis for comparing the models on specific points than was possible when considering "neurotic" disorders from the psychoanalytic point of view.

The focus of the behavior modification approach is on behavior that is currently observable or reportable rather than on conflicts among intra-psychic forces or inferred components of personality. The term *behavior disorder* has been selected here as a generic designation because it reflects the behavior modifier's conceptual focus, but "behavior disorder" and "behavior problem" have also been used by workers in other traditions to refer primarily to behavior that is annoying or difficult to manage, such as aggressive and destructive behavior.

Some behavior modifiers think of all troublesome behaviors exclusively as behavior disorders, their assumption being that, even if organic anomalies contribute to a disorder, the essential goal is to change the problem behavior. These workers contend that such labels as "organic," "retarded," "neurotic," "autistic," and "psychotic" cloud the issue. Other behavior modifiers use some of the traditional labels and may be guided by them in deciding which techniques of behavior modification to employ. A key difference between most behavior modifiers and psychodynamically oriented workers, however, is that the former label as behavior disorders what the latter call "neurotic symptoms."

LEARNING THEORIES AND EXPERIMENTAL PSYCHOLOGY

The primary theoretical basis for behavioral techniques consists of principles of learning formulated in laboratory studies of human and animal behavior. Pavlov, Bekhterev, Thorndike, Watson, Hull, Guthrie, Skinner, and other laboratory experimentalists were the intellectual progenitors of most current theory and practice in behavior modification. Some workers have equated behavioral treatment solely with the application of learning principles to problem behavior and some have further restricted it to a particular theory of learning (cf. Eysenck, 1959; Ross, 1972; Wolpe, 1969). However, following a period of tremendous growth in the techniques and applications of behavior modification from about 1958 until the 1970s, conceptions of behavior modification as an approach to disordered behavior have become very broad. In one conception:

> The underlying assumption is that clinical problems can best be handled by construing psychotherapy as an extension of general experimental psychology. . . . It is a critical experimental approach to a particular subject area, and not merely the technical aspects of the approach. . . .
> There is an emphasis on operationally defined terms, careful and dispassionate experimentation, a tendency to look for principles in the experimental area rather than in the more speculative portions of contemporary psychology, as well as a recognition that the psychological principles that we are currently attempting to apply are in a continual state of re-evaluation and revision [Davison, Goldfried, & Krasner, 1970, p. 767].[1]

[1] G. C. Davison, M. R. Goldfried, and L. Krasner, "A Postdoctoral Program in Behavior Modification: Theory and Practice," *American Psychologist*, 1970, **25** (767). © 1970 by the American Psychological Association and reprinted by permission.

According to this view, certain learning procedures are believed to be effective in changing behavior, but many other factors, such as social and cognitive processes, should be constantly investigated in order to improve the effectiveness of behavior modification and broaden its range of application.

Kanfer and Phillips (1970) have summarized the basic features of the general behavior modification approach as follows:

What is novel in the behavior therapies is their adoption of methods that shift from laboratory to clinic and back to the laboratory in self-conscious testing of the utility and validity of their operation, and with a data-oriented, hypothesis-testing frame of reference within the treatment setting itself. . . .

. . . Behavior therapists tend to select specific symptoms or behaviors as targets for change, to employ concrete, planned interventions to manipulate these behaviors, and to monitor progress continuously and quantitatively. A patient's early life history is largely ignored, except as it may provide clues about such factors as currently active events which maintain symptoms, or hierarchies of reinforcers. Behavior therapists tend to concentrate on an analysis of particular symptoms. They devote far less attention than other clinicians to subjective experiences, attitudes, insights and dreams. Their tools include electronic equipment and devices which permit precise measurement of behavior. Their programs tend to give less consideration to evidence based on empathy than on observations. Their 'show me' attitude puts the burden of proof on the outcome of an attempted therapeutic move rather than on the social preconceptions of what should be beneficial for a person [pp. 16–18].[2]

CONDITIONING

Pavlovian Conditioning

Despite the apparent open-endedness of current conceptions of behavior modification, most applications have stressed the utilization of learning principles. Among the most fundamental learning principles are those derived by the Russian physiologist Pavlov from animal studies he began in 1899. Pavlov's basic procedure was to sound a tuning fork as powdered meat was placed on a dog's tongue. The meat, of course, caused the dog to salivate. After this procedure was repeated several times, the sound of the tuning fork alone elicited salivation. Salivation to the tone was referred to as a *conditional (conditioned) reflex* because elicitation of salivation by the tone was *conditional* on the pairing of the tone with a stimulus (food on the tongue) that had elicited salivation without prior learning. Food on the tongue was an *unconditional (unconditioned) stimulus* because it elicited the reflex *unconditionally*, without training. The tone was a *conditional (conditioned) stimulus* because its power to elicit salivation was

2 F. H. Kanfer and J. S. Phillips, *Learning Foundations of Behavior Therapy* (New York: John Wiley & Sons, 1970). © 1970 by John Wiley & Sons and reprinted by permission.

conditional on its prior pairing with food. Pavlov's procedure became known as *Pavlovian, classical,* or *respondent conditioning.*

Instrumental Conditioning

Pavlov's rival, Bekhterev, another Russian physiologist of the same period, concentrated on what has come to be considered the second fundamental form of conditioning, designated as *instrumental* or *operant conditioning.* In this type of conditioning, a motor response rewarded under certain circumstances will continue to be made under those circumstances. For example, a hungry rat receiving food when it operates a lever will continue to operate the lever. In his book, *Objective Psychology* (1907), Bekhterev proposed that complex habits were created through the chaining of responses that had been rewarded.

The Law of Effect. At about the same time in the United States, E. L. Thorndike was conducting experiments with animal learning that independently led him to a formulation similar to Bekhterev's. Finding that animals repeated responses that had resulted in rewards and failed to repeat punished responses, Thorndike proposed what he called the *Law of Effect.* This stated that responses that led the animal to a "satisfying state of affairs" tended to be repeated, while those that led to an "annoying state of affairs" tended not to be repeated (Thorndike, 1913). Thorndike maintained that the effect a response has previously had determines whether it will be repeated, without any necessity for the intervention of conscious thought.

Watsonian Behaviorism

In the same vein, John B. Watson proposed that human behavior could be formulated in stimulus-response terms similar to those applied to animal behavior, without resort to introspection or notions of consciousness. In his 1913 article, "Psychology as the behavorist views it," Watson maintained that the proper subject of psychology was observable behavior and how it was learned. After reading translations of Bekhterev's work in 1915, he became convinced that conditioning was the basic process in learning and that chains of conditioned covert vocal responses constituted the basis of thinking. He argued that abnormal as well as normal behavior and emotional responses resulted from conditioning.

THE EARLY DEVELOPMENT OF BEHAVIOR MODIFICATION

The Case of Albert

The application of learning principles to the explanation and removal of undesirable behavior is often dated from Watson's work, especially his experimental creation of a phobia in a child named Albert (Watson & Rayner, 1920). Albert was reported to be an especially calm and fearless infant. As shown on motion picture records of his behavior, he responded without fear to stimuli including a white rat, rabbit, dog, monkey, masks, cotton, and burning newspapers.

Watson's experiment began when Albert, at age 11 months, was presented with a white rat, to which he had not previously shown fear. As Albert began to reach for the rat, a steel bar was struck with a hammer immediately behind the child. Albert jumped violently and fell forward. The bar was struck again on a number of other occasions when Albert reached for the rat. Soon, whenever the rat was presented without the bar being struck, Albert withdrew his hand, whimpered, fell over, and crawled away. He showed similar but slightly milder reactions to a rabbit, dog, fur coat, cotton, Santa Claus mask, and Watson's hair. However, he showed no negative reactions to his blocks when they were presented between conditioning trials and between presentations of the other stimuli. Watson interpreted Albert's phobia in terms of classical conditioning whereby pairing of the previously neutral white rat with the fear-arousing sound caused the emotional response of fear to become conditioned to the stimulus of the rat. The apparent transfer of Albert's fear to other objects was interpreted as indicating that the fear response generalized to similar objects but that this generalization was not indiscriminate because it did not transfer to objects such as blocks.

Although Albert moved away before Watson could treat the conditioned fear, Watson proposed three treatments that could have been employed:

1. Repeatedly presenting the feared stimulus without the sound in order to bring about habituation, or "fatigue" of the fear response.
2. Reconditioning by presenting the feared stimulus while creating positive sensations through stimulation of the lips, nipples, or sex organs or by feeding.
3. Building up "constructive" activities around the feared stimulus by getting Albert to imitate unfearful behavior and by using Albert's hand to manipulate the rat.

The Case of Peter and the Rabbit

Some of Watson's proposals for removing children's fears were put to work by Mary Cover Jones (1924b). She reported that presenting a child with a feared stimulus in the presence of a child who was not afraid sometimes promoted imitation by the fearful child and helped reduce his fear on later occasions as well. However, this method occasionally backfired when the unafraid child imitated the responses of the fearful child.

The most effective method appeared to be that of Watson's second proposal, reconditioning through providing pleasurable experience in the presence of the feared stimulus. Jones (1924a) reported the application of this method in a case study that has become nearly as famous as the case of Albert. It is, in fact, often confused with Albert's case because the presenting symptoms were so similar to the ones conditioned in Albert.

The study of Peter began when he was 2 years 10 months old. Peter was very afraid of a white rabbit and slightly less afraid of white rats, fur coats, cotton, feathers, and similar stimuli but not of objects such as wooden blocks. Changes in Peter's behavior during treatment were analyzed into a series of steps representing 17 degrees in his toleration of the rabbit. The first technique was to put Peter with other children who liked the rabbit and petted him. With seven brief sessions spread over several days, Peter progressed nine steps on the scale: From showing fear when the caged rabbit was anywhere in the room to tolerating it at progressively closer distances, tolerating it when it was uncaged, touching it while the experimenter held it, touching it while it was free in the room, and defying it by spitting and throwing things at it. Peter's progress is depicted on the chart in Fig. 10–1.

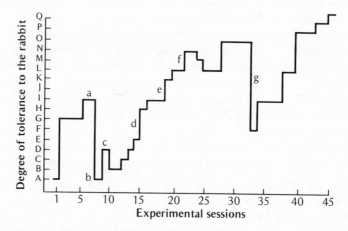

Fig. 10–1. The removal of Peter's fear of the rabbit through reconditioning. Point a = interruption due to Peter's illness; b = renewal of experiment after Peter was frightened by dog; c, d, e, f = sessions in which a nonfearful child or well-liked adult was present; g = Peter scratched while helping to carry the rabbit. From Jones, in Eysenck (1960), p. 48. © 1960 by Pergamon Press and reprinted by permission.

The experiment was interrupted after the seventh session when Peter became ill and was quarantined for nearly two months (point a on the chart). Just before his return for treatment, he and his nurse were severely frightened by a large dog that jumped at him. Upon his return, his fear of the rabbit was back to its original level (point b on the chart). A new form of treatment, called "direct conditioning," was then begun. Peter was given food that he liked while the experimenter brought the caged rabbit as close as she could without disrupting Peter's eating. Improvements in Peter's tolerance were most apparent in the presence of another child or adult who was either well liked by Peter or who was affectionate with the rabbit (points c, d, e, f on the chart). A relapse occured when Peter received a slight scratch while helping to carry the rabbit (point g on the chart), but he recovered and in the forty-fifth session he reached the final step on the scale, allowing the rabbit to nibble his fingers. He also showed no fear despite the presence of another child who was markedly disturbed by the rabbit.

In interviews with Peter during treatment, he at first made no mention of the rabbit. On several later occasions he said, "I like the rabbit." In a follow-up interview after treatment, he showed fondness for the rabbit and a total absence of fear to cotton, fur coats, and feathers. He was also willing to carry a box of rats and a fur rug with a stuffed head that he had previously feared.

Jones concluded that the study was incomplete because the stimulus with which the fear had originated was unknown and it was unknown whether removing the rabbit phobia had influenced the original fear, if there was one. Moreover, Peter's future welfare was much in doubt because of very bad home conditions, including a disturbed mother who frequently suggested fears to the boy, saying, for example, "Come in Peter, someone wants to steal you [p. 315]."

As with Freud's case of "Little Hans," the case of Peter is not only of historical interest as a detailed report of the application of a new theory and treatment paradigm to a child, but because it reveals many critical aspects of the paradigm as it has persisted into the present. Some critical features of the behavioral paradigm illustrated in the case of Peter include:

1. The assumption that the fear of a particular class of stimuli, rather than an inferred intrapsychic conflict, was the essential problem.
2. The assumption that the class of feared objects was determined by stimulus generalization, from one object that had originally been associated with pain or fear, to objects that the child viewed as similar, rather than to objects that were symbols of the original stimulus situation.
3. The structuring of the attempt at amelioration as an experiment for which data on behavior change were recorded and reported as a function of experimental manipulations occurring over time, rather than structuring it as a clinical case history in which events and interpretations are often indistinguishable from one another.
4. The attribution of behavior change to a specific learning process ("conditioning"), although many other processes could have been involved in the situation (e.g., imitation, habituation).
5. The tendency to regard the specific problem behavior as the focus of treatment and the child's life situation as a separate, though possibly ominous, issue.

Other Early Developments

In the same year that Jones (1924a, 1924b) reported her experiments, William Burnham published *The Normal Mind,* a book that reviewed and attempted to evaluate both behavioral and psychoanalytic approaches.

Burnham concluded that psychoanalysis had some genuine value as a placebo because of the interesting tasks in which it engaged the patient. However, he maintained that significant behavioral change was more directly brought about by engaging the client in meaningful tasks that could lead to social reinforcement of new responses to replace the undesirable ones. Burnham also outlined specific procedures for behavior modification that did not become widely used until the late 1950s.

Subsequent textbooks in psychology continued to invoke learning principles as explanations for undesirable behavior and to espouse the application of these principles to the removal of such behavior. For example, Dunlap's (1932) text, *Habits: Their Making and Unmaking,* outlined procedures called *negative practice* for the cure of stammering, tics, nail-biting, and masturbation (which Dunlap considered to be potentially injurious). The client who wished to remove these behaviors was to engage in them repeatedly on a voluntary basis until fatigue built up to the point where the behavior became painful and avoiding it became rewarding. Dunlap implied that such treatment had generally been found successful, but he did not provide details of its application or effects.

Holmes's Experiment. Holmes (1936) questioned the range of application of Watson and Jones's methods for classical conditioning because few children's fears were focused on objects like white rabbits that could be conveniently presented to the child while he was eating. She cited common fears of the dark, heights, bogeymen, and entering the water as being inappropriate for removal by Watson's suggested reconditioning with food. Instead of Watson's procedures, she advocated inducing the child to cope actively with the feared situation and then rewarding him for such behavior. In effect, she was proposing an *instrumental* conditioning paradigm.

In her experiment, Holmes induced nursery school children who feared the dark to enter a dark room in search of a luminescent light pull with which they could turn on a light. If a child was too frightened to search for the light pull alone, Holmes entered the room with the child but constantly encouraged him to search for the light pull on his own. After the child found the pull, Holmes played a game with him in the room as a reward. Most children appeared so highly rewarded by finding the pull and overcoming their fear that the game-playing was superfluous. The dark-fear of 13 out of 14 children seemed to disappear after several experimental trials, although there was no assessment of generalization outside the experimental situation.

Mowrer and Mowrer Study. One of the most significant experimental studies done between the initiation of behavior modification in the 1920s and its revival in the 1950s was Mowrer and Mowrer's (1938) application of a conditioning technique to nocturnal enuresis, a problem very common in child guidance caseloads. After surveying unsuccessful remedies from many cultures, the Mowrers concluded that, while organic factors and severe emotional disturbance contributed in some cases, many cases of enuresis resulted from faulty habit training with or without contributions from emotional factors.

The Mowrers designed a device consisting of an electrically wired pad to be placed on the child's bed and a bell that rang when the pad became moist. The conditioning strategy was as follows: The stimulus of bladder distention caused the reflex of sphincter relaxation and urination. The bell was intended as both an awakening stimulus and a stimulus to sphincter contraction, which inhibited urination. Pairing the awakening-inhibiting bell stimulus with the reflex of sphincter relaxation over several trials caused the child to awaken and inhibit urination when his bladder distended to the point where urination had previously begun.

The Mowrers reported 100 per cent success with 30 children aged 3 to 13 who were residing in a temporary children's home. No evidence of symptom substitution or negative personality effects was found, although relapses occurred in some children when they returned to bad home situations.

LATER DEVELOPMENTS

Government programs to care for the psychological casualties of World War II brought a tremendous increase in training and facilities for the treatment of psychopathology during the 1940s. However, most of the treatment was oriented around the then dominant medical and psychodynamic models. There are a number of reasons why little attempt seems to have been made to extend behavioral methods. One reason is that behavioral methods had been developed and described almost exclusively by specialists in educational and experimental psychology whose work was not familiar to clinical practitioners. A second reason is that the behavioral methods had been applied mainly to children, while the new programs supported by the government were aimed at treatment of adults. A third reason is that psychotherapy as an enterprise seemed to have acquired a life of its own, or *functional autonomy*, as Astin (1961) put it, i.e., the professional training, practice, and career system developed for psychotherapy had become independent of the original reason for its existence, which was to change pathological behavior. The system functioned autonomously, even in the absence of any proof that it was indeed changing behavior.

Especially compelling evidence for the functional autonomy of psychotherapy is the fact that, when attempts were again made to bridge the gap between experimental research and therapeutic practice, the efficacy of psychotherapy was not questioned, although it was entirely unproven. Instead, attempts to bridge the gap were aimed primarily at translating into laboratory learning terms the prevailing concepts and practices of psychotherapy, especially those of psychoanalysis. Such attempts were surprisingly numerous and included works by Cameron and Magaret (1951), Mowrer (1950), Shaffer (1947), Shaw (1946, 1948), and Shoben (1949).

Dollard and Miller

The most prominent attempt at bridging the gap between experimental psychology and psychotherapy was the book *Personality and Psychotherapy*, by John Dollard and Neal Miller (1950). Dedicating their book to "Freud and Pavlov and their students," Dollard and Miller sought "to combine the vitality of psychoanalysis, the rigor of the natural-science laboratory, and the facts of culture [p. 3]." They called psychotherapy a "window to higher mental life" and "the process by which *normality is created* [pp. 3, 5]." Neurotic behavior was viewed as being learned and psychotherapy as providing conditions for the unlearning of neurotic habits and the learning of nonneurotic ones.

Dollard and Miller adopted the Freudian definition of neurosis as an unconscious conflict in which repression was used to keep anxiety-arousing thoughts from consciousness and symptoms were produced in order to avoid further anxiety. However, they translated many of the Freudian concepts into terminology derived from laboratory research on animal and human learning and into a conceptual structure based largely on Clark Hull's (1943, 1951) learning theory.

The four factors Dollard and Miller considered most important in learning were *drive, response, cue,* and *reinforcement.* Drives were hypothetical constructs not very different from Freud's constructs of the instinctual drives of sex and aggression. Hunger, thirst, sex, pain, cold, and other physiologically based need states were regarded as *primary drives.* The reduction of a drive state was said to be rewarding, so that any *response* that reduced a drive was said to be *reinforced,* i.e., the probability was increased that the response would be repeated when the drive was again high, especially if the *cue* (stimulus) conditions were similar. Many of the cue conditions that became associated with drive reduction were viewed as eventually becoming the objects of learned motives, referred to as *learned* or *secondary* drives. For example, an excessively strong desire for money by an adult could be considered a learned drive arising from socialization practices that had caused the lack of money to produce discomfort and the acquisition of money to reduce discomfort.

Fear was portrayed as a learnable drive that could motivate behavior which, in turn, was strongly reinforced if it succeeded in reducing the fear. The learnable drive characteristics of fear were illustrated in an experiment in which rats were shocked in one compartment of a box, but could escape the shock by running to another compartment. The rats' escape behavior continued after shock was no longer administered. When placed in the shock box with the door closed, the rats showed great agitation and soon learned to turn a wheel to open the door. Rats repeatedly placed in the box speedily turned the wheel to escape, indicating that reduction of the learned fear reinforced their wheel-turning response. *Anxiety* was defined as fear for which the specific cues were vague or obscured by repression. *Repression* was defined as avoiding thinking about and remembering a source of fear, in effect preventing the verbal labeling of the fear.

Dollard and Miller also provided extensive reinterpretation of specific symptoms and Freudian defense mechanisms such as phobias, compulsions, obsessions, hysterical paralyses, displacement, projection, regression, hallucinations, and delusions. Most of their reinterpretations appear to be true to the psychoanalytic descriptions of such behavior and the circumstances under which they occur, while dispensing with metatheoretical concepts like id, ego, superego, libido, and cathexis. Their illustration of the defense mechanism of projection provides an example:

. . . Mrs. A. . . . had intense anxiety about any verbal expression of sexual desires. On several occasions as a small girl she had "been taken advantage of" by older boys or men. Later she frequently went into situations where she was likely to be taken advantage of. Instead of any thoughts about having sexual desires of her own, she was afraid that the man wanted to do something to her.

According to our analysis, being taken advantage of reduced this girl's fear of sex because it meant that she was not to blame. She was able to get some satisfaction in those situations that she was not able to get otherwise. These experiences attached learned reward value for the sex drive to the cues of being alone with a man in a provocative situation and to the cues produced by the thought "he wants to take advantage of me." This learned reward value reinforced the responses of going into those situations and thinking those thoughts. Since such intense anxiety had been attached to labeling her own sexual desires, any thought that she wanted the man to make advances was repressed. . . . Such a thought might have kept her out of the sex situation entirely. The thought "he wants to do something to me" also helped to . . . keep anxiety-provoking thoughts about her own desires out of her mind. This was an additional source of reinforcement for that thought [Dollard & Miller, 1950, pp. 182–83].

Along with their application of learning theory to Freudian concepts, Dollard and Miller provided interpretations of how psychotherapy works. One dimension of therapy was helping the patient to acquire verbal labels for anxiety-arousing thoughts and emotions that had been repressed. The original anxiety responses could then be unlearned under the guidance of the therapist who encouraged the patient to express tabooed feelings and thoughts. Expression of these thoughts and feelings without punishment allowed the anxiety responses to be extinguished.

The second therapeutic dimension was what Dollard and Miller called "real-world aspects of therapy." This involved the patient's recognition of the distortions produced in his current life by his neurotic symptoms and his attempts to perform new responses outside the therapy situation. For therapy to be beneficial, Dollard and Miller regarded it as essential that the therapist encourage generalization of verbal responses made in treatment to activity outside therapy. It was also necessary that the therapist move the patient toward new behavior at a rate that would avoid too great an increase in anxiety while permitting sufficient reinforcement for the new behavior to be learned.

Evaluation of the Dollard-Miller Approach. As a *tour de force* in translating psychoanalytic concepts and practices into another theoretical language, *Personality and Psychotherapy* is certainly a significant work. It had the major benefit of showing how psychodynamic lore might be effectively conceptualized in other terms and of creating a basis for rapprochement betwen researchers and clinical practitioners. Many of the specific proposals in the book have continued to provide conceptual models for understanding personality and psychopathology, as exemplified in Mahl's book *Psychological Conflict and Defense* (1971).

On the other hand, the Dollard and Miller book has not had much effect in increasing the rigor of prevailing psychoanalytic formulations or in generating research on psychoanalysis. Nor has it directly led to new ways of *doing* therapy, although it may have provided impetus in this area by (1) popularizing the application of behavioral terminology and analysis to therapy, and (2) demonstrating that even a highly sophisticated synthesis of psychoanalysis and learning theory was insufficient by itself to advance treatment techniques significantly. Meehl has commented thusly on the lack of resulting innovation:

> Even such a powerful and illuminating work as Dollard and Miller's *Personality and Psychotherapy* suffers from the traditionalism with which we are all infected. It is a brilliant rendition, in the learning-theory frame, of a fairly orthodox view of therapy. It might be even more illuminating if the authors applied these principles without being constantly guided by the tradition. It seems odd that the learning formulation apparently suggested so few innovations in therapeutic strategy and tactics as appear in that admirable book [Meehl, 1955, p. 375].

Stronger exception to the "translation" approach has been taken by Bandura and Walters (1963):

> The net effect of these translations has . . . been to entrench more firmly assumptions and concepts that have accumulated over the years through the uncontrolled trial-and-error experiences of practicing clinicians [p. 29].

B. F. Skinner

Beginning with his Harvard PhD dissertation in 1931, B. F. Skinner carried on the behaviorist tradition in a fashion reminiscent of Watson. However, Skinner went further than Watson in declaring that, for purposes of psychology, the concept of the organism could be replaced by the notion of an unopenable black box. The subject matter of Skinner's psychology was to be merely the functional relations between stimuli impinging on the black box and responses emitted by it, without any hypotheses about covert activity, internal drive states, or the like to link the stimuli and responses.

Like Watson, Skinner was eager to extrapolate laboratory behavioral analysis and the findings of animal learning studies to complex human behavior outside the laboratory. In "Baby in a Box" (1945), he described a boxlike apparatus designed to provide a controlled environment for infants so as to avoid the inconvenience and the harmful stimulus-response contingencies involved when a human mother has to take full-time care of her baby. Skinner's novel, *Walden Two* (1948), described a Utopia in which the rational programming of reinforcements replaced the haphazard reinforcement contingencies supporting so much harmful behavior in the real world, and his book, *Beyond Freedom and Dignity* (1971), argues the need for careful environmental planning. He has also applied operant conditioning principles to the design of teaching machines and programmed educational materials.

Many behavior modifiers who favor Skinnerian techniques regard Skinner's book *Science and Human Behavior* (1953) as a significant milestone in the revival of behavioral approaches to psychopathology in the 1950s (Ullmann & Krasner, 1969). The book was primarily an extrapolation, unsupported by data, of Skinnerian principles to a variety of issues in psychology and society at large. Skinner discussed psychotherapy as one among many social institutions for controlling people's behavior. He criticized the psychodynamic emphasis on inner illness and its rejection of behavior as a subject matter in its own right. In effect, his criticism of the dynamic tradition was more radical than Dollard and Miller's because he denied the need to retain in any form the psychodynamic constructs that Dollard and Miller had translated into Hullian learning theory.

However, even Skinner seemed to accept the efficacy of traditional psychotherapy while explaining it in his own terms. He maintained that its effectiveness depends upon the fact that the therapist constitutes himself as a nonpunishing audience who permits the patient to emit previously punished words and other behavior. The repeated emission of such behavior in the absence of punishment reduces the effects of previous aversive conditioning. Stimuli generated by the patient's behavior become less aversive and less likely to generate negative emotional reactions in the patient himself. Consequently, the patient is less likely to engage in operant behavior designed to escape from his own negative emotional reactions.

CONTEMPORARY BEHAVIOR MODIFICATION METHODS

Wolpe's Psychotherapy by Reciprocal Inhibition

The new dawn of behavior modification was heralded mainly by the publication of Joseph Wolpe's book, *Psychotherapy by Reciprocal Inhibition* (1958). Wolpe, a South African psychiatrist, reports that he had originally been "a staunch follower of Freud," but that he became skeptical of the universality of the Oedipus complex and of the efficacy of psychoanalysis beyond its production of comforting insights. Studies of outcome in the treatment of neurosis (such as those summarized in Table 9–2) had also convinced him that psychoanalysis was no more effective than simpler treatments.

Wolpe turned primarily to Pa.lov and Hull for alternatives to the repression theory of neurosis that dominated psychotherapeutic practice. He at first induced experimental neuroses in cats by shocking them under various conditions. Depending upon the conditions of shock and individual differences among the cats, anxiety symptoms appeared that resembled those of various human neuroses. As an example, one cat exhibited the "hysterical" symptom of jerking his shoulders every few seconds whenever Wolpe approached. The jerks may have been aborted jumping movements originating on the first shock when the cat jumped through a hatch in the cage that inadvertently had been left open.

After creation of the experimental neuroses, Wolpe tried out various procedures for eliminating the cats' anxiety and neurotic symptoms. Wolpe's basic strategy was to produce inhibition of anxiety responses by conditioning other responses to the same cue conditions. One technique was to feed the cats in the presence of the cues previously associated with shock, much as Jones (1924a) had fed Peter in the presence of the rabbit. Since Wolpe maintained that two incompatible responses, like eating and physiological anxiety reactions, cannot be made simultaneously, the new responses, when sufficiently strong, caused *reciprocal inhibition* of the old anxiety responses. When the new responses had been strongly enough conditioned to the previously frightening cues, the old anxiety responses to those cues were believed to be permanently weakened.

In applying his reciprocal inhibition principles to humans, Wolpe defined neurotic behavior as:

. . . any persistent habit of unadaptive behavior acquired by learning in a physiologically normal organism. Anxiety is usually the central constituent of this behavior, being invariably present in the causal situation. . . . By anxiety is meant the autonomic response pattern or patterns that are characteristically part of the organism's response to noxious stimulation [pp. 32–34].

Wolpe portrayed the etiology of human neuroses primarily as the conditioning of anxiety responses and/or other specific responses such as hysterical symptoms in the presence either of stimuli directly evoking anxiety or of ambivalent stimulation that resulted in high anxiety. He acknowledged that some people may be especially predisposed to neurosis either because of physiologically based high emotional reactivity or because prior learning has already resulted in conditioned anxiety responses to stimuli that happen to be involved in the neurosis-producing situation. Figure 10–2 portrays Wolpe's representation of the etiology of most human neurotic behavior.

Special predisposing preconditions (not essential)

↓

Subject exposed either to stimuli directly evoking anxiety or to ambivalent stimulation so that anxiety of high intensity is evoked. (Many variables are involved, e.g., degree of constriction of psychological space [limitations of response possibilities], strength of anxiety at each exposure, number of exposures, degree of stimulus constancy at different exposures.)

↓

Conditioning is established
of

high-intensity
anxiety responses   and/or   other responses
e.g., hysterical responses

to

specific stimuli   and/or   pervasive stimuli
("free-floating" anxiety)

Secondary anxiety-relieving behavior may ensue:

a) Physical avoidance of stimuli conditioned to anxiety
            and/or
b) Displacement of attention
            and/or
c) Drug-taking
            and/or
d) Anxiety-relieving obsessions

Modifications in the constitution of neurotic responses following their evocation in contiguity with certain other responses

Fig. 10–2. Wolpe's representation of the etiology of most neuroses. From Wolpe (1958).

Unlike earlier applications of learning principles to psychotherapy, Wolpe's did not stop with theoretical analyses or with the treatment of a few demonstration cases. On the contrary, he applied his principles in various ways to a broad range of neurotics who came to him for treatment. In his 1958 book, he summarized data from 210 cases treated by reciprocal inhibition techniques.

In his initial interviews with a patient, Wolpe obtains details about the symptoms, anything the patient can tell him about their origins, and the patient's life history. However, he emphasizes to the patient that the past is less important than finding out what stimuli evoke the symptoms at the present time. A questionnaire is also administered on which the patient indicates how frequently he experiences various kinds of anxiety reactions. Thereafter, Wolpe explains to the patient that his problems are due to excessive learned fearfulness and the generalization of this fearfulness to benign situations resembling the original fear-producing situation. The objective of therapy is to replace the anxiety responses with other emotional responses.

Wolpe maintains that interviewing by itself brings the benefits of reciprocal inhibition to some patients because the interview situation elicits responses incompatible with the anxiety originally aroused by the topics discussed. This factor, plus fortuitous changes in life circumstances, may account for improvement in approximately two-thirds of neurotics, the proportion reported improved by most traditional treatment methods. However, for more efficient and direct removal of symptoms in these patients and in patients not benefitted by interviewing alone, Wolpe's primary methods include the conditioning of assertive responses antagonistic to anxieties arising out of relations with other people, sexual responses antagonistic to sexual anxieties, and relaxation responses antagonistic to anxieties arising from a variety of phobic situations.

Assertive responses are trained by first inducing the patient to behave more assertively in situations acted out with Wolpe during therapy and by later encouraging similar behavior in the patient in progressively more threatening real-life situations. Sexual responses designed to be incompatible with sexual anxiety, frigidity, impotence, and premature ejaculation are trained by inducing the patient to lie nude with his sexual partner on several occasions without attempting intercourse. Intercourse is attempted only when anxiety has been reduced enough so that normal sexual desire and responses predominate. Relaxation involves training the patient to create muscle tension, to be aware of the accompanying feelings of tension, and then gradually to untense the muscles while attending to the resulting sensations. Wolpe contends that deep muscle relaxation is antagonistic to anxiety responses. He teaches relaxation to most of his patients as a supplement to the more direct conditioning methods and it is the basis for what is probably his most original method, *systematic desensitization*, to be described next.

Wolpe's Systematic Desensitization. In the method most closely paralleling the feeding of cats in the presence of increasing "doses" of anxiety, Wolpe asks the patient to make a list of everything that makes him anxious, ranked in order from most to least anxiety-arousing. Wolpe then scans the patient's *anxiety hierarchy*—as he calls the rank-ordered list—for thematic categories and has the patient rank the items again within each thematic subdivision of the hierarchy. After the patient has been trained in relaxation over several sessions, the first desensitization session begins with hypnosis of the patient and induction of deep relaxation. The patient is then asked to imagine scenes, one by one, beginning with the least threatening scene in one subdivision of his hierarchy. He is to raise his hand if he feels disturbed by any scene. This procedure is repeated for several sessions, gradually moving up the anxiety hierarchy as the patient learns to tolerate progressively more threatening scenes. Patients who cannot be hypnotized are said to be able to progress in a similar but slower fashion without hypnosis. Verbalization of the scenes has been found to be an adequate substitute in patients who cannot effectively visualize them.

Wolpe's Initial Results with Reciprocal Inhibition Methods. The outcome statistics reported by Wolpe were probably the most important reason for his impact in helping to reopen the field of behavior modification. Wolpe attempted to evaluate the outcome of treatment according to the five criteria proposed by Knight (1941) for the evaluation of psychoanalytic treatment:

1. symptomatic improvement;
2. increased productiveness;
3. improved adjustment and pleasure in sex;
4. improved interpersonal relationships;
5. ability to handle ordinary psychological conflicts and reality stresses.

However, for Wolpe to judge any patient as improved, the patient's symptoms had to have been alleviated, not just through changes that enabled him to avoid stimuli that previously elicited the symptoms, but in situations that previously elicited the symptoms. Changes in the anxiety questionnaire score were also considered in determining whether a patient had improved.

Of the 210 patients diagnosed neurotic who had received what Wolpe considered an "adequate" trial of therapy, 89.5 per cent were judged to be cured or much improved. Mean scores on the anxiety inventory for 34 patients taking it before and after treatment showed substantial drops in self-reported anxiety. The average number of interviews was 34.8 for the entire sample (cf. Lazarus, 1961). Two- to seven-year follow-ups were possible on 45 patients. Of these patients one of the "much improved" was found to have relapsed to a moderate degree. Due to the lack of controlled assessment procedures, the specific figures are, of course, subject to some of the same criticisms as Knight's (1941) figures on the effects of psychoanalysis.

Subsequent Developments in Systematic Desensitization

By 1960, there were enough articles on behavioral approaches to warrant a book of readings entitled *Behavior Therapy and the Neuroses* (Eysenck, 1960). Approaches other than Wolpe's were represented, but a fairly large proportion of the reports of clinical applications were by Wolpe and his colleagues. Since then, numerous approaches besides Wolpe's have emerged. Many of these are aimed at producing specific new adaptive responses to replace maladaptive responses rather than at reducing the learned fears hypothesized by Wolpe to be at the root of most neuroses.

In principle, the concept of reciprocal inhibition—the inhibition of old responses to certain stimuli by new responses to the same stimuli—is so general as to explain almost any behavior change. However, many behavior modifiers have taken issue with Wolpe's theory of neurosis, the need for relying on the construct of anxiety, and the concept of reciprocal inhibition. Be that as it may, Wolpe's conceptual framework and his desensitization techniques appear to have received more attention and clinical application than any other behavioral approach to date. Consequently, recent work employing desensitization will be discussed first, followed by a rundown of other behavioral techniques.

Increasing the Precision of Desensitization

Wolpe himself has continued to introduce technical refinements into desensitization procedures, although his basic theory and methods remain essentially unchanged. Several of his innovations are aimed at specifying in more precise ways the degrees of anxiety elicited in a patient by various stimuli and the degrees of anxiety reduction achieved by successive desensitization sessions. Precise specification is important because ascending an anxiety hierarchy too quickly may elicit stronger anxiety responses than the patient can inhibit with relaxation responses. Precise specification is also important for obtaining a proper rank-ordering of fears so that the desensitization sequence can proceed gradually rather than alternating unpredictably between severe and mild fears.

Wolpe (1969) believes that, within a properly constructed anxiety hierarchy, the reduction of a certain number of anxiety units associated with a mild stimulus in the hierarchy will cause reduction of a similar number of anxiety units for each of the more severe stimuli in the hierarchy. For example, in Fig. 10–3, if Stimulus A originally elicited one unit of anxiety and this anxiety is reduced to zero units, then the amount of anxiety elicited by each of the Stimuli B, C, D, and E will also be reduced by one unit.

Subjective Anxiety Scale. To aid in obtaining an anxiety hierarchy of items spaced evenly enough to allow systematic desensitization, Wolpe employs what he calls a *Subjective Anxiety Scale*. This is constructed by asking the patient to assign the number 100 to the worst possible anxiety he can imagine. The patient is then asked to subjectively rate his other anxieties in numbers ranging up to 100. The units of anxiety are referred to as *suds* (*subjective units of disturbance*).

Desensitization is not usually begun until a patient feels no more than about 25 suds when in a state of deep muscle relaxation in the interview setting. Tranquilizing drugs or brief inhalations of carbon dioxide are employed to reduce anxiety in patients who cannot learn to relax sufficiently. Once desensitization begins, the patient is asked to raise a finger when he feels an increase of more than 10 suds of anxiety. The therapist then proceeds no further up the hierarchy until the patient can relax suffi-

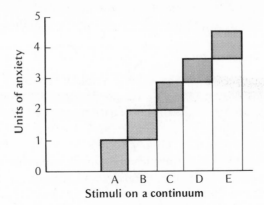

Fig. 10–3. Reducing by one unit the anxiety elicited by stimulus A causes a reduction of one unit in the anxiety elicited by each of the more severe stimuli on the continuum, and so on. From Wolpe (1969), p. 98. © 1969 by Pergamon Press and reprinted by permission.

ciently to inhibit the anxiety aroused by imagining the scene eliciting the 10-sud increase. He also asks the patient to tell him exactly when visualization of the feared scene begins and varies the length of visualization according to the degree of expected anxiety arousal. Scenes expected to elicit high anxiety are induced for one or two seconds at first and later lengthened to five or six seconds, thus providing another means for regulating anxiety exposure.

Fear Survey Schedule. Wolpe has stressed that his conception of neurosis applies not only to specific and isolated dimensions of fear, but also to "complex" neurotic states as well. He considers it possible for a neurosis to be complex in several different ways:

1. Multiple families of stimuli may be conditioned to neurotic reactions.
2. The reactions may include unadaptiveness in important areas of social behavior (e.g., sexual deviations, "character neuroses").
3. The neurosis may have somatic consequences (e.g., asthma).
4. The neurosis may include obsessional behavior.
5. There may be pervasive anxiety in addition to that associated with specific stimuli (Wolpe, 1969, p. 228).

Wolpe maintains that failure to discover and treat all a patient's neurotic fears may be responsible for treatment failures in complex neuroses. In order to explore fully a patient's repertoire of fears, he and P. J. Lang (cf. Wolpe, 1969) have constructed the Fear Survey Schedule (FSS), an extensive list of common fears, many rather subtle. The patient is to indicate on the list how often he experiences each fear. Other questionnaires and extensive interviewing are also employed to obtain an exhaustive record of the patient's fears and the stimulus situations eliciting them. Wolpe believes that behavioral treatment of complex neuroses should almost always succeed if a complete hierarchy of fears is properly handled.

Automation of Desensitization

Tape-recorded instructions have been employed in attempts to demonstrate that personal relations with the therapist are not essential to the treatment and to make treatment more efficient and less expensive. Migler and Wolpe (1967) reported a case study in which the patient's chief complaint was a public-speaking phobia serious enough to keep him from attending important staff meetings where he might be called upon to speak. After construction of an anxiety hierarchy and training in relaxation, the patient was helped to make a tape on which his own voice provided instructions for visualizing the successive anxiety stimuli plus relaxation instructions. A special tape recorder allowed the patient to switch on relaxation instructions immediately following instructions for any anxiety stimulus in the hierarchy. The patient took seven sessions to complete successfully all items in his anxiety hierarchy. A week later he attended a staff meeting, was asked to speak, and made a long speech disagreeing with all the previous speakers. He felt elated and proud of himself and his new ease in speaking at staff meetings generalized to other public speaking situations.

A somewhat similar procedure was used in an experiment comparing the effectiveness of recorded relaxation and desensitization instructions with desensitization treatment by graduate student therapists (Kahn & Baker, 1968). Subjects were college students who had a variety of subclinical but troublesome fears. Those in the automated group received a phonograph record with anxiety items designated as Number 1, 2, etc. The subjects mentally substituted anxiety items from hierarchies they had constructed with the help of a therapist. Five of the six subjects in the automated group were rated as cured or much improved, compared to three out of seven in the therapist-treated group. Although the numbers were too small for meaningful statistical tests, the results suggest that the automated procedure is at least as good as desensitization by relatively inexperienced therapists.

Group Desensitization

Lazarus (1961) divided phobic patients into groups according to the nature of their phobias. Some of the patients with each type of phobia then received either a group desensitization procedure, group interpretive therapy, or group interpretive therapy followed by instructions in relaxation. Members of the desensitization groups were asked to construct personal anxiety hierarchies. Lazarus then made up a group anxiety hierarchy from common elements found in the hierarchies of all the patients with a particular phobia. For example, the hierarchy for patients with acrophobia (fear of heights) contained items beginning with looking out a window 10 feet above ground level. Desensitization then proceeded just as with individual patients. Movement up the hierarchy was halted if any patient in a group signaled distress.

One month after treatment, patients who claimed to have recovered were required to undergo fear tests. The acrophobic patients, for example, were required to climb 50 feet up an outside fire escape and to count passing cars for two minutes while looking down from the roof of an eight-story building. Patients were considered recovered if they passed their tests with outward tranquility and reported no signs that their phobias persisted in other life situations.

Of the patients treated by group desensitization 13 out of 18 met the criteria for recovery, while none of the 9 treated by interpretive therapy and two of the eight treated by interpretation plus relaxation did. Follow-ups averaging nine months showed evidence of relapse in 3 of the 13 who had recovered through desensitization and in 1 of the 2 recovering through interpretation plus relaxation.

Drugs in Densensitization

Wolpe has advocated the use of drugs for inducing relaxation in a few patients who cannot relax by other means. The use of drugs has been carried further by Friedman and Silverstone (1967). They dispensed with relaxation training in favor of intravenously injecting a drug (Brietal) to reduce anxiety whenever a patient reported anxiety during the course of a desensitization session. They reported that all 20 phobic patients treated in this way showed marked improvement or cure. After a follow-up period averaging 10.5 months, 15 of the 18 patients who could be assessed had retained their much improved status.

Application of Desensitization to Children

Although early behavior modification techniques were tried out mainly on children (e.g., Holmes, 1936; Jones, 1924a; Mowrer & Mowrer, 1938), children have been underrepresented among recipients of desensitization treatment. This is perhaps understandable in light of the requirements that the patient clearly formulate his complaints, cooperate effectively in the relaxation and desensitization procedures, and accurately report his anxiety and the stimulus scenes he visualizes. However, Lazarus (1960) applied reciprocal inhibition techniques with 18 phobic children, aged 3 to 12. The average number of treatment sessions was 9.4. All 18 children were reported as recovering or being much improved and as maintaining their status at follow-ups ranging from six months to two and one-half years.

As an illustration, in treating an eight-year-old boy who developed an extreme fear of moving vehicles after being in an auto accident, Lazarus (1960) adopted a procedure reminiscent of Jones's (1924a) treatment of Peter's fear of rabbits. Lazarus first talked with the boy, John, about trains, planes, buses, and other vehicles. Even this evoked anxiety at first, but whenever John made a positive comment, he was casually offered some of his favorite chocolate. After increasing willingness to talk about moving vehicles without anxiety, John was engaged in play with toy cars that became involved in accidents. The anxiety evoked by these accidents soon diminished in response to chocolate. Later he sat with the therapist in a stationary car while discussing the original accident and receiving chocolate. Finally, at the seventeenth session (less than six weeks after therapy began), he willingly entered a car accompanied by a complete stranger and rode to a store to buy chococlate. For a short time afterward, he refused to ride with his parents unless given chocolate, but he soon began to enjoy riding for pleasure.

In another case, Lazarus applied relaxation and desensitization procedures with a nine-year-old girl, Carol, who had developed enuresis, fear of the dark, various psychosomatic ailments, and severe abdominal pains every time she went to school. These symptoms had begun following the drowning of a friend, the death of a playmate from meningitis, and a fatal auto accident she witnessed, all within a few weeks. In addition, Carol's mother had begun treating her coldly after reading that being affectionate with nine-year-olds could interfere with the development of maturity.

Interviews and projective tests indicated that Carol's chief fear was of separation from her mother because she was afraid the mother might die. Inducing the mother to be affectionate again did not result in improvement. Thereafter, an anxiety hierarchy was constructed with items ranging from imagined separation from the mother for five minutes to imagined separation for one week. Standard relaxation training and desensitization enabled Carol to reach the imagined one-week separation within five sessions spaced over 10 days. Carol then willingly returned to school. A 15-month follow-up revealed occasional enuresis but otherwise satisfactory adjustment.

In a later report, Lazarus and Abramovitz (1962) described the use of *emotive imagery* as a substitute for feeding and relaxation in the treatment of children's phobias. The procedure begins with construction of an anxiety hierarchy. However, the therapist then engages the child in conversation to determine what the child's favorite heroes and fantasy situations are. When these have been ascertained, the child is asked to imagine a sequence realistic enough to be credible but in which a story concerning his favorite hero or fantasy is interwoven. When the child's emotions reach a highly positive level, the therapist begins to introject into the fantasy the lowest items in the anxiety hierarchy. The child is told to raise his finger if he feels unhappy, afraid, or uncomfortable. The procedure is extended and repeated until the highest item is reached. Lazarus and Abramovitz described one case as follows:

Stanley M., aged 14, suffered from an intense fear of dogs, of 2½–3 years duration. He would take two buses on a roundabout route to school rather than risk exposure to dogs on a direct 300-yard walk. He was . . . trying to be cooperative, but sadly unresponsive—especially to attempts at training in relaxation. In his desire to please, he would state that he had been perfectly relaxed even though he had betrayed himself by his intense fidgetiness. Training in relaxation was eventually abandoned, and an attempt was made to establish the nature of his aspirations and goals. By dint of much questioning and after following many false trails because of his inarticulateness, a topic was eventually tracked down that was absorbing enough to form the subject of his fantasies, namely racing motor-cars. He had a burning ambition to own a certain Alfa Romeo sports car and race it at the Indianapolis "500" event. Emotive imagery was induced as follows: "Close your eyes. I want you to imagine, clearly and vividly, that your wish has come true. The Alfa Romeo is now in your possession. . . . It is standing in the street outside your block. . . . Notice the beautiful, sleek lines. You decide to go for a drive with some friends of yours. You sit down at the wheel and you feel a thrill of pride as you realize that you own this magnificent machine. You start up and listen to the wonderful roar of the exhaust. You let the clutch in and the car streaks off. . . . You are out in a clear open road now . . . the speedometer is climbing into the nineties; you have a wonderful feeling of being in perfect control; you look at the trees whizzing by and you see a little dog standing next to one of them—if you feel any anxiety, just raise your finger. . . ." An item fairly high up on the hierarchy: "You stop at a cafe in a little town and dozens of people crowd around to look enviously at this magnificent car and its lucky owner; you swell with pride; and at this moment a large boxer comes up and sniffs at your heels. . . ."

After three sessions using this method he reported a marked improvement in his reaction to dogs. He was given a few field assignments during the next two sessions, after which therapy was terminated. Twelve months later, reports both from the patient and his relatives indicated that there was no longer any trace of his former phobia [Lazarus & Abramovitz, 1962, p. 192].

An application of group desensitization to children in Czechoslovakia was reported by Kondas (1967). His subjects were 11- to 15-year-old children who feared school examinations, especially oral ones, as evidenced by teachers, self-reports, and scores on Wolpe's Fear Survey Schedule (FSS). One group was given only relaxation training, a second was given systematic desensitization employing a group anxiety hierarchy, a third received hierarchy items without relaxation, and a fourth group served as a nontreatment control. Posttreatment interview data, scores on the FSS, and tests of palmar sweating during an exam showed the greatest improvement in the desensitization group, less in the other two experimental groups, and no improvement in the control group.

OPERANT CONDITIONING

The reciprocal inhibition approach is grounded in Pavlovian and Hullian concepts of "classical" or "respondent" conditioning. The other most widely used behavioral approach is grounded in the second major conditioning paradigm, *operant* conditioning, as originally proposed by Bekhterev and extended by Skinner. The essence of operant conditioning is summed up by Thorndike's (1913) "Law of Effect": A response which produces a satisfying effect will tend to be repeated while a response which produces an annoying effect will tend not to be repeated. More specifically, an *operant* is a response that *operates* on the environment to produce an effect. The tendency for an operant to be repeated is stated in terms of an increase in its probability of emission under the conditions in which it first produced the satisfying effect. Finally, the satisfying effect is referred to as a *reinforcer* of the response. A reinforcer is defined as any effect which is empirically found to increase the probability of occurrence for the response that preceded it.

As applied to behavior modification, operant conditioning paradigms are generally stated in terms of procedures for increasing the probability of specific operants by providing reinforcement or in terms of *extinguishing* (eliminating) operants through removal of reinforcement they had previously obtained. The creation of aversive effects (punishment) has also been employed as a technique for decreasing certain operants, but punishment is considered by many operant conditioners to disrupt or inhibit behavior temporarily rather than to extinguish it (Skinner, 1953). The use of aversive effects to eliminate undesirable behavior will be discussed further in the section on "aversion therapy."

Beside Skinnerian methods for analyzing complex behaviors into operants and reinforcers, laboratory studies on the effects of stimulus fading, on various reinforcement schedules, and on the shaping of new operants have been major sources of operant conditioning techniques. In stimulus *fading*, the organism first learns that he will obtain a reinforcer when he responds to one clearly discriminable stimulus. After the initial discrimination is learned, the clearly discriminable stimulus is gradually faded out so that another stimulus that has been paired with the initial one comes to elicit the same reaction. For example, after training psychotic children to attend to and imitate an experimenter, Lovaas (1967) began training them to speak words by presenting a stimulus the name of which was to be learned. As soon as the child looked at the stimulus, the trainer spoke the name of the stimulus loudly and clearly. Whenever the child imitated the word, he was given food or whatever had proved to be an effective reinforcer with him. The training stimulus was then removed and presented again. On successive trials the prompt offered by the trainer was gradually faded out by saying the word progressively more softly, whispering it, and eventually making only inaudible mouth movements until the child spoke the word in the presence of the training stimulus without prompting from the trainer.

Laboratory research on the effects of various *schedules of reinforcement* has shown that providing *partial* reinforcement (reinforcement after only some, as opposed to all, emissions of an operant) or *intermittent* reinforcement (reinforcement at set time intervals if the operant is being emitted) makes a response much more resistant to extinction than providing reinforcement every time the response is made. This is especially important in the conditioning of new behavior in humans because even behavior that earns a person new rewards in the real world is likely to do so only on a partial or intermittent reinforcement basis.

Shaping of behavior refers to the training of new responses, usually ones that are complex or are part of a long chain of behavior, by reinforcing successive approximations to them. For example, a rat can be taught to pull a chain in a Skinner box by first releasing a pellet into the rat's food tray whenever he approaches the chain. Next, a pellet is provided each time he rears up slightly; then when he rears up more; then when he leans toward the chain while rearing, and so forth until he is pulling the chain. Figure 10–4 portrays a complex response sequence shaped in a rat named Barnabus.

An analogous demonstration of the shaping of human behavior was carried out by Haughton and Ayllon (1965) with a 54-year-old woman diagnosed as schizophrenic. The woman had been hospitalized for 23 years and did little but smoke. The shaping experiment began after she had been deprived of cigarettes for a time. Her behavior was then shaped by giving her a cigarette for holding a broom in successive approximations to an upright position. When she began to hold the broom consistently in an upright position, her schedule of reinforcement was changed to a *variable interval intermittent* schedule whereby she received a cigarette at varying time intervals if she was holding the broom. The result was that she engaged in broom-holding for long periods. The behavior was later extinguished by terminating reinforcement of broom-holding and a two-year follow-up showed no recurrence of broom-holding. However, before extinction was begun, psychiatrists unaware of the woman's conditioning history were asked for their clinical evaluations of her behavior. One evaluated her behavior as follows:

> Her constant and compulsive pacing holding a broom in the manner she does could be seen as a ritualistic procedure, a magical action. When regression conquers the associative process, primitive and archaic forms of thinking control the behavior. Symbolism is a predominant mode of expression of deep seated unfulfilled desires and instinctual impulses. By magic, she controls others, cosmic powers are at her disposal and inanimate objects become living creatures.
>
> Her broom could be then:
>
> 1. a child that gives her love and she gives him in return her devotion;
> 2. a phallic symbol;
> 3. the sceptre of an omnipotent queen.

Her rhythmic and prearranged pacing in a certain space are not similar to the compulsions of a neurotic, but because this is a far more irrational, far more controlled behavior from a primitive thinking, this is a magical procedure in which the patient carries out her wishes, expressed in a way that is far beyond our solid rational and conventional way of thinking and acting [Haughton & Allyon, 1965, pp. 97–98].

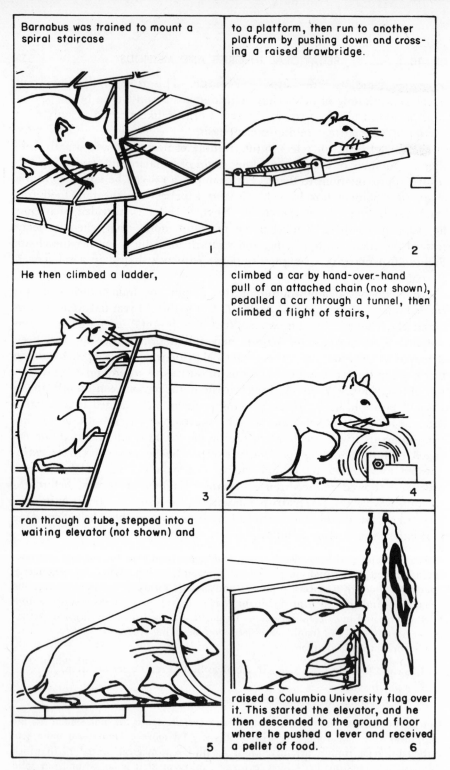

Fig. 10-4. A complex response chain trained through shaping. From Pierrel and Sherman (1963); adapted by Ferster and Perrott (1968), p. 183.

Applications of Operant Conditioning Techniques to Children

Operant conditioning techniques have been much more widely applied to children's behavior than have desensitization techniques. This is partly because desensitization techniques are explicitly aimed at ameliorating "neurotic" behavior that is assumed to result from anxiety. Operant approaches, by contrast, are aimed at changing many other problem behaviors found in children but not readily explainable in terms of anxiety. In fact, operant conditioners tend to be the most radical in eschewing concepts like anxiety. Unlike Wolpe, who retains the terms "neurosis," "patient," "treatment," and "cure," operant conditioners generally prefer to restrict their analyses to specific observable responses, the environmental contingencies maintaining them, and the learning of new operants by the "client" or "subject." A second reason for the wider application of operant conditioning to children is that it can be done under a variety of conditions without requiring the active cooperation of the child.

Many studies have demonstrated the reinforcing effects of adult attention on children's behavior. Excessively immature, inactive, and withdrawn behaviors in preschool children have often been found to elicit extra attention from parents and nursery school teachers. Making adult attention contingent on more appropriate behaviors can. decrease inappropriate behaviors and increase appropriate ones (Baer & Wolf, 1968; Harris, Johnston, Kelley, & Wolf, 1964; Johnston, Kelley, Harris, & Wolf, 1966).

The effects of making adult attention contingent on appropriate rather than inappropriate behavior have been documented by following an *ABAB sequence:* The first *A* refers to a period of observation preceding any intervention to change reinforcement contingencies—the frequencies of the targeted undesirable and desirable behaviors are recorded during this period to provide a *baseline* against which to measure change; the first *B* refers to a period when an intervention is implemented—if the intervention is successful the frequency of the undesirable behavior decreases while that of the desirable behavior increases; the second *A* refers to a period when the intervention is temporarily halted; and the second *B* is a period in which the intervention is reinstated. If the behaviors return approximately to their baseline levels during the second *A* period and return to their first *B* levels during the second *B* period, it can be concluded with considerable certainty that the intervention rather than extraneous factors or the passage of time has been responsible for the behavior change.

The *ABAB* approach is well illustrated in a study of a four-year-old nursery school girl who isolated herself from other children and employed elaborate techniques for obtaining adult attention (Allen, Hart, Buell, Harris, & Wolf, 1964). The girl, Ann, also displayed a number of mild ticlike behaviors. The strategy adopted for changing behavior was to give Ann maximum adult attention whenever she played with another child and minimum attention when she engaged in self-isolating behavior or interactions with an adult alone. Observers recorded in ten-second intervals whether Ann was near an adult or child, or interacting with an adult or child.

Baseline data for the percentage of Ann's interactions with children and adults were obtained over five days (the first *A* period). Teachers' attention was then made contingent on interaction with other children for six days (the first *B* period); the contingencies were reversed again for five days (the second *A* period); and the intervention was reinstated for nine days (the second *B* period). In order to make the new social behavior resistant to extinction, reinforcement during the last nine days was made increasingly intermittent. Figure 10–5 depicts the rises and falls in Ann's social behavior under the different reinforcement contingencies during the *ABAB* sequence. Follow-up periods on Days 31, 38, 40, and 51 indicated that Ann maintained a high rate of social interaction, although the interaction decreased on Day 38, a day when Ann's mother was in the class. Other effects noted were a rise in the volume, tempo, and pitch of Ann's speech, a drop in complaints about minor ills, and a general increase in happiness and confidence.

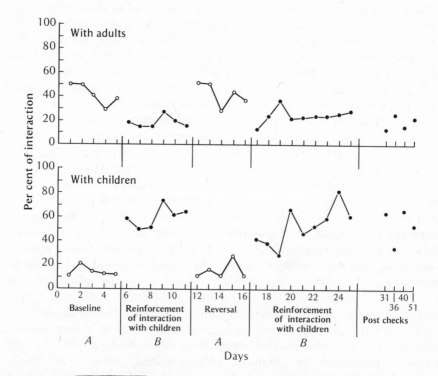

Fig. 10–5. Percentages of nursery school time Ann spent in interaction with adults and children during *ABAB* sequence and postintervention follow-ups. From Allen et al (1964), p. 515. © 1964 by the Society for Research in Child Development and reprinted by permission.

Token Systems. Token systems involve reinforcers (e.g., poker chips, holes punched in a ticket, points on a tally sheet) that are themselves of little value, but that can be exchanged later for valuable reinforcers. The latter are called *back-up* reinforcers. The basic principles of a token system are like those of the money systems existing in most human societies. Under certain circumstances, token reinforcement has several advantages over other forms of reinforcement. One advantage is that different numbers of tokens or tokens having different values can be awarded for various types of desired behavior, thus permitting precise regulation of reinforcement according to the significance or difficulty of specific behavior. Tokens can also be awarded for elements in a chain of behavior so that each step is, in effect, reinforced by the potent reinforcer for which the accumulated tokens can eventually be exchanged.

A second advantage is that the tokens are more convenient to employ than most other forms of reinforcement because they can be easily dispensed (even by machine) and the recipient can store and keep track of them in preparation for later exchange. This also means that human dispensers of the reinforcements need not be either well trained or highly attractive to the recipients of the tokens—they need only dispense prescribed numbers of tokens for specific behavior, although praise accompanying the dispensing of tokens is often considered an important component of token systems.

A third advantage is that token systems allow the recipient to choose from a number of reinforcers the one he will ultimately obtain. This means that an effective reinforcer is more likely to be obtained than if the trainer unilaterally determines which reinforcer is to be provided after emission of a given behavior.

A fourth advantage is that the person who receives the tokens may not only emit the desired behavior, but may learn to direct his behavior to more distant goals such as those earned by the tokens.

Potential disadvantages of token systems include the disadvantages of money economies in general. For example, theft and hoarding can occur unless tokens are individualized and limitations are imposed on when they can be spent. Problems can also arise in getting token-reinforced behavior to be supported by other reinforcement such as social approval and in getting new behavior to generalize to real-world situations where tokens are not dispensed.

Some of the most thoroughgoing applications of token principles have been made with chronic mental patients. A pioneering book by Ayllon and Azrin, *The Token Economy: A Motivational System for Therapy and Rehabilitation* (1968), details the development of a token system and its successes and failures in a mental hospital. Token systems have also been set up in prisons and in institutions for delinquent, retarded, and disturbed children.

Besides their use in residential settings, token systems have been used with children in school programs. In one study, the teacher of a second-grade class selected seven disruptive pupils for observation (O'Leary, Becker, Evans & Saudargas, 1969). Each child was first observed for 20-minute classroom periods by an observer and a reliability checker who recorded various categories of disruptive behavior.

The experiment had eight phases:

1. Baseline observation period;
2. Classroom rules;
3. Educational structure;
4. Praising appropriate and ignoring disruptive behavior;
5. Tokens and back-up reinforcement;
6. Return to Phase 4 with withdrawal of token system;
7. Return to Phase 5 token system;
8. Follow-up.

Classroom rules, introduced in Phase 2, consisted of instructions written on the blackboard, such as "We sit in our seats; we raise our hands to talk," etc. These were restated each morning and afternoon by the teacher. Educational structure, introduced in Phase 3, involved the teacher's organizing her class instruction into four 30-minute periods in the afternoon, e.g., spelling, arithmetic, reading, science. Praising appropriate and ignoring disruptive behavior was added in Phase 4. In Phase 5, the experimenter told the children they would receive from 1 to 10 points during each of the four class instruction periods for following the classroom rules, participating effectively in classroom discussions, and being accurate in their arithmetic and spelling. The points were placed in booklets on each child's desk and were exchangeable for back-up reinforcers including candy, toys, and comics. Progressively longer delays for purchase of back-up reinforcers were arranged, from purchase on each day to purchase after three days, during which period children could accumulate their points to obtain more valuable reinforcers.

Both the teacher and experimenter rated the children, although the teacher assigned the final points on the basis of amounts of improvement in a child's behavior. After the first week, the teacher alone administered the system.

In Phase 6, the token system was withdrawn, while the rules, educational structure, and praising and ignoring remained in effect. The token system was restored in Phase 7. It was withdrawn again in Phase 8 and replaced with a star-chart system in which well-behaved children received stars that could be accumulated to obtain a gold star on a wall chart.

Figure 10–6 portrays the percentage of disruptive behavior by each of the seven subjects and all seven combined during the eight phases of the experiment. Statistical tests showed that disruptive behavior was significantly less during the token phases and the follow-up phase than during any of the other phases.

Although the O'Leary et al study was not designed rigorously to assess changes in academic performance or attendance, scores on standardized

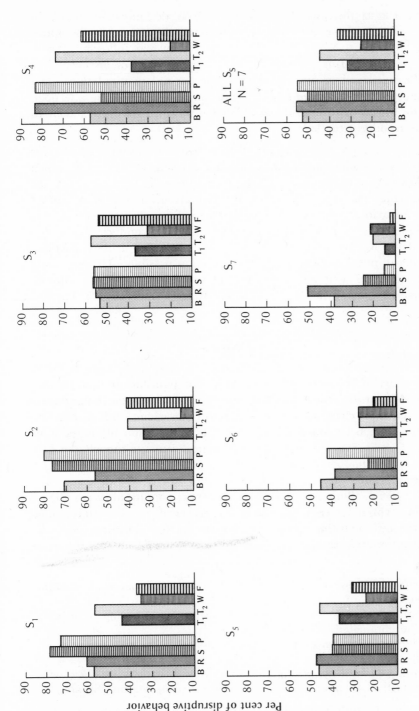

Fig. 10–6. Percentage of disruptive behavior for each of seven children (S_1 to S_7) and all seven combined during eight conditions: Base-line (B), Rules (R), Educational Structure (S), Praise-Ignore (P), Token 1 (T_1), Withdrawal (W), Token 2 (T_2), and Follow-up (F). From O'Leary et al (1969), p. 11. © 1969 by the Society for the Experimental Analysis of Behavior and reprinted by permission.

achievement tests increased from an average grade-equivalent of 1.5 in October to 3.0 in June, and average attendance by the seven disruptive children increased to 99 per cent during the token and follow-up phases, from 86 per cent during the other phases. Observations of disruptive behavior during the mornings, when the experimental manipulations were not in effect, showed no significant improvements related to the afternoon conditions, illustrating the problem of getting token-reinforced behavior to generalize to other situations.

Phase Systems. A related approach in which maintenance of behavior change is less dependent upon continuation of artificial reinforcers is known as the *phase system* approach. In a phase system, individuals work for reinforcers that may include tokens, but, by achieving and maintaining desirable behavior, they can earn promotion to more advanced phases that entail higher level reinforcers, plus new standards of conduct. When the new standards are met, promotion to still more advanced phases is possible, eventuating in phases that are as nearly normal as possible. This approach has been successful with very disruptive adolescents who did not improve under token systems (Martin, Burkholder, Rosenthal, Tharp, & Thorne, 1968).

AVERSION THERAPY

Due in part to Skinner's (1953) opinion that punishment is ineffective in promoting learning, there was for a time a general reluctance to employ painful stimuli for changing behavior. However, various kinds of aversive stimulation have been found effective in the modification of undesirable behavior. Certain aversive methods raise ethical issues, although the fact that some cause temporary physical discomfort makes them no different from uncomfortable medical procedures if they can be shown to be ultimately beneficial. Both respondent and operant conditioning paradigms have been invoked for conceptualizing the effects of aversive stimulation, but the theoretical distinctions between them are less clear than in techniques using positive reinforcers. The four chief models of aversive control are:

1. Removal of positive reinforcement following a response to be eliminated.
2. Application of aversive stimuli (punishment) following a response to be eliminated.
3. Removal of aversive stimuli to reinforce an escape or avoidance response.
4. Making neutral or positive stimuli aversive by pairing them with events that are already aversive (classical aversive conditioning).

Many aversive techniques can be interpreted as conforming to more than one of the models. For example, *time-out from reinforcement* is a method widely employed by operant conditioners with disruptive children for whom contingent application of adult attention or other positive reinforcers is insufficient to change behavior. Time-out usually consists of temporarily closing a child in a room by himself each time he engages in undesirable disruptive behavior.

According to Model 1, the effect of time-out is to cut off all possibilities for positive reinforcement. Thus, any positive reinforcements previously supporting the behavior are removed and the behavior should extinguish. However, the effects of time-out are also interpretable under Model 2, the contingent application of aversive stimuli (punishment), because being closed in a room and losing positive reinforcers are both aversive. According to Model 3, time-out may result in the conditioning of nondisruptive responses to whatever stimuli previously elicited disruptive responses because the new responses are reinforced by avoidance of isolation or escape from it if termination of time-out is contingent on cessation of disruptive behavior.

The probable existence of covert responses to painful aversive stimuli (e.g., "anxiety," autonomic responses) further complicates the question of just how behavior is affected by aversive consequences. Experimental studies have revealed a number of unexpected effects of aversive stimulation—e.g., increases in some punished behavior (cf. Kanfer & Phillips, 1970)—that have not been well explained theoretically. Be that as it may, certain applications of aversive methods appear to produce good results and these are discussed below.

Time-out from Reinforcement

In a typical application of time-out procedures, Wahler (1969) made detailed *ABAB* analyses of two cases in which parents were trained to use time-out in the home. The subjects were five- and six-year-old boys whose parents had sought help at a clinic because of the children's severe oppositional and destructive behavior. One of the boys was also oppositional and destructive at school. His parents attributed his oppositional behavior to distractibility. The other boy was an only child whose parents acknowledged being oversolicitous and giving him anything he wanted because they had lost several previous babies through miscarriages.

Observers first went to the homes to record the number of 10-second units of oppositional behavior during baseline sessions. The parents were then trained to isolate the child in his room for five minutes whenever he began being oppositional. If the child tantrumed while in his room, he was to stay there until the tantrum ceased. The parents were to reinforce the child with praise and attention whenever he showed cooperative behavior. Both children's oppositional behavior dropped sharply during the first *B* (training) period. A temporary return to the pretraining conditions (second *A* period) brought a sudden increase in oppositional behavior, while reinstatement of the training conditions (second *B* period) eliminated oppositional behavior almost completely.

A test of the parents' effectiveness as reinforcers of the child's behavior in a standardized experimental task was administered at the end of each period in the sequence. For both children, the parents' effectiveness as reinforcers was lowest following the first *A* period and next lowest following the second *A* period. It increased following the first *B* period and was highest following the second *B* period. This indicated that, besides affecting the specific target behavior, the intervention had increased parental influence on other aspects of the children's behavior as well.

Electrical and Chemical Aversive Techniques

Both electric shock and drugs producing unpleasant reactions have been used to remove undesirable behavior. Drugs have been used primarily with adults, especially in the treatment of alcoholism. Beginning in the 1930s, Pavlovian approaches were tried in which alcoholics were injected with a drug and given alcohol just as nausea and vomiting induced by the drug began. A report on 4,096 alcoholics who had voluntarily committed themselves to a private sanatorium showed that 60 per cent remained abstinent for at least a year after drug-aversion treatment, 51 per cent for at least two years, 38 per cent for at least five years, and 23 per cent for at least 10 years (Lemere & Voegtlin, 1950). Booster treatments in cases of relapse also produced renewed abstinence. The results are considerably superior to those reported with other treatments for alcoholism, but baselines for spontaneous remission and relapse are unknown for alcoholics in similar socioeconomic circumstances and a marked reluctance to return for booster treatments was noted (cf. Rachman & Teasdale, 1969).

Chemical aversion therapy has also been applied to sexual perversions. One of the first applications was with a man who was sexually aroused by women's handbags and babies' perambulators (Raymond, 1956). He obtained a release of tension by attacking them and had been arrested and hospitalized several times as a result. He had not benefitted from previous treatment including psychoanalysis (despite the obvious symbolism of the fetish objects). However, he developed a revulsion to handbags and perambulators after receiving drug-aversion treatment to them. A 19-month follow-up showed no more fantasies or undesirable behavior related to the fetish objects, greatly improved sexual relations with his wife, and no evidence of symptom substitution.

Electric shock, usually to the finger tips, has been more widely employed than drug aversion with sexual perversions. Shock is made contingent on presentation of fetish objects, words referring to the sexual practices to be changed, the sexual fantasies, or the acts themselves. After training, the client is sometimes given a device with which he shocks himself.

Plethysmographic measures of penis erections in males to the originally conditioned stimuli as well as changes in fantasy life and overt symptomatology have been used as indices of improvement. In a review of the literature, Rachman and Teasdale (1969) report varying effects, but, in cases whose symptoms were successfully removed, there was evidence of improved general adjustment and no evidence of symptom substitution.

Electric shock has also been used with a variety of other adult symptoms, especially hysterical symptoms wherein cessation of small shocks is made contingent on cessation of the hysterical symptom. Kushner (1970) has detailed several cases successfully treated in this way, ranging from paralysis of the lower body to a highly publicized case of constant sneezing by a 17-year-old girl who had unsuccessfully undergone a variety of medical, hypnotic, and psychiatric therapies.

Applications to Children.   Electrical shock has been used in a variety of ways with children, although it remains one of the most controversial techniques. Lovaas (1967) has used electric shock for a number of purposes in the conditioning of severely disturbed children. One purpose has been to suppress self-destructive behavior such as self-biting and head-banging so severe as to be life-threatening. Painful shock contingent on these behaviors was found to suppress the behaviors within minutes, with no recurrence for 11 months.

A second purpose for shocking psychotic children has been to establish social reinforcers by pairing them with pain reduction. For example, psychotic children were shocked on an electrified floor with an adult nearby. Shock was terminated contingent on their going to the adult. It was reported that not only did the children learn to go the adult and to seek adult physical contacts under other conditions, but they also showed social smiles and molded themselves onto the adult's bodies, which they had never been known to do before. When adult attention has become reinforcing through pairing with shock cessation, it has been possible to use the adult attention as a reinforcer for training new behavior.

A third purpose for using shock has been to train severely disturbed children to respond to speech (Bucher & Lovaas, 1968). This has been done by placing a child on the electrified floor, commanding him to come to an adult, and terminating shock when he does so. Other applications to speech training have involved shocking a child whenever the word "No!" was given and shocking him for failing to imitate speech sounds produced by a trainer. In most of Lovaas's severely disturbed cases, shock has been employed primarily at the beginning of training. Thereafter, shock is replaced with food, attention, praise, and other reinforcers as they become effective.

A very different application of shock was undertaken with an infant who manifested a syndrome known as *ruminative vomiting* (Lang & Melamed, 1969). In this syndrome, the child persistently vomits his food and chews the vomitus. Vomiting began when the child was five months old. After the failure of all attempts at treatment, vomiting reached the point where the child was in danger of dying.

The conditioning procedure involved shocking the infant's leg whenever vomiting activity began, as observed by a nurse and indicated by electromyographic recordings taken around the child's throat. By the sixth session, the infant no longer vomited during training sessions. A slight recurrence later was eliminated in three sessions. The child's weight and activity increased steadily, he became more interested in his environment, and he smiled and reached out to be held by visitors. Five-month and one-year follow-ups showed normal weight and behavior and no recurrence of vomiting.

Covert Sensitization

Reversing Wolpe's desensitization approach, Gold and Neufeld (1965) introduced a technique known as _covert sensitization_. Their patient, a 16-year-old boy convicted of homosexual solicitation in public toilets, was trained to relax and to imagine circumstances like those in which he had previously solicited but with negative features, such as physical repulsiveness in the men he imagined. This was succeeded by imagining more attractive men but with policemen standing nearby. Later, the patient was induced to imagine male and female alternatives, with positive verbal reinforcements being given for choosing the female alternative. At the end of a one-year follow-up period, the patient was reported to have formed a relationship with a girl and to have remained free of homosexual symptoms.

Kolvin (1967) has reported similar treatment procedures with a 14-year-old fetishist and a 15-year-old addicted to sniffing gasoline. In each case, the patient was first asked to list his dislikes. During relaxation, Kolvin then told a colorful story leading up to the symptomatic behaviors. When the patient was excitedly enjoying the fantasy, aversive imagery from the patient's list of dislikes was vividly introduced. Seventeen- and thirteen-month follow-ups, respectively, revealed no recurrence of the symptomatic behaviors in either case. Covert sensitization has also been used in the treatment of sadistic fantasies in a college student (Davison, 1968a), of pedophilia and homosexuality in adult men (Barlow, Leitenberg, & Agras, 1969), and of alcoholism (Ashem & Donner, 1968).

IMPLOSIVE THERAPY

Stampfl and Levis (1967) have proposed an approach to therapy which they regard as "a learning theory-based psychodynamic behavioral therapy." Known as _implosive therapy,_ this approach is psychodynamic in the sense that it assumes that neurotic anxiety and symptoms are caused by early traumatic experiences which become associated with a variety of other thoughts and cues, largely according to psychodynamic principles. The defensive maneuvers of the patient are regarded as being designed to avoid ideas and cues associated with the traumas. Thus, anxiety and defense mechanisms are retained as central concepts in the explanation of psychopathology and in guiding the course of therapy.

Implosive therapy is based on learning theory in the sense that it seeks to extinguish conditioned anxiety responses by presenting the conditioned stimuli eliciting them but without the feared painful consequences. By repeatedly presenting the anxiety-arousing stimuli without painful consequences, it is assumed that the anxiety responses will weaken and extinguish.

In practice, implosive therapy generally begins with having the patient report the things that make him most anxious. It is assumed that the real basis for the anxiety and the cues most strongly associated with it are avoided at first through repression and other defenses. The fact that the avoided cues are rarely exposed means that there is little opportunity for anxiety responses to them to be extinguished without therapy. During therapy, the therapist helps the patient to imagine vividly the frightening situations, working up to cues that the therapist believes are even more anxiety-provoking than the ones initially specified by the patient. The expected result is that repeated elicitations of anxiety responses without painful consequences will extinguish the anxiety responses. The reduction in anxiety is assumed to generalize to real-life situations.

Although resembling desensitization in conception, implosive therapy is at variance with Wolpe's desensitization approach in that it exposes the patient quickly to large amounts of anxiety without training new responses to inhibit the anxiety reciprocally. Implosive therapy with various kinds of adult disorders has produced mixed results (cf. Bandura, 1969a; Morganstern, 1973). However, two applications to children's phobias appear to have been successful. In one case (Ollendick & Gruen, 1972), the client was an eight-year-old boy with a severe phobia for a large variety of cues associated with injury, especially bleeding. The boy, Tommy, was also subject to insomnia five to seven nights per week, hives, and asthmatic bronchitis for which no allergin was found. The phobia had apparently begun several years earlier when a mentally retarded sister was born with a blood disease that prevented her blood from clotting. A concomitant factor was that Tommy's bed was moved out of the parents' room and the new sister was moved in.

Following three interviews to establish rapport and to elicit relevant fear-provoking cues, Tommy was seen for two therapy sessions in which he was asked to imagine a sequence of scenes commencing with cutting his head by falling on a rock and climaxing with being attacked by rats that fed on his blood and tore him apart. These scenes evoked extreme anxiety. After each session Tommy was assured that he was all right and was given brief relaxation training. He was then seen bimonthly for follow-ups.

Despite the fact that his grandmother died during the third posttreatment month and that he had to be fed intravenously for a short period because of internal injuries sustained in an accident during the fourth month, Tommy's sleepless nights dropped to one per month in the fourth posttherapy month and none in the fifth and sixth posttherapy months. Tommy was also reported to play more with his retarded sister and to have more fun at school, as well as having no recurrence of hives or bronchitis.

Smith and Sharpe (1970) reported similar success in six implosive therapy sessions with a 13-year-old boy whose severe school phobia prevented him from staying in school. In both studies, the authors remarked that implosive therapy seemed well suited to children because their high suggestibility made induction of the feared scenes especially effective. However, most other therapeutic viewpoints imply that provoking intense fear in children is a very risky procedure.

MODELING AND IMITATION

Imitation is an important technique whereby children acquire new behavior under natural conditions and it has been put to work in changing undesirable behavior. Following a series of studies in which the parameters of imitative behavior were experimentally studied in normal children, Bandura and his colleagues have applied similar procedures to the treatment of children's phobias.

In one study (Bandura, Grusec, & Menlove, 1967), nursery school children who were afraid of dogs observed another child successively approach, pet, feed, and interact with a dog over a series of four sessions. Posttreatment and one-month follow-up measures of performance in a graded series of interactions with dogs showed that children who had viewed the model were significantly superior to children who had seen the dog without the model and children who had enjoyed a party between pretests and posttests but had seen neither the dog nor the model.

In another study, Bandura, Blanchard, and Ritter (1969) found that live modeling plus guided participation in handling snakes eliminated snake phobias in nearly all adolescent and adult subjects, while filmed modeling plus relaxation training was more effective than desensitization, although desensitization was significantly better than no treatment. Fear inventory responses also showed the greatest decreases under the live-modeling-with-participation condition. A one-month follow-up revealed generalization to real-life situations that the subjects had previously avoided.

Group modeling with guided participation has also been found to be effective in the treatment of children's snake phobias (Ritter, 1968). In two sessions of 35 minutes each, 80 per cent of child subjects lost their fear, compared to 53 per cent in a group treated with modeling alone.

In his work with psychotic children, Lovaas has trained imitation of simple tasks by "prompting" the child to follow the trainer's example— e.g., by taking the child's hand and moving it through the desired behavior—and then providing food reinforcers for progressively more complete imitation as the prompts are faded on successive trials. By this means, generalized imitative behavior has been developed in children who had not previously imitated. Personal hygiene, games, drawing, printing, elementary interpersonal skills, and simple speech have then been learned through imitation (Lovaas, 1967; Lovaas, Freitas, Nelson, & Whalen, 1967).

PARENTS AS BEHAVIOR MODIFIERS

One of the innovative characteristics of many behavior modification methods is that they can be applied by people who have not had professional training in the mental-health professions. While the design and evaluation of a behavior modification program may require considerable training and experience, the application of the procedures and recording of behavior change do not necessarily require such background. It has thus been possible for psychiatric aides, volunteer workers, family members, nurses, teachers, and others to carry out behavior modification programs that could not be applied solely by mental-health professionals because there are not enough of them and because they could not play the appropriate roles in the clients' everyday environments.

The use of parents as modifiers of their children's problem behavior is especially promising because the special relationships of children to their parents and the large amount of time they spend together typically make parents the most potent behavior-change agents for their children. Moreover, since most child behavior problems are assumed to originate from learning conditions provided by the parents, modification of the parents' behavior is often a prerequisite for creating and sustaining changes in the child. Other theoretical orientations also emphasize the contributions of parent behavior to child behavior disorders, but few take such a direct approach to analyzing and changing specific parent behavior as does the behavior modification approach, especially the operant conditioning versions of it.

The training of parents to use time-out and contingent positive attention to control disruptive behavior has already been described above (cf. Wahler, 1969). Time-out and contingent reinforcers, such as attention, praise, toys, privileges, and money, have been widely employed in techniques administered by parents. Parents are first taught the basic principles of operant conditioning and are given reading materials on practical applications to children. Observers may then study child-parent interactions in the home and recommend specific behavior modification methods. As the parents attempt to implement these, the observers point out errors and make further suggestions. The parents are also to keep records of the occurrence of the target behavior. After the parents are on their own, they report back periodically on behavior changes. Older children often participate in the design of the behavior modification program of which they are to be the subjects. They may discuss the objectives to be sought and the reinforcements to be given.

As an example, Holland (1969) reported the elimination of a seven-year-old's fire-setting by behavior modification measures taken by the father, without the child ever being seen professionally. Since no therapy time was available, the boy, Robert, had been put on a clinic waiting list, but the fire-setting necessitated immediate action. Three goals were set up which the father agreed to try and achieve, although the mother initially refused to participate. The goals were:

1. to make fire-setting a clearly discriminable situation for punishment;
2. to strengthen the operant behavior of bringing matches to the parents;
3. to strengthen non-striking behavior when matches were available but the parents were not present to receive them.

The first goal was to be achieved by telling Robert that his highly prized new baseball glove would be taken away irrevocably if he set any more fires. At the same time, Robert was told that he was to bring to the father any matches or match covers he found. That evening, the father conspicuously left out an empty match box which Robert then brought him. Robert was given five cents and told he could spend it however he wished. The father continued leaving matches and match covers around and Robert was given varying amounts of money each time he brought them. The father later introduced a partial reinforcement schedule with the money, but social reinforcement was given on every occasion.

A week after the program began, reinforcement for nonstriking behavior was begun. The father told Robert he could strike a full pack of 20 matches under the father's supervision. The father also placed 20 pennies beside the pack and told Robert he would receive one penny for each match left unstruck. On the first trial, Robert struck 10 matches and received 10 pennies. On the second trial he received 17 pennies, and on the third all 20 pennies. A partial reinforcement schedule was then instituted for several more trials.

Within three weeks, the fire-setting behavior had been eliminated and there was no recurrence during an eight-month follow-up. Impressed by the results, Robert's mother began to apply similar principles in her own handling of his disobedience. She gained an increased sense of adequacy in handling him and was able to express more affection for him than she had before. Analogous behavior modification programs have also been set up to train parents in modifying the difficult behaviors of psychotic, brain-damaged, and retarded children in the home (Walder, Cohen, Breiter, Daston, Hirsch, & Leibowitz, 1971; Wetzel, Baker, Roney, & Martin, 1966).

Reprogramming Families

Patterson and Reid (1970) have described an especially ambitious approach to using parents as behavior modifiers in a way that may offer hope for helping the multiproblem families in which so many problem children are found. The focus of their effort was a 10-year-old boy, Sean, who was in a special class for the mildly retarded, was described as a loner, was rejected by his peers, and was accused of lying and stealing. After school, Sean's frequent disappearances from home were followed by fires in parked cars and neighborhood homes. The police accused Sean but his parents denied he was responsible. There were five other children in the family, which resided in a poorly kept house, was marginally supported by the father, and was well known to various social agencies.

Two weeks of baseline observation in the home showed that the family members provided very little reinforcement for one another, either positive or negative. In fact, they spent nearly all their time watching television. When Sean came home from school, he often initiated contacts with family members but was generally ignored. It was then that he usually disappeared from home.

When it was found that the father was illiterate, a tape recording was made of a programmed text on learning principles given by Patterson and his colleagues to parents before interventions are begun. Sean's parents were then trained to record with mechanical counters for a set period each day the frequency of their children's compliance or resistance to requests, the frequency with which the other spouse reinforced adaptive child behavior, and the frequency with which the other spouse received positive reinforcers from the family. Attempts were made to show the parents how increasing positive reinforcement for Sean could control his behavior.

Later, reinforcement was employed to get Sean to talk to his parents, especially telling them when and where he was going. Whenever Sean had initiated a predetermined amount of conversation, a portable signaling device activated by an observer emitted a buzz. This indicated that Sean had earned 10 M & M candies which were to be divided among all the children in the family.

In the next phase of the program, family members were to function as social reinforcers. The mother succeeded in increasing her rate of social reinforcement, but the father never became willing or able to do this effectively. Adding a point system in which the parents awarded Sean points toward a new football proved more effective. The other children in the family were also trained to reinforce the mother with compliments and other positive social initiatives in order to maintain her relatively high rate of social reinforcement of Sean's behavior. Sean's behavior improved markedly at home. There was an increase in social interaction between his mother and himself which appeared mutually pleasurable, he began asking permission whenever he wanted to leave the house, and there was an almost complete disappearance of a variety of aggressive and destructive behaviors recorded by an observer. Sean's behavior outside the home improved and there were no more mysterious fires in the neighborhood.

Intervention was also arranged at school to reduce the isolation that appeared to be central in Sean's deviant behavior there. The best football player in the school agreed to coach Sean in order to provide him with some football skills with which he could win reinforcement from other children. A graded series of skills was set up. Each time Sean improved his score in this series, his classmates were let out five minutes early for recess. This led to a great deal of peer reinforcement and a tremendous increase in the percentage of Sean's time spent interacting with peers.

At a one-month follow-up, Patterson and Reid reported some decline in the improvements, although Sean's behavior was still markedly better than during the baseline period. Patterson and Reid plan further extensions of what they described as their first attempt at applying "stone-age" technology to the overwhelmingly complex problems of poverty families. Much longer follow-up evaluations are especially needed to evaluate the effectiveness of such interventions.

SUMMARY

Behavior modification is becoming a generic term that includes the term *behavior therapy*. The focus of the behavior modification approach is on current problem behavior rather than on conflicts among intrapsychic forces or inferred components of personality. The primary theoretical basis for behavior modification techniques is in the experimental study of learning, but conceptions of behavior modification have broadened to include many techniques that extend far beyond principles derived from learning experiments.

The two most basic paradigms for behavior modification techniques have been *respondent (Pavlovian, classical) conditioning* and *operant conditioning*. John B. Watson was among the first to apply conditioning concepts to the development of psychopathology. He created a phobia in an infant by respondent conditioning and Jones applied Watsonian techniques to the removal of a child's phobia. In another early study, Mowrer and

Mowrer employed a conditioning apparatus to eliminate enuresis in children.

Dollard and Miller and others in the late 1940s and early 1950s attempted to translate psychodynamic concepts into learning theory language, but it was not until Wolpe's book on *reciprocal inhibition* that large-scale applications of new behavioral methods began. Wolpe's reciprocal inhibition methods included the training of assertive responses, sexual responses, and—his most original contribution—*systematic desensitization,* which is aimed at reducing neurotic anxiety and concomitant maladaptive behavior through training of relaxation responses to inhibit anxiety responses.

Operant conditioning, founded mainly on Skinnerian principles of reinforcing desired behavior, has also become a widespread behavior modification technique and has spawned such variants as *token systems* and *phase systems.* Other current behavior modification techniques include *aversion therapy* for removing undesirable behavior; *implosive therapy* for extinguishing excessive anxiety; *modeling* and *imitation* for eliminating phobias; and the use of parents as modifiers of their children's problem behavior.

SUGGESTED READING

Reciprocal Inhibition.   Wolpe's first book, *Psychotherapy by Reciprocal Inhibition* (1958), gives a clear statement of what brought him to try behavioral methods, the theoretical underpinnings for the methods he evolved, and—what may have been most influential—his reports of 90 per cent success in treating neurotics. Other behavior modifiers have questioned the validity of the theory and controlled studies have produced lower success rates, but systematic desensitization is still one of the best researched and validated forms of treatment. Wolpe's more recent book, *The Practice of Behavior Therapy* (1969), is also a worthwhile guide to efforts at refining it further.

Operant Conditioning.   Two recommended basic books on the application of operant principles are *Behavior Principles,* by Ferster and Perrot (1968), and *A Primer of Operant Conditioning,* by Reynolds (1968).

General Handbooks.   Wenrich's *Primer of Behavior Modification* (1970) provides a clear and brief summary of behavior modification concepts and terminology. For more complete analyses, see the books by Bandura (1969a) and Kanfer and Phillips (1970). Ullmann and Krasner's (1969) comprehensive textbook presents abnormal psychology from the behavior modification viewpoint.

11

Clinical Application of
Behavioral Methods

The preceding chapter described a number of specific techniques of behavior modification, including *desensitization, operant conditioning, aversion therapy, implosive therapy, modeling and imitation,* and the use of *parents as behavior modifiers.* Most of these techniques are better suited to certain classes of disorders than to others, although several techniques are often used together in treating the same individual. In the sections that follow, the ways in which behavior modifiers have defined and treated various classes of disorders will be discussed. The range of "behavior" disorders discussed is broad and includes what psychoanalysts would call "psychoneurotic" disorders, plus some that analysts would call "character" disorders, implying that they are enduring personality traits, and others that analysts might regard as "situational reactions," implying that they are reactions to current life stress rather than being based on intrapsychic conflict. Behavioral treatment of psychotic and delinquent children will be discussed in the chapters on psychosis and delinquency.

GENERAL CLASSES OF BEHAVIOR DISORDERS

Phobias

Theoretical differences between the psychodynamic and the behavioral approaches are perhaps most obvious in their portrayals of the origin of phobias. Recall from Chapter 8 Freud's (1926) revised formulation of Little Hans's horse phobia:

1. Hans feared castration by his father as retribution for his sexual desires toward his mother and his aggressive impulses toward his father.

2. Repression alone failed to eliminate his fears, but, because he loved his father, he could not accept thinking of him as a source of danger and a target of aggression.
3. Therefore, the unconscious anxiety was *displaced* onto symbolic substitutes for the father, i.e., horses.
4. Believing a biting horse rather than a castrating father to be the source of his anxiety enabled Hans to avoid recognizing the conflict between his positive and negative feelings toward his father.
5. Thinking of horses as the source of his anxiety also made it possible for Hans to avoid further anxiety by avoiding horses.

The essence of a phobia is thus portrayed by psychodynamic theory as being a repressed intrapsychic conflict. The phobic object or situation is one symbolically associated in the patient's mind with the conflict and the fear is displaced onto the symbolic object because recognizing the true source of the fear is too threatening. According to this view, treatment must be oriented toward relieving the unconscious conflict which generated the fear that was displaced onto the phobic object. If unconscious conflict is not resolved, it is assumed that the fear will remain intact, ready to produce substitute symptoms if fear to the phobic object is reduced.

Behavioral formulations have portrayed phobias as fears learned through the pairing of a painful or fear-evoking situation with a previously neutral object or situation. If the painful or fear-evoking situation is intense enough or if it is frequently enough paired with the neutral object or situation, then the neutral object itself becomes capable of evoking the same fearful reaction as the noxious situation. Stimuli that resemble the newly conditioned phobic object or that have frequently accompanied it are also likely to elicit anxiety reactions in degrees proportional to the strength of the associations they have with the phobic stimulus. Thus, a child bitten by a particular dog may be panicked by the sight of that dog and dogs closely resembling him, slightly less afraid of dogs of other sizes, still less afraid of a dog's bark in the distance, of other furry animals, etc. However, the child may also develop elaborate behavior to avoid situations in which he might meet a dog. This behavior may be reinforced by the relief experienced when the child feels he has avoided dogs but it may also interfere with his development in significant ways such as preventing him from playing with other children. This, in turn, can lead to new problems such as a sense of inadequacy with regard to his skills, excessive dependence on adults, etc. For this reason, it is rare that a child is brought for treatment solely because of a phobia. More typically, the child has a variety of symptoms of which a phobia may be one, although behavior modifiers, especially those who follow Wolpe, may consider many of the problems to be secondary to one or more phobias learned through classical conditioning.

An aspect of the etiology of phobias emphasized by Eysenck, Rachman, and Wolpe is constitutional disposition to anxiety. While these researchers all define phobias as learned fears, they hypothesize that individuals differ constitutionally in their dispositions to react with anxiety to the same objective circumstances.

Eysenck has proposed a general theory of personality according to which people vary along two primary constitutional dimensions (Eysenck & Rachman, 1965). One dimension is *neuroticism,* ranging from normal people whose emotional reactions are relatively stable, weak, and difficult to arouse, to neurotic people whose emotional reactions are labile, intense, and easily aroused. The other dimension is *extroversion-introversion,* ranging from people who are outgoing, sociable, impulsive, optimistic, and not easily conditioned, to people who are quiet, introspective, cautious, serious, and easily conditioned.

On the basis of factor analysis of measures of these two dimensions, Eysenck has concluded that different neurotic syndromes represent different positions on the dimensions. Figure 11–1 portrays the positions of patients diagnosed as anxiety-state, obsessional, hysteric, psychopathic, and psychosomatic. Note that obsessional and psychopathic patients are both considered to be high on emotional reactivity (neuroticism), but obsessional patients are introverted while psychopathic patients are extroverted. Obsessional and anxiety-state patients are regarded as being the most susceptible to phobias because they are the most reactive *and* the most readily

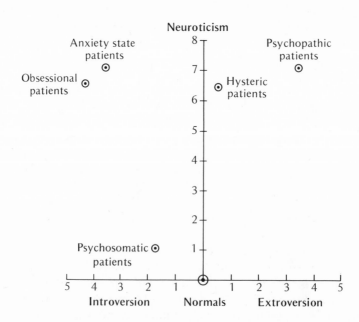

Fig. 11–1. The basic dimensions of personality according to Eysenck's theory. Various patient groups are located according to the average scores they obtain on measures of the two dimensions. Adapted from Eysenck and Rachman (1965), p. 21. © 1965 by R. R. Knapp and reprinted by permission of the publisher.

conditioned. When they encounter a frightening situation, they are the most likely to learn new fears from it. Despite the fact that Eysenck, Rachman, and Wolpe emphasize constitutional predispositions to learn fears, they believe that behavior therapies are the best way to remove these fears once they have been acquired.

The most widely used behavioral treatments for phobias have been desensitization and other reciprocal inhibition procedures for training new responses incompatible with anxiety responses to phobic objects. Various modifications of these techniques have been used to treat children's fears of water (Bentler, 1962), hospitals and ambulances (Lazarus & Rachman, 1957), dogs (Lazarus & Abramovitz, 1962), moving vehicles (Lazarus, 1960), school (Lazarus & Abramovitz, 1962), and school examinations (Kondas, 1967). Other methods of treating children's phobias have included modeling and imitation (Bandura et al, 1967; Bandura & Menlove, 1968), operant conditioning (Patterson, 1965), and implosion (Ollendick & Gruen, 1972; Smith & Sharpe, 1970).

School Phobia.   Fear of going to school, often accompanied by crying, nausea, vomiting, and other somatic symptoms when the child does go, is among the most frequent of childhood problems. Most children experience such fears at some time in their school careers, especially when beginning school for the first time, when beginning a new school, after absences from school, and when facing difficult classes or exams. Those who reach the point of being called phobic may express eagerness to attend school but are seized with terror when the time comes. There is a vast literature on school phobia and a number of theories and treatments have been proposed (cf. reviews by Berecz, 1968; Frick, 1964). Most authors agree on three points:

1. The fear is not so much of school itself but of separation from the mother.
2. The behavior of the parents is crucial in that they may inadvertently encourage the child to stay home.
3. Returning the child to school as quickly as possible is of utmost importance.

The case of Frankie (Bornstein, 1949), presented in Chapter 9, illustrates the psychoanalytic view of the complex psychodynamics underlying a school phobia.

While agreeing that separation rather than the school may be feared, most behavior modifiers focus treatment directly on getting the child into school, reducing his anxiety about staying, and reducing reinforcements or "secondary gain" provided by the parents for staying home. A number of behavior modification methods have been used with apparent success. The cases of a nine-year-old girl treated with desensitization (Lazarus, 1960) and a 13-year-old boy treated with implosive therapy (Smith & Sharpe, 1970) were mentioned in Chapter 10. *In vivo* desensitization has been described in the case of a nine-year-old boy whose therapist accompanied him during gradually increasing exposures to school while distraction, humor, emotive imagery, and rewards were being provided (Lazarus, Davison, & Polefka, 1965). In treating a seven-year-old boy, Patterson (1965) shaped the child's doll play and conversation by reinforcing him with candy whenever the child dolls played away from the parent dolls or the boy made statements expressing independence. The mother was also coached in reinforcing the child for playing outside and for increasing his mobility and independence.

Kennedy (1965) has reported the application of a rapid behavioral treatment to 50 school phobic children. An important aspect of his approach was a diagnostic distinction made between young children whose primary problems seemed to be the school phobia and a related concern about the mother's health, and older children who had previous episodes of school phobia and whose parents were disturbed and difficult to work with. The focus of Kennedy's treatment was on the first group, while the second group was considered to be in need of more intensive treatment.

The treatment began with interviewing of the parents to assess the problem and apprise them of the treatment plan. The father was then to take the child to school, by force if necessary, without procrastination or prolonged advance discussion with the child. The school principal or attendance officer insured that the child stayed in the classroom, while the mother remained in the school hallway for a time if necessary. The child was praised for whatever length of time he was able to remain in school. The stay in school was lengthened on the next day, with the goal being symptom removal by the third day. Before or after the first school day, the therapist met with the child to present him with stories on the advantages of going on in the face of fear and to stress the transitory nature of the phobia. Kennedy reports that all 50 children treated in this way lost their symptoms and remained symptom-free for follow-up periods ranging from two to eight years.

Obsessions and Compulsions

Like the psychoanalytic literature, the behavior modification literature contains few reports of treatment of obsessions and compulsions in children. This may be partly a function of the relatively small percentage of children observed to have obsessions and compulsions (Achenbach, 1966; Judd, 1965), but it may also be due to a general lack of success in treating such symptoms (cf. Solyom, Zamanzadeh, Ledwidge, & Kenny, 1971).

The psychodynamic view emphasizes that obsessions and compulsions help to avoid or reduce anxiety by controlling, avoiding, or neutralizing anxiety-arousing impulses. Behavior modifiers such as Wolpe (1958) agree that some obsessions and compulsions function to reduce anxiety because they help to avoid or reduce fear. Wolpe (1964) reports a case of this sort in which an 18-year-old student had a severe washing compulsion. The basis of the compulsion was an obsessive fear of contamination by urine which led him to take morning showers lasting four hours, to spend 45 minutes washing his genitals after urinating, and to follow this with two hours of hand washing, plus other rituals to avoid contamination. Coming to the conclusion that getting up was not worth the effort, the patient finally began spending most of his time in bed.

The obsessions and compulsions had evidently resulted from the fact that the patient had been forced to share a bed with his older sister until he was 15. He became very guilty and ashamed about his sexual responses toward her and angry toward his parents. Horrified at his destructive fantasies about his parents, he had come to regard himself as despicable. Desensitization treatment began with imagining an unknown person putting his hand into a trough of water containing one drop of urine. Treatment climaxed with *in vivo* desensitization which included having the patient handle his own urine. After treatment he was able to return to school, handwashing was reduced to three minutes and showering to 20 minutes.

Although some obsessions and compulsions may be reinforced because they reduce anxiety, others appear to become relatively autonomous of anxiety. Another behavioral approach to the elimination of obsessions and compulsions of both the autonomous and anxiety-reducing variety has been to prevent the patient from engaging in the behavior, thus demonstrating that the feared consequences do not occur. This has been done with obsessions by interrupting the obsessional thoughts with a disruptive stimulus such as a buzzer or the command "Stop!" (Wolpe, 1958). It has been done with compulsions by preventing the patient from carrying out his rituals (Meyer, 1966).

In certain cases, obsessions and compulsions themselves are considered to be anxiety-arousing rather than anxiety-reducing. In a study of adult obsessive-compulsives, it was found that 37 per cent of obsessive experiences were clearly anxiety-provoking (Solyom et al, 1971). In the same study, behavioral treatment was undertaken by having the patients tape record their obsessional thoughts and then playing the tapes back to the patients. Electric shocks were administered to the patients' finger tips during silent periods interposed before anxiety-arousing sequences and obsessive thoughts. The patients could terminate the shocks by pushing a button. As they terminated a shock, an anxiety-arousing sequence or obsession was played to them. The onsets of the anxiety-arousing stimuli were thus paired with relief from the aversive shock. This aversion-relief therapy produced improvement in 73 per cent of the patients, all of whom had been unsuccessfully treated by other methods.

In one of the few applications of behavior modification to compulsive behavior in a young child, Humphrey and Rachman (cited by Eysenck

& Rachman, 1965, p. 137) used a satiation procedure similar to that suggested by Dunlap (1932). The subject, a four-year-old boy who compulsively tore and chewed curtains, sheets, and pillow slips, was required to tear newspapers into smaller and smaller strips for 20-minute treatment sessions without pausing, despite obvious fatigue. The problem behavior disappeared after three weeks of treatment.

Somatic Dysfunctions

A variety of behavioral formulations and treatments have been proposed for somatic dysfunctions not caused by organic abnormalities. While some behavior modifiers employ traditional diagnostic categories such as hysteria for certain of these dysfunctions, others concentrate on devising procedures for eliminating specific symptoms rather than emphasizing generic differences among them. However, the following four classes of somatic dysfunctions have been conceptualized more or less generically by most behavior modifiers.

Hysterical Symptoms. Ullmann and Krasner (1969) have presented what they call a sociopsychological formulation of hysteria that contrasts with the psychodynamic conception of hysterical "conversion" of unconscious conflicts into somatic forms. According to Ullmann and Krasner's view, hysterical symptoms are on a continuum with reactions to hypnosis, placebo, suggestion, role expectations, and incentives to malinger in that social and other influences cause the person to act as if he had a certain organic condition. The hysteric is not regarded as "deliberately" or "consciously" faking organic dysfunction, but the cues and reinforcements most salient for him provide stronger inducements to manifest such dysfunctions than to avoid them. This is especially likely if the person has previously experienced genuine organic problems or observed others with organic problems from which were derived secondary gains in the form of attention, avoidance of aversive situations, etc. An important implication of this model is that hysterical symptoms may be removed by manipulating the factors like suggestion, reinforcement contingencies, and aversive consequences that helped to create or maintain them in the first place.

One approach consistent with the Ullmann and Krasner model has been to attach aversive consequences to the hysterical symptom. Kushner (1970), for example, has reported several cases in which cessation of small shocks was made contingent on cessation of hysterical symptoms such as paralyses and persistent sneezing.

In another approach, two hysterically blind patients were given the task of pressing a button at intervals in order to gain positive reinforcements, although they were not told how they could judge the intervals (Brady & Lind, 1961; Parry-Jones, Santer-Westrate, & Crawley, 1970). The patient could always push the button at the correct instant by attending to a flashing light set before him. In both cases, the patients eventually attended to the light cue and completely regained their sight.

Behavioral shaping was successfully used in the case of a 13-year-old girl who had barely spoken above a whisper for seven years (Bangs & Freidinger, 1949). Praise was the reinforcer used in getting the girl first to do breathing exercises, then to exhale and hum, and then to hum easy consonants such as "m," "n," "z," and "v." Thereafter, her vocalizations were shaped in small steps toward vowels, vowel-consonant combinations, words, reading, and finally conversation. The steps culminated in the restoration of normal speech within 10½ weeks. No relapses or new symptoms occurred over a two-year follow-up period.

Gardner (1967) has reported a case in which changes in contingencies for parental attention eliminated psychogenic seizures in a 10-year-old girl. During a baseline period, seizures and other somatic complaints occurred six to eight times per week. Then the parents were counseled to act "deaf and dumb" to somatic complaints and seizures while rewarding more appropriate behavior with attention. The somatic complaints dropped to normal levels and the seizures disappeared entirely. In the twenty-sixth week of follow-up, the parents were instructed to reinstate attention to the girl's somatic complaints. Within 24 hours, her somatic complaints increased to about one per hour and she manifested a seizure. When the parents again began ignoring the deviant behavior, it disappeared.

Psychophysiological Reactions. Various psychophysiological reactions and theories as to their etiologies were described in Chapter 6. It has been known since Pavlov's work that physiological responses can be classically conditioned to a neutral stimulus by pairing the stimulus with an unconditioned stimulus, such as food or shock, that already elicited the responses. Pavlov and others have also shown that words, especially under hypnosis, can elicit physiological reactions such as salivation and GSR, even without prior pairing with an unconditioned stimulus. Recent research has demonstrated that heart rate, vasodilation and constriction, EEG waves, and GSRs can be operantly conditioned as well (Scott, Peters, Gillespie, Blanchard, Edmundson & Young, 1973; Ullmann & Krasner, 1969). The typical procedure for conditioning such responses is to reinforce the subject whenever the response of interest reaches a certain level as indicated on a meter or signaling device. The subject then learns to bring these responses under voluntary control.

Systematic desensitization and other forms of reciprocal inhibition therapy have been used to reduce anxiety believed to trigger psychophysiological asthmatic attacks in children and adults (Cooper, 1964; Moore, 1965; Walton, 1960a), ulcers (Wolpe, 1958), and adolescent anorexia nervosa (Hallsten, 1965). Differential application of positive attention has also been used to treat a skin disorder (Walton, 1960b) and anorexia nervosa (Bachrach et al, 1965) by withholding attention that sustained behavior related to the symptom.

Enuresis. Bed-wetting is a problem found in many children who are never brought for treatment, as well as in many who are. Lovibond and Coote (1970) report that about 20 per cent of all four- and five-year-olds in western societies wet their beds often enough to be considered management problems and that two to three per cent are still wetting at the age of 14. Besides creating practical problems and tensions for their parents, enuretic children often suffer humiliation, lowering of self-esteem, and restriction of activities such as camping and overnight visiting because of their problem.

Psychodynamic theorists hold that enuresis is a manifestation of intrapsychic conflict or anxiety arising primarily out of interactions with the parents and that cure requires resolution of these problems (cf. Achenbach & Lewis, 1971). Behavior modifiers tend to emphasize failures of proper conditioning in enuresis, but they acknowledge that these failures can come about because physiological or emotional factors make it especially hard for some children to learn not to wet the bed.

Several studies have employed variants of the alarm apparatus invented by Mowrer and Mowrer (1938) to awaken the child just as he begins to wet the bed. Lovibond (1964) has pointed out that, although the alarm method purports to involve classical conditioning, many children successfully treated with the apparatus quickly learn to sleep through the night without wetting. Rather than being conditioned to awaken in response to bladder tension, Lovibond maintains that they simply learn to avoid urinating in bed because it has been followed by the aversive alarm bell awakening them.

Be that as it may, results with the conditioning apparatus have been much better than results with other treatments. Lovibond and Coote (1970) reported that 98 per cent of enuretics treated with the alarm method reached a criterion of two dry weeks, while Baker (1969) reported the same result for 89 per cent of his subjects. DeLeon and Mandell (1966) found that 86.3 per cent of children treated with a conditioning device reached a criterion of 13 successive dry nights, while only 18.2 per cent of a group receiving 12 weeks of psychotherapy and 11.1 per cent of an untreated control group did so. A four-year follow-up showed that 81 per cent of children successfully treated by conditioning were wetting less than once a year, while the other 19 per cent were wetting much less frequently than before conditioning (DeLeon & Sacks, 1972).

Novick (1966) compared the effects of the conditioning treatment on boys identified as "persistent" enuretics who had never had dry periods and boys identified as "acquired" enuretics who had begun wetting after having been dry for an average of two years. The groups were similar in age, socioeconomic status, intelligence, frequency of enuresis, and degree of maladjustment. More acquired than persistent enuretics responded favorably to a trial of traditional supportive therapy, including record-keeping and encouragement. Of those acquired and persistent enuretics who did not benefit from supportive therapy, almost 90 percent reached a cure criterion of 14 consecutive dry nights after conditioning. However, during a 10-month follow-up, the acquired group showed more frequent wetting after cure and showed significantly more new symptoms than the persistent group, although both groups showed a decrease in anxiety. This suggests that faulty conditioning may indeed be the basic problem for most persistent enuretics, while current life stress may be significant in causing acquired enuresis.

Some relapses occurred in virtually all the studies, but reconditioning was usually more rapid than original conditioning. An "overlearning" procedure whereby the child being conditioned drinks extra liquid before bed has been found to reduce relapses significantly (Young & Morgan, 1972). Despite the commercial availability of the conditioning apparatus for many years, Eysenck (1957) reported that no child guidance clinics in Great Britain used the conditioning treatment. In a survey of 72 pediatricians at the Montreal Children's Hospital, Werry (1966) found that few had ever had contact with it and only 10 per cent approved of it. The basis for the pediatricians' objections to the conditioning treatment ranged from psychodynamic concepts of symptom substitution to the feeling that it was "bad for the child's nerves [Werry, 1966, p. 227]."

Hyperactivity. Hyperactive behavior in children is often considered to be a sign of brain damage, but many hyperactive children have no other signs of brain damage and many nonhyperactive children have strong evidence of brain damage (cf. Chapter 6). Whether or not organic damage predisposes a child to hyperactive behavior, environmental factors are likely to play a role in eliciting, shaping, and suppressing such behavior.

On the assumption that environmental contingencies can influence hyperactive behavior even in children known to be brain-damaged, Patterson and his colleagues have reinforced attending, nonhyperactive behavior in school children. In one study, a hyperactive child known to be brain-damaged was told that he would receive candy and other reinforcers each time he heard a buzz in a small earphone placed in his ear (Patterson, Jones, Whittier, & Wright, 1965). After training outside the classroom, he returned to the class and the other class members were informed that they too would earn reinforcers when the experimental subject succeeded in sitting still in his seat. An observer in an adjoining one-way observation room used a radio transmitter to signal the subject after each 10-second interval in which no nonattending behavior occurred. The experimental subject showed a marked drop in nonattending behavior that was significantly greater than the slight drop observed in a control subject in the same class. The difference between the experimental and control subject was maintained during a one-month follow-up period, although some nonattending responses, such as leg, arm, and chair movements, rose again, while others, such as "fiddling" and "distraction," continued to drop.

Other studies have shown that social reinforcement by the teacher can increase task-relevant behavior in hyperactive children (Allen, Henke, Harris, Baer, & Reynolds, 1967; James, cited by Patterson et al, 1965). Taking another approach, Doubros and Daniels (1966) successfully controlled children's hyperactive behavior by positively reinforcing nonhyperactive behavior in a playroom situation.

Aggressive Behavior

Behavioral approaches to aggression have included manipulation of specific environmental contingencies to eliminate specific behaviors, more complex programming to change multiple aspects of aggressive children's behavior, and attempts to develop general models for how aggressiveness is trained and maintained as a behavioral trait. Bernal, Duryee, Pruett, and Burns (1968) have described a parent-training technique used with an eight-year-old boy manifesting the "brat syndrome" of diverse obnoxious, aggressive, demanding, and controlling behavior. The boy, Jeff, had received diagnoses ranging from adjustment reaction of childhood to schizophrenia, and the possibility of brain damage had also been raised.

Jeff's interactions with his mother were recorded on audiotape at home and on videotape in sessions at the clinic. The mother was observed to have a high rate of indiscriminate response, constantly responding to Jeff in a meek, soft monotone even when correcting him. Using the videotapes and a cue light that could be flashed to the mother while she was interacting with Jeff in an experimental room, the mother was first trained to reduce her verbal output and to ignore Jeff's abusive behavior. If ignoring did not stop a particularly abusive behavior, she was to express anger and order Jeff to stop. If he did not stop, she was to spank him, having already provided clearly discriminable cues of anger that could become conditioned negative reinforcers after being followed several times by punishment. The third step was for the mother to identify Jeff's acceptable behaviors, specify them to Jeff, and praise him warmly when they occurred.

Observation showed that the mother ignored 11 per cent of Jeff's abuses during a pretreatment session but that this rapidly jumped to 100 per cent after training. The percentage of her commands that Jeff obeyed went from zero to 100 per cent and the percentage of time she was affectionate went from zero to 20 per cent. Jeff's general behavior improved, but, when a playmate was present, the mother tended to retreat to her old behavior and Jeff's behavior deteriorated. The playmate was brought in for videotape sessions with the mother and Jeff, and the mother was successfully trained to handle Jeff in the presence of the playmate. The mother's self-confidence improved as a result of the training and she and Jeff grew more mutually affectionate.

Patterson and Brodsky (1966) applied a four-faceted treatment program to Karl, a five-year-old who had been expelled from kindergarten because of his extremely aggressive brat behavior and who, in addition, manifested many immaturities and severe anxiety at being separated from his mother. The four facets of the program were:

1. Extinction and counterconditioning of temper tantrums through forcible time-outs.
2. Extinction and counterconditioning of separation anxiety by reinforcing Karl for doll play and conversation expressing independence.
3. Providing tangible and social reinforcers to Karl and his classmates for play in which Karl did not hurt other children.
4. Retraining Karl's parents to reinforce nonfearful, cooperative, and mature behavior.

Dramatic improvements were brought about in Karl's behavior and most were maintained over a two-month follow-up period.

Behavioral Analyses of Aggression. Based on painstaking home observations of the interactions of aggressive and nonaggressive boys with their families, Patterson and Cobb (1971) have provided a general analysis of aggressive behavior. They suggest that coercive behaviors such as crying, screaming, and kicking have survival value for the infant because they get the parents to meet the infant's needs. As the child grows older, parents typically punish coercive behavior and reward prosocial behavior. Nevertheless, coercive behavior may continue to be used as a means for dealing with aversive stimuli. If there are many aversive stimuli and if coercive behavior is reinforced by compliance on the part of the victims, then coerciveness may become a general behavioral trait.

In a study of aggressive boys, Bandura and Walters (1959) found that the parents of these boys used physical punishment much more than parents of nonaggressive boys. The latter tended to use withdrawal of love as a means of punishment. Based on this and other differences in the personalities and families of the aggressive and nonaggressive boys, Bandura and Walters concluded that the behavioral models provided by the parents contributed significantly to the boys' aggressive behavior.

Learning Disabilities

Operant conditioning methods, programmed learning materials, teaching machines, and computer hook-ups based on experimental analyses of learning are being increasingly used in schools. As is evident from studies already cited, behavior modification methods have also been used to control problem behaviors, such as aggressiveness, disruptiveness, and hyperactivity, that are incompatible with school learning. Some of the studies have documented improvements in school achievement, while others have provided no data on achievement.

School learning problems would appear to be a natural target for learning-based behavior modification. However, few studies have as yet reported results of behavior modification methods with children whose primary problem is difficulty in acquiring specific academic skills. Even among children with ostensibly adequate home environments, many become educationally handicapped in one or more areas. A comparison of such children with their nonhandicapped siblings and unrelated control children has revealed at least five overlapping groups (Owen, Adams, Forrest, Stolz, & Fisher, 1971):

1. Children suspected of having subtle medical-neurological problems.
2. Children having verbal aptitude scores much lower than their performance aptitude scores due apparently to familial patterns of poor verbal aptitude.
3. Children having IQs notably lower than other members of their families, especially in verbal areas.
4. Children with relatively high IQs whose poor school learning may result from personality maladjustment.
5. Socially deviant children with behavior disorders, police records, and disorganized families.

Given the facts that learning disabilities have diverse causes and that, once a child has a learning problem, the causes can rarely be undone by either schools or treatment agencies, there is a great need for powerful techniques by which to inculcate skills in children for whom teaching methods geared to their peers have failed.

Operant conditioning methods have predominated in behavioral approaches to learning disabilities. In one of the best-documented operant conditioning programs for children with retarded reading skills, Haring and Hauck (1969) arranged a special classroom in which third- through fifth-grade boys sat at desks equipped with mechanical counters and an intercom connected with the teacher's desk. After precise evaluation of what words the boys could read, they were given programmed reading materials to study and respond to by circling the correct word or picture, filling in missing letters, writing a whole word, and reading words and sentences orally to the teacher through the intercom. The teacher answered questions and gave prompts when necessary.

The programmed materials were used without external reinforcement during a two-week baseline period in order to obtain data on each child's rate of correct responding and time spent reading. Thereafter, a token system was introduced in which each child's counter recorded points given for various kinds of correct responses. The points could be exchanged for back-up reinforcers including edibles and material items. An important facet of the program was that, as the child advanced from the programmed material to regular school books, he was reinforced only for correct oral reading of increasingly larger units, beginning with single words from a word list and reaching complete stories from books of his own choosing. The child silently practiced reading a unit until he decided he was ready to read for the teacher. He was then reinforced only after correctly reading it aloud.

All four boys showed large increases in the number of correct responses made from the baseline to the reinforcement conditions. After five months of daily 65-minute sessions, the boys had progressed one and one-half to four years in reading skills and were returned to regular classrooms where they continued to be awarded exchangeable points for accurate reading.

Other applications of operant conditioning have been made in programs where older learning-disabled children operantly conditioned younger learning-disabled children (Drass & Jones, 1971), where low-achieving disadvantaged children attended an after-school remedial program (Wolf, Giles, & Hall, 1968), and where nonprofessional volunteers taught reading to retarded and disadvantaged junior high school children (Staats, Minke, Goodwin, & Landeen, 1967). Hewett (1968) has provided a detailed behavioral program for educating emotionally disturbed children, including methods for controlling problem behavior, teaching specific subject matter, promoting social behavior, and evaluating results, plus outcome studies of his own application of these methods.

EVALUATION OF BEHAVIOR MODIFICATION APPROACHES

The foregoing rundown of disorders shows that behavior modification approaches are multiple and diverse. Moreover, despite the use of methods, concepts, and terminology derived from experimental psychology, and the frequent avowal of "learning theory," most behavior modification procedures are a far cry from the animal learning research upon which they are purportedly based. There is no doubt that animal learning research constituted an important stage in the development of concepts now applied to changing troublesome human behavior, but behavior modification in practice involves considerably more than direct extrapolation of findings on animal learning to humans. The role of language in most behavior modification procedures and the lack of any clear analogues for spoken language in most animal research makes the stimulus-response-reinforcement relations in human behavior modification differ in unknown ways from those in animal learning.

Considerable controversy has arisen over whether laboratory-based learning principles are sufficiently well established to provide explanations or treatments for psychopathology. Critics have claimed that success with behavior modification may depend heavily upon suggestion, transference, and psychodynamic factors unwittingly influenced by behavior modifiers

(Breyer & McGaugh, 1965; Klein, Dittman, Parloff, & Gill, 1969; Weitzman, 1967; cf. replies by Rachman & Eysenck, 1966; Wiest, 1967). Others have maintained that behavior therapy, especially Wolpe's, is not truly "behavioristic" because it focuses on the clients' perceptions of their emotions and their mental representations (Locke, 1971).

Perhaps due partly to criticism and partly to the apparent success of so many different variants of behavior modification that are in no obvious way predictable from "learning theory," there has been a lessening of dogmatic assertions that behavior modification is the application of "modern learning theory" and is the antithesis of all traditional methods. London (1972) has proposed that the learning theory ideology has served a useful purpose in providing metaphors, paradigms, analogies, and a sense of theoretical identity for behavior modifiers, but that a technological orientation is becoming more appropriate than an ideological orientation. By this he means that the technology of behavior modification, in terms of both mechanical gadgetry and therapeutic techniques, is developing faster than any single theoretical viewpoint capable of integrating it all. As a result, the current needs are not to show how each innovation is derivable from laboratory learning principles, but to find useful guides wherever they are—for inclusion in other treatment modalities, for examining concepts underlying modification procedures found successful in order to derive new ones, and for improving the measurable effectiveness of behavior modification.

The position taken by London appears to be shared by an increasing number of behavior modifiers. For example, Lazarus, one of the foremost of early behavior modifiers, now advocates an "antipanacea" approach focused upon finding the best possible combination of techniques to use with each patient rather than translating everything into S–R terms (Lazarus, 1971, pp. xi–xii). Lazarus, London, and other behavior modifiers (e.g., Davison, 1968b) have also pointed out that the efficacy of a treatment does not prove that a disorder was caused in the way specified by the theory that generated the treatment. Problems arising from organic causes can sometimes be modified by behavioral means, while problems arising from learning can sometimes be modified by organic means, e.g., drugs to reduce anxiety.

Insofar as the attitudes expressed by Lazarus and London are representative of the direction behavior modification is taking, the evaluation of behavior modification does not depend upon proof that learning theories correctly "explain" behavior disorders or that the effectiveness of behavior modification techniques depends solely upon principles of learning. Instead, the more important question is that which must be asked of all treatments: Is there objective evidence that the treatment works? Leaving this question exclusively to the intuitions of theoreticians and practitioners has in the past led to the persistence of such treatments as bloodletting for mental patients well into the nineteenth century and exposure to cold air for pneumonia patients well into the twentieth century.

In evaluating whether a treatment for psychopathology or behavior disorders works, the criteria for improvement are often in dispute. Kanfer and Phillips (1970) express the general behavior modification view as follows:

Frequently clinicians feel rewarded in their work by the "insights" and "empathy" they achieve, mistaking private intellectual pleasures for accomplishments of actual goals and mistaking untested hypotheses for confirmed data. Such pleasures have their hazards. They may, for one thing, support the clinician in persisting on a false approach to the patient's difficulties. They may cause the clinician to regard *insight*, or understanding of the causes of his behavior by the patient, as a *sine qua non* of treatment, instead of seeking removal of symptoms. The argument for understanding and unraveling as a goal of therapy states, in effect, that to prevent future difficulties, all relevant determinants of the individual's complex behaviors must be explored. If such prolonged treatment were possible and effective, it would still be questionable whether the clinician's job should be extended to encompass a total evaluation and change of the patient's life pattern when the specific problem for which help is requested can be attacked more directly. The multiplicity of factors relating to a given problem, therefore, requires that the clinician limit his efforts toward some predetermined goal by manipulating whichever variables are practical and effective. Behavior change, not understanding, is the clinician's main goal [p. 29].[1]

Beside focusing on changing behavior as the primary goal of treatment, behavior modifiers tend to share a common set of values regarding the verification of such changes. In terms of the distinction between the *context of discovery* and the *context of confirmation, or justification,* (detailed in Chapter 4), most behavior modifiers emphasize the importance of moving their ideas from the context of discovery into the context of justification where the ideas are subjected to objective test.

. . . once a set of testable hypotheses is established, be it a treatment plan or a research design, the behavioral clinician strives to operate within the strict rules of the context of justification, which he shares with the scientist. It is at this stage of the clinical enterprise, therefore, that the focus is shifted to observable responses, specifiable operations, and objective measures.

The general format of the behavioral clinician's plan of conduct can be compared with the steps usually described for the experimental psychologist. They consist of (1) formulation of the problem, (2) design of operational procedures that test the hypotheses stated in (1), (3) execution of the treatment, (4) analysis of the data, and (5) evaluation of the implications of the results for the problem. In clinical procedures, the steps in this process are less discrete. The last step may simply lead to a repetition of the cycle, if the results of a single treatment procedure do not resolve the original problem. Nevertheless, the formulation of a research

[1] F. H. Kanfer and J. S. Phillips, *Learning Foundations of Behavior Therapy* (New York: John Wiley & Sons, 1970). © 1970 by John Wiley & Sons and reprinted by permission.

problem and the design of a procedure in terms of available treatment methods (independent variables) and behaviors selected for modification (dependent variables) are parallel activities. Similarly, the analysis of experimental data is comparable to the clinician's evaluations of the effect of treatment. In both cases the relevance of the findings must be related to the original statement of the problem [Kanfer & Phillips, 1970, p. 27].

Do Behavior Modification Techniques Work?

With the possible exception of client-centered therapy for adults (e.g., Rogers, 1967; Rogers & Dymond, 1954), no approach to the treatment of psychopathology or behavior disorders has been subjected to nearly as much systematic evaluative research as the behavior modification approach. It may be recalled from Chapter 9 that only two uncontrolled studies (Masserman, 1963; Knight, 1941) and one controlled study (Heinicke, 1969) of the effect of psychoanalysis on neurotic disorders have been published. The latter study, the only study with children, showed little clear difference between the effects of four-times weekly psychoanalysis and once-weekly psychotherapy. By contrast, in a review of the effects of behavior modification on children, Pawlick (1970) listed 54 studies published between 1965 and 1969 alone. The methodology of many of these studies was insufficiently objective, but 32 of them might be regarded as controlled studies because they included control groups and/or a combination of an objectively specified baseline for the problem behavior and systematic variations of treatment or follow-ups to demonstrate behavioral changes from the baseline.

When behavior change is rigorously evaluated against a baseline, preferably with controlled variations in treatment (e.g., *ABAB* procedures) and follow-ups, analyses of single cases and small groups without control groups have an important place in illustrating new techniques. Such studies also constitute paradigms for context-of-justification evaluation of treatment in everyday practice. However, single case and small group studies without control comparisons usually leave unanswered the questions of how typical the cases are and what proportion of the authors' other cases have shown similar outcomes. Single case and small group studies without control group comparisons, therefore, constitute an insufficient basis for evaluating how well a treatment typically works. For this reason, our examination of the results of behavior modification procedures will deal only with studies employing control groups.

Systematic Desensitization

Clinical Studies. Table 11-1 summarizes six studies in which the effectiveness of desensitization with clinical patients have been objectively compared to the effectiveness of other treatments with control groups of patients. All six studies included both self-report and objective observa-

TABLE 11-1

Controlled studies comparing desensitization with other treatments in clinical groups.

Study	Patients and problems	Comparison treatment	Length of treatment	Length of de-sensitization	Superior treatment
1. Gelder & Marks (1966)	Adult agoraphobic inpatients	Individual psycho-therapy	19 weeks	23 weeks	No significant difference
2. Gelder, Marks & Wolff (1967)	Adult phobic outpatients	Individual psycho-therapy	12 months	9 months	Desensitization
		Group psycho-therapy	18 months	9 months	Desensitization
3. Marks, Gelder, & Edwards (1968)	Adult phobic outpatients	Suggestion and hypnosis	12 weeks	12 weeks	Desensitization
4. Miller, Barrett, Hampe, & Noble (1972)	Child phobic outpatients	Individual psycho-therapy	24 sessions	24 sessions	No significant difference
		Waiting list (no treatment)	*	24 sessions	a. Desensitization superior with children aged 6–10 b. No significant difference with children aged 11–15
5. Moore (1965)	Child and adult asthmatic out-patients	Relaxation	8 sessions	8 sessions	Desensitization
		Relaxation with suggestion	8 sessions	8 sessions	Desensitization
6. Zeisset (1968)	Adult neurotic and psychotic inpatients, treated for interview anxiety	Relaxation	4 sessions	4 sessions	No significant difference
		Attention-placebo	4 sessions	4 sessions	Desensitization
		No treatment	*	4 sessions	Desensitization

* No-treatment control groups received pre- and posttreatment evaluations at the same times as treated gorups.

tional measures of improvement. Of the 12 comparisons made within the six studies, desensitization was found to be significantly superior in eight and equal to another treatment in four.

Although desensitization was more effective than other treatments in reducing anxiety, "cures" were not frequently produced by any method in most studies. The Zeisset (1968) study was explicitly oriented only toward reducing severely disturbed patients' anxiety in interviews rather than curing them. The three studies by Gelder, Marks, and their colleagues showed that severe agoraphobia (fear of open places) was especially resistant to cure by either desensitization or three comparison treatments—individual and group psychotherapy and suggestion-hypnosis (Gelder & Marks, 1966; Gelder, Marks, & Wolff, 1967; Marks, Gelder, & Edwards, 1968). A rough baseline for the long-term effects of traditional outpatient psychotherapy on phobias was provided by Errera and Coleman (1963) who reported that phobic symptoms persisted in 18 out of 19 adults followed up 23 years after clinic contacts. Most of the former patients led severely restricted lives.

In the only study of a substantial number of child patients, the subjects were phobic children aged 6 to 15 (Miller, Barrett, Hampe, & Noble, 1972). After screening by a social worker, the parents and children were interviewed by a clinician (the "primary evaluator") who was not to serve as a therapist. A behavioral test of each child's reactions to the feared object or situation was made, parents and teachers filled out descriptive inventories of the children's behavior, parents were called on five consecutive days to get reports of the children's fear behavior for those days, and psychological testing was done. On the basis of all the data, the primary evaluator rated the severity of each child's phobia on a seven-point scale. The reliability of the ratings was checked by another clinician who made a similar rating from the data plus videotapes of the primary evaluator's interviews with the children and their parents. There were no significant differences between the ratings of the two clinicians. The 67 children whose ratings showed them to be severely phobic were then randomly assigned to receive individual desensitization, psychotherapy, or to serve as waiting-list controls.

The children who received treatment were seen three times weekly for eight weeks. At the end of eight weeks, all three groups were reevaluated by the primary evaluator through repetition of the pretreatment procedures. They were reevaluated again at follow-up, six weeks later. Figure 11–2 portrays the severity scores at pretreatment, posttreatment, and follow-up evaluations.

All three groups improved significantly and there were no significant differences among the conditions, although the waiting list controls improved nonsignificantly less than the two treatment groups. There was also no significant difference between children treated by experienced and inexperienced therapists. Taken alone, the parents' ratings showed signifi-

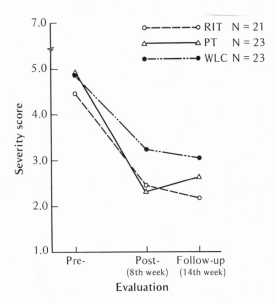

Fig. 11–2. Mean primary evaluator severity score for reciprocal inhibition (RIT), psychotherapy (PT), and waiting list control (WLC) Ss at pretreatment, post-treatment, and follow-up. From Miller et al (1972). © 1972 by the American Psychological Association and reprinted by permission.

cantly more improvement for treated than for control children, but, as the authors point out, this could be due to parental expectations that therapy would be helpful.

Despite the implication that phobic children improve with or without treatment, an analysis by age groups showed that most of the successes (cases whose fears dropped below three on the seven-point severity scale) were in the 6- to 10-year range and that both treatments were significantly more effective than no treatment for these children. Among the 11- to 15-year-old children, only 45 per cent receiving treatment and 44 per cent not receiving treatment were successful, compared to 96 per cent with treatment and 57 per cent without treatment among the 6- to 10-year-olds. Desensitization was nonsignificantly more successful (56 per cent) than psychotherapy (36 per cent) with the older children.

If the above findings are reliable, they indicate that young children's phobias are readily removable by either desensitization or psychotherapy, but that older children's phobias are not readily removable by either treatment. Thus, more research is needed to develop effective treatments for older phobic children. The effectiveness of one or both treatments may have been limited by the duration of treatment (24 sessions over eight weeks), but this is more than the average number of sessions provided in typical child guidance clinics (cf. Miller, et al, 1972).

TABLE 11-2

Controlled studies comparing desensitization with other treatments in nonclinical groups.

Study	Subjects and problems	Comparison treatment	Length of treatment	Length of de-sensitization	Superior treatment
1. Bandura, Blanchard & Ritter (1969)	Snake phobic adolescents and adults	Filmed modeling & relaxation	4½ hours	6 hours	Filmed modeling & relaxation
		Live modeling & guided participation	3½ hours	6 hours	Live modeling & participation
		No treatment	*	6 hours	Desensitization
2. Crighton & Jehu (1969)	Exam-anxious students	Group nondirective psychotherapy & relaxation	24 sessions?	24 sessions?	No significant difference
3. DiLoreto (1971)	Students having interpersonal anxiety	Group nondirective psychotherapy	11 hours	11 hours	Group desensitization
		Group rational-emotive therapy	11 hours	11 hours	Group desensitization
		Placebo (attention)	11 hours	11 hours	Group desensitization
		No treatment	*	11 hours	Group desensitization

Study	Population	Control condition	Control sessions	Treatment sessions	Treatment
4. Kamil (1970)	Snake phobic students	No treatment	*	12 sessions	Desensitization
5. Lang, Lazovik, & Reynolds (1965)	Snake phobic students	Individual hypnotic pseudotherapy or no treatment	16 sessions	16 sessions	Desensitization
6. Paul (1966, 1967)	Public-speaking-anxious students	Individual insight-oriented psychotherapy	5 sessions	5 sessions	Desensitization
		Individual attention & placebo drug	5 sessions	5 sessions	Desensitization
		No treatment	*	5 sessions	Desensitization
7. Paul & Shannon (1966), Paul (1968)	Public-speaking-anxious students	Individual insight-oriented psychotherapy	5 sessions	5 sessions	Group desensitization
		Individual attention & placebo drug	5 sessions	5 sessions	Group desensitization
		No treatment	*	5 sessions	Group desensitization

* No-treatment control groups received pre- and posttreatment evaluations at the same times as treated groups.

Studies with Nonclinical Groups. Controlled studies of desensitization have been conducted with college students and other volunteers having anxiety that had not led them to seek clinical treatment. Some of these studies have compared desensitization to other forms of treatment, while others have compared full-scale desensitization to various components of the desensitization procedures. These studies have generally attained greater precision than the studies in clinical settings, although it is difficult to determine whether the findings are validly generalizable from subjects who would not otherwise be undergoing treatment to actual candidates for clinical treatment. Some workers have suggested that the generalizability of findings with college students is limited because simply instructing them to deal with the phobic object or situation may be effective in overcoming their fears (Cooper, Furst, & Bridger, 1969; Jacobs & Wolpin, 1971).

Table 11–2 presents the overall findings from seven studies comparing desensitization with other treatments in nonclinical groups. Among the 16 comparisons made in the seven studies, desensitization was found to be superior in 13 and equal to a comparison treatment in one. Desensitization was slightly inferior to one treatment for phobias—filmed modeling with relaxation—and markedly inferior to a second—live modeling with guided participation (Bandura, et al, 1969).

In a number of other studies, attempts have been made to determine whether certain components of the desensitization procedures, such as relaxation or experience with the graded anxiety hierarchy, are the crucial therapeutic elements. If certain components have as much effect as the entire treatment, then therapy can concentrate on those components, and theoretical implications can be drawn and tested that may further enhance the effectiveness of treatment.

Among the studies of matched nonclinical groups receiving desensitization or components of desensitization, most have found the entire desensitization procedure to be more effective than any of the components alone (Davison, 1968b; Folkins, Lawson, Opton, & Lazarus, 1968; Hyman & Gale, 1973; Kondas, 1967; Lomont & Edwards, 1967; Rachman, 1965). However, some studies have indicated that the specific combination of relaxation and desensitization does not alone account for the effectiveness of treatment. Instead, such factors as therapeutic instructions and reinforcement for tolerating the fantasied phobic situations may also play important roles (Cooke, 1968; Leitenberg, Agras, Barlow, & Oliveau, 1969; Oliveau, 1969; Oliveau, Agras, Leitenberg, Moore, & Wright, 1969).

In summary, there is evidence from controlled studies that systematic desensitization is more effective than most other brief treatments for phobic anxiety in clinical and nonclinical groups of adults. Many of the studies also reported that the benefits were maintained during follow-up periods ranging up to several years. However, in the only well-controlled study of desensitization with a substantial number of children, desensitization and psychotherapy were equally effective with 6- to 10-year-olds, but neither was effective with 11- to 15-year-olds. While further controlled studies of the effects of both psychotherapy and desensitization with children are needed, these findings suggest that:

1. Results with adults are not automatically generalizable to children.
2. Results with children in one age range are not automatically generalizable to another age range.
3. An effective treatment for early adolescent phobias of clinical magnitude may remain to be found.

Modeling and Imitation

The one form of treatment found superior to desensitization was modeling, as employed with snake phobias by Bandura, et al, (1969). Although the subjects, aged 13 to 59, had not otherwise applied for clinical treatment, their snake phobias were severe enough to restrict their recreational, social, and/or occupational activities. One group was trained in relaxation that they could then employ as they viewed filmed models engaging in a graduated sequence of interactions with snakes. The subjects regulated the film so that they could stop and reinduce relaxation whenever anxiety increased. A second group viewed live models engaging in graduated sequences of interaction with snakes. The subjects were then guided in approaching, touching, and interacting with the snakes. A third group received Wolpean desensitization, while a fourth group served as an untreated control. Treatments continued twice weekly until subjects reached the most advanced level within their treatment for up to a maximum of 5.25 hours beyond initial relaxation training.

Subjects in all three treatment groups improved significantly more than control subjects on behavioral, attitudinal, and anxiety measures relating to snakes, as well as showing some improvements on an inventory of other fears. However, the live-modeling-with-participation treatment was far superior to the other treatments on nearly all measures, while filmed modeling was superior to desensitization on some measures and inferior on none.

In related studies, snake-phobic 5- to 11-year-olds given modeling and guided participation improved significantly more than children given modeling alone who, in turn, improved significantly more than children receiving no treatment (Ritter, 1968), and dog-phobic preschool children witnessing live or filmed modeling improved significantly more than children receiving no treatment (Bandura, et al, 1967; Bandura & Menlove, 1968). Taken together, the modeling studies indicate that graduated modeling is an effective treatment for animal phobias in nonclinical groups and that guided participation is more effective than either filmed modeling with relaxation or Wolpean desensitization.

It is important to note that graduated modeling and guided participation are not incompatible with the conception of desensitization. The main difference between the two is that the former employ the actual feared stimuli, while desensitization relies primarily on the client's mental representations of them. In fact, Ritter (1968) referred to her procedures as "vicarious and contact desensitization," although the same procedures were referred to as "modeling and guided participation" in her work with Bandura (Bandura, et al, 1969). An obvious conclusion from the comparison of the modeling and desensitization studies is that, if the phobic object can be conveniently presented for graduated contact, this is probably superior to desensitization through graded fantasy, at least in nonclinical groups without other serious problems. Further evidence for the beneficial effects of real-life graduated exposure to the feared stimulus was obtained by Sherman (1972) who showed that graduated exposure to water produced better effects in aquaphobics receiving partial or complete desensitization procedures or no formal treatment than in similar groups not given water exposure.

Operant Conditioning

There have been few published comparisons of operant conditioning with other treatments in matched control groups. This may be due largely to the operant conditioners' preference for own-control evaluations in which changes in a subject's performance are measured during a series of changes in reinforcement contingencies (e.g., *ABAB*). When precisely executed, this is a powerful technique for testing the effects of a treatment for an individual subject. However, by itself, this technique is not sufficient for comparing the effectiveness of operant conditioning with other treatments. Even though behavior may change in response to changes in reinforcement contingencies, this does not prove that other treatments could not be more effective or economical. Moreover, unless behavioral improvement results in the development of permanent new skills or in new reinforcements from the natural environment, the fact that problem behavior returns when interventions are withdrawn indicates a lack of the enduring effects that most treatments seek to produce.

P. W. Clement and his colleagues have carried out one of the few programs of comparisons between operant and other treatments for children. The subjects have been elementary school boys identified by their teachers as being withdrawn, anxious, friendless, and introverted. In a study by Clement and Milne (1967), one group of boys received play therapy, a second group received play therapy plus tokens exchangeable for back-up reinforcers whenever they engaged in prosocial behavior, and a third group met in a play group without a therapist. All groups met for 14 weekly sessions.

In the second study (Clement, Fazzone, & Goldstein, 1970), three groups were similar to those in the first study, but there was also a control group of boys who engaged in solitary play at the clinic. All the boys attended 20 weekly sessions. In the third study (Clement, Roberts, & Lantz, 1970), the following six groups met for 24 sessions:

1. A therapy group.
2. A therapy group that also received token reinforcement for prosocial behavior.
3. A therapy group that received token reinforcement plus films of well-adjusted boys modeling prosocial behavior.
4. A therapy group that saw the films but received no token reinforcement.
5. A group that received only the films, without a therapist or tokens.
6. A control group that met without a therapist.

In all three studies, mothers were seen in small guidance groups while their sons were attending the clinic.

The overall results of the three studies showed that the groups receiving therapy with token reinforcement improved more than any of the other groups on various posttreatment and follow-up measures. This was true even when the therapy-plus-reinforcement condition was provided by a psychoanalytically oriented psychiatrist who opposed behavioral methods (Clement et al, 1970).

In another study of operant conditioning, Wolf et al, (1968) compared school grades and achievement scores obtained by disadvantaged children participating in an after-school token program of remedial education with grades and scores obtained by peers who received no special program. After one year of the remedial program, the latter, who might be considered an untreated control group, showed significantly smaller gains in grades and achievement test scores than did the token-reinforced remedial group.

Behavioral Treatments for Enuresis

Numerous studies have reported high rates of success in treating nocturnal enuresis with pad-and-bell apparatus like that designed by Mowrer and Mowrer (1938; see Lovibond, 1964, and Lovibond & Coote, 1970 for reviews). Table 11–3 presents five studies that made controlled comparisons with other treatments. In all eight comparisons within the five studies, conditioning produced more "cures" and improvements than other treatments and this superiority was maintained in the five follow-up comparisons. The evidence is thus consistent in showing that conditioning procedures eliminate enuresis more effectively than any other treatment that has been subjected to a controlled comparison.

Symptom Substitution

One of the primary objections raised by psychodynamically oriented workers to behavior modification is their belief that removing a neurotic symptom without relieving intrapsychic conflicts may lead to the substitution of new and potentially more harmful symptoms (Bookbinder, 1962; Cahoon, 1968; Spiegel, 1967; Yates, 1958, 1962). However, outcome and follow-up studies of behavioral treatment have reported little evidence for symptom substitution (e.g., Gelder & Marks, 1966; Gelder, et al, 1967; Ken-

TABLE 11-3

Controlled studies comparing conditioning with other treatments for nocturnal enuresis.

Study	Comparison treatment	Duration of treatment	Duration of conditioning	Superior treatment	Follow-up Length	Follow-up Superior treatment
1. Baker (1969)	Wake-up	10 weeks	10 weeks	Conditioning	6 mos.	Conditioning
	Waiting list (no treatment)	10 weeks	10 weeks	Conditioning	6 mos.	Conditioning
2. DeLeon & Mandell (1966), DeLeon & Sacks (1972)	Psychotherapy	12 weekly sessions	12 weeks	Conditioning	(4 year follow-up of successfully conditioned Ss— 81% still dry)	
	Kept record of wetting (no treatment)	12 weeks	12 weeks	Conditioning		
3. Forrester, Stein, & Susser (1964)	Amphetamine drugs	Up to 6 months	Up to 6 months	Conditioning	No follow-up	
4. Werry & Cohrssen (1965)	Psychotherapy	6–8 sessions	Up to 4 months	Conditioning	No follow-up	
	Waiting list (no treatment)	4 months	Up to 4 months	Conditioning	No follow-up	
5. Young (1965)	Various drug treatments	5 months	2 months	Conditioning	1–19 mos.	Conditioning

nedy, 1965; Lazarus, 1971; Nolan, Mattis, & Holliday, 1970; Paul, 1967; Werry & Cohrssen, 1965). In the few cases where new symptoms have been reported, they were attributed to conditions arising subsequent to treatment. Some new symptoms were successfully treated by reapplication of behavioral techniques.

Since new symptoms may bear only a chance relationship to any particular treatment, the most informative studies of symptom substitution are those in which symptoms and adjustment are compared in treatment and control groups during follow-up periods. Two studies of enuresis were especially designed to do this. In Baker's (1969) six-month follow-up of 18 children whose enuresis was eliminated by conditioning, three children developed new symptoms (encopresis, dependency, and eye-blinking) but these seemed related to new stress and they disappeared quickly. As for general adjustment, the cured enuretics showed greater improvements than unimproved enuretics and nonenuretic controls in scores on a neuroticism inventory and a self-image questionnaire. Parents' ratings also showed significant improvement for cured enuretics on a measure of general adjustment and a list of specific symptoms.

In the second study, Novick (1966) found that a much larger percentage of "acquired" enuretics (dry for an average of two years before becoming enuretic) than "persistent" enuretics (never previously dry) became dry through supportive encouragement alone and that the remaining acquired enuretics became dry more quickly than the persistent enuretics when a conditioning apparatus was used. However, during follow-ups ranging up to a year, the "cured" acquired enuretics also showed a much greater rate of relapse, new symptoms, and behavior deterioration than the "cured" persistent enuretics. This suggests that current emotional problems may have played a greater role in acquired enuresis than in persistent enuresis. Together with Baker's (1969) findings on children who were nearly all persistent enuretics, the Novick findings indicate that persistent enuretics are optimal candidates for conditioning while acquired enuretics may need help of a more general sort. The lack of controlled follow-up studies of psychodynamic treatment precludes any conclusion as to whether it is followed by more or fewer new symptoms than behavioral treatment.

FUTURE PROSPECTS FOR BEHAVIOR MODIFICATION

Since the late 1950s, application of and research on behavioral approaches to psychopathology have grown at a tremendous rate. A rapid increase in the number of behavioral treatment centers and training programs, especially in clinical psychology, makes it likely that the proportion of disturbed people receiving behavior modification will continue to increase. The already demonstrated possibilities for using nonprofessional workers, parents, peers, and patient groups as supervised behavior modifiers also make it likely that the reach of mental health workers can be extended far beyond that of the traditional one-professional-to-one-patient therapies.

Still more crucial is the fact that controlled studies have demonstrated that some behavior modification techniques produce measurable benefits. The readiness of many behavior modifiers to continue objectively evaluating their methods and to change them in order to get better results represents perhaps the biggest breakthrough of the "behavior modification movement."

While more and better evaluative studies are needed, and while such studies will no doubt show that initial enthusiasm for some techniques was unwarranted, the measure of the long-term impact of the behavior modification approach will be in the degree to which it spreads attitudes of scientific objectivity in the study of psychopathology and its treatment. This does not mean that behavioristic concepts or explanations are intrinsically more "scientific" than any others. It simply means that constant testing of hypotheses by means of objective observations should be a hallmark of work in psychopathology, be it basic research into etiologies or everyday treatment of individual patients, by whatever means, behavioral or otherwise.

While behavior modification techniques often appear simple, the human realities to which they are applied are usually complex. For this reason, appropriate training for professional behavior modifiers must be intensive and must provide considerable experience in actually trying out and evaluating the effectiveness of various techniques. Ullmann's (1971) summary of concepts to be taught professional behavior modifiers reflects many of the basic attitudes advocated by current behavior modifiers:

The first thing a behavior therapy trainee must learn . . . is a new view of people. This means that the target behavior is a normal, appropriate, reasonable outcome of past and continuing experience. This is a very therapeutic thing in and of itself. It leads the behavior therapist to address his client as a normal individual and one to be respected for the strengths he manifests in the majority of his activities. Such strengths are not defenses or reaction formations. The person's difficulties are not the outgrowth of his totally distorted psyche and are not the result of a compromise between intrapsychic conflicts. The person is a unique person and not a label or a diagnostic categorization. Specifically, we no longer deal with phobics who require a total overhaul, but with people who under limited and specifiable circumstances emit phobic behavior. We deal with responses to those circumstances, and we do not use peoples' occasional phobic responses to justify an excursion into their unconsciouses [Ullman, 1971, p. 369].

It is interesting to contrast Ullmann's statement with one by Irving Bieber (1973), in his presidential address to the American Academy of Psychoanalysis:

Behavior therapy has made rapid gains because of its claims of a quick cure. The get-cured-quick type of climate has tended to produce a therapeutic polarization: quality therapy, which is psychoanalysis at one end—and, on the other, the poor man's therapy, which can be almost anything else [p. 51].

Thus, as Bieber views it, psychoanalysis is the only "quality therapy" and almost anything else is, "the poor man's therapy." However, even in many cases where psychodynamic concepts appear to be relevant for understanding the etiology of symptoms, psychoanalytic treatment is neither available (partly due to cost) nor desirable because the initial magnitude of a child's problems do not warrant casting him in a "patient" role for the amount of time analytic treatment requires. Yet, if allowed to persist, many symptoms can interfere with development to an extent far exceeding their initial seriousness.

The following is an illustration of behavioral methods with a child who developed a phobia under conditions suggesting determinants like those emphasized by psychoanalysts but for whom analytic treatment was out of the question:

Until Kirsten was 3½, she had slept in a room adjoining her parents' room. However, when her mother became pregnant for the second time, Kirsten's parents began to make plans to move Kirsten to an upstairs bedroom. The house had two bedrooms on the first floor and two on the second, making it impossible for both children and the parents to have rooms of their own on the same floor. With Kirsten's help, the upstairs bedroom was decorated and her toys were gradually moved up to it. Some months before the baby's arrival, Kirsten's bed was moved to her new room. The transition was facilitated by the timely arrival of a stray cat which Kirsten "adopted" and which slept with her at night.

Shortly before the baby's birth, Kirsten began to express fear that the roof beams of the house might break—the house was an old one with exposed beams in Kirsten's room. Kirsten's parents re-assured her about the beams and made a little model of the house to show just how the beams held up the roof.

Just before the baby's arrival, Kirsten was taken to her grandparents. She expressed fear that the beams in their house might break, although they had no exposed beams. Kirsten came home from her grandparents the night before her mother returned from the hospital. Although her other grandparents were now staying in the room next to hers, Kirsten was very reluctant to sleep, expressed fear of the beams, and woke up crying several times. After the baby came home, she continued to express fear of the beams and wanted to sleep downstairs. Whenever she finally did consent to sleep upstairs, she came to her parents' bed during the night crying in fear of the beams.

In view of her distress, Kirsten was allowed to sleep downstairs, first in the baby's room and then in the living room. She was also given extra attention and was allowed to help with the baby as much as possible, although she occasionally betrayed her ambivalence—e.g., by "handing" the baby a toy with considerably more force than necessary and by getting rough with her cat to the point of pushing it down the stairs.

After several weeks, Kirsten appeared to have relaxed about the baby and was in many ways her old self again. Nevertheless, she seemed more determined than ever to keep sleeping downstairs. Since this meant that she often went to sleep quite late, was awakened when her parents got up to tend the baby, and interfered with her parents' use of the living room, her parents tried various methods of reasoning and interpretation to induce her to return to her room. Being quite immovable when determined, Kirsten was not persuaded. Punishment was ruled out because it was recognized that Kirsten was dealing with strong feelings about the baby's arrival and perhaps about the possibility of her parents engendering more babies. On the other hand, her parents felt that allowing Kirsten to have her way over a long period on this issue would create further difficulties for her as well as for them.

After all else failed, it was decided to try a token reinforcement system. A piece of cardboard was ruled off into 30 squares on which Kirsten could paste an S & H Green (trading) Stamp each time she went to bed upstairs without resistance and another stamp each time she stayed there all night, whether or not going to bed had been sufficiently cooperative to earn a stamp. Since she had been talking about wanting a new doll, the doll was to be the back-up reinforcer.

With some trepidation, Kirsten's parents introduced the plan to her, telling her that they wanted to help her overcome her fear. To their relief, she eagerly exclaimed, "You mean I can *earn* stamps for a doll? Can I start tonight?" She did start that night and earned all 30 stamps in slightly more than the 15 days that would have been required for perfect performance. Kirsten was warmly praised whenever she earned a stamp. She expressed no more fear of the beams and proudly showed her stamp card to friends. She also began to ask about the number of stamps, learned to count higher than previously by counting them, and noticed the similar arrangements of the cells of the card and the numbers on her calendar. This prompted curiosity about the days of the months, when to turn the calendar page, etc.

After Kirsten had earned her doll, there were no further problems with fear of going to bed, but she asked if she could go on earning stamps. Her parents offered to let her earn stamps for getting dressed in the morning and undressed at night, with the back-up reinforcer being a doll high chair. When Kirsten wanted to continue the stamp system after that, she was offered a trip to the zoo in return for asking for things nicely rather than whining and for picking up her room. She decided that the latter was more than she cared to bargain for, but the change in her way of asking for things eventually earned her the trip to the zoo. However, both Kirsten and her parents began to lose interest in the stamp system during the last phase. Her parents forgot to award the stamps when they were due and Kirsten did not bother to remind them or to paste the stamps on her card when they were awarded.

Briefly stated, the determinants of Kirsten's beam phobia appeared to be as follow: Kirsten's anxiety was due to the arrival of a new sibling, the parents' rejection of her that this signified, the need to compete for parental attention, and, possibly, the fear that the parents would engender more babies if they were left alone at night to do so. Being alone upstairs in her room at night while the baby was downstairs in her old room near her parents was the most concrete source of fear. While visiting friends several months earlier, Kirsten heard them jokingly describe how an exposed beam in their house had once cracked. Kirsten's new room was distinguished from the downstairs rooms by having exposed beams. Thus, the frightening fact that exposed beams sometimes crack and the fact that such beams existed in a situation already frightening to her but not in her old room made the beams good candidates for becoming phobic objects. The influence of fear of separation on the beam phobia was indicated by (1) Kirsten's fear of beams at her grandparents' where there were no exposed beams but where she was separated from her parents while they were with the baby, and (2) Kirsten's lack of fear when she could sleep downstairs unseparated from her parents, despite the exposed beams upstairs. Once the phobia had developed, it was reinforced by its success in earning Kirsten the privilege of sleeping near her parents.

Even though Kirsten's fear was complexly determined, it did not seem possible to overcome it through interpretation, working through, etc. Instead, the course finally selected was intended to take advantage of Kirsten's ability to look ahead in time and her conscious desires to master new skills and responsibilities. In fact, the particular technique appeared to mesh well with her current capabilities. She not only succeeded in mastering her fear, but became very proud of her new accomplishments in "earning" (as she called it), sleeping in her "apartment," counting, and understanding the calendar. In the second phase of the system, she also became very proud of dressing herself.

The point of the above case is not to show that token systems are in any sense a panacea. On the contrary, the green stamp system might have been totally inappropriate for a younger or older child and, as often happens with token systems, it eventually became inappropriate in this case merely because both the child and her parents tired of it. Nor is the point to show that the symptom was purely an outcome of learning or that the token system induced new learning—the only new behaviors learned by Kirsten (counting higher, calendar reckoning) were indirect byproducts of the token system. Rather, the point of the case is to show that a typical but troublesome and complex symptom in a child can often be handled by motivating behavior that will enable the child to resume the developmental progress he is capable of, instead of attempting to unravel all the possible determinants in search of insight that the child may be incapable of translating into action. Kirsten was approached at the level of her conscious understanding of a situation and she was helped to direct her behavior toward new conscious goals. Some of the brightest prospects for behavior modification techniques with children appear to be of precisely this nature, where future-oriented behavior is facilitated with the conscious participation of the child in order to help him achieve developmental progress.

SUMMARY

The behavioral formulation of *phobias* contrasts with the psychodynamic formulation in that the former portrays phobias as learned fears while the latter portrays them as symbolic substitutes for fears associated with repressed intrapsychic conflicts. Despite their contention that specific phobias are learned, most behavior modifiers believe that differences in constitutional factors and previous experience cause people to differ in their predispositions to learn new fears.

Eysenck has presented evidence for two fundamental dimensions in personality, *extroversion-introversion* (high conditionability versus low conditionability) and *neuroticism-normality* (high emotional reactivity versus low emotional reactivity). Because personality tests show that people diagnosed as having obsessional or anxiety neuroses are high on introversion and high on neuroticism, Eysenck maintains that they are more likely to acquire conditioned fears than are people who are extroverted and/or low on neuroticism.

Behavioral methods for treating phobias have included desensitization and other reciprocal inhibition procedures, modeling and imitation, operant conditioning, and implosion.

Behavior modifiers agree with psychodynamic theorists that some *obsessions* and *compulsions* function to reduce anxiety, but they have presented evidence that other obsessions and compulsions become relatively autonomous, while still others actually increase anxiety. Desensitization, forcible prevention, aversive conditioning, and satiation procedures have been used to eliminate obsessions and compulsions.

Various *somatic dysfunctions* have been treated behaviorally: *Hysterical* symptoms have been removed with aversive and operant conditioning; *psychophysiological reactions* have been alleviated with desensitization to reduce the anxiety believed to trigger them and with operant conditioning to change the reinforcement contingencies related to the reactions; *enuresis* has been eliminated with several variants of a conditioning apparatus; *hyperactivity* has been reduced by operant conditioning.

Behavioral treatment of *aggressive* behavior has consisted primarily of operant conditioning. Behavior modifiers have also evolved models for the learning of aggressiveness as a general behavioral trait.

Operant conditioning has been used to overcome *learning disabilities* and to improve academic performance.

Because it is increasingly acknowledged that behavior modification methods represent a new technology of treatment, rather than being simply an application of laboratory-based learning theory, the most appropriate evaluation of behavioral methods is not a test of learning theory principles, but controlled comparisons of each method with other possible methods for treating specific disorders in specific types of clients. Controlled comparisons have shown desensitization to be equal or superior to most other treatments for anxiety or phobias except modeling-with-guided-participation in specific phobias. Desensitization and psychotherapy were both found to be highly effective for treating phobias in 6- to 10-year-olds, but neither was effective with 11- to 15-year-olds.

There have been few controlled comparisons of operant conditioning with other treatments, but it has been found more effective than other treatments with introverted, withdrawn boys. The conditioning apparatus method has been found superior to all comparison treatments in eliminating enuresis.

Numerous follow-up studies have reported little evidence for *symptom substitution* after removal of symptoms by behavioral methods, although there is evidence that *acquired enuresis* is a reaction to emotional stress that is more likely to lead to relapse and new symptoms after behavioral or supportive therapy than is *persistent enuresis*.

SUGGESTED READING

Clinical Applications. Rachman's book, *Phobias: Their Nature and Control* (1968) provides a comprehensive picture of the behavioral theory and treatment of phobias, primarily from the viewpoint of desensitization. A broader picture, though also heavily influenced by the behavioral approach, is presented by Marks (1969). Lovibond (1964) and Lovibond and Coote (1970) provide surveys and analyses of the nature and treatment of enuresis. The detailed history of a project for providing broad-gauged behavioral treatments for children where few other clinical services were available and where nonprofessionals played an essential role is presented in Tharp and Wetzel's book, *Behavior Modification in the Natural Environment* (1970). Histories of applications of behavioral principles to institutionalized groups, along with the realities of institutional resistances and other complexities, are contained in Ayllon and Azrin's book, *The Token Economy: A Motivational System for Therapy and Rehabilitation* (1968), dealing with a mental hospital, and Thompson and Grabowski's, *Behavior Modification of the Mentally Retarded* (1972), dealing with an institution for the retarded.

Evaluation of Behavior Modification. A volume entitled *Behavior Therapy: Appraisal and Status,* edited by C. M. Franks (1969), contains a number of informative papers by a wide range of contributors on the evaluation and future prospects of current behavior modification methods.

The Broadening Conception of Behavior Modification. In his article, "The end of ideology in behavior modification," London (1972) has made the case that the behavior modification approach represents a body of technology rather than an application of a unified and verified learning theory and that acknowledgment of this will facilitate development of constructive interaction with other approaches, as well as progress toward the creation and validation of more successful treatment methods. Arnold Lazarus (1971) expresses similar sentiments and offers practical guides to what he calls a "flexible or personalistic system of psychotherapy."

12

Psychotic Disorders

In reference to adults, "psychosis" is almost synonymous with the legal term "insanity." It refers to the condition of a person who is considered to be "out of contact with reality" or whose "reality-testing" is so poor that his misinterpretations of ordinary situations grossly interfere with his adaptation. Adult psychosis, manifested by *delusions* (bizarre ideas), *hallucinations* (perceptions of nonexistent objects or sounds), and bizarre behavior, have been described in virtually every culture for thousands of years.

EARLY INTEREST IN CHILDHOOD PSYCHOSIS

Although anecdotal reports of "insanity" in children had previously appeared, it was only in the late nineteenth century that interest in child psychopathology rose to the point where the question of childhood psychosis was given serious consideration. Efforts to identify psychotic syndromes of childhood were at first met with opposition by those who refused to acknowledge the existence of childhood "insanity," but, by the early twentieth century, there was considerable evidence for psychotic symptoms in children (cf. Kanner, 1971). As interest in childhood psychosis developed, Kraepelin's system of classification for adult disorders was simply extrapolated downward to cover children. Kraepelin's category of *dementia praecox* ("early insanity," i.e., insanity beginning in adolescence or early adulthood) became the basis for a new category, *dementia praecocissima* ("very early insanity").

Bleuler's "Four A's"

In 1911, the Swiss psychiatrist Eugene Bleuler published his conclusion that *dementia praecox* included a variety of disorders all of which involved a "splitting" or disharmony of feeling and thought. He proposed the name *schizophrenia* ("split mind") to designate the inner splitting or coming apart which he observed in *dementia praecox*. (Note that "schizophrenia" does not refer to "split" in the sense of "multiple" personality, although it is often incorrectly used in this way.)

Bleuler specified the primary symptoms of the various schizophrenic disorders in terms of what became known as *Bleuler's four A's:*

1. *Autism,* i.e., excessive absorption in the self, detached from outer reality.
2. Fragmentation and lack of continuity in mental *associations.*
3. *Affective* disturbance and disharmony.
4. Marked *ambivalence.*

Delusions, hallucinations, and peculiar motor behavior were considered to be secondary to these primary symptoms. Bleuler believed that the basic splitting of feeling and thought in schizophrenia was caused by organic factors, but that the ultimate form of the disorder was influenced by the particular environment to which a person with the schizophrenic defects had to adapt. Although he had little clinical experience with children, Bleuler reported that four per cent of adult schizophrenics had begun to manifest problems during childhood.

Types of Childhood Psychosis

By the 1930s, the concept of childhood schizophrenia had been generally accepted. It represented primarily an application to children of Bleuler's criteria for adult schizophrenia. Potter (1933) is often credited with presenting explicit criteria for the diagnosis of childhood schizophrenia, which he restricted to disorders beginning before puberty. Potter's criteria were:

1. A generalized retraction of interests from the environment.
2. Dereistic (unrealistic) thinking, feeling, and acting.
3. Disturbances of thought—manifested through blocking, condensation, perseveration, incoherence, and diminution of speech, sometimes to the extent of mutism.
4. Defects in emotional rapport.
5. Diminution, rigidity, and distortion of affect.
6. Alterations of behavior, with an increase of motility, leading to incessant activity, or a diminution of motility, leading to complete immobility, or bizarre behavior with a tendency to perseveration.

A 30-year follow-up of 12 children originally diagnosed schizophrenic by Potter showed that, in adulthood, nine were diagnosed schizophrenic and three mentally retarded (Bennett & Klein, 1966).

Manic-depressive psychosis, the other major adult psychotic disorder, which is characterized by extreme swings of mood from energetic ebullience to deep depression, was also reported in a small number of children by the 1930s (e.g., Kasanin and Kaufman, 1929).

Despite the relative specificity of Bleuler's and Potter's criteria for diagnosing adult and childhood schizophrenia, respectively, the term "childhood schizophrenia" rapidly became almost a synonym for childhood psychosis. In fact, childhood schizophrenia is the only category provided for severe childhood disturbance in both the 1952 and 1968 editions of the American Psychiatric Association's *Diagnostic and Statistical Manual of Mental Disorders.*

Because many children considered to be psychotic do not closely resemble the picture of childhood schizophrenia presented by Potter, one of the greatest sources of confusion in the study of childhood psychosis has been lack of agreement on diagnosis. Some early efforts were directed at differentiating among psychotic children on the basis of age and manner of the disorder's onset. A distinction was frequently made between children who seemed to have been very abnormal since infancy, those who had long presented behavior problems that rather suddenly took on psychotic proportions, and those who had appeared relatively normal until they suddenly became psychotic in late childhood or early adolescence (Despert, 1938; Symonds & Herman, 1957).

Another approach was to delineate specific subtypes of psychotic children within or in addition to the general category of childhood schizophrenia. For example, Leo Kanner (1943) described a syndrome he designated as *early infantile autism,* which he considered to be "an inborn autistic disturbance of affective contact." Margaret Mahler (1952) proposed the category of *symbiotic psychosis* which she portrayed as a failure of the infant to develop an identity independent of his mother. On the basis of psychological, neurological, and family history data on children diagnosed schizophrenic, William Goldfarb (1956, 1961) concluded that there are at least two major groups, those with signs of organic dysfunction and those who lack signs of organic dysfunction but who come from difficult home situations.

Unfortunately, the attempts at distinguishing among types of severely disturbed children have not greatly increased conceptual clarity because many workers use the diagnostic terms without much regard for the specific characteristics on which they are supposed to be based. Thus, "autism," "schizophrenia," and "symbiotic psychosis" are used almost interchangeably by some workers. The confusion has been further compounded by the addition of a still broader term, *atypical development* (Rank, 1949), to refer to a general class of disturbed children many of whom would be called "schizophrenic," "autistic," or, at least, "psychotic" by other workers.

Meanwhile, attention of child workers to manic-depressive psychosis has all but disappeared. This may be partly due to the fact that diagnostic fashions in adult psychopathology have changed so that many adults who once might have been diagnosed manic-depressive are now diagnosed schizophrenic or schizoaffective. In light of this change, reassessment of early published reports of manic-depressive psychosis in children has led to the conclusion that this diagnosis was unfounded and that manic-depressive psychosis has not been demonstrated in prepubertal children (Anthony &

Scott, 1960). However, the apparent benefits of an adult antimanic medication (lithium) with children having manic symptoms suggest that the debate is about to be reopened (Feinstein & Wolpert, 1973).

THE GAP CLASSIFICATION

In its proposed classification of psychopathological disorders of childhood, the Group for the Advancement of Psychiatry ("GAP", 1966) offers the following general description for childhood psychotic disorders:

> Psychotic disorder is revealed often by (1) severe and continued impairment of emotional relationships with persons, associated with an aloofness and (2) a tendency toward preoccupation with inanimate objects; (3) loss of speech or failure in its development; (4) disturbances in sensory perception; (5) bizarre or stereotyped behavior and motility patterns; (6) marked resistance to change in environment or routine; (7) outbursts of intense and unpredictable panic; (8) absence of a sense of personal identity; and (9) blunted, uneven or fragmented intellectual development. In some cases, intellectual performance may be adequate or better, with the psychotic disorder confining itself to other areas of personality function [p. 251; numbers added].

The GAP report goes on to *interpret* psychosis primarily in psychoanalytic terms of an extreme distortion of ego development. However, the above *description* of the disorder is one that has found fairly wide acceptance since the time it was originally proposed in similar terms by a British group (Creak, 1961). In reviewing studies of symptomatology in children diagnosed psychotic, Goldfarb (1970) concluded that virtually all the primary behavioral symptoms were embodied in the nine points of this description, although few children manifested all the symptoms and no symptom by itself could be regarded as diagnostic of psychosis.

Among childhood psychoses, the GAP classification distinguishes three major categories as follows:

1. *Psychoses of infancy and early childhood,* including
   a. *early infantile autism;*
   b. *interactional psychoses*—symbiotic psychosis plus others that involve a pathological tie to the mother or a family member;
   c. *other psychoses of infancy and early childhood,* which do not conform closely to the pictures of either autism or interactional psychoses.
2. *Psychoses of later childhood,* including
   a. *schizophreniform psychotic disorder*—believed to begin between the ages of six and 12, these psychoses are considered to resemble adult schizophrenia but to differ in ways related to the developmental stage of the child and not necessarily to develop into adult schizophrenia;
   b. *other psychoses of later childhood.*

3. *Psychoses of adolescence,* including
   a. *acute confusional state*—described as having an abrupt onset, with acute anxiety, depression, confusion, and a sense of depersonalization;
   b. *schizophrenic disorder, adult type;*
   c. *other psychoses of adolescence.*

The proposed classification appears to provide a workable guide for diagnosis and research on etiology, treatment, and prevention, but continuing disagreements as to whether early infantile autism is really an early form of schizophrenia, whether schizophrenia often begins between the ages of six and 12, etc., may prevent the classification from being put to use. As this classification system has not yet been used on any scale, the present chapter is organized as much as possible around only the categories that have received the most attention, i.e., childhood schizophrenia, autism, and symbiotic psychosis. As will be repeatedly evident, the lack of standardization of terminology and of objective description has resulted in considerable overlap even among these three categories.

Incidence of Childhood Psychosis

The lack of terminological standardization and of objective description interferes with obtaining accurate estimates of the frequency of psychotic disorders in children, although all studies concur that such disorders occur in no more than about 6 out of every 10,000 children (Werry, 1972). Werry's review also shows that all studies report an excess of boys over girls classified psychotic, with the ratios running from about 1.7:1 to 9.5:1. However, disproportionate numbers of boys manifest most other psychopathological and physical disorders as well.

For the sake of comparison with adult psychoses, studies in Europe, Asia, and North America (Yolles & Kramer, 1969) report that the proportions of adults identified as psychotic range from 380 per 10,000 population in Germany and Formosa, to 2,350 per 10,000 in rural Sweden. The rates for adults are thus between 63 and 392 times as great as the highest estimated rates for children. Since methods for diagnosing and determining the incidence of adult psychosis are only slightly better than those applied to child psychosis, the precise figures should be taken with a grain of salt. However, they do indicate that childhood psychosis is rare not only in absolute terms, but also in relation to adult psychosis.

CHILDHOOD SCHIZOPHRENIA

In the absence of a widely accepted alternative definition for childhood schizophrenia, the GAP (1966) definition for *schizophreniform psychotic disorder* will be employed.

Schizophreniform psychotic disorder: This reaction ordinarily is not seen until the age period between six and twelve or thirteen years. Onset may be gradual, neurotic symptoms appearing at first, followed by marked and primitive denial and projection, looseness of association in thought processes, concretistic thinking, low frustration tolerance, hypochondriacal tendencies, and intense temper outbursts. Later developments may include marked withdrawal, intense involvement. in fantasy, autistic behavior, emotional aloofness, true disorders in thinking, and a breakdown in reality testing. In other instances, more acute and sudden eruptions at this developmental phase may involve crises accompanied by intense anxiety, uncontrollable phobias, and marked withdrawal leading to autistic behavior and distorted reality testing.

* * *

. . . Bizarre behavior and stereotyped motor patterns, such as whirling, are frequently present. Some children show sudden and wild outbursts of either aggressive or self-mutilating behavior, inappropriate mood swings, and suicidal threats and attempts. Ideas of reference, dissociative phenomena, somatic delusions, catatonic behavior, paranoid thinking, and other manifestations seen in adults may occur [pp. 254–55].

A poignant portrayal of a boy who fits the picture of childhood schizophrenia can be found in *Jordi*, a short novel by Theodore I. Rubin (1968).

Family Characteristics

During the 1940s and 1950s, there was a prevalent tendency to blame childhood psychosis—schizophrenia in particular—on the behavior of the child's mother. Rank (1949) and Despert (1947) were especially avid proponents of the view that psychosis was caused by mothers who were immature, narcissistic, overintellectual, and incapable of mature emotional relationships. The *schizophrenogenic mother* became a commonplace of clinical lore and has continued to be employed by some writers to explain psychosis even though they may acknowledge the possibility of constitutional vulnerability in children who become psychotic. The schizophrenogenic mother theme has also been extended to include mothers who "wish that [their] child should not exist [Bettelheim, 1967, p. 125]" and "parents [who] inadvertently hated one another and used the child emotionally [Wolman, 1970, p. vii]."

There are numerous studies of pathology in the families of adult schizophrenics, but most suffer the disadvantage that their data are retrospective, largely recalled by the parents or the schizophrenics themselves after the disorder had become evident. An exception is a study by Ricks and Berry (1970) in which the child guidance clinic records of individuals who later became schizophrenic were compared with the records of individuals who later had other diagnoses or were considered socially adequate. "Schizophrenogenic" mothers were found in all groups but *least* frequently for individuals who later became chronic schizophrenics. Studies of relatively objective factors such as family poverty and loss of parents through death, divorce, desertion, or illness have not generally shown greater frequencies of these factors in the childhoods of adult schizophrenics than of normal controls, although parental psychosis was somewhat higher in the families of schizophrenics (Oltman, McGarry, & Friedman, 1952; Schofield & Balian, 1959).

Demographic Characteristics. A study by Lowe (1966) roughly parallels some of the adult studies in that objective demographic characteristics of the parents of schizophrenic children were compared with those of parents of other psychotic children and of nonpsychotic emotionally disturbed children, although evidently no attempt was made to match the children in each group on variables such as age, race, or sex. Lowe found that fathers of both the schizophrenic and other psychotic children had significantly higher educational and occupational levels than fathers of the nonpsychotic emotionally disturbed children. Also, schizophrenic and other psychotic children came from broken homes much *less* frequently than did nonpsychotic children.

Maternal Attitudes. Klebanoff (1959) assessed the child-rearing attitudes of mothers of schizophrenic, brain-damaged retarded, and normal children by having them fill out the Parental Attitude Research Instrument (PARI), a widely used questionnaire designed to tap attitudes related to childrearing and family life. It was found that mothers of the brain-damaged retarded children manifested significantly more pathological attitudes than mothers of schizophrenic children who, in turn, manifested more pathological attitudes than mothers of normal children. Since the most pathological attitudes were found among mothers of brain-damaged children, whose defects could not be blamed on their mothers' behavior, it was suggested that the intermediately pathological attitudes found in mothers of schizophrenic children were—like the pathological attitudes of mothers of brain-damaged children—*results* rather than causes of the problems presented by their children. Other studies have also failed to find exceptionally pathological attitudes among mothers of schizophrenic or "psychotic" children (Pitfield & Oppenheim, 1964; Zuckerman, Oltean, & Monashkin, 1958).

Maternal Speech. On a different tack, two studies have demonstrated differences in the tape-recorded speech of mothers of psychotic and nonpsychotic children. In one study, the mothers of schizophrenics were rated as being significantly inferior to mothers of normals in general speech and language, communication of meaning, and communication of mood (Goldfarb, Goldfarb, & Scholl, 1966).

In the second study, clinicians rated mothers of psychotic children significantly less likable, less treatable, and more pathogenic than mothers of nonpsychotic disturbed children (Rice, Kepecs, & Yahalom, 1966).

Parental Psychological Characteristics. In another attempt to identify characteristics of parents of schizophrenic children, mothers and fathers of schizophrenic (also referred to by the authors as "autistic") and nonpsychotic neurotic children were given the Rorschach inkblot test, the Minnesota Multiphasic Personality Inventory (MMPI), and the Thematic Apperception Test (TAT; Block, Patterson, Block, & Jackson, 1958). The test protocols were evaluated by three clinical psychologists who made Q-sorts describing their impressions of each parent. (A Q-sort consists of sorting a large number of descriptive statements about a person into groupings ranging from "very characteristic of" the person to "very uncharacteristic of" the person.) No significant differences were found between the Q-sort placements of any of the 108 statements describing the parents of schizophrenics and the placement of these statements describing the parents of neurotic children.

In the same study, six psychiatrists were asked to make Q-sorts describing their conceptions of typical schizophrenogenic mothers and fathers. The average correlation between Q-sorts by each pair of psychiatrists for the "typical" schizophrenogenic mother was .56, while for the typical father it was .18. The psychiatrists' Q-sorts for the idealized schizophrenogenic mother and father correlated no more highly with the Q-sorts for the real parents of schizophrenic children than with the Q-sorts for the parents of nonschizophrenic children. Together, these findings indicate that the psychiatrists' conceptions of typical parents of schizophrenic children agreed neither with each other nor with descriptions of parents who really did have schizophrenic children.

Following up reports that parents of adult schizophrenics showed conceptual disorganization on an object-scoring test, Schopler and Loftin (1969a) found conceptual disorganization in the object-sorting performance of parents of psychotic children who were undergoing psychodynamic evaluation and treatment. However, parents of psychotic children tested in the context of interviews about their *normal* children did not show conceptual disorganization (Schopler & Loftin, 1969b). This was interpreted as indicating that parental disorganization was likely to result from anxiety generated by being evaluated in relation to their disturbed child.

Family Interactions. In a study designed to investigate interactions between schizophrenic boys and their parents, recordings were made of family discussions of topics about which each family was to make a joint decision (Lennard, Beaulieu, & Embrey, 1965). Interchanges in families having a schizophrenic son were compared with those in families having only normal children. Since many measures did not significantly differentiate the two groups of families, and, since the normal "control" families were apparently not closely matched to the schizophrenics' families on demographic variables, the significant differences found were no more than suggestive of unusual patterns of interactions between parents and their schizophrenic son. However, the most evident pattern seemed to be one in which the father engaged in minimal interchange with his son, while the mother was more active, especially in discussing the feelings of other family members. Other studies of family interactions in standardized situations have failed to reveal systematic differences between parental treatment of young adult schizophrenics and their normal siblings (Sharan, 1966; Waxler & Mishler, 1971).

Summary of Family Characteristics.   There is no clear evidence for a predominance of any one set of attitudes, personalities, or behavior patterns in the parents of schizophrenic children, although there is evidence that the fathers of schizophrenic and other psychotic children have higher educational and occupational status than fathers of nonpsychotic disturbed children. This will be taken up in later sections where it is pertinent to certain etiological theories.

There is also evidence that the speech of mothers of psychotic children is poorer and makes them sound less likable, less treatable, and more pathogenic than mothers of nonpsychotic children. The etiological significance of these findings is uncertain, however, because the speech samples were taken from clinical interviews in which the topics involved the mother's child-rearing. There is no way of knowing whether the negative characteristics of the mothers' voices under these conditions resulted from anxiety about their possible contribution to their child's psychosis or whether they reflected long-standing characteristics of the mothers that may have etiological significance. The former possibility is supported by evidence that the object-sorting performance of parents of psychotic children is more disorganized in contexts relating to their disturbed child than in more neutral contexts.

Neurobiological Characteristics

The sections that follow are divided into the two general categories of neurological and biochemical factors. These categories are by no means mutually exclusive, as a biochemical abnormality may cause neurological damage or vice versa. Neither are they incompatible with research on family characteristics, because unusual characteristics of other family members could result from the same biological abnormality as schizophrenia in the child, or family characteristics could adversely influence a child who is biologically vulnerable.

Neurological Factors.   Lauretta Bender has, since the 1930s, held as her major thesis that both child and adult schizophrenia are due to genetically determined vulnerability in the nervous system. Supporting her conviction that child and adult schizophrenia share the same genotype, Bender has reported a follow-up showing that 96 per cent of children she diagnosed as schizophrenic were still schizophrenic in adulthood, although her criteria for schizophrenia are quite broad (Bender & Faretra, 1972).

According to Bender, children with the basic schizophrenic vulnerability manifest different syndromes depending on the age at which organic or psychological stresses precipitate a schizophrenic breakdown. She describes three basic developmental syndromes:

1. The *pseudodefective* syndrome, resembling severe retardation and characteristic of children who break down during the first three years of life.
2. The *pseudoneurotic* syndrome, involving severe anxiety and defenses against it, especially obsessions and phobias, and characteristic of children who break down in early and middle childhood.
3. The *pseudopsychopathic* syndrome, involving paranoia and aimless antisocial behavior, and characteristic of children who break down around the age of 10 or 11.

Unfortunately, Bender has specified neither the precise nature of schizophrenic vulnerability nor the defining symptomatology in ways that are reliably usable by other workers. Since she subsumes so many different patterns under schizophrenia—including pseudodefective, pseudoneurotic, pseudopsychopathic, autistic, symbiotic, and certain nonpsychotic conditions—it is difficult to know just where the limits lie for her generalizations about schizophrenic vulnerability.

Barbara Fish, one of Bender's students, has attempted to identify vulnerable infants on the basis of unusual combinations of performance on Gesell infant tests. In one study, three out of 14 children receiving developmental and neurological examinations at the age of one month were predicted to be especially vulnerable to schizophrenia (Fish, Shapiro, Halpern, & Wile, 1965; Fish, Wile, Shapiro, & Halpern, 1966). At the age of nine years, each child was interviewed by a psychiatrist and tested by a psychologist, both of whom were blind to the predictions of vulnerability made at age one month.

The psychiatrist diagnosed as schizophrenic the child who had been rated most vulnerable at age one month, while he diagnosed all the other 13 children as having neurotic reactions or character disorders. There was no significant relation between infant vulnerability ratings and the psychiatrist's judgments of severity in the children he diagnosed as nonschizophrenic.

On the basis of intelligence, perceptual-motor, and projective tests, the psychologist identified all three "vulnerable" children as grossly pathological, while she diagnosed two other children as having moderate neurotic problems and the remaining nine as being within the "normal" range.

The degree of agreement between the diagnosis of vulnerability and the blind assessments at age nine, especially the psychologist's, suggests that the signs of neurological vulnerability were good predictors of severe disturbance existing nine years later. The study does not conclusively show, however, that neurological vulnerability is either a necessary or sufficient cause of childhood schizophrenia, because other factors, such as the infant examiner's knowledge that the most vulnerable child's mother had long been severely schizophrenic, may have influenced her judgment of vulnerability. Also, the numbers were small, only one of the three vulnerable children appeared to be clearly schizophrenic by age nine, and the family situations of all the children were so bad that any basic vulnerability would have been likely to produce severe consequences. Despite these reservations, the potential significance of this type of study for both the theory and prevention of childhood schizophrenia is so great as to cry out for replication on a larger scale with appropriate methodological improvements.

William Goldfarb (1961) has made one of the most thorough attempts to identify neurological abnormalities in children diagnosed as schizophrenic. Unfortunately, no distinction was made between autistic and schizophrenic children, and Goldfarb (1970) later reported that some of the subjects fit his syndrome of early infantile autism.

Thorough neurological evaluations revealed various subtle abnormalities in 17 of the 26 subjects. The existence of many more prenatal and perinatal complications in the birth histories of the schizophrenics than in those of their siblings or of normal controls suggested that early neurological damage was a major source of the organic abnormalities (Taft & Goldfarb, 1964).

The children diagnosed organically impaired were compared on a large number of measures wih the other schizophrenic children and with normal children matched for age and sex. On 93 per cent of the neurological, perceptual, behavioral, and conceptual test measures, the normals were superior to the "nonorganic" schizophrenics who were, in turn, superior to the "organic" schizophrenics. As an example of the differences between the two subgroups of schizophrenics, the average IQ of the nonorganics was 92, compared to 62 for the organics.

Because Goldfarb hypothesized that childhood schizophrenia can result either from organic defects or from adverse psychosocial factors, he compared "family adequacy" scores for the normals, organic schizophrenics, and nonorganic schizophrenics. The family adequacy score was the sum of 46 separate ratings on family interaction made by an observer who spent a three-hour session in the home of each family when the schizophrenic or normal control child was present. It was found that the families of the normals were nonsignificantly more adequate than the families of organics but significantly more adequate than the families of the nonorganics. The results were interpreted as supporting Goldfarb's hypothesis of two distinct groups of schizophrenic children, one in which organic defects play a primary etiological role, and a second in which family inadequacy plays a primary role.

In a related study, Meyers and Goldfarb (1961) investigated what they called "maternal perplexity," which was scored on the basis of spontaneity of maternal interaction, decisiveness, consistency of emotional relatedness, appropriate mode of relating to child, appropriate control of child, appropriate anticipation of physical needs, and appropriate meeting of child's demands.

Consistent with the scores for family adequacy in the Goldfarb study, Meyers and Goldfarb found the least maternal perplexity in the normal control group, somewhat more in the organic schizophrenic group, and the most in the nonorganic schizophrenic group. As an illustration of maternal perplexity, the following is quoted from an interview with the mother who received the highest score for perplexity:

When asked about her maternal feelings, Mrs. A. responded, "My maternal feelings were of responsibility, not of joy, because I was so overanxious. I remember once I was so strict to my schedule that I gave Betty [schizophrenic child] a bath when she was sleeping. . . .

In response to a question about how her husband cooperated in the feeding of the children when they were infants, she said. "We were both afraid to touch her. We thought that she would break. Both of us got up in the night and one gave her the bottle and one held the baby. I put a handkerchief in his hand to hold the baby's head because I was afraid that if he would touch her with his bare hand her head would dilapidate. . . ."

When asked how she handled temper tantrums, Mrs. A. said, "Then I got a temper tantrum too. I don't want to hit Sam because you can sometimes hit him harder than you want. Betty I hit a lot. Now I lock Sam up in a room, but only in the daytime; if it is in the evening I put on the light, naturally, and I try to make it as short as possible. . . ."

Mrs. A's perplexity over handling sexual play between her children is openly revealed in the following: "Oh yes, she has a terrible effect on him. She plays with his sex organ and then she shows him [her genitals]. Then she plays with his sex organs and he plays with hers and they laugh like it is low, not nice. I just cry that it should be over, but I don't say 'Don't do it.' Am I acting the right way? I don't know why but everything she says [about sex] is like it is low. It is a low thing to own sex organs, the way she puts it. She teaches him low feelings. They laugh together and their laugh is also low, like it wouldn't be nice to have sex organs. . . . He never asked me about sex organs. Just this week he mentioned why did he have them, so I said—I didn't want to name it, I just said—so he asked me, 'Do you use it to urinate with?' and I said yes. I can't tell him this is the way a man has intercourse with his wife because he wouldn't understand [Meyers & Goldfarb, 1961, pp. 561-62].[1]

In a further study by Meyers and Goldfarb (1962), the parents and siblings of 45 schizophrenic children were interviewed in order to determine how many appeared schizophrenic. Again, the schizophrenic children were subdivided into organic and nonorganic categories, although they appear to have been heterogeneous in other respects, e.g., other workers might have classified some as autistic or symbiotic. The criteria for schizophrenia in the parents and siblings were also broad, including borderline, pseudoneurotic, latent, and "compensated" schizophrenia, the last of which might be classified as "schizoid personality" by other workers. According to these criteria, 44 per cent of the mothers, 8 per cent of the fathers, and 14 per cent of the siblings of nonorganic and 21 per cent of the mothers, 15 per cent of the fathers, and 4 per cent of the siblings of organic schizophrenics were considered to be schizophrenic.

[1] D. I. Meyers and William Goldfarb, "Studies of Perplexity in Mothers of Schizophrenic Children," *American Journal of Orthopsychiatry*, 1961, **31**, 3 (551–64). © 1961 by the American Orthopsychiatric Association, Inc., and reprinted by permission.

Meyers and Goldfarb viewed the greater incidence of schizophrenia in mothers of nonorganic schizophrenic children as tentatively supporting their two-group approach, but the difference between the two groups in total frequency of family schizophrenia appears too small to be conclusive. The relatively low rates of sibling schizophrenia may be misleading because some of the siblings might have developed schizophrenia as they grew older. Moreover, the group differences are compatible with a genetic hypothesis as well as with Goldfarb's hypothesis of two separate etiologies. The genetic hypothesis would state that a strong genetic-familial disposition to schizophrenia—as manifested by a large number of schizophrenic family members —can cause a child to become schizophrenic even if he has no detectable neurological abnormalities to precipitate additional stress.

Figure 12–1 summarizes Goldfarb's conceptual model for the study of childhood schizophrenia. Note that he regards both parental inadequacy *and* constitutional deviance in the child as being possible primary etiological factors that then prevent normal ego development.

Goldfarb's work seems to have demonstrated that, in his samples of schizophrenic children, those with detectable organic abnormalities have less "perplexed" parents than those without organic abnormalities. This strongly suggests that both organic abnormalities and parental perplexity can be *contributory causes* of childhood psychosis, but it does not show that these

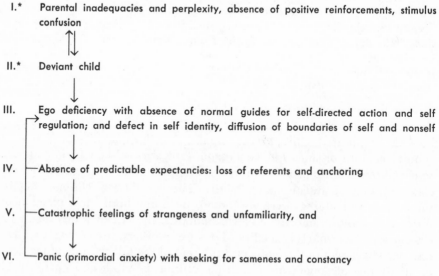

I.*   Parental inadequacies and perplexity, absence of positive reinforcements, stimulus confusion

II.*   Deviant child

III.   Ego deficiency with absence of normal guides for self-directed action and self regulation; and defect in self identity, diffusion of boundaries of self and nonself

IV.   Absence of predictable expectancies: loss of referents and anchoring

V.   Catastrophic feelings of strangeness and unfamiliarity, and

VI.   Panic (primordial anxiety) with seeking for sameness and constancy

* I and II may be either primary or secondary.

Fig. 12–1. Goldfarb's conceptual model for childhood schizophrenia. From Meyers and Goldfarb (1961), p. 552. © 1961 by the American Orthopsychiatric Association and reprinted by permission.

factors are either *necessary* or *sufficient causes* for childhood schizophrenia. On the one hand, Goldfarb's failure to distinguish among symptom syndromes (e.g., autistic, symbiotic, schizophreniform) leaves open the possibility that organic or environmental factors contribute differentially to different syndromes. On the other hand, the data do not rule out the possibility that a genetic predisposition is a *necessary* and/or *sufficient* condition for schizophrenia and that organic or psychological stresses may influence only the timing, form, or severity of the disorder in people who have the genetic predisposition.

In a comparison of 76 children diagnosed schizophrenic and/or autistic with 113 of their siblings, Pollack, Gittelman, Miller, Berman, and Bakwin (1970) found that 76 per cent of the psychotic children, compared to 17 per cent of their siblings, had signs of neurological abnormality; the mean IQ of the psychotics was 71 compared to 112 for their siblings; and the mean Vineland Social Maturity Quotient was 75 for the psychotics and 112 for their siblings. Ten of the siblings were retarded, while one was psychotic. On the basis of his own data and his reviews of other studies, Pollack concluded that the high incidence of prenatal, perinatal, and neurological abnormalities, the low but stable IQs, and the low incidence of severe psychopathology (except retardation) in siblings of psychotic children argued against both a familial-genetic and a psychogenic etiology for childhood psychoses (Pollack, 1967; Pollack & Woerner, 1966). Instead, he proposed that the childhood psychoses comprise a heterogeneous group of syndromes resulting from various kinds of brain damage.

The findings of little family pathology in Pollack's samples and those of the studies he highlights contrast with the findings of Meyers and Goldfarb (1962). While Pollack and many of the studies he cites used the term "schizophrenia," they did not generally distinguish among types of psychotic children. It is thus difficult to know whether the heterogeneity of organic etiologies inferred by Pollack might result from the heterogeneity of the samples he reviews or whether syndromes such as childhood schizophrenia and autism each result from heterogeneous organic etiologies.

In a study of 97 schizophrenic pupils from a special day school, Gittelman and Birch (1967) reported a number of findings similar to those of Pollack. Unfortunately, some of the same children may have been included in the sample studied by Pollack et al (1970), because the same school was a source of children in both studies, although no indication is provided as to whether the samples overlap. Consistent with Pollack's findings, Gittelman and Birch found that many of the children had low IQs (82 per cent below IQ 90), signs of neurological dysfunction (75 per cent), and prenatal or perinatal complications (35 per cent). IQ was also found to be very stable, the test-retest correlations being .90 for Binet IQs and .82 for WISC IQs over periods averaging three and one-half years. Among ex-pupils followed up over an average period of six years, those who improved had relatively high initial IQs and showed a further increase averaging four points from initial to final testing. Diagnoses had changed for 39 per cent of the children, mostly to primary mental retardation or organic damage.

Of the families of children still attending the school, 30 per cent contained at least one other member diagnosed as mentally ill. However, unlike Goldfarb's (1961) finding, there was no significant tendency for children without neurological signs to come from the more disturbed families. Gittelman and Birch concluded that their findings argued against a psychogenic etiology or even a continuum from psychogenic to organic etiology as proposed by Goldfarb.

High rates of neurological signs have also been reported in two studies that made finer distinctions among syndromes than did the foregoing studies. In one study, White, DeMyer, and DeMyer (1964) reported abnormal EEG records in 57 per cent of children diagnosed autistic or symbiotic, 46 per cent of those diagnosed schizophrenic, 57 per cent of those having nonpsychotic behavior disorders, 10 per cent of those having neurotic disorders, and none of those in a normal comparison group. Although the normals and neurotics cannot really be considered controls because they were not closely matched to the other groups, both these groups had significantly fewer EEG abnormalities than the psychotic and behavior disorder groups. While the high percentage of abnormalities is consistent with the previously cited studies, the fact that they were also found in the nonpsychotic behavior disorder group suggests that they bear no specific relation to schizophrenia or autistic-symbiotic psychoses.

In the second study, extensive medical, psychiatric, and psychological examinations of 32 psychotic children led to the conclusion that two were autistic with no signs of neurological abnormality, six were schizophrenic, two of whom had neurological signs, and the remaining 24 were brain-damaged, with psychosis being secondary (Menolascino, 1965). Again, the picture is one of a high rate of organic problems in psychotic children, although a clear differentiation seems to have been possible between those in whom brain damage was most prominent and those, mostly without organic signs, who fit the schizophrenic or autistic syndromes. A low proportion of children with prominent organic damage had very pathological families, but the pathology of most of the other families was interpreted as being reactive to the problems created by the child.

High Risk Children. Further evidence comes from a longitudinal study that may ultimately yield a great deal of valuable information about schizophrenia, at least adolescent-adult schizophrenia (Mednick & Schulsinger, 1965). Being studied for 20 to 25 years are Danish children known to have a high risk for schizophrenia because they have severely schizophrenic mothers. A closely matched control group of children with nonschizophrenic parents is also being followed. The study began with extensive testing of the children at an average age of 15, before any had had mental breakdowns.

So far, the first 20 to have mental breakdowns have been compared with 20 matched high-risk subjects who have not broken down (Mednick, 1970; Mednick & Schulsinger, 1972). Most of those who broke down have been hospitalized with diagnoses of schizophrenia. Compared to high-risk subjects who have not broken down, those who have broken down lost their mothers prior to hospitalization, were disciplinary problems in school, were more erratic on word association tests, and had galvanic skin responses (GSRs) that were especially sensitive to the onset and termination of stress. Seventy per cent of the subjects who broke down had suffered serious pregnancy or birth complications, compared to 15 per cent of the high-risk subjects who had not broken down, and 33 per cent of the normal control group.

On the basis of these findings and studies of the effects of ablation in different areas of animal brains, Mednick (1970) has hypothesized that early damage to the hippocampal region of the brain, especially through deprivation of oxygen prenatally or perinatally, may lead to the oversensitivity to stress observed in the GSRs of the breakdown group. He suggests that a damaged hippocampus may play a vital predispositional role in schizophrenia by exerting a less than normal inhibitory influence on the brain. However, comparison of a new sample of children of schizophrenic parents with children of nonschizophrenic parents, all of whom had pregnancy and birth complications, has indicated that pregnancy and birth complications were significantly correlated with poor performance on infant development tests *only in the children of schizophrenics* (Mednick, Mura, Schulsinger, & Mednick, 1971; Mednick & Schulsinger, 1972). This was interpreted as indicating that the children of schizophrenics already had a genetic vulnerability that was exacerbated by prenatal and perinatal injuries that did not produce significant effects in children of nonschizophrenics.

Until Mednick's high risk subjects are past the usual ages for the development of schizophrenia, it will not be known whether pre- and perinatal complications play a crucial role in adult schizophrenia or whether they merely hasten it and make it more severe in individuals otherwise predisposed. In order to obtain a more complete picture of the developmental spectrum of schizophrenic disorders, Mednick also plans studies of preadolescent children of schizophrenics and of attempts to prevent schizophrenia in children whose mothers are schizophrenic (Mednick & McNeil, 1968; Mednick & Schulsinger, 1972).

Another study of high risk children has been undertaken by Anthony (1972). It entails clinical, experimental, and physiological comparisons between children having a schizophrenic parent, children having normal parents, and children having a parent who suffers an organic illness such as tuberculosis. Preliminary analyses have suggested the presence of the following types of reactions among the children of schizophrenics:

1. *Parapsychotic*—disturbed thinking and behavior occurring in children engaged in an early close relationship with a schizophrenic mother. This syndrome is believed to be determined primarily by the environ-

mental influence of the disturbed parent and is alleviated by severance of the close tie to the parent.

2. *Nonpsychotic*—neurotic and behavior disorders occurring in children as reactions to stress created in the home by the schizophrenic parent, but not reaching bizarre proportions.

3. *Prepsychotic*—hypersensitivity to minor stresses, accompanied by repeated "micropsychotic" episodes in children who appear to be constitutionally vulnerable to psychosis, regardless of which parent is schizophrenic.

Anthony provides the following example of a micropsychotic episode:

. . . a girl of nine . . . noted a small blemish on her skin and became extremely upset. She accused her mother of putting things in her food in order to poison her. She also began to notice that she was becoming forgetful in response to the toxic substance and falling behind in her classwork. She thought that the doctor who examined her with negative findings was in league with the mother, and she observed that some of the patients sitting in his waiting room had similar blemishes so that he was the center of a wider conspiracy. In three months the . . . micro-paranoidal system cleared up completely, and she was her apparently normal self again [Anthony, 1972, p. 404].[2]

Anthony's study has not yet reached the stage where his findings can be systematically compared with Mednick's, but Anthony (1972), like Mednick, has reported high physiological reactivity in children of schizophrenic parents. However, among the 36 families with one schizophrenic parent studied by Anthony so far, none of the 137 children is regarded as a childhood schizophrenic, despite the evidence for prepsychosis and parapsychosis in some. Mednick also has not reported any childhood psychoses among the 207 children of schizophrenic mothers he is studying. Similarly, Biermann (1966) found no childhood schizophrenia among the 180 children of 100 Swiss and German families having a schizophrenic parent. These findings do not necessarily conflict with Meyers and Goldfarb's (1962) report of high rates of schizophrenia in the parents of children diagnosed schizophrenic, because they started with child cases rather than parent cases. Even if childhood schizophrenia is somehow related to adult schizophrenia, the rarity of childhood schizophrenia may mean that a much smaller percentage of schizophrenic parents have offspring who develop schizophrenia in childhood than who develop schizophrenia in adulthood. It is surprising, however, that out of a total of 524 children of schizophrenic parents in the Anthony, Mednick, and Biermann studies, *none* was apparently regarded as a childhood schizophrenic, although between 10 and 20 per cent were expected to become schizophrenic in adulthood (Anthony, 1972; Mednick, 1970). It should, therefore, be noted again that we can consider childhood psychosis

[2] E. J. Anthony, "A Clinical and Experimental Study of High Risk Children and Their Schizophrenic Parents," in *Genetic Factors in "Schizophrenia,"* A. R. Kaplan (Ed.). (Springfield, Ill.: Charles C. Thomas, 1972). © 1972 by Charles C. Thomas and reprinted by permission.

in relation to adult schizophrenia only with the proviso that they may in fact be very different disorders.

Biochemical Factors. Any biochemical abnormalities in schizophrenia may well be linked to neurological abnormalities either because biochemical abnormalities may create neurological dysfunctions or neurological dysfunctions may create biochemical abnormalities. Whichever comes first, a vicious circle may be created that puts the schizophrenic in an abnormal physiological state which, in turn, affects his subjective experiences, reactions to stress, and learning from experience. For example, according to Mednick's (1970) hypothesis, the damaged hippocampus may fail to inhibit secretion of ACTH, a pituitary hormone that triggers protective physiological reactions during stress. The oversupply of ACTH circulating in the blood may then keep the individual in a hyperaroused state during stress. This would explain the oversensitivity to stress observed in the GSRs of high-risk subjects who later became schizophrenic.

A great many other hypotheses involving biochemical abnormalities have been tested and biochemical differences between adult schizophrenics and normals have often been reported. However, many studies finding such differences have compared unhospitalized normal subjects with hospitalized schizophrenics whose diets, daily schedules, activity levels, exposure to infectious illness, moods, drug consumption, and treatments such as electroconvulsive shock could account for the differences found. According to recent reviews, no firm evidence for a specific biochemical etiology has yet been found in adult schizophrenia, much less in childhood schizophrenia where there has been little biochemical research (Friedhoff, 1972; Kety, 1969; Weil-Malherbe & Szara, 1971). Biochemical research on childhood psychosis has begun to increase, but it has been directed mainly at early infantile autism, to be discussed later in the chapter. Although biochemical variables can often be dealt with more precisely than behavioral, experiential, or neurological variables, the vast numbers of possible biochemical variables and interactions among them make it likely that biochemical research will be most productive when it is guided by hypotheses closely related to behavioral and neurological data.

Summary of Neurobiological Characteristics. A number of studies agree in finding elevated frequencies of neurological signs and pre- and perinatal complications in children diagnosed schizophrenic and in high-risk children who later break down mentally. High long-term stability in the IQs of schizophrenic and other psychotic children has also been found. However, the lack of consistency in diagnostic criteria makes it difficult to be certain how specific these findings are to a particular diagnostic entity.

Evidence for neurological abnormalities has been used to support several hypotheses related to the role of early neurological damage in the etiology of schizophrenia. These include Bender's hypothesis of a pervasive inherited vulnerability beginning prenatally and being manifested in excessive unevenness in development; Goldfarb's hypothesis of two general types of etiology, one being almost purely organic and the other being almost purely psychological; Pollack's hypothesis that childhood psychosis, including schizophrenia, comprises a heterogeneous group of syndromes produced by a variety of early organic damage; and Mednick's hypothesis that schizophrenia, at least adult schizophrenia, results from genetic vulnerability exacerbated by early damage to the hippocampal region of the brain that later interferes with normal suppression of arousal to stress.

Genetic Factors

Many organic hypotheses hold that genetic factors are responsible either for specific biological abnormalities causing schizophrenia or for biological vulnerabilities that make schizophrenia likely if the individual encounters organic or psychological trauma. Most genetic research has been on adult schizophrenia, although researchers are increasingly focusing on the developmental dimension from birth through adulthood. Because the question of whether child and adult schizophrenia are etiologically related remains unanswered, it is not known whether genetic hypotheses and findings pertaining to adult schizophrenia are applicable to childhood schizophrenia. However, in our present state of ignorance, it seems prudent to consider genetic research on adult schizophrenia along with the meager existing genetic research on child schizophrenia. At the outset it can be said that chromosomal studies have pretty well ruled out major chromosomal abnormalities as a significant cause of childhood schizophrenia (Böök, Nichtern, & Gruenberg, 1963).

Genetic hypotheses have taken many forms, but they fall into the following two major categories (Rosenthal, 1970a).

1. *Monogenic-biochemical hypotheses* that hold that a single gene or set of genes leads to a specific metabolic error that causes schizophrenia. According to this view, schizophrenia exists in a qualitative fashion like color blindness, although degrees of severity in schizophrenic phenotypes may result from degrees of severity in the basic metabolic defect. Monogenic models derived from family and twin studies include that of a single, partially dominant gene (Slater, 1972), a single recessive gene (Hurst, 1972), and a pair of genes that must both be inherited together in a certain form to result in schizophrenia (Karlsson, 1972).

2. *Diathesis-stress hypotheses* hold that a general predisposition to schizophrenia rather than a specific abnormality is inherited, probably on the basis of polygenic rather than single or paired gene mechanisms. (The word *diathesis* literally means "a bodily condition predisposing to a disease.") Given the bodily predisposition, a person who has other physical liabilities and/or severe life stress will develop schizophrenia while a person who has other physical assets and/or benign life experience will not develop

schizophrenia, although he may develop milder abnormalities such as schizoid personality.

As theories have become more complex in order to take account of increasingly diverse data, the distinctions between monogenic-biochemical hypotheses and diathesis-stress hypotheses have become blurred, with most genetic hypotheses invoking some form of heredity-environment interaction to explain schizophrenia. Mednick's (1970) hypothesis that early hippocampal damage plays a causal role in individuals already genetically disposed to schizophrenia is a diathesis-stress hypothesis, as is Gottesman's (1968) hypothesis that schizophrenia is jointly determined by polygenic and environmental factors.

Comparisons of MZ and DZ Twins. Numerous studies have compared *concordance rates* for schizophrenia in monozygotic (MZ; "identical") and dizygotic (DZ; "fraternal") twins as a way of estimating the *heritability* of schizophrenia (see Chapter 5 for the rationale and techniques for estimating heritability). Table 12–1 presents a summary of 12 studies from nine countries in which heritability indices can be calculated from MZ and DZ twin rates. The figures for heritability in Table 12–1 have been calculated by the present author using the formula

$$H = \frac{\% \text{ MZ concordant} - \% \text{ DZ concordant}}{1 - \% \text{DZ concordant}}$$

Insofar as could be determined from each study, concordance rates based on only those cases definitely diagnosed as schizophrenic were employed, although many studies based their heritability estimates on cases diagnosed schizoid or borderline schizophrenic as well as those diagnosed schizophrenic. Many of the studies have also increased the concordance figures found for young adult schizophrenics by adding a percentage based on the number of nonschizophrenic individuals expected to become schizophrenic by the age of 45, the oldest age at which people are generally diagnosed schizophrenic for the first time. Although age corrections of this type are defensible (cf. Rosenthal, 1970a), these corrections, plus other corrections that tend to raise concordance and heritability estimates, were eliminated wherever possible in calculating the *H* values for Table 12–1. The values in Table 12–1 should thus be considered minimal and some are lower than those reported by the original authors.

Note in Table 12–1 that the four most recent studies yielded lower *H* values than any of the eight earlier studies. The four recent studies initially identified twins from files of large numbers of twins ("twin registers") and then tracked them down to determine which ones were schizophrenic, while the earlier studies began with individuals who were already diagnosed schizophrenic in hospital settings and then attempted to determine whether these individuals had twins who were schizophrenic. Two possible byproducts of the latter procedure are that high proportions of very severe

TABLE 12–1

Major twin studies of schizophrenia.

Study	Country	MZ Pairs		DZ Pairs		H[a]
		N	Per cent concordant	N	Per cent concordant	
Luxemburger, 1928	Germany	17	60	33	0	.60
Rosanoff, Handy, Plessert, and Brush, 1934	U. S. A., Canada	41	61	101	10	.57
Essen-Möller, 1941	Sweden	11	55	27	15	.47
Kallmann, 1946	U. S. A.	174	69	517	10	.66
Slater, 1953	England	37	68	115	11	.64
Kallmann & Roth, 1956 (Preadolescents)	U. S. A.	17	71	35	17	.65
Inouye, 1961	Japan	55	36	17	12	.27
Gottesman & Shields, 1966	England	24	42	33	9	.36
[b]Kringlen, 1968	Norway	45	27	69	4	.24
[b]Tienari, 1968	Finland	16	6	21	5	.01
[b]Fischer, Harvald, & Hauge, 1969	Denmark	21	24	41	10	.16
[b]Allen, Cohen, & Pollin, 1972	U. S. A.	95	27	125	5	.23

[a] Only cases diagnosed schizophrenic are included, although many studies added schizoid personalities, etc., in their calculations of concordance. The formula

$$H = \frac{\% \text{ MZ concordant} - \% \text{ DZ concordant}}{1 - \% \text{ DZ concordant}}$$

has been used despite the fact that formulas yielding higher H values were used in some studies (cf. Allen, Cohen, & Pollin, 1972). H values are thus minimum values for the data and lower than reported in some of the studies from which data are derived.

[b] Located twins through twin registers rather than beginning with hospitalized twins. See text for implications of this approach for producing lower concordance rates.

chronic cases were included and that twin pairs concordant for schizophrenia were more likely to be found than pairs discordant for schizophrenia. A high proportion of severe cases could maximize concordance rates because severe cases may have the highest genetic loadings for schizophrenia and/or the types of environmental backgrounds most influential in producing schizophrenia. Location of concordant pairs is also more likely if the primary sources of data (hospital records) concern people who have schizophrenia rather than people identified merely as being twins, whether or not they develop schizophrenia. Both factors could have produced greater concordance rates in the earlier studies.

On the other hand, the twin register method may miss severe and concordant cases, as the twin register study that produced the lowest concordance rates (Tienari, 1968) located well under half of the twins born in the

target population. However, both types of studies are unanimous in yielding higher concordance rates in MZ than DZ twins.

A further step taken in one of the recent twin studies was to compare the
heritability indices for schizophrenia with those for a number of organic
diseases in the same sample of twins (Pollin, 1972, employing data from the
subjects studied by Allen, Cohen, & Pollin, 1972). Although the actual H
for schizophrenia was low, H was lower still for all the organic diseases,
some of which (e.g., duodenal ulcer and diabetes) have been previously
shown to be genetically influenced. This indicates that, while the heritability of schizophrenia in this sample was low, genetic factors do play some sort
of role.

The only study of preadolescent schizophrenics yielded the second highest heritability estimate of all the studies (Kallmann & Roth, 1956), although
the exact figure is subject to the same criticisms as the figures obtained in
other early studies. When concordance rates in that study were based on all
individuals who eventually became schizophrenic, rather than on just those
who became schizophrenic by age 15, the MZ concordance rate rose to 88
per cent and the DZ rate to 23 per cent, yielding an H of .84, by far the
highest of all the studies. Unfortunately, the published report failed to
present details as to the source of the subjects, age of onset, and specific
syndromes, but the children were presumably disturbed severely enough to
have been hospitalized.

Studies of Foster Children. Another strategy for studying the relative
strength of genetic and environmental influences on schizophrenia is to compare the incidence of schizophrenia in children of schizophrenics and children of nonschizophrenics when the children are reared by foster parents.
In one study of this type, Heston (1966) followed up children who had been
born to schizophrenic women in mental hospitals. The study included only
infants who appeared normal in weight and condition at birth, who were
separated from their mothers within three days after birth, and who had
never lived with their maternal relatives. Control children from the same
foundling homes as the experimental subjects were matched to the experimental subjects for sex, type of eventual foster placement, and length of
time in child-care institutions. In addition to obtaining information from
psychiatric institutions, police, physicians, etc., it was possible to make firsthand assessments of most subjects, based on personal interviews, Minnesota
Multiphasic Personality Inventory (MMPI) scores, IQ, and social class data.
Two psychiatrists blind to the origins of the subjects made diagnoses and
rated all the data for degree of psychosocial disability.

Although agreement on precise diagnosis did not always occur, it was possible to obtain complete agreement on four general diagnostic categories:
schizophrenia, mental retardation, sociopathic personality, and neurotic personality disorder. Table 12–2 presents adult characteristics of the 47 experimental and 50 control subjects who could be located for evaluation.

It is clear from Table 12–2 that substantially more psychopathology, in-

TABLE 12–2

Characteristics of foster children born to schizophrenic and nonschizophrenic mothers.

Characteristics	With schizophrenic mothers	With nonschizophrenic mothers
Mean psychosocial disability [a]	65.2 **	80.1
Schizophrenia	10.6% *	0%
Mental retardation (IQ < 70)	8.5% *	0%
Sociopathic personality disorder	19.1% *	4%
Neurotic personality disorder	27.7% *	14%
Persons spending > 1 year in penal or psychiatric institution	23.4% **	4%
Convicted felons	14.9% *	4%
Psychiatric or behavioral discharges from armed forces	17.5% *	2%
Mean IQ	94.0	103.7
Never married > 30 years old	19.1%	8%

[a] Low score indicates much disability.

$* p \leq .05$
$** p < .01$ } for difference between groups

NOTE.—From Heston (1966).

cluding the only five cases of schizophrenia, occurred in the group having schizophrenic mothers than in the group having nonschizophrenic mothers. Altogether, 55.3 per cent of the experimental subjects showed serious psychosocial disability, compared to 18 per cent of the control group. However, of the 44.7 per cent of the experimental subjects who showed no psychosocial impairment, more had colorful life histories and creative occupations than did their control subjects.

In a further study, Heston and Denney (1968) compared the experimental and control subjects who were raised in foster families with the experimental and control subjects who were raised mainly in child-care institutions. No significant differences were found between institutionalized and family-reared groups on any of the variables listed in Table 12–2. Three of the five experimental subjects who developed schizophrenia had been raised primarily in institutions while two had been raised in families. Even the average MMPI profiles were nearly identical for the home- and institution-reared groups. The facts that all measures showed more pathology in the experimental than control group and that institutional versus family rearing seemed to make little difference were interpreted as supporting the hypothesis that genetic factors play a significant role in schizophrenia and that other forms of psychopathology are also related to the same genetic factors.

NIMH Studies. Two adoption studies have been carried out in Denmark by a group from the National Institute of Mental Health (NIMH; Rosenthal, 1972). In the first study, adoption and hospital records were used to identify individuals who were adopted and who were later diagnosed schizophrenic or borderline schizophrenic. Nonschizophrenic adoptees were then matched to the schizophrenic adoptees for sex, age, preadoption history, and socioeconomic status of the adoptive family. In the second study, the records of parents who had given up their children for adoption were searched to identify any who had been diagnosed schizophrenic (Rosenthal, Wender, Kety, Welner, & Schulsinger, 1971). The offspring of these parents, plus adopted individuals matched for sex, age, age at adoption, and socioeconomic status of adoptive parents, were assessed by interviewers blind to the status of the biological families. Both studies revealed higher frequencies of schizophrenia in individuals whose biological forebears included schizophrenics, regardless of whether schizophrenia was present or absent in the adoptive families.

Monozygotic Twins Discordant for Schizophrenia. If two individuals have identical genotypes, but only one develops schizophrenia, the two can be compared in order to determine what nongenetic characteristics differentiate them in such a way as possibly to account for the development of schizophrenia in one but not the other. Exactly this strategy is being pursued in a study at the National Institute of Mental Health (Pollin, Stabenau, Mosher, & Tupin, 1966).

It was possible to locate 11 sets of adolescent and adult twins who met the following criteria:

1. one twin had been diagnosed schizophrenic or borderline schizophrenic while the other twin was apparently not schizophrenic;
2. monozygosity was established on the basis of concordance in 28 different blood group factors;
3. both twins had been raised by their biological parents;
4. both the parents and twins were able to live temporarily at the NIMH;
5. no identifiable neurological syndrome or mental deficiency was present.

Despite their being nonschizophrenic, eight of the 11 nonschizophrenic twins were diagnosed as having fairly significant nonpsychotic personality disorders, two as having less obvious pathology, and only one as showing no evidence of psychopathology.

So far, several differences of possible etiological significance have emerged. One is that, in all 11 pairs, the schizophrenic twin weighed less at birth than the nonschizophrenic twin. Although other studies have not revealed unusually low birth weights in schizophrenics, it is generally assumed that the lower birth weight member of a twin pair was more poorly placed and received less oxygen *in utero* than the heavier twin.

A second finding was that, in nine of the 11 pairs, the mother felt that the smaller twin "needed more," fed him first, and generally gave him more praise and attention, thus treating him as if he were more vulnerable and helpless. Other findings were that the schizophrenic twins had more physical illness and injuries, especially during infancy, and showed more "soft" (equivocal) signs of neurological dysfunction than did their nonschizophrenic cotwins during adulthood. In nine of the 11 pairs, the nonschizophrenic twin was the dominant member of the pair, more competent, better organized, and more successful in school, job, home, and peer activities than his schizophrenic cotwin.

Taken together, the findings suggest that an initial biological disadvantage present at birth may have led to unusual patterns of life experience for the schizophrenic twins, beginning with more intensive but anxious mothering, greater susceptibility to physical illness, and the development of less competence and a poorer self-image.

In an attempt to identify the physiological mechanisms related to the greater vulnerability of the schizophrenic twin, Pollin (1971) has compared the twins' concordance on biochemical substances excreted in the urine while both twins were living under hospitallike conditions at the NIMH. Compared to normal controls living under the same conditions, both members of the pairs discordant for schizophrenia excreted significantly higher levels of several substances (dopamine, norepinephrine, epinephrine). However, compared to normals *and* to their nonschizophrenic cotwins, the schizophrenic twins also excreted a significantly higher level of another type of substance, 17-hydroxysteroids.

Although the evidence is in no way conclusive, Pollin interpreted his findings as tentatively suggesting that the substances found to be significantly elevated in both the schizophrenic and nonschizophrenic cotwins are related to the genotype for schizophrenia, while the substance that significantly differentiated the schizophrenic from the nonschizophrenic cotwins related to the life experience, including early organic damage, that actually precipitates schizophrenia in a genetically vulnerable individual. Later work by the same group has revealed other biochemical differences between normal control subjects and both the schizophrenic and nonschizophrenic members of the discordant twin pairs (Wyatt, Murphy, Belmaker, Cohen, Donnelly, & Pollin, 1973).

Summary of Genetic Factors. Most research on genetic factors in schizophrenia has employed adolescent and adult subjects. It is unknown whether childhood schizophrenia and adolescent-adult schizophrenia are etiologically related. The one large-scale study of twin concordance rates for preadolescent schizophrenia yielded a heritability estimate as high as similar studies of adolescent-adult schizophrenia and the highest heritability estimate of all such studies when cotwins who became schizophrenic after age 15 were counted in the concordance rates. Conflicting data have been reported on the percentage of schizophrenics among the parents of childhood schizophrenics.

Consistent evidence for genetic influences on adolescent-adult schizophrenia has come from a large number of twin studies and from studies of foster children. Two general classes of genetic hypotheses have been proposed, the *monogenic-biochemical hypotheses* and the *diathesis-stress hypotheses*. Evidence from longitudinal studies of the offspring of schizophrenic parents and from comparisons of MZ cotwins discordant for schizophrenia appears to be converging on a diathesis-stress etiology in which a combination of genetic vulnerability and early organic damage interferes with psychological development in such a manner as to produce schizophrenia in adolescence or adulthood. Whether childhood schizophrenia can be accounted for by greater genetic vulnerability, more severe organic damage, and/or more debilitating psychological stresses, or whether it is not an early form of adult schizophrenia remains to be seen.

EARLY INFANTILE AUTISM

Next to childhood schizophrenia, early infantile autism is the category of childhood psychosis that has received the most attention. It was first proposed as a distinct syndrome by Leo Kanner in 1943 after he had seen 11 children manifesting characteristics that he summarized as follows:

1. *Inability to relate* to people from the beginning of life.
2. *Extreme autistic aloneness* that ignored and shut out stimuli by treating them as if they were not there unless they reached painful proportions.
3. *Failure to assume an anticipatory posture* in preparation for being picked up.
4. *Failure to use speech to convey meaning to others*—even in the eight out of 11 autistic children who did speak, language was used primarily for naming objects and for repetition of phrases, rhymes, songs, etc.
5. *Excellent rote memory* for names, pictures, tunes, etc.
6. *Echolalia*—the literal repetition ("echoing") of phrases the child had heard.
7. *Extreme literalness* in the use of words. For example, a child who learned to say "Yes" when his father promised to put him on his shoulders if he said "Yes" then used the word yes only to mean he wanted to be placed on his father's shoulders.
8. *Reversal of personal pronouns* so that the child referred to himself as "you" and to other people as "I".
9. *Eating difficulties,* including vomiting and food refusal, during the first year of life.
10. *Extreme fear of certain loud noises and moving objects* such as vacuum cleaners, egg beaters, tricycles, elevators, etc.

11. *Monotonously repetitious noises and motions by the child.*
12. *Anxious desire for sameness* such that the child became upset when furniture, clothing, etc., was changed.
13. *Minimal variety in spontaneous activity.*
14. *A good relation to objects* such that the child could play happily with them for hours.
15. *Apparently good intellectual potential* as suggested by average or better performance on some items of intelligence tests and by intelligent facial expressions.
16. *Facial expressions* that were typically serious but showed tenseness in the presence of others and placid smiles when alone with objects.
17. *Normal physical condition.*

Kanner presented case histories of the 11 autistic children, as exemplified by the following excerpts from parental reports on Donald, a child whom Kanner first saw at the age of five years:

At the age of 1 year he could hum and sing many tunes accurately. Before he was 2 years old, he had an unusual memory for faces and names. . . . He was encouraged by the family in learning and reciting short poems, and even learned the Twenty-third Psalm and twenty-five questions and answers of the Presbyterian Catechism. The parents observed that he was not learning to ask questions or to answer questions unless they pertained to rhymes or things of this nature, and often then he would ask no question except in single words. . . . He became interested in pictures and very soon knew an inordinate number of pictures in a set of *Compton's Encyclopedia.* He knew the pictures of the presidents and knew most of the pictures of his ancestors and kinfolks on both sides of the house. He quickly learned the whole alphabet backward as well as forward and to count to 100.

It was observed at an early time that he was happiest when left alone, almost never cried to go with his mother, did not seem to notice his father's homecomings, and was indifferent to visiting relatives. . . . Donald even failed to pay the slightest attention to Santa Claus in full regalia.

He seems to be so self-satisfied. He has no apparent affection when petted. He does not observe the fact that anyone comes or goes, and never seems glad to see father or mother or any playmate. He seems almost to draw into his shell and live within himself. We once secured a most attractive little boy of the same age from an orphanage and brought him home to spend the summer with Donald, but Donald has never asked him a question nor answered a question and has never romped with him in play. . . .

In his second year, he developed a mania for spinning blocks and pans and other round objects. At the same time he had a dislike for self-propelling vehicles . . . tricycles, and swings. He is still fearful of tricycles and seems to have almost a horror of them when he is forced to ride. . . . This summer we bought him a playground slide and on the first afternoon when other children were sliding on it he would not get about it, and when we put him up to slide down it he seemed horror-struck. The next morning when nobody was present, however, he walked out, climbed the ladder, and slid down, and he has slid on it frequently since, but slides only when no other child is present. . . .

When interfered with, he had temper tantrums, during which he was destructive. He was dreadfully fearful of being spanked or switched but could not associate his misconduct with his punishment [Kanner, 1943, pp. 217–18].

In formulating a conception of a strange new syndrome such as autism and in beginning to search for the etiology and appropriate treatment, one of the first questions to arise is, what typically happens to the children as they grow older? In order to throw some light on this question, Kanner and his colleagues have reported follow-ups of 96 children diagnosed autistic (Eisenberg, 1956; Kanner, 1971; Kanner, Rodrigues & Ashenden, 1972). Most of the children ended up under varying degrees of custodial care, but 11 achieved adequate social adjustment. Three of the 11 obtained college degrees, three junior college educations, one was doing well in college, and the other four did not go beyond high school or special education. Their occupations included bank teller, lab technician, duplicating machine operator, accountant, and several types of unskilled work.

The outcomes showed no relation to whether psychiatric treatment had been received. The best single predictor of good outcome was the development of useful speech by age five. Neither the 10 males nor the one female showed spontaneous interest in the opposite sex or in marriage, although several had unsuccessfully experimented with very limited dating.

Kanner et al interpreted the attempts at dating as being related to the one thing that appeared to differentiate the 11 from the other autistic children who had useful speech by age five, viz., that the 11 underwent an apparent change during their early to middle teens. They all seemed to become aware of their peculiarities and to make a conscious effort to do something about them. Realizing, for example, that young people were expected to have friends, they made use of their obsessive preoccupations and specialized abilities to try to win approval from others, particularly in hobby clubs and special interest groups. Kanner et al interpreted their sporadic attempts at dating as stemming from the same sense of obligation to conform, although failures to achieve any real involvement apparently did not cause displeasure.

Donald, the boy whose case was described above, showed one of the best outcomes of all:

In 1942 [when he was nine], his parents placed him on a tenant farm. . . . When I visited there in May 1945, I was amazed at the wisdom of the couple who took care of him. They managed to give him goals for his stereotypies. They made him use his preoccupation with measurements by having him dig a well and report on its depth. When he kept collecting dead birds and bugs, they gave him a spot for a "graveyard" and had him put up markers; on each he wrote a first name, the type of animal as a middle name, and the farmer's last name, e.g.: "John Snail Lewis. Born, date unknown. Died, (date on which he found the animal)." When he kept counting rows of corn over and over, they had him count the rows while plowing them. . . . It was obvious that Mr. and Mrs. Lewis [the farm couple] were very fond of him and just as obvious that they were gently firm. He attended a country school where his peculiarities were accepted and where he made good scholastic progress.

The rest of the story is contained in a letter from Donald's mother, dated April 6, 1970:

"Don is now 36 years old, a bachelor living at home with us. . . . Since receiving his A.B. degree in 1958, he has worked in the local bank as a teller. He is satisfied to remain a teller, having no real desire for promotion. He meets the public there real well. His chief hobby is golf, playing four or five times a week at the local country club. . . . Other interests are Kiwanis Club (served as president one term), Jaycees, Investment Club, Secretary of Presbyterian Sunday School. He is dependable, accurate, shows originality in editing the Jaycee program information, is even-tempered but has a mind of his own. . . . He owns his second car, likes his independence. His room includes his own TV, record player, and many books. In College his major was French and he showed a particular aptitude for languages. Don is a fair bridge player but never initiates a game. Lack of initiative seems to be his most serious drawback. He takes very little part in social conversation and shows no interest in the opposite sex.

"While Don is not completely normal, he has taken his place in society very well, so much better than we ever hoped for. If he can maintain status quo, I think he has adjusted sufficiently to take care of himself [Kanner, 1971, pp. 121–22]." [3]

The Problem of Definition

Kanner's Syndrome. Strict adherence to the descriptive criteria provided by Kanner for identifying cases of early infantile autism (also known as *Kanner's syndrome*) should have made possible the clear communication among workers that is necessary for the accumulation of data leading to discoveries of etiology and methods for prevention and treatment. Such was the case with Down's syndrome, where workers could at least agree on whether they were discussing children having the same descriptive characteristics, whether or not they agreed with Down's theory that the syndrome represented an evolutionary throwback to the "mongol race."

Unfortunately, such clarity of communication did not follow upon the beginning made by Kanner. As we have seen in the discussion of childhood schizophrenia, the term "autism" has been used by many authors as a virtual synonym for childhood schizophrenia and childhood psychosis in general. Kanner (1943) himself mentioned that some of the characteristics of early infantile autism resembled childhood schizophrenia, but he explicitly pointed out ways in which it appeared to differ from "all other known instances of childhood schizophrenia [p. 248]." These differences included extreme aloneness from the very beginning of life, as contrasted with a *change* from relatively normal behavior considered to characterize schizophrenia; the purposeful and "intelligent" relation to objects but exclusion

[3] L. Kanner, "Follow-up Study of Eleven Autistic Children Originally Reported in 1943," *Journal of Autism and Childhood Schizophrenia*, 1971, 1 (121–22). © 1971 by the Scripta Publishing Corporation and reprinted by permission.

of people; and the extreme desire for sameness, coupled with extraordinary memories for how things were arranged, no matter how disorganized the arrangements.

One problem in attempting to employ a new category such as Kanner's is that of determining whether all the characteristics are necessary before a child should be regarded as belonging to the category. In the case of Kanner's syndrome, the age at which a child is evaluated obviously plays a role in determining which characteristics are relevant. For example, if the child is below the age of about two, the presence or absence of speech cannot be a very telling criterion. If he is above the age of about three, but does not speak, peculiarities of speech such as echolalia and reversal of personal pronouns are not relevant criteria.

Kanner has been concerned with these problems and has designated two characteristics as the cardinal symptoms of early infantile autism:

1. *Extreme self-isolation, present from the first years of life,* and,
2. *obsessive insistence on the preservation of sameness* (Eisenberg & Kanner, 1956).

All the children Kanner has diagnosed as autistic have also had distortions in language, ranging from lack of speech or delayed onset of speech through echolalia, pronominal reversal, and highly metaphorical language, apparently employed with little communicative intent, but Kanner (1954) believes that the speech peculiarities may be secondary to the two cardinal symptoms. Another aspect of Kanner's definition of the syndrome is that none of his cases had organic pathology considered sufficient to account for the behavioral syndrome.

Other Attempts to Delineate Early Infantile Autism. Although the American Psychiatric Association's *Diagnostic and Statistical Manual* (1968) does not make provision for any child psychoses other than childhood schizophrenia, the GAP classification system includes the following description of early infantile autism, which generally follows the lines of Kanner's descriptions:

Early infantile autism appears to have its onset during the first few months or the first year of life, with failure on the part of the infant to develop an attachment to the mother figure. The infant remains aloof, showing little apparent awareness of human contact, and is preoccupied with inanimate objects. Speech development is delayed or absent; when it appears, speech is not employed appropriately or for purposes of communication. The child shows a strong need for the maintenance of sameness and tends to resist change, responding with marked outbursts of temper or acute and intense anxiety when routines are altered. Sleeping and feeding problems are often severe. Stereotyped motor patterns, often bizarre or primitive in nature, are frequent. Intellectual development may be normal or advanced or it may be restricted and uneven in many areas [p. 253].

Several workers have devised checklists in order to obtain more precise delineation of the autistic syndrome and more reliable discrimination of autistic children from other abnormal children. One of the most widely used checklists of this type is designed to be filled out by the child's parents (Rimland, 1964). The items include many specific variants of the characteristics originally noted by Kanner (1943). The checklist is scored by subtracting the number of responses considered to be uncharacteristic of autistic children from the number of responses considered to be characteristic of them.

Rimland (1971) has reported an analysis of checklists filled out for 2,218 psychotic children who had been diagnosed autistic in over 30 different countries. He found that only 215 (9.7 per cent) met his criterion for autism, a score of 20 or more (i.e., 20 more autistic than nonautistic characteristics). The finding that only about 10 per cent of the children seemed to be "truly autistic" agreed with Kanner's impression that only about 10 per cent of the children sent to him as autistic actually fit his syndrome of early infantile autism. Many of the children had received a large variety of diagnoses, including deafness, schizophrenia, symbiotic psychosis, retardation, brain damage, and "emotionally disturbed," and there had been little agreement among diagnosticians.

DeMyer, Churchill, Pontius, and Gilkey (1971) have compared scores on Rimland's checklist and two others (Lotter, 1966; Polan & Spencer, 1959) for children who had independently been classified as autistic, schizophrenic, or nonpsychotic (brain-damaged or retarded emotionally disturbed). The DeMyer et al criteria for autism were:

1. Emotional withdrawal from people before age three.
2. Lack of speech for communication.
3. Nonfunctional, repetitive use of objects.
4. Failure to engage in role play alone or with other children.

These criteria differ from Kanner's fundamental criteria in including children whose withdrawal begins as late as age three and in omitting obsessive insistence on preservation of sameness. DeMyer et al also divided their autistic group into what they designated as "primary or higher functioning autism" and "secondary or lower functioning autism."

DeMyer et al found that the correlations among the Rimland, Lotter, and Polan-Spencer checklists ranged from the .40's to the low .60's, indicating just a moderate degree of agreement among them. Only Rimland's checklist produced mean scores that were highest for DeMyer et al's primary autistic group, next highest for their secondary autistic group, third highest for their schizophrenic group, and lowest for their nonpsychotic group, the ordering that best indicates agreement between classification by DeMyer et al and the checklist scores. However, even DeMyer et al's primary autistic children received a mean score on Rimland's checklist of only 1.63, far below his suggested cutoff point of 20. As DeMyer et al concluded, good agreement is still lacking among even the more objective approaches to the descriptive definition of autism and further work must be aimed toward making descriptions of children diagnosed autistic as explicit and objective as possible.

Family Characteristics

Parental Education and Occupation. The most striking family characteristics noted by Kanner in his reports on autistic children were that all the parents were highly intelligent, most were very obsessive, and few were really warmhearted. Among the fathers of his first 100 cases were 31 businessmen, 12 engineers, 11 physicians (including five psychiatrists), 10 lawyers, 8 tradesmen, 5 chemists, 5 military officers, 5 PhD's, 4 writers, 2 teachers, 2 rabbis, and one each a psychologist, dentist, publisher, professor of forestry, and photographer (Kanner, 1954).

Kanner also noted that there was remarkably little severe mental illness or marital disruption in the families of the autistic children. As will be discussed in later sections, the questions of parental intelligence, attainments, pathology, and marital stability figure prominently in various theories of etiology. It is, therefore, important to consider systematic research designed to assess Kanner's findings.

Four studies have reported that the educational levels of parents of autistic children were well above those for comparison groups of other severely disturbed children (Lowe, 1966 [1]; Lotter, 1967; Rimland, 1968; Treffert, 1970), but not nearly to the degree Kanner reported for his first 100 cases.

However, a fifth study showed no significant differences between the occupational, educational, or income levels of parents of autistic and other disturbed children (Ritvo, Cantwell, Johnson, Clements, Benbrook, Slagle, Kelly, & Ritz, 1971). One possible explanation is that the diagnosis of autism in the latter study was not based primarily on Kanner's criteria but on evidence of "perceptual inconstancy" which the authors hypothesized to be the fundamental characteristic of a wide range of childhood psychoses (Ornitz & Ritvo, 1968).

Intellectual Abilities and Values of Parents. Kanner's impression that the parents of autistic children were of exceptional intelligence has been borne out to some degree by Lotter's (1967) finding that parents of autistic children were superior to those of nonautistic disturbed children on both a vocabulary test and a nonverbal measure of general intelligence. Although the differences were related to the higher social-class status found for the parents of autistic children, there were also differences favoring the parents of autistic children within social-class groups.

In another study, the verbal IQs of the fathers of autistic children were found to be nonsignificantly higher (mean IQ $= 116$) than those of fathers of normal children matched for socioeconomic status (mean IQ $= 108.9$), but significantly higher than those of fathers of brain-damaged disturbed

[1] Lowe included some symbiotic children in her autistic group.

children not matched for socioeconomic status (mean IQ = 100.5; Allen, DeMyer, Norton, Pontius, & Yang, 1971). Mothers of autistic children had nonsignificantly higher scores (mean = 109) than mothers of either of the other groups (mean IQs = 108.9, 103.8, respectively). Few of the parents in either group were found to be idea-oriented, intellectual people, and there were no differences among the groups in this respect.

Marital Stability. Lowe (1966) reported that 11 per cent of autistic children came from broken homes, compared with 15 per cent of schizophrenic children, and 50 per cent of other emotionally disturbed children. Schain and Yannet (1960) found that 10 per cent of the parents of autistic children were separated, although they made no comparisons with other groups. While not as high as reported by Kanner, marital stability among parents of autistic children thus appears to be relatively high, but this may be a byproduct of the high occupational and educational status of the parents.

Mental Disorders in Parents and Relatives. Kanner's (1954) estimate that less than five per cent of the close relatives of autistic children were psychotic or severely neurotic has been generally supported by Lotter (1967) and Treffert (1970), although their comparisons with other groups do not necessarily support Kanner's contention that this rate of mental disturbance is exceptionally low. The rate of serious mental illness in relatives of Lotter's comparison group of nonautistic handicapped children was only .005 per cent, compared to 3.2 per cent for the autistic children. No siblings of nonautistic children were seriously disturbed, compared to 4.8 per cent for the autistic group. Treffert found the percentage of parents who had some kind of psychiatric treatment to be greater in his autistic group (23 per cent) than in his nonautistic psychotic group (19.1 per cent) or organically handicapped disturbed group (13.5 per cent), although the percentage of parents seriously enough disturbed to have *inpatient* treatment was lower in the autistic group (7.1 per cent) than in either of the other groups (13.4 per cent and 9.4 per cent, respectively). Schain and Yannet (1960) reported that four per cent of the parents of autistic children had been diagnosed psychotic and that four per cent of the siblings had some form of mental retardation, while Weber (1970), in Germany, found 2.3 per cent of the parents to be psychotic, but no comparisons with other groups were made in either study.

Child-rearing Practices. Extensive parent interviews on child-rearing practices and early infant characteristics have been carried out as part of a large-scale comparison of autistic children with matched normal and brain-damaged children (DeMyer, Pontius, Norton, Barton, Allen, & Steele, 1972). The sample included 26 children diagnosed autistic and seven diagnosed schizophrenic who had developed severe autistic symptoms before their third birthday, although no separate breakdowns of results for the autistics and schizophrenics were provided.

It was found that all three groups of parents provided at least average warmth, attention, and stimulation to their children during infancy, although the parents of the brain-damaged children were significantly lower than the other two groups in these characteristics. The parents of autistic children were next lowest but they were more like the parents of normal children than of brain-damaged children and they did not differ significantly in total scores from parents of normal children. However, in ratings based on reports of the child's early behavior, both the autistic and brain-damaged children scored significantly lower than the normal children on a factor-analytically derived dimension of sociability. This dimension included cuddliness, strength of reaction to weaning, raising arms to be picked up, need for attention, and alertness. Thus, while behavior of the parents of autistic children was apparently like that of parents of normal children, the behavior of autistic infants was like that of brain-damaged infants.

Parental Psychological Characteristics. Singer and Wynne (1963) carried out an intriguing comparison of the Rorschach and Thematic Apperception Test (TAT) responses of parents of 20 children, most diagnosed as autistic (the rest as schizophrenic) and 20 neurotic children matched to the "autistic" group for demographic characteristics. A psychologist blind as to which couples had autistic or neurotic children correctly classified 17 out of 20 couples in each group on the basis of their test responses. The outstanding characteristics of the responses of autistic children's parents were their cynical outlooks, passivity and apathy about interacting with other people, superficiality, obsessive intellectual distance, and dissatisfaction. While the possibility remains that these parental themes arose as *reactions* to having an autistic child, the fact that they were sufficiently conspicuous to permit blind differentiation from responses of matched parents who also had difficult children suggests that they are enduring characteristics of the parents of autistic children.

Singer and Wynne interpreted their findings as indicating that, when unempathic autistic-type parents have an infant with low innate capacity to elicit responsiveness, a crippling of ego development will begin at birth, resulting in autism. However, the data are also consistent with the hypothesis that the characteristics of the parents are not *causal* in the child's autism, but are milder manifestations of a basic defect in relatedness with which they too were born.

Another study has shown significant differences between the Rorschach responses of the parents of autistic (and symbiotic) children and the parents of normal children (Ogdon, Bass, Thomas, & Lordi, 1968). However, the authors acknowledged that the responses by parents of autistic children did not necessarily imply that parental behavior causes autism. In fact, two Rorschach indices showed the parents of autistic children to be slightly *less* perfectionistic and obsessive and to have *less* interpersonal anxiety and social isolation than the parents of normal children.

Summary of Family Characteristics. Kanner has stressed the following characteristics of parents of autistic children: exceptionally high intelligence and educational and occupational achievement; obsessiveness and coldness; exceptionally low rates of marital disruption and of serious mental illness. Later studies have confirmed that parents of autistic children tend to be higher in occupation and education, perform better on intelligence tests, and have lower rates of marital disruption than do parents of other severely disturbed children, although the parents have not been as exceptional in these respects as Kanner reported. Low rates of severe mental illness in the families of autistic children have also been found, but these rates have not been very different from those in the families of other severely disturbed children.

Parents of autistic children have not been found to differ in child-rearing practices from parents of normal children, although both groups were more attentive, warm, and stimulating than parents of emotionally immature brain-damaged children.

Compared to responses by parents of neurotic children, projective test responses by parents of autistic children have suggested more cynicism, apathy about interpersonal relationships, obsessive intellectual distance, and dissatisfaction. Projective test responses by parents of autistic children have also been found to differ significantly from responses by parents of normal children, but not to indicate more obsessiveness or isolation in personal relationships than for parents of normals. There is no evidence that the personality characteristics of the parents play a causal role in autism.

Neurobiological Characteristics

Kanner (1943) concluded his original report as follows:

> We must . . . assume that these children have come into the world with innate inability to form the usual, biologically provided affective contact with people, just as other children come into the world with innate physical or intellectual handicaps. If this assumption is correct, a further study of our children may help to furnish concrete criteria regarding the still diffuse notions about the constitutional components of emotional reactivity. For here we seem to have pure-culture examples of *inborn autistic disturbances of affective contact* [p. 250; italics original].

Despite his clear statement that he assumed a basically biological etiology for autism, Kanner has often been incorrectly cited as blaming autism on the "refrigerator" characteristics of the parents. Psychogenic theories that blamed autism upon the refrigerator personalities of the parents held sway until the early 1960s (e.g., Despert, 1951; Rank, 1949). However, the research reported above on family characteristics has cast doubt both on the universality of such characteristics in parents of autistic children and on the possibility that such parental characteristics could be exclusively responsible for a condition as unusual and severe as autism. The fact that autism rarely occurs in more than one child of a family casts further doubt on a purely psychogenic hypothesis. Even the most avid proponents of psychogenic hypotheses now suggest that a constitutional vulnerability may be a necessary condition for the development of autism (e.g., Bettelheim, 1967). However, agreement that biological factors may be necessary or that autism results from some kind of organism-environment interaction does not by itself tell us what the specific etiological factors may be, how to prevent them, or how to help the afflicted children.

Neurological Factors. Like Kanner, Lotter (1967) and Treffert (1970) found low frequencies of birth complications, abnormal EEGs, and other evidence for neurological damage, as compared with other groups of severely disturbed children. Schain and Yannet (1960) reported that eight per cent of their autistic children definitely had neurological abnormalities, although there was little definite evidence for organic damage in the rest. However, an unexpected finding was that 42 per cent had seizures at some time during their lives, compared to an expected rate of about seven per cent among children in general.

Weber (1970) found definite evidence of brain damage in 41 per cent of her cases, although this evidence probably included seizures, since these were not reported separately. Both the Schain-Yannet and Weber studies differ from the former ones in dealing only with institutionalized groups, in having no direct comparison groups, and in finding much smaller boy–girl ratios (about 1.5:1) than the 3 to 4:1 ratio typically reported. The restriction of the samples to institutionalized groups could account for the finding of a higher proportion of seizures and other signs of damage, since children with these problems would be most likely to be institutionalized. The lower boy–girl ratios might also suggest that, among the children most difficult to manage and most likely to be damaged, girls are more frequent than among children with the less difficult-to-manage degrees of the disorder and less evidence of neurological damage.

Three other studies have reported high rates of seizures or other evidence for neurological damage in children referred to as "autistic," but the descriptions of the children indicate that many did not manifest Kanner's syndrome (Bender, 1969; Gubbay, Lobascher, & Kingerlee, 1970; Rutter & Bartak, 1971).

Taking another approach, Chess (1971) ascertained the incidence of autism in 243 children who were known to have been infected with rubella (German measles) *in utero*. Seventy-nine per cent had major birth defects, including visual, hearing, neurological, and cardiac handicaps. Ten of the children, all with organic defects, were diagnosed autistic, for a rate of 412 per 10,000—far above the rates found in general populations, which have ranged from .7 per 10,000 (Treffert, 1970) to 2.1 per 10,000 (Lotter, 1966). Another nine children were diagnosed as "partially autistic."

Since Chess's diagnoses of autism appear to have followed Kanner's criteria quite closely, and since the rate of autism was so much higher than generally found, it appears that congenital organic defects *can* play a role in the etiology of autism. However, since most autistic children in other studies have not manifested obvious organic defects like those of the children with rubella, the findings do not tell us whether prenatal central nervous system damage is a necessary and/or sufficient causal factor in autism.

Biochemical Factors. Studies of biochemical variables in autistic children have only recently begun and no findings with confirmed etiological significance have yet been reported. However, a few studies have reported findings that may in some way be related to the etiology of autism. One such finding was that, under certain well-controlled conditions, blood *platelets* (colorless discs carried in the blood) of 11 out of 13 autistic children scoring above 20 on Rimland's scale gave off a chemical amine (5-hydroxy-tryptamine) at much higher rates than did the platelets of normals or of psychotic children scoring lower on Rimland's scale (Boullin, Coleman, & O'Brien, 1970; Boullin, Coleman, O'Brien, & Rimland, 1971). The finding was interpreted as suggesting that defective binding of this amine in the brain may be related to the etiology of autism.

It has also been found that the nervous systems of a group of "autistic" children showed responses unlike those of either normals or schizophrenics to certain chemical substances in such a way as to suggest an underlying cerebral defect that is aggravated by normal chemical responses to stress and by dietary characteristics (Goodwin, Cowen, & Goodwin, 1971). However, all the children in this study had evidence of organic damage and it is not clear whether they fit Kanner's criteria in other respects.

Summary of Neurobiological Characteristics. With broad samples of autistic children matching Kanner's criteria, standard indices of neurological damage, such as pre- and perinatal difficulties, neurological signs, seizures, and abnormal EEGs, have generally supported Kanner's impression of low rates of abnormality. Studies employing Kanner's criteria but restricted to institutionalized children have reported higher rates of neurological dysfunction and lower boy-girl ratios. Still higher rates of neurological dysfunction have been reported in studies that have not adhered closely to Kanner's criteria for autism. An exceptionally high rate (4 per cent) of autism in children known to be prenatally afflicted with rubella suggests that an organic factor of this type can lead to autism. Some recent studies have obtained biochemical differences between autistic children and normal and other psychotic children, but no etiological role has been confirmed for these differences.

Genetic Factors

Chromosomal studies have not revealed pathological abnormalities in autistic children (Judd & Mandell, 1968; Weber, 1970). The extreme rarity of autism has precluded large-scale twin studies of heritability and the low frequency of severe psychiatric disorder in the siblings and families of autistic children has suggested that it is not transmitted via simple

Mendelian mechanisms. Reports on small numbers of twins have indicated that most, but not all, MZ twins are concordant for autism (Judd & Mandell, 1968; Weber, 1970).

A number of genetic hypotheses have been proposed. Several have postulated that autism involves an aberration related to genes for the high intelligence often reported in parents of autistic children. Rimland (1964), for example, has proposed that intelligence depends upon the volume of blood circulating in the brain. He contends that infants who have inherited genes for exceptionally high blood circulation in the brain may be vulnerable to brain damage caused by atmospheric oxygen and even more so to the high concentrations of oxygen used medically with newborns. Rimland has suggested that the damage caused by oxygen in such cases is limited to areas of the brain, particularly the reticular system, that may be responsible for the integration of certain classes of stimulation.

One possible genetic model for an intelligence-related disposition to autism is highly compatible with a polygenic model for IQ in which intelligence-enhancing alleles have additive effects (cf. Chapter 7). If autism is assumed to depend upon a genotype comprising a very high proportion of intelligence-enhancing alleles, then two parents, each of whose alleles for intelligence are nearly all intelligence-enhancing, would be the most likely people to produce an autistic child. Only a small proportion of the children of such parents would have the autistic genotype because only a small proportion would inherit the maximum number of intelligence-enhancing alleles. Such parents would not be the only ones who could produce a child with the autistic genotype, because, as demonstrated in Chapter 7, parents with smaller proportions of intelligence-enhancing alleles can occasionally produce offspring with exceptionally high proportions of intelligence-enhancing alleles.

Such a model is supported by what now seem to be well-established findings that the mean level of intellectual accomplishment among parents of autistic children is above average, that some parents of autistic children are not above average, and that autism in more than one child of a family is rare. A somewhat analogous model has been proposed for schizophrenia by Karlsson (1972) on the basis of genealogical studies in Iceland. Karlsson hypothesizes that nonschizophrenic people carrying part of the genotype for schizophrenia are likely to be especially talented, while those with the complete genotype are likely to develop clinical schizophrenia.

Bio-behavioral Studies

Such striking behavioral characteristics as lack of eye contact, insistence on sameness, and preference for inanimate objects over humans have recently begun to receive systematic study in order to determine how primary they are and how they may be related to organic or psychological abnormalities in autistic children. To minimize a persistent source of confusion, only those studies in which the subjects clearly met Kanner's criteria will be discussed.

Levels of Physiological Arousal. S. J. and Corinne Hutt and their colleagues have carried out some of the most extensive bio-behavioral studies of children who appear to fit Kanner's criteria. In one study, autistic and nonautistic disturbed children were individually observed when alone in an empty room, when alone with colored blocks, when with the blocks plus a familiar woman who sat passively in a corner, and when the woman tried to engage the child in building a standard design with the blocks (Hutt, Hutt, Lee, & Ounsted, 1965).

Except in the empty room, the autistic children showed significantly shorter visual fixations and durations of manipulatory activity than the nonautistic children. The autistic children also spent much of their time scanning the environment rather than fixating on anything in particular and showed much less constructive block play and approached and fixated on the adult less than did the nonautistic children. Using telemetric methods whereby a tiny radio transmitter attached to the child's collar sent EEG data to recorders, it was found that the autistic children's EEG patterns became progressively more indicative of high arousal and behavior became more stereotyped as the environment became more complex from the first to the third condition.

In a later study, Hutt and Hutt (1970) observed the behavior and monitored the telemetered EEG of another autistic child as he was introduced to an unfamiliar room. When first placed in the room, the child "froze" motionless, staring straight ahead. He then made repetitious sterotyped motions with his fingers. After 20 minutes in the room, his flat irregular EEG began to give way to a more normal, rhythmic pattern and he began to move slowly around the room. After 10 30-minute sessions in the same situation, more regular EEG activity occurred even when the child first entered the room, but stereotyped gestures and desynchronized EEG activity continued to reappear if an adult entered the room.

Autistic children were also observed to avoid systematically a new toy and to increase their stereotyped behavior after it was placed in a room with them. They increased their stereotyped behavior as environmental complexity increased, while retarded children showed less stereotyped behavior as environmental stimulation increased. The authors suggested that the stereotyped behaviors and the disorganized EEGs in novel situations indicated that autistic children may be in a chronic state of high physiological arousal that is exacerbated by novelty. The stereotyped activity may be an attempt to cope with the excessive arousal.

The possibility that autistic children are in chronic states of abnormal arousal has received considerable attention and it has been hypothesized that much of their behavior (e.g., apparent insensitivity to sights, sounds, and people, insistence on preservation of sameness, repetitive activity) consists of defensive maneuvers against further arousal. However, in contrast to Hutt and Hutt's suggestion that chronic high arousal is a central problem, it has also been suggested that autistic children are abnormally *hypo*aroused (*under*aroused) because of a combination of a biologically determined barrier to stimulation and a lack of stimulation from parents (Schopler, 1965).

Combining the two possibilities of over- and underarousal, DesLauriers and Carlson (1969) have suggested that *some* autistic children suffer from chronic *hyper*arousal while others suffer from chronic *hypo*arousal. On the basis of Routtenberg's (1968) proposal that two neurological systems reciprocally regulate consciousness and levels of arousal, DesLauriers and Carlson have hypothesized that those autistic children who are hyperactive and irregular in eating and sleeping are defective in the limbic-midbrain arousal system. This system is believed to mediate reward and positive affect and to suppress the activity of the other arousal system, the ascending reticular activating system (ARAS). The ARAS is hypothesized to be the source of drive energy and activation in the brain.

According to DesLauriers and Carlson, hypoactive autistic children, often described as exceptionally "good" and placid babies, are defective not only in the limbic-midbrain system that normally inhibits the activity of the ARAS, but are defective in having an ARAS that is subnormal in its activity. Thus, like the hyperactive children, they are defective in the arousal system that mediates affect, but they are also defective in the arousal system that mediates attention and alertness. An effect common to both types of children is that there is a barrier to normal levels of affective stimulation, although the hyperaroused group may experience nonaffective stimulation as excessive while the hypoaroused group is relatively unaware of any kind of stimulation.

The existence of two types of arousal defect might explain Hutt and Hutt's (1970) finding that, once autistic children approached a novel toy that could be made to emit sounds by manipulating a lever in a certain way, they chose to manipulate the lever to produce the sounds. Similarly, Metz (1967) found that, when left alone with a lever-operated apparatus that could produce sounds of different volume, autistic children chose significantly higher volumes than schizophrenic or normal children. Perhaps the autistic children in both studies were predominately of the hypoactive type who sought more stimulation.

Gaze Aversion. One of the most striking characteristics of children who clearly meet Kanner's criteria is that they systematically avoid looking directly into other people's eyes. On the rare occasions when they do look toward a person's face, they appear to be looking "through" or beyond him rather than looking right at him as normals do.

In an experiment designed to determine whether certain facial configurations elicited more avoidance than others, the five models shown in Fig. 12–2 were mounted on stands around the periphery of an empty room familiar to the subjects (Hutt & Ounsted, 1970). Autistic and nonautistic

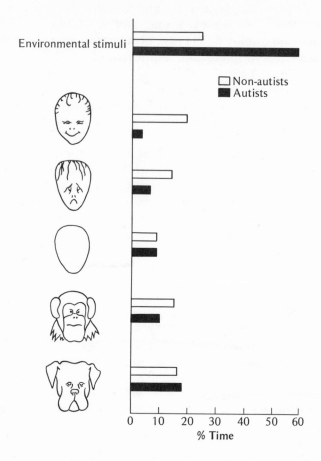

Fig. 12–2. Percentage of time spent by autistic and nonautistic disturbed children inspecting face models and environmental stimuli (e.g., room fixtures). From Hutt and Ounsted (1970), p. 107. © 1970 by Pergamon Press and reprinted by permission.

disturbed children were individually observed in the room with the model faces for a 10-minute session. As Fig. 12–2 indicates, the autistic children spent significantly less time than the nonautistic children looking at the human faces and significantly higher proportions of their time looking at fixtures in the room (lights, windows, faucets) than looking at the facial stimuli.

In another experiment, Hutt and Ounsted (1970) found that autistic children made more approaches to a model face having no eyes than one having no mouth. On the basis of ethological evidence for the importance of eye contact in social communication among humans and members of other species, Hutt and Ounsted concluded that autistic children's avoidance of eye contact has a severely disruptive effect on their social relations with other people and that it may be a technique for avoiding exacerbation of their hyperaroused state.

The systematic avoidance of eye contact and faces in general may help to explain another interesting finding. Small, DeMyer, and Milstein (1971) recorded EEG responses in autistic and normal children as slide photographs of an unfamiliar woman, an unfamiliar child, the subject's mother, and the subject himself were projected. EEGs of normal children showed different responses to the different stimuli, while the EEGs of autistic children did not. The finding was interpreted as being compatible with both hyper- and hypoarousal hypotheses, because hyperarousal might have precluded further measurable arousal when the stimuli were presented, while hypo- arousal might have made the child unaware of the stimuli. However, an- other possibility is that the autistic children simply avoided attending to the facial stimuli, although this may in turn have resulted from an abnormal state of arousal.

Perceptual Handicaps. Another line of bio-behavioral thinking is that autistic children may have some kind of perceptual defect. This possibility is suggested by the fact that many autistic children are thought to be deaf because of their lack of responsiveness to sounds during infancy. Other autistic children show unusual behavioral mannerisms like those observed in blind children. Figure 12–3 illustrates mannerisms characteristic of blind children—eye-rubbing, rolling the eyes to the extremes of their sockets, and walking on tip-toe—occurring in a blind child and in autistic children.

Despite showing behavioral characteristics of perceptually handicapped children, autistic children have not generally been found to be impaired on standard tests of hearing and vision. Research on their responses to stimuli in a single sensory modality has also failed to reveal significant defects, al- though performance in associating cues in one modality with cues in an- other sensory modality is poor (Bryson, 1970; Lovaas, Schreibman, Koegel, & Rehm, 1971). Whether this difficulty in cross-modal association is a pri- mary factor in autism or secondary to other abnormalities is unknown.

Summary of Bio-behavioral Studies. Various kinds of data have been interpreted as indicating that autistic children are in abnormal states of arousal, either hyper- or hypoarousal, or, according to DesLauriers and Carlson, hyperarousal in some autistic children and hypoarousal in others. The arousal hypotheses have in common that they attribute many odd be- haviors of autistic children to a blocking out of normal stimuli, especially social stimuli, although autistic children have been found to select rela- tively high-volume sounds when given a choice. Systematic aversion to faces and models of faces has been demonstrated. Despite behavioral similarities to blind and deaf children, autistic children have not been found defective in vision or hearing, although their association of cues from one sense modality with those of another sense modality appears poor.

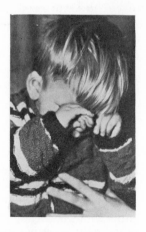

(a) Blind, nonautistic child

(b) Elisabeth, aged 3 years,
7 months, autistic

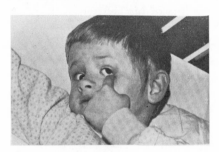

(c) Diana, aged 5 years,
10 months, autistic

(d) Holger, aged 3 years,
8 months, autistic

(e) Cornelia, aged 3 years,
2 months, autistic

Fig. 12–3. Autistic mannerisms resembling those of blind children. From Weber (1970), pp. 55, 56, 63, 74.

SYMBIOTIC PSYCHOSIS

The concept of *symbiotic psychosis* was first proposed by Margaret Mahler (1952). She defined it as a failure of the child to move beyond the symbiotic relationship with his mother which normally prevails during infancy. Employing a psychoanalytic approach, Mahler hypothesized that the child fails to develop a mental representation of the mother as a separate, outside object. Instead, the representation of the mother remains fused with that of the self as part of a delusion of omnipotence. Mahler reported that the symbiotic child appears relatively normal during the first year of life, but his disturbance becomes apparent at points when maturation of the ego would normally enable him to master new aspects of reality independent of his mother. When his own development challenges him with separation from his mother, the child's illusion of symbiotic omnipotence is threatened and he reacts to separation with panic, usually between the ages of two and one-half to five years.

Mahler believes that infantile psychoses, whether autistic or symbiotic, usually involve a constitutional predisposition toward inherent ego deficiency, although they may in some cases result from repeated severe traumas during early infancy (Mahler, 1952, 1965; Mahler & Furer, 1972). The ego deficiency causes the child to remain alienated from reality or to be able to adhere to reality only through delusional symbiotic fusion with his mother image. Mahler also believes that parent behavior can play a role by interfering with the separation and individuation process that normally ends infantile symbiosis, but that the degree of parent contribution is difficult to ascertain in individual cases. Mahler (1965) contends that autistic symptoms in many cases are actually secondary formations aimed at restoration of omnipotent oneness with the symbiotic mother.

Although the concept of symbiotic psychosis has gained a place in the literature on child psychopathology, there has been little systematic research on it and the number of cases reported is very small. One prominent child psychiatrist has stated that few psychiatrists use the diagnosis and that he has himself seen only one child who might be considered a case of symbiotic psychosis (Eisenberg, 1967). Only two cases were found among 676 disturbed children evaluated at a children's psychiatric hospital (McDermott, Harrison, Schrager, Lindy, & Killins, 1967). Since Mahler's concept of symbiotic psychosis includes children with autistic symptoms, children who might be considered by some to be primarily autistic and by others to be primarily symbiotic are sometimes lumped together as "autistic and/or symbiotic" (e.g., Lowe, 1966).

The category designated as *interactional psychotic disorder* in the GAP classification system probably represents the most general consensus as to the description of symbiotic psychosis, although again little research has been done on this broader conception. GAP defines *interactional psychotic disorder* as follows:

Interactional psychotic disorder: This category covers children with symbiotic psychosis; the group referred to is a wider one, however, embracing other cases with somewhat different features, and symbiotic parent-child relationships may be seen in disorders other than psychoses. Many of these are children who by their histories seem to have developed reasonably adequately for the first year or two of life, with awareness of or attachment to the mother figure appearing during the first year. Subsequently the child may show unusual dependence upon the mother in the form of an intensification and prolongation of the attachment, apparently failing to master successfully the step of separation and individuation.

In the second to fourth or fifth year, the onset of the psychotic disorder occurs, ordinarily in relation to some real or fantasied threat to the mother-child relationship. The young child often rather suddenly shows intense separation anxiety and clinging, together with regressive manifestations, the latter frequently including the giving up of communicative speech. The picture is usually one of gradual withdrawal, emotional aloofness, autistic behavior, and distorted perception of reality, to a point which may resemble infantile autism. Rarely, the father or another family member may become the interactional partner, as the result of a shift in parental or familial roles [pp. 253–54].

TREATMENT

Several approaches to treatment for psychotic children have evolved. These can be roughly categorized as *educational, milieu* (provision of a special environment), *psychoanalytic, behavioral,* and *organic.*

Educational Approaches

Some approaches focusing primarily upon the education of the child might be considered to represent an educational model, although education also has a role in each of the other four approaches to treatment, being especially central in the behavioral and milieu therapy approaches. Many facilities for psychotic children are explicitly called "schools," but the variations in schooling generally follow the philosophies of one of the other treatment approaches or of traditional special education rather than representing a distinct and separate approach.

In one of the few attempts at objective evaluation of a more-or-less traditional special education approach, Havelkova (1968) found little difference in outcome for schizophrenic and autistic children who received a special nursery school program and those who did not. The special program began with a one-to-one relationship between the child and his nursery therapist. The child's activities included pleasurable contacts with the therapist, instruction in dressing, eating, and toileting, and trips into the community. After one to two years, the child moved gradually into a normal nursery school where his therapist accompanied him for as long as was deemed necessary. A social worker also met with the parents each week to help them understand their child.

Havelkova concluded that children who were least severely disturbed and began to show improvement before the age of four and one-half had the best outcomes, while those who were most severely disturbed and did not improve before the age of five and one-half had poor outcomes, regardless of treatment. Enduring intellectual deficits were found even in many of the children whose social behavior improved.

Milieu Therapy

"Milieu therapy" refers to provision of a therapeutic milieu or environment for the child. The emphasis in most milieu therapy is upon full-time socialization of the child by engaging him in interactions with others, helping him to adapt to structured routines, and encouraging him to develop educational, creative, and practical skills. However, milieu therapy often overlaps with one of the other approaches to a considerable degree in that the milieu and the specific treatment provided within it are designed to achieve goals based upon psychoanalytic, behavioral, or organic assumptions. Thus, many special environmental settings referred to as providing milieu therapy may be found to differ along the lines of the other treatment approaches.

Goldfarb, Goldfarb, & Pollack (1966) have compared the effects on schizophrenic children of full-time milieu therapy with the effects of a day-treatment program similar in most respects to the full-time program except that the day-treatment children spent nights, weekends, and vacations at home. Dividing the children into "organic" and "nonorganic" groups on the basis of Goldfarb's (1961) criteria—outlined earlier in the chapter—the authors found that the most severely disturbed children benefitted from neither type of treatment. However, among the less severely disturbed children, improvements in educational achievement, IQ, and ratings on "ego status" were approximately equal for organic children receiving both kinds of treatment, but greater for nonorganic children receiving residential treatment than for those receiving day treatment. It was suggested that protection from harmful family dynamics was an important advantage for the nonorganic children in residential treatment.

A comparison of the effects of three milieux on autistic (Kanner's syndrome) children produced results slightly at variance with those of Goldfarb et al (Wenar, Ruttenberg, Dratman, & Wolf, 1967). Children spending a year in a day-treatment program were found to improve in ratings of relationships to people, attempts at mastery, and psychosexual development, while children spending a year in either of two full-time treatment settings actually declined on these measures. However, one of the two full-time settings was purely custodial and both had older children, poorer child/staff ratios, more staff turnover, and less involvement of the staff with the children than did the day-treatment setting. The purely custodial institution produced somewhat better results in certain respects than the other residential institution where there was the most staff turnover and the least staff involvement with the children. None of the settings produced much improvement in communication or vocalization by the children.

Often overlooked is the fact that nonprofessional child-care workers in residential settings are likely to have much more effect than the therapists, who see the children for only a few hours a week at most. This fact has been demonstrated in a study wherein disturbed inpatient children were found to imitate child-care workers significantly more than they imitated therapists (Portnoy, 1973).

Psychoanalytic Approaches

Psychoanalytically oriented workers generally portray childhood psychosis as a failure or fragmentation of ego development resulting from extreme disturbances in the early mother-child relationship. While most psychoanalytic theorists acknowledge that constitutional factors may make a child especially vulnerable to psychosis, they tend to focus on maternal behavior and emotions as the most readily identifiable cause of childhood psychosis. According to Bettelheim (1967), Mahler (1965), and Rank (1949), a first goal of therapy must be to create for the child a loving, accepting relationship with an attentive, permissive mother figure who will provide the ego support that the child's own mother failed to provide. It is assumed that achievement of such a relationship—which may take years—is a prerequisite for later stages of treatment. The later stages of treatment resemble the uncovering and working through of unconscious conflicts done in psychoanalytic treatment of neurotic disorders.

As for evaluation of the effects of psychoanalytically oriented treatment, Bettelheim (1967) has reported that 42 per cent of the children with "infantile autism" treated as long-term inpatients at his Orthogenic School showed good improvement. Unfortunately, no data as to method of appraisal were provided and descriptions of some of the children suggest that they did not resemble either Kanner's syndrome or the more broadly defined autistic syndromes described by other workers.

Brown (1960) conducted a follow-up study of children diagnosed as having "atypical" development (autism or schizophrenia; cf. Rank, 1949) and receiving psychoanalytically oriented outpatient treatment. Comparing the 20 who made the most progress over several years with the 20 who made the least progress, Brown found that the more severely disturbed a child was initially, the worse the final outcome. Children having the best outcomes did not differ significantly from those having the worst outcomes on any treatment variables, including age of child at beginning of treatment, number of years of treatment, number or experience of therapists for child or mother, or treatment of father.

In a later follow-up, Brown (1963) compared 15 "atypical" children who received no treatment with 109 who received at least six months of individual therapy or at least a year of small group treatment (e.g., at Bettelheim's Orthogenic School). Again, treatment appeared to have little effect on the outcome.

In a study somewhat similar to Brown's (1960) first study, the 10 most improved and the 10 least improved were selected from a group of 40 schizophrenic children who had received psychoanalytic psychotherapy for an average of four to five years in day care, inpatient, and outpatient settings in conjunction with special schooling and group programs (Kaufman, Frank, Friend, Heims, & Weiss, 1962). Unlike Brown's study, no effect of initial severity was found, although severity in this study was judged according to inferred personality factors rather than according to overt behavior. Length of treatment was *inversely* related to improvement, with the least improved group receiving an average of 58 months of therapy compared to 36 months in the most improved group. Frequency of treatment appeared to have no effect, although the least improved children had more numerous therapists, therapists who were less regular in keeping appointments, and therapists who had less emotional involvement with the children.

Behavioral Approaches

Although behavioral approaches to the treatment of psychotic children began much more recently than any of the other major approaches, there has been considerably more documentation of the effects of behavioral methods on psychotic children. Ferster and DeMyer (1961) were among the first to demonstrate that the behavior of psychotic children could be systematically shaped by operant conditioning using food as reinforcement.

Lovaas (1967, 1968) has carried out a number of more elaborate applications of operant conditioning with psychotic children who had been rejected for other types of treatment because of their very low levels of functioning. It was noted that self-mutilation and other psychotic behaviors increased whenever demands were made on the children, but removing the demands appeared to reinforce the psychotic behavior. Temporary isolation was found to eliminate self-mutilation in some children, while brief painful electric shock was found to eliminate it in those whose self-destructive behavior (e.g., biting flesh from their own bodies) was too dangerous to be allowed to continue long enough for the isolation treatment to be effective. Case studies by Risley (1968) and by Baroff and Tate (1968) have also demonstrated success in eliminating self-destructive behavior with electric shock after other methods had failed. In both cases, no adverse effects were detected and the elimination of self-destructive behavior permitted successful treatment of other behavior.

Shock has also been used to make people effective reinforcers for children who previously showed no response to social stimuli. Lovaas, Schaeffer, and Simmons (1965) showed that psychotic children who learned to terminate shock from a floor grid by running to adults soon smiled at and molded themselves to the bodies of their adult rescuers. However, pairing food reinforcement with praise and physical contact has generally replaced shock as a means for making adults more reinforcing for psychotic children.

Operant conditioning of speech has been a primary focus of behavior therapy with psychotic children. Lovaas (1967) reported that reinforcement for appropriate speech and withdrawal of reinforcement following echolalia decreased echolalic speech. With mute children, imitation of single words in response to conspicuous prompts by an adult is at first reinforced. Once imitation of the adult has become a well-learned response, simple vocabularies and sentence forms have been successfully taught (Lovaas, 1968; Risley & Wolf, 1967).

Imitation of other adult behavior has also been reinforced in order to aid the teaching of self-help skills, athletics, play, drawing, and writing. Training of imitation must sometimes begin with prompts such as moving the child through the motions to be imitated and reinforcing him for the slightest attempt at spontaneous imitation. Several studies have demonstrated that generalized imitation could be learned by extremely disturbed autistic and schizophrenic children (Hewett, 1965; Hingtgen, Coulter, & Churchill, 1967; Lovaas et al, 1967).

Many aspects of operant conditioning have been taught the parents of psychotic children to enable them to continue training their children at home (e.g., Risley & Wolf, 1964; Wetzel et al, 1966; Wolf, Risley, & Mees, 1964). Churchill (1969) has noted that providing parents with effective techniques for training their disturbed children can help relieve the vicious cycle of hostility, rejection, and guilt experienced by such parents in reaction to the problems presented by their children.

With children who fail to make eye contact, reinforcement of attention and eye contact must precede reinforcement of imitation. Blake and Moss (1967) have described a novel procedure in which the child subject, Dolly, was seated in a dark booth. Every five seconds, the trainer opened a shutter to the booth and turned on the lights, saying, "Hi, Dolly—look at me!" Dolly was given a spoonful of ice cream whenever she did look. Within 75 trials, Dolly always responded with eye contact when the trainer said "Look at me!" and continued to make eye contact after the training session.

Token reinforcement of school behavior has been used with some success with autistic children (Martin, England, Kaprowy, Kilgour, & Pilek, 1968). Tokens were first given reinforcing value by rewarding the child with food whenever he handed a token to the trainer. The tokens were then used to reinforce sitting quietly at a desk, imitating words when prompted, identifying objects, answering simple questions, and matching pictures. It was eventually possible to shift to a group classroom situation in which the children sat quietly and responded to commands and questions from the teacher.

In a study of classroom education in sensory-motor skills, Fischer and Glanville (1970) found that psychotic children could progress in a small group setting using training procedures like those of Lovaas in which the child is reinforced for following conspicuous prompts by the teacher. However, the rate of progress indicated that 10 years of training would be required before the children could begin a regular primary school course.

Extended reports on operant conditioning of relatively complex behavior in autistic and other psychotic children have been published by Browning and Stover (1971) and by Hamblin, Buckholdt, Ferritor, Kozloff, and Blackwell (1971). The latter authors have reported on 17 autistic children who were initially without useful language. The children underwent one to three years of operant conditioning, beginning with the conditioning of eye contact and leading up to speech, social behavior, reading, and other school activities. Unlike Lovaas, these workers eliminated disruptive and self-injurious behavior by ignoring it and by reinforcing behavior incompatible with it rather than by punishment. Corroborating a demonstration by Churchill (1971) that high success/failure ratios reduced disruptive behavior in psychotic children, they found that disruptive behavior could be avoided by providing learning conditions geared so closely to the child's abilities that no errors occurred. Nearly all the mothers of the autistic children were successfully trained as assistant teachers.

Preliminary evaluation showed that 35 per cent of the children achieved good adjustments, i.e., acquired functional linguistic syntax and were able to function well in public school regular or special classes; 30 per cent achieved fair adjustments, i.e., functioned well in a special lab school and at home and continued to make progress in speech; and 35 per cent made poor adjustments. The special significance of age five for autistic children was again apparent in that only one of the 11 children beginning treatment by age five showed a poor outcome, while five of the six children beginning treatment after age five showed poor outcomes. The remaining child showed a fair outcome.

In one of the very few studies comparing the effects of different types of treatment in well-matched groups of psychotic children, Ney, Palvesky, and Markely (1971) provided 50 sessions of psychoanalytically oriented play therapy, followed by 50 sessions of operant conditioning for schizophrenic boys. Exactly the reverse sequence was provided for schizophrenic boys matched to the first group for age, signs of organicity, amount of speech, and Vineland Social Maturity Scale scores. The play therapy was guided by the premise that play activities symbolize the child's conflicts and provide a means for expressing his thoughts. A warm, accepting therapist interpreted recurrent play themes to the child. The operant conditioning involved candy and verbal reinforcement of behavior related to self-awareness, emotional relationships, imitation of adult behavior, and communication.

Tests of intellectual, communicational, sensory-motor, and personal-social functioning showed statistically significant improvements after operant conditioning but not after play therapy. Direct comparison of the two treatments showed that operant conditioning was superior to play therapy whether it came first or second, but that the difference in favor of operant conditioning was significant only when it came second.

Organic Approaches

Electroconvulsive Shock Treatment. Lauretta Bender (e.g., 1960) has advocated shock treatment for psychotic children on the basis of her theory that childhood schizophrenia results from excessive plasticity in embryonic stages of organic development. She maintains that shock treatment stimulates biological maturation, patterns primitive embryonic plasticity, mobilizes anxiety in apathetic children, and reduces anxiety in pseudoneurotic children. Bender reports that follow-ups of more than 500 children treated with shock between 1942 and 1955 revealed no adverse effects and that over 50 per cent showed social improvement, especially if they received shock treatment before the age of seven. The specific effects of shock are difficult to determine, however, because evidently no controlled comparisons have been made.

Drug Treatments. Tranquilizers and antipsychotic medications are widely used to suppress difficult behavior in psychotic children, but there are few adequate studies of their effectiveness (see Werry, 1972, for a brief review). In one of the best-controlled studies, Fish, Shapiro, and Campbell (1966) formed two groups of two- to six-year-old "schizophrenic" children matched for degree of impairment in linguistic and social functioning. During a three-week baseline period all the children participated in an intensive therapeutic nursery program, were given an inactive placebo drug, and were rated on structured scales for language, social awareness, and mood. Thereafter, all the children continued in the nursery program, but one group received the drug trifluoperazine while the control group continued on placebos.

Ratings by a psychiatrist blind to the drug conditions showed that, of the eight children who had been speaking during the baseline period, the four who received the placebo improved significantly, while the four receiving trifluoperazine worsened, showing depression, lethargy, and decreases in speech. By contrast, the seven most severely disturbed children receiving trifluoperazine showed significantly greater improvement than their severely disturbed controls, who appeared to benefit little from the therapeutic nursery program alone. The complex outcome of the study illustrates how essential it is that treatments, drug or otherwise, be evaluated on matched groups who can be classified on variables such as severity of behavioral deficits.

In another drug study, two autistic identical twin boys were alternated between a placebo drug and LSD-25 (Simmons, Leiken, Lovaas, Schaeffer, & Perloff, 1966). Under LSD, the children showed increases in eye contact, laughter, smiling, and movements toward adults, while they decreased in self-stimulatory behavior and movements away from adults. It was concluded that LSD might be a useful adjunct to other therapies because it increased the children's attentiveness and social interactions. Other studies have not shown positive changes in psychotic children under LSD, but the lack of standardized diagnostic criteria makes it difficult to reconcile the positive findings of Simmons et al. with the negative findings of other studies (e.g., Freedman, Ebin, & Wilson, 1962; Rolo, Krinsky, Abramson, & Goldfarb, 1965).

Alteration of Stimulation. On the basis of the hypothesis that autistic behavior functions as a defense against exacerbation of a hyperaroused state, Stroh and Buick (1970) evaluated the effects of placing two autistic children in relative sensory isolation. Each child spent several sessions of three to four days in a windowless, soundproofed room, alternating with four to six days in a transitional condition of graduated stimulation. During the isolation sessions, a child-care worker spent approximately five hours a day caring for the child, but he was left alone for the rest of the day.

Both children showed decreases in rocking and running and increases in attentiveness to visual and auditory stimuli that previously had been ignored. Exploration, vocalization, seeking of contact with the child-care worker, and looking at her also increased. The authors interpreted their findings as supporting the hypothesis that much autistic behavior constitutes defensive reactions against excessive stimulation.

Also starting from the premise that autistic children are in abnormal states of arousal—some hyperaroused, but some hypoaroused—DesLauriers and Carlson (1969) adopted the *opposite* treatment strategy. Instead of isolating the child from stimulation, they provided one-to-one experiences with an adult who systematically intruded upon the child, attempting to "humanize" him by providing a maximum of pleasurable sensory and affective stimulation through gamelike activities.

At first, stimulation was primarily tactile, kinesthetic, and proprioceptive, but this was followed by increasing concentration on visual and auditory stimulation. Once the child began to respond to affective stimulation, reciprocal communication was to be established between the child and his therapist. Eye contact was established, for example, through a game in which the therapist repeatedly threw a towel over the child's head and placed himself so the child would be looking right into his eyes when the towel was removed. Although DesLauriers and Carlson viewed their approach as having an affinity with the behavioral approach, they did not attempt to condition discrete bits of behavior. Instead, they sought to provide catalysts for "awakening" the children affectively, thereby creating the conditions under which they could reinforce spontaneous initiative, curiosity, and mastery that might cause learning to generalize to new situations. They maintained that effective "reinforcement" involves an organic arousal condition within the child and that it is not equivalent to giving specific rewards for specific behavior. As a child improved, his parents were encouraged to provide highly affective stimulation at home.

Assessments of intellectual and social functioning showed gains for five autistic children, although it is difficult to know how much of the gains can be attributed to spontaneous development and, on the intelligence tests, to repeated experience with the test items. One-year follow-ups of four children showed that none had regressed into autistic isolation, but all had fairly severe problems in adjustment. Neither the parents nor school personnel seemed able to continue providing the special stimulation and tolerance prescribed by DesLauriers and Carlson.

SUMMARY

"Psychosis" refers to the condition of people who are "out of contact with reality" or whose "reality-testing is poor." When severe mental disorders in children were first recognized, they were regarded as early forms of adult psychosis, especially of schizophrenia. Terminological confusion has been an obstacle to communication because the terms "childhood schizophrenia," "childhood psychosis," "autism," and "atypical personality development" have often been used interchangeably. Despite the confusion, there seems to be justification for separating at least three main types of disorder:

1. *childhood schizophrenia,* involving a decline or arrest after a period of relatively normal development in children who have some degree of useful language and relatedness to others;
2. *early infantile autism* (Kanner's syndrome), involving self-isolation and lack of relatedness from infancy onward, an obsessive insistence on sameness, and disorders of speech ranging from mutism to echolalia;
3. *symbiotic psychosis,* involving a failure to develop an identity separate from the mothering person.

It is unknown whether these disorders comprise homogeneous classes or are etiologically related to each other or to adult psychosis.

Research on childhood schizophrenia has yielded no consistent evidence for the etiological role of parental behavior and there is conflicting evidence on the incidence of schizophrenia in the families of schizophrenic children.

Findings of high rates of pre- and perinatal complications and of neurological signs in schizophrenic children have led to the hypotheses that schizophrenia is a genetically based disorder of embryological development (Bender); that early organic damage plays a causal role in some children, while psychogenic factors may be more important in others (Goldfarb); and that childhood schizophrenia is a heterogeneous grouping of organic syndromes (Pollack). Longitudinal study of offspring of schizophrenic mothers has shown much higher rates of pre- and perinatal complications in offspring who break down in adolescence and early adulthood than in those who do not break down. This has also suggested a critical role for early organic damage in adolescent-adult schizophrenia (Mednick).

Twin and adoption studies have consistently produced evidence for a genetic disposition to adolescent-adult schizophrenia, although they also show that genetic factors are unlikely to be the only determinants. Genetic hypotheses can be divided into *monogenic-biochemical* and *diathesis-stress* hypotheses, but the distinctions between them are becoming blurred as research increasingly focuses on specific genetic and stress mechanisms. One of the most powerful strategies for unraveling the genetic and nongenetic contributions is the study of *MZ twins discordant* for schizophrenia. Partly due to the paucity of cases, there has been little genetic research on childhood psychosis and it is unknown whether the evidence for genetic factors in adolescent-adult schizophrenia applies to childhood schizophrenia.

More attempts have been made to make the diagnosis of early infantile autism objective and reliable than has been the case with other childhood psychoses, although communication is still hampered by the tendency of some workers to apply the diagnosis loosely. Research has borne out Kanner's impressions that parents of autistic children are above average in occupation, education, and intelligence, and that they have low rates of marital instability and mental illness, although they are not as exceptional in any of these respects as Kanner reported.

Autistic children rarely show evidence of neurological abnormality, but elevated frequencies of autism in rubella-damaged children and unusual biochemical characteristics in autistic children have been found. Various hypotheses have attributed autistic behavior to abnormal arousal states that cause the child to be refractory to normal stimulation.

Symbiotic psychosis is extremely rare and little research has been done on it.

Treatment of childhood psychosis has included *educational, milieu, psychoanalytic, behavioral,* and *organic* approaches. No treatment approach has produced major improvements in large percentages of psychotic children. A repeated finding is that autistic children who begin to improve by the age of five have much better prognoses than those who fail to improve by this age, regardless of treatment. The very few well-designed studies tend to show complex interactions between the effect of a treatment and the type or severity of disorder such that a treatment may help some children while not helping others or making them worse.

Behavioral approaches have received the most extensive documentation and have demonstrated that adaptive behavior can be systematically substituted for maladaptive behavior in most psychotic children, although progress is often very slow.

SUGGESTED READING

Portrayal of Psychotic Children. T. I. Rubin's (1968) book *Jordi/Lisa and David* poignantly portrays the experience of a schizophrenic boy, Jordi, as inferred by one who has much experience with psychotic children. Although it is fiction, it has a ring of truth about how such a child might experience the world. The other story in the book, *"Lisa and David,"* is also worth reading as a portrayal of two very disturbed adolescents. An excellent movie, entitled "David and Lisa," was made from the story. *I Never Promised You a Rose Garden* (Green, 1964) is also a moving portrayal of the experience of a psychotic adolescent, this time as an autobiographical novel.

Genetic Research.   David Rosenthal's (1970a) book is a good introduction to genetic concepts, research, and findings in relation to psychopathology. It contains an extended treatment of genetic research on schizophrenia, although there is little to report on child psychosis. A book edited by A. R. Kaplan, *Genetic Factors in "Schizophrenia"* (1972), contains papers on research by a wide variety of experts in the field.

Overview of Research and Theories.   William Goldfarb's (1970) paper on childhood psychoses is one of the more complete reviews available in which most theoretical viewpoints are well represented. *The Journal of Autism and Childhood Schizophrenia,* published by Scripta Publishing Company since 1971, now provides a forum devoted exclusively to current research and theories on severe disturbances of childhood.

Parents of Autistic Children.   Following the founding of the Association for Parents of Autistic Children by Rimland, there has been a considerable amount of parental activity directed at locating and creating services for autistic children and finding better ways to live with such children. John Kysar (1968), a psychiatrist, has described his own ordeals in attempting to get education and treatment for his autistic son while being blamed for the child's condition at almost every turn. Lorna Wing (1972) has written a guide for parents of autistic children ("autistic" broadly conceived) which stresses our lack of knowledge as to etiology and provides parents with suggestions for educational resources, organizations, and ways for maintaining their own equilibrium while living with a difficult child.

Schizophrenics Anonymous.   For adult schizophrenics, there is a mutual aid organization similar to Alcoholics Anonymous, with chapters in many cities. In the absence of firm knowledge about etiology and treatment, such an organization may be of great help to people who might otherwise suffer more than necessary from loneliness, isolation, and despair. Literature can be obtained from: Schizophrenics Anonymous, P. O. Box 913, Saskatoon, Saskatchewan, Canada.

13

Antisocial Behavior and Juvenile Delinquency

Juvenile delinquency is in certain respects even more problematic than the topics presented in earlier chapters. Since a given behavior may be legally delinquent at one age but not at another, may be delinquent if associated with one motive but not with another, may be delinquent if preceded by a previous police record but not in the absence of such a record, and may be delinquent if the child is caught but not if he gets away with it, the purely legal definition of delinquency provides a poor starting place for understanding and treating behavior that may indeed be dangerous to the child or others, maladaptive, self-defeating, or "pathological."

It is widely acknowledged that delinquency that reaches the notice of juvenile courts constitutes only an unrepresentative tip of a much larger iceberg. Many other illegal acts are committed by officially adjudicated delinquents as well as by children who are never adjudicated delinquent. Lack of uniformity in defining and reporting crime also blurs the picture of juvenile delinquency. In practice, the purely legal definition is thus applied only to a small and haphazard sample of the relevant behavior. Moreover, the legal categories applied to children's behavior often bear little relation even to the most obvious characteristics of children's problems. For example, a judge may adjudicate a child delinquent for an extremely minor offense simply to pressure the parents into taking more responsibility for the child who, the judge feels, is being neglected.

Because adjudication as a delinquent is usually an advanced step in a long sequence of problem behavior, antisocial behavior in general is likely to provide a more appropriate conceptual starting place than do behavioral acts that happen to push certain children over the threshold of the juvenile court. It is only recently that the development of aggression and other antisocial behavior has begun to be studied in its own right, as a problem logically prior to the manifestation of delinquent behavior. In considering antisocial behavior, the focus will be upon behavior that is injurious or threatening to the property or well-being of other people. Political activity that may meet these criteria, but may be considered by some to be promoting prosocial goals, will not be considered because it is rare before the age of about 18.

RESEARCH ON THE DEVELOPMENT OF AGGRESSION

Much antisocial behavior involves direct or indirect aggression. Viewpoints on the problem have ranged from the position that aggression is inevitable because the human species is innately aggressive to the position that aggression will disappear when social conditions are improved and human reason prevails.

As for psychological theorizing, Freud at first held that aggression was merely a response to the blocking of libidinal expression. However, impressed by the violence of World War I, he revised his earlier instinct theory to include an instinctual aggressive drive as one of the two basic motivators of behavior, the sex drive being the other. While sexual and aggressive impulses are still regarded by analysts as being the most fundamental motivators of behavior, Freud's (1922) elaboration of the concept of an aggressive drive into a "death instinct" (*Thanatos*), that competes with the sex or life instinct (*Eros*), has not generally been accepted.

At the opposite extreme, Watson's limitation of innate motives to hunger, thirst, sex, and a few specific fears such as loud sounds left the explanation for aggression exclusively to learning.

The Frustration–Aggression Hypothesis

One of the first systematic attempts to study the determinants of aggressive behavior was carried out by Dollard et al (1939). In their theoretical formulation, Dollard et al were influenced by Freud's concepts of aggressive impulses and the expression of these impulses in various substitute forms. However, Dollard et al rejected the instinct concept in favor of the theory that aggression is a response elicited by frustration. *Aggression* was defined as a sequence of behavior having the objective of injuring the person toward whom it is directed, while *frustration* was defined as the blocking of an ongoing goal-directed activity. The fundamental hypothesis was that aggression is always a response to frustration, i.e., that frustration always leads to some form of aggression and that aggression is produced only by frustration.

Dollard et al also specified a number of subsidiary principles that enabled them to integrate a variety of data on sequences of frustration presumed to instigate aggression. One principle was that the probability of an aggressive act is jointly determined by the amount of frustration and the strength of punishment anticipated if the aggressive act is emitted. Dollard et al also held that the inhibition of aggression constitutes an additional frustration that instigates further aggression, especially aggression displaced onto different targets and expressed in modified forms. Following Freud, they hypothesized that any act of aggression is a *catharsis* that reduces the strength of other aggressive impulses.

Dollard et al suggested that a large number of factors found to be statistically correlated with criminal behavior could be understood in terms of the frustration–aggression model. For example, low economic, educational, and vocational status, youth, membership in disadvantaged minority groups, and lack of a stable marital relationship could be viewed as conditions that would create high frustration in various spheres. These conditions are also likely to minimize fear of punishment for overt aggression because they mean that an individual has less to lose through punishments like imprisonment. Thus, the frustration–aggression model appeared to make possible a psychological integration of diverse empirical relationships.

Frustration is still widely considered to be a source of aggression and several studies have demonstrated that children may become more aggressive following experimentally induced frustration (e.g., Block & Martin, 1955; Mallick & McCandless, 1966; Miller & Bugelski, 1948; Otis & McCandless, 1955). Some of these studies have also taken account of the effect of personality variables on the frustration–aggression relationship. For example, Block and Martin found that children rated as having weak ego controls indeed responded aggressively to frustration, but children rated as "over-controllers" responded with constructive play. These and other factors might be fit into the strict frustration–aggression model, but only at the risk of resorting to extremes of post hoc redefinition in terms of frustration and aggression.

A further illustration of conceptual problems with the strict frustration–aggression model is that, if somebody deliberately tromps on one's toes, the response is likely to be aggressive, but how can the toe-tromping be treated as the blocking of a goal-directed activity? A characteristic solution designed to save the strict frustration–aggression formulation has been to explain the aggressive response by inferring that the toe-tromping "interfered with the internal response oriented toward the preservation or attainment of security and comfort [Berkowitz, 1962, p. 30]." Other problems include the questions of why aggression is a prepotent response, how to measure degree of frustration and strength of anticipated punishment, and what individual differences exist in threshold for frustration.

Recent animal evidence indicates that aggression may be an innately determined response to noxious stimuli in many species. For example, after no previous rewards for aggression, young rhesus monkeys separated from their mothers, rats shocked electrically, and pigeons receiving no food when pecking a stimulus that previously produced 100 per cent food reward, all attacked innocent members of their own species (Azrin, Hutchinson, & Hake, 1966; Hutchinson, Ulrich, & Azrin, 1965; Seay & Harlow, 1965).

Sears's Studies of Child Aggression. Robert Sears and his colleagues attempted to test the frustration–aggression hypothesis by calculating the correlations between behavioral, fantasy, and teacher-report measures of aggression in nursery school children and measures of prior frustration (e.g., severity of feeding scheduling, weaning, toilet training; Sears, Whiting, Nowlis, & Sears, 1953). No nonchance relations were found between the measures of early frustration and later aggressive behavior. Similarly, no nonchance relations were found between aggressive behavior and current frustration (eating problems, sickness, danger, maternal demands for orderliness and cleanliness).

A later study using questionnaire measures indicated that very aggressive five-year-olds tended to have mothers who were highly permissive of aggression but who administered severe punishment when aggression did occur (Sears, Maccoby, & Levin, 1957). In a follow-up of the same children at age 12, it was found that high maternal permissiveness for aggression at age five was still positively related to aggression, but that *low* punishment rather than severe punishment for aggression was now positively related to antisocial aggression (Sears, 1961). Thus, if the measures of aggression can be trusted, low permissiveness for aggression is successful in inhibiting aggression throughout childhood, while high punishment encourages aggression early in childhood but inhibits it later.

Stability of Aggession Throughout Development

Despite Sears's evidence for changes in the relation of child-rearing practices to aggression, there is also evidence for stability in aggressiveness as a behavioral trait over the course of development. In their analysis of behavioral characteristics of children in the Fels Institute longitudinal study, Kagan and Moss (1962) found statistically significant correlations between ratings of various aggressive traits made during several periods of childhood. For example, the correlation for indirect aggression toward peers at ages 3 to 6 and 10 to 14 was .51. Some prominent sex differences were observed in the correlations, with "behavioral disorganization" (violent crying, tantrums, uncontrolled destructive activity) at ages 3 to 6 and 10 to 14 correlating .52 for boys, but only —.03 for girls.

Kagan and Moss interpreted the general lack of positive relations between early and later aggression in females as reflecting cultural pressures on females to be nonaggressive. An analogous interpretation was applied to the complementary finding that childhood dependency scores correlated significantly with adult dependency scores in females but not in males, i.e., cultural pressures censure males for dependency just as they censure females for direct aggression. Women were also found to be more conflicted about expressing and recognizing aggression, while men were more conflicted about dependency, thus supporting a cultural interpretation for the discontinuity between child and adult aggresssion in females and dependency in males. However, Kagan and Moss acknowledged the possibility that constitutional differences could interact with cultural factors to shape the sex differences with respect to aggression and dependency.

Whatever the source of the sex differences in manifest aggression, their consistency is apparent in Feshbach's (1970) review of over 50 studies comparing aggression in boys and girls. Boys were found to be more aggressive in nearly all comparisons. In the few comparisons showing no sex difference or girls being more aggressive, the measures were generally of verbal or indirect aggression. Feshbach has proposed that the difference between males and females in overt aggression may be partially accounted for by the same factor that may account for the repeated finding of a positive correlation between muscularity and aggression in boys, i.e., greater muscularity is likely to make aggression more successful as an instrumental behavior in achieving the child's goals, thereby reinforcing aggression. However, characteristics of temperament that are correlated with greater muscularity may also enhance aggressive tendencies (Cortes & Gatti, 1972).

Learning Analyses of Aggression

Reinforcement for Aggression. Although the frustration–aggression formulation, Sears's studies, and the Fels Institute longitudinal study all make provisions for the role of learning, later studies have attempted to delineate more precisely the parameters of learning in aggressive behavior. One approach has been to study reinforcement for aggression. Buss (1966) has argued that frustration by itself is not a very potent instigator to aggression. Instead, he maintains that aggression occurs primarily if it has instrumental value, i.e., if it can get the individual what he wants or can eliminate noxious stimulation. In experiments where college student subjects believed they were shocking another person to aid him in learning a simple concept, Buss found that frustrating the subjects did not increase the intensity of shock they used, but that being told intense shock speeded learning did cause them to increase the intensity. Thus, perceived instrumental value of aggression appeared to increase it while frustration did not. Other laboratory studies have demonstrated that reinforcement for aggression could also increase aggressive behavior by children in standardized situations (e.g., Walters & Brown, 1963).

Through systematic observations of children in nursery school, Patterson, Littman, and Bricker (1967) found that aggressive behavior was frequently reinforced by the consequences provided by the victim or teacher. Behavioral change over 26 weeks showed increases in aggression for socially active children, who typically passed through sequences of being victimized by aggressive children, successfully counterattacking, and initiating aggression.

Aggressive behavior among socially inactive children, however, remained low.

Observational studies of institutionalized delinquents and families of aggressive children have generally shown that there are many natural reinforcements for aggression (Patterson & Cobb, 1971). Delinquents, for example, provide a great deal of social acclaim for one another in the recounting of past misdeeds. The families of aggressive children provide much aversive stimulation which can be temporarily terminated by aggressive responses. Patterson and Cobb postulated a "coercion trait" stemming from the continued reinforcement of coercive behaviors like screaming and kicking that infants normally use to get their parents to remove noxious conditions such as hunger, cold, wetness, etc.

If aggressive behavior is, like other instrumental responses, reinforced by favorable consequences, then it may also be subject to extinction or replacement by other rewarded responses. Several studies have demonstrated that training in constructive, nonaggressive behavior could reduce aggression in young children, even after frustration (Brown & Elliot, 1965; Chittenden, 1942; Davitz, 1952; Updegraff & Keister, 1937). On the other hand, the contrasting hypothesis put forth by Freud and Dollard et al (1939) that free expression of aggression reduces subsequent aggression has not been supported. For example, Mallick and McCandless (1966) found that children experimentally frustrated and allowed to engage in aggressive play did not subsequently show less aggression toward their frustrator than did children not given the opportunity for "cathartic" aggression. Similarly Kahn (1966) found that experimentally frustrated college students who engaged in cathartic expression of anger later expressed *more* dislike for their frustrator and *higher* physiological arousal than did frustrated subjects who had not been given the opportunity for catharsis.

Identification, Imitation, and Modeling. *Identification with the aggressor* was proposed by Freud to account for his observation that the child resolved his Oedipal conflict partly by identifying with the same-sex parent from whom he feared punishment for his desires toward the opposite-sex parent. In effect, by imagining himself to *be* the same-sex parent the child symbolically achieved his goal of possessing the opposite-sex parent at the same time as he eliminated his fear of the same-sex parent as an external aggressor. Besides accounting for the disappearance of Oedipal behavior, the appearance of conscience and strongly sex-typed behavior, and the behavioral resemblances between children and their same-sex parents, identification with the aggressor came to be counted among the defense mechanisms that can continue to be employed throughout life (A. Freud, 1936).

In the learning theory tradition, Miller and Dollard (1941) portrayed *imitation* as an instrumental response that was acquired through reinforcement. For example, a child seeing an older sibling obtain a reward for a certain behavior might then imitate the behavior and be similarly rewarded.

Consequently, not only the specific behavior, but imitation as a generalized response disposition was reinforced.

In their attempts to reconcile psychoanalytic and learning theory concepts, Miller, Dollard, Sears, and their colleagues placed imitation on a continuum with identification. Their basic position was that identification involved a persisting disposition or learned drive to imitate not only the behavior but the values and feelings of the model, who was usually a parent.

While the instrumental value of imitation may indeed lead to extrinsic reinforcement as Miller and Dollard held, it is unlikely that instrumental learning exclusively accounts for children's strong propensity to imitate. The author has observed that some infants as young as three weeks of age will distinctly imitate a model who repeatedly sticks out his tongue. Gardner and Gardner (1970) have published evidence for imitation of tongue and mouth movements in a six-week old infant.

Whatever its initial source, imitation appears to play a role in the acquisition of many human behaviors. Bandura has experimentally demonstrated that children readily imitate the aggressive behavior of live and filmed models, although Bandura prefers the term *modeling* for the acquisition of behavior through observing and replicating the behavior of another person (Bandura, 1965; Bandura, Ross, & Ross, 1963). Bandura (1969a, 1969b) has analyzed the process of modeling in terms of the child's coding of the model's behavior in verbal and other symbolic form and reproducing the behavior if the model is positively valued by the child, has high status, is perceived as being similar to the child, is not punished for his behavior, or if the child is given incentives for reproducing the model's behavior.

"Identification" is regarded by Bandura as an instance of modeling that may, like other modeling, be governed by the factors just mentioned. In a comparison of the attitudes and family backgrounds of antisocial aggressive adolescent boys and a matched control group of nonaggressive boys, Bandura and Walters (1959) uncovered numerous group differences with which they sought to explain the failure of the aggressive boys to identify with and internalize societal standards for behavior. Two major etiological factors appeared to be (1) the fathers' general hostility toward their sons, and, (2) the mothers' rejection and discouragement of their sons' dependency needs.

It was also found that the parents of the aggressive boys had significantly more often encouraged aggression and had presented aggressive models in their attitudes and in their more frequent use of physical punishment and deprivation of privileges, as opposed to reasoning and punishment through withdrawal of love (e.g., refusing to speak to the child, ignoring him). From what could be gathered about the aggressive boys' early life history, aggression had long been a problem and had become more serious during adolescence mainly because of the boys' increased size, physical maturity, and independence, rather than beginning for the first time in adolescence.

McCord, McCord, and Howard (1961) found nearly all the same differences as Bandura and Walters between aggressive and nonaggressive boys living in a high delinquency area who were studied over a five-year period, from the ages of nine to 14. However, they found that not only aggressive behavior, but all forms of overt deviance, including alcoholism, criminality, psychosis, sexual promiscuity, and desertion, were more frequent among the fathers of aggressive boys. Parents of disturbed children manifesting aggressive symptoms have also been found to have significantly more overt social problems and more deviant MMPI test scores than parents of disturbed children manifesting nonaggressive symptoms (Achenbach, 1966; Anderson, 1969).

The Eron, Walder, and Lefkowitz Study. Eron, Walder, and Lefkowitz (1971) attempted to examine simultaneously the effects of numerous variables considered important in the learning of aggression by children. Their subjects included all of the approximately 900 third-grade children in a semirural county of New York. The data included objectively scored parent interviews, newspaper reports of parental arrests, peer and teacher ratings of aggression and other antisocial behavior in school, child guidance clinic records, and data from experimental studies of aggression.

Physical punishment, rejection, lack of nurturance, marital discord, and aggressiveness by parents were all again found to be positively related to aggression in the children. More detailed analyses showed, however, that boys who identified strongly with their fathers were less aggressive the more they were punished for aggression, while, among boys who did not identify with their fathers, punishment increased aggression. Since *most* boys did *not* identify strongly with their fathers, the general effect of severe punishment was to increase rather than decrease aggression.

Another finding was that children of fathers with high occupational status tended to be more aggressive than children of fathers with low occupational status, although parental education showed a negative correlation with aggression. These inverse relations of parental occupation and education to aggression probably resulted from the fact that fathers who achieved high occupational status with low education were especially aggressive. A supplementary finding was that, among the children of fathers with high occupational status, the positive relation between punishment and aggression was most pronounced. Thus, the severely punished upper-class children were rated the most aggressive by their peers. Whether these relations would also hold in urban groups is unknown.

Data collected by Eron, Walder, and Lefkowitz made possible one of the first direct tests of the long-term effects of television violence on aggression. The original study, like many others, showed that aggressive children preferred to watch violent TV programs. Unfortunately, the direction of causality cannot be inferred with certainty from a correlation of this sort, because it cannot be determined whether the children's exposure to TV violence caused their aggressiveness or whether their aggressiveness caused them to prefer violent TV.

However, in a follow-up study ten years later, when the children averaged 19 years in age, 427 of the original third graders were given MMPIs and were interviewed to obtain peer ratings and self ratings on current aggression (Eron, Huesmann, Lefkowitz, & Walder, 1972). For males, aggression as measured by peer and self ratings and the MMPI at age 19 all correlated significantly with preference for violent TV in third grade, no matter how aggressive the boy already was in third grade, how much parental nurturance, disharmony, rejection, punishment, or aggression there was, how much the boy identified with his parents, what the father's occupational status was, or how much the boy watched television. In fact, except for the boy's rated aggression in grade three, none of the other variables predicted aggressiveness at age 19 as well as preference for violent TV in third grade.

The direct *causal* role of TV seems apparent from findings that experimental exposure of children to violent TV, regardless of their preferences, results in more aggressive behavior and more willingness to hurt other children than does exposure to neutral or prosocial programs (Murray, 1973). The behavioral effects are especially marked for children who are already aggressive and those who enjoy violent programs. Eron et al (1972) attributed the lack of long-term influence of TV violence on aggression among girls to the paucity of aggressive female models on TV and other cultural pressures against aggression in women.

MORAL DEVELOPMENT

Both psychoanalytic and learning theory approaches to antisocial behavior focus upon acquisition by the child of behavioral norms from people around him, especially his parents. According to psychoanalytic theory, the superego is formed largely through identification with the values and traits of the same-sex parent at the termination of the Oedipal period. According to most learning theory approaches, reinforcement and punishment of antisocial behavior, degree of parental permissiveness, warmth, and nurturance, and the models presented by others influence the degree to which a child internalizes socially prescribed controls over his behavior. In both approaches, the discomfort of guilt feelings is assumed to become a major factor in controlling the older child's behavior.

Early studies of moral knowledge, cheating, and other forms of dishonesty revealed little correlation among various types of moral behavior in various situations (Hartshorne & May, 1928–30). Later studies and reanalyses of the Hartshorne-May data have revealed somewhat more individual consistency in honesty, although situational differences were still prominent in children's resistance to temptation (Burton, 1963; Nelson, Grinder, & Mutterer, 1969; Sears, Rau, & Alpert, 1965).

The Piagetian Approach

Another approach to moral development has been to study the kinds of judgments made by children in their answers to questions on the rules of games, the nature of justice and punishment, and stories posing moral dilemmas. From data gathered in this way, Piaget (1932) inferred a series of stages that correspond roughly to stages of cognitive development. The primary dimensions along which the stages vary are the individual's conception of justice and his conception of rules of social order. In early stages of moral development, children feel that rules are absolute and unalterable. They view behaviors as totally right or wrong and judge the wrongness of an act by the severity of its consequences. For example, in response to the question of who was naughtier, a boy who accidentally broke 15 cups while obeying his mother, or a boy who broke one cup while sneaking some jam, young children reply that the boy who broke 15 cups was naughtier because the damage was greater. Children up to the age of about eight also believe in immanent justice, i.e., that a punishment or misfortune will automatically befall a wrongdoer, no matter what the nature of the transgression. They do not clearly distinguish justice from obedience to rules laid down by an adult, and they believe that unvarying punishment for disobedience is the essence of justice.

By the age of about 11 or 12, children begin to make judgments in terms of more relativistic views of rules and justice. Rules are viewed as being dependent upon functional goals and mutual agreements among people, while justice is viewed as depending upon the constructive versus destructive intentions of the wrongdoer, individual circumstances, degree of responsibility for adverse consequences, and restitutions to victims of transgressions. The cognitive developmental trends in the child's changing moral judgments manifest his decreasingly egocentric and increasingly abstract, logical thinking. Piaget maintains that social interaction is also an important source of changing moral views because it increasingly requires the child to take other people's points of view.

In a review of research on moral development, Hoffman (1970) reported that age was positively correlated with Piaget's stages in 20 out of 21 studies comparing children of different age groups in western societies. Piaget's stage sequence was also found in studies of West African children and Hopi Indians, but not in some other American Indian tribes. Among children from industrial societies, IQ and social class were positively and independently related to moral development, while specific parental child-rearing practices tended not to be. The effects of IQ and social class suggest that both high cognitive ability and the general characteristics of higher social-class environments facilitate development of higher stages of moral judgment. A study by Hoffman (1971) also showed that boys with no father in the home were significantly lower on several moral indices and higher in overt aggression than matched boys with fathers in the home, although paternal absence made no significant difference for girls.

Kohlberg's System

Lawrence Kohlberg (1969, 1971) has attempted to provide a more detailed portrayal of cognitively based moral development. He has enumerated 25 aspects of moral judgment that can be scored to place an individual at one of six hypothetical stages of moral development. For example, Stage 1 is described as "Obedience and punishment orientation; egocentric deference to superior power or prestige, or a trouble-avoiding set." Stage 6 is described as "Conscience or principle orientation. Orientation not only to actually ordained social rules but to principles of choice involving appeal to logical universality and consistency; orientation to conscience as a directing agent and to mutual respect and trust [Kohlberg, 1969, p. 376]."

Using Kohlberg's scoring system, trained raters can score responses to hypothetical moral dilemmas with moderate reliability. Qualitatively similar answers to a standard set of moral dilemmas have been found in a number of cultures and the ordering of the stages is similar in the various cultures, although the higher stage responses are positively related to IQ, socioeconomic status, and residence in western cultures.

The question of how stages of moral judgment relate to antisocial behavior has not been clearly answered. Experimental tests of resistance to temptation were not found by Grinder (1964) to relate significantly to Piaget's measures of moral development nor by Nelson, Grinder, and Challas (1968) to Kohlberg's measures, although Krebs (1968) did find a positive relation to Kohlberg's measures. In the absence of more data on the relation between antisocial behavior and moral judgment, it appears that a child's level of moral judgment may be constrained by his level of cognitive development. Judgmental level may, in turn, be a significant factor in determining what sort of socialization techniques a child is amenable to, but there is little to indicate that a child's behavior is very much constrained by the level of moral judgment he is capable of verbalizing.

JUVENILE DELINQUENCY

The foregoing sections dealt with the development of antisocial behavior and moral judgment in broad samples of children who had not necessarily been adjudicated delinquent. Many of the children may indeed have committed crimes at some time in their lives, but the objective of most studies of antisocial behavior by children who are not necessarily delinquent is to find antecedents of antisocial behavior in general rather than in the subset of children who happen to cross the threshold of the juvenile court. A virtue of this strategy is that its portrayal of the development of antisocial behavior may be less influenced by the effects of police and court action on the child and his family than is a strategy that begins with children who have been arrested. A disadvantage is that, unless children who become delinquent are singled out, etiological factors may be missed that separate this relatively extreme group from other children whose antisocial behavior does not become so extreme.

Arrests of Juveniles

Children who are known to be delinquent represent the tip of the iceberg that is the focus of public concern. Because of lack of uniformity in reporting practices, lack of consistent distinctions among reasons for adjudication as delinquent (e.g., seriousness of crime by child versus perceived need for court supervision because of parental neglect), and varying definitions of crime depending upon the age of the individual, an accurate portrayal of even the tip of the iceberg is difficult. However, the FBI's annual *Uniform Crime Report* and the U.S. Children's Bureau's *Juvenile Court Statistics* provide a general index of juvenile crimes that receive official notice.

According to the FBI's *Uniform Crime Report* (U. S. Dept. of Justice, 1972), juveniles under 18 were arrested for 28 per cent of the major offenses considered to have been solved in 1971. (The major crimes comprising the FBI's Crime Index are murder, manslaughter, forcible rape, robbery, aggravated assault, burglary, larceny, and auto theft.) The percentages of offenses cleared by arrests of juveniles ranged from 5.4 per cent of the murder cases to 40 per cent of the larceny and auto theft cases. Many juveniles were also arrested for offenses peculiar to their age groups, such as truancy, vandalism, and violation of omnibus statutes pertaining to "delinquent tendencies." Over 640,000 juveniles below the age of 18 were arrested for Crime Index crimes and over 1.7 million for all offenses during 1971.

As indicated in Fig. 13–1, the Crime Index showed a marked rise during the late 1960s, far outstripping the rise in population during the same period. Because only about 20 per cent of Crime Index crimes are considered to be cleared by arrest, it is difficult to determine what percentage of the increase was caused by juveniles. However, all indices of juvenile criminal activity (e.g., arrests, juvenile court cases) suggest that much of the increase in Crime Index crimes was attributable to juveniles.

Juvenile Courts

Origins. Until the nineteenth century, juveniles who broke laws were generally treated in the same way as adult offenders. During the nineteenth century, most states established "reform" schools for young lawbreakers. These schools were little more than prisons where hard work and rigid discipline were relied upon to reform the children. In 1899, however,

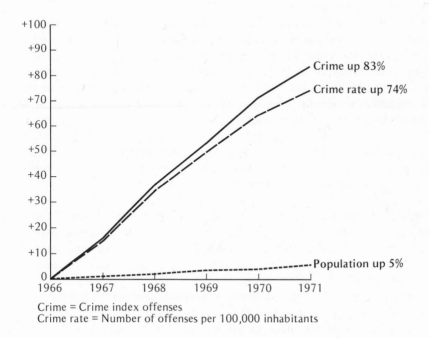

Crime up 83%

Crime rate up 74%

Population up 5%

1966   1967   1968   1969   1970   1971

Crime = Crime index offenses
Crime rate = Number of offenses per 100,000 inhabitants

Fig. 13–1. Percentage of change in population and major crimes between 1966 and 1971. From United States Department of Justice (1972), p. 2.

Illinois passed a law specifying that delinquents were to be treated in the same way as neglected or dependent children. The law also provided for the establishment of a juvenile court in Chicago, the first in the country. The function of the juvenile court was to protect and provide treatment for children who were neglected, dependent on public support, or delinquent.

In order to reduce the stigma associated with courts, the juvenile court proceedings were to be informal and oriented toward investigation, diagnosis, and treatment of children rather than toward punishment. The term "petition" was substituted for "complaint," "hearing" for "arraignment," "adjudication of involvement in delinquency" for "conviction," and "disposition" for "sentencing." The judges were given broad discretionary powers to apply laws according to individual circumstances and to attempt to work out the best possible arrangements for preventing further misdeeds. In 1909, an explicitly clinical approach was adopted by the Chicago Juvenile

Court with the establishment of the Psychopathic Laboratory for clinical evaluation of delinquents.

Current Status. There is now a juvenile court in every American legal jurisdiction, although they vary greatly in facilities, procedures, degree of overcrowding, and maximum age limits. In many states juvenile court records are not supposed to constitute criminal records and are to be destroyed once the child passes the age of the juvenile court's jurisdiction, which is generally 16 to 18 years. There has recently been a strong movement to give juveniles the rights of legal counsel and to apply the standards for evidence, testimony, etc., that prevail in adult courts, although most juvenile courts retain their informal, highly discretionary procedures.

Surveys of juvenile courts have revealed that most do not function as intended because they have far too many cases for the number of judges, probation officers, and social workers, they lack psychiatric and psychological services, and dispositional alternatives such as foster homes, group homes, work programs, etc., are rarely available (cf. Gibbons, 1970). The President's Task Force on Juvenile Delinquency (1967) has reported that the average probation officer supervises between 71 and 80 cases, excluding prehearing case studies that take at least half the time of most probation officers. The amount of time juvenile court judges spend on each case averages between 10 and 15 minutes.

Figure 13–2 presents the number of juvenile court delinquency cases and the total child population from 1940 through 1971. While it has become a truism (perhaps at all times in all societies) that delinquency is getting worse, Fig. 13–2 indicates that, over the 30 years from 1940 through 1971, there were some marked changes in rate. There was a marked *drop* in delinquency between 1947 and 1950, although it did not reach the low level of 1940 to 1942.

The practice begun in 1957 of reporting traffic offenses separately (see Fig. 13–2) indicates that the rates have recently increased rapidly whether or not traffic offenses are included, although the absolute figures are somewhat lower when traffic offenses are excluded. In 1971, 970,000 children, representing 2.9 per cent of all American children aged 10 to 17, were referred to juvenile courts for nontraffic offenses (U. S. Children's Bureau, 1972). The increase in the most serious crimes (homicide, forcible rape, aggravated assault, robbery) has been outdistancing that for other crimes, amounting to a 193 per cent increase from 1960 to 1971. It is estimated that approximately 20 per cent of all children will be referred to a juvenile court at some time in their lives. The rate of delinquency, as measured by court referral, has also increased steadily since the 1950s in many other industrialized countries, with Sweden apparently having about the highest rate (Tunley, 1962).

Studies of continuous juvenile court records in Cleveland show that a peak of 6.6 per cent of the juvenile population was referred in 1919. A low of 2.1 per cent was reached in 1939, after which a rise has occurred to over

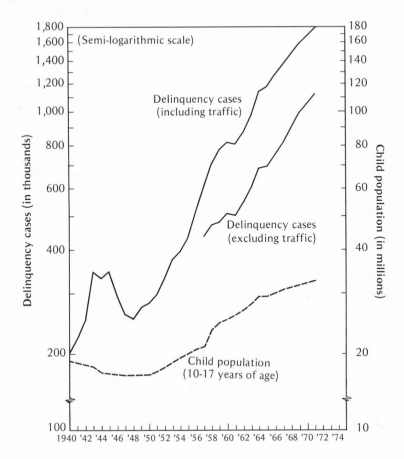

Fig. 13–2. Juvenile court delinquency cases involving children aged 10 to 17 years from 1940 through 1971, presented on a semilogarithmic scale. From United States Children's Bureau (1969, 1972).

3 per cent in the 1960s, corresponding to the national rise (Kessler, 1966). Detailed analyses of delinquency among various ethnic groups in Chicago have shown the highest rates to be among the children of the most recently immigrated group, beginning with Germans and Irish in the first decades of this century and followed by Polish, Italian, black, and Spanish-speaking immigrants to the city (Shaw & McKay, 1969).

Going back further in our history, Tunley (1962) relates accounts of eighteenth- and nineteenth-century delinquency that have a familiar contemporary ring. In the mid-nineteenth century, however, the youth gangs roaming New York were composed of children of English, Irish, and German immigrants, and carried such names as Plug Uglies, Roach Guards, Slaughter Housers, Dead Rabbits, and Forty Thieves. Contrast these with the more genteel names of current gangs such as the Young Lords, Viceroys, and Crusaders.

Hidden Delinquency

There is no doubt that official statistics underestimate the amount of crime committed by juveniles. The degree of underestimation in a high delinquency area is suggested by the finding in a longitudinal study that only 40 out of 101 fairly serious delinquents were ever arrested (Murphy, Shirley, & Witmer, 1946). Moreover, out of 616 serious crimes, only 68 (11 per cent) were prosecuted and out of 4,400 minor offenses, only 27 (0.6 per cent) were prosecuted.

Anonymous questionnaire surveys of adolescents also show that many who are not classified as delinquent have committed illegal acts. Table 13–1 presents data from one such survey in which the responses of high school students in small midwestern towns and small western cities were compared with those of adolescents incarcerated in western training schools.

STRATEGIES FOR CLASSIFYING DELINQUENCY

It is all too easy to conjure up a stereotyped image of The Delinquent. In such an image, many undesirable characteristics may be lumped together —gang activities, sexual licentiousness, irrational violence, vandalism, mugging, carefully planned robberies and burglaries, poor school work, truancy, bad home conditions in a slum neighborhood, hate for the police and society at large, alienation, drug addiction, etc. It is also easy to supplement the stereotype with stereotyped explanations for delinquency and the treatment that ought to be implemented. Depending upon one's predispositions, the assumed causes and treatment might range from moral, genetic, or cultural inferiority treatable only by "get-tough" policies such as the death penalty or long-term incarceration at one extreme, to poverty or discrimination treatable with more boys' clubs, social workers, and welfare benefits at the other extreme.

Among workers who study delinquency, stereotypes have occasionally been given more elaborate theoretical rationales in terms of *anomie* (normlessness), gang culture, "crime from a sense of guilt," superego lacunae, etc. However relevant these concepts may be to *some* delinquents, the tendency has been very strong to generate from them stereotypes that may be plausible, but that have not been demonstrated to match many children whose behavior is actually delinquent. Because the lure of the stereotype is so strong in the popular (and professional) imagination, any meaningful study of the nature, origins, and possible methods for treatment and prevention of delinquency must begin with empirical attempts to identify individual characteristics of children who commit crime.

TABLE 13-1

Percentage of high school students and delinquents in training schools who anonymously admitted committing certain offenses more than once or twice.

Type of offense	Boys			Girls		
	Midwest	West	Training school	Midwest	West	Training school
Skipped school	24.4	23.8	85.9	10.1	12.2	66.3
"Run away" from home	2.8	2.4	37.7	1.0	1.0	51.8
School probation or expulsion	2.1	2.9	31.3	0.3	0.2	29.3
Taken little things (worth less than $2) that did not belong to you	18.5	12.9	65.1	5.7	3.5	48.1
Taken things of medium value ($2–$50)	3.8	3.8	61.4	1.0	0.6	29.6
Taken things of large value ($50)	1.1	2.1	47.7	1.7	0.9	10.1
Used force to get money from another person	2.4	—	35.5	0.3	—	21.5
Taken part in "gang fights"	6.7	5.2	47.4	1.7	1.1	27.7
Taken a car for a ride without the owner's knowledge	4.5	4.0	53.4	1.0	0.6	20.7
Bought or drank beer, wine, or liquor (outside your home)	21.1	—	75.0	10.8	—	75.3
Deliberate property damage	17.5	8.2	49.7	5.7	1.6	32.1
Used or sold narcotic drugs	0.7	1.6	12.6	0.3	0.3	23.8
"Beat up" on kids who hadn't done anything to you	3.1	2.8	26.2	1.0	0.9	18.3
Had sex relations with a person of opposite sex	20.3	19.9	73.4	4.1	4.8	81.5

NOTE.—From Short & Nye (1958).

Despite the large number of studies in which antecedents and correlates of delinquency have been sought, surprisingly few have attempted to distinguish among clusters of behavioral and psychological characteristics that may differentiate specific subgroups of delinquents. Far too many studies have simply treated the legal definition of delinquency as if it encompassed a homogeneous class of individuals whose backgrounds could be investigated to reveal why delinquency in general occurs.

Behavioral Clusters

When attempts have been made to differentiate objectively among types of delinquency, the main approach has been to record behavioral and personality characteristics of delinquents in a standardized format and then to apply the statistical techniques of cluster analysis or factor analysis to the correlations among all pairs of variables. The result is a number of clusters that represent dimensions or types of delinquent behavior or personality. Children can be grouped according to their scores on the dimensions or their resemblance to the clusters thus obtained. Antecedent factors and effects of various treatments can then be ascertained for children who resemble one another on the empirically derived clusters or dimensions.

As an example, in Quay's (1964) factor analysis of behavioral traits among institutionalized delinquent boys, the following characteristics correlated highly with one another: Accepted by delinquent subgroup, bad companions, engages in gang activities, stays out late at night, and strong allegiance to selected peers. This cluster was given the label "socialized-subcultural delinquency." A second cluster of characteristics included: Irritable, verbally aggressive, assaultive, feels persecuted and that others are unfair, defies authority, quarrelsome, and unable to profit by praise or punishment. This cluster was given the label of "unsocialized-psychopathic delinquency." A third cluster, given the label "disturbed-neurotic delinquency," included: Sensitive, worries, timid, shy, and has anxiety over own behavior.

Personality Clusters

Factor analyses of questionnaire responses by delinquents have also produced dimensions like those labeled by Quay as socialized-subcultural, unsocialized-psychopathic, and disturbed-neurotic delinquency. Items found by Peterson, Quay, and Tiffany (1961) to represent the socialized-subcultural dimension included:

When I was going to school, I played hooky quite often. In school I was sometimes sent to the principal for cutting-up. My folks usually blame bad company for the trouble I get into. When I was a little kid, I was always doing things my folks told me not to [p. 362].

Items representing the unsocialized-psychopathic dimension were:

The only way to make big money is to steal it. It's dumb to trust older people. A lot of times it's fun to be in jail. The only way to settle anything is to lick the guy. I go out of my way to meet trouble rather than try to escape it. I would have been more successful if people had given me a fair chance. I'm really too tough a guy to get along with most kids. A person is better off if he doesn't trust anyone. I hardly ever get excited or thrilled [p. 361].

Items representing the neurotic-disturbed dimension were:

I don't think I'm quite as happy as others seem to be. I just don't seem to get the breaks other people do. It seems as if people are always telling me what to do, or how to do things. I often feel as though I have done something wrong or wicked. It is hard for me to act natural when I am with new people. I seem to do things that I regret more often than other people do. People often talk about me behind my back. I get nervous when I have to ask someone for a job. It seems as if I've been caught in every lie I ever told [p. 361].

Factor analysis of personality responses by a broad range of junior high school students has yielded similar dimensions, indicating that the personality dimensions are not confined to delinquents, but that delinquents are differentiated by being more extreme on the dimensions (Quay & Quay, 1965).

Correlates of the Behavioral and Personality Clusters

Since the cluster- and factor-analytic studies appear to have reliably identified distinct behavioral and personality types among delinquents, the next question is whether these empirically derived types relate to different antecedents and correlates. A typology or classification system has value only if its categories are correlated with other important variables. Several studies have shown that socialized delinquents have lower IQs and socioeconomic status, less overt parental rejection, less adequate father figures, better relations with their mothers, and less deviant MMPI (Minnesota Multiphasic Personality Inventory) profiles than solitary delinquents (Brigham, Ricketts, & Johnson, 1967; Hewitt & Jenkins, 1946; Jenkins & Boyer, 1968; Randolph, Richardson, & Johnson, 1961; Shinohara & Jenkins, 1967). Studies that have distinguished between disturbed-neurotic delinquents and unsocialized-psychopathic delinquents have also found differences between them in MMPI profiles (Shinohara & Jenkins, 1967) and in parental attitudes and family interactions in experimental problem situations (Hetherington, Stouwie, & Ridberg, 1971).

Although it bears only incidentally on subclassification of delinquency, a study by Monachesi and Hathaway (1969) has demonstrated the power of personality traits measured by the MMPI to predict delinquency. In two samples totaling over 15,000 ninth graders, boys and girls with high MMPI scores on psychopathy, schizoid tendencies, and mania had the highest rates of delinquency over the next several years. These scores were also the highest ones in the studies comparing MMPI profiles in the various types of delinquent boys (Randolph et al, 1961; Shinohara & Jenkins, 1967).

Taken together, the evidence on personality and behavioral characteristics of different types of delinquents suggests that the socialized-subcultural delinquent is a relatively normal person who happens to live in a family and community environment that enhances the learning of delinquent rather than nondelinquent norms, values, and ways of having fun. The unsocialized-psychopathic delinquent, by contrast, appears to be a relatively abnormal person who does not have good social relations even with delinquent peers and who actively seeks out trouble rather than seeking to make adaptive adjustments to his community (delinquent or otherwise). The third syndrome, disturbed-neurotic delinquency, has been less systematically researched and may represent a heterogeneous class of individuals who have personality or organic problems that happen to lead to delinquency, but who differ from unsocialized-psychopathic delinquents in having high rather than unusually low anxiety.

This "typology" should be taken with a grain of salt because most offenders may at times manifest behavior of all three general kinds. Also, various factors may interact so that, for example, a neurotic child is more likely to become delinquent if he lives in a neighborhood subculture where peers and other factors facilitate delinquency than if he lives where conditions make delinquency less attractive. The potential strength of culture in preventing or facilitating delinquency is illustrated by the extremes of the traditional Eskimo culture, where there is reputedly no delinquency at all, and the Mafia subculture of Sicily, where boys in Mafia families have virtually no choice but to participate in family crime (Cavan & Cavan, 1968).

In addition to the three types of male delinquents, female delinquents will be considered together as a group. Evidence exists that they, too, fall into categories like those of the males (e.g., Hetherington et al, 1971), but there has been much less research on female delinquency, perhaps because girls are arrested for less threatening offenses and many fewer are brought into court.

There is some cluster-analytic evidence that a syndrome characterized primarily by drug use is beginning to appear in delinquent populations (Stein, Sarbin, & Kulik, 1971), but the problem of drug abuse has become so massive in this country and it cuts across so many aspects of problem behavior that it warrants a chapter of its own, whether or not it represents a discrete category of delinquent personality.

SOCIALIZED-SUBCULTURAL DELINQUENCY

The first cash register I ever rang was in a drugstore on Broadway. There was one man at a long counter. Butch had picked this spot out for me because it was so easy and I hadn't done it before. Butch told me to wait until he did something to make the man come down to the far end of the counter. I watched Butch from inside the telephone booth. He walked up the aisle until he got to the candy display, then he stumbled forward, knocking over the candy and chewing gum display. The man came running out from behind the counter. As he came out, I came out of the telephone booth, went behind the counter, and within a matter of seconds was at the other end of the aisle helping Butch and the counterman pick up the stuff. Butch would pick it up and drop it again until he saw me coming. After we had picked up everything, the man thanked us and went back to his duties, and I walked out with his money [Brown, 1965, p. 31.] [1]

. . . the shoplifting experiences were alluring, exciting, and thrilling. . . . I was in the grip of the bunch and led on by the enticing pleasure which we had together. There was no way out. The feeling of guilt which I had could not overbalance the strong appeal of my chums and shoplifting. At first I did not steal for gain nor out of necessity for food. I stole because it was the most fascinating thing I could do. It was a way to pass the time, for I think I had a keener adventurous spirit than the other boys of my age, sort of more mentally alert. I didn't want to play tame games nor be confined in a schoolroom. I wanted something more exciting. I liked the dare-devil spirit. I would walk down between the third rails on the elevated lines in the same daring spirit that I stole. It gave me a thrill and thrilled my chums in turn. We were all alike, daring and glad to take a chance [Shaw, 1930, p. 7].[2]

In the United States, the highest delinquency areas are generally slum neighborhoods populated by recent immigrant groups. Poverty, large families, parents born abroad or in other regions of the country, parental (especially paternal) inadequacy, criminality and other social problems in the family, low IQs, poor school work, and youth gangs have been repeatedly found to characterize high delinquency areas. Impulsivity, frustration, lack of future-orientation, *anomie* (normlessness), and failure to internalize societal standards have been postulated as psychological causes of delinquency in these environments.

Despite the abundance of potential causes for delinquency in such areas, a major problem in identifying causal factors in socialized-subcultural delinquency is to distinguish between specific factors that would make life hard for any child and more general cultural factors that support delinquent solutions to such problems. In other words, are delinquency rates high among lower-class inner city children because the hardships of parental inadequacy, poverty, large families, etc., specifically cause delinquency, or is there something about the learning regime provided in their environments that makes delinquent behavior especially rewarding?

While adult crime is beyond the scope of this book, it might also be inquired whether middle-class culture specifically promotes certain types of adult crime that may be far more expensive to our society than is lower class crime. The invocation of "executive privilege" by politicians to prevent investigation of white collar crime at the highest levels of our government stands in marked contrast to the vehemence with which the same politicians vowed to punish "crime in the streets." Official tolerance of white collar crime is further illustrated by the action of the Internal Revenue

1 Claude Brown, *Manchild in the Promised Land* (New York: Signet Books, 1965). © 1965 by Claude Brown and reprinted by permission of The Macmillan Co., New York, and Jonathan Cape, Ltd., London.

2 C. R. Shaw, *The Jack Roller* (Chicago: University of Chicago Press, 1930). © 1930 by the University of Chicago and reprinted by permission.

Service pertaining to damages paid to customers whom 29 electrical manufacturers had jointly defrauded of $300 million. The IRS permitted the electrical companies to deduct the damages they paid as ". . . ordinary and necessary business expenses [Berg, 1967]."

Sociological Perspectives

Since studies of high delinquency areas in the United States almost inevitably focus upon minority or recent immigrant groups, it is instructive to turn for a moment to England where most high delinquency groups are neither recent immigrants nor members of ethnic minorities. In a comparison of delinquency in middle and lower socioeconomic groups, McDonald (1969) began by determining whether the differences between the groups were as great when delinquency was measured with anonymous questionnaires filled out by adolescents in school as when it was measured by police and court statistics. McDonald found that more lower-class boys did admit to delinquency and that they admitted to many more delinquent acts than middle-class boys, especially delinquencies involving damage and violence.

More importantly, across social classes, no significant associations were found between delinquency and several factors often believed to influence delinquency, including broken homes, working mothers, number of siblings, part-time jobs, youth club membership, religion, or church attendance. Thus, while these factors may have differentiated delinquents from nondelinquents *within* a social class, they were unlikely to have influenced the etiology of delinquency to anywhere near the same extent as social class did. Something about social status per se appears to have been operating to determine which children would become delinquent in the presence or absence of each of the other factors.

Sociological Theories.   The above findings were interpreted as being consistent with two different sociological theories of subcultural delinquency:

1. The *anomie theory,* first proposed by the nineteenth-century French sociologist Emile Durkheim and applied to American society by Robert Merton (1957). This theory holds that lower-class people share the same basic values and material goals as middle-class people. However, when their access to these goals by legitimate means such as education is blocked, they abandon the prescribed social norms for behavior and attempt to achieve their goals by delinquent means. "Anomie" refers to the state of lawlessness or normlessness characterizing such people. Merton maintained that anomie is an especially critical factor in American society because the goals of material acquisition are held out to everyone in greater measure than in most countries.

2. The *lower-class culture theory* (Miller, 1958) holds that the values and norms inculcated in lower-class children are different from those inculcated in middle-class children. Lack of reward for obeying rules and delaying gratification, less moral training, high esteem for "tough-

ness," etc., all combine to create delinquent rather than nondelinquent norms for behavior.

Merton's version of the anomie theory and Miller's version of the lower-class culture theory represent somewhat extreme positions in that they attempt to explain lower-class delinquency exclusively in terms of normlessness or the delinquent nature of lower-class culture, respectively. However, many current sociological concepts regarding delinquency are derived from one or the other of these positions. For example, in their widely cited book, *Delinquency and Opportunity,* Cloward and Ohlin (1960) inferred from anomie theory that various types of delinquent subcultures develop as substitutes for the dominant culture that has been rejected by the lower-class youth who finds his access to legitimate means blocked.

According to Cloward and Ohlin, one type of delinquent subculture is the *criminal subculture* organized primarily around stealing and other criminal activities for profit, often in liaison with adult criminals. In a criminal subculture, the material goals of the larger society continue to be pursued, but by illegitimate means. A second type is the *conflict subculture,* characterized chiefly by a search for status through violence. According to Cloward and Ohlin, the conflict subculture is most common in neighborhoods that are insufficiently stable to support the close social bonds necessary for organized crime. The resort to violence is, therefore, a result of being frustrated in the pursuit of both conventional *and* criminal opportunities for material gain. A third type, the *retreatist subculture,* centered primarily in drug taking, is hypothesized to represent a response to failure either to move on to successful adult criminal activities or to adopt other adult roles once the activities of a conflict group lose their attractiveness during late adolescence.

In order to assess Cloward and Ohlin's anomie-based theory of specialized delinquent subcultures, Short, Tennyson, and Howard (1963) attempted to find gangs in Chicago that exemplified the criminal, conflict, and retreatist subcultures. In over a year of searching, no group typifying the criminal subculture and only one group resembling a retreatist subculture could be found, although conflict-oriented gangs were abundant. Workers who infiltrated the gangs were able to secure considerable information on 598 members of 16 gangs, although gang structures and definitions of membership were found to be extremely fluid.

Through acquaintance with gang members, it was possible for the workers to judge whether each member had participated in each of a large number of specific delinquent and nondelinquent activities (e.g., hanging around the street corner, drinking, sexual intercourse, joy riding, gang fighting, theft, truancy, vandalism, narcotics, rape). Reliability checks on reports by pairs of workers who infiltrated the same gangs and checks against police records indicated considerable consistency in the ratings for each youth.

Factor analysis of the items showed that the primary dimension of behavior was most strongly characterized by conflict items, including individual fighting, group fighting, carrying concealed weapons, and assault, but that virtually all other delinquent activities were positively correlated with this dimension as well. The second most prominent dimension was characterized by sports, social activities, joy riding, truancy, and hanging around on the corner.

Thus, among the Chicago gangs, there was little evidence for the delinquent subcultural specialization hypothesized by Cloward and Ohlin. Instead, it appears that among lower-class socialized-subcultural delinquents the gang serves largely as a focus for adolescent peer group identification and for the organization of fighting among youths who engage in a large variety of delinquent activity independent of, as well as in conjunction with, the gang's activities.

Taking a different approach to the questions of anomie and lower-class culture, Rosenberg and Silverstein (1969) interviewed adolescent slum dwellers in high delinquency areas of New York City, Chicago, and Washington, D.C. In each city, a well-defined neighborhood was chosen where the young people knew one another and expressed a deep sense of localism in that they rarely associated with people from other neighborhoods, even when they were physically away from their own neighborhood. People who had moved to other parts of the city also returned frequently to participate in the life of the neighborhood. The population in New York was predominantly Puerto Rican, in Chicago southern white, and in Washington southern black.

Each interviewee was asked to let his imagination run loose with respect to the kind of job, income, and residence he would like to have. Most seemed to have aspirations in line with their realistic expectations, as illustrated by the following examples:

PUERTO RICAN YOUTH IN NEW YORK
Do you want very much to get ahead in the world?
Yeah.
What do you mean by get ahead?
Well, I'd have a good job.
Suppose you had any one of your choice—this is heaven now—any kind of job. What would you pick?
If I had any kind of job?
Yes.
I would get an office job.
You'd like to work in an office? Doing what?
Maybe typing or . . .
That would be the best job you could imagine? Typing?
No, it wouldn't be the best.
What's the best you can imagine? Dream.
That's kind of hard.
Can't you think of any?
No.

Well, what do you think you will wind up doing? . . .
Maybe something that has to do with stock work in department stores and things like that.
How much do you think you'll earn?
I won't make too much. Maybe about eighty or something [pp. 128–29].

BLACK YOUTH IN WASHINGTON

What kind of work would you like to do for the rest of your life?
Wash dishes.
Wash dishes in a restaurant?
I think that's clean. More clean, like, that's clean work.
Anything else you would like to do?
Cook. Cooks make pretty good money [p. 129].

WHITE YOUTH IN CHICAGO

What kind of work would you like for the rest of your life?
It's hard to say. I wouldn't mind working . . . I don't even mind pumping gas. I like anything that has to do with a car, put it that way. I'll go sit and look at a car all day long. I'm not sure what I'll do. I may get a job and just keep it, even if I don't like it. I mean if it's easy, I'll keep it. If it isn't, then I'll find a way to get fired [p. 131].

Less than 25 per cent stated high aspirations. Of those who did, some were realistically attempting to take the necessary steps toward them and had engaged in little delinquency. For example, a young black man from Washington said:

Success? That's a very large word as far as I'm concerned. Well, so far, let's just say after I've gotten out of high school, say when I got this job right here, I made a little success in attaining my goal. I have myself a good job now. I can, let's say, more or less get me anything I want because I don't have any responsibilities whatsoever. . . . I think I have been successful. . . . All I have to do is get into college right there. I think that's on the way to success.
What kind of work would you like to be doing the rest of your life?
The rest of my life? Well, that's why I'm trying to go to school now—to be a student first, then a lawyer second. That's what I really want to be—a lawyer. I think I'll be a pretty darn good one . . . I know first it takes four years of college, possibly three or four years of law school—because I want at least three years of law school [pp. 125–26].

Others of the 25 per cent with high fantasy aspirations were less optimistic but seemed content to settle for expectations more typical of their group, as exemplified by an adolescent in Chicago:

Why would you like to be a lawyer?
I don't know. I guess cause they talk a lot. I fit in there perfectly.
Do you have any idea what a lawyer does?
Yes. I have an idea of what a lawyer does. He makes good money, I can assure you of that.
What kind of thing does he have to do on his job?
He . . . either condemns 'em or. . . . In other words, helps 'em to get locked up, or maybe even sent to the death house, maybe even be the one who executes

'em. Or he could be the one that gets 'em out of an execution. But, it depends on whose side you're on, who hires you for the best price, or whatever. That's just like, say people out here hire you for a job and they don't tell you what you're running up against. That's the same way with a lawyer. He never knows what he runs up against until he's right there.

What kind of work do you think you'll do for the rest of your life?

Digging ditches mostly. . . . Or I'll be running machines. . . . Not too good of jobs, but jobs, you know. Enough today, at least it's a job [pp. 126–27].[3]

Rosenberg and Silverstein interpreted their findings as failing to support the anomie theory that delinquency results from the blocking of legitimate means to fulfilling high aspirations. If anything, there was an inverse relation between high aspiration and delinquency. However, the authors also concluded that basic differences in patterns of delinquency among the three ethnic groups studied cast doubt upon the theory that there is any *single* lower class culture that causes delinquency.

Delinquents and Nondelinquents in High Delinquency Areas

The Glueck Studies. The fact that by no means all boys in high delinquency areas become delinquent weakens any explanation resting solely upon subcultural hypotheses. The question of what distinguishes delinquents in a high delinquency area has generally been addressed by comparing delinquents to nondelinquents from the same neighborhood. One of the most ambitious attempts to do this has been carried out by Sheldon and Eleanor Glueck (1950, 1970). The Gluecks began with samples of 500 persistent delinquent boys and 500 nondelinquent boys from the same high delinquency neighborhoods matched for age, IQ, and ethnicity. Through extensive physical and psychological examinations and investigations of home backgrounds, the Gluecks found the following to be significantly more frequent among delinquents than nondelinquents: mesomorphic (muscular) body build; lower verbal than performance IQ; delinquency, alcoholism, emotional disturbance or serious physical ailment in parents; family dependence on welfare; poor management of family income; erratic employment of mother; crowded or disorderly home; broken home; lack of family cohesiveness; indifference or hostility of parents or siblings toward boy; unsuitable supervision, discipline, or punishment by parents. Other studies have confirmed the higher frequencies of these characteristics among delinquent than among nondelinquent boys in slum neighborhoods (cf. Peterson & Becker, 1965).

The Gluecks have employed their findings to construct actuarial tables designed to predict at younger ages which children will become delinquent in adolescence. The actuarial tables are similar in form to those used by

---

[3] Bernard Rosenberg and Harry Silverstein, *The Varieties of Delinquent Experience* (Waltham, Mass.: Blaisdell, 1969). © 1969 by Xerox Corporation and reprinted by permission.

insurance companies for predicting death rates and other phenomena in order to set premiums for various types of policies. The Glueck prediction tables weight the various background factors according to the strength of their relations to delinquency in the original samples of 500 delinquents and 500 nondelinquents. Thus, children who possess several of the heavily weighted characteristics will receive higher scores for potential delinquency than children who have few heavily weighted characteristics.

The Gluecks have cited numerous studies in which the scores for known delinquents exceeded the scores for boys who were not delinquent (e.g., Glueck & Glueck, 1959). However, in one of the few tests of the tables' *predictive* power, predictions from the tables were not more accurate than predictions from base rates for the neighborhood as a whole (Voss, 1963). (In a *base rate prediction*, the percentage of boys becoming delinquent in a neighborhood is used to make predictions for each boy individually. Thus, if 10 per cent of the boys in a neighborhood typically become delinquent, the base rate prediction for each boy is that he will not become delinquent because his probability of delinquency is only 10 per cent.) While some of the variables isolated by the Gluecks are undoubtedly related to delinquency, the failure of the prediction tables to improve upon base rate prediction indicates that the exact combinations derived *post hoc* from their samples do not relate inexorably to delinquency in new samples.

Cambridge-Somerville Youth Study. The Cambridge-Somerville Youth Study was begun in 1937 as an attempt to prevent delinquency in the slums of Cambridge and Somerville, Massachusetts. Treatment and control groups were formed of boys averaging 11 years in age and matched for health, intelligence, emotional adjustment, home backgrounds, neighborhood, and delinquency prognosis. Each member of the treatment group was assigned a counselor who visited the boy and his family, took trips with the boy, arranged when necessary for psychotherapy, medical, dental, and welfare assistance, and helped coordinate contacts with various agencies, summer camps, etc. The boys and their families were encouraged to attend church, clergymen were alerted to their problems, and police departments were kept in touch with the project.

The intervention of World War II, its effects on counselor turnover, and other practical problems prevented the project from being carried out as planned with the entire group. By the end of the project in 1945, only 75 of the original 325 boys remained in the active treatment group. Psychological testing, assessments of school adjustment, police and court records, and juvenile court judges' ratings of the seriousness of the boys' crimes showed little difference between the treatment and control groups at the end of the project or in subsequent follow-ups (Powers & Witmer, 1951).

By 1955, 41 per cent of the boys from the treatment group and 37 per cent of those from the control group had court convictions for nontraffic criminal offenses, the numbers and types of convictions were similar, and the tendency for crime to taper off in later years was similar in both groups

(McCord, McCord, & Zola, 1959). The negligible benefit of reform school was also evident in both groups, as 74 per cent of the treatment boys and 83 per cent of the control boys who had been sent to reform school were later convicted of major crimes. Analysis of numerous child, parent, neighborhood, and treatment variables showed no evidence that treatment was very effective for any particular subgroup of children. The only evidence for positive benefit occurred among 12 boys who had especially intensive relationships with a counselor for at least two years and whose counselor had frequent interviews with parents and had been able to remedy obvious material, medical, or educational handicaps. Only six of these boys, as compared to 11 of their 12 control boys, became delinquent $(p < .05)$.

While the Cambridge-Somerville Study evidently failed to prevent much crime, the vast amount of information accumulated on the boys and their families has made it possible to look for etiological factors in the data collected prior to and concurrently with the development of delinquency (McCord et al, 1959). Certain combinations of home characteristics were found to produce extreme rates of delinquency. For example, of the boys having parents who were quarrelsome, neglectful, and lax in discipline, 100 per cent became delinquent, as compared to only 14 per cent of boys with quarrelsome neglectful parents who used consistent love-oriented discipline, e.g., refusing to speak to the child. Across all types of homes, the rate of delinquency among boys receiving consistently punitive discipline was lowest (21 per cent), with love-oriented discipline being next (27 per cent), lax discipline being next (50 per cent), and erratic discipline being the highest (56 per cent).

The roles of parental deviance and love were examined together by assigning one point for each parent who was overtly deviant (criminal, alcoholic, sexually unfaithful) and one point for each parent who was unloving. Thus, a family's score could range from zero (neither parent deviant or unloving) to four (both parents deviant and unloving). The rate of delinquency showed an increasing progression for each point on this scale, from 28 per cent for boys whose parents were both loving and nondeviant, to 81 per cent for boys whose parents were both unloving and deviant. However, the biggest single factor appeared to be the mother's personality. Even when complicated by overprotective attitudes, anxiety, or neurosis, high maternal love generally led to low rates of crime.

It is difficult to extract any coherent picture of a single type of family constellation that alone produces delinquency in slum areas. Instead, it appears that several prominent factors having to do with parental laxness, inconsistency, deviance, quarrelsomeness, neglect, and hostility each increase the likelihood of delinquency in a boy living in a high delinquency area. The more factors present, the more likely the boy is to be delinquent. However, even among boys whose families did not appear to present the delinquency-enhancing conditions, approximately 20 to 30 per cent became delinquent anyway, indicating perhaps the pull exerted by the sheer fun of delinquent activities for boys who do not have strong scruples against them or competing sources of nondelinquent fun.

The "Good Boy" in High Delinquency Areas.   Another approach to delinquency in high crime areas is to single out boys who do not become delinquent.   This was done in a study in which teachers were asked to nominate 12-year-old boys in their classes whom they believed would not get into trouble with the law (Scarpitti, Murray, Dinitz, & Reckless, 1960).   Police records were searched to eliminate any of the boys who had already been in trouble.   Structured questionnaires were then administered to the boys and their mothers.

In a follow-up four years later, teachers were asked for nominations of "good boys" from the group who were now 16 years old, police records were searched, and the boys and their mothers were again interviewed.   Four of the original 103 "good boys" had acquired police records, although all were for minor offenses.   Teachers again nominated nearly all the same boys as likely to stay out of trouble.   The new nominations by teachers and the police records thus showed that the predictions made at age 12 held good for four years.

The questionnaire results showed that the boys were exceptionally good citizens, admitted to very little delinquent behavior of any sort, had favorable attitudes toward the police, felt that they were accepted by parents, and felt that their parents employed the right amount of discipline.   They were also favorably disposed toward school, were nearly all in the academic program (though not necessarily outstanding in grades or attendance), expected to finish high school, stayed away from boys who were delinquent, and said they would give up a friend if he were leading them into trouble.   Comparison with a parallel group of boys nominated by teachers as being headed for trouble at age 12 showed large differences in both the questionnaire measures and police records.   Although both groups came from the same neighborhoods and socioeconomic status, the proportion of delinquent acts for the later group was far higher over the four-year period studied (Dinitz, Scarpitti, & Reckless, 1962).   The findings indicated that a firm nondelinquent self-image developed by the age of 12 could insulate a boy against delinquency through his most vulnerable years, even in a high delinquency area.

UNSOCIALIZED-PSYCHOPATHIC DELINQUENCY

He lied so plausibly and with such utter equanimity, devised such ingenious alibis or simply denied all responsibility with such convincing appearances of candor that for many years his real career was poorly estimated. Among typical exploits with which he is credited stand these: prankish defecation into the stringed intricacies of the school piano, the removal from his uncle's automobile of a carburetor for which he got 75 cents, and the selling of his father's overcoat to a passing buyer of scrap materials.

Though he often fell in with groups or small gangs, he never for long identified himself with others in a common cause. . . . With several others he broke into a summer cottage . . ., stole a few articles, overturned all the furniture, and threw rugs, dishes, etc., out of the window. He and a few more teenage boys on another expedition smashed headlights and windshields on several automobiles, punctured a number of tires, and rolled one car down a slope, leaving it . . . battered and bogged in a ditch.

At 14 or 15 years of age, having learned to drive, Tom began to steal automobiles with some regularity. Often his intention seemed less that of theft than of heedless misappropriation. A neighbor or friend of the family, going . . . to where the car was parked . . . would find it missing. Sometimes . . . [Tom] would leave the stolen vehicle within a few blocks . . . of the owner, sometimes out on the road where the gasoline had given out. After he had tried to sell a stolen car, his father consulted advisors and, on the theory that he might have some specific craving for automobiles, bought one for him as a therapeutic measure. On one occasion while out driving, he deliberately parked his own car and . . . stole an inferior model which he left slightly damaged on the outskirts of a village some miles away [Cleckley, 1964, p. 86].[4]

The second behavioral-personality cluster found among delinquents has much in common with the traditional psychiatric diagnosis of psychopathic personality. This diagnosis grew out of the concept of "moral insanity," coined in 1835 by the English physician J. C. Pritchard to describe those in whom "the moral and active principles of the mind are strangely perverted and depraved; the power of self-government is lost or greatly impaired; and the individual is . . . incapable, not of talking or reasoning upon any subject proposed to him, but of conducting himself with decency and propriety."

By the late nineteenth century, "moral insanity" was replaced by the more clinical terms "psychopathic inferiority" and "constitutional psychopathy." The somewhat more neutral term "sociopathic personality" came into use in the twentieth century to avoid the implication of a constitutional etiology. In the latest edition of the American Psychiatric Association's *Diagnostic Manual* (1968), this term has been replaced by the term "antisocial personality," applied to:

individuals who are basically unsocialized and whose behavior pattern brings them repeatedly into conflict with society. They are incapable of significant loyalty to individuals, groups, or social values. They are grossly selfish, callous, irresponsible, impulsive, and unable to feel guilt or to learn from experience and punishment. Frustration tolerance is low. They tend to blame others or offer plausible rationalizations for their behavior [p. 43].

While most diagnosticians would hesitate to stigmatize a child as a psychopath, sociopath, or antisocial personality, the behaviors, personality test responses, and MMPI profiles reported earlier in the chapter as occurring in

---

4 Hervey Cleckley, *The Mask of Sanity*, 4th ed. (St. Louis: The C. V. Mosby Co., 1964). © 1964 by The C. V. Mosby Co., and reprinted by permission.

the "unsocialized-psychopathic" cluster have all the earmarks of the adult syndrome, whatever one prefers to call it. Not only are the behaviors delinquent, but the lack of sustained relations with others—even other delinquents, the persistent defiance of authority, the failure to respond to praise or punishment, the active seeking out of trouble, and the lack of strong emotions despite trouble-seeking, all suggest a personality constellation like that described for adult antisocial personalities.

Continuity Between Child and Adult Sociopathy

Longitudinal evidence on the continuity between childhood and adult sociopathic behavior is available from a study by Robins (1966). Robins attempted to locate 524 persons 30 years after they had been seen in a child guidance clinic, plus 100 normal control subjects from the same neighborhoods. Adult records were obtained from family members, neighbors, employers, police, etc., on 98 per cent of the sample and interviews were obtained with 82 per cent.

Two psychiatrists diagnosed each subject on the basis of all data available between the time the subject was 18 and the time of the study, when the subjects averaged 43 years of age. Eighty per cent of the former clinic patients were considered to be psychiatrically disturbed, with the largest single group (22 per cent) diagnosed as sociopathic. By contrast, only two per cent of the control group were diagnosed sociopathic. Ninety-four per cent of the sociopathic group as compared to only 17 per cent of the control group had been arrested for nontraffic offenses. The median number of nontraffic arrests uncovered was eight for the sociopaths.

Ninety-five per cent of the sociopaths had been originally referred to the clinic for antisocial behavior. The sheer number of antisocial symptoms listed in the child's clinic record was strongly related to later sociopathy in that none of the child patients without at least six kinds of antisocial behavior, four episodes of antisocial behavior, or an episode serious enough to warrant court referral was diagnosed sociopathic in adulthood. Thus, all the adult sociopaths had shown childhood antisocial behavior of at least moderate degree and the most prominent types of childhood antisocial behavior were the same as those regarded as pathognomonic of sociopathy in adulthood.

Information on family backgrounds indicated that social class per se was less strongly related to the later diagnosis of sociopathy than it is to juvenile delinquency. The number of antisocial symptoms exhibited by the child and diagnosis of the child's father as sociopathic were both far stronger predictors of adult sociopathy than was social class. Moreover, fathers who were rated especially cold had children with exceptionally *low* rates of sociopathy, and broken homes did not produce significantly higher rates of sociopathy than of other kinds of disorder. Thus, lack of warm, cohesive family relations did not appear to be so major a factor in sociopathy as it is in subcultural delinquency. However, as with subcultural delinquency, good parental discipline produced exceptionally low rates of adult sociopathy.

In reviewing 23 other studies on the relations between child and adult antisocial behavior, Robins (1970) concluded that his own findings were supported in that antisocial behavior in childhood generally portended antisocial behavior in adulthood, whether or not psychotherapy was provided. There thus appears to be considerable continuity between childhood and adult antisocial behavior, and sociopathic behavior in childhood is linked to the syndrome of sociopathy in adulthood.

Research on Sociopathic Personalities

Anxiety in Sociopaths. Although there has been little systematic research on unsocialized-psychopathic delinquency in childhood, a growing body of research on adults diagnosed as sociopathic (psychopathic, antisocial) is yielding a picture of a distinctive pattern that apparently dates well back into childhood. Beginning with a study by Lykken (1957), it has been repeatedly demonstrated that people diagnosed sociopathic show less anxiety on various objective measures than do normals or nonsociopathic criminals. Lykken's sociopathic subjects were adolescents and young adults confined in state penal institutions. One of his control groups was composed of prisoners diagnosed as neurotic, while the second control group was composed of normal high school and college students.

The subjects received a questionnaire measure of anxiety in which preferential choices had to be made between frightening activities and onerous activities equated to the frightening activities for general unpleasantness (e.g., making a parachute jump versus digging a big garbage pit). The subjects were also given two experimental tasks designed to measure learning as a function of painful consequences. On one task, the subject's job was to learn the correct "path" through a "mental maze" programmed into an apparatus having four switches. Operation of the switches in a certain sequence constituted the correct path through the maze. Whenever the correct switch for a choice point was pressed, a green light flashed and the program advanced to the next choice point. At each of the choice points, operation of one of the incorrect switches produced a shock. The subject was not told of the experimenter's interest in determining how well the shocked switches came to be avoided.

The second experimental task involved recording galvanic skin responses (GSRs) while the subject periodically heard two different buzzers. An unpleasant shock was administered after one of the buzzers. Extinction trials were then provided in which the buzzers but no shocks were presented.

Lykken found that the sociopaths differed significantly from the normals in more frequently choosing the frightening tasks over the onerous tasks, making proportionally more shocked than nonshocked errors on the mental maze, and showing smaller GSRs to the shocked buzzer. The neurotic criminals were intermediate between the normals and sociopaths on all three measures. Experimental measures similar to Lykken's but employing other noxious stimuli have also revealed poor avoidance learning by sociopaths (e.g., Gendreau & Suboski, 1971).

Emotional Reactivity in Sociopaths. Schachter and Latané (1964) sought to test directly the hypothesis that defects in emotional reactivity underlie the failure of sociopaths to learn from painful experience. Sociopathic and nonsociopathic ("normal") prisoners were given Lykken's mental maze task under two conditions, half receiving each condition first. Under one condition, the prisoners were given an injection of adrenalin (epinephrine), causing increases in blood pressure, heart rate, respiration, tremor, and flushing. Under the other condition, they were injected with an inert placebo.

The groups of prisoners did not differ in total number of maze errors, nor did the two injection conditions have an effect on total errors. However, under placebo, the normal prisoners showed a marked decline in proportion of shocked errors from the beginning to the end of a session, but the sociopaths showed little decline in their proportion of shocked errors to unshocked errors. Under adrenalin, the groups showed exactly the reverse patterns, that is, the normals did not decrease their proportion of shocked errors as a session progressed, while the sociopaths markedly decreased their shocked errors.

The findings were interpreted as indicating that sociopaths do not respond with avoidance to normal levels of pain-induced arousal, but that they can respond with avoidance when physiological arousal is greatly heightened by the injection of adrenalin. On the other hand, such high arousal levels disrupt performance by normals, who typically learn to avoid pain at much lower levels of arousal.

Pain Thresholds in Sociopaths. To test the hypothesis that sociopaths' low reactivity to pain under normal conditions might be due to their having higher thresholds for the *perception* of pain, Hare administered several levels of very mild shock to sociopathic and nonsociopathic prisoners. When a subject's threshold for the detection of shock had been identified, shocks close to that threshold were paired with certain stimuli and the prisoner was asked to identify the stimulus that had been followed by a shock. Using a boring version of the shock detection task, Hare (1968) found that sociopaths had significantly higher thresholds for the perception of shock than did nonsociopaths. However, when a much less boring version of the procedure was used, Hare and Thorvaldson (1970) found no differences between the shock perception thresholds of sociopaths and nonsociopaths.

Hare and Thorvaldson also asked their subjects to rate more intense shocks on a five-point scale ranging from "uncomfortable or unpleasant, but not painful" to "stop: don't wish to go any higher." When Level 5 was reached, the subject was told that he would receive two cigarettes for every further level of shock intensity he was willing to tolerate. There was no significant difference between the groups in the intensities tolerated without incentives (Level 5), but sociopaths tolerated significantly more shock than nonsociopaths when the cigarettes were offered. This indicated that they were especially willing to face pain in order to obtain something they wanted.

Effects of Various Punishments. In a comparison of the effects of various kinds of punishments, Schmauk (1970) administered Lykken's mental maze task under three punishment conditions to sociopathic prisoners and a normal control group. In the *physical punishment* condition, subjects were shocked for activating the punished switches. In the *social punishment* condition the experimenter said "wrong" in a disapproving tone when a subject activated a punished switch. In the *tangible punishment* condition, the subject lost a quarter from a pile of forty quarters whenever he activated a punished switch. Figure 13–3 portrays the effects of each type of punishment on avoidance learning by each type of subject. (The avoidance learning scores were calculated by subtracting the ratio of punished errors from 1 so that a high score indicates a small proportion of punished to unpunished errors.)

As in previous studies, it was found that sociopaths were significantly poorer in learning to avoid the punished switches when the punishment was shock. Likewise, the sociopaths' avoidance learning was significantly poorer than that of the normals under the social punishment condition. However, under the *tangible punishment* condition, the sociopaths' learning was slightly *better* than that of the normals! Likewise, the sociopaths' GSRs anticipatory to the pushing of a punished switch were significantly lower

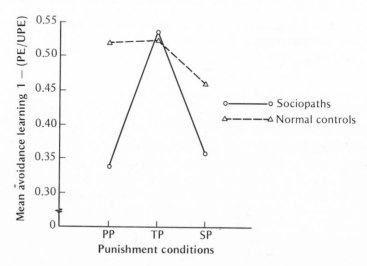

Fig. 13–3. Mean avoidance learning scores plotted for two groups across three punishment conditions (PP = physical punishment; TP = tangible punishment; SP = social punishment). Adapted from Schmauk (1970). © 1970 by the American Psychological Association and reprinted by permission.

than normals' in the physical and social punishment conditions, but not in the tangible punishment condition. The sociopaths in the tangible punishment condition also rated their anxiety higher and showed more awareness of the punishment contingencies than in either of the other punishment conditions. Thus, according to all measures, it appears clear that sociopaths were minimally affected by either physical or social punishment, but that they were as strongly affected as normals by the tangible punishment of monetary loss.

The implication of Schmauk's finding is that there is nothing unusual about the sociopath's nervous system that makes him incapable of experiencing anxiety. On the contrary, he is fully capable of experiencing anxiety and learning to avoid actions that produce it, but his scale of values may differ from that of the normal person so that he does not feel anxious in response to all the same events as a normal. On the basis of Schmauk's experiment, one kind of punishment that does appear effective is the immediate forfeiture of tangible assets.

DISTURBED-NEUROTIC DELINQUENCY

While the socialized-subcultural and unsocialized-psychopathic clusters each appear to represent relatively unitary groups of delinquents, there is little evidence that delinquents classified as disturbed-neurotic have much in common with one another beside, perhaps, unhappiness. Little research has been done on these children as a group and they may well include neurotic, psychotic, retarded, and brain-damaged children whose personal pathology and environmental circumstances happen to result in delinquent behavior, but whose delinquent behavior is only a small part of a larger picture of disturbance. Most of the evidence on this group is only indirect, comprising primarily findings of elevated frequencies of pathology in heterogeneous samples of delinquents.

EEG Findings

One of the most widely reported pathological findings in delinquent and aggressive children is an elevated frequency of EEG abnormalities. For example, Assael, Kohen-Raz, and Alpern (1967) found that 62.5 per cent of fairly severe delinquents in Israel had abnormal EEGs, while Bayrakal (1965) found lying, stealing, and hostility to be significantly more frequent among disturbed children with abnormal EEGs than among disturbed children with normal EEGs. Unfortunately, the lack of a control group in the first study and the lack of matching for age and other characteristics of the two groups in the second study make inference hazardous.

The 6- and 14-per-second Spike. High frequencies of a particular EEG abnormality, known as the *6- and 14-per-second spike,*[5] have also been re-

---

[5] A sharp, spike-like wave suggestive of an epileptic focus and occurring at recording points that normally produce 6 waves and 14 waves per second.

ported in individuals with aggressive behavior disorders (e.g., Kurland, Yeager, & Arthur, 1963; Schwade & Geiger, 1960). In a controlled comparison of patients aged 5 to 20 having normal EEGs, EEGs with 6- and 14-per-second spikes, EEGs with 6- and 14-per-second spikes plus other abnormalities, or other EEG abnormalities without 6- and 14-per-second spikes, it was found that only the group with 6- and 14-per-second spikes *plus* other EEG abnormalities showed significantly more aggressive behavior than the groups without 6- and 14-per-second spikes (Walter, Colbert, Koegler, Palmer, & Bond, 1960). The children with 6- and 14-per-second spikes plus other EEG abnormalities seemed to be distinguished from socialized-subcultural and sociopathic delinquents especially by their outbursts of extreme rage and violent acts with minimal provocation, as illustrated by the following case:

. . . this 13-year old boy impulsively shot and killed his mother. There is no history of illness or accidents. His social adjustment and school progress were excellent.

* * *

Prior to the shooting the mother had threatened to deprive this boy of his only meaningful relationship, his boy friend. When studied there was a lack of affect, some confusion, and total lack of ability to describe the tragedy in detail. At the time of the act he stated that he seemed to have to do it and could not resist. While in the detention home there were two aggressive outbursts without obvious cause. One was described as the boy being "at white heat with hands shaking." After he was in the State School there were several violent outbursts which he described as "They are just there. Then they are gone." They occurred when he was frustrated and lost status thereby [Schwade & Geiger, 1960, p. 618].

The XYY Syndrome

Another type of delinquent in which an organic factor may play a role is the male having the XYY chromosomal complement (detailed in Chapter 5). The incidence of XYY's in the population at large appears to be about .11 per cent as compared to about two per cent in mental-penal settings (Hook, 1973). This means that the probability of an XYY man being incarcerated in a mental-penal institution at any given time is 18 times greater than that for an XY man. It has also been found that XYY men tend to have severe acne, below-average IQs, and above-average heights, although the fact that tall XY males are not overrepresented in penal institutions indicates that height alone is not a critical predisposing factor (e.g., Hook & Kim, 1971).

The proportions of XYY men in other types of penal settings appear to be lower than those in mental-penal institutions, the absolute proportion of XYY men who become incarcerated is low, the crimes they commit are not especially aggressive, and the total proportion of crime that they account for is low. Hence, while longitudinal research is needed to determine why XYY boys are more likely than XY boys to be incarcerated, the XYYs do not appear to play a very significant role in the general picture of delinquency. In fact, spectacular publicity has greatly exaggerated the XYY phenomenon. For example, Richard Speck, convicted of murdering eight nurses in 1966, was repeatedly portrayed in the press as having an XYY chromosome complement, although the only laboratory to perform studies of his chromosomes found him to have the normal XY complement (Engel, 1972).

A few studies of criminal behavior in twins have revealed somewhat higher concordance rates for identical (monozygotic) than for fraternal (dizygotic) twins, but problems of sample bias, of definition of criminality, and of zygosity determination weaken the evidence for genetic factors other than the XYY chromosome complement (cf. Rosenthal, 1970a).

Other Findings

Collections of case history material on specific kinds of criminal deviance have sometimes suggested that certain types of crimes arise from particular types of psychopathology. For example, in a review of 80 adolescent boys arrested for sexually molesting younger children, "the adolescent child molester" was described as a loner who has no social peer group activity with youths his own age, prefers playing with much younger children, is immature and sexually naive, identifies with an overprotective and dominant mother, has a passive father, and is invariably an academic underachiever (Shoor, Speed, & Bartelt, 1966). Unfortunately, the lack of adequate control groups in studies of this sort makes it impossible to determine which of the foregoing characteristics are more typical of child molesters than of other adolescent delinquents or nondelinquents. Until such controlled comparisons are made, little can be said with confidence about subtypes of personality disturbance or neurotic motivation leading to specific crimes.

JUVENILE DELINQUENCY AMONG GIRLS

Perhaps because the offenses are generally less threatening to other people and less frequent than those of males, crime among females has received far less publicity and study than crime among males. However, since 1965, juvenile court cases involving girls have risen twice as fast as those involving boys, causing the former ratio of more than four boys to each girl to drop to three boys for each girl seen in juvenile courts (U. S. Children's Bureau, 1972). The disproportionate increase in female cases has occurred in urban, suburban, and rural jurisdictions, and has also been reported in European countries. Since an increase of such generality is unlikely to be caused by changes in specific court or police practices, it probably reflects a change in female role expectations such that delinquent behavior is becoming a more acceptable part of the self-concept of more girls.

The most frequent offenses for which girls are arrested and committed to state facilities are running away, incorrigibility, and sex delinquency, although the first two are often euphemisms for the third (Wattenberg & Saunders, 1954). Boys, by contrast, tend to be arrested and committed most often for auto theft, burglary, assault, and vandalism. Questionnaire studies of admitted delinquency by high school students have shown that the rank order of types of delinquent acts, as measured by the percentage of students admitting each act, is similar for the two sexes (Short & Nye, 1958, cf. Table 13-1; Wise, 1967), although higher percentages of boys admitted to each act and to repetitions of the acts. The sex differences in the statistics on arrests and commitments may thus exaggerate the differences in the types of offense committed by each sex. Sexual offenses and behavior associated with them appear more likely to result in commitment for a girl, while various forms of thievery are more likely to result in commitment for a boy.

Sexual Delinquency

The risk and actuality of unwed pregnancy are primary reasons for the greater judicial concern with sexual offenses by girls than by boys. Many girls adjudicated delinquent are, have been, or appear likely soon to become pregnant. Rapidly increasing rates of unwed pregnancy may account for some of the disproportionate increase in delinquency statistics among girls (Mueller, 1966). However, unwed pregnancy among adolescent girls is a highly variegated phenomenon that may have little more specific significance by itself than, say, theft, among adolescent boys.

There is little adequate research differentiating among types of girls, background factors, and subsequent behavior in adolescent girls who become pregnant, but what little there is suggests that cultural factors associated with race give unwed pregnancy a different significance among blacks than among whites. The rates of unwed pregnancy are far higher among blacks than whites and a far smaller proportion of out-of-wedlock black babies are given up for adoption (Mueller, 1966). The latter fact may be partly due to the lack of adoptive families for black babies, but the result is that a much higher proportion of black babies grow up without legally responsible fathers.

A comparison of unmarried pregnant black girls under 17 years of age with a control group of nonpregnant black girls has shown that about the only evident "pathogenic" factors more characteristic of the pregnant girls was a lower amount of punishment by parents and more mothers employed outside the home (Gottschalk, Titchener, Piker, & Stewart, 1964). The pregnant black girls had fewer broken homes, less sickness, less problems around menstruation, and fewer neurotic symptoms than the nonpregnant black girls.

Among white girls of similar socioeconomic status and similar neighborhoods, the ones who were pregnant had also received less punishment from parents, but had more broken homes and more neurotic symptoms than the nonpregnant white girls. This suggests that the black pregnant girls were relatively more normal than the white pregnant girls as compared to their respective control groups. However, a study of lower socioeconomic black girls in a special assistance program for unwed adolescents showed that those who became pregnant a second time shortly after their first delivery were less well adjusted and came more often from broken homes than girls who did not quickly become pregnant again (Barglow, Bornstein, Exum, Wright, & Visotsky, 1967).

Personality Characteristics

As a group, girls manifest far fewer problems of overt aggression than do boys. For example, in a factor-analytic study of children's psychiatric symptoms, Achenbach (1966) found for each sex a symptom cluster that was given the label "externalizing symptoms" and that included disobedience, stealing, lying, fighting, and destructiveness. For both sexes, there was also a cluster labeled "internalizing symptoms," that included phobias, stomachaches, pains, worrying, obsessions, fearfulness, withdrawal, and vomiting. Twice as many boys were found to have the externalizing cluster as the internalizing cluster, while girls showed exactly the reverse pattern.

Analogous to the findings on symptom patterns, a study of adolescents' responses to pictorially portrayed frustrating situations showed that boys gave significantly more aggressive responses than did girls (Rosenzweig, 1970). At both the levels of overt problems and projective responses to frustrations, then, aggression appears to be more dominant in boys than in girls. The stronger general propensity toward aggression by boys, for whatever reasons—cultural and/or biological, may account to some extent for the large sex differences in delinquency. Moreover, it appears that emotional difficulties may play a bigger role in promoting delinquency among girls than among boys. Wattenberg and Saunders (1954), for example, found that 59 per cent of girl delinquents came from broken homes, as compared to 44 per cent of boy delinquents. Higher percentages of girl delinquents also reported marked quarreling at home and intense hostility toward parents. In addition, more girl delinquents were classed as being friendless "lone wolves," hostile toward teachers and other adults, and unable to get along with their neighbors.

Personality Types

There is some evidence for personality types among girl delinquents analogous to those found among boy delinquents. Hetherington et al (1971) divided institutionalized delinquent boys and girls into groups of unsocialized-psychopathic, socialized-subcultural, and neurotic-disturbed on the basis of their scores on personality questionnaires designed to measure these three dimensions. Nondelinquent control groups of each sex were also selected from high delinquency areas. The interactions between each adolescent and his family were then observed in a structured task where they were asked to reach solutions to hypothetical family problems.

For both sexes, maternal dominance was found to be associated with neurotic-disturbed delinquency. The neurotic-disturbed delinquents themselves were found to be relatively passive and inactive in family interactions. The unsocialized-psychopathic and socialized-subcultural girls were more assertive and disruptive in interacting with their parents, particularly their fathers, than were any of the other groups, including the boys. The mothers of the unsocialized-psychopathic girls were the weakest in any group, although the fathers did not effectively control their families either. Furthermore, the parents of the unsocialized-psychopathic girls were the least warm of all the parents. While it is difficult to be certain how much of the parental behaviors and attitudes reflected *reactions* to their children's delinquent behavior rather than *causes* of it, the differences in family constellations found for delinquent girls differing in personality type suggest that a typology resembling the one employed for boys may be productive.

A factor analysis of personality test responses given by girls in a California training school substantiated the above typology to some extent, although the exclusion of subcultural delinquent girls from the population precluded identification of a socialized-subcultural cluster (Butler, 1965). Of the three clusters identified, one was labeled "disturbed-neurotic" and clearly resembled the category of this type found for boys and employed for both sexes by Hetherington et al (1971). The other two clusters appeared to represent subtypes of the psychopathic pattern. One cluster, labeled "immature-impulsive," was characterized mainly by aggressiveness, impulsiveness, and overt manipulation. The other cluster, labeled "covert manipulation," was characterized by an externally conforming· appearance coupled with continuous covert manipulation and reactions of aggression and hostility when the manipulative activities are discovered. Further refinement of these first attempts at objectively discriminating among types of delinquent girls may make it possible to identify differential etiologies, prognoses, and appropriate treatments.

In the meantime, clinical reports seem to leave little doubt of a female psychopathic type similar to that found among males. In his classic descriptions of psychopathy, Cleckley (1964) includes two females. One, Roberta, is described as having begun her career with repeated thefts, truancy, and straight-faced lying early in childhood. Her family was financially secure and could find no reason for her behavior. Despite her ingenuity in deliberately hiding her misdeeds, she reacted to discovery as if she felt people were just overdoing trivial incidents that she herself did not regard as important. Following psychiatric hospitalization and treatment, a series of jobs and placements were obtained for her in various localities. Her letters to her psychiatrist portrayed a remarkable cure:

You and Doctor ———— have given me a new outlook and a new life. This time we have got to the very root of my trouble and I see the whole story in a different light. I don't mean to use such words lightly and, of all things, I want to avoid even the appearance of flattery, but I must tell you how grateful I am, how deeply I admire the wonderful work you are doing. . . . If, in your whole life you had never succeeded with one other patient, what you have done for me should make your practice worthwhile. . . . I wish I could tell you how different I feel. How different I am. But, as I so well realize now, it isn't saying things that counts but what one actually does. I am confident that my life from now on will express better than anything I can say what you have done for me. . . . It is good to feel that as time passes, you can be proud of me and as sure of me as I am sure of myself . . . whether I go on to college or follow up my old impulse and become a nurse; if I become a business girl or settle for being just a normal, happy wife, my life will be fulfilling and useful. . . . If it had not been for you, I shudder to think what I might have become . . . [Cleckley, 1964, p. 73].

Despite her letters, Roberta was continually getting into trouble as serious as before, including theft, turning her quarters into a brothel, obtaining money under false pretenses, etc. Moreover, she frequently requested letters of recommendation from her psychiatrist whom she knew had been informed of her continuing escapades. She seemed blissfully certain that he would recommend her in the most glowing terms.

TREATMENT

The traditional "treatment" for crime has been punishment. The traditional motive for punishment has probably been revenge more than anything else, although it may be rationalized as deterrence, protection for society, correction, or rehabilitation, despite the lack of evidence that the traditional punishments deter, protect, correct, or rehabilitate.

Since the advent of juvenile courts at the turn of the century, the principal options open to judges have included informal court supervision by a caseworker or probation officer, official court supervision in the form of probation, and incarceration in a training school or other detention facility. Because courts rarely have enough caseworkers and probation officers to provide more than token supervision, the basic form of treatment for juvenile delinquents, as for adult criminals, is incarceration and the threat of incarceration. Although there had been a slight decrease from previous years in the number of juveniles in training schools, forestry camps, and temporary detention centers, over 49,000 juveniles resided in such facilities in 1970 (U. S. Children's Bureau, 1971). Close to 300,000 others were under court supervision in the community, primarily on probation or parole (Gibbons, 1970).

Traditional Institutionalization

Most institutions for juvenile offenders are "open" in that they are not walled and escape is relatively easy (and frequent). Superintendents have typically been appointed through the political spoils system. Token educational, vocational, and psychotherapeutic programs exist, but the orientation is primarily custodial. Major concerns include keeping costs down and avoiding disturbances and escapes that might bring community and political repercussions. Tacit agreements often exist between the staff and an inmate power structure dominated by the tougher, more experienced juveniles who exercise control over other inmates for purposes of extortion, homosexual practices, and scapegoating. The regimented institutional mentality frequently afflicts the staff as well as the inmates and there is little attempt to take account of individual inmate differences that may have bearing on prospects for rehabilitation (Gibbons, 1970; Street, Vinter, & Perrow, 1966).

Preparation and help are rarely provided for adoption of noncriminal occupations and life styles upon an inmate's release. Likewise, the inmates have little need for constructive thinking or initiative because nearly every detail of their daily living is structured according to regulations imposed by the staff. Rather than providing a positive socialization influence, the negative approach of traditional penal institutions appears to leave to the inmate subculture the task of socializing new arrivals. A delinquent's account of his incarcerations illustrates the form this socialization generally takes:

In the Detention Home, and in every institution where criminals are confined, the inmates always talk about their experiences in crime. That is the main topic of conversation. . . . Every fellow tries to impress upon everybody else what a great criminal he is and how many big deals in crime he has pulled off. Anything in the underworld like scandals, murders, robberies is interesting and talked about. Every fellow tries to tell the biggest exploit and make the other fellows look up to him as a big shot and a daring gunman.

They talk about the outside and how they're going to get by the next time. They talk against the police, and the older guys tell the young fellows how to get by in the racket and not get caught. The fellow who is timid and cries is razzed and made fun of. If there's anything that makes a young crook miserable, it's to be razzed by a big shot for being a coward [Shaw, 1930, p. 12].

It should not be surprising that the "cure" rate of the traditional treatment for delinquency is not high. Follow-up studies of boys released from training schools generally show that only 20 to 30 per cent avoid being rearrested within the next few years (Cohen & Filipczak, 1971; Gibbons, 1970; McKay, 1967). There is less information on the success rate with girls, but it appears that as many as 80 per cent of girls avoid rearrest within a few years after release, perhaps because they reach ages where the behavior for which most of them were incarcerated is no longer of concern to the law. The sex difference and the fact that most juveniles already have extensive police records before being sent to training schools suggest that the schools themselves do not actually cause further delinquency, but neither do they appear to prevent it very effectively.

In one of the few controlled comparisons between the effects of community treatment and incarceration, California delinquents who would otherwise have been sent to training schools were instead kept in the community to receive either individual therapeutic and vocational counseling or group therapy and supervision. Twenty-nine per cent of the subjects in the community groups had their paroles revoked within 15 months, compared to 48 per cent of the matched controls released from a state training school. However, the community groups committed an average of 2.81 known offenses compared to 1.61 for the training-school group. The higher rate of offenses among the community groups may have been because their parole officers were more likely to find out about their offenses than about the other group's. However, comparison of the seriousness of offenses showed that training-school parolees were more likely to have their paroles revoked for less serious offenses, while the community group had their paroles revoked only for serious offenses (Gibbons, 1970; Lerman, 1968). In short, it appears that community treatment led to a different sort of relationship with the parole officers, but there was no clear-cut evidence that training-school placement actually increased crime over community treatment. Nevertheless, it is clear that the traditional methods do little to prevent subsequent crime.

Psychotherapy. The addition of more than token psychotherapy to traditional training school programs has produced mixed results. Guttman (1970) compared parole violations by boys receiving psychiatric treatment in two California training schools with violations by boys from the same schools receiving no therapy. Treated boys from one school had fewer violations than untreated boys, while treated boys from the other school had more violations than untreated boys. The apparently negative effect of psychotherapy in the second school was attributed to the greater age of the boys and staff hostility toward the psychiatric unit in that school.

In another California training school, intensive individual and group therapy were provided for high- and low-anxiety boys (Adams, 1962). Upon follow-up, treated high-anxious boys were found to have the fewest parole violations, while treated low-anxious boys had more than untreated boys. Taken together, the studies suggest that psychotherapy may be a beneficial addition to training-school programs for some boys but harmful to others.

Pharmacotherapy. The finding that amphetamines seem to reduce hyperactivity and aggression in young children suggests that amphetamines might also be beneficial to some kinds of delinquents. This hypothesis was tested in a training school by providing amphetamines, a placebo drug, or no drug to boys who had been identified as especially difficult (Eisenberg, Lachman, Molling, Lockner, Mizelle, & Conners, 1963). The boys receiving amphetamines showed the greatest improvement in their behavior as measured by symptom checklists and sociometric ratings by peers and by the subjects themselves. Within three weeks after the end of drug treatment, however, the differences among the groups became negligible. Current concerns over drug abuse may militate against extensive therapeutic use of amphetamines with delinquents, but further follow-ups of the Eisenberg et al findings might contribute to a better understanding of the origins and possible control mechanisms for at least some aspects of troublesome behavior among delinquents.

Therapeutic Milieux

As an alternative to training-school incarceration, many mental-health workers favor the concept of the *therapeutic milieu*. Redl and Wineman (1957) have extensively described their early attempts to create a therapeutic milieu for delinquent children. Although their project, Pioneer House, came to a premature end for lack of funds, and no formal evaluation of its effects was made, their descriptions of impulse-ridden children have become classics in the field.

Maxwell Jones (1953) introduced the concept of the "therapeutic community" in which patients and staff participate as equals in governing the community and in continuous group therapy. Other forms of therapeutic milieux, including that advocated by Redl and Wineman (1957), emphasize democratic self-government and total staff participation less than does Jones's model, but they have in common an emphasis on group interaction directed toward improved socialization of the patients.

A comparison of the effectiveness of a self-governing therapeutic milieu like that of Jones with a more standard authoritarian system was carried out in England by Crafts, Stephenson, and Granger (1964). The patients were sociopathic males, aged 13 to 26, who were under court orders to have residential treatment. A council composed of all the patients and staff ran the self-governing unit. Each patient also joined an intensive therapy group. Patients in the more authoritarian unit were told that they would receive a therapy program designed especially for their needs. Noise and disarray were not tolerated and offenders were to be put to bed, fined, or deprived of privileges. Patients stood up when senior staff entered and monthly convocations were held at which notices were read and offenders were sentenced. Not enough nursing and psychiatric time was allotted for more than superficial psychotherapy. The rules made visits to nearby towns much more difficult than for patients in the self-governing unit.

Tests given at admission and discharge showed that the boys in the authoritarian unit improved significantly in IQ and in Porteus Maze measures of impulsivity and carelessness, generally found to be high in delinquents. Overall personality profiles did not change in either group, although the test results and test-taking behavior indicated that the boys from the authoritarian unit became more concerned with producing a good impression, while the boys from the self-governing unit became more carefree and abusive.

During follow-up periods averaging 14 months, the boys from the self-governing unit committed significantly more offenses, were more often in need of reinstitutionalization, and were rated less improved than the boys from the authoritarian unit. No differences were found between the groups in neurotic traits at follow-up. Contrary to the authors' predictions, it was concluded that the authoritarian unit produced better results than the self-governing unit. For this particular group, then, it appeared that the milieu having the more therapeutic effect was the one in which considerably less energy was put into psychotherapy and self-government.

Highfields. The Highfields program was set up in New Jersey to try out a concept of *guided group interaction* in the treatment of delinquents (McCorkle, Elias, & Bixby, 1958). About twenty boys were housed in the mansion of Charles Lindbergh's former estate, known as Highfields. Rules were at a minimum, but staff members could mete out punishment by assigning extra work during leisure hours and boys could be returned to court if they continued to misbehave. On weekdays the boys worked as laborers at a nearby mental institution. Weekends were taken up with house chores, recreation, and visitors.

The focus of guided group interaction was in group therapy sessions held five evenings per week. The topics were each boy's "problem" and the progress he was making on it. Guided group interaction was designed to provided socializing experiences in which the delinquent could discuss, examine, and understand his problems without the threats common in his previous experience.

Results. The effects of Highfields treatment were evaluated by comparing outcomes for Highfields boys with state training school boys who met criteria for admissions to Highfields (Weeks, 1958). Unfortunately, the groups could not be made entirely comparable because those who went to Highfields did so at the discretion of judges and as part of a voluntary condition of probation.

The results showed that 63 per cent of the Highfields boys completed their stays (usually four months) and were not reinstitutionalized for at least a year following discharge. This compared with 47 percent of the training school boys not being reinstitutionalized within eight months of discharge. (The difference in lengths of follow-up is partly due to the longer terms spent in the training school.) The difference in recidivism (relapse into crime) was especially pronounced for blacks: 59 per cent of those from Highfields completed their stay and were not reinstitutionalized, compared to 33 per cent from the training school. For whites, the corresponding figures were 64 per cent and 59 per cent.

Personality and attitude tests administered to the Highfields and training school boys at admission and discharge did not show major differences. However, within each facility, boys initially showing the most positive attitudes toward law enforcement had the best long-term outcomes.

Essexfields. The apparently greater effectiveness of Highfields in shorter time and at lower cost than the training school led the state of New Jersey to establish other group homes with similar programs. Another variant, known as Essexfields, differs from Highfields in that it is situated in an urban area and the boys return home at night.

Comparison of Approaches. A comparison was made between boys who went to Essexfields and similar groups placed on probation, sent to Highfields or other group homes, or sent to the training school. Recidivism during a two-year follow-up was 15 per cent for those on probation, 41 per cent for those from group homes, 45 per cent for those from Essexfields, and 53 percent for those from the training school (Stephenson & Scarpitti, 1969). When "treatment failures" (generally those who recidivated before their treatment was finished) were included, the recidivism rate rose to 32 per cent for those on probation, but it is not clear what it was for Essexfields and the group homes. In a somewhat similar comparison of a private institution (Boy's Republic) and a group home where boys returned to their own homes on weekends, Empey and Lubeck (1971) found 12-month recidivism rates of 44 per cent for the institution boys and 40 per cent for the group home boys.

The rather small differences among recidivism rates for the treatments other than probation do not show that any is much more successful than the others. Nevertheless, Stephenson and Scrapitti's examination of a number of predictor variables—including socioeconomic status, delinquency record, and race—indicated that boys who were generally poor risks (lower socioeconomic blacks with long delinquency records) often did better in Essexfields and the group homes than in the other treatments. This suggests that funneling certain types of high-risk delinquents into Essexfields and the group homes may improve the success rate with this group.

Halfway Houses. While there is no strong evidence that group homes markedly reduce recidivism for delinquents in general, the concept of a treatment situation intermediate between probation and incarceration has grown popular and many states have implemented it in one way or another. Perhaps the most general term for this type of facility has become the "halfway house," although this term also covers a variety of analogous facilities for mental patients, adult criminals, and drug abusers. The concept of the halfway house extends to people on their way out of an institution as well as to people in danger of being committed.

It is in helping to bridge the gap between institutional and community living that halfway houses may prove most useful, although the few existing evaluation studies have not shown that release from institutions to halfway houses reduces recidivism greatly (Keller & Alper, 1970). Nevertheless, even if "coddling" delinquents by giving them humane treatment does not reduce recidivism, the evidence so far that it does not *increase* recidivism either might make such treatment preferable to traditional incarceration, which is far more expensive.

Behavior Modification

It is only recently that reward for good behavior has been systematically applied as an antidote to antisocial behavior. The use of positive rewards by behavior modifiers should not be confused with approaches that offer reward or freedom noncontingently, as in the English experiment with the self-governing unit for sociopathic adolescents (Crafts et al, 1964). Instead, rewards are offered on an explicit contractual basis as motivators for the acquisition and utilization of behavior that can substitute for antisocial behavior. Behavioral approaches to the modification of antisocial behavior also use punishment, especially through deprivation of reward. However, rather than indiscriminately applying punishment once a person has crossed the threshold defining him as delinquent, behavioral approaches direct specific punishments toward reduction of specific, potentially modifiable behavior. As detailed in Chapter 11, various behavior modification techniques, especially token systems, have been applied to antisocial behavior in educational programs for institutionalized retarded delinquents (Burchard, 1967), institutionalized delinquent girls (Meichenbaum, Bowers, & Ross, 1968), and noninstitutionalized hyperaggressive boys (Hamblin et al, 1971). Application of behavioral methods in therapy of delinquents with their families has also shown a significant reduction of recidivism as compared to client-centered or psychodynamic family therapy or no treatment (Alexander & Parsons, 1973).

CASE-II-MODEL Project. One of the most thorough applications of behavioral methods with delinquents was undertaken at the National Training School (NTS), a Federal Government reform school (Cohen & Filipczak, 1971). Known as the CASE-II-MODEL project (Contingencies Applicable to Special Education–Motivationally Oriented Designs for an Ecology of Learning), it was implemented for one year following a pilot test (CASE-I).

A point system was set up in which each point represented one cent. Upon arrival, a new inmate, referred to as a "student educational researcher," was temporarily allocated a private sleeping room and was given IQ and achievement tests. The student was paid one point for every correct answer on the tests. Thereafter, he could earn further points for studying and passing tests. Points tallied by a staff member were employed in preference to tokens, which might be stolen.

The points could be used to purchase entrance to the recreational lounge, better food than the usual institutional fare, clothes, items in the store ranging up to TV sets, merchandise from mail-order catalogues, telephone calls, transportation home, and—after a free introductory period—continued use of a private sleeping room and private shower. Not being required to work for points, students could instead choose to go on "relief," which meant receiving regular NTS treatment such as sleeping in a group room and receiving standard institutional food and clothing.

The major objective of the program was to develop adaptive academic skills in boys who were so academically deficient that they would not have been able to obtain the most menial jobs. As opposed to the isolation and punishment philosophy of traditional institutions, CASE-II sought to motivate the boys positively to learn new behavior necessary for success in the outside world. Most educational instruction was done with programmed materials and teaching machines so that students could operate at their own rates and levels. They received payoffs in points whenever they succeeded in passing tests more advanced than the level from which they began.

Normal social behavior was also encouraged. Over the objection of the Chief Chaplain of the Federal Bureau of Prisons, the boys were allowed to purchase magazines like Playboy and to hang pin-ups in their rooms. They could also purchase admission to coed social events and could earn weekend passes during which they were encouraged to date. Unlike the traditional NTS policy of discouraging, ridiculing, and punishing masturbation and preventing solitude when it might occur, provision of private rooms and showers (when earned) made masturbation as acceptable as for non-institutionalized boys.

Results. Most students increased several grade levels on most achievement measures and mean IQs increased from 93 to 105.

Follow-ups showed that the students who had spent at least 90 days in CASE and were released directly from CASE had a recidivism rate of 27 per cent in the first year and 36 per cent by the end of two years. Of the students who had gone into other penal programs after CASE was terminated, 63 per cent recidivated in the first year, and 69 per cent by the end of two and one-half years. Previous NTS data had indicated a recidivism rate of 76 per cent for similar juveniles in the first year, although no matched control group was evaluated. The new Robert F. Kennedy Youth Center, built in Morgantown, West Virginia, to replace the National Training School, is maintaining much of the CASE program (Cohen & Filipczak, 1971).

DIFFERENTIAL TREATMENT

Despite the evidence cited earlier in the chapter for several different behavioral-personality types among delinquents and the evidence that most treatment programs do not succeed with many delinquents, only a few attempts have been made to find optimal matches between types of delinquents and types of treatment. Juvenile court judges may intuitively attempt to individualize the justice they dispense, but their limited range of treatment options, lack of objective criteria for identifying types of delinquents, and lack of follow-ups make this a haphazard business at best, although many judges appear loath to give it up (cf. Dean & Repucci, 1973).

California Youth Authority Studies

The most systematic attempt to establish and evaluate differential treatment has been carried out in the California corrections system, guided largely by Warren's (1969, 1972) concept of stages of interpersonal maturity. According to Warren, there are seven stages of interpersonal maturity, ranging from interpersonal reactions like those of the newborn infant, to an ideal of social maturity that is seldom reached in our culture. Adolescent delinquents generally range from Level 2 to Level 4. Within each level are subtypes characterized by specific kinds of behavioral reactions. For example, an individual at Maturity Level 2 is primarily involved with demands that the world take care of him. He sees others as either "givers" or "withholders," he cannot effectively explain, understand, or predict the behavior of others, and he is not interested in things outside himself except as sources of supply. The subtypes at this level of maturity are the *Asocial Aggressive*, who responds with active demands and open hostility when frustrated, and the *Asocial Passive*, who responds with whining, complaining, and withdrawal when frustrated.

People at Maturity Level 3 understand others better, but they perceive the world on a power dimension and manipulate their environments for short-term gains. The subtypes at Level 3 are the *Immature Conformist*, who responds with immediate compliance to whomever seems to have the power at the moment; the *Cultural Conformist*, who responds with conformity to his delinquent peers; and the *Manipulator*, who attempts to undermine the power of authority figures and/or usurps power for himself.

Individuals at Maturity Level 4 have internalized a set of standards by which they judge behavior. They are concerned about status and have rigid "good–bad" standards with no tolerance of ambiguity. The subtypes at Level 4 are the *Neurotic Acting-Out* delinquent who responds to underlying guilt with attempts to avoid conscious anxiety; the *Neurotic Anxious* delinquent who responds with symptoms of emotional disturbance to conflicts produced by feelings of inadequacy and guilt; the *Situational Emotional Reaction* subtype who responds to crises by acting out; and the *Cultural Identifier*, who identifies with a deviant value system and deliberately lives out his delinquent beliefs (Warren, 1969, 1972). Note that Maturity Level 2 is somewhat analogous to the psychopathic personality-behavioral cluster, Level 3 to the subcultural cluster, and the first two Level 4 subtypes to the neurotic-disturbed cluster.

In a long-term programmatic test of various treatments for the delinquent subtypes, delinquents committed to the California Youth Authority were first sent to diagnostic centers where classification was made on the basis of interviews and observation. The delinquents were then assigned to various treatments, many of which were community-based programs. One finding was that careful matching of delinquent subtypes with group home workers having styles appropriate to those subtypes reduced recidivism during a two-year follow-up. A second finding was that grouping by subtypes within a living unit resulted in fewer rule infractions, peer problems, and transfers to closer confinement, especially for Manipulators, Cultural Conformists, and Acting-Out Neurotics. These same groups were also found to benefit most from treatment in a community setting, while Cultural Identifiers were more effectively handled by incarceration. Another finding was that a behavior modification program was especially appropriate for the two types of asocial delinquents and for the Cultural Conformists. On the other hand, guided group interaction appeared to be most appropriate for Acting-Out Neurotics.

Kennedy Youth Center

Another approach to differential treatment has been taken at the new Robert F. Kennedy Youth Center, the successor to the National Training School. The physical plant was specially designed to facilitate application of the CASE-II system. A behavior checklist, self-report questionnaire, and life history checklist are employed to classify delinquents according to dimensions derived factor-analytically by Quay (1964). The primary dimensions are inadequate-immature, neurotic-conflicted, psychopathic-aggressive, and socialized-subcultural (cf. Dean & Repucci, 1973).

The primary treatment program is operant conditioning based on the CASE-II model, but the students are assigned by subtype to a cottage staffed by people best suited to handle the particular subtype. Treatment goals and point payoffs are worked out by each student with his cottage staff. Various other treatments, such as guided group interaction, are employed according to a student's particular characteristics. There are three levels within the token economy—*trainee, apprentice,* and *honors.* Promotion to each higher level requires attainment of the goals set for the preceding lower level. Pay and privileges are greater at the higher levels, although fines for violations are also greater. Prior to release, honors students move to prerelease cottages where they gain additional privileges. If the Kennedy Center operates as planned, it should provide a strong test of whether the institutional implementation of contemporary psychological treatment methods can be more effective than traditional institutional methods.

PREVENTION

If effective treatment programs for identified delinquents are difficult to create and evaluate, prevention programs are still more difficult, because populations containing potential nondelinquents as well as potential delinquents must be the targets and none of the subjects is under court order to participate in treatment. Nonetheless, one of the first large-scale attempts to deal with delinquency was an attempt at prevention, the Cambridge-Somerville Youth Project, described earlier in the chapter (McCord et al, 1959; Powers & Witmer, 1951).

The basic strategy was to compare the rates of later delinquency in initially matched groups of Cambridge-Somerville children receiving either no intervention or the long-term assistance of an adult counselor. While the implementation of the intervention varied greatly from counselor to counselor and child to child, these variations were considered less important than the benefit of the friendship-counseling-understanding relationship to be provided each child. The fact that a significantly lower arrest rate occurred for a small group who had especially intense long-term relations with their counselors suggests that counseling could make a difference, although, even in this group, 6 out of 12 of the children were eventually arrested. However, there seems little reason to doubt the general conclusion that nonspecific friendship-counseling-understanding, idiosyncratically implemented, did not reduce delinquency (McCord et al, 1959).

Taking gangs rather than individual boys as the target for intervention, Miller (1962) conducted a study in which detached streetcorner workers became involved with adolescent gangs whose values and behavior the workers then tried to influence. Seven gangs received intensive attention, seven superficial attention, and seven no attention. Upon follow-up, the number of court appearances was found to be almost identical for all three groups of gangs.

An unusual variant of preventive intervention was tried by Schwitzgebel (1964). He paid adolescents who had been delinquent at some time to serve as subjects in an "experiment" where their sole responsibility was to talk into a tape recorder during set hours each week. Over a period of nine to 12 months, the subjects' talk became progressively more focused on their own problems and seemed to reveal increasing insight. The subjects also developed friendships with the "experimenter" and became punctual and regular in their attendance. A three-year follow-up showed significantly fewer arrests and fewer months of incarceration in the experimental group than in a control group, although the numbers incarcerated were not very different (7 out of 20 experimentals, 9 out of 20 controls).

The heavy concentrations of deliquency in lower-class neighborhoods suggests that improvement of status for lower-class people may reduce delinquency in the long run. Unfortunately, public policies are rarely maintained consistently over long enough periods to demonstrate results of this sort. Isolated gestures like erecting public housing, for example, have never been shown to change suddenly the behavior of people toward whom the gestures were intended, and there is no reason to believe that stop-and-go actions of this sort will materially reduce crime. Moreover, larger changes in social attitudes often appear to outweigh concrete environmental changes in determining the overall volume of crime, as illustrated by recent upsurges in middle-class and female delinquency. Within the conditions set by the culture at large, however, specific familial factors appear to play significant roles in determining which individuals will become delinquent. Prevention at the level of the family will depend most upon the identification and modification of criminogenic child-rearing practices and attitudes.

SUMMARY

Early psychological explanations for aggression included Freud's concept of an aggressive instinctual drive and Dollard et al's hypothesis that frustration causes aggression. The latter hypothesis generated much research which has shown that frustration often leads to aggression, but that there are other reactions to frustration and other instigations to aggression.

Variables that appear to increase aggression include parental permissiveness and encouragement of aggression; reinforcement for aggression by compliance of the victim; imitation of aggressive models; parental deviance, quarrelsomeness, and rejection; and preference for violent TV programs. Severe punishment for aggression is positively correlated with aggression in early childhood but negatively correlated with aggression in later childhood. "Cathartic" aggression does not seem to reduce subsequent aggression and may increase it. Aggressiveness is relatively stable from childhood to adulthood in males, but not in females.

Children's moral behavior is highly influenced by situational variables, but their moral judgments are strongly related to their level of cognitive development.

Juvenile crime has risen rapidly since about 1950. Three personality-behavioral clusters have been repeatedly replicated in studies of male delinquents: *Socialized-subcultural* delinquency is especially characteristic of lower-class boys from broken, disorganized homes with deviant parents; *unsocialized-psychopathic* delinquency occurs among people of all social classes and is characterized by poor peer relations, low fear of punishment, and chronic misbehavior; *disturbed-neurotic* delinquency probably comprises a heterogeneous group of disturbed and organically damaged youth.

Female delinquency has risen twice as rapidly as male delinquency since 1965, although there are still three times as many boys as girls arrested. Girls are most frequently arrested for sexual delinquency, running away, and incorrigibility. They show much less aggression than boys, but there is some evidence for three personality-behavioral clusters among females like those among males.

Informal supervision, probation, and incarceration are the treatment options typically open to juvenile courts. Recidivism following incarceration generally runs between 70 and 80 per cent. Psychotherapy and various therapeutic milieux have produced mixed results. Compared to incarceration, group homes may cut recidivism somewhat for certain types of delinquents and are much cheaper.

Attempts to evaluate various treatments for various subtypes of delinquents have indicated that some treatments benefit certain subtypes while harming others. Little is known about how to prevent delinquency.

SUGGESTED READING

Development of Aggression.   Feshbach (1970) gives a thorough review of theories and research on the development of aggression in children. Most empirical research on variables influencing childhood aggression has dealt with it from the learning point of view. Examples include Bandura and Walters' (1959) comparison of aggressive and nonaggressive boys and their parents; Eron, Walder, and Lefkowitz's (1971) study of family characteristics relating to aggression; and Patterson and Cobb's (1971) analysis of reinforcement for aggression occurring in children's interpersonal interactions. A psychoanalytically oriented portrayal of extremely aggressive children is provided by Redl and Wineman (1957).

Subcultural Delinquency.   Some good firsthand accounts of what it's like to be young in a high delinquency slum can be found in Claude Brown's (1965) autobiographical book, *Manchild in the Promised Land*, and in Rosenberg and Silverstein's (1969) accounts of youth attitudes in three ethnically different high delinquency communities.

Psychopathy.   A classic book on psychopathy (sociopathy, antisocial personality) is Cleckley's, *The Mask of Sanity* (4th ed., 1964). Cleckley presents many fascinating case histories including those of a psychopathic scientist, businessman, physician, and psychiatrist, along with his hypothesis as to the underlying nature of psychopathy. Hare (1970) provides an extensive review of theories and empirical research on psychopathy.

Treatment.   Street et al (1966) report a sociological comparison of six residential settings for delinquents, including traditional penal settings, educational settings, and treatment-oriented settings. An extensive description of the Highfields guided interaction program can be found in Mc-Corkle et al (1958) and a report of the evaluation of this program in Weeks (1958). Cohen and Filipczak (1971) describe in detail the CASE-II behavioral program at the National Training School. Warren (1969) presents the rationale for and some findings with her system of differential diagnosis and treatment of delinquents by the California Youth Authority.

14

Drug Abuse

The use of drugs to promote pleasurable feelings for nonmedicinal purposes has a history as old as human civilization. What some may view as a scourge unique to the youth of our times might be more rationally approached if it is seen as a form of behavior manifested by people of many ages in many societies and historical epochs. Contrasts in percentages of people using drugs for pleasure, the drugs selected, the social significance of usage, and the nonphysiological consequences of usage can best be understood in terms of specific sets of psychosocial conditions.

As an example, in England during the early nineteenth century, an opiate-based patent medicine, Dr. Godfrey's Cordial, was widely recommended for young children "that are weakly and restless . . . and those that are greatly troubled with gripes, vomitings, or loosenesses [Wilson, 1968, p. 141]." A large teaspoonful was prescribed for one-year-olds, half that for six-month-olds, and so forth according to age. Contemporary accounts are available of the huge quantities of the cordial sold and of its obviously addictive effects. A surgeon of the time stated that such drugs were a frequent cause of death among children and that he considered informing the coroner of deaths that he knew had resulted from the drugs, but their use was so widespread he doubted if he could make an impression (Wilson, 1968).

At the turn of this century there were estimated to be 240,000 opiate addicts in the United States, a far greater proportion of the population than is now believed to be addicted, even according to the most liberal current estimates (Boyd, 1971). Many of the addicts were women who employed opiate-based patent medicines like Dr. Godfrey's Cordial for various aches and ailments. Little social censure or crime appeared to be associated with the use of such medicines despite their physiological and behavioral effects. In fact, opiate addiction was regarded as less serious than alcoholism and some physicians proposed to cure alcoholism by substituting opium for alcohol. Heroin was considered to be still less harmful as it appeared to be a cure for morphine addiction and was substituted for other opiates in tonics and cough medicines. Medical journals stressed its nonaddictive properties (Nyswander, 1963). Following the Harrison Narcotics Act of 1914, banning opiates for nonmedical use, the number of addicts decreased markedly, especially among women, while the association between crime and narcotics increased because many of the remaining addicts were men who engaged in criminal activities to obtain their now illicit drugs.

TYPES OF DRUGS AND THEIR EFFECTS

Before examining psychosocial characteristics related to drug abuse in present-day adolescents, it is important to distinguish among types of drugs and their effects. The biochemical and pharmacological properties of the drugs are beyond the scope of this book, but Table 14–1 presents the major categories of habit-forming drugs subject to fairly widespread abuse, their effects, and current beliefs as to whether they cause physical as well as behavioral dependence.

All the drugs in Table 14–1 are *psychoactive* in the sense that they cause alterations in subjective feeling states by affecting the central nervous system. A drug is usually considered to cause *physical dependence* if it induces a physiological state that requires continued ingestion of the drug to prevent physiological withdrawal symptoms. Some drugs, whether or not they produce physical dependence, induce an increased *physical tolerance,* meaning that increasing doses are necessary to produce a given subjective effect. Among the drugs that produce marked tolerance without physical dependence are LSD and related hallucinogens. Amphetamines produce marked tolerance accompanied by a questionable type of physical dependence. Opiates produce enormous tolerance, plus strong physical and psychological dependence, resulting in a continuously increasing drive to get larger quantities of the drugs.

Although physical withdrawal symptoms were traditionally used as criteria for classifying a drug as addictive, *psychological dependence* appears to be a more central factor in addiction than does physical dependence. Some drugs, such as cocaine, result in no physical dependence or tolerance, but very strong psychological dependence. Moreover, the strong physical dependence and tolerance produced by drugs such as the opiates appear to have greater psychological than physiological significance in maintaining addiction—relieving withdrawal symptoms by taking the drug strongly reinforces the behavior of drug-taking, but, even after complete physical withdrawal, appropriate stimuli such as the sight of another addict may elicit conditioned withdrawal-type symptoms in an exaddict, thus motivating him to resume taking drugs (Isbell, 1972). As a consequence, physical with-

TABLE 14–1

Some Commonly Abused Addictive Drugs.

Type of dependence	Drug	Usual toxic effects	Effect on central nervous system
A. *Psychological*	1. Organic solvents [a] (e.g., acetone, benzene contained in glue)	Mild	Depressant
	2. Tobacco	Mild	Depressant
	3. Cannabis (marijuana, hashish)	Mild	Hallucinogenic
	4. Mescaline (peyote)	Moderate	Hallucinogenic
	5. Psilocybin	Moderate	Hallucinogenic
	6. Cocaine	Severe	Stimulant
	7. LSD	Severe	Hallucinogenic
	8. STP	Severe	Hallucinogenic
B. *Psychological & mild or questionable physical dependence*	1. Amphetamines (e.g., Benzedrine, Dexedrine, Methedrine)	Moderate	Stimulant
C. *Psychological & physical dependence*	1. Alcohol	Mild	Depressant
	2. Barbiturates (e.g., Pentobarbitone, Amylobarbitone, Phenobarbitone)	Moderate	Depressant
	3. "Minor" tranquilizers (e.g., Librium, Doriden)	Moderate	Depressant
	4. Opiates (e.g., opium, morphine, heroin)	Severe	Depressant
	5. Synthetic Opiate-like drugs (e.g., Methadone, Pethidine)	Severe	Depressant

[a] Pharmacological properties of solvents give them potential for physical addiction, but type of usage, generally inhalation by young boys on a binge, make physical dependence unlikely, although large doses can be fatal.

NOTE.—From Boyd (1971) and Isbell (1972).

drawal may often be followed by readdiction because many of the old conditioned cues and reinforcers for drug-taking behavior have not lost their potency.

Tobacco

Identifying specific patterns of drug use is essential since any generalizations about the use of relatively inexpensive legal drugs enjoying strong social support, such as alcohol and tobacco, are unlikely to be valid for expensive illegal drugs subject to severe legal sanctions, such as heroin. In terms of sheer quantity of juvenile delinquency, the former drugs are much more significant than the latter drugs. Many states have laws against the purchase of tobacco by minors under a specified age, often 16 or 18 years. Most parents and school officials also object to smoking by young people and illicit use of tobacco by juveniles has many of the earmarks of other early delinquencies in that it is begun as a sign of toughness, adultness, disregard for authority, camaraderie with other youth, etc. However, the fact that tobacco is so widely condoned and available and that its harmful effects are long-term physiological debilitation rather than intoxication or physiological dependence mean that its use is rarely regarded as a significant delinquency. Even the anonymous questionnaire studies, cited in Chapter 13, concerning self-admitted offenses that were not all technically illegal have completely omitted questions on tobacco and there is no firm data on the percentage of children who smoke or whether smoking is significantly associated with other delinquency (Short & Nye, 1958; Wise, 1967).

Alcohol

In some respects, alcohol occupies a category intermediate between tobacco and other addictive drugs. Like tobacco, it is illicitly used by a large proportion of adolescents, but, because its greater cost and more stringent control make it more likely to be obtained illegally and because it produces intoxication that is more conspicuously related to antisocial behavior, alcohol is a greater focus of concern in relation to juvenile delinquency. Despite adult social support for drinking, abuse of alcohol is also a far larger problem than is abuse of illegal drugs. There are estimated to be at least 6,000,000 alcoholics and several million other problem drinkers in the United States. It has been estimated that over 50 per cent of fatal traffic accidents involve at least one drunken driver. Adding the large number of crimes committed under the influence of alcohol to the upwards of 30,000 annual traffic deaths involving drunkenness, the amount of personal grief brought to children and spouses of alcoholics, and the physical debilitation resulting from alcoholism demonstrates that alcohol abuse should probably be regarded as our Number 1 drug problem.

Statistics on arrests suggest that alcohol abuse also constitutes a numerically larger problem than other forms of drug abuse by juveniles. In 1971, there were over 81,000 arrests of persons under 18 for violation of liquor laws and over 47,000 for drunkenness, compared to 88,000 for all violations of narcotic drug laws. Since simple possession of liquor is less likely to result in arrest than is possession of other drugs, the disparity in usage is likely to be even greater than indicated by the ratio of 128,000 arrests for alcohol violations to 88,000 for other drugs. However, the rate of increase in arrests for alcohol-related offenses has been far smaller than for other drug offenses. California statistics, for example, show an increase of over 2,000 per cent in nonalcoholic drug arrests between 1960 and 1969, from 1,616 to 35,965 (Fraser, 1972).

Illicit Drugs

Despite the fact that offenses related to alcohol are numerically more common among the young and that abuse of alcohol may cost our society more than drug addiction, abuse of other drugs is of much greater current concern and probably has a more direct relation to other serious crime among the young than does alcohol abuse. Moreover, the tremendous increase in the extent and variety of abuse of drugs other than alcohol during the 1960s and early 1970s has caused widespread alarm that has created major political issues and had ramifications at every level of our society.

Drug Abuse in Other Developed Countries. While the total quantity of drug abuse among young Americans appears to be higher, or at least better publicized, than in most other countries, large increases in drug abuse have occurred in other developed countries as well (cf. Btesh, 1972). The United Kingdom, which has long permitted physicians to prescribe opiates and cocaine for addicts, witnessed an increase from 437 known addicts in 1960 to 2,782 in 1968 (Beedle, 1972). This increase appeared due largely to the rise of a general drug culture among youths who first obtained narcotics from addicts and others posing as addicts who had been given prescriptions by physicians (James, 1969). The fact that the "British system" of prescribing drugs for addicts had successfully stabilized the number of addicts for four decades, but was unsuccessful when a new set of values arose among the young, demonstrates the influence of cultural factors on drug use regardless of the official mechanism for handling drugs. However, treatment programs, compulsory registration of addicts, and limitations on the number of physicians allowed to dispense drugs brought a decline in known British addicts to 1,430 in 1970.

Illegal amphetamine abuse in Britain showed an increase from 958 convictions in 1965 to 3,603 in 1969. Convictions for illegal use of cannabis went from 663 in 1963 to 7,250 in 1970, while LSD convictions went from 159 in 1969 to 757 in 1970 (Beedle, 1972).

Studies in Sweden provide about the best picture of drug use among the young of any country because they are based upon questionnaire surveys of large proportions of the nation's youth (Goldberg, 1972). In a 1967 survey of 16-year-olds in greater Stockholm, 19.6 per cent admitted illicit drug use at some time. Cannabis was by far the most frequently used drug. Some important findings of the survey were that drug abuse was correlated with broken homes, enrollment in nonscholastic school courses, and heavy consumption of alcohol and tobacco. The first two factors suggest that drug abuse in Sweden is correlated with the same types of home and school factors reported in Chapter 13 for delinquency in general.

The correlation of illicit drug abuse with alcohol and tobacco consumption suggests that illicit drugs do not function as substitutes for the legal ones, but that youths who use one type heavily also use the other type heavily.

Cannabis. This section will focus primarily upon marijuana, the most widely used illicit drug and the crux of the greatest controversy. Much that is said of marijuana can also be said for hashish, which comes from the same plant (*Cannabis sativa,* "Indian hemp"). Marijuana—also known as "grass," "pot," "weed," "bush," "tea," "joint," "boo," "Mary Jane," and "dope"—is typically a mixture of crushed cannabis leaves, flowers, and twigs, while hashish ("hash") is made from the more potent resin of the plant. The principal active chemical compound is *Tetrahydrocannabinol* (THC), which is sometimes taken in pure form to obtain stronger effects than those gained by smoking cannabis.

Use of cannabis for production of hemp and for medicinal, ceremonial, and intoxicating purposes began in many cultures long before the birth of Christ. Marijuana smoking spread in the southwestern United States and especially in New Orleans around 1910, largely as a result of contact with Mexicans, who had begun using it widely during the late nineteenth century. The word marijuana is itself Mexican. Black jazz musicians, their fans, and lower-class urban blacks were the first identifiable groups in the United States to use marijuana on a large scale. During the 1920s and 1930s, New Orleans served as the major distribution center from which marijuana was shipped up the Mississippi to other urban areas. A committee appointed by New York Mayor Fiorello LaGuardia reported in 1944 that there were at least 500 individual marijuana peddlers in Harlem and 500 "tea pads" where marijuana was sold (Commission of Inquiry into the Nonmedical Use of Drugs, 1972—hereafter cited as CINUD).

An increase in white middle-class use of marijuana apparently occurred after World War II when soldiers who had begun using it in the service returned to college campuses under the G.I. Bill. This increase was augmented in the 1950s by the endorsement given marijuana by popular Beat writers such as William Burroughs, Allen Ginsberg, and Jack Kerouac.

In the middle and late 1960s, usage burgeoned due in part to the spread of the psychedelic youth culture in which the popular rock music groups sang drug-related lyrics and touted drug-induced ecstasies. Drugs also became a prominent youth symbol in the traditional conflict between generations that was enormously heightened by the Vietnam war. The Vietnam war was itself a direct cause of the spread of marijuana usage among Americans because many American servicemen first began using marijuana in Vietnam, where it is abundantly available in potent form. By the early 1970s, it was conservatively estimated that between 50 and 60 per cent of soldiers stationed in Vietnam had at least experimented with marijuana, most while they were stationed in Vietnam (U. S. House Committee on Armed Services, 1971).

The total number of Americans using marijuana at least once is estimated at between eight and 25 million, with about a million "potheads" maintaining chronic marijuana intoxication (U. S. Public Health Service, 1972). Between 35 and 50 per cent of high school and college students are believed to have tried marijuana and 35 per cent of these have used it more than 10 times (Benson & Wallace, 1972). The widespread availability of marijuana has made it unnecessary to become part of a special group or to go to great lengths to get the drug. Most Americans first try marijuana out of curiosity at the urging of friends (CINUD, 1972).

Marijuana has been classed as an hallucinogen in Table 14–1 because heavy doses induce hallucinations, thought disorder, and delusions. In the more typical smaller doses, the subjective effects are a feeling of being "high," mild intoxication, loosening of inhibitions, increase in self-confidence, and uncontrollable hilarity or crying. Under intermediate doses, there is a rush of thoughts, sights and sounds seem more vivid, and there may be an illusion that one is thinking better. Judgment and memory become impaired, and confusion, disorientation, and mood variation occur.

As with most psychoactive drugs, the effects of marijuana depend a great deal on the circumstances of administration and the user's personality and expectations. Initial usage rarely produces positive experiences. These usually come only after training in inhalation procedures and guidance by veteran users as to the drug's various effects. Between 20 and 50 per cent of users are estimated to discontinue after a few trials (CINUD, 1972). Those who continue moderate to heavy usage appear to restrict their associations to other users, partly in order to maintain secrecy, although the need for special contacts with dealers and fear of arrest now appear minimal. Heavy long-term users acquire many of the characteristics of mental inertia found in chronic alcoholics (Boyd, 1971), and emotionally vulnerable individuals may be precipitated into acute panic, paranoia, or psychosis.

While there are indications that the frequency of psychopathology is higher in chronic cannabis users than in nonusers, it is not known whether cannabis leads to psychopathology through neurological, emotional, or psychosocial effects, or whether psychopathology contributes to cannabis usage.

The same problem as to causal direction exists with respect to determining reasons why there appears to be a statistical association between cannabis consumption and other forms of crime. It is unknown whether such an association is due primarily to the fact that an individual willing to break any given law (e.g., by using cannabis) is more likely than average to commit other offenses, or whether the lessening of inhibitions through cannabis consumption makes an individual more likely to commit crime. There are a few reports of crimes committed under the influence of cannabis and of crimes committed in order to obtain cannabis (CINUD, 1972).

Marijuana produces a number of minor short-term physiological effects, such as increases in pulse rate, bloodshot eyes, puffing around the eyes, drying of the mouth, throat, and nasal passages, stimulation of the appetite, nausea, and drowsiness. Long-term effects have not been well studied, although the cancer-producing potential of marijuana smoking is probably equal to that of tobacco. Both yield similar amounts of tar and the typically lower frequency of marijuana than tobacco smoking is offset by the deeper inhalation and longer retention of marijuana smoke. Conflicting results have been obtained in EEG studies of cannabis users. The highest rates of EEG abnormalities and other signs of neurological damage have been reported in cannabis users who also used other drugs such as LSD and amphetamines (Campbell, Evans, Thomson, & Williams, 1971; CINUD, 1972).

Marijuana, Hard Drugs, and Social Problems. One of the most frequently used arguments against legalization of marijuana is that its use "leads to" the use of more dangerous drugs, especially heroin, amphetamines, and LSD. It has been found that marijuana was the first drug, other than tobacco and alcohol, used by many users of more dangerous drugs (e.g., Fraser, 1972), although these users also made exceptionally heavy use of alcohol and tobacco.

The epidemic use of marijuana by white, middle-class adolescents has not been in progress long enough to test a causal relationship between the adolescent use of marijuana and the later use of other drugs by this group, but there is some evidence on this relationship among urban black males who were adolescents at a time when marijuana was already plentiful in their neighborhoods. In a follow-up study of boys in St. Louis, Robins, Darvish, and Murphy (1970) interviewed over 200 black males averaging about 33 years in age. Information on the men was also obtained from police, Federal Bureau of Narcotics, and hospital records. Almost half the men reported using marijuana at some time and a third had begun before their twentieth birthday.

Comparisons of the marijuana users with men who had used no drugs showed that more of the users had failed to graduate from high school and college; married spouses who had previous marriages or illegitimate children; reported their own marital infidelity and the fathering of illegitimate children; earned less than $4,000 per year; worked at low-status jobs; suffered unemployment; received financial aid; had adult police records for nondrug offenses; drank heavily enough to create social or medical problems; and reported violent behavior. Even when Robins et al controlled for dropping out of high school, nondrug juvenile delinquency, and early drinking, the above differences between users and nonusers on the other variables remained.

Although it could not be conclusively proved that adolescent marijuana use *caused* the relationships found, more subjects who began using marijuana in adolescence than in adulthood eventually went on to amphetamines, barbiturates, and opiates, to opiate addiction, and to heavy drinking, medical or social problems with alcohol, and alcoholism. Of those who had begun using marijuana in adolescence, those who continued to use it for more than five years also showed higher frequencies of nearly all the social problems studied than did those who used it for less than five years.

Whether adolescent marijuana usage is an index of other personal problems or whether it is a fundamental cause of problems cannot be determined with certainty from the Robins et al data, but the existence of a strong relationship between early marijuana usage and later overt social problems seems well established for this group of black urban males. Moreover, the evidence conclusively shows that marijuana does not function as a substitute for alcohol or other drugs and that users are not less violent than comparable nonusers. In fact, marijuana use was positively correlated with the use of alcohol and other drugs and with violent behavior. There was also some indication that early marijuana use was likely to interfere with the solving of typical adolescent social problems so that the users were less prepared for adulthood and, therefore, more likely to continue seeking refuge in drugs, including alcohol and hard drugs.

Legal Controls. In recognition of the fact that marijuana is probably a less serious threat than hard drugs, federal laws were rewritten in 1970 to classify the possession and sale of marijuana as misdemeanors rather than felonies, although the penalties for these offenses still range up to a year in prison and/or a $5,000 fine. More severe penalties are provided for second offenses and for giving marijuana to minors under 18 years of age. Marijuana currently presents many of the same dilemmas that alcohol and tobacco present: All three are demonstably harmful to the well-being of users and are potentially harmful to the well-being of nonusers. Free access to any, especially alcohol and marijuana, by adolescents is likely to interfere with their solving developmental tasks in ways that contribute toward adequate adult adjustment. However, the drugs are enjoyed by such a large proportion of the population and they can be so easily obtained illegally that total prohibition seems as likely to fail and as likely to bring other harmful effects as the prohibition of alcohol in the 1920s. About the only thing clearly distinguishing marijuana from alcohol and tobacco is that the number of people using it is far smaller and can probably be kept that way if it is not legalized.

Other Hallucinogens. LSD (lysergic acid diethylamide, "acid") is the best known and probably most widely used hallucinogen beside cannabis. Others include mescaline ("peyote"), psilocybin ("mushrooms"), and STP (4-methyl-2, 5-dimethoxyalphamethyl phenethylamine). While these drugs, especially LSD, were prominent in the middle-class youth culture of the mid 1960s, their use seems to be decreasing, perhaps in response to the stricter controls on their distribution, to fears of chromosomal and other organic damage, and to accumulated evidence that "bad trips" can be extremely harmful to many people (Kifner, 1968). The most conspicuous harmful effects have been LSD-precipitated psychoses and dangerous behavior that have led to accidental deaths. There is also evidence of increased birth defects, chromosomal breakage, and spontaneous abortion in the offspring of people who have used LSD and of inhibition of disease-combatting antibodies in the users themselves (Maugh, 1973). The decline of the psychedelic youth culture and of availability of the extreme hallucinogens as well as the lack of much sentiment for legalizing them mean that they will probably play a decreasing role in future drug abuse.

Stimulants. Amphetamines and cocaine are the two major stimulants subject to large-scale abuse.

Amphetamines. Amphetamines ("speed," "pep pills") have been legally prescribed by physicians for ailments ranging from obesity and depression to stuffiness caused by head colds. They are also prescribed for hyperactive children whose hyperactivity they, paradoxically, seem to reduce. However, they have been subject to widespread dependency-producing abuse by people who obtain them through prescription as well as by those who obtain them illegally. The most commonly abused amphetamines are Benzedrine ("bennies"), Dexedrine, and Methedrine. Federal action was taken in 1973 to limit drastically the availability of diet drugs containing amphetamines (Schmeck, 1973).

Moderate doses of amphetamines produce feelings of self-confidence, alertness, and well-being for a few hours and are often used by truck drivers and students to ward off fatigue. Heavy doses cause withdrawal, irritability, disorganized thinking, and paranoid psychoses. The psychoses are apparently direct products of the drugs rather than being precipitated by the drugs only in vulnerable individuals. Because there is an increasing tolerance for amphetamines, increasing doses are needed to produce a given effect. Moreover, withdrawal of the drug produces depression reaching suicidal proportions. These factors combine to drive the heavy user toward ever larger, more continuous, and more direct dosing, especially intravenous administration ("shooting" speed), and to the use of depressant drugs (barbiturates, heroin) to blot out the effects of the "crash" that comes when amphetamines wear off.

Experiencing pleasure from large doses and continuing their use appear to be greatly enhanced by the presence of other users who provide social support and advice on effects and techniques. Smith's (1972) study of adolescent users in the Haight-Ashbury district of San Francisco documents the progression from an initial curiosity about various drugs to the abandonment of old life styles and adoption of the alliances, rhetoric, and attitudes of the speed culture, along with criminal activities required to support the habit.

Steadily escalating levels of violence seem particularly characteristic of the speed culture because of the kinds of behavior directly promoted by the drugs, the inexperience of middle-class users in stable, profitable, and nonviolent crime, and the inability of speed addicts to plan and carry out systematic criminal activities like burglary, which is a mainstay of heroin addicts. The murder of dealers suspected of being "burn artists"—those who sell adulterated or phony drugs—seems especially common. Many deaths attributed to accidental overdoses may really be murders by means of deliberate injections administered by dissatisfied customers (Smith, 1972). Whether amphetamines contribute similarly to crime and violence outside of subcultures like those in the Haight-Ashbury is not known, although the disastrous effects they have on users seem to insure that they will present a major problem unless changes in drug fads and availability significantly reduce the number of new users.

Cocaine. Cocaine produces many of the same effects as the amphetamines, but it is physiologically more toxic. It can produce extreme excitement, confusion, headache, nausea, vomiting, abdominal pain, aggression, and psychosis with delirium, convulsions, and coma. It is typically sniffed or injected intravenously and is often taken with opiates that serve as "downs" to counteract the "up" caused by the cocaine. The "speedball" is an especially vicious combination of cocaine and heroin. Perhaps because its negative physiological effects are more conspicuous and immediate and it is generally less available, cocaine appears to be less widely used than amphetamines among American adolescents.

Depressants

Organic Solvents. Sniffing of organic solvents contained in some glues, cleaning fluids, and aerosol sprays tends to be confined to young boys who use it to produce a temporary feeling of being high. The effects of small doses do not last long and they do not appear to cause addiction, although there have been cases of compulsive glue sniffing. Mild asphyxiation is responsible for much of the high feeling. Convulsions and death can be caused by prolonged asphyxiation through sniffing of highly concentrated solvents. The recent addition of mustard and other unpleasant smelling additives to these solvents has been designed to deter sniffing, although many other widely available volatile substances can produce a high through sniffing.

Barbiturates and Minor Tranquilizers. Barbiturates (e.g., Phenobarbital, Pentobarbital, Amylobarbital, Seconal; "barbs," "goof balls," "candy"), and "minor" tranquilizers (e.g., Librium, Doriden) have been medically prescribed in large quantities to help people relax and sleep. Their primary effect in small doses is sedative. However, in higher doses, they produce intoxication, confusion, staggering, anger, irritability, and impairment in thinking and emotional control. Combining them with alcohol or other drugs heightens their effects. Overdoses of barbiturates are a prominent cause of death, both accidental and deliberate. Like alcohol, barbiturates produce physical dependency that cannot be effectively ended simply through abrupt withdrawal. Because abrupt withdrawal can be fatal, withdrawal must be gradual or counteracted by other drugs. Many barbiturate abusers are adults who obtain them on prescription from their physicians and who probably engage in little drug-related crime, although they may risk automobile accidents and death through overdose. Among younger people, barbiturates are obtained illegally and taken in combination with amphetamines, heroin, and alcohol, greatly multiplying their intrinsic hazards.

Opiates. Since about 1910, opiate addiction has been considered the most serious form of drug abuse in western countries. Opium is obtained from the juice of the poppy seed and has served as a pain killer and narcotic for thousands of years. Each grain of opium contains a tiny amount of morphine. Heroin ("H," "horse," "junk," "snow," "joy powder"), made by heating morphine in acetic acid, is the most widely abused derivative of opium, although morphine, paregoric, and codeine are also abused. Opiate addiction sometimes begins with oral ingestion, sniffing, and injection under the skin, but intravenous injection ("mainlining") of heroin is by far the most common and serious form.

The effects of opiates include reduction of the hunger, thirst, and sex drives, a relaxed, worry-free euphoria, and a high in which the user feels very self-confident, followed by a period of inactivity bordering on stupor. Physical dependence, enormous increases in tolerance, the pleasant feelings, fear of withdrawal symptoms, assimilation into the subculture of users, and the need for continuous criminal activity to raise funds all combine to produce a tremendous psychological dependence that is not eliminated by withdrawal, even though opiates can be withdrawn more safely and quickly than can barbiturates and alcohol. The extreme psychological dependence can be effectively understood in terms of conditioning—since the narcotic anesthetizes drive stimuli, any increase in a drive, including hunger and thirst, becomes a conditioned stimulus for the response of taking heroin (Nichols, 1965). Physical illness is endemic among heroin addicts because hunger and thirst are abnormally suppressed, withdrawal effects and overdoses are common due to the varying purity of street heroin, and unsterile needles transmit tetanus and hepatitis.

The implementation and enforcement of national and international regulations against nonmedical use of opiates early in this century greatly reduced the number of addicts in the United States. Most of the remaining addicts have been urban blacks and Puerto Ricans, concentrated especially in New York City (Rasor, 1968). The total number of American opiate addicts was believed to have reached a low point of about 43,000 in 1958—down from about 240,000 in 1900, but it has risen rapidly since then to the point where current estimates range from 100,000 to over 700,000 addicts in the country as a whole. Age of addiction is also getting younger and heroin usage has become the leading cause of death among 15- to 35-year-olds in New York City (Boyd, 1971). Many deaths from heroin addiction have also been reported among children under 15. Worse yet, infants born of addicted women are physiologically addicted at birth and may die unless given withdrawal treatment.

The exact reasons for the recent increases in addiction are not known, although some of the increase among middle-class youth may have resulted from the psychedelic drug culture that helped glamorize all types of drug experience. The role of cultural factors of this sort seems quite apparent in Britain and there is little reason to believe they did not contribute in the United States. In addition, as with marijuana, many American servicemen began using cheap and potent heroin in Vietnam. The government's policy of dishonorably discharging those who were caught, thereby excluding them from further government treatment and benefits, has probably contributed to the rise in addiction as well.

PSYCHOSOCIAL CHARACTERISTICS OF DRUG ABUSERS

Many studies have been done on personality and background characteristics of drug abusers. Unfortunately, because almost all of them focus upon drug abusers after they have been identified as abusers—often after they have been arrested in connection with their abuse—it is difficult to be certain that some of the characteristics are not results of drug abuse rather than predating or causing it. However, the availability of some longitudinal data and the consistency of some of the findings regarding people selected after they have become abusers make tentative conclusions possible.

Adolescent Alcohol Abusers

Personality characteristics of alcohol abusers have probably been the best studied and data from a longitudinal study beginning in childhood (Jones, 1971) corroborate the findings of studies beginning after drinking started. A recent review of the relevant studies reports that adolescent problem drinkers, especially males, are generally lacking in personal controls, as indicated by relatively high aggressiveness and impulsiveness (Braucht, Brakarsh, Follingstad, & Berry, 1973). The problem drinkers also show relatively low self-esteem, high anxiety, depression, and a lack of success in the attainment of life goals. Background characteristics of adolescent problem drinkers include parents who drink heavily and peer groups in which high alcohol use is encouraged (Braucht et al, 1973).

Adolescent Abusers of LSD, Amphetamines, and Marijuana

LSD, amphetamines, and, recently, marijuana have come to be used predominately by middle- and upper-class youth who identify with the psychedelic drug culture. LSD users in particular have parents with high occupational and educational status (Smart & Fejer, 1969). A positive correlation has also been found between drug use by high school students and use by their parents of drugs including alcohol, tobacco, tranquilizers, barbiturates, and amphetamines. More mothers than fathers were reported to use psychoactive drugs and the students tended to use the same drugs as their parents (Smart & Fejer, 1972).

A clear picture of the personality characteristics of users of these drugs is harder to achieve. Despite an enormous number of popular writings, unsupported generalizations, and uncontrolled studies, there has been little research employing representative samples with adequate controls. Themes commonly stressed by the literature in relation to college users include the following:

1. alienation and search for meaning;
2. disillusionment and rebellion;
3. need for stimulation;
4. lack of self-definition;
5. need for interpersonal relations;
6. escape from sexuality;
7. hedonism;
8. relief of anxiety and tension;
9. curiosity.

Of course, these concerns are by no means unique to drug users.

A number of studies have revealed high rates of serious psychopathology such as schizophrenia and borderline psychosis in users, especially multidrug users, although the pathology may predispose an individual to drug usage rather than result from it (Braucht et al, 1973). It is possible that the faddish nature of preferences among the hallucinogens and amphetamines has caused them to be used temporarily by a large variety of adolescents, rather than being chosen only by a limited range of personality types.

Adolescent Opiate Abusers

Background factors strongly related to adolescent opiate usage include membership in ethnic minorities, especially black and Puerto Rican, impoverished urban environments, broken homes, and delinquent peers from whom drugs are readily available (Braucht et al, 1973). Comparisons of white, Puerto Rican, and black adolescent heroin users and nonusers from similar neighborhoods in New York has also shown that the users in each ethnic group had less cohesive families, based on an index of family quarreling, degree of joint participation in celebrations and mealtimes, behavior when a family member was ill, etc. (Chein, Gerard, Lee, & Rosenfeld, 1964). Comparisons of socioeconomic deprivation within the three ethnic groups, however, showed that only among blacks were the users more deprived than the nonusers. Among the whites and Puerto Ricans, the users were *less* deprived than the nonusers.

Although Chein et al found that most of the users and nonusers had known of heroin use in their neighborhoods at an early age and many had been offered the opportunity to try it, the users freely accepted the opportunities while the nonusers did not. Moreover, the nonusers deliberately avoided groups who used drugs. Boys who were nonusers and not delinquent in other respects were clearly "square" by their neighborhood standards. They expressed more interest in books, school, organized activities, future plans, and long-term friendships than did the "cats" who were willing to try drugs. The cats who tried drugs engaged in other delinquency, spent most of their time hanging around, and were preoccupied with immediate acquisition of cars, clothes, etc.

Most of the cats who became regular users had been casually offered heroin by peers at around the age of 15 or 16. Very few had spontaneously sought out heroin. The age of 16 seemed especially critical in that the percentage of boys accepting offers of heroin and quickly becoming addicted was greater at that age than at earlier or later ages. The facts that most who tried it had quit school by 16, that they had acquired working papers, and that they thought of themselves as more independent at that point probably contributed to the significance of the age of 16 for addiction.

Most of those who tried heroin had positive reactions on their first try. Ninety per cent of those who eventually became regular users did so within one year of the first try, the rest within two years. Among a group of 50 delinquents in the Chein study who were nonusers, four had tried heroin but did not continue beyond the first try. It thus appears that, for most but not all the youth from the areas studied, the road from an experimental first try to regular use is traveled with great speed.

Studies employing personality tests generally agree in showing opiate addicts to be immature, insecure, irresponsible, and egocentric (Braucht et al, 1973). MMPI profiles of adult and teenage addicts resemble those of sociopathic personalities, although there are subgroups who show neurotic and schizoid features in addition to sociopathy (Gilbert & Lombardi, 1967; Hill, Haertzen, & Glaser, 1960). A comparison of MMPI responses by nonaddict criminals, opiate addicts, and alcoholics showed only small differences among them in degree of sociopathy, with the alcoholics being somewhat more neurotic and depressed than the other two groups.

TREATMENT

"Treatment" for drug abuse raises more diverse questions than does treatment for any other form of behavior considered in this book. Not only is more basic research needed to expose the causes and antidotes for drug abuse, but the problems presented by drug abuse also concern the relations among medical, legal, behavioral, and ethico-moral dimensions to a greater extent than do most other forms of psychopathology. In no other area of psychopathology do the public passions run higher in support of so many opposing viewpoints. Other forms of delinquent behavior raise some of the same questions concerning prevention, punishment, treatment, deterrence, and self-protection, but drug abuse additionally raises fears of epidemic contagion to one's own children, irrational violence, the weakening of the nation, and intergenerational conflict, not to mention questions about such cornerstones of adult social relations as tobacco and alcohol.

Considering the lack of agreement on whether to formulate the problem of drug abuse as primarily medical, legal, behavioral, moral or social, and considering the vicissitudes of public policy and funding, it should not be surprising that no treatment methods have demonstrated large-scale success. Where success has been substantiated, it is with drugs such as tobacco that create the smallest social problems for adolescents and for which "treatment" or simply quitting is usually undertaken only by people who are spontaneously motivated without external pressure. Alcoholism has probably been treated for the longest period and by the greatest number of methods, but, as mentioned in Chapter 10, even potent aversive methods have not achieved high rates of long-term cure and relapsed alcoholics are reluctant to undergo them a second time (Lemere & Voegtlin, 1950). Alcoholics Anonymous appears to help some highly motivated alcoholics, although it is unknown what percentage of those who join succeed in staying dry and how representative they are of alcoholics in general.

There appears to be little in the way of systematic treatment programs specifically for usage of cannabis, LSD, other hallucinogens, and amphetamines, except for psychotherapy, support, restraint, and hospitalization when pathological behavioral reactions occur. The lack of physiological dependence on these drugs makes medical withdrawal treatments unnecessary, although treatment for hepatitis and tetanus transmitted by unsterile needles and for malnutrition may be necessary following amphetamine abuse.

Transcendental Meditation

A "treatment" that appears to have reduced all drug use, especially the use of nonopiates, is Transcendental Meditation, an Indian mental technique taught by instructors certified by Maharishi Mahesh Yogi (1966).

Practitioners are asked to abstain from drug abuse for 15 days prior to starting Meditation. Following formal instruction, the program entails practicing the technique for two 15- to 20-minute periods per day. Benson and Wallace (1972) have reported a questionnaire survey of drug use among practitioners of Meditation in California. The survey showed a decline from 78 per cent of the respondents using cannabis before starting Meditation to only 12 per cent using it after 22 or more months of practicing Meditation. LSD showed a decline from 48 per cent using it before Meditation to only 3 per cent after 22 or more months. Users of amphetamines declined from 32 per cent to 1 per cent. Harder drugs showed similar declines, although the percentages initially using them were small.

In the absence of a control group and data on drop-outs and on the validity of the questionnaire responses, the findings require confirmation through a controlled prospective study. However, the apparent degree of success is so much greater than in most drug-control programs that systematic assessment of Transcendental Meditation certainly seems warranted. While most of the users were not physiologically addicted and may have been able to give up drugs spontaneously without too much difficulty, those using Meditation appear to have been differentiated from more typical users by becoming strongly motivated to abstain.

Treatment of Opiate Addiction

Although an almost exclusively punitive approach to narcotics addiction was taken with the passing of the Harrison Narcotics Act in 1914, the somewhat more enlightened view that narcotics addiction may be like a disease came to dominate official pronouncements concerning addicts themselves, if not their criminal activities or the nonaddicted criminal controllers of the narcotics trade. Beginning in 1935, treatment was offered addicts at the U. S. Public Health Service Hospital in Lexington, Kentucky. Treatment at Lexington consists of physical detoxification, plus short-term vocational rehabilitation and psychotherapy aimed at helping the addicts meet stress without recourse to drugs. Thereafter, the addicts are returned to their home communities—to become readdicted, as follow-up studies have demonstrated.

Most studies of addicts discharged from Lexington have shown relapse rates of approximately 90 per cent. Furthermore, 90 per cent of the relapses occur within six months after treatment (O'Donnell, 1965). Chein et al (1964) have reported similar rates and rapidity of readdiction among young addicts receiving hospital treatment in New York City. The influence of being with other addicts is suggested by the fact that the highest relapse rates for Lexington dischargees have been found for addicts from New York City who return there, where the number of addicts is far greater than elsewhere in the country (O'Donnell, 1965). By contrast, some upper socioeconomic addict groups, such as physicians, who have much higher rates of addiction than other professionals, show rates of re-addiction as low as 8 per cent (Jones, 1958).

There is a tendency for addicts to give up their habit as they grow older. A general decrease in the strength of primary drives or other physiological factors may be responsible, as older experimental animals have also been found to become less strongly addicted than younger animals. Hunt and Odoroff (1962) found that Lexington dischargees over the age of 30 were more likely to remain abstinent than those under 30. Contrary to popular beliefs, nonvoluntary patients (probationers and those under threat of prison) were more likely to remain abstinent than voluntary patients, perhaps because the voluntary patients more often left before physiological withdrawal could be completed. Spontaneous motivation may be a big factor in overcoming other forms of drug dependency, but Chein et al (1964) found that lower-class opiate addicts spend most of their free time thinking about drugs and rarely have sufficient spontaneous motivation to do anything about quitting, beyond enunciation of good intentions. In summary, the follow-up studies show that the traditional form of hospital treatment with psychotherapy is an almost complete failure for the majority of addicts, although not all addicts relapse. Those who are older and have high occupational status relapse least frequently.

Synanon

Synanon is an organization founded in 1958 by an ex-alcoholic, Charles Dederich. Dederich describes the "family structure" of Synanon as having an autocratic overtone that demands that the members of the family take directions in helping with the preparation of meals, house cleaning, etc. The supervising family members—all ex-addicts—attempt to implant spiritual concepts and values that will result in self-reliance.

"Synanon" is a word coined to describe another major aspect of the organization, a kind of three-time-weekly group psychotherapy session moderated by a "Synanist," an addict who has successfully given up drugs or who is making good progress toward that goal. The Synanon sessions are intended to provide an emotional catharsis and to trigger an atmosphere of truth-seeking.

Synanon has rapidly become a national organization with local residential units run by ex-addicts and providing the Synanon form of group therapy, noontime educational seminars, cultural activities, and a work program. Yablonsky and Dederich (1965) report that, of the addicts who stay at Synanon for more than the three-month trial period, 70 per cent remain free of drugs. Dederich also has data on the total percentage of addicts coming to Synanon who relapse before, as well as after, the three-month trial period. However, he refuses to release the data on the grounds that addicts, "like emotional children," will use the failure rate as a rationalization for continuing drugs. Instead of emphasizing the size of the relapse rate, Dederich prefers to emphasize the success of the program in terms of the number of "clean man-days"—the number of days on which an addict is free of criminal behavior and all drugs, including alcohol.

An innovative feature of Synanon is that it creates new social roles for many of its members as Synanon executives, Synanists, and workers with addicts in prison. The fact that Synanon offers upward mobility within its own organization and does not attempt to return the addict to the outside world may be a major strength, because the addict is thus enabled to stay away from the conditions that supported his addiction in the first place.

Another major factor in Synanon's apparent success may be its extremely difficult entrance "exams." When an addict arrives begging for help, token roadblocks—such as appointment times, fees, and ridicule—are thrown up in his way by ex-addict "experts." The addict is viewed as an emotional infant whose silly plots and rationalizations need to be exposed and who needs to be given a job commensurate with his limited ability. The following is an excerpt from an interview with an addict "prospect" whom Synanon had decided to accept. "J. H." is ex-addict Jack Hurst, Resident Director of the Westport, Connecticut, Synanon House.

J.H.: You'll be the new element in the family. You'll be kind of like the new baby. . . . You'll be told when to get up, you'll be told what to do when you do get up. You'll be told when to go to Synanon, what kind of work to do, when to go to seminars. You'll be told when to talk and when not to talk. . . .

I guarantee you that if you go through the motions that we describe and prescribe for you you'll end up being a man, not the sniveling whining brat that you are now. You'll be a man!

Prospect: What makes you think I'm a sniveling brat? You only know me for five minutes and . . .

J.H.: You see, people that use drugs, people that live with their sisters, people that steal hubcaps, people that go in and out of jails, the people that go to nut houses for help, these are sniveling brats in my opinion and my opinion carries a lot of weight in this house. Get that gut level. My opinion is pretty Goddamn certain to be valid as a salad. Try to understand that, if you don't understand it, act as if you understand.

When you make a lot of noise in our environment it's not very nice to listen to. Arguments are something we save for Synanons. You can argue your ass off in a Synanon. When you're being talked to around here, and when you're in my office or in my dining room you kind of behave yourself and keep your big mouth shut. Listen to what's going on around you, you might learn something. Don't be so frightened to learn something. You see, you almost learned something a moment ago—the fact that you are a whining, sniveling brat. But you fight it. . . .

Now you're not going to be expected for a couple of, three-four months, to do our banking, for instance. This would be like asking a four-year-old child to carry a hundred-pound suitcase like a man. You're not going to be expected to do our shopping. You're not going to be expected to get into our car and go to Bridgeport to pick up donations. . . . What you're going to be expected to do is wash the toilets, wash the floors, do the dishes, anything that we feel that you should be doing.

As you learn how to do these things *well, well* mind you, then you will gradually get to more and better things, or let's say, more responsible jobs. You'll graduate up the power structure, pretty soon you know in a couple of years, maybe even a year, you just might be a big shot around here—or Santa Monica or Reno (Yablonsky & Dederich, 1965, pp. 201–2).

One effect of the initial reception may be to increase the motivation of some addicts, as attested to by the reaction of one:

I couldn't figure it out. I figured there must be a gimmick. I didn't really want to stop being a dope fiend. I wanted to rest awhile. First, I began to look for the connection in the joint. They laughed at me. I think I stuck around at the beginning cause I couldn't believe it was true. Live dope fiends not shooting dope— behind an open door, with no screws to keep them locked up! (Yablonsky & Dederich, 1965, p. 200).

Another effect of the entrance hurdles and the three-month trial period may be to exclude a large proportion of addicts who are poor prospects. This makes the overall effectiveness of the Synanon model difficult to evaluate as a treatment for addiction. Be that as it may, Synanon and similar organizations, such as Daytop Village and Phoenix House, have come to offer hope for at least some addicts, especially since they offer new long-term social roles that enable the addict to avoid returning to the psychosocial conditions that previously supported his drug use.

Odyssey House

The Odyssey House program in New York offers something of an intermediate alternative between the traditional medical approach and the Synanon community run by ex-addicts (Rohrs, Murphy, & Densen-Gerber, 1972). Odyssey House is a "therapeutic community" in which ex-addicts serve in important positions, especially in the handling of newly admitted addicts. As in Synanon, there is a strong emphasis on group process. The addict is not given the opportunity to generate interpersonal conflicts with other individuals. However, professional psychotherapists are also used, especially in later stages of treatment, and the ex-addict is encouraged to reintegrate himself gradually into the outside world rather than to assume a permanent role in the organization. The professional staff of Odyssey House believes that important distinctions among treatments for types of addicts are necessary and that programs that do not make these distinctions do irreparable damage. An especially important distinction, they believe, is between sociopathic addicts, whose improvement may depend on the development of stressful anxiety and guilt, and schizophrenic addicts for whom increases in anxiety may be disastrous.

In a survey of 2,500 Odyssey House patients, 1,000 of whom were between 9 and 18 years of age, 45 per cent were reported to have left during their first week due to lack of motivation. About 40 per cent of those entering completed the 12- to 18-month program. Of the initial 41 graduates during the first three years of operation, 96 per cent remained drug free, although the length of the follow-up periods for these 41 is not stated (Rohrs, et al, 1972).

Methadone Maintenance

During the mid 1960s, it was discovered that methadone, a synthetic opiatelike drug, blocked the craving for heroin and heroin's euphoric effect. Methadone itself is highly addictive, but, because it can produce its effect when taken orally, it can be cheaply manufactured, and it maintains its effects for 24 hours (compared with 2 to 4 hours for heroin), it may be a desirable substitute for heroin. Furthermore, many addicts appear willing to use it, as indicated by the rapid growth of methadone maintenance programs to the point where over 12,000 American addicts were enrolled by 1971 (Jaffe, 1972). Despite some public, legal, and medical resistance to substituting one addiction for another, methadone programs have been widely implemented as at least a stopgap measure against the crime generated by heroin addiction. Methadone is also being employed in Britain as a substitute for the prescription of heroin by physicians, because the British drug epidemic of the 1960s demonstrated that the heroin given addicts to take at home could easily fall into the wrong hands once a demand existed. Furthermore, intravenously injected heroin risks more medical complications than does orally ingested methadone.

Methadone maintenance is not without its problems, as users have sold excess amounts obtained from private physicians, and deaths from overdoses have been reported. To prevent illicit sales, the handling of methadone by private physicians is being limited and many programs now require participants to obtain and consume their daily dose at a clinic. Methadone maintenance by itself does not lead to a change in the life style of addicts, some of whom may continue their criminal activities and increase their use of alcohol, amphetamines, and barbiturates.

In a study of addicts voluntarily admitted to a methadone program in New York (Eddy, 1970), it was found that few dropped out. Of 544 males in the program, 28 per cent were gainfully employed and 40 per cent were on welfare at the time af admission. After five months, 45 per cent were employed and after 24 months 85 per cent were employed or in school, while only 15 per cent were on welfare, although it is not clear whether there were selective factors differentiating those who remained 24 months from the rest of the sample. None of the patients remaining in the program became readdicted to heroin, but 11 per cent repeatedly used amphetamines or barbiturates and 5 per cent had chronic alcohol problems. Participants in the methadone program showed much lower rates of arrest than a matched comparison group admitted to an ordinary detoxification unit (Eddy, 1970). Other studies, however, have reported much higher rates of alcohol abuse among addicts maintained on methadone (Liebson & Bigelow, 1972).

Behavior Modification

Although analyses of addiction in terms of conditioning principles have frequently been made, only a few studies have reported behavioral treatment of addiction. In one of the few studies employing more than one addict, O'Brien et al, (1972) applied aversive conditioning, relaxation training, and systematic desensitization with two young adults who had begun using drugs in adolescence and had become extremely heavy users of heroin supplemented by other drugs. After detoxification with methadone, the clients were told dramatic stories using their own jargon and stringing in sequence all their usual cues for needing a fix. At crucial points in the stories they were given painful electric shocks to injection sites on their bodies. They were also shocked at the sight of items used in preparing and injecting heroin. Unpleasant verbal associations supplied by the addicts gradually replaced shock as the aversive stimulus paired with thoughts of heroin use. Relaxation and desensitization were used to counteract feelings that had previously motivated the clients to use heroin.

One patient remained heroin-free for a 14-month follow-up period, while the second gave up heroin but refused to continue aversive conditioning. He remained heroin-free for a six-month follow-up period, after which he refused further contacts.

It is surprising that behavioral methods have not been more widely applied to drug addiction, although the reaction of the patient who refused to continue aversive conditioning suggests that this form of behavior therapy is not likely to succeed on a very large scale. One likely direction for further experimentation is the use of nonaversive behavioral techniques to help shape positive adaptive behavior in addicts whose addiction continues to be blocked by methadone or who are prepared to seek out new social roles after treatment by organizations like Synanon.

PREVENTION OF DRUG ABUSE

Education

Prevention is among the most talked about but least researched approaches to drug abuse. Numerous films, lectures, and reading materials have been offered young people in hopes of heading off drug abuse. However, there is little evidence that any educational programs prevent drug abuse or, if any do, which approaches are the most effective. Chein et al (1964) found that lower percentages of adolescent heroin users than nonusers from the same neighborhoods reported knowing the dangers of drugs before they were given the opportunities to try them. Although the subjects were growing up in the 1950s before publicity about drugs had reached its current crescendo, it is difficult to believe that the "square" nonusers were actually so much better informed than the "cats" who tried drugs, when almost all of both groups had reported seeing addicts in their neighborhoods. Casting further doubt on sheer ignorance as a major contributor to drug abuse is the fact that drug abuse has grown tremendously during a period when knowledge of its dangers has become more widespread than ever.

One benefit of drug education programs, whether or not they completely prevent drug abuse, may be to make young people more discriminating and cautious in their choice of drugs. Thus, the decline in LSD usage and the growth of marijuana usage may be partly due to the dissemination of the increasing evidence for the dangers of LSD and the relative safety of marijuana. Moreover, drug education has a role to play in preventing abuse of drugs legally available over the counter or by prescription. Some abuse of barbiturates, amphetamines, and tranquilizers almost certainly results from public ignorance of their effects. Unless more stringent controls are exercised on the prescription, production, and advertising of commercial psychoactive drugs, public wariness will be the only way to reduce drug abuse encouraged by massive advertising of drugs.

Law

Stricter laws, law enforcement, and penalties are probably the most popularly advocated measures against drug abuse. This approach seems to have been effective in some situations. In Japan, for example, amphetamines were widely used during World War II to ward off pilot and worker fatigue. By 1954, two million Japanese were using amphetamines intravenously and 600,000 were chronic users. Strict laws and an all-out educational campaign reduced arrests from 55,000 in 1954 to 271 in 1958 and there has been no recurrence of epidemic amphetamine abuse. A heroin epidemic in Japan was controlled by similar measures between 1955 and 1962. American legal efforts against opiates also reduced addiction considerably after 1914, but, despite strict laws, the number of addicts has remained so large that a purely legal approach seems unlikely to succeed here. The amount of crime generated by Prohibition and the foothold given to criminal syndicates through sale of illegal liquor also suggest that a purely legal approach may do more harm than good.

Socioeconomic Changes

The proposition that the only successful preventive measures will be slum clearance, elimination of economic disadvantage, and a general improvement in conditions for disadvantaged minorities may have some validity for heroin users, but Chein et al (1964) found that white and Puerto Rican heroin users were somewhat more economically advantaged than their nonuser counterparts from the same neighborhoods. Also, most of the growth in other types of drug abuse has occurred among relatively advantaged youth. They, too, may be suffering from the lack of family cohesiveness, poor parental examples, etc., that appear to be the most critical factors in drug abuse among disadvantaged adolescents (Chein et al, 1964), but no foreseeable changes in social conditions are likely to remove these contributors to drug abuse.

Just as massive drug usage grew partly out of the ethos of a new fad in the youth culture, so future fads will no doubt bring other expressions of the desire of adolescents to find new identities for themselves. Maybe Transcendental Meditation, maybe a back-to-nature movement, maybe alcohol, or who knows what will be rediscovered by the next adolescent generation as a reaction against the drug movement that preceded them. However, many of the present-day speed freaks, barbiturate addicts, pot and acid heads, and especially the heroin addicts will need more than a change of youth fads to help them.

SUMMARY

The significance of psychoactive drug usage depends upon the way it is viewed in a society. All psychoactive drugs, legal as well as illegal, are potentially harmful. *Physical dependence,* most strongly induced by alcohol, barbiturates, and opiates, is generally a less significant factor in addictions than is *psychological dependence* that may cause readdiction even after physical dependence is terminated by withdrawal. *Physical tolerance,* produced by LSD, amphetamines, marijuana, and opiates, requires a user to increase the doses needed to obtain a given subjective effect.

Adolescents often begin their illicit use of tobacco and alcohol in the same manner as illegal drugs. The enormous volume of abuse, traffic deaths, and crimes associated with alcohol make it the most problematical drug in the United States.

Adolescent abuse of illicit drugs spiraled in most developed countries during the 1960s. *Cannabis* is the focus of greatest controversy because it has been used by the largest number of people and appears to be the least harmful of the illicit drugs. It is unknown whether the statistical association between psychopathology and cannabis usage occurs because cannabis usage causes psychopathology or vice versa. Cannabis does not function as a substitute for alcohol or other drugs, nor does it reduce violent behavior. There is evidence that use of cannabis by black urban males during adolescence increases the probability of later social problems, including excess use of alcohol and other drugs, although the relations between cannabis use and later problems by other groups of adolescents have not been investigated. LSD and related hallucinogens have produced serious psychopathological reactions as well as possible organic damage.

Amphetamines, legally prescribed for sleepiness, obesity, head colds, and children's hyperactivity, are illicitly taken intravenously in large doses to produce very strong stimulative effects. The stimulative effects are often followed by suicidal depression, disorganized thinking, and paranoid psychosis. Groups of amphetamine users seem especially prone to violence. *Cocaine* produces similar but more powerful and toxic effects.

Sniffing of *organic solvents* contained in household products can depress central nervous system functioning enough to produce mild intoxication. High doses of *barbiturates* and *"minor" tranquilizers* are used to produce more extreme central nervous system depression. Their effects become especially potent when mixed with alcohol or other drugs.

Opiates, especially *heroin,* produce some of the most extreme forms of addiction by anesthetizing organic drive stimuli and producing euphoria. Even after elimination of physical dependence through withdrawal, new withdrawal symptoms can be elicited by the sight of another user. The number of heroin users has risen sharply since 1958 and the age of addiction has become progressively younger.

Adolescent alcohol abusers tend to be characterized by low self-esteem, high anxiety, depression, and parents and peers who use alcohol heavily. No clear-cut personality constellations have been verified for LSD, amphetamine, and marijuana users, although they tend to be middle class. Fairly high rates of psychopathology are found among them.

Heroin users tend to be minority group members from poor urban neighborhoods, broken homes, and peer groups who readily provide drugs. Lack of family cohesiveness seems especially pronounced among users, although socioeconomic deprivation is not necessarily greater than among nonusers from the same neighborhoods. Most users quickly become addicts after their first experience with heroin. Personality tests indicate that immaturity, irresponsibility, insecurity, and egocentrism are prominent traits of heroin users. The MMPI profiles of users resemble those of sociopaths, although there are subgroups who show neurotic and schizoid features.

Traditional hospital treatment and psychotherapy for lower-class heroin addicts are generally followed by readdiction. Fewer addicts from upper socioeconomic groups relapse. Synanon, Daytop Village, and Phoenix House are communities of ex-addicts that seek to create new social roles for the addict. Odyssey House is intermediate between traditional treatment and the community-of-addicts approach in that it has a staff of professional psychotherapists and attempts to return addicts to the outside world. *Methadone* is being widely used to block the craving for heroin, although methadone is addictive and does not directly alter the addict's life style.

Like treatment, preventive approaches have not been demonstrated to be highly effective. Strict legal approaches have cut drug abuse greatly in some countries, but the example of Prohibition suggests that they cannot be completely successful in the United States.

SUGGESTED READING

One of the main problems in studying drug abuse is to keep up with the latest fads and literature. Since the burgeoning of illicit drug use by the young of many countries, a great many conferences have been held and numerous publications have appeared. The growth of drug abuse and the changes in preferred drug combinations have prevented programmatic research on the effects of the drugs from keeping pace and have made many sociological pronouncements obsolete before they appeared in print.

Overviews. Mensh (1970) and Brecher (1972) provide substantial reviews of drug abuse, while Braucht et al (1973) offer a review of psychosocial correlates of deviant drug use specifically in adolescence. Papers from two international conferences on drug abuse, edited by Btesh (1972) and Zarafonitis (1972), present broad coverage of medical findings, treatment models, and usage patterns in many countries.

Marijuana. The controversy over legalization of marijuana has produced several well-researched volumes. Two that distinctly favor decriminalization have been written by Goode (1970) and Kaplan (1970). Kaplan is a law professor who served on an advisory group appointed by the California legislature to make recommendations concerning drug laws. When the group tentatively recommended treating marijuana use as a vice rather than a felony, all the members were fired. The most thoroughly researched and scientifically documented report on cannabis has been issued by The Commission of Inquiry into the Non-medical Use of Drugs (1972), appointed to advise the Canadian Government. This report is especially useful because it contains two opposing views. The view of the majority of the Commission favors penalties for sale but not for possession or cultivation of cannabis for private use. The minority view favors government production and marketing of cannabis under regulations similar to those governing alcohol. Unlike the California advisory group, the Canadian Commission was not fired for its recommendations.

Opiates. Before the recent blossoming of the drug culture, heroin was the illicit drug that received the most attention. Chein et al's (1964) book, *The Road to H,* is a worthwhile source of data on adolescent addiction in the slums of New York, although the data are sometimes buried in the verbiage. A series of papers edited by Wilner and Kassenbaum (1965) provides diverse information from many sources on opiate addiction, including a description of Synanon by Yablonsky and Dederich. Yablonsky (1965) presents a more extended treatment of the Synanon story in a book entitled *The Tunnel Back: Synanon.* A thorough and authoritative portrayal of the prevalence and distribution of opiate addiction among various groups in the United States is contained in a collection of papers edited by Ball and Chambers (1970).

15

Classification of
Psychopathology

As we have considered each general category of pathology, we have been confronted again and again with the need to make distinctions among syndromes of behavior, types of individuals, levels of functioning, and possible outcomes. Explicitly or implicitly, we have been faced with problems of classification—of grouping together individuals who have something in common, whether it be low IQ scores, genetic anomalies, phobic symptoms, autistic behavior, criminal records, or addiction to heroin. The groupings we have employed are clearly imperfect as guides to etiology, treatment, management, or prognosis, but they are representative of present-day custom in the mental-health fields.

CURRENT CLASSIFICATION SYSTEM

The official embodiment of present-day custom in classification is the system contained in the *Diagnostic and Statistical Manual* of the American Psychiatric Association ("DSM-II," 1968) which was outlined in Chapter 3. However, this system was designed primarily for categorizing adult psychopathology and it fails to take account of some of the most salient characteristics of child psychopathology. For example, its only provision for children's psychotic disorders without known organic etiology is the category of "Schizophrenia, Childhood Type." In view of the increasing evidence for marked differences between disorders beginning early in infancy (e.g., Kanner's syndrome, see Chapter 12) and those developing later in childhood, the blanket application of the term schizophrenia to all of them interferes with more than it facilitates communication and the search for etiologies and treatments.

One reaction to the faults of the official classification system has been to condemn all classification. Yet classification occurs whenever human beings make judgments about anything, whether it be to decide that another human is "sick," "conflicted," "defensive," "high in ego strength," "phobic," or "in need of systematic desensitization." In each such judgment, something is being abstracted from everything that could be known or stated about the individual and he is being assigned to a class of individuals who, despite all their differences, are assumed to have in common the characteristic of being "sick," "conflicted," "defensive," or the like.

In effect, any act of classification, implicit or explicit, involves a compromise between (1) treating every bit of new information about a client as if it were totally unique, and (2) attempting to identify similarities between the client and others with whom experience has previously been gained. Although "diagnosis" and "classification" lie along the same conceptual continuum, *diagnosis* generally refers to the information-gathering process during which all relevant information is gathered to form a picture of the client and his problems; *classification* generally refers to an endproduct of the diagnostic process, i.e., a conclusion that serves as a shorthand link to other clients with whom experience has been gained.

Because virtually all acts of judgment involve at least implicit classification, the problem of classification cannot be escaped simply by rejecting a specific type of classification such as that found in the DSM-II. The basic question is not *whether* to classify, but *how* to classify. Since classification is not an end in itself, *how* to classify should be dictated by the goals of the classifier. The similarities sought out among clients should be those that will best guide an effective course of action. If the classifier is a diagnostician trying to decide whether a client needs treatment, he looks for characteristics like those of other clients who improved without treatment, grew worse without treatment, improved with treatment, and grew worse with treatment. If treatment has already been decided upon, the diagnostician looks for characteristics like those of other clients who have done well or poorly with each available type of treatment.

The characteristics on which the diagnostician bases his judgments may include laboratory tests for organic disorders, life history data, the client's free associations, his overt behavior, IQ, age, affect and mood, external appearance, etc. For some disorders, the findings of laboratory tests may prove decisive, e.g., if the client's Wassermann Test is positive, this crucial similarity with clients classed as having syphilis will make penicillin a likely treatment, regardless of the client's differences from other clients having syphilis. On the other hand, the absence of organic findings requires a search for other types of similarities with previous clients. If the decision concerns type or level of education to be provided for the client, the client's current level of knowledge and intellectual functioning rather than his particular disorder or its etiology may be among the relevant criteria for classifying him. Because different systems of classification are needed for different purposes, the same client may be classified according to etiology for purposes of medical treatment, but by intellectual level for purposes of education.

Reliability of Current Classification

In our present rudimentary state of knowledge about psychopathology, an official classification system such as that of the DSM-II represents so many compromises and embodies so many different functions and principles that the system as a whole is likely to serve only the most general purposes of communication. How well this system facilitates communication is open to empirical test by determining the degree of agreement *(reliability)* between diagnosticians in assigning clients to the categories of the system. Many studies were made of the reliability of the system contained in the DSM-I (American Psychiatric Association, 1952), the immediate predecessor to the DSM-II. Except for some changes in terminology and the addition of more categories, the DSM-II does not differ greatly from the DSM-I.

Nearly all studies of the reliability of the DSM-I showed that agreement between clinicians classifying adult cases was moderately high for categories assumed to have organic etiologies (e.g., Chronic Brain Syndrome with Central Nervous System Syphilis; Chronic Brain Syndrome with Senile Brain Disease), lower for psychotic disorders without known organic etiologies (e.g., Schizophrenia, Manic-depressive Psychosis), and lowest for personality and neurotic disorders. Classification was also most reliable when it was restricted to a very few broad categories (e.g., organic versus psychotic versus neurotic or personality disorder), but grew more unreliable as specificity increased, becoming very unreliable at the level of specific personality and neurotic disorders (e.g., Beck, Ward, Mendelson, Mock, & Erbaugh, 1962; Sandifer, Pettus, & Quade, 1964; Schmidt & Fonda, 1956).

There was little point in studying the reliability of DSM-I with respect to children's disorders, as the only categories listed were "Adjustment Reaction" (of Infancy, Childhood, and Adolescence) and "Schizophrenic Reaction, Childhood Type." While adult categories could also be applied to children, the fact that 70 per cent of children seen in clinics were either unclassified or classified as having adjustment reactions made for high but useless reliability (Rosen et al, 1964).

Validity of Current Classification

The *validity* of a classification system is defined as the degree to which assignment of people or disorders to its categories is correlated with whatever characteristics the classification system is supposed to index. For example, if a classification system is supposed to index the etiologies of disorders, then one way to validate classification of clients as brain-damaged or non-brain-damaged would be through autopsies when the clients eventually died. The system would be highly valid if all those who had been classified as brain-damaged were eventually found on autopsy to have damaged brains, while those classified as non-brain-damaged were found to have undamaged brains. Of course, high validity could not be achieved unless the classification were also reliable—even a system that accurately defined symptoms of brain damage could not achieve a high correlation with autopsy findings if users of the system could not agree on when the appropriate combinations of symptoms were present. Thus, reliability sets a limit on validity. However, high reliability does not guarantee validity—a classification system could be based on characteristics that are easy to identify, but the characteristics might not relate to anything else important.

A classification system whose classes validly relate to etiologies of disorders is useful because knowledge of etiology is likely to be helpful in devising methods for treatment and prévention. Where effective treatment and prevention are not yet possible, knowledge of etiology may at least be helpful in determining prognosis and appropriate management techniques. However, in the areas of psychopathology where etiologies are generally unknown, classification may provide provisional guides to research in epidemiology, etiology, treatment, prevention, prognosis, and management. The test of the validity of such classifications cannot, therefore, be a comparison with a more direct assessment of etiology (as at autopsy), because the etiology is unknown. Instead, the appropriate measures of validity may be diverse and imprecise—an omnibus classification like the DSM-II for disorders not known to have organic causes may at best be hoped to facilitate communication, so that all trained practitioners know precisely what behavioral syndrome is represented by each diagnostic label, and to provide leads for research on etiology, treatment, prevention, prognosis, and management.

The studies cited above indicate that the reliability of classification of adult disorders is high enough to facilitate communication for broad categories, but not very high for specific categories of disorders having no known organic cause. The value of the categories of the present system for providing leads for research on etiology, treatment, and prevention will only be known by the results of such research—if causal factors specific to schizophrenia are discovered, for example, then the category "schizophrenia" will have been shown to be a good one. The genetic evidence cited in Chapter 12 suggests that schizophrenia may indeed be a valuable category for classifying adult disorders, but not for child disorders, where developmental and other characteristics may provide better etiological leads than the current diagnostic category of "Schizophrenia, Childhood Type."

The Present System as a Guide to Treatment

The worth of the present system as a guide to treatment has been investigated by comparing the treatments received by clients having similar diagnoses with clients having different diagnoses. Bannister, Salmon, and Lieberman (1964) studied the relations between treatment and three levels of classification employed by English psychiatrists with 1,000 adult clients. Diagnostic Level I comprised three broad categories: Psychotic, neurotic, and organic. Level II comprised more specific categories, such as schizophrenia, organic senile psychosis, anxiety state, hysteria, personality disorders, and addictions. Level III comprised the major categories of the International Classification of Disease, on which the DSM-II is based. None of the levels of classification was found to predict the treatments actually employed for more than about 33 per cent of the patients.

WHO NEEDS TREATMENT?

In the absence of knowledge of etiologies, of the most appropriate treatments, and of prognoses for disorders with no known organic causes, a fundamental question arises as to who should be considered in need of treatment and who should not. Long the subject of philosophical dispute between various schools of thought and between clinicians trying to decide for specific cases, the problem of how mental-health professionals distinguish the mentally "ill" from the mentally "healthy" has recently been investigated empirically.

Pseudopatients. Rosenhan (1973) carried out a study in which a graduate student in psychology, three psychologists, a pediatrician, a psychiatrist, a painter, and a housewife voluntarily entered 12 different mental hospitals as pseudopatients, unbeknown to the hospital staffs. Each pseudopatient arrived at the hospital's admissions office complaining that he had been hearing voices that seemed to be saying "empty," "hollow," and "thud." These symptoms were chosen because they suggested existential symptoms of a concern about the meaninglessness of one's life, although no report of an existential psychosis had ever been published. Each pseudopatient falsified only the above symptoms, his name, and his occupation. All life history data, current behavior, etc., were reported accurately.

While hospitalized, each pseudopatient behaved normally and cooperatively, especially after hospital personnel made it clear that these were the chief criteria for release, and nearly all the pseudopatients quickly became eager for release. They took extensive notes on their observations, but found that no precautions were necessary to hide notetaking, since no one cared anyway. Later examination of hospital records showed that the pseudopatients were diagnosed schizophrenic in 11 hospitals, all state run, and manic-depressive in the twelfth, a private hospital. There was no indication in any record that any pseudopatient's status was suspect to the staff. However, of 118 real patients on the 12 admissions wards, 35 voiced suspicions, some vigorously accusing the pseudopatients of being there to check up on the hospital. Length of hospitalization ranged from 7 to 52 days.

All patients were eventually released with the diagnosis of schizophrenia or manic-depressive psychosis "in remission."

The Effect of Pathological Labels. The wholesale and unquestioned labeling of the pseudopatients as psychotic certainly raises some fundamental questions about the validity of current diagnostic-classificatory procedures as they are actually employed. The lack of objective criteria for distinguishing mental "health" from mental "illness" in the current approach has been further demonstrated by two studies of the effects of prior labeling upon the judgments of diagnosticians. In one study, psychiatrists, clinical psychologists, and graduate students in clinical psychology were asked to diagnose a tape-recorded interviewee who was actually a professional actor trained to sound like a person of exceptionally good mental health (Temerlin, 1968). One group of clinicians first heard the interviewee described by a prestigious confederate as "a very interesting man because he looks neurotic, but actually is quite psychotic." Control groups of clinicians heard the same tape following a confederate's statement affirming the interviewee's mental health or with no prior suggestions. The clinicians were then asked to circle one of 30 possible diagnoses, including "normal or healthy personality."

All the clinicians in the "healthy" control group and 57 per cent in the "no-suggestion" control group diagnosed the interviewee as healthy, while none diagnosed him as psychotic. By contrast, in the "psychotic" condition, none of the psychiatrists, 12 per cent of the psychologists, and 11 per cent of the graduate students diagnosed the interviewee as healthy, while 60 per cent of the psychiatrists, 28 per cent of the psychologists, and 11 per cent of the graduate students diagnosed him as psychotic.

In a second study, a videotaped interview of a young male job applicant was shown to groups of clinicians who were either behaviorally or psychodynamically oriented (Langer & Abelson, 1974). The clinicians were asked to write brief descriptions of the interviewee, his gestures, attitudes, and the factors that probably explained his outlook on life. The instructions to all the clinicians were the same except that the word "patient" was substituted for "job applicant" in the instructions given to half the clinicians of each type. The clinicians' descriptions were later rated on a scale of 1 ("very disturbed") to 10 ("very well adjusted") by raters blind to the conditions and hypotheses.

Under the condition where the interviewee was described as a job applicant, the descriptions by both the behavioral and the psychodynamic clinicians received mean ratings of 6.3 on the 10-point scale, indicating relatively good adjustment. However, under the condition where the interviewee was described as a patient, the psychodynamic clinicians' descriptions were rated significantly lower (mean = 3.8), while the descriptions by the behavioral clinicians were rated nonsignificantly lower (mean = 6.1). Both the Temerlin and Langer-Abelson studies thus demonstrate that prior labels have a powerful influence on the diagnostic-classificatory behavior of clinicians, especially those with a traditional orientation toward psychopathology.

ALTERNATIVES TO THE PRESENT SYSTEM

The fact that most of the problems illustrated above concern the diagnostic classification of adults does not mean the situation is more satisfactory with respect to childhood disorders. On the contrary, the paucity of evidence on the classification of children's disorders reflects more the lack of systematic evaluations of current practices than satisfaction with them. The almost total absence of differentiation among childhood disorders in DSM-I may help to account for the fact that alternative proposals were more frequent than were attempts to evaluate the DSM-I system. The greater differentiation of the DSM-II system reflects these alternative proposals to some extent, but the system's effectiveness has not yet been well evaluated. The child categories of the DSM-II are not much more objectively specified than the adult categories and they are likely to suffer many of the same inadequacies. What follows are accounts of several alternatives to the DSM system for childhood disorders.

The GAP Classification System

The Committee on Child Psychiatry of the Group for the Advancement of Psychiatry (GAP) has proposed what is perhaps the most ambitious alternative to the DSM system for the classification of children's disorders (GAP, 1966). Categories of the proposed system have been cited earlier in this book, especially in reference to the psychotic disorders.

Acknowledging that an ideal classification scheme would include clinical description, psychodynamic and psychosocial factors, etiology, prognosis, and the appropriate method of treatment for each disorder, the GAP Committee opted for a "clinical-descriptive" system that could be used by workers from varying schools of thought to insure more uniform collection of data. It was hoped that this system would, in turn, eventually lead to a more ideal classification. The proposed system is outlined in Table 15–1. Note that an important innovation is the inclusion of a category entitled "Healthy Responses." The committee listed this category first in order to emphasize the need for assessing the strengths of the child and the possibility that what seems to be abnormal may really be a normal reaction. Examples include developmental crises such as the anxiety infants begin to show around six to eight months of age whenever their mothers disappear; phobias among preschool children; compulsive behavior in school-aged children; identity crises in adolescents; and grief reactions to the death of loved ones.

The GAP Committee maintained that its definitions of the various categories were as operational as possible, entailing what was regarded as an irreducible minimum of inferences. While all attempts at classification involve some inference, the degree of inference involved in the GAP system varies considerably from category to category. Category 4, Psychoneurotic

TABLE 15–1

Outline of the classification system proposed by the G.A.P. (1966).

I. **Healthy Responses**
   A.   Developmental crisis
   B.   Situational crisis
   C.   Other responses

II. **Reactive Disorders**

III. **Developmental Deviations**
   A.   Deviations in maturational patterns
   B.   Deviations in specific dimensions of development (Motor, sensory, speech, cognitive, social, psychosexual, affective, or integrative)

IV. **Psychoneurotic Disorders**
   A.   Anxiety
   B.   Phobic
   C.   Conversion
   D.   Dissociative
   E.   Obsessive-compulsive
   F.   Depressive
   G.   Other

V. **Personality Disorders**
   A.   Compulsive
   B.   Hysterical
   C.   Anxious
   D.   Overly dependent
   E.   Oppositional
   F.   Overly inhibited
   G.   Overly independent
   H.   Isolated
   I.   Mistrustful
   J.   Tension-discharge disorders
      1. Impulse-ridden
      2. Neurotic personality
   K.   Sociosyntonic
   L.   Sexual deviation
   M.   Other

VI. **Psychotic Disorders**
   A.   Psychoses of infancy and early childhood
      1. Early infantile autism
      2. Interactional psychotic disorder
      3. Other
   B.   Psychoses of later childhood
      1. Schizophreniform psychotic disorder
      2. Other
   C.   Psychoses of adolescence
      1. Acute confusional state
      2. Schizophrenic disorder, adult type
      3. Other

VII. **Psychophysiologic Disorders**
   (Specific sites are listed)

VIII. **Brain Syndromes**
   (Acute, chronic)

IX. **Mental Retardation**

X. **Other Disorders**

Disorders, for example, is defined almost exclusively in terms of psychoanalytic theory, as

. . . disorders based on unconscious conflicts over the handling of sexual and aggressive impulses which, though removed from awareness by the mechanism of repression, remain active and unresolved. . . . The anxiety, acting as a danger signal to the ego, ordinarily sets into operation certain defense mechanisms, in addition to repression, and leads to the formation of psychological symptoms which symbolically deal with the conflict, thus achieving a partial though unhealthy solution [GAP, 1966, pp. 229–30].

The border between description and inference is often vague, but nonpsychoanalysts might question the degree to which the committee's goal of a descriptive system, based on operational, minimally inferential definitions, was achieved for the category of psychoneurotic disorders.

Reliability of the GAP System.   An empirical study of the reliability of the GAP system has been made in Australia by Freeman (1971).   Forty-four case histories were submitted to 20 child psychiatrists for diagnostic classification according to the GAP system.   All 20 psychiatrists agreed in their placement of 2 out of the 44 cases into one of the major diagnostic categories, while 16 to 19 psychiatrists agreed in their placement of another 8 out of the 44 cases.

When each case was classified according to the major category used by the most psychiatrists (i.e., the modal category), it was found that only six categories were needed to classify all the cases—Reactive Disorders, Psychoneurotic Disorders, Developmental Deviations, Personality Disorders, Psychotic Disorders, and Brain Syndromes.   Considering only the six popular categories, the average degree of agreement among psychiatrists was 59 per cent, which is about the same degree of agreement found for classification of adult patients according to the major DSM categories (e.g., Beck et al, 1962; Sandifer et al, 1964; Schmidt & Fonda, 1956).   The degree of agreement for specific subcategories was not reported, although analysis of specific subcategories within major categories indicated that overall agreement on specific subcategories was quite low.

"Test-retest" reliability was assessed by having the psychiatrists rediagnose six of the case histories three months after they had made their original diagnoses.   The average agreement between all the psychiatrists' first diagnoses and their second diagnoses was 72 per cent for the major categories.

Taken together, the findings of the study indicate that the GAP system is used with about the same degree of reliability as the DSM system for adult patients.   The fact that the innovative categories of Healthy Responses and Developmental Deviations were used rarely and with very high rates of disagreement suggests that the GAP system was applied in roughly the same manner as the adult system.   Whether it was due to the influence of the adult categories on the thinking of the child psychiatrists, previous experience, lack of training with the GAP system, or the paucity of cases actually fitting the new categories, the GAP system does not appear to have introduced much new clarity to the diagnostic classification of children by the Australian psychiatrists participating in Freeman's study.

Experience with the GAP system in an American child guidance clinic showed that the new categories of Healthy Responses and Developmental

Deviations were employed for 8.7 and 14.9 per cent of the clients, respectively, although objective assessment of reliability was not made (Bemporad, Pfeifer, & Bloom, 1970). Some of the GAP system's new categories for personality disorder—such as Overly Dependent, Oppositional, Overly Inhibited, and Tension-Discharge Disorders—were also used fairly frequently. Comparison with diagnoses from other clinics suggested that the more differentiated GAP system had made possible a large reduction in diagnoses of Adjustment Reaction.

Empirical Clustering Approaches

Both the DSM and GAP systems were created by committees of psychiatrists who established the diagnostic categories through discussion and the polling of colleagues. The categories with clear organic features are, like disorders in the rest of organic medicine, defined according to their organic features. Types and severity of mental retardation are generally categorized according to the system contained in the 1961 edition of the American Association on Mental Deficiency's *Manual on Terminology and Classification in Mental Retardation* (Heber, 1961). Since most of the organic syndromes and the types of mental retardation have been delineated through research that has yielded relatively objective indices of the disorders (e.g., physical features, laboratory and IQ tests, health histories, family characteristics), there has been little reason to propose radical alternatives to these categories. Instead, alternative procedures for devising classifications have been directed primarily at disorders not having known organic features.

One of the chief alternative approaches has been to determine empirically what characteristics tend to occur with what other characteristics. The rationale for this approach is that disorders sharing a cluster of characteristics may be similar in etiology, amenability to treatment, prognosis, or the like. The pronouncements of the DSM and GAP committees are consistent with this approach in that they emphasize *description* as a basis for the classification of disorders with unknown etiologies. Nevertheless, as illustrated above in the GAP's definition of the psychoneurotic disorders and as shown by the low reliability in clinicians' use of the "descriptive" categories, the committee efforts have not produced categories that function well as objective descriptions. Whether this is because the categories fail to correspond to the actual disorders or because the descriptions lack clarity is not certain.

Since the number of possible behavioral variables and combinations of them is so enormous, many workers have recently looked to statistical and computer technology to aid in the search for behavioral clusters. The chief statistical technique used in these studies has been *factor analysis,* although related techniques known as *cluster analysis* may also be used. A factor-analytic study begins with the recording of data on specific items concerning each individual in a group of interest. Decisions as to what kinds of data to record about the individuals are made on the basis of prior theory, hunches, previous experience, types of information available on the individuals, level of skills of the people who record the data, degree of precision with which the data can be scored, etc. Thus, a factor-analytic study may begin with items at various levels of inference and specificity, including reports by observers, test scores, demographic information, and so forth. A psychoanalytically oriented investigator may choose variables such as "ego strength," "castration anxiety," "repression," and "denial," while a behaviorally oriented investigator may choose variables such as "cries during interview," "hits brother," "throws food," and "fears dogs."

Most factor-analytic studies of disturbed children have employed behavioral and self-report variables rather than variables requiring a great deal of inference. However, the level of inference and specificity of the variables has ranged from items such as "Anxiety symptoms, somatic or psychic" (Collins, Maxwell, & Cameron, 1962), to items like "picks nose" (Dreger et al, 1964). Needless to say, studies employing items as general as the first usually have a far shorter list to be scored for each child than do studies like that of Dreger et al, which employed 229 different items.

Since factor analysis is based upon *correlations* of every item with every other item, the items must be subject to some type of quantification. The type of quantification has included simply scoring a 0 if a child does not manifest the item and a 1 if he does manifest it; a 0–1–2 system in which a score of 1 represents a moderate or ambiguous degree of the item; and systems employing scales with several. steps representing degrees of intensity or frequency for each item. After each item has been scored for each child, correlations are calculated among all the items.

A "Mental" Factor Analysis. Consider for a moment how we might employ correlations among items to identify clusters without using a formal statistical technique such as factor analysis. To begin our "mental" factor analysis, a look at the correlations among individual items might show that *phobias* and *stomachaches* correlate .60; *phobias* and general *fearfulness* correlate .49; *stomachaches* and *fearfulness* correlate .47; *phobias* and *pains* (other than stomachaches) correlate .32; *stomachaches* and *pains* correlate .41; *fearfulness* and *pains* correlate .27; *phobias* and *disobedience* correlate −.65; *stomachaches* and *disobedience* correlate −.43; *fearfulness* and *disobedience* correlate −.51; and *pains* and *disobedience* correlate −.27.

From the preceding correlations we could conclude that phobias, stomachaches, fearfulness, and pains all tend to occur together, while disobedience tends not to be reported for children who show the other symptoms. Thus, a rough approximation to a descriptive category might be the combination of phobias, stomachaches, fearfulness, and pains, in the *absence* of disobedience.

It may already have occurred to the reader that the varying degrees of correlation between the items suggest that, because they are not all equally correlated with one another, they may not be equally important to the cluster derived from their intercorrelations. The fact that *phobias* correlates most highly with all the other symptoms suggests that *phobias* is particularly important in this cluster and that the presence or absence of *pains*, which has the lowest correlations, may be much less crucial. Consequently, it may be decided that a child should be classified according to this cluster if he has, say, three of the four symptoms, as long as the three include *phobias*.

Except for the quantification of the basic observational data and the calculation of correlations between each item of data, our mental factor analysis has so far proceeded in much the same way as the traditional clinician proceeds when he attempts to identify clusters of characteristics that may enable him to begin developing hypotheses about etiologies, treatments, prognoses, etc. Of course, quantitative representation of the degree of correlation between each variable has made our task easier than that of the clinician who works only from memories and impressions of how often he has seen each characteristic together, in what intensities, and whether some characteristics only occurred in a negative relationship to certain other characteristics (e.g., phobias and disobedience). The quantitative correlations have also enabled us to rank the degrees of relationship among the variables rather than having to guess at the relative degrees of relationship once we have decided that there are relationships. Rank ordering of the correlations has shown us, for example, that *phobias* occurs more consistently with the other three symptoms of our cluster than does *pains*.

The task of identifying a cluster among five symptoms by "mental" factor analysis of correlation coefficients is not really too difficult, at least not when the symptoms were deliberately selected for their simplicity, positive correlations among four of them, and negative correlations between these four and the fifth. However, if, as is more typical, the items had not happened to form such a nice pattern of correlations, and if some of the items that correlated positively with phobias had also correlated *positively* rather than negatively with *disobedience,* we would have been faced with many more decisions about how to define a cluster or whether the data held any evidence for a clustering of items.

These obstacles are, of course, not insurmountable and a kind of mental factor analysis, even without the benefit of quantitative correlations, has served well in the identification of many syndromes in the history of psychopathology—including Down's syndrome (mongolism), general paresis, Klinefelter's syndrome, Turner's syndrome, and phenylketonuria. Each of these syndromes was originally identified on the basis of a small number of relatively clear-cut organic features. However, when we consider the number of characteristics that may form clusters among children who do not manifest organic anomalies, the failure of traditional clinical experience to yield a reliable and valid classification system becomes understandable.

The Hewitt and Jenkins Study.   Our selection of five symptoms to illustrate mental factor analysis forced us to deal with 10 intercorrelations. The number of variables needed to describe children's disorders more realistically is illustrated by the fact that the first attempt to employ a kind of mental factor analysis to intercorrelations among children's symptoms involved 94 symptom items (Hewitt & Jenkins, 1946). The 94 items were scored as present or absent in each of 500 child clinic case records, but the authors retained for analysis only 45 of the items, chosen on the basis of high frequency or "obvious clinical importance."

The 985 correlations among the 45 items were inspected to detect three clusters that the authors expected in advance. When clusters resembling those expected by the authors were identified, a combination of statistical and subjective criteria were employed to determine which items would be used to define each cluster in order to classify children's disorders. A symptom was considered to belong to a cluster if it correlated at least .30 with "most" of the other symptoms in the cluster and if it fit the "clinical picture" suggested by the cluster. The three clusters thus formed were labeled as representing the *Overinhibited Child,* the *Unsocialized Aggressive Child,* and the *Socialized Delinquent Child.* The latter two clusters, refined through more advanced statistical techniques applied to data from delinquent children, have since provided a basis for identifying subtypes of delinquents (see Chapter 13).

Formal Factor Analysis. It was not until the 1960s that formal factor-analytic procedures, made easy by the advent of computers, were used to identify symptom clusters in broad samples of children. Because it uses objective mathematical criteria for identifying the clusters or dimensions among correlations, factor analysis avoids the need for mentally subdividing large numbers of correlations and avoids many (but not all) of the subjective, often arbitrary, decisions that would have to be made in the course of a mental factor analysis. Moreover, because the number of correlations among items grows much more quickly than the actual number of items, the magnitude of a mental factor analysis becomes prohibitive with far fewer descriptive items than are required for an adequate description of disturbed behavior. One of the first factor-analytic studies of child behavior disorders, for example, employed a relatively short list of only the most frequently reported items in clinic records. This list included 58 items, among which there were 1255 correlations (Peterson, 1961). The 229 items in the Dreger et al (1964) study, cited earlier, produced 26,106 correlations.

The outcome of a factor analysis is not simply a series of clusters in which each item appears once.[1] Rather, the outcome is a series of factors (dimensions) with which every item has a correlation. The correlation of an item with a factor is called the *loading* of that item on that factor. The items with the highest loadings (positive or negative) are used to define the factor.

---

[1] The mathematical procedures for factor analysis will not be dealt with here. Good introductions can be found in Fruchter (1954) and Comrey (1973), and advanced presentations in Harman (1967) and Mulaik (1972). The availability of prepared programs for factor analysis in most computer centers makes it unnecessary for users to perform the mathematical operations.

A group of items with high loadings may be treated as if they formed a cluster. Individuals may then be sought whose characteristics resemble that cluster.[2] A single factor may have both a group of items with high positive loadings and a group of items with high negative loadings. This would mean that the two clusters at the opposite poles (ends) of the factor correlate negatively with one another, i.e., an individual having the characteristics clustering at one pole is unlikely to have the characteristics clustering at the opposite pole.

Recall now the five symptoms presented for the illustration of mental factor analysis. These symptoms were included on a symptom checklist of 91 items employed in a factor-analytic study of 300 boy and 300 girl psychiatric clinic clients who showed no evidence of organic features (Achenbach, 1966). Various sources in each child's record (e.g., parents, physicians, teachers, self-reports) provided the information for scoring each symptom as present or absent.

When the intercorrelations of the items were factor-analyzed, separately for each sex, the factor found to account for the largest proportion of the relationships among the items ("first principal factor") was composed of a group of items with high positive loadings, a group with low positive and negative loadings, and a group with high negative loadings. For the boys, *phobias, stomachaches, fearfulness,* and *pains,* reported earlier as having positive correlations with one another, had the highest loadings on one pole of the first principal factor, while *disobedience,* the symptom having negative correlations with the others, had the highest loading at the other (negative) pole of the first principal factor.

Table 15–2 presents the items from both poles of this "bipolar" factor for the boys. Only those items having loadings as high as ±.25 are included in Table 15–2. The items having loadings between +.25 and −.25 on this factor have been omitted. Because the symptoms at the positive pole of the factor seemed to consist of problems within the self, this cluster was given the shorthand label of *Internalizing* symptoms. By contrast, the symptoms at the negative end of the factor seemed to involve conflict with the outside world and were given the shorthand label of *Externalizing* symptoms. A very similar bipolar factor was found for the girls' symptoms. Other factor-analytic studies of the behavior problems of nonclinic as well as clinic children have revealed dichotomous clusters like those labeled Internalizing and Externalizing, even though other symptom checklists and factor-analytic methods were employed (e.g., Collins et al, 1962; Kohn & Rosman, 1972; Miller, 1967; Peterson, 1961; Quay & Quay, 1965).

Relations Among Levels of Factorial Classification. Achenbach's (1966) study had several purposes beside the empirical identification of symptom

---

[2] Another approach is to calculate a *factor score* for each subject. This is done by multiplying the subject's score on each item by the loading the item has on a factor. The factor score is a *quantitative* measure of how high or low the subject is on the dimension presumably reflected in the factor rather than a *qualitative categorization* of individual subjects as having or not having a particular cluster of characteristics.

TABLE 15–2

Symptoms having loadings as high as ±.25 on the first principal factor found for disturbed boys.

"Internalizing" symptoms	"Externalizing" symptoms
+.53 Phobias	—.63 Disobedient
.42 Stomachaches	.56 Stealing
.38 Fearful	.51 Lying
.36 Pains	.49 Fighting
.34 Worrying	.45 Cruelty
.34 Withdrawn	.45 Destructive
.34 Nausea	.40 Inadequate guilt feeling
.34 Obsessions	.40 Vandalism
.33 Shy	.37 Truancy
.33 Vomiting	.36 Fire-setting
.30 Compulsions	.34 Swearing
.30 Insomnia	.32 Running away
.27 Crying	.28 Temper tantrums
.26 Fantastic thinking	.28 Showing off
.26 Headaches	.27 Hyperactive
.26 Seclusive	
.25 Apathy	

NOTE.—Symptoms with loadings between +.25 and —.25 are omitted from the table. From Achenbach (1966).

clusters. One purpose was to determine whether there was a hierarchy of clusters such that some were subtypes of others. The findings of earlier factor- and cluster-analytic studies, especially of adult symptoms, had differed as to whether there were a few very general clusters or many specific ones. Since the particular factor- or cluster-analytic method chosen could influence the degree of specificity in the factors found, Achenbach combined several methods by first factor-analyzing the data using the method that produced the general factor portrayed in Table 15–2. Next, factor-analytic methods were applied that yielded many specific clusters. Table 15–3 presents the shorthand labels for the seven specific factors found for boys and the 11 specific factors found for girls.

When all the factors had been obtained, each of the 300 boys and 300 girls was classified according to his or her resemblance to the clusters at each pole of the first principal factor. This was done by classifying a child as an Internalizer if 60 per cent or more of his symptoms came from the Internalizing pole of the first principal factor or as an Externalizer if 60 per cent or more of his symptoms came from the Externalizing pole. If at least 60 per cent of his symptoms were not represented at either pole, he was left unclassified.

After all the children were categorized as Internalizers, Externalizers, or

TABLE 15-3

Labels given specific symptom clusters found among disturbed children.

1. Aggressive behavior
2. Anxiety symptoms (girls only)
3. Delinquent behavior
4. Depressive symptoms (girls only)
5. Enuresis and other immaturities (girls only)
6. Hyperreactive behavior
7. Neurotic and delinquent behavior (girls only)
8. Obesity (girls only)
9. Obsessions, compulsions, and phobias
10. Schizoid thinking and behavior
11. Sexual problems (boys only)
12. Somatic complaints

NOTE.—From Achenbach (1966).

unclassified on the first principal factor, they were classified by the same procedure according to their resemblance to the specific factors obtained for their respective sex. Thus, for example, if 60 per cent or more of a boy's symptoms came from the "Somatic Complaints" factor for boys, he was classified under that heading.

Lastly, the relationships between classification by the first principal factor and by the specific factors were examined to determine whether any of the specific factors were clear-cut subtypes of the more general factors. Figure 15-1 shows that certain specific clusters for the boys were almost entirely subsumed by the categories of the first principal factor, while some other clusters, especially the one labeled "Schizoid Thinking and Behavior," included boys who were not restricted to one category on the principal factor.

Figure 15-2 shows the picture for girls to be complicated somewhat by their greater number of specific factors. Nevertheless, the specific factors clearly subsumed by either the Externalizing or Internalizing cluster for the boys are similarly subsumed for the girls. "Aggressive Behavior" and "Delinquent Behavior" are both subsumed by the Externalizing cluster and "Obsessions, Compulsions, and Phobias" and "Somatic Complaints" are both subsumed by the Internalizing cluster. The specific cluster labeled "Anxiety Symptoms," and occurring only for girls, was also subsumed by the Internalizing cluster. Thus, these syndromes appear to be distinct subtypes of the types represented by the more general Externalizing and Internalizing clusters, while "Schizoid Thinking and Behavior" does not appear strongly related to the Internalizing-Externalizing dichotomy.

Correlates and Theoretical Implications of the Factorial Classification.
While a descriptive classification based on empirical groupings of symptoms

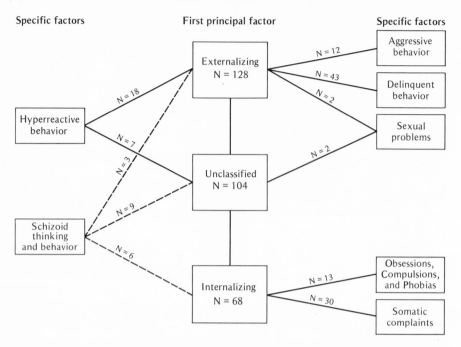

Fig. 15–1. Classification of disturbed boys by first principal and specific factors. One "obsessive" and two "somatic" boys came from the Unclassified group. From Achenbach (1966). © 1966 by the American Psychological Association and reprinted by permission.

might improve communication and reliability, its value would be greatly enhanced if important correlates of the classes could be discovered. Besides the intrinsic value of discovering correlates of the classes, such correlates, together with the hierarchical relationships found, might suggest research-able hypotheses as to why symptoms cluster as they do and what causal variables might be involved in the different clusters. Examination of bio-graphical characteristics showed Externalizers of both sexes to differ signifi-cantly from Internalizers in having poorer school performance, more pre-vious problems (police, psychiatric, school expulsion, school failure), parents with more overt social problems (alcoholism, divorce, neglect, desertion, illegitimate children, criminal records, psychiatric histories), parents who were less concerned about their child's problems, and homes that more often lacked at least one of the biological parents.

The patterns of differences suggested that the Internalizing and External-izing clusters were at least partly a product of the children's socialization histories. As a result of having relatively stable homes with concerned parents who did not have overt social problems, Internalizers had been so-cialized in such a way that their reactions to stress were manifested in unag-gressive symptoms of intraself conflict. The background characteristics of

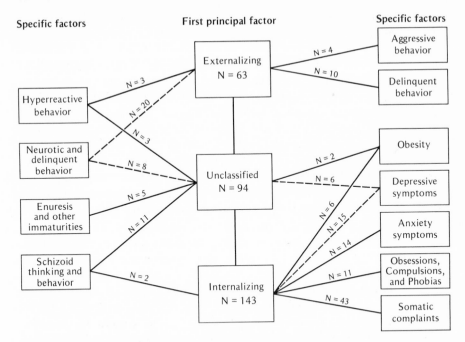

Fig. 15–2. Classification of disturbed girls by first principal and specific factors. One "obsessive" and one "anxiety" girl came from the Unclassified group; one "enuresis" girl came from the Externalizing group; one "enuresis" and one "neurotic and delinquent" girl came from the Internalizing group. From Achenbach (1966). © 1966 by the American Psychological Association and reprinted by permission.

the Externalizers, by contrast, suggested that their socialization experiences had not suppressed aggressive, extrapunitive reactions to stress. The fact that twice as many girls were Internalizers as were Externalizers, while the ratio of Internalizers to Externalizers among boys was almost exactly the opposite (see Figs. 15–1 and 15–2), suggests that the suppression of aggressive reactions is typically more effective for girls than for boys, and/or that biological characteristics make girls more likely to react to stress with Internalizing rather than Externalizing symptoms.

The fact that all the children classified according to the Aggressive Behavior and the Delinquent Behavior factors for both sexes were also classified as Externalizers implies that all of them had backgrounds that failed to suppress aggressive behavioral reactions, but that their specific reactions (Aggressive or Delinquent) were determined by other variables. Similarly, the fact that virtually all children classified according to the Somatic Complaints and Obsessions Compulsions, and Phobias factors for both sexes and the Anxiety Symptoms factor for girls were also classified as Internalizers suggests that all these children shared backgrounds that suppressed Externalizing reactions to stress, but that their specific reactions (e.g., Somatic; Obsessive; Anxiety) were determined by other variables.

Children whose symptoms matched the Schizoid Thinking and Behavior factor, by contrast, were categorized as Internalizers, Unclassified, and, for the boys, Externalizers. This suggests that what these children had in common was not primarily related to socialization, but, instead, may have been something such as an organic or basic psychological abnormality. In further support of the possibility that schizoid children may have *either* internalizing *or* externalizing symptom patterns, Mednick and Schulsinger (1968) found that ratings by teachers and psychiatrists showed children of schizophrenic mothers to be *either* more passive and nervous *or* more aggressive and disruptive than normal control children. Some of the other specific factors shown in Figs. 15–1 and 15–2 to relate to more than one category derived from the principal factor may also signify commonalities which, like the schizoid cluster, are not so strongly indicative of a particular socialization history as are the specific factors clearly subsumed by the Internalizing and Externalizing categories.

Examination of the background characteristics of children matching the specific factors revealed some further patterns that may aid in discovering the etiology of each symptom cluster. One type of pattern was developmental: Nearly all the girls classified by the Enuresis and Other Immaturities factor were four or five years old, the mean age being 4.3 years. This cluster thus appears characteristic of young girls and is not likely to be found at later ages. For both sexes, the Hyperreactive Behavior factor classified predominately young children, the mean ages being 7.3 years for girls and 7.8 for boys. This cluster may be characteristic of young children because it is an age-specific way of reacting to stress or because it is a manifestation of undetected organic damage that may not produce hyperreactivity at later ages. All the girls classified by the Obesity factor, found only for girls, were between the ages of 10 and 14, indicating that it represents a syndrome associated with puberty. Similarly, almost all the girls classified by the Neurotic and Delinquent Behavior factor were between the ages of 12 and 15.

Another pattern occurred with respect to IQ and social class: Children classified by the Obsessions, Compulsions, and Phobias factor had higher social-class status and mean IQs (112 for boys and 115 for girls) than did children classified by any other specific factor. At the other extreme, children classified by the Aggressive Behavior factor had the lowest social-class status, the lowest mean IQ for boys (87), the second lowest mean IQ for girls (96), and parents with the most social problems of all the children classified by specific factors.

Validation of the Factorial Classification.   The Internalizing-Externalizing factor has been replicated with new samples of children in different clinical settings (Achenbach & Lewis, 1971; Shechtman, 1970a), although replication of the more specific factors has not yet been attempted. Classification of new samples of children according to their resemblance to a number of the factor-based clusters has also been found to discriminate the children on numerous variables. Butcher (1966) found that fathers of adolescent Externalizing boys attending a clinic had significantly higher scores for psychopathy on the MMPI than did fathers of Internalizing boys. Similarly, Anderson (1969) found that both parents of clinic boys classified by the Aggressive Behavior factor had significantly more deviant MMPI profiles than did parents of boys classified by the Obsessions, Compulsions, and Phobias factor. Again, the fathers of the Aggressive boys (all these boys being, of course, Externalizers) were especially deviant on the psychopathy scale of the MMPI.

Tests administered to clinic children classified as Externalizers have shown that they were more impulsive, less able to delay gratification, and less foresightful than clinic children of similar socioeconomic status who were classified as Internalizers (Weintraub, 1973). In another study, Externalizing boys were also rated more impulsive and more aggressive by a psychiatrist, while Internalizing boys were rated as having a more passive orientation, using more babyish speech, being more ready to relinquish the care of their bodies, and having mothers and fathers who professed to protect their sons' masculinity. Furthermore, mothers of Internalizers were rated as exercising more strict control over their sons and Internalizers remained longer in psychotherapy and were rated as improving more than Externalizers (Achenbach & Lewis, 1971).

In a study comparing Internalizing and Externalizing children with children of schizophrenic and Internalizing mothers, Rolf (1972) found that their classmates rated Externalizing children lower than any of the other children on various traits of competence and desirability and higher on traits concerning badness, fighting, temper, and bullying. Teachers also rated the Externalizers as the lowest of all the groups on academic behavior and various social-emotional characteristics, although Externalizers were rated higher than Internalizers on "positive extroversion."

The factorial findings have been put to use in the evaluation of relations between school children's Internalizing and Externalizing behavior, as judged by teachers, and the children's reports of their parents' child-rearing behaviors (Armentrout, 1971). Fifteen items representing Internalizing behavior and 15 representing Externalizing behavior were derived from the clusters found by Achenbach and two very similar clusters ("Conduct Problem" and "Personality Disorder") found by Peterson (1961). Armentrout asked teachers to rate each of their pupils on the 30 behavioral items. Reliability, as indicated by ratings repeated two to three weeks later, was .89 for the Internalizing items and .92 for the Externalizing items.

The teachers' ratings on both the Internalizing and Externalizing items were found to correlate significantly with children's reports of being rejected by their parents, while the ratings on only the Externalizing items correlated significantly with children's reports of being excessively controlled by their parents. Without independent verification of the parents' actual behavior, the most parsimonious view of these findings is probably that feeling rejected is part of both kinds of syndrome, while feeling excessively controlled is a component only of the Externalizing syndrome.

The symptom checklist employed by Achenbach has also been employed in epidemiological studies in which nonclinic children have been compared to demographically matched clinic children for frequency of symptoms. Shechtman (1970b) reported that, among white children, those attending a clinic had nearly twice as many symptoms as those not attending clinics and 21 specific symptoms occurred significantly more frequently in the clinic group. Among blacks, however, the difference in mean number of symptoms for clinic and demographically matched nonclinic children was not significant and only three specific symptoms occurred significantly more frequently in the clinic group (Shechtman, 1971). Coupled with Shechtman's finding that only five per cent of the black parents had initiated their children's clinic contacts, while the rest were referred by schools and other agencies, this suggests that the behavior of white children seen in clinics tends to be considerably more deviant from that of their white peers than is true for black clinic children.

Other Approaches to Classification

Numerous other approaches have been proposed for the classification of child psychopathology. Anna Freud's (1965) Developmental Profile was described in Chapter 8 and Eysenck's system for classifying adult disorders along the dimensions of extroversion-introversion and neuroticism was described in Chapter 11 (Eysenck & Rachman, 1965). Little research on the Developmental Profile has been published beyond illustrative case histories. The lack of objective criteria for assessing the numerous variables associated with the Profile and for scoring individuals according to their standing on these variables makes it difficult to see how the Profile can be used with adequate reliability or how its validity can be assessed.

Eysenck's system, by contrast, classifies individuals objectively according to the scores they obtain on personality tests and the loadings these tests have on the extroversion-introversion and neuroticism factors. However, the system was designed for the classification of adult disorders and most of the tests are not usable with children. Eysenck (1953) has interpreted children's symptom clusters like the Internalizing and Externalizing clusters as representing introversion and extroversion, respectively, but Eysenck's system makes no provision for specific clusters that are not direct functions of his two primary dimensions. It is, therefore, difficult to see how the system could accommodate developmental differences in symptoms, even if it is assumed that all specific clusters could be positioned along the two basic dimensions.

Anthony (1970) has attempted to integrate developmental concepts into a general schema for developmental psychopathology. Anthony's aim was

TABLE 15-4

Anthony's proposed diagnostic classification for developmental psychopathology.

Ages	Psychosexual stages (Freud)	Psychosocial stages (Erikson)	Cognitive stages (Piaget)	Affective stages (Jersild)	Psychopathology
0–1½	Oral	Basic trust vs. Mistrust	Sensorimotor	Fears of: Dark Strangers Aloneness Sudden noise Loss of support	Autism Anaclitic depression Feeding and sleeping problems
1½–3	Anal	Autonomy vs. Doubt, shame	Symbolic	Separation Desertion Sudden movements	Symbiosis Negativism Constipation Shyness & withdrawal Night terrors
3–5	Genital Oedipal	Initiative vs. Guilt	Intuition, Representational	Animals Imaginary creatures Injury	Phobias Nightmares Speech problems Enuresis Encopresis Anxiety states
6–11	Latency	Industry vs. Inferiority	Concrete operational	School failure Ridicule Loss of possessions Disfigurement Disease Death	School problems School phobias Obsessions Conversion symptoms Tics
12–17	Adolescent— recapitulation of earlier conflicts	Identity vs. Role confusion	Formal operational	Being different physically, socially, intellectually Sexual fears Loss of face	Identity diffusion Anorexia nervosa Delinquency Schizophrenia

NOTE.—Adapted from Anthony (1970, p. 730). © 1970 by John Wiley & Sons and reproduced by permission.

to portray disorders "in terms of the psychosexual, psychosocial, psychocognitive, and psychoaffective operations at work during any particular stage [p. 731]." As can be seen from Table 15–4, he has listed roughly parallel stages put forth by Freud, Erikson, Piaget, and Jersild, plus the approximate ages and some pathology thought to be typical of each stage.

As Anthony points out, his schema cannot be expected to do more than generate hypotheses, but it may be a useful way of summarizing the multiple psychological dimensions along which development has been hypothesized to proceed and the multiplicity of factors that might be needed to form a complete picture of a child at any given age. Important questions are, however, whether each of the theoretical portrayals of development is valid, whether they are effective ways of conceptualizing developmental changes, and whether each adds anything meaningful to what is already portrayed by one of the others.

A more ideal classificatory schema for developmental psychopathology would move beyond rough parallels between existing theories to objectively defined stages, dimensions, symptom clusters, etc., that serve as indices of etiology and guides to epidemiology, treatment, management, and prognosis. To make possible such a system for the disorders without organic features, it will no doubt be necessary to concentrate on both the objective delineation of specific pathological reactions and on the elucidation of developmental processes and their aberrations. The enormous changes children undergo from birth to maturity mean that no specific reaction is likely to be found at all developmental periods nor to have exactly the same determinants and significance at each of the several developmental periods at which it might occur. On the other hand, there may well be dimensions of pathology that characterize certain children throughout the course of development, even though the successive manifestations of the pathology differ from one developmental period to the next.

SUMMARY

Classification refers to an endproduct or conclusion of the diagnostic process. It provides a shorthand link to other clients with whom experience has been gained. Although the faults of the official DSM classification system have led some to condemn all classification, the fact that human judgments inevitably involve classification means the basic question is not *whether* to classify but *how* to classify psychopathology.

Methods of classification should be dictated by the goals of the classifiers. The same person may be classified according to one criterion (e.g., etiology of disorder) for one purpose and according to another criterion (e.g., level of functioning) for another purpose.

In the absence of firm knowledge about etiology, treatment, and prognosis, classification of psychopathology can at best serve to facilitate communication and to guide research on epidemiology, etiology, treatment, and prognosis. However, the low *reliability* and *validity* of the official classification system and the strong influence of suggestion on the use of the system by traditional clinicians indicate that it does not function effectively.

The innovations of the proposed GAP system for the classification of childhood disorders include categories for healthy responses, developmental deviations, and highly differentiated categories for childhood psychoses and personality disorders. Although it is intended to be a descriptive system, the GAP system relies heavily on psychoanalytic inferences in the definitions of some disorders. Reliability of usage appears to be about the same as that for the DSM system.

Empirical clustering approaches, primarily employing factor analysis, have been undertaken to identify clusters of characteristics as they actually occur among children. Two general clusters, labeled Internalizing and Externalizing or Personality Problems and Conduct Problems, have been found in many samples of children. More specific clusters have also been found, some of which are subsumed by the general clusters, while others are peculiar to certain developmental periods. The hierarchical relations among the specific and general clusters, as well as other characteristics of the children classified by the various clusters, have suggested etiological differences among the symptom patterns embodied in the clusters.

Other approaches have included Anna Freud's Developmental Profile, Eysenck's two-dimensional schema, and the parallel specification of pathologies and developmental stages for each age period. It is likely that both the objective specification of symptom patterns and a better understanding of developmental processes will be necessary in order to create a comprehensive system for the classification of childhood psychopathology.

SUGGESTED READING

Classification Systems. Despite the proliferation of proposals for classification, there has been much less research on or theoretical analysis of the general functions of classification for child psychopathology than for adult psychopathology. The GAP's (1966) proposed classification is worth examining as an expression of how a committee of child psychiatrists conceived of the problems of classification and how they arrived at a solution. Both the DSM-I (American Psychiatric Association, 1952) and DSM-II (American Psychiatric Association, 1968) are also worth examining because, not only are they the official American classification systems, but as products of psychiatric consensus, they embody what are, in effect, the lowest common denominators of prevailing psychiatric concepts. Comparing the two editions will provide a view of how psychiatric thinking changed between 1952 and 1968.

Conceptual Issues. A widely cited paper entitled "Psychiatric Diagnosis: A Critique" (Zigler & Phillips, 1961) provides a clear analysis of many of the fundamental issues in diagnostic classification, issues that are often obscured by the theoretical preconceptions underlying particular proposals for classification. Numerous viewpoints on the role and methodology of classification in psychopathology are presented in a book edited by Katz, Cole, and Barton (1965). Rosenhan's (1973) report of the experiences of pseudopatients who were all classified as psychotic and committed to mental hospitals without the slightest reservation is a startling reminder of how fallible are even the most gross current distinctions between mental "illness" and "health." For 15 letters from professionals expressing critical reactions to Rosenhan's study and for Rosenhan's reply, see *Science*, 1973, 180, pp. 356–69.

16

Diagnosis and Assessment
of Psychopathology

Diagnosis literally refers to the process of "distinguishing" or "knowing apart" (from Greek *dia* = "apart," *gignoskein* = "to know"), especially the "knowing apart" of diseases. As discussed in Chapter 15, "diagnosis" and "classification" occupy two points on the same conceptual continuum. "Diagnosis" refers to the process of assembling information about a client in order to form a comprehensive picture of him and his problems. "Classification," by contrast, refers to an endproduct of this process whereby the client is linked to other people with whom experience has already been gained. Because medical models for etiology, classification, and treatment of psychopathology are much in dispute, many workers now prefer the more neutral term "assessment" to the disease-oriented term diagnosis.

Like classification, diagnosis (assessment) is not an end in itself but a means to an end. How the end is defined depends upon the goals of the diagnostician. If a satisfactory classification system were available—a reliable system based on characteristics validly related to etiology, management, prognosis, and/or treatment—diagnosis would primarily involve determining what class of the system a child matched, plus identifying any important idiosyncracies of the child that were not taken into account by the classification system. The diagnostic process would thus consist of whatever procedures were necessary to determine which class a child or disorder belonged to. The classification system would serve as the primary guide to action to be taken with respect to the child.

In the absence of a satisfactory and widely accepted system of classification, there has been much dispute over the appropriate role and nature of diagnosis in psychopathology. However, until we have a classification system that serves as an effective guide for action, it would appear that diagnostic procedures can best be evaluated according to their effectiveness as partial guides to action. A diagnostic procedure is most valuable if it helps to reduce uncertainty about what to do to help a child. In order to reduce uncertainty, the diagnostic procedure must reveal something important about the child that we do not already know. "Important" items of information are those that enable us to maximize the accuracy of our predictions about the child's future behavior.

The most useful "important" items of information are those that enable us to predict a child's future behavior under each of several possible treatment conditions, including no treatment. Accurate prediction of behavior under various treatments requires, of course, that the effects of each of the possible treatments have already been evaluated for other children who are in some way like the child being considered. Hence, diagnosis cannot be a really effective guide to action unless we have previously evaluated the effects of various actions with other children.

Notice that we have come full circle to the problem of classification again: Once we link characteristics of new cases to previous cases about whom we have gained knowledge, we are engaged in classification. The important point is that diagnosis, classification, treatment, and the evaluation of treatment are integral parts of the process of attempting to help people— the specific procedures employed at each step should be determined in part by procedures at other steps and by overarching conceptions of what is wrong and how it can be remedied. It is only because our present knowledge is so rudimentary that procedures for diagnosing, classifying, treating, and evaluating outcomes must be dealt with in a fragmentary manner.

The sections that follow deal with the major foci of current psychodiagnostic practices as they are applied to children—Infant Development, Intellectual Functioning, Personality, Behavioral Assessment, Family Characteristics, and Organic Dysfunction. These sections will be followed by an illustration of a diagnostic work-up typical of current practice in child psychopathology.

INFANT DEVELOPMENT

Some revisions of the early Binet intelligence scale included items for testing infants, but the first test specifically designed for assessing infant development was published by Gesell in 1925. Other infant tests have appeared since then, although the later revisions of Gesell's scales remain among the most widely used. The Gesell scales consist of a series of motor, adaptive, language, and personal-social items assessed by eliciting behavior from the child in a standardized manner (Gesell & Amatruda, 1947). They are supplemented by parent reports on behavior which is not readily elicited in the testing situation. Norms are provided for four-week intervals up to the age of one year, three-month intervals to the age of two years, and six-month intervals to the age of three years. Four Developmental Quotients

(DQs) are calculated by dividing the child's scores on each of the four types of items by the child's chronological age and multiplying by 100, analogous to the calculation of an IQ score. Table 16–1 presents examples of items from the Gesell scales.

TABLE 16–1

Some sample items from the Gesell Scales of Infant Development.

Area	Age		
	4 weeks	**24 weeks**	**52 weeks**
Motor	Moves hand to mouth Both hands fisted	Sits in chair Grasps cube	Walks with 1 hand held
Adaptive	Watches ring if placed in line of sight	Holds ring with 2 hands	Attempts block tower
	Drops rattle placed in hand	Grasps & fingers rattle	Tries to put pellet in bottle
Language	Impassive face Small, throaty noises	Growls, grunts Vocalizes to mirror	2 words Understands "give"
Personal-Social	Activity diminishes when regarding face	Discriminates stranger	Cooperates in dressing
	Stares indefinitely at surroundings	Spontaneous social vocalization	Gives toys to mother

NOTE.—From Gesell and Amatruda (1947).

Other infant scales include Cattell's (1960) Mental Test for Infants and Young Children, the Bayley Scales of Infant Development (1969), the Griffiths Scale (1954), and the Denver Developmental Screening Test (Frankenburg & Dodds, 1968). The Bayley Scales are the only ones based on large representative national samples.

It was at first hoped that infant test scores would predict later IQ test scores, but longitudinal studies have repeatedly demonstrated negligible and even *negative* correlations between infant test scores before the age of about 18 months and later IQ test scores (see Bayley, 1970). Since IQ tests largely measure manipulation of symbols (especially linguistic symbols), which infants appear totally incapable of, it is not surprising that infant test scores do not predict later IQs.

In view of their lack of correlation with later IQ tests, infant tests have come to be used primarily as screening devices. Exceptionally *low* scores may indicate organic damage, disease, or severe environmental deprivation which might be remediable; *uneven* performance, such as large disparities between motor, language, and social development, may indicate specific handicaps—e.g., deafness, emotional disturbance, or autism. Studies cited in Chapter 6 have demonstrated fairly strong relationships between retarded performance on infant tests and various signs of pre- and perinatal organic damage (e.g., Harper et al 1959; Stechler, 1964a), while studies cited in Chapter 12 have indicated a relation between uneven infant test performance and later psychopathology (Fish et al, 1965; Fish et al, 1966).

ASSESSMENT OF INTELLECTUAL FUNCTIONING

IQ Tests

The IQ tests most widely used in clinical settings are the Stanford-Binet and the Wechsler tests—the Wechsler Preschool and Primary Scale of Intelligence (WPPSI); the Wechsler Intelligence Scale for Children (WISC); and the Wechsler Adult Intelligence Scale (WAIS). The nature of these tests and the history of their development were reviewed in Chapter 7, as was evidence on the stability of IQ scores and on the degree to which they predict academic performance. The evidence is consistent in showing that the rank ordering of most children's IQ scores on the individual tests becomes fairly stable by about the age of six, although the precise scores continue to fluctuate a bit for most children and a great deal for some children. The evidence is also consistent in showing that both individual and group test scores predict academic grades fairly well and predict achievement test scores quite well.

Clinical-Diagnostic Use of IQ Tests

Beside yielding an estimate of a child's academic potential and mental age, individual IQ tests are used diagnostically to form hypotheses about specific problem areas. Such hypotheses are based upon observation of the ways in which a child deviates from the responses typically given by children his age.

Response Style. A child's approach to IQ test items and his style of responding to them may be as informative as the content of his answers. For example, if a child frequently gives incorrect answers without stopping to think, the examiner may ask the child to stop, think, and see if he can give another answer after each quick but incorrect answer. If the child frequently gives correct answers on the second try, it may be inferred that impulsivity rather than lack of ability interfered with his performance. This can be noted in the test report and one IQ score can be calculated on the basis of the child's initial answers, while a second IQ is calculated on the basis of his second answers. The two can be contrasted in the test report to demonstrate the possible difference between the child's typical current functioning and his potential functioning when his impulsivity is reduced.

In contrast to impulsivity, a response style characterized by unusually lengthy detailing of answers may suggest an obsessive-compulsive concern with knowledge and correctness.

Patterns of Performance. Another diagnostic use of the IQ test is to compare the child's performance on various types of items. The Wechsler tests lend themselves to this approach especially well because they are divided into subtests, each of which is administered to each child and each of which is normed separately. The WISC, for example, includes Vocabulary, Arithmetic, Information, Comprehension, and Similarities subtests, which yield the Verbal IQ score, and Picture Completion, Picture Arrangement, Object Assembly, Block Design, and Coding subtests, which yield the Performance IQ score (see Chapter 7 for details).

While all children show some disparity among their scores on the various subtests, exceptionally low scores on one or two subtests may suggest a weakness in a particular area, while exceptionally high scores on one or two subtests may suggest a special strength. Since chance or momentary factors may cause even very large disparities, such disparities should be the basis for *hypotheses* rather than for *conclusions* about the child. The hypotheses should be tested by gathering other data about the child from parent and school reports, medical examinations, observation of the child, and other tests to see whether the child is consistently weak in a particular area and whether the basis for such a weakness can be found.

One pattern of IQ test performance that frequently alerts examiners is a markedly poorer performance on items requiring visual-motor coordination than on verbal items. Examples of these items are the copying of a square and a diamond on the Stanford-Binet and the puzzlelike tasks on the Block Design and Object Assembly subtests of the WISC. If the examiner notices especially poor performance on these items and if performance does not improve when the child is asked to repeat them more slowly, a likely hypothesis is that the child's functioning in areas requiring visual-motor coordination is below his functioning in more purely intellectual areas.

The general hypothesis of a weakness in visual-motor functioning can be further tested by giving the child other tests specifically designed to assess visual-motor functioning and by observing how the child walks, grasps objects, etc., in order to detect any gross peculiarities in coordination. Specific hypotheses as to etiology might include poor vision, slow perceptual-motor maturation, damage or disease in the nervous system, or excessive anxiety about overt physical activity. The organic possibilities can be tested by ophthalmological, neurological, and medical examinations, and by gathering life history data to identify any events that might have been responsible for organic damage. In the absence of positive evidence for organic damage, the anxiety hypothesis can be tested further by observing the child in various situations, administering personality tests, and interviewing the child and his parents.

Another potentially significant pattern involves exceptionally low scores on the Information and Arithmetic subtests. Such a pattern may suggest environmental deprivation or poor school learning in a child whose ability is adequate. Exceptionally high scores on these subtests may suggest a background of environmental and academic enrichment in a child whose basic ability is not especially high.

Nature of Incorrect Responses. Besides subtest patterning, another aspect of test performance that alerts an examiner is the nature of a child's incorrect responses. As was noted long ago by Piaget, children's incorrect answers to adult questions do not merely reflect a lack of knowledge as to the content of correct answers. Instead, children's answers often reflect a qualitatively different way of thinking about a problem and a set of assumptions different from those of the adult. While most IQ test items are not explicitly designed to reveal the qualitative levels of a child's thought, certain incorrect answers are consistently given by children whose overall level of thinking is developmentally below that required for a correct answer. For example, on the Binet, the question, "What makes a sailboat move?" is often answered "The water," by children below the mental age of seven.

A child whose incorrect answers are consistently like the incorrect answers of other children is probably thinking in a way that is normal for children of a cognitive level below the level of the questions he is being asked. However, answers that are not only incorrect but extremely unusual may suggest the hypothesis that the child has a peculiar and possibly bizarre way of thinking. The response, "A unit in the sky," to the Binet vocabulary word "Mars," for example, was sufficiently peculiar to alert one psychologist to the possibility of a thinking disorder in a person who was later concluded to be schizophrenic.

Incorrect answers to easy items interspersed with correct answers to difficult items can also indicate that anxiety or some other factor is interfering with the child's intellectual performance.

Specialized Tests of Ability

A widely used nonverbal test is Raven's Progressive Matrices (1960), which can be administered to people in any language and even to deaf mutes. The matrices consist of a series of designs and patterns from which one component is missing. The subject is to select the missing component for each item from a multiple-choice array. The test's major clinical function is to provide a quick estimate of intellectual level, especially with people who may be linguistically handicapped on standard IQ tests. The test can also be administered in group form and has been widely used for cross-cultural research on intellectual functioning.

Other tests designed to minimize the influence of linguistic factors include the Leiter International Scale (Leiter, 1948), the Porteus Mazes (Porteus, 1965), and the Goodenough Draw-a-man Test (Goodenough, 1926). In the latter test, the child is merely asked to draw a person and the drawing is scored according to norms for children aged three to 14 (Harris, 1963). Performance on this task correlates moderately well with IQ, although it is typically used only as an "ice-breaker" at the beginning of testing, as a very rough index of ability, and as a basis for general inferences about personality.

At the other extreme from the tests having no verbal content are the Peabody Picture Vocabulary Test (Dunn, 1965), which requires the child to point to a picture corresponding to a word spoken by the examiner, and the Illinois Test of Psycholinguistic Abilities (ITPA; Kirk, McCarthy, & Kirk, 1968), which yields several highly differentiated indices of verbal functioning in children aged two to 10. The ITPA has been used as an educational diagnostic instrument and for evaluating the progress of children in special educational programs for the disadvantaged, especially programs focusing on the enhancement of linguistic skills. It was found in one study to have a higher correlation with achievement tests administered two years later ($r = .72$) than did the Stanford-Binet ($r = .60$; Hirshoren, 1969).

Achievement Tests

Despite the fact that most children seen in clinical settings have school problems, precise clinical evaluation of children's academic strengths and weaknesses is rare. Individual tests, such as the Wide-Range Achievement Test (Jastak & Jastak, 1965) and Gray Oral Reading Test (Gray, 1963) are occasionally administered, but diagnosis is often restricted to "clinically relevant" characteristics rather than including specific academic weaknesses that may be contributing to a child's overall maladjustment. Even the diagnosis of "learning disability" is often a global one implying a fundamental block in learning that must be overcome by therapeutic measures, after which the child is expected to progress normally in school. Yet, whatever the original reason for a child's poor school progress, the gap between what he has mastered and what his agemates have mastered is unlikely to be closed merely by a new surge of psychological health. Instead, a child who is behind in school is likely to need specific help from teachers, tutors, or parents in addition to therapeutic measures. In some cases, enhancement of school progress may serve as a primary therapeutic measure, both in terms of improving the child's self-esteem and in aiding him to employ developmentally more advanced methods for dealing with his problems and the world around him.

For the foregoing reasons, precise assessment of a child's academic weaknesses and precise techniques for remedying them deserve more attention than they have traditionally received in clinical settings. A child's subtest scores on group achievement tests (e.g., Stanford Achievement, Iowa Tests, California Achievement) administered annually in most schools offer a rough index to his specific academic strengths and weaknesses, although they neglect artistic and musical talents.

Behavior modifiers have recently employed programmed teaching materials in conjunction with achievement tests to provide a continuous process of diagnosis and remediation whereby children are rewarded for the acquisition of specific new responses at progressively more advanced levels of achievement (see Chapter 11, e.g., Haring & Hauck, 1969; Chapter 13, Cohen & Filipczak, 1971). The Vineland Social Maturity Scale, described in Chapter 7, is also used as an index of deficits and progress in self-help skills, especially with the retarded, although more detailed behavioral indices are now being devised for guiding behavior modification with the retarded (e.g., Baker, 1973).

ASSESSMENT OF PERSONALITY

Most approaches to the diagnosis and treatment of psychopathology are based on personality theories. In practice, "personality" is probably the single most general concept linking together views of psychopathology, diagnostic procedures, psychotherapeutic methods, and goals of treatment—once mental retardation and organic dysfunction have been ruled out, it is the personality of the client that is typically regarded as malfunctioning, that is the object of diagnosis, and that treatment is intended to influence. Unfortunately, the lack of consensus as to the best way of conceptualizing and measuring personality precludes a single generally acceptable definition of personality, beyond, perhaps, "the total functioning of the person."

One very gross distinction between conceptions of personality is the distinction between *psychodynamic theories* and *trait theories*. The wellspring of most psychodynamic concepts is, of course, psychoanalytic theory. Basic psychodynamic theory portrays behavior as a resultant of the interplay between motives and defenses that oppose and modify the expression of the motives. The favorite diagnostic tools of the psychodynamic approach are relatively unstructured situations in which the client's motives, conflicts, and defenses can be freely exposed. Unstructured interviews in which the possibilities for free association are enhanced, unstructured play sessions assumed to function for children like unstructured interviews for adults, and projective tests, such as the Rorschach and Thematic Apperception Test, are the most widely used techniques for psychodynamic diagnosis.

Trait theories (e.g., Cattell, 1957; Eysenck, 1957) portray personality in terms of lasting dispositions of a person to act in a certain way. Traits are usually assessed by psychometric methods, including standardized personality tests and structured interviews from which the client's responses can be quantified. Quantified response measures on projective tests, such as the Rorschach and TAT, and structured observations from free play are occasionally used as well. A person's standing on a trait is best judged from his scores over several measures, although the more typical clinical procedure is to judge a person's standing by his score on one or two tests that have previously been shown to correlate with other measures. Anxiety is perhaps the most frequently inferred and measured personality trait, but introversion-extroversion, aggression, hostility, passivity, depression, and traits corresponding to diagnostic categories such as hysteria and psychopathy are also of widespread interest.

In clinical practice, the results of psychodynamically oriented assessments are often integrated with trait measures in such a way as to give the diagnostician or therapist a feeling of understanding his client. Unfortunately, the feeling of having an accurate picture of another person's personality is difficult to validate. An unusual approach to validating an integrated personality picture was taken by Ulrich, Stachnik, and Stainton (1963) who administered a trait measure (Bell Adjustment Inventory) and a projective measure (House-Tree-Person Test) to college students. The students who took the tests were later given a psychologist's written interpretation of their personalities, as exemplified by the following:

You have a strong need for other people to like you and for them to admire you. You have a tendency to be critical of yourself. You have a great deal of unused capacity which you have not turned to your advantage. While you have some personality weaknesses, you are generally able to compensate for them. Your sexual adjustment has presented some problems for you. Disciplined and controlled on the outside, you tend to be worrisome and insecure inside. At times you have serious doubts as to whether you have made the right decision or done the right thing. You prefer a certain amount of change and variety and become dissatisfied when hemmed in by restrictions and limitations. You pride yourself as being an independent thinker and do not accept others' opinions without satisfactory proof. You have found it unwise to be too frank in revealing yourself to others. At times you are extroverted, affable, sociable, while at other times you are introverted, wary, and reserved. Some of your aspirations tend to be pretty unrealistic [p. 832].

The students were asked to rate the interpretations of their personalities on a five-point scale of accuracy, ranging from Excellent to Very Poor, and to write down additional comments regarding the interpretations. Fifty-three of the 57 student subjects rated the interpretations of their own personalities as either good or excellent, the top two steps on the scale, while three rated the interpretations as average, one rated them as poor, and none rated them as very poor. Some typical comments by subjects were as follows:

". . . I agree with almost all your statements and think they answer the problems I may have."

"On the nose! Very good. I wish you had said more, but what you did mention was all true without a doubt. I wish you could go further into this personality sometime."

"The results have brought out several points which have worried me because I was not sure if I had imagined these to be personality traits of mine. Tests like this could be valuable to an individual in helping him to solve some of his own problems."

"The interpretation is surprisingly accurate and specific in description. I shall take note of many of the things said."

"I feel that the interpretation does apply to me individually. For the first time things that I have been vaguely aware of have been put into concise and constructive statements which I would like to use as a plan for improving myself [Ulrich et al., 1963, p. 833]." [1]

The evidence that the personality interpretations corresponded to the students' actual feelings about themselves certainly appears to substantiate the validity of the tests—unless one is troubled by the fact that all the students were given *exactly the same interpretation,* the one quoted above. Another study produced similar results (Forer, 1949).

The tendency of people to accept generalized personality interpretations may stem from the fact that almost everybody has almost every identifiable personality characteristic in *some* degree and that certain statements are probably true of almost everybody. The compelling plausibility of generalized personality interpretations has come to be called the *Barnum Effect* in honor of P. T. Barnum, the famous showman who enthralled customers with his off-the-cuff personality interpretations.

The power of the Barnum Effect should serve as a warning that the intrinsic plausibility of personality interpretations is not an adequate test of their validity for discriminating among people with respect to characteristics related meaningfully to etiology, treatment, or prognosis. Satisfying as a personality description may be to the clinician who writes or reads it, it is useless unless it adds information with which to make decisions that will benefit the client.

Since many of the personality-diagnostic methods to be described in the following sections are used by workers differing in their approaches to personality, the methods will be evaluated in terms of the functions assigned them by the varying approaches. Besides the psychodynamic and trait approaches, the behavioral approach employs some of the personality measures to be described, although behaviorally oriented workers tend to think in terms of specific facts about a person rather than in terms of a global conception of personality.

Interview Procedures

Of all methods of assessment, the interview is the most universally used and the one considered most indispensible by clinicians. Indeed, it is unlikely that the interview will ever be entirely superseded as a source of diagnostic data. A fundamental question is, however, what data can best be obtained by interviews? Basic facts about the client's appearance, manner of speaking, his views of his problems (insofar as he is willing to share them), certain demographic data (age, education, occupation, family constellation) if the client is competent to relate them, and arrangements for further procedures are likely to be obtained primarily through face-to-face interviews.

Behaviorally oriented interviewers generally include structured ques-

[1] R. E. Ulrich, T. J. Stachnik, and N. R. Stainton, "Student Acceptance of Generalized Personality Interpretations," *Psychological Reports,* 1963, *13* (831–34). Reprinted by permission of authors and publisher.

tions about the specific nature of the client's problems, their duration and cause, and the client's readiness to accept behavioral methods. Psychodynamically oriented interviewers usually expect to obtain a sketch of the client's childhood and an impression of underlying dynamics based upon the client's free associations and his emphasis on or avoidance of certain topics. In effect, the psychodynamically oriented diagnostic interview functions like the uncovering process carried on in psychoanalysis, although interpretations are unlikely to be given except perhaps as "trial balloons" to see how the client reacts. A diagnostician with more of a trait orientation may use both the behavioral and psychodynamic approaches to rate the client on traits such as anxiety and to make some initial judgments as to what personality measures should be given later.

Despite the central importance of interviewing in all diagnostic approaches, there is relatively little research on the reliability or validity of the interview as a diagnostic procedure. Studies cited in Chapter 15 indicated that diagnostic classifications made from traditional psychiatric interviews were not very reliable (e.g., Beck et al, 1962). Furthermore, suggestion caused a significant bias toward severe pathology in diagnoses made by traditional clinicians from interview observations (Rosenhan, 1973; Temerlin, 1968), although suggestion did not significantly affect diagnoses by behaviorally oriented clinicians (Langer & Abelson, 1974).

A detailed analysis of clinicians' judgments has been carried out by Stoller & Geerstma (1963) using a filmed psychiatric interview with a typical therapy patient. The original purpose of the film was to constitute an exam for testing medical students' skills in evaluating a patient for psychotherapy.

A pool was formed of 565 clinically descriptive statements to be rated on a scale of 0 to 5 as to their applicability to the filmed patient. Eight "nonsense" items were also included to catch the more naive students, e.g., "At this point the patient's depreciation of the introjected father's penis is revealed;" "inability to distinguish between anal, oral, and phallic rage;" "excessive parental transfiguration;" "the loss of a boy friend is painful for the patient because it reawakens her secondary envy of mother's breast." Statements eliciting high agreement among psychiatrists were to serve as questions on the exam.

Twenty-seven highly experienced psychiatrists served as judges. Correlations among the psychiatrists' ratings over the 565 items averaged .37. On only one of the 565 items did as many as 90 per cent of the psychiatrists use the same rating category, while on only 17 items did as many as 90 per cent use only two categories. Little agreement was obtained on the remaining 97 per cent of the items. Even the nonsense items, which were expected to be readily dismissed by the psychiatrists, elicited a great deal of disagreement. On only one of the eight nonsense items were 90 per cent of the psychiatrists' judgments within even four categories of each other.

To eliminate the effects of individual differences in using the 0–5 scale, judgments were also divided into a simple no–yes dichotomy (categories 0, 1, 2, versus categories 3, 4, 5). Scored in this way, 17 per cent of the items were agreed to be present or absent by at least 80 per cent of the psychiatrists.

Analysis of specific items showed that the greatest agreement occurred for items deemed inapplicable to the patient: The one item eliciting agreement from 90 per cent of the psychiatrists was that the client was *not* expressing elation at a point in the interview where she was talking of sadness and losing an important person. There was little agreement on which positive statements regarding feelings, etiology, psychodynamics, diagnosis, prognosis, or need for treatment *were* applicable to the patient. Fortunately for the medical students, the lack of agreement among the experts led the authors to conclude that their approach would not yield a satisfactory exam.

Interviews with Children

If the diagnostic value of interviews with adult clients is questionable, the diagnostic value of interviews with children may be even more questionable because children rarely have either the motivation or the ability to contribute actively to the diagnostic process. To have any potential for validity, child interview data must be related to developmental norms for child behavior. Unless the interviewer is thoroughly familiar with the range of behavior typically displayed by children of various age, intelligence, and socioeconomic levels in interview settings, he may mistake normal withdrawal, anxiety, fear, or boisterousness for pathological symptoms. The range of data considered by the interviewer of children must also extend beyond that considered for adults. The way a child separates from and returns to his parents and what he does with objects in the interview setting may be more informative than what the child says.

One of the few systematic appraisals of the reliability and validity of diagnostic interviews with children has been carried out by Rutter and Graham (1968). They conducted a standardized interview in a room containing several toys for the child's use. The first part of each interview was unstructured in order to get the child relaxed and talking freely. In later parts of the interview, the child was systematically asked about his fears, worries, unhappiness, irritability, temper, and peer relationships. The exact wording was left to individual interviewers, but observations were to be recorded in predetermined categories. Attention span, persistence, and distractibility were assessed by asking the child to do some age-appropriate tasks, such as drawing a man, naming the days of the week forwards and backwards, and doing simple arithmetic.

In one of the studies reported by Rutter and Graham, nonclinic children were interviewed by different interviewers on two occasions averaging 12 days apart. The two interviewers rated each child as showing *no* psychiatric abnormality, *some* abnormality, or *definite* abnormality. The correlation between their ratings on this three-point scale was .84, but similar three-point ratings showed much lower agreement for specific items, especially items concerning emotions.

In a second study, either Rutter or Graham interviewed child psychiatric patients while the other observed. In this case, interrater agreement on specific items increased, but the correlation between the two psychiatrists' ratings on overall psychiatric state declined to .74. In a third study, test-retest reliability for disturbed children was assessed by each author interviewing child psychiatric patients at one- to four-week intervals. With variability in the child as well as in the interviewers being factors, agreement on specific items was lower than in the second study, as was agreement on overall psychiatric state, where the ratings correlated .61. In general, overall reliability thus appeared to be highest when normal children were interviewed, as in the first study, and lowest when disturbed children were interviewed, especially when they were interviewed by different psychiatrists at different times.

In a fourth study, the validity of the interview procedure was assessed by applying it to children judged either normal or disturbed on the basis of teacher and parent reports. Blind to the teacher and parent reports, the interviewers diagnosed as abnormal only 25 per cent of the boys and 43 per cent of the girls in the "abnormal" group, although this was significantly more than the proportion they diagnosed abnormal in the normal group (3 per cent of the boys and 0 per cent of the girls). A number of the specific interview items also significantly differentiated between the "abnormal" and "normal" criterion groups.

A correlation of .45 between parent questionnaire reports of pathology and psychiatric interview ratings for degree of disturbance in clinic children, and a correlation of .31 for nonclinic children, have also indicated a low degree of validity for judgments based on psychiatric interviews in a study by Sherwin, Schoelly, Klein, Schwartz, & Kahn (1965).

Taken together, the findings of Rutter and Graham and of Sherwin et al indicate that moderately reliable and valid judgments of gross degree of pathology *can* be obtained through standardized interview procedures with children. However, little attempt has been made to study the reliability and validity of the much more typical practice of drawing elaborate clinical inferences from unstandardized interviews with children.

Projective Techniques

The concept of *projection* was originally used by Freud in reference to the defensive process whereby a person ascribes to other people unconscious motives of his own that are too threatening for him to recognize in himself. In 1939, L. K. Frank formulated the position that projective techniques for personality assessment are analogous to techniques in the physical sciences and medicine (e.g., X-ray photography) that reveal hidden structures without dissecting or oversimplifying them, as measures of quantitative dimensions do. With the justification that they function like X-rays of the personality, projective techniques rapidly became the most popular and glamorous ways of assessing personality.

As some specialists in projective techniques have pointed out, the aspects of the individual's private world revealed by his response to minimally structured materials may not be unconscious, unacceptable, negative, nor entirely concerned with his own characteristics (Murray, 1959). Rather, such techniques may merely provide a way of evoking "images, fantasies of inter-actions, and dramatic improvisation . . . [which] constitute one of several forms of behavior"—only certain parts of the responses elicited by a projective technique can "be called projective, *grain* for the analyst of personality. The rest is *chaff.* . . . Hence, the great question is this: By what signs can one differentiate grain from chaff? [Murray, 1951, p. xiii–xiv]"

The problem of separating the grain from the chaff is still paramount in the use of projective techniques. This is so not only because diagnostic methods of all types are justified only if they aid in making valid decisions about how to help people, but also because projective techniques are based on the assumption of behavioral determinism. Users of projective techniques assume that a subject's responses are neither random nor expressions of free will, but are systematically determined by underlying characteristics from which other behavior can be predicted. Projective techniques must thus be evaluated according to the reliability and validity of the predictions they yield, just as is true of other psychodiagnostic methods.

The Rorschach Technique.   Interest in people's responses to inkblots has a long history. During the 1890s, Binet employed the number and type of responses to inkblots as a measure of imagination. Dearborn, in the United States, employed them to study the contents of consciousness, while others used them to study perceptual development (cf. Zubin, Eron, & Schumer, 1965).

In 1911, Hermann Rorschach, in Switzerland, began experimenting with colored geometric cut-outs to test fantasy, but he found that inkblots produced more encouraging results. By the time of his death in 1922, he was concentrating primarily on the perceptual aspects of inkblot responses rather than on their content. The Rorschach Test, consisting of 10 standard ink-blots printed on cards, became popular in the United States during the 1920s and soon spawned an enormous literature. By the 1940s, great confidence was placed in the value of the Rorschach for revealing the way a person sees and handles the world, his anxieties, needs, hurts, likes and dislikes, motivations, intellectual efficiency, emotional maturity, acceptance of reality, the configuration of his personality, and organic or nonorganic basis for his problems (e.g., Lindner & Seliger, 1945).

In the 1950s, efforts were made to relate Rorschach responses to research on perceptual and personality functioning, but the lack of standardization in administration, scoring, and interpretation has made reconciliation of the myriad conflicting findings difficult. The typical clinical procedure is to hand each of the 10 cards to the client, one at a time in a standardized order, and to write down each response, the response time, and any turning of the card by the client. After all the cards have been responded to, they are given to the client so that he may indicate where he saw each percept. With young children, the inquiry as to response locations is usually done right after the child has given his response. The examiner marks the location of each percept on reproductions of the blots printed on a record sheet. The instructions to the client and the length and depth of the inquiry about the client's responses vary greatly.

Rorschach responses can be scored according to various systems based on the number and proportions of percepts involving human or animal movement, dominance of color versus form, reliance on the whole blot versus small details, well-differentiated versus global images, etc. (e.g., Klopfer, Ainsworth, Klopfer, & Holt, 1954). Children's responses are often judged for levels of development by comparing them with responses given by children of various ages, although the available normative samples are small and unrepresentative (e.g., Ames, Learned, Metraux, & Walker, 1952).

There are many hypotheses about the meaning of the various scores, relations among them, and the content of responses. Clinicians vary in the way they use scoring methods, popular rules of thumb, their own personal experience, and other knowledge about the client to arrive at interpretations of his personality. Full scoring and the writing of an interpretation of a Rorschach protocol often take up to 10 hours.

Reviews of the enormous Rorschach literature have revealed little evidence for the validity of personality descriptions or predictions based on responses to the Rorschach (Suinn & Oskamp, 1969; Zubin et al, 1965). Among the few Rorschach measures found by Suinn and Oskamp to have received adequate support are certain scores that discriminate early or mild schizophrenics from nonschizophrenics and others that discriminate brain-damaged from non-brain-damaged patients, although many scores purported to identify schizophrenia and organicity have not been validated.

Juvenile delinquents have been found to obtain higher scores than non-delinquents on Rorschach scores for anxiety and hostility, and the scores for these traits have been found to correlate with other measures of anxiety and hostility in nondelinquent groups. Mixed positive and negative results have been obtained in attempting to predict adults' continuation and improvement in psychotherapy, but the results with children have been uniformly negative.

In the reviews by Suinn and Oskamp and by Zubin et al, the authors comment on the paradox that the Rorschach's enormous popularity, the great amount of time expended on it, and the thousands of publications it has stimulated are all based on so little evidence for its validity. A further paradox is that its proponents stress its value for idiographically portraying personality, but the most prominent students of the Rorschach (e.g., Beck, 1952; Klopfer, et al, 1954; Piotrowski, 1956) are those who have invented quantitative, quasi-psychometric scoring systems for it. Similarly, virtually the only well-validated predictions and discriminations made from the Rorschach have been made on the basis of these quasi-psychometric scoring systems. Unfortunately, even the findings with these systems are tenuous because the lack of standardization in administration procedures and the well-documented effects of examiner behavior on Rorschach responses (cf. Zubin et al, 1965) make for low reliability. Low reliability, in turn, makes it unlikely that valid predictions from data obtained by one examiner will be replicated by other examiners.

Other tests have been designed to improve on research with the inkblot technique. One is the Holtzman Inkblot Test, which consists of two sets of 45 blots each (Holtzman, Thorpe, Swartz, & Herron, 1961). The client gives only one response to each blot, thus simplifying administration and scoring. Another test is the Behn-Rorschach, which is designed as an alternate form for the Rorschach (Behn, 1956). However, the availability of these tests appears to have had little impact on the Rorschach literature.

One probable reason for the continued popularity of the Rorschach is that the general approach and the massive clinical lore about it fit in so nicely with other aspects of traditional clinical practice—the clinician's feeling of understanding a client is enhanced by Rorschach data and this feeling of understanding is a primary criterion for determining what methods will be employed. While the clinician's feeling of understanding a client's underlying personality may be important for his own self-satisfaction, the lack of evidence that Rorschach responses provide an X-ray of the personality suggests that they should be used for other purposes, if at all.

One alternative approach is simply to use Rorschach responses as a sample of the client's verbal behavior that may correlate with other behavior and that may suggest hypotheses about his thinking or other behavior. However, these hypotheses are only useful if they are actually tested with other data—if the client gives unusual or bizzare responses to the Rorschach that might suggest peculiar thought processes, can evidence for these thought processes be elicited in other situations and is his other behavior consistent with the hypothesis of a thought disorder?

When viewed merely as one source of hypotheses based on verbal responses from a client, the use of the Rorschach must be compared with other possible methods for generating hypotheses that will aid in the treatment of the client. If other techniques suggest hypotheses that are more relevant to the treatment of a client and/or more readily put in testable form, then they should displace the Rorschach. On the other hand, if there are situations in which the Rorschach adds information not readily obtainable in easier ways, and if this information increases the validity of decisions made about clients, then the use of the Rorschach is justified.

The Thematic Apperception Test. The main difference between the Thematic Apperception Test (TAT) and the inkblot tests is that the TAT provides pictures for which the subject is to make up stories, rather than inkblots that the subject is to interpret as images. Thus, the subject is to *apperceive* (interpret) the TAT stimuli in terms of dramatic themes.

Although there were a few other early attempts to use pictures as projective stimuli, Henry Murray's Thematic Apperception Test was the first complete test of this type (Morgan & Murray, 1935). The last version of the test (Murray, 1943) consists of 30 black-white reproductions of paintings and drawings, plus one blank card. Only about 10 of the cards are usually given to a client. Some cards are especially intended for boys, girls, men, or women, but the examiner often decides which cards to administer on the basis of expectations he has about the client. The client is asked to make up a story about each card, telling who the people are, what they are doing, thinking, and feeling, what led up to the current situation, and what the outcome will be.

Murray assumed that the stories reveal needs or motives, and he postulated a number of basic needs, such as achievement, affiliation, succorance, and power, the strength of which could be inferred from TAT stories. Later research by others has produced fairly reliable systems for scoring the strength of some of these motives in TAT responses (cf. Atkinson, 1958). McClelland, in particular, has stimulated a great deal of research on need for achievement (n Achievement), as scored from TAT protocols (e.g., McClelland, 1955, 1961). This research demonstrated numerous low but statistically significant relations between TAT scores for n Achievement and behavior in other situations.

As the research became more sophisticated, however, concern arose about motives to *avoid* certain situations as well as to achieve. For example, achievement *behavior* came to be viewed as a joint function of n Achievement and need to avoid failure. The latter might keep a person from actually attempting to achieve. McClelland (1966) has more recently formulated the view that TAT imagery is an index of a person's concern with a particular topic rather than an index of needs to strive in a particular direction. Thus, high achievement imagery might indicate high concern about achievement, but does not necessarily indicate whether a person will engage in achievement activity or avoid it.

Findings that adolescent *activities* rather than adolescent TAT imagery predicted adult TAT imagery in a longitudinal study have indicated that a particular kind of activity may increase imagery related to that activity rather than the other way around. Consequently, McClelland suggested that TAT imagery may represent an index of a person's previous activity instead of a predictor of his future activity. This hypothesis is by no means incompatible with the theory of projective techniques, which implies merely that a person's mental concerns are revealed in his responses to ambiguous stimuli.

Although the goal of clinical projective testing has been to make predictions about people on the basis of their current fantasies, there is no reason to believe that such fantasies, even if accurately tapped by projective tests, portend future behavior. Thus, the low predictive validity found for projective measures may result from the fact that people's fantasies are at least partly products of their past behavior rather than their future behavior being a product of their current fantasies. If this is the case, projective measures are unlikely to be direct predictors of anything, although they may help in classifying a person on the basis of his past. If such classification is related to different etiologies and/or to differential prognoses under various treatments, then increases in the validity of classification provided by projective measures would justify their use.

Clinical Use of the TAT. Much of the research on the TAT, especially the research based upon formal scoring of motives, has been more sophisticated than the research on the Rorschach. In clinical practice, however, the TAT is usually used to infer themes and conflicts in a person's fantasies without being formally scored for the strength of specific needs. The clinical-diagnostic use of the TAT has received considerably less validation than its use as a research instrument for measuring *n* Achievement and other formally scored needs. Among the clinical findings that have been validated, however, is the finding that deviant themes, deviant emotional tones, poor quality of story organization, and incongruous story elements appear in the responses of schizophrenic and neurotic adults more than in the responses of normal adults (Suinn & Oskamp, 1969). Furthermore, the number of aggressive stories, aggressive stories to cards rarely eliciting them, and aggressive impulses have all been found to be greater in the TAT responses of overtly aggressive and delinquent adolescents than of nonaggressive adolescents in several studies (Suinn & Oskamp, 1969).

In one of the very few comparisons between judgments based on clinicians' subjective interpretations of the TAT and judgments based on objective scoring of TAT signs, Lindzey (1965) found that a clinician correctly discriminated between homosexual and nonhomosexual college students in 95 per cent of his judgments, while three methods of *post hoc* scoring of objective signs did somewhat worse. In samples of homosexual and nonhomosexual prisoners, one clinician reached 80 per cent accuracy, while a second reached 60 per cent accuracy. The formulas derived from the college student samples accurately identified only 57 per cent of the homosexuals, not significantly above the chance level of 50 per cent. The findings thus indicated some advantages of expert clinical interpretation in the identification of homosexuality. However, the fact that the clinician who reached only 60 per cent accuracy in the second sample was the one who reached 95 per cent accuracy in the first sample suggests that not only statistical methods of prediction, but clinicians, as well, may decrease in accuracy when they deal with new samples of individuals.

In another study which made a rough comparison between clinical and statistical approaches, Cox and Sargent (1950) applied a large number of fairly objective scoring categories to the TAT responses of emotionally disturbed and normal boys. Surprisingly, the normals had significantly *higher* scores on most categories, including feelings of frustration, anxiety, negativism, and depression, need for security, fears of death, disaster, and domination, positive and evasive actions, and story outcomes involving failure. The disturbed boys, by contrast, significantly more often showed an *absence* of feelings, needs, fears, actions, or outcomes involving either success or failure. The finding that normal boys were more expressive of feelings, fears, needs, etc., may explain the fact that clinicians given the protocols of 15 normals to judge classified 11 out of the 15 as disturbed. This again points up the tendency of clinicians who lack an objective baseline of judgment to focus upon negative or pathological-appearing information, which, indeed, was relatively abundant in the responses of the normal boys.

Variants of the TAT for Children. One of the best known TAT-type tests designed for children is the Children's Apperceptive Test (Bellak, 1954). The CAT consists of 10 pictures of animals in situations suggestive of psychosexual conflicts assumed to be important for children between the ages of about three and 10. For example, one picture portrays an adult dog sitting with one paw raised over the rear end of a puppy stretched over the adult dog's knee, with a toilet nearby. Animals were employed as the key figures in the belief that they would be easier for children to identify with than would the mostly adult figures of the TAT.

Some normative data on CAT responses have been collected, although there has been little attempt at validating interpretations made from the CAT. Several studies have indicated that children tell longer stories, express more feelings, and give other evidence of greater identification in their responses to human pictures than to CAT pictures, thus casting doubt on the greater clinical value of the CAT approach (Zubin et al, 1965).

The Michigan Picture Test (MPT) was constructed as another alternative to the TAT for children (Andrew, Hartwell, Hutt, & Walton, 1953). The authors pretested nearly a thousand pictures on children aged eight to 14 in order to obtain a final collection of 15 pictures, plus a blank card. The pictures are photographs that are much more realistic than those used in other projective tests. They portray scenes such as a schoolroom, a family of four engaged in various activities at a table, and a streak of lightning on a black background. On the basis of normative samples, the authors have identified MPT response variables that correlate with teacher ratings and other criteria of maladjustment. In general, the MPT norms provide a much more adequate baseline against which to compare children's responses than do most other projective tests.

Another variation of the TAT used with children is the Make-A-Picture Story (MAPS) Test (Shneidman, 1960). The child selects figures from an array of 67 cut-outs to make a scene against each of 22 background pictures and tells a story for each scene. Unfortunately, the intended strength of the test in allowing great freedom as to the stimuli to be responded to has proved to be a source of weakness for the accumulation of normative data and the assessment of reliability and validity. Some clinical signs have been found to differentiate significantly certain groups in some studies, but, because every subject is responding to different stimuli, generalizations and cross-validations have been nearly impossible (Zubin et al, 1965).

Rosenzweig Picture-Frustration Study. The Rosenzweig Picture-Frustration Study (P-F Study) consists of 24 cartoonlike pictures, each portraying two people in a frustrating situation (Rosenzweig, 1960). One figure is shown as saying something that is either frustrating to the second figure or describes the frustration of the second figure. The client is instructed to write in or tell what words should fill the empty "balloon" above the second figure.

Direction of aggression is scored as *extrapunitive* (directing aggression outward), *intropunitive* (directing aggression against the self), or *impunitive* (no aggression is expressed). Type of aggression is scored as *obstacle-dominance* (responses focusing on the barrier that causes frustration), *ego-defense* (responses referring to ego-threats in the situation), and *need-persistence* (responses emphasizing the solution of the frustrating problem). Samples from many countries show a steady decrease with age in extrapunitiveness and an increase in both intro- and impunitiveness, indicating that this represents a general developmental dimension.

In many respects, the P-F Study is psychometrically better than most other projective tests. Administration procedure is standardized, rules for scoring are explicit, interrater agreement in scoring has been over 80 per cent in several studies, the results can be compared with normative samples by age, and the hypotheses derived from the results are quite specific. Test-retest reliability—practically nonexistent for other projective measures—has generally ranged between about .30 and .60. Since projective techniques may be assumed to be influenced by short-term changes in the client, it is not certain whether higher test-retest reliability would be considered an unmitigated blessing. However, if a projective technique primarily reflects the momentary state of a client, what useful information can it provide about the more stable characteristics of the client that may need to be known in order to help him?

Although research on the validity of the P-F Study has been extensive, it does not resolve this dilemma. A number of studies have found no difference in P-F scores of normals and assaultive or delinquent subjects (cf. Zubin et al, 1965) and at least one study has found that delinquent boys showed significantly *lower* aggression scores than normals on the P-F (Lindzey & Goldwyn, 1954). Rosenzweig (1963) has attempted to account for these negative findings by maintaining that level of personality and degree of overtness in the subjects' responses were not taken into consideration, but this hardly resolves the problem of *how* one can determine the relation between a momentary measure of what is presumed to be fantasy and important behavior outside the testing situation.

Evidence for the relation of P-F scores to other types of variables has been summarized by Rosenzweig (1960). He reports significant relations between P-F scores and various patterns of behavior in children; higher extrapunitive scores in child guidance clinic children than in normal children; and greater accuracy in teachers' identification of their pupils' responses to the P-F than to parallel questionnaire items.

It would appear that one of the most likely avenues for future research with this instrument would be to determine the basis for the consistent decrease with age in extrapunitiveness and increases in intro- and impunitiveness found in cultures as diverse as American, French, Italian, German, Japanese, Indian, Congolese, Finnish, Sicilian, and Dutch. A possible explanation for the developmental trend is that it results from the cognitive changes revealed by Piaget's measures of moral development.

Drawing Techniques. The simplest and most widely used projective technique involving the child's drawing is the Draw-A-Person test. According to a procedure outlined by Machover (1949), the child is first asked to draw a person and then a second person of the sex opposite to the first. Machover (1960) also suggests 33 questions to be asked about each figure, such as, "What is he/she doing?" "How old is he/she?" "Is he/she married?" "Is he/she somebody you know?" The questions provide an opportunity to explore the child's thinking beyond what is assumed to be revealed in the drawings.

Interpretations of the figures are based on the assumption that they represent projections of the child's image of his own body and various concerns and ideals he has for himself. Machover (1960) has presented composite descriptions of "typical" drawings for each sex from age four through 12, but there is no systematic way to assess deviations from the composite descriptions.

Research on human figure drawings has shown that clinical judges could not discriminate between the drawings of physically handicapped and normal children, thus suggesting that the drawings are not good guides to children's body images (Silverstein & Robinson, 1956). Moreover, drawing skill appears to be a significant determinant of the characteristics included in the human figure (Woods & Cook, 1954). Certain characteristics of adults' figure drawings have been shown to discriminate between schizophrenics and normals, although neurotics could not be discriminated from schizophrenics, and interpretations of personality from human figure drawings have not correlated with other personality tests (cf. Suinn & Oskamp, 1969).

In a slightly more elaborate test, the child is first asked to draw a house, then a tree, then a person, and, lastly, a person of the sex opposite to the first person (Buck, 1966). The drawings are followed by questions such as "What is the person doing?" "How old is the tree?" "Is the tree alive?" The drawing of the house is interpreted as revealing the child's associations concerning his family, e.g., smoke pouring from the chimney represents a hot and turbulent home situation. The tree is believed to portray the child's deeper unconscious feelings about himself, while the person reveals the child's more conscious view of himself and his relations to his environment (Hammer, 1960). However, H-T-P drawings and responses to questions about the drawings have not been found to differentiate physically handicapped from normal children (Wawrzaszek, Johnson, & Sciera, 1958).

Sentence Completion Tests.   In the early 1900s, Jung made up a list of words to which clients were asked to respond with their first associations. From the responses and variations in reaction times to each stimulus word, Jung attempted to infer the client's unconscious complexes in psychoanalytic fashion.   While word association tests of this sort are still sometimes used in clinical settings, they have generally been replaced by tests in which the client is asked to provide endings for incomplete sentences.   The advantage of the incomplete sentence method is that the stimuli can be more precisely focused on specific problem areas and the responses are likely to be more revealing with less inference than are simple word associations.   Some typical incomplete sentence items are: "I am . . ." "I wish my father . . ." "People always . . . " "One should never . . ."

Even with stimuli more focused than those in the classical single-word association tests, sentence completion tests present the typical problems of projective techniques for assessing the reliability and validity of their results and for comparing the results with normative data.   On one sentence completion test, however, Rotter's Incomplete Sentence Blank (ISB), each item is scored on a seven-point scale for degree of conflict (Rotter & Rafferty, 1958).   Scores on this test have been fairly successful in discriminating between maladjusted and normal children and adults (Suinn & Oskamp, 1969). Since the test is primarily intended to be administered in group form, it may be useful for picking out individuals in schools or other settings who are likely to need special assistance.

Objectively Scored Tests

A contrast is often made between *projective* and *objective* tests.   The latter generally include yes-no, multiple-choice, and other structured questionnaires in which the possible responses are limited to those provided in advance by the test.   Since it can rarely be known whether the subject's responses accurately reflect his true behavior or feelings with respect to the questionnaire items, the "objectivity" of these tests does not lie in their assessment of the subject's personality.   Their objectivity is in the *scoring* of his responses to the standardized content of each question.   Overall scores for such instruments are thus based on the total number of each type of answer, scored according to a predetermined scheme that guarantees that all scorers will obtain the same result for a given subject, barring clerical errors.   The ultimate question to be asked of the scores on objective tests is, therefore, the same as the question to be asked of projective test responses, i.e., whether the subject's responses correlate with anything meaningful that could not be readily learned about him in other ways.

Certain tests using projective-type stimuli are "objective" because they offer objectively scored response choices.   The Blacky Test (Blum, 1960), for example, consists of a series of cartoon pictures of dogs drawn to suggest various psychosexual conflicts. The subject is asked to select from a multiple-choice array of answers describing each scene. These answers are scored objectively for various personality traits. TAT pictures have also been administered in multiple-choice formats. Even though the rationale of the stimulus materials in both these techniques is "projective," the scoring system makes them as "objective" as virtually any objective test of personality.

In practice, most objectively scored tests also differ from projective tests in that their more limited numbers of possible response dimensions put greater constraints on the degree of individuality that can be manifested in the scores. However, some projective tests, such as the Rotter Incomplete Sentence Blank, are deliberately designed to yield a single dimensional score intended to discriminate between adjusted and maladjusted subjects. Likewise, the Rorschach is most commonly used to discriminate between psychotic and nonpsychotic people. On the other hand, the most widely used objectively scored test, the Minnesota Multiphasic Personality Inventory, yields a large number of dimensional scores whose *configuration* is typically *interpreted* to obtain a diagnostic picture of the subject. Thus, objectively scored tests do not necessarily differ from projective tests in the degree to which they portray individual patterns of responses subject to idiographic interpretation.

Children's Anxiety Scales. Of the few questionnaire-type tests widely used with children, most have been developed as offshoots of tests originally designed for adults. Among these are several tests of anxiety modeled after adult scales such as the Manifest Anxiety Scale (Taylor, 1953). One is the Children's Manifest Anxiety Scale (CMAS; Castaneda, McCandless, & Palermo, 1956), while a second is the General Anxiety Scale for Children (GASC; Sarason, Davidson, Lighthall, Waite, & Ruebush, 1960). The CMAS contains items like "I blush easily" and "I worry most of the time." The GASC contains items like, "Are you afraid of spiders?" and "Do you worry that you are going to get sick?" Another version of the latter is the Test Anxiety Scale for Children, which is designed to identify children whose anxiety about being tested may interfere with their intellectual performance in school (Sarason et al, 1960).

Significant correlations have been found between the CMAS and GASC filled out by children and by their parents as pertaining to the children (Hafner, Quast, Speer, & Grams, 1964). Psychiatrists' ratings of the children's anxiety did not, however, correlate significantly with the childrens' or parents' ratings, although the number of symptoms checked by psychiatrists on symptom checklists for the children did correlate significantly with the children's anxiety scores.

The results thus suggest that both scales are getting at similar characteristics, but that these characteristics are not the same as what psychiatrists identify as anxiety in their evaluations of children. Finding that CMAS scores also failed to correlate with psychologists' or teachers' ratings of children's anxiety, Wirt & Broen (1956) suggested that the CMAS measures "willingness to say deviant things about the self," rather than the clinical concept of anxiety. The finding in the Hafner et al (1964) study that anxiety test scores correlated with the number of symptoms checked by psychiatrists is consistent with this hypothesis.

Minnesota Multiphasic Personality Inventory (MMPI). The MMPI is the most widely used objectively scored personality test (Hathaway & McKinley, 1951). Devised primarily for adults, it has been used in studies of parents of disturbed children and has had some use with adolescents as young as the age of 12. A tape-recorded version of the MMPI has been constructed for use with poor readers (Baughman & Dahlstrom, 1968). Because of the large number of items (566), the fact that they are designed to be read by the subject, and the morbid and sexual content of some of them, it is unlikely that the MMPI will ever be widely used with young children. However, the method by which it was constructed, the highly differentiated personality profiles which it yields, and the large number of statistically significant relations found between it and other variables make it worth considering here.

The test was constructed in a manner similar to the original Binet Intelligence Scale and the Strong Vocational Interest Inventory (Strong, 1943), a test used in vocational counseling to determine whether a person's interest pattern is like that of people who are successful and satisfied in each of a variety of occupations. Construction of all three of these tests began with a large pool of items thought to be related in some way to the variable to be measured—academic potential for the Binet, vocational interests for the Strong, and personality traits for the MMPI. Each potential item was then administered to appropriate subjects and correlations were calculated between their responses and certain criterion variables—age, scholastic performance, and teachers' ratings for the Binet; occupational group for the Strong; and psychiatric diagnosis for the MMPI.

From the original MMPI pool of thousands of items, 566 were found to discriminate between normals and various diagnostic groups well enough to be kept in the final test. The items are single-sentence statements to be answered as "true," "false," or "cannot say." Responses to each item are scored on one or more scales to yield a personality profile based mainly on the Kraepelinian diagnostic categories that provided the external criteria against which the items were originally validated. The clinical scales based on these diagnostic categories include Hypochondriasis, Depression, Hysteria, Psychopathic Deviate, Paranoia, Psychasthenia (obsessive-compulsive syndrome), Schizophrenia, and Mania.

The MMPI also contains a Masculinity-Femininity scale and several scales designed to indicate whether the subject's scores are likely to be valid. These include the number of items answered "Cannot say," a lie scale composed of extremely strait-laced moralistic items, a scale reflecting the degree to which a person tends either to deny or exhibit personal problems, and a scale composed of peculiarities and inconsistencies rarely endorsed even by psychiatric patients. The latter scale is intended to identify tests that are invalid because of randomness or inconsistency in responding, due possibly to poor reading skills, inattention, or crude attempts to invalidate the results. If a person's score on any of the validity scales is higher than a certain level, the scores on the clinical scales are considered invalid.

Because there are many items on each scale, no single response has much influence in determining a person's scores. Hence, a person may respond "true" to the item "I am easily awakened by noise," and "false" to the item "Once in a while I laugh at a dirty joke." Both of these responses count toward the score for Depression, but the subject may still obtain an extremely low score for Depression because there are 60 items on the scale.

What constitutes an abnormally high or low score for each scale is determined by the scores of normal people on whom the test was standardized. A score is considered to be abnormally high only if it is above about the ninety-eighth percentile of the normative sample. In the case of the Depression scale, for example, a woman must answer 30 or more of the 60 items in the directions scored for depression to reach the ninety-eighth percentile. (The distributions differ for men and women on many of the scales.)

While the ninety-eighth percentile cut-off point is considered to be important for each of the clinical scales, it alone is not considered to be diagnostic of psychopathology. Rather, the particular *configuration* of scores on the various scales has been found to correlate more highly with other criteria for particular types of psychopathology than have scores on individual scales. For example, test profiles in which the Psychopathic Deviate and Manic scores are the highest are frequently found among people diagnosed psychopathic according to other criteria and among people who are described by acquaintances as being overactive, impulsive, irresponsible, untrustworthy, shallow, and superficial in their relationships (Dahlstrom & Welsh, 1960). However, men who have this pattern, plus a moderately high score for femininity on the masculinity-femininity scale are often active social reformers, in accord with the endorsement of prosocial values characterizing responses keyed in the feminine direction on the masculinity-femininity scale.

Besides the enormous number of personality correlates found for adult MMPI profiles (cf. Butcher, 1969; Dahlstrom & Welsh, 1960; Welsh & Dahlstrom, 1956), there is now a growing body of evidence for correlations between adolescent MMPI profiles and behavior, and for correlations between the behavior of children and the MMPI profiles of their parents. Some of the evidence on the ability of the MMPI scores of ninth graders to predict later delinquency was presented in Chapter 13 (Monachesi & Hathaway, 1969).

Parents of child clinic patients in general have been found to have MMPI profiles more deviant than normal adults, but less deviant than adult psychiatric patients. The Hysteria and Psychopathic Deviate scores have been especially elevated in some but not all samples of parents of child guidance clinic clients (Hafner, Butcher, Hall, & Quast, 1969). However, a probable source of inconsistency in findings on parental MMPI has been the absence of clear-cut criteria with which to group the children. The use of more homogeneous groupings of children's disturbances may permit conclusions to be drawn about specific parental characteristics that shape the patterns of children's disturbances. For example, studies of the MMPIs of parents whose children were objectively classified by symptom patterns have shown that fathers of clinic boys with Externalizing symptoms had significantly higher scores on the Psychopathic Deviate scale of the MMPI than did fathers of boys with Internalizing symptoms (Anderson, 1969; Butcher, 1966; cf. Chapter 15). Moreover, using as a criterion therapists' Q-sort descriptions of child patients whom they had seen for 10 hours, Marks (1961) found that other clinicians who saw *only* the *parents' MMPI profiles* were able to make Q-sort descriptions as accurate as clinicians who saw the children several times for a traditional work-up.

ASSESSMENT OF FAMILY CHARACTERISTICS

Because the child is dependent on his family, controlled by them, directly involved in their conflicts, shaped by the models, rewards, and punishments they provide, and usually brought for help only at their initiative, his problems cannot be assessed in isolation from his family context. One prominent exponent of the role of the family goes so far as to state, "The emergence of psychiatric disorder in a child is regularly preceded by family conflict" (Ackerman, 1968, p. 513). Ackerman's statement may be correct simply because there are probably no families without conflict, but this does not establish a *causal* role for family conflict in all child psychopathology—conflict exists in the families of children who do not develop psychiatric disturbance as well as in those who do. Moreover, there is evidence that the role of family conflict per se may be minimal in the etiology of some disorders, such as childhood psychosis (see Chapter 12).

The view that the family plays a crucial role in the etiology and treatment of most child psychopathology has long been manifest in the traditional child guidance "team" approach whereby the parents are seen by a social worker at least as often as the child is seen by his therapist. The purpose of this arrangement is to enable the social worker to gather information about the child and to advise and treat the parents in order to reduce their contributions to the child's problems. In practice, the mother is usually seen much more frequently than the father and her behavior often becomes the main focus of the social worker's contact with the family. This generally occurs because mothers bring the child for treatment and fathers are less willing and available to participate, although there is ample evidence that fathers' behavior, as well as mothers', shapes child psychopathology (Becker, Peterson, Hellmer, Shoemaker, & Quay, 1959; Peterson, Becker, Shoemaker, Luria, & Hellmer, 1961).

Despite the emphasis on the family context in child psychopathology, few techniques have been developed and validated for assessing the roles of family interaction in a specific child's problems and how these interactions can be changed to help the child. Many of the diagnostic techniques already reviewed attempt to assess the child's feelings and fantasies about his family, but they cannot identify the actual events in the home that support these feelings and fantasies, nor can they reveal actual family interactions that may be subject to change in order to help the child. Unless specific patterns of childhood disorder are consistently demonstrated to occur only in the presence of specific patterns of parental behavior, inferences from a child's fantasies, statements, and problems to etiological factors in family behavior are no more than guesses.

As has previously been mentioned, one approach has been to analyze the relations of children's symptom patterns to parental MMPIs, parents' attitudes toward their children's problems, and problems manifested by the parents themselves (see Chapter 15). Other research (Britton, 1969) has shown relations between classification of children as having "neurotic" or "conduct" disorders (parallel to the Internalizing-Externalizing distinction) and the diagnoses received by those of their mothers who had previously received psychiatric treatment. In this research, most mothers who had been diagnosed neurotic or depressed had children with neurotic disorders, while most mothers who had previously been diagnosed "inadequate personality" had children with conduct disorders. Likewise, children of neurotic and depressed mothers significantly more often had phobias and anxiety symptoms, while children of mothers diagnosed "inadequate personality" significantly more often had symptoms including lying, firesetting, and aggressiveness. Thus, the type of pathology in disturbed mothers appears to be an important determinant of whether their children will show "neurotic" or "conduct" symptoms.

Parental Reports

Most of the information collected about a child and his family usually comes from his parents. Yet, this information is subject to the typical biases of human observers, compounded by the facts that the parent is likely to be intimately involved in the child's problems and that his motivation in bringing the child to treatment may include securing treatment for himself, trying to blame the other parent for the child's problems, responding to pressure from school authorities, trying to prevent the child's incarceration for a crime, etc. Even without the duress associated with seeking treatment, parents' reports of their children's behavior histories have been shown in longitudinal studies to be inaccurate (e.g., Thomas, Chess, & Birch, 1968).

In one of the few studies designed to assess the adequacy with which data relevant to child psychopathology could be collected in parent interviews, Graham and Rutter (1968) made up an interview schedule to elicit a full description of children's abnormalities from their mothers. After the mother's spontaneous comments had been expressed, the interviewer asked questions concerning 36 symptom areas.

It was found that two raters could reliably rate the interview schedules for degree and general type of emotional disturbance, but that agreement was poor between data based on two separate interviews with the same mothers one week to one month apart. Moreover, the degree of disturbance the mothers perceived in their children did not agree well with psychiatrists' judgments of disturbance and the correlation between ratings of mothers' judgments of the degree of disturbance at the two interviews was only .43. Agreement between ratings of the two interviews was generally highest for items concerning overt behavior such as bed-wetting, soiling, temper tantrums, and overactivity. Agreement was lowest for items requiring more inference, such as miserableness and poor relationships with parents.

It should be noted that the assessment of agreement between the two interviews was based on psychiatrists' ratings of their content and not on mothers' own ratings of the problems. This procedure is representative of current procedures, because inferences by professionals from unstructured parent reports typically constitute the basis for clinical judgments. However, it is possible that the degree of agreement between the two interviews would have been higher if the mothers themselves had made ratings of their children's problems on each occasion.

Parent interviews will never be completely supplanted by other methods, but having parents fill out structured rating forms describing their children's behavior may improve the reliability and validity of the data upon which inferences and diagnostic conclusions are predicated. Wimberger and Gregory (1968) have tried out a procedure in which parents fill out a behavioral checklist under supervision just prior to their initial clinic interview. The checklist consisted of 66 symptoms scored on four-point scales ("Very often," "frequently," "seldom," and "never"), plus any items the parent wished to add.

Total scores on two checklists filled out by parents thirty days apart correlated .84, indicating much higher test-retest reliabilities than found for most diagnostic procedures. Of the 53 separate items checked frequently enough for statistical analysis, all showed highly significant ($p < .001$) agreement on the two ratings. Agreement between parents' and therapists' ratings for individual items was also high.

Another finding was that the number of symptoms checked far exceeded the number reported in diagnostic interviews, indicating that the checklist could provide a more complete report of the child's symptoms than interviews typically do. Besides providing more adequate initial information, checklists filled out by both parents can be used to identify differences between the parents in what they consider to be the child's problems and to evaluate changes in behavior in treated and control groups (Wimberger & Millar, 1968).

BEHAVIORAL ASSESSMENT

Chapters 10 and 11 presented illustrations of behavioral assessment as it relates to behavior modification. These illustrations included counting the frequency of specific behaviors that are targets for modification, observing the interactions of children with their parents, siblings, peers, and teachers in the home and school, observing parent-child interaction in a laboratory setting, having children indicate their specific fears on a Fear Survey Schedule, observing children's behavior in the presence of feared objects, and having children enact their problems in role-playing scenes.

A fundamental difference between traditional and behavioral paradigms is that traditional diagnosis is directed toward the understanding of underlying personality characteristics while the behavioral approach is directed toward assessment of behavior in the situations where behavioral change is desired (Goldfried & Kent, 1972). Psychodynamic interviewing and personality tests reviewed earlier are generally designed to obtain responses that are viewed as *signs* of underlying characteristics that, in turn, are hypothesized to predict criterion behavior outside the test situation.

Behavioral assessment, by contrast, is designed to obtain *samples* of the actual problem behavior. Parents often come with a variety of vaguely expressed complaints that can be refined by having the parents keep structured records of problem behaviors in the settings where they occur, having trained observers record the child's behaviors in such settings to identify possible instigating circumstances and reinforcers, and by interviewing the child. Standardized tests, especially reading and achievement tests, are also used if they measure behavior closely related to the target behaviors.

On the basis of data obtained in these ways, an attempt is made to define the child's problems in terms of specific responses and the environmental contingencies controlling them. Attempts are then made to modify the behavior by changing the environmental contingencies, often by advising teachers or parents to change their behavior toward the child. Sometimes the child is taught new behavior in a one-to-one situation with a therapist, or his parents are directly guided in changing their behavior toward the child, e.g., by being instructed via earphone by an observer behind a one-way glass while the parent is interacting with his child. Nonoperant behavioral methods such as systematic desensitization also involve changing specific problem behaviors identified in advance through direct observation and through reports by the child and people around him.

Besides being aimed at initially sampling the problem behaviors, behavioral assessment is intended to continue over the course of treatment as problem behavior is monitored to identify changes in response to specific interventions. Failure of the behavior to change when its assumed determinants are changed can lead to a new diagnostic formulation and alteration of treatment procedures. Thus, a trial of a particular kind of behavioral treatment may be part of the assessment process. Trying out specific instructional methods ("diagnostic teaching") is also gaining popularity as a strategy with children for whom the global IQ score is not very helpful in identifying the precise level at which educational intervention should begin, the optimal method of intervention, or the rate of progress that can be expected (e.g., Severson, 1971).

Direct versus Indirect Measures

Although the goal of sampling the specific problem behaviors differs from the traditional psychodiagnostic goal of portraying personality, there are some points on which their effectiveness can be compared. Well-designed comparisons of the effectiveness of behavioral and traditional diagnostic approaches for selecting and guiding treatment have not been carried out, but Scott and Johnson (1972) have reported several comparisons of direct and indirect measurements of personality characteristics. The *direct* measures consisted of questionnaires containing statements for which subjects were to indicate their degree of agreement. The *indirect* measures consisted of subjects' responses to TAT cards, predictions of outcomes of hypothetical events, completions of stories by selecting from alternative endings, judgments of the prevalence of certain disapproved orientations within their peer groups, and judgments of the effectiveness of arguments for and against various attitudes. The subjects included college students and incarcerated delinquents, while criterion measures consisted of ratings on these subjects by people who knew them well.

For nearly all comparisons on a large number of opinions, attitudes, motives, and personal characteristics, the correlations of the criterion ratings with the direct measures were higher than with the indirect measures. All measures correlated higher with the criterion ratings when the responses were anonymous than when subjects identified themselves, but the direct measures were equally superior to the indirect measures under both conditions.

Because the utility of information yielded by a particular diagnostic method depends upon one's conception of pathology and the kinds of treatment one is willing to apply, there is no absolute basis for comparing the utility of behavioral and traditional methods. Unless one believes that personality must be understood exclusively in terms of unconscious motives and structures, however, information from behavioral assessment is likely to be helpful in determining a baseline for the child's current problems against which the effects of treatment can be measured. Furthermore, it has repeatedly been found that the best predictors of behavior in specific criterion situations are behaviors in situations most like the criterion situations (Weiss, 1968).

Information from traditional personality tests may also be helpful to behavior modifiers insofar as the information discriminates between types of individuals who may and those who may not benefit from specific types of behavioral technique. For example, the evidence cited in Chapter 13 on the responses of MMPI-diagnosed sociopaths to various types of punishment suggests that their misbehavior may not be treatable in the same way as the misbehavior of nonsociopathic delinquents (e.g., Schmauk, 1970).

ASSESSMENT OF ORGANIC DYSFUNCTION

The research on neurobiological development reviewed in Chapter 6 indicates that one-to-one relationships between organic damage and behavioral abnormality are rare. The behavioral effects of a specific type of damage in a specific area of the nervous system depend upon the age at which the damage occurs and a multiplicity of other organic and psychological characteristics of the child and the situations he confronts. The effects can also change over the course of development, some being conspicuous during early childhood and disappearing later, others being inconspicuous in early childhood and becoming prominent later in life.

Assessment of the source and effects of organic damage is usually a rather imprecise business because autopsy findings are about the only ultimate criterion against which to validate assessment procedures and even autopsy findings are not likely to reveal the functional effects of most organic anomalies. Organic assessment procedures such as the EEG, skull X-rays, and neurological examination were discussed in Chapter 6. In practice, these are often used in conjunction with perceptual-motor performance on psychological tests, behavioral observations, interviews, and personal histories to form a judgment as to whether a child has an organic dysfunction, whether there is progressive deterioration (e.g., due to a malignant tumor or neurological disease), and whether surgery or other medical procedures are warranted. Since each of the diagnostic methods is imprecise in most cases, a conclusion is usually based upon a composite of the various findings.

The possibility of organic dysfunction should be considered in every child referred for psychological diagnosis. Many children's problems may be influenced by undetected organic dysfunction that is first suggested by their performance on psychological tests and other behavior during a diagnostic work-up. In some cases, the dysfunction may consist merely of visual or auditory defects that can be tested further and remedied by specialists in vision or audition. In other cases, the dysfunction may be an early sign of a progressive disorder requiring medical attention. In the majority of cases, however, specific organic causes are not found for dysfunctions suggested by performance during a psychological examination. Rather, the results of the examination are used, along with life history and medical data, to infer that brain damage, slow maturation, or poor neural organization may be creating a handicap for the child and that expectations for the child should take account of that handicap.

The function of diagnosis with respect to organic dysfunction should not be merely to label a child as damaged or undamaged, but to identify specific strengths and weaknesses that can guide future treatment. Organic damage is just one factor that influences a child's behavior, and the child with organic damage is just as much influenced by other factors, such as his learning history, motivation, and family pressures, as any other child. However, most tests in current use have been validated only against gross diagnoses of organic damage versus no organic damage. Only the third test to be described here, the Frostig Developmental Test of Visual Perception, is aimed at providing a differentiated profile of performance. Even with the Frostig Test, a variety of other test performance and diagnostic teaching is needed to obtain an adequate guide for helping most organically handicapped children.

Bender Gestalt Test

The most widely used test of visual-motor dysfunction in both children and adults, the Bender Gestalt Test, consists of nine figures printed on separate cards. These figures were originally selected by Lauretta Bender (1938) from configurations designed by the *Gestalt* psychologist Max Wertheimer (1923) to illustrate various principles of visual-perceptual organization. Bender hypothesized that children's ability to copy the various *Gestalten* (configurations) reflected their levels of perceptual-motor maturation. The figures include a circle attached to a diamond, a straight line of dots, a series of small circles arranged in short parallel lines, complex patterns of dots, and straight and wavy lines.

The child is asked to copy each of the designs in succession. If a child rotates the figures, seems confused, makes major alternations, or produces inferior copies for his age, he may be asked to repeat his drawings in order to see whether he can recognize and improve upon his errors.

Bender provided no norms or scoring procedures, but Koppitz (1964) has devised a scoring system based upon specific distortions, rotations, failures of integration, and other errors in Bender drawings by children between the ages of 5 and 10. Interrater reliabilities are in the .90s and test-retest reliabilities over four-month intervals have been reported to be in the .50s and .60s. Normative data show a steady improvement in scores from the ages of 5 to about 9. The developmental nature of Koppitz's scoring of the Bender is also reflected in the fact that scores correlate highly with MA, correlating up to .85 in retardates.

Because Bender performance has such a strong relationship to intellectual development, a child's general level of ability must be considered when evaluating his performance for perceptual-motor handicaps. A child having a low level of cognitive development, as indicated by a low MA, cannot be expected to perform well on the Bender even if he has no perceptual-motor

malfunction or emotional disturbance. In studies controlling for MA, however, Koppitz's scoring system, used in combination with assessment of the
qualitative nature of a child's errors, his ability to improve upon them, and
other aspects of his performance, has effectively identified children diagnosed
as brain-damaged by a consensus of other criteria. Koppitz emphasizes that
low scores for a given MA merely *suggest* brain damage and that all other
data about a child should be considered together in arriving at a diagnosis.

Graham-Kendall Memory-for-Designs Test

The Graham-Kendall Test (Graham & Kendall, 1946, 1960) follows principles similar to the Bender, except that the subject is asked to draw each
design from memory after having seen it for five seconds. The designs are
all straight-lined figures selected for ease of scoring and effectiveness in discriminating between normal and brain-damaged people in the standardization samples. Scoring is highly reliable and data on a variety of groups
show that test performance discriminates fairly well between normal and
brain-damaged subjects ranging in age from nine to 60. For this age range,
level of intellectual development appears less influential than on Bender
performance for ages five through nine. Evidence from normative samples
for both tests suggests that, after an MA of about 10 is reached, further
intellectual development does not improve perceptual-motor functioning
much. However, the scoring system of the Graham-Kendall does permit a
correction for developmental level by subtracting the scores for a subject's
age and vocabulary level.

Frostig Developmental Test of Visual Perception

The Frostig Test was designed to provide a profile of a child's performance in five different areas believed to reflect organic dysfunction (Maslow,
Frostig, Lefever, & Whittlesey, 1964). The five areas are eye-hand coordination, figure-ground perception, form constancy, position in space, and spatial
relationships. Various drawing tasks tapping the five areas have been standardized on large samples of children aged three to nine. A perceptual age
level and a perceptual quotient (PQ), analogous to the IQ, are calculated
for a child in each of the five areas on the basis of his resemblance to the
performance of children his age in the standardization sample. The five
areas of functioning are believed to be fairly independent of one another
and, indeed, the correlations among the five PQs are low. Scoring is objective and test-retest reliabilities for PQs over several weeks have been about
.80 (Frostig & Orpet, 1972).

As to validity, significant correlations have been found between Frostig
scores and teachers' ratings of classroom adjustment, motor coordination,
and intellectual functioning, Goodenough Draw-a-man scores, and reading
scores. Marked scatter among scores and low total scores have also been
found in children diagnosed as neurologically impaired. One of the pur-

poses of the perceptual profile is to guide Frostig's educational program for improving perceptual-motor functioning. Controlled studies have shown that Frostig's procedures do improve PQ scores on her test, but that these improvements do not necessarily improve reading or other aspects of school performance (Rosen, 1966).

AN ILLUSTRATIVE DIAGNOSTIC WORK-UP

Not all diagnostic procedures are used with all children and no single diagnostic work-up can illustrate all aspects of diagnosis. However, the following illustrates diagnostic procedures typically used in a traditional child guidance setting with a fairly typical case.

RALPH W.

Ralph W. was first seen by a private psychiatrist when he was six years old. He had been referred by his pediatrician primarily because of encopresis (bowel incontinence without organic cause), distractibility, and uncontrollable behavior in school, despite good academic performance. Because the parents could not afford private psychiatric treatment, they were referred to a public child guidance clinic with a sliding fee scale based on income.

Social Worker's Interviews with Parents

Ralph's parents described Ralph, now seven years old, as being tense and high strung, as having considerable conflict with his younger sister, and as being prone to temper tantrums when he failed to get his way. He was also reported to be very involved in fantasies about the H-bomb and the end of the world and to believe and be frightened by other children's fantasies. Although his parents did not consider it a problem, Ralph had recently been wetting his bed every night.

Ralph's physical coordination was so poor that he could not catch a ball nor pour without spilling, although he liked to climb and jump from heights. He could not get along well with other children because he fought with them, and he was often uncontrolled and destructive at home, although his parents made little effort to prevent this. Both parents were artistically inclined, cultured people who greatly valued Ralph's apparently precocious intellect and creativity, despite finding him a bit difficult to live with.

Developmental history revealed that Ralph had been born nearly two months prematurely, had weighed less than five pounds, and had been in critical condition at birth due to a breathing difficulty.

Psychiatric Interviews with Ralph

During the first psychiatric interviews, Ralph was given a neurological examination because his difficult birth history, poor coordination, and distractibility were all suggestive of organic dysfunction. The neurological findings were largely negative, although neurological abnormalities could not be ruled out. During the exam, Ralph became irritated, raised his voice, and clenched his fists as if he were about to have a temper tantrum but then appeared to think better of it and calmed down.

Ralph's doll play in the interview situation showed a great deal of conflict between a boy doll and a younger girl doll. In one sequence, he said, "She's gentle when I hit her and she's rough when she hits me." During another episode, the girl doll hid from the boy and had a bowel movement under the bed so she wouldn't get caught going to the bathroom.

During his play, Ralph occasionally said "Good grief," and eventually commented on how much he is like Charlie Brown in Peanuts. On another occasion, he brought in a Mr. Magoo doll which, like his comment on Charlie Brown, was interpreted as suggesting that Ralph viewed himself as an inept, clumsy figure. On the other hand, he consistently picked out games intended for much older children and became upset when he could not play them well. The therapist was impressed by Ralph's advanced verbal output and the imaginativeness of his play.

Psychological Testing

The WISC, Draw-a-man, Rorschach, TAT, Bender Gestalt, and two drawing items from the Stanford-Binet were administered. Ralph was cooperative and highly motivated, but also quite distractible and impulsive. Although the testing room was rather bare, he examined and asked about almost everything in sight. He was very concerned about his performance and asked the examiner if he tested other children from Ralph's school. He even asked about several of his schoolmates by name.

IQ Testing. On the WISC, Ralph often answered test questions quickly without careful thought, but did not improve his answers much when given a second try. He became quite frustrated on the Object Assembly subtest (a series of puzzlelike tasks) and on the Block Design subtest (forming colored blocks into designs to match those printed on a card). He said these items were too hard, he couldn't do them, and he wished someone else would do them for him. However, his score on the Block Design was well above average for his age and higher than his score on any other subtest of the WISC Performance Scale. His score on the Object Assembly subtest was his lowest on the Performance Scale, but still only slightly below average for his age.

His reactions to both these tasks suggested an awareness of the weakness in perceptual-motor functioning that had been emphasized by his parents, but the fact that he did so much better on the one which offered a concrete model for imitation (Block Design) than on the one which offered no model (Object Assembly) suggested that he could perform well in this area if a guiding structure were available. His total Performance Scale IQ was 120.

On the WISC Verbal Scale, Ralph's scores were very high on the Arithmetic, Vocabulary, and Information subtests, but about average on the Comprehension and Similarities subtests, which are assumed to involve more abstract reasoning than the others. He often gave high-sounding answers which he could not justify on further questioning. This and the fairly large disparity between the first three and latter two subtests were interpreted as suggesting that he had benefitted from his intellectually enriched home and excellent schooling, but that his basic reasoning abilities were not exceptional. His Verbal Scale IQ was 128 and Full Scale IQ 126. His performance on the Draw-a-man test received a score roughly equivalent to an IQ of 110, slightly above his level of performance on the Similarities and Comprehension subtests.

Bender Gestalt. Ralph's performance on the Bender Gestalt, as scored by the Koppitz system, was better than average for his chronological age and almost exactly what would be expected for the mental age of about 8.8 years represented by his IQ of 126 on the WISC. Ralph had difficulty in copying one Bender design, a design resembling a Christmas tree composed of dots and lying on its side. His first attempt at this design was much poorer than his other designs. A second attempt was still worse. This suggested difficulty in integrating a complex array of small units, but his good performance on all the other Bender designs, coupled with his average to very good scores on the WISC perceptual-motor subtests, and his age-adequate performance on Stanford-Binet drawing items all indicated that any perceptual-motor handicap was not likely to interfere much with school-type tasks.

Rorschach. As on the IQ test, Ralph's responses to the Rorschach were often impulsive. In the inquiry he was frequently unable to justify percepts which had been loosely suggested by the inkblots. His 13 responses included a jet plane with a hole in it, a jet plane with the cab on fire, a tiny rocket with enormous exhaust, and an explosion, in all of which he emphasized the "blaze" of fire, smoke, and "stuff that comes out." He also mentioned several times that the ink looked like it had fallen or been spilled with great force to produce the image he saw. Although not uncommon for seven-year-old boys (Ames et al, 1952), these responses were interpreted as indicating preoccupation with rebellion, struggles for control, and, in particular, his encopresis. Ralph also saw two images of the insides of the human body, suggesting concern about something being wrong inside. Other than that, most of what he saw consisted of spiders, bats, birds, and other animals seen in the blots by many children his age.

TAT. Five of Ralph's 11 TAT stories contained themes of transgression and retribution. In most cases somebody actually did something wrong and was then punished for it. In one case, a bad boy only dreamed that "they" would kill him if he continued being bad and grumpy, so he started being good. Another story dealt with a painter who drank too much liquor and went crazy. His wife restrained him, called the police and hospital, and they cured him. The succeeding story dealt with the boy Rembrandt painting his first picture and being told he'd grow up to be a famous painter, which he did.

Taken together, these stories were interpreted as indicating that Ralph had internalized the great expectations for intelligence and creativity that his parents had for him and that he felt he was bad when he didn't live up to these expectations. If only he could be helped to gain control of himself, either by being punished, restrained, or cured, he could live up to the standards set for him.

Interpretive Summary and Recommendations

While the overall interpretations of a diagnostic work-up are often quite elaborate in terms of unconscious motivations, fantasies, and traits, only the conclusions most obviously justified by the foregoing data seemed necessary for guiding recommendations to the parents and for defining the goals of treatment. These were as follows:

1. Ralph is indeed clumsy and this may have resulted from perinatal organic damage. He is also concerned about his clumsiness, excessively fears failure in tasks requiring perceptual-motor coordination, and thinks of himself as a bumbling awkward figure. However, his perceptual-motor coordination on tasks related to

school performance is quite adequate. His fear of failure, clumsiness, and bumbling self-image are likely to interfere with his performance in sports, which could further reduce his self-esteem, but patient help from an adult (preferably his now somewhat distant father) in acquiring basic skills for ball playing, etc., may minimize further frustration and may increase his self-esteem.

2. Ralph's intellectual performance shows that he has done well in acquiring academic knowledge and that he has the ability to perform well in school, but that he should not be expected to be intellectually outstanding.

3. Ralph's behavior in interviews and his concern about intellectual performance indicate that he shares his parents' very high standards for intelligence and creativity.

4. Ralph's Rorschach responses suggest that he harbors explosive anger which may be partially expressed in his encopresis. His TAT responses suggest considerable concern with being bad and its possible consequences in punishment. However, they also suggest that he feels some of his own badness may be beyond his control and that being restrained and ultimately cured will enable him to become the great creative artist he and his parents expect him to be.

5. Since a major source of Ralph's anger and feeling of badness appears to be his inability to be as superior and creative as he feels he must be, his parents should try to treat him more like a seven-year-old boy than a budding genius. The parents' *laissez faire* attitude toward Ralph's uncontrolled behavior may stem in part from their values and from the nature of their marital relationship, but work with the parents should focus on how this prevents Ralph from getting the firm adult help he needs to develop self-control.

6. The diagnostic work-up also suggested that treatment should aim to help Ralph establish more realistic expectations for himself, to build his self-esteem by praising him when he meets these more realistic expectations, to overcome the specific symptoms of enuresis and encopresis which will otherwise continue to damage his self-esteem, and to help him develop self-control so that he will not react to frustration with temper tantrums and other uncontrolled behavior.

SUMMARY

Diagnosis and the less disease-oriented term *assessment* refer to the process of assembling information in order to form a comprehensive picture of a person and his problem. The most useful diagnostic procedures are those that lead to classification which in turn guides selection of the most effective treatment. Such a sequence implies that a reliable and valid classification system is available and that the effects of various treatments on the various classes of disorders are known. In our present rudimentary state of knowledge, diagnosis, classification, treatment, and evaluation of treatment remain fragmented from one another in many areas of psychopathology.

Infant development tests are designed to identify infants who are organically damaged, diseased, deprived, or suffering from severe emotional disturbance. They do not correlate with later IQ tests, probably because they cannot measure manipulation of symbols, which is what IQ tests primarily measure.

Besides yielding a global score predictive of school performance, individually administered IQ tests can provide information about a child's response style, patterns of performance, and types of errors. More specialized tests of intelligence tap nonverbal functioning and specific patterns of verbal performance.

"Personality" is the primary focus of many diagnostic procedures, although there is little agreement on what personality is. Two approaches to personality diagnosis are the *psychodynamic* and *trait approaches.* The global portrayal of personality often sought from personality test data is difficult to validate and may yield a false sense of understanding due to factors like the *Barnum Effect.*

Interviews are the most universally used diagnostic procedures, but inferences from unstructured interviews are highly unreliable, even when made by clinicians observing the same interview. More structured interviews employing predetermined systems for making judgments can yield adequate reliability and validity with children and their parents.

Projective techniques have enjoyed widespread popularity, but there is little evidence for the reliability or validity of most of the interpretations made from them. The most reliable and best validated inferences from them have been obtained by applying quasi-psychometric techniques in order to make specific predictions rather than global personality portrayals.

Objectively scored personality tests have been used much less than projective tests with children, although children's anxiety scales have been developed and the MMPI has been shown to predict delinquency among adolescents. Children's symptom patterns have also been shown to relate to the MMPI profiles of their parents.

There are few systematic procedures for assessing family dynamics. Developmental histories obtained from parents are often inaccurate, although parents' responses on symptom checklists have been found to be reliable and to yield more information about their child's symptoms than interviewing typically does.

Behavioral assessment attempts to *sample* behavior as nearly as possible in the situations where change is desired. To a greater extent than other approaches, behavioral assessment is integral with treatment because the problem behavior is monitored during treatment in order to determine whether modification of the assumed determinants of the behavior is indeed changing the behavior. Since their goals differ, there has been little systematic comparison of traditional and behavioral diagnostic procedures, but there is evidence that direct self-reports are more accurate than projective and other indirect measures.

Psychodiagnostic tests for organic dysfunction generally consist of drawing and copying tasks. With mental age partialled out, they are fairly effective in identifying children diagnosed as having organic damage by a consensus of medical indices.

SUGGESTED READING

Clinical versus Statistical Prediction. An issue which was explicitly stated in Chapter 4, but which implicitly concerns many of the problems of validating the diagnostic approaches discussed in the current chapter was formulated in 1954 by Paul Meehl in terms of "clinical versus statistical prediction." *Clinical prediction* refers to the traditional procedure of formulating a global impression of a personality on the basis of everything known about him and then deducing from this mental construct what the person is likely to do under various circumstances. *Statistical prediction,* by contrast, employs a prediction formula based on the relations betwen diagnostic data and outcomes in one sample of people to make predictions about new but similar clients. In a 1965 article, Meehl reviews later work and assesses what appears to be the only instance of superiority for clinical over statistical procedures, namely, Lindzey's (1965) study of clinical judgments of homosexuality from TAT protocols, reported in the current chapter. Another paper relevant to this controversy is by Sawyer (1966) who adds the mode of data *collection* (clinical versus mechanical) to the question of mode of data *combination* (statistical versus clinical) and reviews the literature to identify the most successful approaches.

Projective Tests. Although the volume of literature on projective tests is too enormous to be comprehensively reviewed, two books (Suinn & Oskamp, 1969; Zubin et al, 1965) provide good overviews and critiques of findings relating to the major projective tests. The latter book also provides an analysis of how projective tests might be put to better use if they are to be retained at all.

New Approaches to Diagnosis. Books by Mischel (1968) and Peterson (1968) and an article by Goldfried and Kent (1972) state the case for drastically revising traditional approaches to personality assessment for clinical purposes. They point out many problems in the traditional approaches and propose new approaches, largely behavioral, which reflect new criteria for what diagnosis should do.

17

Issues in the Treatment
of Psychopathology

The ultimate goal in studying developmental psychopathology is, of course, to create effective methods of treatment and prevention. The purposes of this chapter are to discuss some treatment modalities that have not been detailed earlier in the book; to present general issues involved in all efforts at treatment, especially in the treatment of disadvantaged children, who offer the most significant challenges to traditional conceptions of treatment; to deal with the conceptual intricacies and empirical results of the evaluation of treatment effects; and to attempt an overview of where we currently stand with respect to the treatment and prevention of psychopathology in children.

NONDIRECTIVE PLAY THERAPY

In nearly all forms of nonorganic therapy with preadolescent children, play materials and the opportunity to play in the presence of the therapist are provided. The assumption is that children feel more comfortable and are better able to express themselves in play than in a purely verbal interview situation. Psychoanalytically oriented therapists regard the child's play as symbolically expressing his unconscious thoughts and conflicts, just as free association does in adults. Some behavior therapists also use the play situation as a way of getting at problems that the child is not initially willing or able to discuss verbally, but thereafter they tend to employ play as an instrument for behavior change, e.g., by reinforcing the child for dealing with certain problems in new ways through play and by supporting the child's self-esteem. In neither the psychoanalytic nor the behavioral approach is play *per se* considered to be the *therapy*—in both cases, play is an instrument used by the therapist to aid in carrying out his therapy. By contrast, in nondirective play therapy, the child's play in the presence of the therapist is viewed as the essential instrument of therapy.

Nondirective play therapy is an extension to children of Carl Rogers' (1951) nondirective client-centered therapy for adults. Virginia Axline (1969), one of the chief proponents of nondirective play therapy, has expressed the basic assumptions of nondirective therapy as follows: All behavior is caused by a "drive for complete self-realization." When external pressures block this drive, the individual either fights outwardly to establish his self-concept in external reality or he turns his struggle inward and begins separating himself from reality. An individual is maladjusted when he lacks the self-confidence to grow in self-realization in the real world and fails to channel this drive into constructive positive directions. Axline regards daydreaming, withdrawal, compensation, identification, projection, regression, and repression as means by which the child who is turning inward attempts to achieve his self-concept. The greater the disparity between the inner self-concept and the outer behavior, the greater the maladjustment.

Since it is assumed that the individual has within himself the drive toward self-realization and the ultimate ability to solve his own problems, the goal of nondirective therapy is to provide the opportunity for the client to be himself. By conveying unconditional positive regard for the client, even when he expresses thoughts censured by others, and by reflecting back to the client the feelings he states, the therapist helps the client to accept and clarify his feelings without loss of self-esteem and to reorient himself to coping constructively with reality. The therapist's role is to create the conditions under which the client directs his own course rather than to interpret what the client says in psychodynamic terms or to modify the client's behavior by manipulating external contingencies.

As with most extensions of adult therapy downward to children, play in nondirective therapy is assumed to serve the same function that words do with adults. Thus, the play therapist's role is to create conditions under which the child can express his feelings in play, face them, and learn to control or abandon them. The play room is portrayed as a secure place where the child is the most important person and where he can achieve a sense of power to be an individual in his own right. Since the child's self-directed expressive activity is considered crucial, Axline recommends that therapy rooms be equipped with simple toys that children can use creatively, rather than with mechanical toys or competitive games.

According to Axline, play therapy can be successful without changes in the behavior of adults who are contributing to a child's problems. Although counseling or therapy for the significant adults in a child's life may be helpful in many cases, the play therapist's primary alliance is with the child and he or she does not work with the parents. If play therapy is successful, the child may develop new and effective ways for coping with the negative influences of adults. Axline (1969) has provided some excellent case illustrations of play therapy and a full-length case history entitled *Dibs: In search of self* (1964).

Effects of Nondirective Play Therapy

During the development of nondirective therapy for adults, Carl Rogers stressed the need for evaluating the effects of therapy and he coordinated research that demonstrated positive benefits from client-centered therapy (Rogers & Dymond, 1954). To some extent, concern for research on the effects of therapy has carried over into the development of play therapy. Controlled studies have shown greater improvement on several personality measures by children receiving play therapy than by untreated control children, even without the involvement of the treated children's parents (e.g., Cox, 1953; Dorfman, 1958). However, controlled comparisons of behavior reinforcement procedures and play therapy with boys having conduct disorders have shown that reinforcement procedures produced greater improvements in such disorders than did play therapy (Perkins, 1967).

Filial Therapy

A variant on play therapy, called *filial therapy,* has been tried out by Guerney (1964). Filial therapy involves training parents to conduct play sessions with their emotionally disturbed children. The parents initially meet in groups with therapists who teach them the principles of nondirective play therapy and who continue to meet weekly with them. Besides benefitting the child directly, filial therapy is intended to reveal the parents' problems with their children so that these can be discussed in the group sessions and to help the parents implement changes in their attitudes and behavior toward their children. A study in which observers rated parents' empathy, degree of involvement, allowance of self-direction, and reflection of feeling in play sessions with their children showed that parents improved significantly on all these measures after training and improved still further in three posttraining play sessions (Stover, Guerney, & O'Connell, 1971).

GROUP THERAPY

J. L. Moreno is often credited with having initiated group psychotherapy, in Vienna about 1911. He began by having children act out dramatic plays, but soon allowed them to act out their problems without a prepared script. After he came to the United States in 1927, Moreno applied this technique, known as *psychodrama,* with prisoners and reform school inmates. His work helped to instigate a tremendous upsurge of interest in group psychotherapy. Some of the main assets of group therapy are considered to be its stimulation of social behavior among group members and its creation of a situation in which several people share their problems and support one another in their reality testing and attempts to solve their problems. While group therapy is assumed to have functions different from individual therapy, it is sometimes used as a supplement to individual therapy or as a substitute for it when a client's finances or a shortage of therapists make individual therapy unavailable.

Several different forms of group therapy are used with preadolescent children who are too young for adolescent-adult forms of discussion group therapy. One is the *activity group* in which up to about eight children meet together in a room containing a variety of toys, art materials, etc. The children are free to pursue their own interests, but they also have a refreshment period and may take trips together. The therapist exerts as little leadership or control as possible, but he praises good work and behavior and provides a model of thoughtfulness, courtesy, and self-control with which the children can identify. Slavson (1952), one of the pioneers of group therapy for children, maintains that activity groups can be especially beneficial in socializing children with mild hyperactivity and aggressiveness, constricted personalities, poor sex-role identification, low self-esteem, and mild neuroses.

Another variant is the *activity-interview group*, which combines the activity group approach with the approach taken in individual psychoanalytically oriented therapy. Beside permitting the children to behave pretty much as they wish, the therapist encourages communication and interprets the children's behavior to them, with the goal of promoting insight.

A third variant of child group therapy is *nondirective group play therapy*, which generally follows the principles of individual play therapy except that the children meet in groups. An early report showed a positive effect of nondirective group play therapy on retarded readers (Bills, 1950), but a much better controlled study has shown no differences between a treated group and a nontreated control group at the end of therapy or after a one-year follow-up, either on measures of social adjustment or on reading scores (Elliot & Pumfrey, 1972). An eclectic combination of group play and discussion has been found to be about as effective as individual therapy with children considered to have high ego strength, but neither group nor individual therapy significantly improved the behavior of children low in ego strength (Novick, 1965).

One of the latest innovations in group therapy is the application of behavior modification methods. As reported in Chapters 10 and 11, group modeling, desensitization, and reinforcement techniques have all shown significant effects with children (e.g., Clement & Milne, 1967; Ritter, 1968), and Rose (1972) has provided a handbook of behavior modification techniques for children in therapy groups. The groups he describes are designed to take advantage of both small group dynamics and specific behavioral methods to achieve well-defined goals, with constant monitoring of the child's behavior outside the group to determine whether the goals are being met. An advantage of this approach is that the effects of treatment can be evaluated in terms of predefined goals, although there have as yet been few systematic comparisons between the effects of the group treatments Rose outlines and other forms of treatment or no treatment.

CONJOINT FAMILY THERAPY

Most approaches to psychotherapy with children emphasize the need for work with the child's family. The traditional approach to treatment, in which a social worker sees the parents while the child is seen by his therapist, is frequently referred to as "family therapy." However, the 1950s saw the introduction of treatment in which all members of a family meet together with a single therapist or two cotherapists. This form of treatment is referred to as *conjoint family therapy*. It is based on the assumption that the family is a social system and that each member's behavior is a function of pressures existing in the system. The symptoms of a child brought for treatment are thus not regarded primarily as manifestations of the child's pathology, but as manifestations of the family's pathology. Moreover, the child's symptoms are regarded as having a definite function in the family, so that their disappearance without other changes in the family may produce new symptoms in other family members or a dissolution of the family system. Consequently, the child is referred to as the "identified patient"—i.e., the one identified as a patient by the other family members—but the family is viewed as the appropriate unit of treatment.

Conjoint family therapists may make use of psychodynamic concepts, but they tend to apply them at the level of the family rather than individual functioning. Similarly, they may make use of behavioral concepts, but the focus for behavioral change is the total set of interactions among all family members rather than the alteration of contingencies affecting the identified patient or the one-to-one interaction between other family members and the identified patient. Differences between the viewpoints of family therapists and those of psychoanalysts and behavior modifiers can be seen in a family therapist's interpretation of Freud's (1909) case of "Little Hans" presented in Chapter 8 and reanalyzed from a behavioral point of view by Wolpe and Rachman (1960) in Chapter 9:

> If we view Hans' family as a gestalt, we will then not only analyze Hans' oedipal fantasies but also attempt to understand what impact his parents had on their development. . . .
> Children's developmental problems activate unresolved childhood conflicts of their parents so that when a parent seeks assistance from a therapist in relation to his child, he is also presenting a part of himself which seeks help. When Hans' father went to Freud, he may have been unconsciously communicating that "I, Hans' father, have Oedipal difficulties of my own which I can't resolve. They are being stimulated constantly by my son. Please help me." It is of interest that concurrent with Hans' developing sexual curiosity, we find his father curious about the sexual

theories of Freud and attending his lectures on sex. . . . Based on his quests for sexual information . . . one may reasonably speculate that the father was having some sexual difficulties of his own.

If our hypothesis concerning the sexual difficulties that Father was experiencing with his wife is correct, and if we consider the dearth of communication that transpired between the mother and father throughout the case, it would follow that Hans' sexual curiosity could not be discussed by Mama and Papa together, either with or without Hans present. Apparently, Hans' burgeoning sexual curiosity and attendant fantasies induced considerable anxiety in both parents and in turn, exacerbated their withdrawal from each other. Intensified were Hans' erotic desires towards Mother because he sensed an increased availability of her by virtue of Father's withdrawal from her. Furthermore, Father, who attended lectures on sex in his spare time and did not spend very much time with his wife, emerged throughout the story as a tender, maternal man, one whose lack of aggressiveness could strengthen a boy's Oedipal guilt. Hence, Papa and Mama avoided each other, avoided discussing sexual questions about Hans with each other, and interestingly, Hans developed a symptom which had as its major feature, avoidance. Because there was a dearth of verbal communication in the interdependent triangular relationship of sex, Hans squelched his feelings and thoughts on the subject and displaced his conflicts on to an object that could not verbally communicate at all, namely, a horse.

* * *

The relationship between Hans' father and Freud became recapitulated in the father's treatment of Hans; childhood sexuality was again the topic of discussion. Since these therapeutic encounters transpired almost daily, we can tentatively conclude that the sexual discussions provided both partners with some sexual stimulation and gratification. . . . As Freud, himself, has taught us, when an Oedipal conflict in a boy is strong, a common defense is to repress his competitive aggression toward the father and deny the love attachment towards the mother. The boy then submits to father in a homosexual manner, his hostility goes underground, and a love and beloved relationship between father and son is formed. Father's sexual talks with Hans apparently seduced the boy into a submissive relationship with him, and Hans became more and more positively suggestible to his father's interpretations. To please his father, Hans gave up the fear of horses, which was Father's main objective. It will be recalled that as the case material unfolded, and not prior to the therapy, Hans became increasingly effeminate and submissive. He began to have fantasies of becoming a woman and dreamed that he had given birth to a baby. Like his mother who had given birth to Hans' baby sister during his pre-Oedipal phase, Hans became, psychologically, his father's wife and surrendered his own virility.

As we know, Mother was excluded and probably excluded herself from the consultations with Freud. . . . Is there a possibility that the rage she felt in being a loner was conveyed to Hans when she admonished him for his masturbatory activity by threatening him with the loss of his "widdler"? . . .

As family therapists have demonstrated, when the family member with the presenting problem improves, other family members exhibit distress and/or the family unit can possibly be threatened with dissolution. Hans' phobia was the displayed expression of family conflict and held the family together, preserving its equilibrium. When Hans, the family member with the presenting problem, improved, the parents' marriage soon after was dissolved. The mutual avoidance pattern of both parents towards each other reinforced Father's attachment to his son wherein Hans became his father's wife. As mother became further alienated from her husband and son, Hans and his father drew closer. Father evolved into both a mother and father for Hans, was ascribed strong omnipotence by the latter, and the patient was cured through love. Hans, in his submission to father, complied with his father's prescription that was received from Freud, namely, that "the phobia is nonsense and ridiculous to keep" [Strean, 1967, pp. 230–32].

Application of Conjoint Family Therapy

Family therapists vary greatly in the specific procedures they use. Some, such as Satir (1967), generally see the parents first for a couple of sessions and then the children with the parents for most of the rest of the sessions, unless the children are under four. Satir also takes an extensive family history in order to inform herself about the family and to provide the family some initial structure that may help in overcoming the fears they have of the therapy situation. Other therapists see all family members from the beginning to the end of therapy, while still others see only the parents and the child who is the identified patient. Many do not take detailed family histories because they believe this sets a pattern of having the therapist ask questions and the family answer them.

Nearly all family therapists are in agreement as to the necessity for avoiding taking sides with particular family members. Certain rules are also laid down by most therapists at the beginning of therapy. A primary rule is that anybody can say anything he wants to without being punished afterward, but that nobody has to say anything unless he wants to do so. There is a wide range of disagreement, however, as to the degree to which the therapist should interpret individual psychopathology as opposed to responding only to family dynamics. A questionnaire survey of 300 family therapists of various professions yielded such variety in this respect that it was decided to order therapists along a dimension ranging from A to Z (Group for the Advancement of Psychiatry, 1970).

A therapists are those whose theory and practice is similar to that of individual psychotherapists, except that they use family therapy as a supplement or occasional substitute for individual therapy. *Z* therapists, at the other extreme, think in terms of family systems for all emotional problems and tend to see several family members in all their therapy. The *Z* therapists represent the purer form of family therapy, but they are a small minority.

John E. Bell, in one of the first case illustrations of conjoint family therapy (1961), outlined several phases he generally finds in family therapy. The first phase is the *child-centered phase* in which the therapist builds a relationship with the children by being especially attentive to them, supporting their requests for changes in parental behavior, and tending to ignore parental criticism. In the second phase, the *parent-child interaction phase,* parental complaints about the children are prominent and the parents and children tend to talk *about* each other rather than *to* each other. In the *father-mother interaction phase,* the parents begin to express their conflicts with each other. These conflicts are generally assumed to be the cause of the identified patient's problems. As therapy progresses toward the *termination phase,* emphasis on the identified patient and parental interaction gives way to a focus on the interaction of all family members with one another.

There is no doubt that the situation created in conjoint family therapy brings a family's attitudes and ways of interacting into much sharper focus than can ever be achieved through individual therapy with some or even all the family members. Not only can the *in vivo* behavior of each family member be observed, but the specific stimuli provided by each family member to the others, the responses of other family members to these stimuli, and the continuing succession of stimuli and responses can be observed. In fact, observations on families in therapylike situations are being increasingly used for research on relations between child psychopathology and family behavior (e.g., O'Connor & Stachowiak, 1971).

Effects of Conjoint Family Therapy

Insofar as children's pathology is a function of familial pressures, the family therapy situation would seem to be better for ameliorating those pressures than one-to-one treatment in which a change in the child or a parent is by itself unlikely to alter the family dynamics very much. In conjoint family therapy, the presence of several family members and the focus on family interaction would seem more likely to insure complementary and lasting changes. However, there are so many variables involved, including the therapist's ability to respond effectively to entire families, that the efficacy of conjoint family therapy, like that of all other therapies, must be tested empirically rather than being accepted merely because the concept is inherently attractive.

In what may be the only adequately controlled evaluation of conjoint family therapy, young adolescent delinquents and their families were assigned to one of four treatment conditions (Alexander & Parsons, 1973):

1. behavioral family therapy in which therapists prompted and reinforced all family members for clearly communicating the substance as well as the affect of their thoughts, for clearly presenting their "demands," and for negotiating contractual compromises, e.g., through use of token systems;
2. client-centered family therapy;
3. psychodynamically oriented family therapy;
4. no-treatment control.

Six- to 18-month follow-ups showed the adolescents in the behavioral condition to have a recidivism rate of 26 per cent, significantly less than those in the client-centered condition (47 per cent), psychodynamic condition (73 per cent), and no-treatment condition (50 per cent). Thus, it appears that behavioral family therapy had significant benefits in reducing recidivism while the more traditional forms did not.

PSYCHOEDUCATIONAL APPROACHES

It is ironic that the agencies having the greatest responsibility for the largest number of children for the longest periods of time have traditionally received so little attention from workers in child psychopathology. These agencies are, of course, the schools. The simple facts that almost every child attends school, that educational failure almost automatically precludes normal adaptation in western society, and that most children referred for clinical help are having problems in school all highlight the crucial role of school in children's lives.

The role of the school was recognized very early in the development of clinical services to children. The first psychological clinic in America, founded by Lightner Witmer in 1896, was explicitly intended to help children with their school problems and to train practitioners who would work primarily with children in their schools. Furthermore, what became the cornerstone of psychological assessment, the intelligence test, was created for the purpose of finding appropriate educational placements for children.

Schools began in the nineteenth century to take responsibility for evaluating and educating children diagnosed as mildly retarded. However, theories of adult psychopathology focused attention on "emotional disturbance" as an explanation for problem behavior not attributable to low intelligence. When extrapolated downward to children, these theories implied that school problems were symptoms of personality disorder and that only treatment of the personality disorder could eliminate the symptoms manifested in school. Since clinical treatment of emotional disturbance was considered to be no more a responsibility of schools than was clinical treatment of organic disease, the early attempts to deal with many educational problems directly in the school soon gave way to the conviction that the school's responsibility ended when a child acquired the label of "emotionally disturbed."

A frequent consequence of labeling a child emotionally disturbed is that school personnel, often with the encouragement of clinicians, stop trying to cope with the child's behavior, partly out of fear of aggravating the child's condition. The label often provides a justification for excluding the child from school, or, if the school continues to tolerate his presence, it may stop trying to educate him. Another consequence is that "treatment" is seen as a panacea that will enable the child to rejoin the ranks of "normal" children and require no further special attention in school. While not all school personnel react to the label "emotional disturbance" in this way and not all clinicians encourage the cleavage between matters educational and matters clinical, the gap between the professions is wide enough so that communications between them are often reducible to the teacher's question, "Is the child emotionally disturbed or not?" and the clinician's replies in terms destined more to mystify than to help the teacher cope realistically with the child.

Special Classes for the Emotionally Handicapped

Virtually no locality in the United States has enough clinicians to treat all the children who *could* be labeled emotionally disturbed on the basis of their school problems. Moreover, even where clinicians are relatively plentiful, the gaps in time and effectiveness between the identification of school problems and clinical influence upon them are usually so great as to leave many children educationally handicapped even when the clinical outcome is deemed satisfactory.

During the early 1960s, the federal government and many states began to recognize the enormous disparity between the needs of children with educational problems and the meager resources being employed for meeting these needs. With federal support, many states enacted laws requiring local school systems to provide special instruction for "educationally handicapped" or "emotionally handicapped" children. Thus, the mandate of 60 years earlier that schools should take responsibility for educating the mentally retarded was broadened to include responsibility for children whose problems could not be attributed to low IQ.

Making schools officially responsible for the educationally handicapped was a great step forward. Now, according to the laws of many states, non-retarded children who did not cope well in regular classrooms could not simply be excluded from the educational process. However, the options open to most school systems remained limited—as school systems moved to implement their new mandate, they were faced with an almost total absence of teachers trained to teach the educationally handicapped and a scarcity of private educational settings in which children could be placed by those localities willing to do so. A frequent outcome was that extreme cases who could not be tolerated in school were given "homebound" instruction of perhaps a few hours a week by an itinerant teacher and that the less extreme cases were kept in regular classes but were no longer labeled emotionally disturbed, lest the gap between the mandate and its fulfillment become too obvious.

As more teachers have achieved state certification for teaching the educationally handicapped, more special classes have been set up and more of the most difficult children are being handled in these classes. There is evidence that placement in such classes can be beneficial, both educationally and behaviorally. Vacc (1968), for example, found that disturbed children placed in special classes improved significantly more on achievement tests and behavior rating scales from the beginning to the end of a school year than did well-matched disturbed children in regular classes. The disturbed children in the regular classes actually became somewhat worse, according to the behavior rating scales. A sociometric measure in which children individually chose classmates for positive and negative roles in a hypothetical class play also showed that the disturbed children in regular classes were selected for positive roles much less frequently and for negative roles much more frequently than were their normal peers.

Haring and Phillips (1962) found that a highly structured, academically programmed special class produced significantly greater gains in achievement test scores and behavior ratings for disturbed children than did a permissive special class or regular classes provided with many supportive services, including monthly case conferences with the teacher concerning each disturbed child. Children who returned from the structured special class to regular classes were also found to adapt well. The fact that the children in the permissive class started off at much higher levels than the children in the regular or structured classes makes it difficult to evaluate the differences between this class and the others, but it is clear that the structured special class produced greater benefits than the regular class.

In an exceptionally thorough comparison of the effects of structured but individualized special class programs with the effects of regular class placement for matched groups of disturbed children, Rubin, Simson, and Betwee (1966) found only small advantages for the special classes. However, in an analysis of a large number of diagnostic variables, they found that special classes were very helpful for certain types of children. The children helped most had perceptual-motor weaknesses and excessive inhibitions and withdrawal. The findings pointed to the need for precise diagnostic evaluation of children and adaptation of special programs to their specific needs.

Behavior modification methods for disturbed children in special classes were described in Chapters 10 and 11. Hewett (1968) has published an especially detailed behavioral program for educating emotionally disturbed children, including methods for controlling problem behavior, teaching specific subject matter, promoting social behavior, and evaluating results. He provides designs for optimal physical layouts, desensitization procedures for reducing anxiety about school failure before operant conditioning of new skills begins, and detailed lesson plans to aid the teacher in her role as a "learning specialist." Comparison of Hewett's classroom procedures with control procedures not using tangible reinforcers have shown that the children in the experimental classroom improved significantly more in attentiveness and in arithmetic achievement (Hewett, 1972).

Special Schools

As described in Chapter 12, some day and residential treatment centers for psychotic and other severely disturbed children are known as "schools" and provide programs primarily educational in nature. A broader educational approach for a wider range of disturbed children has been initiated under the name of Project Re-ED (Hobbs, 1966). Project Re-ED basically consists of residential schools in which new concepts of reeducation can be tried out, a new type of mental health professional—the teacher-counselor—can be trained, and the effectiveness of reeducation can be evaluated.

The children in Re-ED, aged 6 to 12, are average or above in intelligence, usually retarded in academic achievement, and not so disturbed or destructive as to require hospitalization, although there would be no other alternative for many of them without Re-ED. The goal of Re-ED is to provide about six months of reeducation that will permit the child to return to his home and school.

The primary "treatment" is not psychotherapy intended to "cure" the child, but ecological structuring intended to help him adapt to the outside world from which he came and to help his family re-establish the child in his own home, school, and community as quickly as possible. Controlling overt symptoms, building trust and a sense of competence, and enhancing cognitive control of behavior are important foci within the school program. To maintain and strengthen the child's relations with the world to which he will return, he spends weekends at home, his parents are involved in school discussion groups and activities, and the school social worker and a liaison teacher help smooth the child's way back into the public school and community. Costs of the Re-ED schools are approximately $25 per day, far less than those of long-term residential institutions emphasizing psychotherapy, where costs run as high as $100 per day over periods of several years.

In an evaluation of the effects of Re-ED, parents and the agencies that referred the children to the schools rated about three-fourths of the children as moderately to greatly improved following their return home (Weinstein, 1969). Symptom checklists filled out by the parents at enrollment and six months after return home also showed significant improvements in symptomatology, as did ratings on several behavioral and personality scales by the children's public school teachers. However, the children remained about as academically retarded as they had been before Re-ED and their public school teachers now rated them as having less ability than before Re-ED, perhaps because they no longer attributed the children's poor performance to emotional problems.

Other Psychoeducational Approaches

The expense of special classes guarantees that they will never become very numerous. The inevitable stigma and other disadvantages of putting children so conspicuously into the category of "emotionally" or "educationally" handicapped also makes it undesirable that children be placed in special classes except as a last resort. For many children who at some time have school problems not attributable to low ability, therefore, special class placement is not a viable option. Just how many children need special help at some time is suggested by a finding that 41 per cent of a broad sample of children in kindergarten through third grade had already repeated a grade, been placed in a special class, received special assistance from a school psychologist, social worker, speech therapist, or tutor, or had been rated by their teacher as having attitudinal or behavioral problems (Rubin & Balow, 1971). Although this 41 per cent included some children considered to be retarded and some with sensory-motor handicaps, it probably included only a small proportion of those who *at some time* in their school careers would have significant problems.

Since the advent of special classes for the retarded, many school systems have employed school psychologists having Masters degrees. The original function of these psychologists was to administer individual IQ tests in order to determine whether a child qualified for placement in a class for the retarded. With the development of personality tests and tests of perceptual-motor functioning, the school psychologist's diagnostic function broadened somewhat, but it remained primarily to make a general recommendation about class placement. Larger school systems often employ PhD level psychologists to do research, supervise pupil placement practices, and render a variety of counseling, diagnostic, and therapeutic services. Many school systems also employ social workers to meet with families whose children are having problems, and part-time medical and psychiatric consultants to make recommendations for children suspected of having organic problems.

Despite the provisions for mental-health personnel, they commonly operate in a rather piecemeal fashion. If, for example, a teacher's concern about a child eventuates in a request for service from one of the mental-health professionals, there is often a long delay before the mental-health worker is available to take up the child's case. Once the child's case has been taken up, the contacts between the teacher and the mental-health worker often consist of written reports, with the final recommendations of the mental-health worker for more individual attention, clinical treatment, etc., being avenues the teacher may have already tried or ones not possible for the teacher to undertake alone.

The Resource Room.   One approach to overcoming the fragmentation of educational and mental-health services for children not placed in full-time special classes is the "resource room." This is a room to which disturbed children go only during the periods of the day when they function least well in regular classes. Although resource-room programs vary greatly, the only controlled study of their effects has been with a behavioral resource-room program employing token and time-out procedures (Glavin, Quay, Annesley, & Werry, 1971). Disturbed children attending the resource room for one or two periods per day showed significantly greater advances in reading and arithmetic achievement, but no more behavioral improvement while in regular classes than did control children not receiving the resource-room program.

Classroom Consultants. A broader-gauged attempt at providing mental health services in schools has been described by a group working at the Yale Psychoeducational Clinic (Sarason, Levine, Goldenberg, Cherlin, & Bennett, 1966). Classroom consultants—psychologists who spent time observing problem children in classrooms—served as the key links in attempting to help children both in school and in treatment at the clinic. After a child was identified by his teacher or by the consultant as having problems, the consultant first attempted to identify classroom influences on the child's behavior. The consultant then met with the teacher to discuss ways of altering the class conditions in order to help the child. If the classroom situation was basically sound or if the teacher was unable to improve her handling of it, the consultant met directly with the child and, occasionally, with the child's parents to discuss ways of altering the child's school behavior. As a last resort, the child was seen at the Psychoeducational Clinic.

The clinic contact was worked out by the therapist and the child with the parents' permission. Unlike most clinic contacts, the child was fully involved in planning it, the nature of the clinic was explained by the consultant in advance, and, in many cases, the child was driven to the clinic by the consultant to prevent the missing of appointments so frequent with the inner-city children who made up the bulk of the clientele. The basic focus of the clinic contact was the child's school behavior, with nondirective therapy and help in schoolwork being used to identify the precise nature of the child's problem and to attempt to build up more adaptive school behavior. The Psychoeducational Clinic was also the site of ongoing group meetings between psychologists and teachers to discuss and attempt resolution of day-to-day school problems.

Although the variety of problems dealt with and the variety of ways in which they were handled precluded adequate controlled evaluation, Sarason et al reported that only one child was expelled from the four inner-city schools involved in the project, a rate significantly below the rate for these schools prior to the project and significantly below the rate for the 10 inner-city schools not involved in the project.

Preventive Measures. Just as schools can potentially play an important role in the treatment of many children, they are also in a position to play a major role in the prevention and early identification of psychopathology before it becomes severe. In one attempt to utilize this potential, all children scheduled to begin school were seen for an evaluation by a psychologist while their parents were interviewed by a psychiatric social worker (Newton & Brown, 1967). The aims of this evaluation were to identify techniques teachers might use with specific children, to make predictions about the children's adaptation to school, to advise the parents, and to provide interventions when necessary before the children actually entered school. Preschool interventions included arranging for needed medical attention, food from the welfare department, supervised group experience, and therapeutic interviews. After the children entered school, a stand-by interventionist was available to assist as soon as problems became evident. A five-year evaluation of children passing through the preventive program was planned.

Although not directly providing preventive services, a study by Bower (1969) was designed to provide tools for the mass screening of elementary school children to identify maladjustment which could, in turn, lead to intervention. Bower first had school psychologists and psychiatrists pick out children they believed to be disturbed. Personality and sociometric measures were then filled out by all the children in the classes of those identified as disturbed and teachers' ratings of adjustment were obtained.

The teachers rated as poorly adjusted 87 per cent of the children identified in advance by the psychologists and psychiatrists. Other children's ratings on the sociometric measure showed that the disturbed children were perceived more negatively than their classmates. A five-year follow-up of children identified as disturbed showed that, compared to classmates initially selected by teachers as having average adjustment, the disturbed children had significantly more police contacts, more referrals to guidance clinics, health services, and school guidance personnel, more school disciplinary actions, and more absences.

Further studies reported by Bower showed that nearly all the children in new samples who were identified as disturbed by teachers and sociometric and self-report measures were found upon individual evaluation to be disturbed, even though the psychologists doing the evaluations were blind to the results of the screening and most of the children had not been otherwise referred for special help. Moreover, a study by Stennett (1966) showed that classification by Bower's screening procedures was reasonably reliable in that 83 per cent of children were classified in the same way in two successive years in different class settings. Thus, if schools possess adequate methods for preventive intervention during the elementary school years, the tools for identifying candidates for such intervention are available.

COMMUNITY MENTAL HEALTH CENTERS

"Community mental health," "community psychiatry," "community psychology," and related terms are rapidly replacing terms like "dynamic," "intensive," and "depth" in many mental health workers' hierarchies of valued words. The 1960s and 1970s have witnessed a flood of publications emphasizing a community approach and the concept has come to cover an enormous range of activities and proposals. Rather than attempting to present everything that is now being tagged with the "community" label, the emphasis here will be primarily on two central foci of community approaches: The community mental health centers initiated by the federal government and the disadvantaged children whose needs present the greatest challenges to traditional mental health services.

Origins of the Centers

It might seem natural that the concept of community mental health centers grew out of the emphasis on community concepts that emerged during the War on Poverty. In fact, however, the governmental initiative that launched the community mental health centers did not originate in a special concern for the poor nor was it an outgrowth of the increased federal help for the poor in the mid-1960s. Rather, the concept of a federal program to create community mental health centers originated with the recommendations of the Joint Commission on Mental Illness and Health, established by Congress in 1955. After five years of research on mental health manpower and needs, the Commission recommended that reliance on large mental hospitals be replaced by a flexible array of local services for the mentally ill (Joint Commission on Mental Illness and Health, 1961). These services were intended to provide treatment at the first sign of serious disorder and to minimize disruptions in a patient's social relations to his family and community.

Several considerations dictated the commission's proposed reform of mental health services. One was the advent of tranquilizing drugs that enabled many patients to return quickly to their homes rather than become long-term hospital residents. Although the drugs did not bring about cures, and relapses occurred, the need to maintain a home, job, and family relations became much more salient than in the era when difficult behavior was treated primarily through continued incarceration. A second consideration was the advent of new concepts of treatment that emphasized the therapeutic properties of the social milieu and the negative effects of "hospitalism."

A third consideration was the commission's finding that mental health facilities were extremely inadequate for all but the very wealthy living in certain favored localities. For example, a survey of mental health resources showed that there were *no* mental health services for children in half the counties of the United States, less than one quarter of the counties had child guidance clinics, most of the existing clinics had long waiting lists, and there was little coordination among the available services (Robinson, DeMarche, & Wagle, 1960). The recognition that only programs initiated at the federal level could make an appreciable dent in such a massive national problem was aided, perhaps, by precedents set in the assumption of government responsibility for the millions of emotional casualties among the servicemen of World War II and the Korean War and by the founding of the National Institute of Mental Health in 1949.

A fourth consideration was the sheer arithmetic of numbers revealed in the commission's surveys. The ratio between the estimated numbers of people needing help and the number of mental health professionals projected for the future demonstrated conclusively that traditional one-to-one treatment could never meet even a significant fraction of the need. As a result of the commission's recommendations, President Kennedy in 1963 delivered the first message to Congress by an American President on the mental health of the nation. Congress responded by appropriating up to two-thirds of the funds necessary for construction and initial staffing of comprehensive community mental health centers by the states. The ultimate goal was to provide one community mental health center for approximately every 100,000 of population, a total of 2,000 centers by 1975. The centers were to offer inpatient and outpatient care and "partial" hospitalization in the form of night care for people who could work during the day, short-term hospitalization, and after-care for people who had been hospitalized. The centers were also to engage in consultation with other agencies in areas of education, research, and prevention.

In order to provide adequate staffing for the centers and for other needs, the National Institute of Mental Health set up a program that by the late 1960s provided up to 10,000 stipends yearly for graduate training in mental health professions. Money was also provided for basic research and for evaluation of programs. The vision of a coordinated national effort to reform the piecemeal and inequitably distributed approaches of the past appeared on the verge of realization. However, political changes in the early 1970s brought a sudden end to much of the federal support for the new efforts. Government stipends for the training of mental health professionals were eliminated as was much of the support for research and the establishment of new facilities.

Although forward momentum has been reduced, it is worthwhile to consider the current status of the several hundred community mental health centers that have been put into operation. A key issue for those interested in children is that the original report and recommendations of the Joint Commission said little about meeting children's needs. Eighty-five per cent of child clinics have waiting lists, as compared to 42 per cent of adult clinics (Rosen, Wiener, Hench, Willner, & Bahn, 1966), and over two-thirds of the 1.5 million children needing immediate care are not receiving it (Joint Commission on Mental Health of Children, 1969). Nevertheless, the emphasis was upon improving treatment for adults, who were already being treated in far greater proportions than were children.

The emphasis on adult treatment is understandable if one begins by viewing mental health problems in terms of the number of existing patients, how they were being treated, what the implications of the prevailing treatments were, and how much it was all costing. Half the hospital beds in the United States were occupied by mental patients. The Joint Commission estimated that the direct cost of mental disorders was a billion dollars a year in 1960 and that indirect costs were another two billion dollars, far more than the costs of any other form of illness. However, the most conspicuous costs were attributable to adult patients. Very few children occupy mental hospital beds (partly because very few beds have ever been allocated for them); few children receive expensive private treatment; no wages are lost by disturbed children; the immediate crime and welfare costs of childhood disorders are minimal; and child psychopathology does not cause the break-up or destitution of families in such obvious ways as does parental psychopathology (although there is evidence that a disturbed child can create family instability in less obvious ways). Moreover, mental health training and practice have been oriented toward adults to such a degree that most professionals have simply been more aware of the unmet needs for adult treatment.

Thus, in a spirit of "first things first," the primary focus of the community mental health centers was on adults. Even where there was an awareness that the community mental health center was an appropriate vehicle for improving services to children, these services were frequently among the first "frills" to be eliminated when the planning got down to the actual dollars and cents available from the federal and state governments.

In practice, some community mental health centers, especially those constituting the only resource in a given community, have provided services for children as well as for adults. Many of the centers have also taken up the challenge of providing new types of services to the poor who became the focus of the War on Poverty. This role has embroiled some centers in political and ethnic conflicts and has broadened their sense of mission beyond providing more-or-less traditional services modified to keep patients functioning in their home communities.

Evaluation of the Centers

While it is difficult to evaluate objectively the impact of a community mental health center on an entire community, many of the centers appear to have succeeded to some degree, both in their mission of preventing long-term hospitalization and in their newer mission of serving the disadvantaged on a broader front. The location of some centers in poor neighborhoods, their use of indigenous paraprofessional staff, and their orientation outward into the community-at-large through storefront branch offices and through neighborhood contacts have enabled them to facilitate the organization of new programs and to serve as intermediaries between warring factions, including local government officials and dissatisfied residents. Some centers have even served as refuges for neighborhood people during riots. They have also originated educational and preventive programs in mental health and drug abuse.

Another facet of the success of some centers, a facet that relates both to their original therapeutic strategy and to their functions on behalf of the poor, is that they have paved the way for new models for the staffing of mental health systems. Partly by design and partly because of the realities encountered, the traditional medical model for delivery of mental health services has been replaced in many centers by one in which medicine is just one of a number of specialties that may be relevant to helping disturbed people. Thus, the chief administrators of many mental health centers and units within them are nonphysicians such as psychiatric social workers, nurses, and psychologists, while physicians are employed by these centers to carry out roles that specifically require medical training, e.g., the prescription of drugs. The practice of choosing administrators according to their skills rather than according to a predefined hierarchy of professional titles has greatly expanded the pool of potential administrators. This practice has spread to other types of mental health systems, including state mental hospitals and departments of mental health, which were once headed exclusively by physicians.

While the early history of many of the centers was marked by uncertainty and turmoil, and the cutting off of funds now appears to have doomed the goal of a national network of well-staffed centers, the net effect of the original federal initiative appears to have been highly positive. However, since services for children have not been greatly benefitted, any new efforts should be directed much more intensively toward helping children, both through applying more systematically the knowledge we already possess and through developing interventions designed to have an impact on more aspects of children's development than our current piecemeal methods do.

DISADVANTAGED CHILDREN

Besides the community mental health centers, the other major focus of community mental health to be considered here concerns helping disadvantaged children, especially with respect to those of their needs that require the development of new perspectives by mental health workers.

The term "disadvantaged" is only one of a variety of euphemisms—including "underprivileged," "deprived," "culturally deprived," and "culturally different"— that have been used to designate children growing up in poverty. Although the term "culturally deprived" has been widely used, it is one of the least satisfactory because it implies that the basic problem of children is a lack of "culture." While a lack of exposure to certain aspects of the dominant American culture may indeed be handicapping in institutions based on that culture (e.g., schools), the term "cultural deprivation" carries the implication that culture is the unique invention of the dominant group and that the poor are without culture.

It has recently dawned on many who would help the poor that the absence of middle-class culture does not mean an absence of a system of values and customs, i.e., a culture. Instead, it is being increasingly recognized that *differences* in cultural values and expectations, rather than deprivation of culture per se, account for many of the differences in behavior between middle-class Americans and those of various poverty groups. However, the substitution of the term "culturally different" is not a satisfactory solution either, because it is not the cultural differences per se, but the facts of poverty, discrimination, and a high concentration of developmental risks, as well as certain cultural differences, that put many poor children at a serious disadvantage for achieving adequate education, health, and eventual self-sufficiency.

As with the other terms, "disadvantaged" can too readily become a euphemism implying a pejorative evaluation of the groups so labeled. However, it is intended here to refer only to the net result of growing up under social and economic conditions that place a child at a severe disadvantage in comparison with children of higher socioeconomic status. The most conspicuous concentrations of disadvantaged children are among the whites of rural Appalachia, the rural South, and certain inner-city areas, the Indians of the Midwest and West, Chicanos of the West, blacks in urban and rural areas of much of the country, Puerto Rican immigrants to the northern cities, and migrant farm workers of various ethnic groups throughout the country. In numerical terms, it has been estimated that one in four American children, over 19 million in all, are living in poverty (Joint Commission on Mental Health of Children, 1969).

The cultures of the various groups having high concentrations of disadvantaged children differ from one another in many ways, but the conditions their children face confront traditional mental health practices with similar challenges. The challenges presented by the problems of these children demand new approaches at the community level. Just as victory over most epidemic diseases has been won not by individual treatment but by public health, educational, and preventive measures—such as water purification, the teaching of sanitary practices, and vaccination—the problems of disadvantaged children are not likely to be met without action on a community-wide front.

Developmental Risks

It is all too easy to conceive of disadvantaged children as a homogeneous group suffering uniformly from the "disease" of poverty. In fact, the children are as varied as those in any other group. Poverty may create certain common experiences and values, just as affluence does, but neither the condition of poverty per se nor the cultures of the various poverty-stricken groups in this country are inherently pathological. The fact that a child grows up in a culture of poor people does not mean he is "sick." Similarly, scoring at the mean for his neighborhood rather than at the mean for a national sample on an IQ test does not automatically indicate that a poor child suffers from mental defect. Many children growing up in poverty actually manifest a great deal of zest, humor, adaptability, and resourcefulness that can hardly be termed pathological, even though some of their behavior deviates from the norms of the dominant culture. Many adults who have grown up in poverty succeed very well in the dominant culture, as the history of successive waves of immigrants conclusively demonstrates.

Nevertheless, there are numerous specific factors that create developmental risks for far greater proportions of disadvantaged than advantaged children. Moreover, most disadvantaged children are subjected to multiple combinations of these risks that may create different net impacts than would be expected from each of the risks encountered singly. Consequently, consideration of these risks in combination is an important prerequisite for formulating ameliorative procedures.

Organic Risks. The sequence of elevated risks for disadvantaged children actually begins long before the children are born. Since the parents of disadvantaged children have typically been raised in poverty themselves, it is important to consider the effects of their developmental history on the risks presented to their offspring. At the biological level, the nutritional and medical history of the mother affects pre- and perinatal risks for the organic development of her offspring. Evidence cited in Chapters 6 and 7 indicates that a poor early nutritional history in the mother increases the risks of difficulties during pregnancy and birth, which in turn can cause neurological damage in her offspring. Moreover, if the child is one of the mother's first, he is likely to be born while she is a teenager, when the immaturity of her reproductive system elevates the risks of birth injury. If the child is born when the mother is older, he is likely to have been preceded by a large number of previous pregnancies, a factor that also increases the risk of pre- and perinatal damage.

No matter where the child comes in the birth line, the poverty of the mother is likely to affect adversely her diet and access to medical care during pregnancy, thereby increasing the risk of prenatal damage. High rates of untreated venereal disease and other illness further increase the prenatal risk to disadvantaged children. Approximately 1,000,000 children are born annually to women who lack medical care during pregnancy or obstetrical care for delivery (Joint Commission on Mental Health of Children, 1969). Opiate dependence in the mother, as occurs among the poor of some urban areas, also creates the risk of prenatal opiate addiction in the child (cf. Chapter 14).

The mother's own experiences as a child in poverty conditions are certain to have shaped her attitudes about her own children. It is likely that her own birth was unplanned and unwanted and that she experienced much competition with siblings in seeking fulfillment of her material needs and needs for affection from her parents. Furthermore, her own mother's behavior is likely to have provided the model for her maternal behavior.

Since the rate of unmarried pregnancy is high among the poor—one inner-city New York hospital reports that 70 per cent of the births there are out of wedlock (Riessman, 1967)—the probability of the child's birth being unplanned and unwanted is high, thereby further increasing the likelihood that the mother will not be eager to care for him. A longitudinal study of young adults has shown that conditions of child-rearing are also likely to grow worse as the number of children in a family increases—the more children the young adults had, the more rejecting their attitudes toward children became, especially among those who had three or more children (Hurley & Hohn, 1971).

Taken at the point of birth then, the average degree of disadvantage already incurred by the child born into poverty is likely to be greater than that of the child born into more affluent circumstances. This does not mean that all poor children are already at a disadvantage, nor that organic disadvantages will inevitably prove to be handicaps in later life. It means only that the *proportion* of children with organic disadvantages is likely to be greater, that the disadvantages are more likely to be multiple, and that the parents' readiness to compensate for the disadvantages with extra effort and flexibility is likely to be minimal.

After birth, the organic risks remain far higher for poor children than for the more affluent. The risk of malnutrition is everpresent. Welfare and food-stamp benefits are received by only about 25 per cent of poor children. Even these benefits are significantly below the actual market costs of meeting minimum federal guidelines for an adequate diet (Joint Commission on Mental Health of Children, 1969). It should not be surprising, therefore, that surveys have revealed rates of anemia and other nutritional disorders as high as 80 per cent in the poor children of Alabama and Mississippi and 65 per cent in Washington, D.C. (Birch & Gussow, 1970).

Malnutrition not only slows growth and produces discomfort and lethargy, it also produces a greater susceptibility to infection and illness. Even if the increased vulnerability to illness does not result in organic damage, it can produce sufficient discomfort and incapacitation to interfere with important developmental tasks such as school learning and formation of good peer relationships. To complete the vicious circle, infection and illness in a person already malnourished can cause further malnourishment by decreasing food intake and increasing the rate at which the body consumes and excretes valuable food elements such as protein and vitamins.

Lack of adequate medical care and unsanitary and dangerous living conditions also increase organic risks for disadvantaged children. A widespread risk that has only recently begun to receive attention is lead poisoning caused by the nibbling of paint peeling from the walls of dwelling units. Lead poisoning directly damages the brain, causing mental retardation and even death. It is estimated the 600,000 children each year suffer lead poisoning and that 6,000 become permanently handicapped by physical or mental impairment (Dept. of Health, Education, and Welfare, 1972).

Physical abuse and neglect are also little recognized risks that, while not confined to the poor, are much more prevalent in poor than in better off families (Young, 1964). Just how appalling the picture is with respect to the organic risks for poor children in the United States and the known effects of these risks on school learning and other behavior is extensively documented by Birch and Gussow (1970).

Psychosocial Risks. The psychosocial risks of growing up in poverty have probably received more attention than the organic risks, but there is less agreement about just what aspects of the psychosocial environment are most critical. Based on findings that severe sensory deprivation in infancy adversely affects the development of experimental animals (see Chapter 6) and that institutional environments appear to retard human infant development, the hypothesis became popular that the below-average intellectual performance of poor children is attributable in part to sensory deprivation. However, visits to the homes of poor children, especially those in urban areas, clearly demonstrate that most of the children are bombarded with more sensory stimulation than children in affluent circumstances. Because large families are crowded into small quarters and crowding often exists in the neighborhood at large, the sheer number of interpersonal contacts is usually greater for the poor child than for the child growing up under less crowded conditions. Televisions and radios typically blare at high volume and street noises are inescapable in many houses.

Thus, with the exception of certain isolated rural children, most poor children are not likely to be suffering from a lack of sensory stimulation. However, the intensity and unpredictability of the sensory stimulation may prevent the child from gradually assimilating and organizing for himself a set of stable associations between his actions, physical objects, individual adults, interpersonal communications, and various forms of sensory input.

The facts that fathers are often absent, there are numerous siblings, and the mother has little time to interact with her child may also deprive the disadvantaged child of stable relationships with adults who encourage, reinforce, and channel his developing capabilities. What the child does learn from adults under these circumstances may be largely through modeling of their behavior, much of which—owing to lack of privacy—is likely to be inimical to the child's developmental needs. Delinquent behavior by adults and older youth also contributes through modeling to the high rates of delinquency found among disadvantaged children (cf. Chapter 13).

Not only relationships with adults but the child's physical surroundings are often transitory and impermanent. The family's emotional investment in its physical surroundings is typically low or negative, moves may be frequent, and there is little opportunity to develop a sense of order, regularity, and pride from one's environment. A poignant expression of a pervasive sense of impermanence can be heard in the conversation of many disadvantaged children for whom "Where you staying?" is the standard way of asking "Where do you live?"

Since the family owns little furniture or is likely to lose the better portion through repossession, there is little reason to think in terms of preserving it for future use. Similarly, whatever toys the child happens to acquire are subject to appropriation and possible destruction by other children in the family.

In sum, the kaleidoscope of sensory experiences and personal interactions experienced by many disadvantaged children is unlikely to provide consistent attention, affection, care, encouragement, reinforcement, and expectations appropriately geared to the child's growing social and cognitive potentials. It should not be surprising, therefore, that many disadvantaged children are ill prepared for the routines, responsibilities, and requirements of the educational system.

Educational Risks. While many disadvantaged children begin school with organic and psychosocial handicaps that might interfere with their adaptation in any event, differences between their cultural backgrounds and the typical school culture can make this adaptation still more difficult. The difference between the language spoken at home by many disadvantaged children and the language of teachers and textbooks has been a primary focus of theories and programs of compensatory education. Some theorists, such as Bereiter and Engelmann (1967), maintain that the primary disadvantage of poor children is that their native language is so impoverished as to prevent them from thinking adequately. According to Bereiter and Engelmann, the speech of poor children is undifferentiated to the point that they speak in word strings amounting to "giant words," rather than in sentences composed of well-differentiated parts of speech representing various logical categories.

Assuming that the absence of a given word in a child's vocabulary means the absence of the concept represented by that word, Bereiter and Engelmann approach remediation by teaching vocabulary words and specific linguistic skills in the hope of conveying the concepts represented by the standard language. However, research with congenitally deaf children, who have learned neither spoken language nor formal sign language, demonstrates that their cognitive development, as measured by nonverbal Piagetian tasks, is not significantly behind that of hearing children, at least through the elementary school years (Furth, 1966). Thus, the assumption that the language of the poor significantly interferes with their cognitive development seems unwarranted.

At the other extreme, Baratz has maintained that a primary reason for the poor school performance of disadvantaged children is that schools do not take account of the *differences* between standard school English and the nonstandard dialects spoken by the children (Baratz & Shuy, 1969). Baratz has, therefore, urged that children initially be taught using books written in their own dialects, with standard English being taught later as a second language. To demonstrate the influence of the differences between standard English and nonstandard black dialect in particular, Baratz (1969) has shown that white children have more difficulty than black children in repeating sentences recorded in black dialect, while black children have difficulty repeating sentences recorded in white standard English.

However, the degree to which black children's *comprehension* of standard English interferes with their school performance is questionable, since no difference has been found in the scores achieved by poor black children on individual IQ tests administered by black examiners speaking black dialect and by black examiners speaking white standard English (Quay, 1971). Moreover, in another study, poor black and poor white children were able to comprehend words spoken by an educated white speaker *better* than those spoken by either uneducated black or uneducated white speakers (Eisenberg, Berlin, Dill, & Frank, 1968).

Thus, linguistic differences do not appear to create significant handicaps for the *comprehension* of a teacher's speech by poor blacks and whites, perhaps because they are exposed to much standard English on radio and television before they enter school. Inability to *speak* white standard English may, however, adversely affect teachers' evaluations of poor children, and lack of practice in any form of English certainly handicaps Indian and Spanish-speaking children unless special efforts are made to teach them English.

Another way in which a poor child may be initially handicapped in school is by his unfamiliarity with school-type materials and lack of motivation to succeed with them. Most poverty-stricken homes have few books or writing materials, the adults in such homes do not spend much time modeling the use of these materials, and the child has little opportunity to gain experience with the rewards attainable from these materials because others do not often read to him nor encourage him to draw, write, or count.

The extremely powerful influence of adult modeling of schoollike activities can be observed very early in homes where reading is a frequent activity —the author has observed a child as young as eight months, not yet able to walk, who climbed laboriously up onto a chair to "read" diligently a magazine, even making the appropriate eye and head movements, in imitation of a nearby adult. Being read to provides an even more direct incentive for learning how to read, as evidenced by the many preschool children who spend hours "reading" stories from books they have learned by heart through hearing them read aloud. Woe be to the parent who attempts to skip a few words in a book familiar to the child!

In the absence of positive incentives in the home to acquire school skills and effective support from the parents once school begins, children who are motivated primarily to get tangible and immediate rewards are unlikely to put up with the frustrations of traditional schooling long enough to begin earning the satisfactions that come with intellectual achievement. Where disadvantaged children are in the majority—a frequent occurrence resulting from segregated housing patterns and the "neighborhood" school—the structures, techniques, and expectations of the traditional school are often hopelessly overwhelmed.

Most teachers cannot cope singlehandedly with the health, family, discipline, and motivational problems that must be dealt with before they can begin doing the teaching they were primarily trained to do. Consequently, the school often becomes the site of the most salient behavior problems of the disadvantaged and a primary source of referral for treatment.

Since effective treatment is rarely implemented, initial difficulties often touch off a vicious circle of frustration for the child as he fails to move ahead educationally, followed by rebellion or copping out which, in turn, interfere with further learning, and, finally, a reaction of anger or despair by the school, which may then terminate its efforts at serious education. The school thus becomes very much part of the poverty cycle and may do as much to perpetuate the disadvantages of many poor children as it does to educate those who are fortunate enough to have broken out of the vicious circle at some point.

Treatment for the Disadvantaged

Lest the foregoing account of risks imply that all disadvantaged children are hopeless bundles of psychopathology, it should be reiterated that many are no more "sick" than most affluent children. In fact, the evidence cited in Chapter 12 indicates that the most severe forms of child psychopathology, especially autism, are more frequent in upper- than in lower-socioeconomic families. However, the gross rates of child psychiatric and adaptive impairment, as revealed in a door-to-door epidemiological study, do increase as one descends the socioeconomic ladder (Langner, et al, 1970). Yet, income alone may not be an adequate index of disadvantage, as both black and Spanish-speaking children had approximately the same rates of impairment in low-income families (18 and 17 per cent, respectively) as they did in high-income families (19 and 15 per cent, respectively). This may have resulted partly from the fact that most of the high incomes in the latter groups depended on both parents working.

The rate of psychopathology in adults has also repeatedly been found to increase as one descends the socioeconomic scale, with an especially high concentration at the lowest level (Dohrenwend & Dohrenwend, 1965). However, several studies have shown that the proportion of disturbed lower-socioeconomic children (and adults) receiving treatment is below that for disturbed upper-socioeconomic people (e.g., Hollingshead & Redlich, 1958; Langner et al, 1970). Lack of ability to pay for private treatment is an obvious obstacle for lower-class children. But, even at clinics providing service on a sliding fee scale, studies have shown the following differences from middle-class clients:

1. Lower-socioeconomic parents are less likely to bring their children unless pressured by schools or law enforcement agencies (Furman, Sweat, & Corcetti, 1965).
2. Psychotherapy is less likely to be offered lower-class children (Harrison, McDermott, Wilson, & Schrager, 1965).
3. When psychotherapy is offered to lower-class children, it is more likely

to be done by trainees and nonpsychiatrists than by highly paid psychiatrists (Baker & Wagner, 1966; Langner et al, 1970).

4. Lower-class children are more likely to miss appointments (Speer, Fossum, Lippman, Schwartz, & Slocum, 1968).

Thus, even if traditional psychotherapeutic approaches for children could be shown to produce strong benefits, disadvantaged children are unlikely to receive those benefits. Furthermore, if the number of professionals doing psychotherapy were increased twentyfold, the economic barriers to treatment were suddenly abolished, and the waiting-list-office-hours-appointment system were replaced by a system in which access to therapy was immediate and not dependent upon parental involvement, even the most intensive forms of traditional therapy would leave the problems of many disadvantaged children untouched. The leverage that can be exerted on disadvantaged children's emotional life in therapy sessions is simply no match for the organic, social, and educational handicaps that continue to affect their lives outside the therapy room.

As a consequence, mental health workers must think in terms of breaking the vicious circle of poverty at every possible point. While many of the needed interventions do not involve direct one-to-one delivery of traditional mental health services, mental health workers should be in the vanguard of those representing the interests of disadvantaged children, since the mental health problems of these children are so often culminations of the multiple developmental risks they experience.

Some examples of vitally needed interventions that have to date been implemented only on a spot basis here and there are:

1. direct provision of nutritional and medical care to disadvantaged pregnant women, plus birth-control services to help them avoid unwanted pregnancies;
2. improved obstetrical services at birth and the provision of medical services and ongoing instruction to the parents in infant care after the child is born;
3. provision of adequate food directly to poor children and enough food stamps to ensure a healthy diet for the entire family rather than depending on parents to purchase food stamps with welfare or other funds;
4. mass screening for lead poisoning among poor children and immediate treatment for those discovered to have high blood-lead levels;
5. strict building code enforcement to eliminate peeling lead paint and other hazards;
6. provision of better housing, preferably in scattered units rather than in large apartment complexes occupied exclusively by low-income people;
7. routine preventive innoculations for the poor;
8. provision of care for the children of mentally ill parents while the parents are hospitalized and after their release—mental hospital in-

take procedures typically make no provision for ensuring that children of patients are cared for (cf. Rice, Ekdahl, & Miller, 1971);

9. greater legal authority for permanent removal of children from neglectful and abusive parents—under present laws, even when the lives of children are in danger, legal action can rarely be taken, few agencies can provide good alternative homes, and courts favor placement with the biological parents (cf. Young, 1964);

10. provision of day care centers offering meals, supervision by trained child-care workers, and educational programs structured to increase motivation for school achievement, to reward children for the constructive behavior necessary to acquire basic academic skills, and to enhance children's sense of intellectual competence;

11. increased usage of the educational potential of television, the effectiveness of which has been demonstrated by Sesame Street (Ball & Bogatz, 1972);

12. public school programs geared to mesh with preschool programs and individualized to maximize effectiveness in thinking and achievement at whatever rate a child is capable of, rather than attempting to raise IQs or to meet national achievement norms for each age—for some children, for example, delaying reading instruction in order to enhance motivation or to await sensory-motor maturation may be preferable to crash programs aimed only at the very early years;

13. provision of school-based recreational and educational activities after school hours and during vacations;

14. provision of a graduated series of mental health services rendered through the educational system so that problems requiring special treatment can be spotted early, dealt with first by consultation between school-based mental health workers and the child's teacher and parents, next through special modification of educational programming, and, as a last resort, through individual, group, or family treatment or behavior modification by mental health workers who work with the child and his family in their home if necessary.

While the foregoing may sound Utopian, all of the specific proposals have been implemented in some localities on at least a small scale or demonstration basis. Furthermore, both Houses of Congress in 1971 passed a $750-million bill establishing parent-child centers to provide many of the services just outlined. The bill was vetoed by President Nixon on the grounds that it threatened the sanctity of the family.

None of the above proposals requires a drastic change in current social and educational structure, although basic and applied research is necessary to develop optimal techniques for identifying, diagnosing, and treating specific educational and behavioral problems of the disadvantaged. Two requirements currently lacking are:

1. A commitment at the federal level to provide the plans, money, and personnel to initiate and coordinate the various facets of the needed interventions on a national scale. Local initiative alone is insufficient,

because localities needing the interventions most are those that can least afford to implement them.

2. The creation of a system of child advocacy agencies, at the state or county level, whose chief function is to make certain that children's interests are really being served.

The Report of the Joint Commission on Mental Health of Children (1969) contains a detailed proposal for a system of child advocacy agencies. While government bodies at all levels currently make laws concerning children and there is an enormous patchwork of services intended for children, the interests of children from multiproblem families almost inevitably become entangled in a web of agencies, laws, rules, regulations, and piecemeal mandates. It is especially to rescue children of multiproblem families from this web that child advocacy agencies, with the legal and financial powers to provide for the interests of children, are needed. In many cases, such agencies may reduce the costs of meeting children's needs by quickly obtaining appropriate services for a child and reducing duplication and competition among the myriad existing agencies, each of which is oriented toward only a narrow class of problems. Child advocacy agencies should be responsible for gathering data on the needs of children in specific localities and for formulating comprehensive plans for services to all children, rather than having responsibilities divided among legal, educational, health, welfare, and other agencies, both public and private.

Besides the need for overall coordination and advocacy on behalf of children, the creation of a full range of services for disadvantaged children would require an expansion of the function of schools to include more provision for the health and welfare, as well as the education, of children. Since schools already exist for children everywhere and school attendance is required by law, the school is a logical locus for expanded services. However, teachers should retain their roles as educational specialists while other workers are placed in the school to provide the additional services. Allowing children to retain the same teacher over more than one year might enable the teacher to become more effective in individualizing the child's educational program and in calling on appropriate supportive services as necessary.

EVALUATION OF TREATMENTS

Throughout the book, emphasis has been placed on the need for evaluating the effects of treatment. Intriguing theories have given rise to treatments that have often made "doing therapy" an end in itself rather than a means to producing measurable benefits for troubled children. Recently, the ideology of community mental health has given consultation to community groups a valued status equal to that once occupied exclusively by doing therapy. Perhaps because accountability to a community is an important facet of the ideology of community approaches, more attention has been paid to evaluating their effects than was true in the early years of individual psychotherapy, and attempts at evaluating community approaches are being made (Roen, 1971). However, the range of activities coming under the "community" umbrella, the short period they have been in progress, and intrinsic difficulties in defining specific targets for evaluation make it difficult to arrive at conclusions about their effects to date.

The picture is somewhat different in regard to the effects of individual and small group treatment. Without minimizing the complexities involved in evaluating these forms of treatment, it can be said that the target of change is the behavior of a specific child and, in many cases, his family. Moreover, despite their differences in interpretation of causes for psychopathology, there is a large area of implicit agreement among child therapists as to what changes are desirable. If therapists were to be polled, they would no doubt agree on the desirability of ameliorating most of the symptoms typically reported during diagnostic evaluations, such as distractibility, feelings of rejection, depression, destructiveness, encopresis, enuresis, excessive fears, fire-setting, nightmares, poor school work, poor peer relationships, etc. Their theoretical differences may cause various approaches to differ in *what else* they seek to accomplish beside symptom removal (e.g., strengthened ego functioning, less restrictive superego, greater sense of competence, more fully functioning personality), but a failure to ameliorate symptoms that interfere with a child's adaptation or reduce his self-esteem must be considered a failure of treatment. In this respect, the goals of nearly all child treatment may be more clearly specifiable than the goals of adult treatment, because many adults seek treatment to increase their sense of self-understanding rather than to ameliorate specific symptoms.

Research Designs for Evaluating Treatment

Since the minimal goals of child treatment are fairly clear, it should be possible to evaluate the relative effectiveness of various treatments according to the *parallel* design illustrated in Fig. 17–1. Three groups of children, Groups 1, 2, and 3, are matched on potentially important variables such as age, sex, race, socioeconomic status, diagnosis, and symptomatology. To compare two treatments with each other and with no treatment, Group 1 receives one treatment, Group 2 the second treatment, and Group 3 no treatment. A given treatment is not rigidly applied in identical manner for all children in a group, but the range of variation within a treatment group is assumed to be only what inevitably arises from therapist differences and from what is required for adapting the treatment to each child. This range of variation is assumed to be less than the variation between treatment groups. For example, if Treatment 1 is psychodynamic and Treatment 2 is behavioral, the therapists using Treatment 1 adapt their approach to each child, within the bounds of typical psychodynamic procedures but these therapists do not use the behavioral methods characterizing Treatment 2.

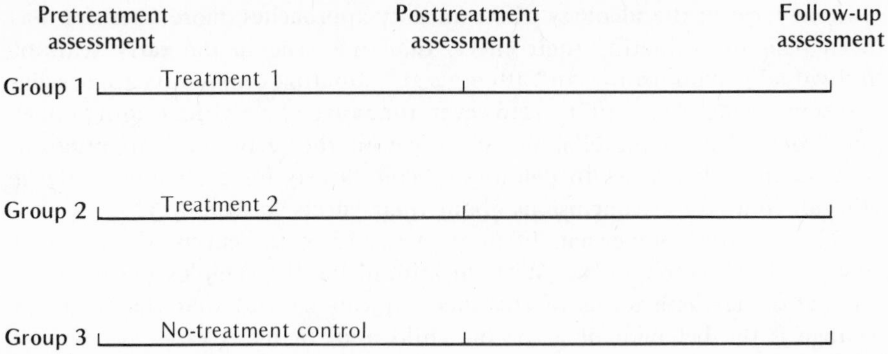

Pretreatment assessment	Posttreatment assessment	Follow-up assessment

Group 1 └───Treatment 1────────────────┴──────────────────────────────┘

Group 2 └───Treatment 2────────────────┴──────────────────────────────┘

Group 3 └───No-treatment control───────┴──────────────────────────────┘

Fig. 17–1. Basic design for comparing the effectiveness of various treatments and no treatment.

Following treatment, the groups are compared as to symptomatology and other relevant variables, e.g., parents' reports of global functioning, personality tests, school reports, and grade averages. They are compared again after a follow-up period of perhaps six months, a year, or two years. The follow-up period is essential because some changes may be only temporary and because some forms of treatment, such as the psychodynamic, are aimed at personality changes that are assumed to have long-term rather than short-term effects. The no-treatment control group is also essential because developmental changes may cause problems to take on new forms or to disappear entirely without treatment. In order to eliminate bias in the evaluation, it is desirable that the pretreatment, posttreatment, and follow-up assessments be done by people who do not know what treatment condition each child received. Since this requirement is usually difficult to fulfill, it is important that assessments be done by techniques that are as objective as possible.

Many variants on the general evaluation design are possible, such as comparing only one treatment group with a no-treatment control group, alternating treatments in opposite orders for two groups (the *cross-over* design), and instituting a treatment to see if it decreases symptoms, removing the treatment to see if the symptoms return, reinstituting the treatment, and so on, as in the *ABAB* design employed by operant conditioners and drug researchers.

Since it is unlikely that all therapists are equally effective with a given method or that a given method is equally effective with all types of children or all types of problems, more sophisticated *factorial* designs can be used to compare more than one therapist using each method and the effectiveness of each method with groups of children differing in various ways (e.g., age, sex, race, IQ, socioeconomic status, symptom pattern). Thus, instead of three similar groups of children receiving three different treatment conditions, as illustrated in Fig. 17–1, three types of children might receive each of three types of treatment in the 3 × 3 factorial design illustrated in Fig. 17–2.

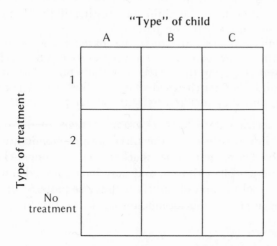

Fig. 17–2. Basic factorial design for comparing the effects of three treatment conditions on three "types" of children. The term "type" could refer to age, socioeconomic status, IQ, symptom pattern, personality pattern, degree of parental involvement, or the like.

Since no one treatment is likely to be equally effective for all children, it is important to determine what possible combinations of treatment, type of child, type of problem, and type of therapist are likely to be most effective, rather than attempting to squeeze each child into the mold of a single type of treatment or to depend on trying a large variety of treatments with each child before finding one that appears appropriate.

The practical difficulties of evaluating various combinations of treatment, child, therapist, and problem are great, but not insurmountable. When such designs are carried out, the results are often surprising and convincingly demonstrate the fallacy of applying a single general type of treatment to broad categories of children. One of the few factorial studies to examine the effects of several variables related to child treatment was detailed in Chapter 11 (Miller et al, 1972). Briefly, it was found that reciprocal inhibition and play therapy, both with experienced and inexperienced therapists, were significantly more effective than no treatment for 6- to 10-year-old phobic children. However, neither treatment, with either experienced or inexperienced therapists, was more effective than no treatment with 11- to 15-year old phobic children.

In one of the few other factorial studies of child treatment, three methods of treatment were assigned to children of three socioeconomic strata who were having school problems (Love, Kaswan, & Bugental, 1972). The three methods of treatment were:

1. child psychotherapy in which the therapists also met with parents and school personnel as they deemed necessary;
2. parent counseling in which only the parents were seen following one initial interview with the child and testing if the clinician felt test information would help the parents;
3. information feedback, in which the parents and school personnel provided their views to a counselor, the family was fed back similarities and differences among themselves and the school in their perceptions of their child, they watched videotapes of their own meetings with the counselor, and they met jointly with school personnel.

Figure 17–3 portrays the effects on grade averages of the three types of treatment for children in each of the three socioeconomic groups. As can be seen from the figure, **parent feedback** benefitted upper-class children, did not affect middle-class children, and may have harmed lower-class children. Parent counseling showed exactly the reverse pattern, while recipients of psychotherapy in all three socioeconomic classes declined in grade average.

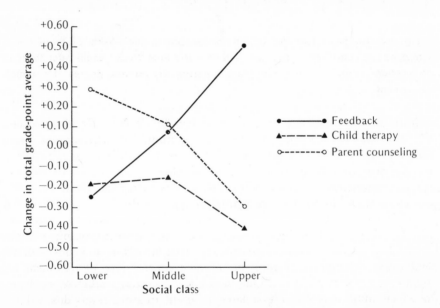

Fig. 17–3. Effects of social class and type of treatment on school performance. From Love et al (1972), p. 355. © 1972 by the American Psychological Association and reprinted by permission.

Although a true no-treatment control group was not included, a group of the subjects' classmates not referred for treatment but participating in a research project at the same clinic showed no changes in grade average. The results appear to demonstrate quite conclusively that psychotherapy was not beneficial for any of the groups and that the effectiveness of the other treatments depended heavily upon the socioeconomic status of the recipients.

Evaluation of Traditional Child Psychotherapy

In practice, psychotherapy of one form or another is by far the most common treatment for virtually all forms of child psychopathology except mental retardation. Evaluations of various types of psychotherapy and other treatments have been reported throughout the book as those treatments were described. However, much of the treatment actually rendered is an eclectic mixture of parental guidance, advice, psychodynamic techniques, and play therapy, couched primarily in psychodynamic terminology. Levitt (1957, 1963, 1971) has reviewed 47 studies evaluating psychotherapy as it is typically applied to heterogeneous groups of children in child guidance clinics. He concluded that an average of 66 per cent of the children had shown moderate or great improvement by the end of treatment and that follow-ups at a median of 4.8 years showed a 78 per cent improvement rate. Surprisingly, a similar review of reports of adult psychotherapy showed almost exactly the same average rate of improvement at the end of treatment, 64 per cent (Eysenck, 1965).

Since most of the studies did not provide control groups, Levitt (1957) attempted to obtain a baseline for outcome under a no-treatment condition by calculating the mean rates of improvement for child guidance clinic "defectors"—children who were accepted for treatment but whose families did not follow through in obtaining it. In studies of defectors, the mean improvement rate was 78 per cent in an 8- to 13-year follow-up (Witmer & Keller, 1942) and 70 per cent in a one-year follow-up (Lehrman, Sirluck, Black, & Glick, 1949). Clearly, the outcomes for the treated groups were not better than for the defector groups. In his review of the results of adult psychotherapy, Eysenck (1965) also cited figures indicating that untreated controls improved as much as or more than people receiving psychotherapy.

To obtain more information on defectors, Levitt, Beiser, and Robertson (1959) followed up treated and matched defector children seen five years earlier in a child guidance clinic. Follow-up evaluation data included psychological tests, the subject's statements about himself, interviewer's judgment of the subject, parents' evaluation of the subject and his symptoms, and objective facts like marriage, military service, institutionalization, and completion of schooling.

No more than chance differences were found between the treated and defector groups on the 26 follow-up variables analyzed. While the authors acknowledged that much of the treatment in their clinic was rendered by relatively inexperienced therapists and trainees, they pointed out that this is typical of most other clinics. Furthermore, length of experience and profession of therapists has been found to be unrelated to outcome of child psychotherapy (Lessing & Schilling, 1966).

As might be expected, Levitt's reports unleashed a storm of critical reaction from defenders of psychotherapy (e.g., Heinicke & Goldman, 1960; Hood-Williams, 1960; see also the 14 different critiques published with Eysenck's 1965 report). One target of criticism was Levitt's use of clinic defectors to provide a control baseline for improvement. It was argued that the parents of defectors had not followed through on treatment because the defectors were less seriously disturbed or had improved while awaiting treatment. Another criticism was that the length of the follow-up periods after which defectors were reevaluated was so great as to obscure any effects clinic treatment or its absence might have had.

Levitt (1960, 1963) rebutted some of the criticisms, but other studies showed that defectors had few problems of long duration and that fewer of them had spent time on a waiting list before being offered treatment (Cole & Magnussen, 1967; Ross & Lacey, 1961). These studies differed from Levitt et al's, however, in that they defined defection as occurring after no more than four or five treatment interviews, while Levitt defined it as occurring after only a diagnostic work-up with no treatment interviews. The minimum number of interviews qualifying as "treatment" was also greater in the latter studies, being 12 in the first study and 16 in the second, as compared to Levitt's criterion of five or more interviews. Thus, these studies compared cases that may have been differentiated more by *length* of treatment than by acceptance or rejection of treatment.

In a more recent study comparing children who received five or more treatment sessions with those who rejected treatment after receiving only an extensive diagnostic work-up (approximately 12 hours of contact time with family members), McAdoo and Roeske (1973) found no differences in parental MMPIs, IQ of child, number of children in the family, distance from clinic, referral source, diagnostic category, presence of brain damage, length of time on waiting list, duration of parents' concern, history of developmental difficulties, or presence of unusual symptoms. The only significant difference was in reported duration of symptoms, with fewer defectors than remainers having symptoms of more than a year's duration. The authors concluded that defectors do constitute an adequate control for evaluating the effects of clinic treatment.

Since McAdoo and Roeske made so many statistical comparisons, the difference in symptom duration could well have arisen by chance. However, this difference was also found in the earlier studies and could indicate greater recalcitrance in the remainers' problems than in those of the defectors. It is possible, for example, that, if the problems of the defectors were less recalcitrant, they improved spontaneously during the diagnostic work-up or the diagnostic work-ups themselves had a beneficial effect.

These possibilities suggest that considerably more attention should be paid to maximizing the therapeutic utility of the initial contacts. A still more important reason for focusing upon the initial contacts, rather than regarding psychotherapy as the primary source of benefits, is that very few children who reach clinics actually receive treatment. Nationally, only about one-third of those who are seen in child clinics eventually receive treatment (National Institute of Mental Health, 1966) and many who apply to clinics may never be seen at all, as 85 per cent of the clinics have waiting lists (Rosen et al, 1966). A breakdown of outcomes among families seen in a typical child guidance clinic has also shown that 24 per cent quit during the intake period, 39 per cent were referred elsewhere, 11 per cent refused treatment after it was offered, 19 per cent entered treatment but withdrew against the therapist's advice, and only 7 per cent received full treatment (R. G. Hunt, 1961).

The Buckinghamshire Study. In order to compare the effects of clinc contacts with no contacts, the problem of whether initial clinic contacts are beneficial can be circumvented by comparing children who have had no clinic contacts with those who have received treatment. As part of an epidemiological study, Shepherd, Oppenheim, and Mitchell (1971) obtained school records and parent questionnaire reports on symptoms displayed by a random sample of over 6,000 children throughout the county of Buckingham, England. From this pool of subjects, children who had symptoms but who had never received psychotherapy were selected as matched controls for children beginning treatment at child guidance clinics in the county. The parents of both the control and clinic children were interviewed in order to obtain a complete picture of their child.

After the clinic children had completed their treatment, the parents of both the clinic and control children were again interviewed and asked to fill out the initial symptom questionnaires. Separate reports based on the original and final interviews were prepared and submitted to clinical judges for assessment of improvement. It was found that 65 per cent of the clinic children were rated as improved, practically identical to the 64 per cent reported in Eysenck's (1965) review of adult therapy and the 66 per cent reported in Levitt's (1971) review of child therapy. Eighteen per cent of the children were rated as unchanged and 16 per cent as worse. Omitting the two who received treatment after the study began, an improvement rate of 62 per cent was found for the untreated children, while 29 per cent were unchanged and 10 per cent were worse. This distribution of outcomes was not significantly different from those for the treated group. Thus, again, the magic number was about two-thirds for those showing improvement in both the treated and untreated groups.

Since there were initial differences between the groups in socioeconomic status, loss of a parent, severity of disturbance, and degree of parental concern (all somewhat greater for the clinic children), it is possible that the clinic group actually had more recalcitrant problems. However, when both groups were divided according to severity of initial problems (mild, moderate, severe), the rate of improvement among the clinic children was found to be *greatest* for those with the most severe problems, while the rate was fairly constant for the nonclinic children at each level of severity. Moreover, division of clinic children into those receiving five or fewer versus six or more treatment sessions showed that, at each level of severity, improvement rates among those receiving *few* interviews were greater than for control children, while improvement rates among those receiving more interviews were less than or equal to those for control children. Thus, increases in amount of traditional therapy did not appear to be beneficial, no matter whether the child was rated mildly, moderately, or severely disturbed. Any benefits of clinic contact appeared to be obtained almost immediately.

Factors Affecting the Outcome of Traditional Psychotherapy

None of the above-cited studies of traditional psychotherapy was methodologically very adequate. Systematic evaluation before and after therapy and at follow-up were rarely made. Where control groups were used at all they were not well matched on all nontreatment variables. Creating *post hoc* control groups, as done by Levitt (1971) and Eysenck (1965) is an especially unsatisfactory procedure because of the large number of unknown ways in which the experimental and control groups may differ. Nevertheless, the uniformity of the findings with respect to the percentage improved under treatment and no-treatment conditions is surprising. Considering the variety of ways in which the studies differed, it is striking that evidence for the benefits of traditional psychotherapy is so meager.

While some workers have shrugged off the findings on the grounds that their own clinical experience tells them therapy *is* beneficial, others have attempted to determine with greater precision what variables affect problem behavior and how these variables can be manipulated. In addition to the introduction of new procedures, especially those broadly subsumed under behavior modification, attempts have been made to tease apart factors influencing the outcome of psychotherapy. Unfortunately, these attempts have so far been confined largely to research on adult psychotherapy. Yet they bear mentioning here because they provide guides for what must be done in order to determine what, if anything, is of value in traditional psychotherapy for children.

One of the most fundamental modifications in strategies for evaluating psychotherapy is a change in the basic question "Does psychotherapy work?" to a set of more specific but related questions: "What kind of treatment rendered by what kind of therapist under what circumstances will have what effects on what kind of client with what kind of problem?" These questions are best evaluated with *factorial* designs, as described earlier, wherein several combinations of clients, problems, therapy, therapists, etc., are evaluated simultaneously.

Re-analyses of the evaluations of traditional therapy have shown that some of the people receiving therapy do improve significantly more than those receiving no therapy, but that some receiving therapy actually get *worse* than those receiving no therapy (e.g., Bergin, 1971). The result is that the *average* degree of improvement for therapy and nontherapy groups appears the same, but that averaging obscures the different effects therapy has on different people. In order to improve treatment effects, it is, therefore, essential to find ways of identifying in advance people who will be harmed and those who will benefit from psychotherapy. If only those who can potentially benefit actually receive therapy, it may be possible to demonstate that traditional therapy is effective, while other treatments will have to be found for those who are harmed by psychotherapy. A repeated finding along these lines is that those who improve most in psychotherapy are the ones who initially have the greatest strengths in terms of adjustment, intelligence, education, socioeconomic status, etc. (Garfield, 1971; Luborsky, Chandler, Auerbach, Cohen, & Bachrach, 1971). This means that the people in greatest need of help are the least likely to benefit from psychotherapy even if they can obtain it.

Furthermore, differentiation of therapists according to their interests and personalities reveals two distinct personality and interest patterns that have been designated as *Type A* and *Type B*. The responses of Type A therapists on the Strong Vocational Interest Blank are like those of lawyers, author-journalists, advertising men, sales managers, life insurance salesmen, and real estate salesmen. Most individuals in these occupations have in common a disposition to "sell themselves," to be persuasive, and to be active and facilitative in interpersonal relationships. Type B therapists, by contrast, tend to have interests more like those in mechanical and engineering occupations. Numerous studies have shown that Type A therapists tend to do best with schizoid patients while Type B therapists do best with neurotic patients. The exact reason for these interactions of patient and therapist type is unknown, but it certainly appears to be a potentially critical factor in determining the outcome of treatment for adults (Razin, 1971). Similar distinctions may be important in child therapy.

One factor much more pertinent to child than to adult therapy is the involvement of the child's parents in treatment. A review of studies attempting to assess the influence of this factor has shown that results tended to improve as the focus of treatment broadened beyond the child himself, from child only to mother only, to mother and child, mother and father, and mother, father, and child (Levitt, 1971). However, these differences in parental participation have arisen spontaneously rather than by experimental design. It is possible, therefore, that the greater improvement found when both parents participated was due to the fact that these parents were more actively committed to helping their children. The extent and form of family participation is a variable that deserves much more study in relation to all forms of child therapy.

WHERE DO WE GO FROM HERE?

Having reviewed so many different aspects of children's problems and ways of understanding and treating them, the person interested in helping children must at last seek a vantage point from which to view prospects for the future. In many ways, the prospects for helping troubled children are brighter than ever before. Adults in many capacities are becoming more aware of the needs of these children and there is a new readiness to help children in new ways, most notably through the educational system. On the other hand, social and economic conditions continue to create developmental risks that can only be ameliorated through action coordinated and supported by the resources of the national government. Without a governmental commitment, it is unlikely that major progress can be made in helping the most needy of our children.

Assuming adequate public support for services to children, new conceptual frameworks and research methodology offer prospects for progress in the development, evaluation, and selective application of more powerful preventive and therapeutic techniques. One of the most significant signs of change is the growth of behavioral methods of treatment. In certain respects, these methods may have an influence on child treatment similar to the influence of drug therapy for adults during the 1950s. While behavioral methods may fall short of the claims of their more dogmatic proponents and they will probably not wipe out mental illness, behavioral approaches have brought a new emphasis on *specificity* in the definition, treatment, and evaluation of problems. They have thereby removed much of the mystique from psychopathology and its treatment and have challenged other approaches to justify their existence on a cost/effectiveness basis.

The extension of clinical services during the 1960s to groups not heretofore reached also created roles that were more readily filled by behavioral approaches than by traditional psychotherapies. Moreover, the simplicity of many behavioral concepts and their applicability in everyday situations make them more readily assimilated by workers outside the mental-health professions, e.g., by educators and those responsible for retarded and delinquent children.

The rapid rise of behavioral approaches and the benefits they may bring to the entire field should not, however, obscure the fact that much remains to be done to determine which methods are effective, with whom, and under what conditions. The evidence reviewed in Chapter 11 shows that, despite the much greater attention to evaluation than has characterized other approaches, only a few behavioral methods have been adequately tested for effectiveness. Unless behavioral methods are evaluated further and long-term follow-ups are done, their net effect may be more to add a new jargon and new dogmas than to help children.

Besides the advent of behavior modification, contributions from other sources are likely to play increasing roles in our ways of helping children. One source is the study of genetics. Research in genetics has already thrown light on a number of syndromes associated with retardation and may enhance our understanding of some forms of psychotic and delinquent behavior (e.g., as in the XYY syndrome). Of more general significance, however, is the light that genetic research may throw on the processes of normal development and on the interactions between specific genetic and environmental factors in producing phenotypic behavior. It may well be that studies of the heritability of traits like IQ, extroversion-introversion, anxiety, and schizophrenia can tell us more about environmental influences than will purely environmental studies. Thus, for example, comparisons of the environmental histories of people who are all believed to possess a genetic disposition to schizophrenia may tell us what *non*genetic characteristics lead to schizophrenic and nonschizophrenic outcomes. Such studies must include research on biochemical and other physical characteristics, as the crucial environmental events may be those producing organic effects, such as perinatal damage.

A Developmental Framework

Most crucial in the utilization of contributions from the various sources of knowledge, both new and old, is a conceptual framework for understanding each child as a whole, integrated, living organism who—unlike each of the specific organic, motivational, genetic, experiential, or behavioral influences—is the essential reality with which we deal. Any child is far more than the sum of the identifiable influences on him. Even when displaying "maladaptive" behavior, he is a highly adaptive organism whose troublesome behavior represents a complex adaptation to many facets of reality and his conception of it.

The study of normal development is most likely to provide the necessary conceptual framework within which to understand specific deviations. We already know enough about normal cognitive and socioemotional development to show that much "disturbed" behavior can be understood in terms of normal adaptive mechanisms that change as development proceeds. Erikson's (1963) outline of psychosocial development highlights the qualitatively different tasks and methods of coping that children display at various ages. Behavior that seems abnormal to an uninformed observer may be quite typical of children at a given age while they wrestle with a developmental task at the interface between societal sanctions and their own unfolding desires, capabilities, and fantasies. Much behavior that *is* indeed abnormal, in the sense that it deviates greatly from the typical developmental course or interferes with the developmental progression, may be an exaggeration of the normal range of coping behavior, due to specific parametric deviations in the child or his environment.

Similarly, the outline of cognitive development provided by Piaget portrays the sequence of changes and continuities in children's ways of knowing about themselves and the world. The basic biological push of all living things to adapt by means of modifying the self (accommodation) and modifying the environment (assimilation) is so obvious in children as to be often overlooked. Children's need to create an understanding of the world at their own level and the qualitative changes occurring in their systems of knowing are inescapable facts that must condition any adult view of child behavior and attempts to modify it.

Given the importance of a developmental framework within which to integrate the study of pathology, certain implications arise for modifying pathological behavior. One of the most important implications is that the accomplishment of specific developmental tasks is essential to the child's well-being in the long run. These tasks include satisfactory resolution of psychosocial conflicts like those outlined by Erikson (trust versus mistrust, autonomy versus shame and doubt, initiative versus guilt, etc.). These tasks also include the maintenance of a sense of competence and pleasure in constructive advance—abundantly evident in the delight healthy infants and young children take in novelty and in meeting the cognitive challenges they create for themselves. More specific developmental tasks include acquisition of the developmentally graded skills needed for adaptation in a given society—appropriate toileting, speaking, dressing, tying shoes, academic skills, and the social skills of making friends, dealing with strong emotions, learning cooperation, etc.

Although the developmental processes can go awry at many points—due to organic and experiential factors, parental behavior, lack of appropriate models, guidelines, and incentives, and unfortunate combinations of vulnerabilities and risks—the general goal of a developmental approach to amelioration is to help the child adapt and move forward through the developmental tasks in the best way possible for him. The best methods of amelioration may include environmental changes, family changes, organic treatments, prosthetic educational techniques to enable the child to learn as much as possible despite handicaps, modification of specific troublesome behavior that may be alienating others or preventing the child from moving ahead developmentally, and verbal counseling or therapy. However, for most children, the "treatment" should take account of the child's conceptions of himself and his problems, and of his potential for consciously striving toward solutions to developmental tasks.

Cognitive Aspects. Behavioral approaches and psychodynamic approaches have both tended to neglect children's capacities for constructive cognitive adaptation and reorganization. This neglect has resulted from assuming that the child's thinking is an epiphenomenon of his reinforcement history or of his unconscious motives and conflicts. Some behavior modifiers have attempted to take account of thinking by including symbolic mediation and self-control techniques in their paradigms (e.g., Bandura, 1969a), while some psychodynamic theorists have attempted to do likewise by proposing a conflict-free sphere of the ego embodying higher thought processes (Hartmann, 1939). However, neither of these solutions appears destined to advance very far beyond translating a few concepts of cognitive psychology into the language of S-R theory or psychoanalysis. While exercises in translation may be useful to show that there is a common ground of interest among diverse viewpoints, they are unlikely to provide an adequate paradigm from which research on the role of thinking per se can proceed.

In the study of many forms of pathology, it may be far more profitable to study thinking as a respectable independent variable that may be correlated with other kinds of independent variables or may itself provide a basis for predicting important behavior. For example, a child's symptom pattern may represent his strategy for coping with "reality" as "reality" is mentally represented by the child. His mental representations are end-products of all his specific organic and experiential parameters, but these representations, rather than the separate effects of each parameter, serve as the most salient guides to his behavior. Constructive modification of his behavior may, therefore, be possible by altering his representations and his strategies for coping.

One means of intervention is at a verbal level through which the child is helped to reorient his representations away from the past in which they were shaped and toward present and future developmental goals. Another line of intervention may be through the direct amelioration of anxiety, fears, and deficits in social or academic skills or the like which contribute to a view of the self that is not oriented toward further development. Still another line of intervention may be through the amelioration of environmental pressures that are constraining the child's opportunities for more constructive adaptation. In most cases, a combination of methods is likely to be needed to give the child the opportunity to change his strategies for coping, to help him make the changes, and to help him acquire new capabilities that will make the new strategies viable as he faces new developmental tasks.

The essential point is that children are biologically and cognitively designed for adaptation and change. Treatments are valuable insofar as they remove obstacles to development and provide support for it. The most promising avenue for the improvement of child treatment may, therefore, be to gear treatment to a child's current strategies and capabilities for adaptation and, as far as possible, to his cognitive representations of his current status. Except in the case of specific organic disorders directly curable by medical means, treatment should then be directed toward reorienting the child toward developmental advancement.

SUMMARY

Nondirective play therapy is an extension to children of Carl Rogers' client-centered therapy for adults. Controlled studies have demonstrated benefits for somewhat maladjusted children receiving play therapy without the involvement of their parents. *Filial therapy* is a variant of play therapy in which parents are trained to conduct play sessions with their own disturbed children. Improvements in parents' therapeutic skills have been found during filial therapy, but changes in their children have not been reported.

Forms of group therapy used with children include *psychodrama, activity groups, activity-interview groups, nondirective group play therapy,* and the application of behavior modification techniques in group situations. The latter have been shown to have significant benefits, but little evaluative research has been done on the more traditional forms of child group therapy.

In *conjoint family therapy,* an entire family meets together for therapy sessions. Based on the assumption that a child's symptoms result from pressures within the family system, the objective is to modify the behavior of the family rather than that of the *identified patient* alone. Despite an increasing number of descriptive works on family therapy, there has been little controlled evaluative research on its effects, although behaviorally oriented family therapy has been found superior to client-centered and psychodynamically oriented family therapy.

Psychoeducational approaches to child psychopathology have included special classes, special schools, "helping teachers," resource rooms, classroom consultants, and procedures for early identification of emotional problems in school. Evaluative research has demonstrated that some of the psychoeducational approaches are effective and that schools can play an important role in prevention and treatment of child psychopathology.

Community mental health has become a prominent focus for the mental health professions. Several hundred community mental health centers were established under a federal program before it was prematurely curtailed in the early 1970s. The centers offer a variety of preventive and short-term treatment programs aimed at avoiding long-term hospitalization, primarily for adults.

Helping disadvantaged children has been another objective of community mental health activities. The high concentration of developmental risks faced by disadvantaged children makes traditional one-to-one treatment methods unlikely to have significant effects. Widespread risks include pre- and perinatal damage, malnutrition, lead poisoning, elevated rates of illness, physical abuse and neglect, lack of concerned adult attention, poor role models, lack of incentives for behavior compatible with school learning, and lack of flexibility and resources in schools for adapting to the needs of the disadvantaged.

While the above disadvantages do not necessarily create severe psychopathology, they do handicap many children during the course of development. Closely coordinated help, beginning with birth control services and nutritional and medical aid for pregnant women, nutritional and medical care for their children from birth onward, day care and early education closely geared to later public school education, and early identification of behavioral and family problems are needed to help break the poverty cycle at all possible points. *Child advocacy agencies* are also necessary to insure that all children receive the services they need without the delays, duplication, and fragmentation that are typical today.

Research designs for evaluating the effectiveness of treatment include the *parallel, cross-over, ABAB,* and *factorial* designs. The factorial design is typically the most powerful for identifying effective combinations of treatment, child, problem, therapist, etc. The few well-controlled factorial studies of child treatment have exposed the fallacy of applying a single general type of treatment to broad categories of children.

Numerous rather crude studies have shown that approximately two-thirds of children and adults receiving traditional psychotherapy improve, while approximately the same proportion not receiving therapy also improve. More detailed analyses have shown that some clients improve significantly more with therapy, while others get worse, that clients with the greatest initial strengths and advantages improve the most, and that certain types of therapists do best with certain types of clients.

It was proposed that understanding and treatment of child psychopathology would benefit from a conceptual framework based on knowledge of normal development and that treatment should help children orient themselves toward the achievement of developmental goals.

SUGGESTED READING

Nondirective Play Therapy. One of its chief exponents, Virginia Axline, has written a detailed presentation of play therapy in diverse contexts (1969) and a full-length case history poignantly portraying a particularly successful case (1964).

Group Therapy. Rose (1972) has provided an extensive and detailed guide to behavioral methods for use with groups of disturbed children. Guides to nondirective group play therapy have been written by Ginott (1961) and by Schiffer (1969).

Family Therapy. There has recently been a small explosion of zealous and fascinating writings on conjoint family therapy, although they are short on objective evaluation of its effects. Satir (1967) offers a detailed presentation of her approach, while books by Ferber, Mendelsohn, and Napier (1972), Haley (1971), and Zuk (1971) include contributions by a wide variety of practitioners.

Community Mental Health. The dimensions of the problems we face in child mental health, the sources of the problems, the inadequacy of the resources for dealing with these problems, and recommendations for government action are contained in *Crisis in Child Mental Health: Challenge for the 1970s,* which is the report of the Joint Commission on Mental Health of Children (1969), originally appointed by Congress in 1965. Many publications have recently appeared on disadvantaged children, but three that provide valuable perspectives on problems of concern to mental health workers are: Baughman and Dahlstrom's (1968) *Negro and White Children,* a detailed empirical study of the personalities and school behavior of children in a poor area of the South from which many migrate to urban slums; Birch and Gussow's (1970) book, *Disadvantaged Children: Health, Nutrition, and School Failure,* which documents the existence and effects of organic risks; and Young's (1964) book, entitled *Wednesday's Children,* a portrayal of just how extreme is the abuse and neglect suffered by many children in this country, not all of them economically disadvantaged.

Some initial efforts at systematic evaluation of community interventions have been reviewed by Roen (1971). Summaries of various issues in the implementation and evaluation of community and preventive mental health activities have been presented in a volume prepared by Division 27 of the American Psychological Association (1971).

Evaluation of Psychotherapy.   Meltzoff and Kornreich (1970) have written a detailed review and critique of studies on the outcome of psychotherapy, although—reflecting the state of the field—it deals almost exclusively with research on adults.   A book edited by Bergin and Garfield (1971) constitutes a good reference source on the empirical evaluation of psychotherapy. It contains papers by a large variety of authors on psychotherapy research, again, almost but not quite, exclusively with adults.

References

Bracketed numbers following each reference are the pages on which the reference is cited in the text.

ACHENBACH, T. M. The classification of children's psychiatric symptoms: A factor-analytic study. *Psychological Monographs,* 1966, **80**(Whole No. 615). [49, 57, 63, 303–304, 378, 470, 501, 555, 558–559]

ACHENBACH, T. M. Conservation of illusion distorted identity: Its relation to MA and CA in normals and retardates. *Child Development,* 1969, **40**, 663–679. [245, 470]

ACHENBACH, T. M. Comparison of Stanford-Binet performance of nonretarded and retarded persons matched for MA and sex. *American Journal of Mental Deficiency,* 1970, **74**, 488–494. (a) [245]

ACHENBACH, T. M. The Children's Associative Responding Test: A possible alternative to group IQ tests. *Journal of Educational Psychology,* 1970, **61**, 340–348. (b) [207, 249]

ACHENBACH, T. M. Stanford-Binet short-form performance of retarded and non-retarded persons matched for MA. *American Journal of Mental Deficiency,* 1971, **76**, 30–32. (a) [245]

ACHENBACH, T. M. The Children's Associative Responding Test: A two-year follow-up. *Developmental Psychology,* 1971, **5**, 477–483. (b) [249]

ACHENBACH, T. M. Surprise and memory as indices of concrete operational development. *Psychological Reports,* 1973, **33**, 47–57. [246]

ACHENBACH, T. M., & LEWIS, M. A proposed model for clinical research and its application to encopresis and enuresis. *Journal of the American Academy of Child Psychiatry,* 1971, **10**, 535–554. [318, 382, 560–561]

ACHENBACH, T. M., & ZIGLER, E. Cue-learning and problem-learning strategies in normal and retarded children. *Child Development,* 1968, **39**, 827–848. [249]

ACKERMAN, N. W. The role of the family in the emergence of child disorders. In E. Miller (Ed.), *Foundations of child psychiatry.* New York: Pergamon Press, 1968. Pp. 509–533. [592]

ADAMS, S. The PICO project. In N. Johnston, L. Savitz, & M. E. Wolfgang (Eds.), *The sociology of punishment and correction.* New York: Wiley, 1962. Pp. 213–224. [505]

AINSWORTH, M. D. S. Object relations, dependency, and attachment: A theoretical review of the infant-mother relationship. *Child Development,* 1969, **40**, 969–1025. [99, 137]

AINSWORTH, M. D. S., & BELL, S. M. Attachment, exploration, and separation: Illustrated by the behavior of one-year-olds in a strange situation. *Child Development,* 1970, **41**, 49–67. [99, 137]

ALEXANDER, F. *Psychosomatic medicine.* New York: Norton, 1950. [181]

ALEXANDER, F., FRENCH, T. M., & POLLACK, G. H. *Psychosomatic specificity.* Vol. 1. Chicago: University of Chicago Press, 1968. [175]

ALEXANDER, J. F., & PARSONS, B. V. Short-term behavioral intervention with delinquent families: Impact on family process and recidivism. *Journal of Abnormal Psychology,* 1973, **81**, 219–225. [509, 613–14]

ALLEN, J., DeMYER, M. K., NORTON, J. A., PONTIUS, W., & YANG, E. Intellectuality in parents of psychotic, subnormal, and normal children. *Journal of Autism and Childhood Schizophrenia,* 1971, **1**, 311–326. [440]

ALLEN, K. E., HART, B., BUELL, J. S., HARRIS, F. R., & WOLF, M. M. Effects of social reinforcement on isolate behavior of a nursery school child. *Child Development,* 1964, **35**, 511–518. [357–358]

ALLEN, K. E., HENKE, L. B., HARRIS, F. R., BAER, D. M., & REYNOLDS, N. J. Control of hyperactivity by social reinforcement of attending behavior. *Journal of Educational Psychology,* 1967, **50**, 231–237. [384]

ALLEN, M. G., COHEN, S., & POLLIN, W. Schizophrenia in veteran twins: A diagnostic review. *American Journal of Psychiatry,* 1972, **128**, 939–945. [428–429]

ALLPORT, G. W. *Personality: A psychological interpretation.* New York: Holt, 1937. [50]

American Journal of Diseases of Children. 1969, 118(2), 22–23. [183]

American Psychiatric Association. *Diagnostic and statistical manual of mental disorders.* Washington, D.C.: American Psychiatric Association, (1st ed.), 1952; (2nd ed.), 1968. [26, 57, 62–68, 178, 437, 492, 542, 544, 565]

AMES, L. B., LEARNED, J., METRAUX, R., & WALKER, R. *Child Rorschach responses.* New York: Harper, 1952. [581, 602]

ANASTASI, A. Heredity, environment, and the question "how"? *Psychological Review* 1958, **65**, 197–208. [137]

ANDERSON, L. M. Personality characteristics of parents of neurotic, aggressive, and normal preadolescent boys. *Journal of Clinical and Consulting Psychology,* 1969, **33**, 575–581. [561, 592]

ANDREW, G., HARTWELL, S. W., HUTT, M. L., & WALTON, R. E. *The Michigan Picture Test.* Chicago: Science Research Associates, 1953. [585]

ANDREWS, J. D. W. Psychotherapy of phobias. *Psychological Bulletin,* 1966, **66**, 455–480. [292]

ANOKHIN, P. K. Systemogenesis as a general regulator of brain development. *Progress in Brain Research,* 1964, **9**, 54–86. [151]

ANTHONY, E. J. The behavior disorders of childhood. In P. H. Mussen (Ed.), *Carmichael's manual of child psychology.* New York: Wiley, 1970, Vol. 1. Pp. 667–764. [562–564]

ANTHONY, E. J. A clinical and experimental study of high risk children and their schizophrenic parents. In A. R. Kaplan (Ed.), *Genetic factors in "schizophrenia."* Springfield, Ill.: Thomas, 1972. Pp. 380–406. [423–424]

ANTHONY, E. J., & SCOTT, P. Manic-depressive psychosis in childhood. *Journal of Child Psychology and Psychiatry,* 1960, **1**, 53–72. [410–411]

ARMENTROUT, J. A. Parental child-rearing attitudes and preadolescents' problem behaviors. *Journal of Consulting and Clinical Psychology,* 1971, **37**, 278–285. [561]

ASCOUGH, J. C., & SIPPRELLE, C. N. Operant verbal conditioning of autonomic response. *Behavior Research and Therapy,* 1968, **6**, 363–370. [177]

ASHEM, B., & DONNER, L. Covert sensitization with alcoholics: A controlled replication. *Behavior Research and Therapy,* 1968, **6,** 7–12. [366]

ASSAEL, M., KOHEN-RAZ, R., & ALPERN, S. Developmental analysis of EEG abnormalities in juvenile delinquents. *Diseases of the Nervous System,* 1967, **28,** 49–54. [497]

ASTIN, A. The functional autonomy of psychotherapy. *American Psychologist,* 1961, **16,** 75–78. [339]

ATKINSON, J. W. *Motives in fantasy, action, and society.* Princeton, N.J.: Van Nostrand, 1958. [583]

AUERBACH, A. H., & LUBORSKY, L. Accuracy of judgments and the nature of the "good hour." In J. M. Shlien (Ed.), *Research in psychotherapy.* Washington, D.C.: American Psychological Association, 1968. Vol. III. Pp. 155–168. [316–317]

AX, A. F. The physiological differentiation between fear and anger in humans. *Psychosomatic Medicine,* 1953, **15,** 433–442. [176]

AXLINE, V. M. *Dibs: In search of self.* New York: Houghton Mifflin, 1964. [608, 649]

AXLINE, V. M. *Play therapy.* (Rev. ed.) New York: Ballantine Books, 1969. [46, 68, 607–608, 649]

AYLLON, T., & AZRIN, N. H. *The token economy: A motivational system for therapy and rehabilitation.* New York: Appleton-Century-Crofts, 1968. [359, 407]

AZRIN, N. H., HUTCHINSON, R. R., & HAKE, D. F. Extinction-induced aggression. *Journal of the Experimental Analysis of Behavior,* 1966, **9,** 191–204. [466]

BACHRACH, A. J., ERWIN, W. J., & MOHR, J. P. The control of eating behavior in an anorexic by operant conditioning techniques. In L. P. Ullmann & L. Krasner (Eds.), *Case studies in behavior modification.* New York: Holt, 1965. Pp. 153–163. [178, 382]

BAER, D. M., & WOLF, M. M. The reinforcement contingency in preschool and remedial education. In R. D. Hess & R. M. Baer (Eds.), *Early education: Current theory, research, and action.* Chicago: Aldine, 1968. Pp. 119–129. [357]

BAKER, B. L. Symptom treatment and symptom substitution in enuresis. *Journal of Abnormal Psychology,* 1969, **74,** 42–49. [382, 400–401]

BAKER, B. L. *READ PROJECT.* Cambridge, Mass.: Behavioral Education Projects, 1973. [574]

BAKER, J. Q., & WAGNER, N. N. Social class and treatment in a child psychiatry clinic. *Archives of General Psychiatry,* 1966, **14,** 129–133. [632]

BALL, J. C., & CHAMBERS, C. D. *The epidemiology of opiate addiction in the United States.* Springfield, Ill.: Thomas, 1970. [541]

BALL, R. S. The predictability of occupational level from intelligence. *Journal of Consulting Psychology,* 1938, **2,** 184–186. [208]

BALL, S., & BOGATZ, G. A. Summative research of Sesame Street: Implications for the study of preschool children. In A. D. Pick (Ed.), *Minnesota Symposia on Child Psychology.* Minneapolis: University of Minnesota Press, 1972. Vol. 6. Pp. 3–17. [633]

BALLER, W. R. A study of the present social status of a group of adults who, when they were in elementary school, were classified as mentally deficient. *Genetic Psychology Monographs,* 1936, **18,** 165–244. [251]

BALLER, W. R., CHARLES, D. C., & MILLER, E. L. Mid-life attainment of the mentally retarded: A longitudinal study. *Genetic Psychology Monographs,* 1967, **75,** 235–329. [193, 251]

BANDURA, A. Influence of models' reinforcement contingencies on the acquisition of imitative responses. *Journal of Personality and Social Psychology,* 1965, **1,** 589–595. [469]

BANDURA, A. *Principles of behavior modification.* New York: Holt, Rinehart, & Winston. 1969. (a) [367, 373, 469, 646]

BANDURA, A. Social-learning theory of identificatory processes. In D. A. Goslin (Ed.), *Handbook of socialization theory and research.* Chicago: Rand McNally, 1969. Pp. 213–262. (b) [469]

BANDURA, A., BLANCHARD, E. B., & RITTER, B. Relative efficacy of desensitization and modeling approaches for inducing behavioral, affective, and attitudinal changes. *Journal of Personality and Social Psychology,* 1969, **13,** 173–199. [368, 394, 396]

BANDURA, A., GRUSEC, J. E., & MENLOVE, F. L. Vicarious extinction of avoidance behavior. *Journal of Personality and Social Psychology,* 1967, **5,** 16–23. [368, 377, 397–398]

BANDURA, A., & MENLOVE, F. L. Factors determining vicarious extinction of avoidance behavior through symbolic modeling. *Journal of Personality and Social Psychology,* 1968, **8,** 99–108. [377, 397]

BANDURA, A., ROSS, D., & ROSS, S. A. Imitation of film-mediated aggressive models. *Journal of Abnormal and Social Psychology,* 1963, **66,** 3–11. [469]

BANDURA, A., & WALTERS, R. *Adolescent aggression.* New York: Ronald Press, 1959. [385, 469, 515]

BANDURA, A., & WALTERS, R. *Social learning and personality development.* New York: Holt, Rinehart, & Winston, 1963. [342, 397]

BANGS, J. L., & FREIDINGER, A. Diagnosis and treatment of a case of hysterical aphasia in a thirteen-year-old girl. *Journal of Speech and Hearing Disorders,* 1949, **14,** 312–317. [381]

BANNISTER, D., SALMON, P., & LEIBERMAN, D. M. Diagnosis-treatment relationships in psychiatry: A statistical analysis. *British Journal of Psychiatry,* 1964, **110,** 726–732. [545–546]

BARATZ, J. C. A bi-dilectal task for determining language proficiency in economically disadvantaged Negro children. *Child Development,* 1969, **40,** 889–901. [629]

BARATZ, J. C., & SHUY, R. W. (Eds.), *Teaching black children to read.* Washington, D.C.: Center for Applied Linguistics, 1969. [629]

BARGLOW, P., BORNSTEIN, M. B., EXUM, D. B., WRIGHT, M. K., & VISOTSKY, H. M. Some psychiatric aspects of illegitimate pregnancy during early adolescence. *American Journal of Orthopsychiatry,* 1967, 37, 266–267. [501]

BARLOW, D. H., LEITENBERG, H., & AGRAS, W. S. Experimental control of sexual deviation through manipulation of the noxious scene in covert sensitization. *Journal of Abnormal Psychology,* 1969, **74,** 597–601. [366]

BAROFF, G. S., & TATE, B. G. The use of aversive stimulation in the treatment of chronic self-injurious behavior. *Journal of the American Academy of Child Psychiatry,* 1968, **7,** 454–470. [455]

BARRON, F., & LEARY, T. F. Changes in psychoneurotic patients with and without therapy. *Journal of Consulting Psychology,* 1955, **19,** 239–245. [328]

BASSER, L. S. Hemiplegia of early onset and the faculty of speech with special reference to the effects of hemispherectomy. *Brain,* 1962, **85,** 427–460. [155]

BAUGHMAN, E. E., & DAHLSTROM, W. G. *Negro and white children: A psychological study in the rural South.* New York: Academic Press, 1968. [590, 650]

BAYLEY, N. Consistency and variability in the growth of intelligence from birth to eighteen years. *Journal of Genetic Psychology,* 1949, **75,** 165–196. [212, 240]

BAYLEY, N. Learning in adulthood: The role of intelligence. In H. J. Klausmeier and C. W. Harris (Eds.), *Analyses of concept learning.* New York: Academic Press, 1966. Pp. 117–138. [252]

BAYLEY, N. Behavioral correlates of mental growth: Birth to thirty-six years. *American Psychologist,* 1968, **23,** 1–17. [33]

BAYLEY, N. *Bayley Scales of Infant Development: Birth to two years.* New York: Psychological Corporation, 1969. [569]

BAYLEY, N. Development of mental abilities. In P. E. Mussen (Ed.), *Carmichael's manual of child psychology.* New York: Wiley, 1970. Vol. I. Pp. 1164–1209. [206, 569]

BAYRAKAL, S. The significance of EEG abnormality in behavior problem children. *Canadian Psychiatric Association Journal,* 1965, **10,** 387–391. [497]

BECK, A. T., WARD, C. H., MENDELSON, M., MOCK, J. E., & ERBAUGH, J. K. Reliability of psychiatric diagnoses. 2: A study of consistency of clinical judgments and ratings. *American Journal of Psychiatry,* 1962, **119,** 351–357. [544, 550, 577]

BECK, S. J. *Rorschach's Test: III. Advances in interpretation.* New York: Grune & Stratton, 1952. [581]

BECKER, B. A. Exogenous drug influences on the developing nervous system: Teratology and perinatal toxicology. In W. A. Himwich (Ed.), *Developmental neurobiology.* Springfield, Ill.: Thomas, 1970. Pp. 613–651. [146]

BECKER, J. It's in the genes X-linked and dominant. Review of G. Winokur, P. J. Clayton, & T. Reich, *Manic-depressive illness. Contemporary Psychology.* 1970, **15,** 629–630. [130]

BECKER, W. C., PETERSON, D. R., HELLMER, L. A., SHOEMAKER, D. J., & QUAY, H. C. Factors in parental behavior and personality as related to problem behavior in children. *Journal of Consulting Psychology,* 1959, **23,** 107–118. [593]

BEEDLE, P. The patterns of drug abuse in the United Kingdom. In S. Btesh (Ed.), *Drug abuse: Nonmedical use of dependence-producing drugs.* New York: Plenum Press, 1972. Pp. 114–117. [520]

BEERS, C. W. *A mind that found itself.* New York: Longmans, Green, 1908; reprinted by Doubleday, 1966. [27, 37]

BEHN, G. *Behn Rorschach Test.* New York: Grune & Stratton, 1956. [582]

BEKHTEREV, V. W. *Objektive Psychologie oder Psychoreflexologie* (1907). German translation. Leipzig: Teubner, 1913. [334]

BELL, J. E. Family group therapy. *Public Health Monograph,* U. S Dept. of Health, Education, and Welfare, 1961, No. 64. [612]

BELLAK, L. *The Thematic Apperception Test and the Children's Apperception Test in clinical use.* New York: Grune & Stratton, 1954. [585]

BEMPORAD, J. R., PFEIFER, C. M., & BLOOM, W. Twelve months' experience with the GAP classification of childhood disorders. *American Journal of Psychiatry,* 1970, **127,** 118–124. [551]

BENDA, C. E. *Down's syndrome: Mongolism and its management.* New York: Grune & Stratton, 1969. [143, 213]

BENDER, L. A visual motor Gestalt test and its clinical use. *The American Ortho-psychiatric Association Research Monographs*, 1938, No. 3. [598]

BENDER, L. Treatment in early schizophrenia. *Progress in Psychotherapy*, 1960, **5**, 177–184. [458]

BENDER, L. A longitudinal study of schizophrenic children with autism. *Hospital and Community Psychiatry*, 1969, **20**, 28–35. [445]

BENDER, L., & FARETRA, G. The relationship between childhood schizophrenia and adult schizophrenia. In A. R. Kaplan (Ed.), *Genetic factors in "schizophrenia"*. Springfield, Ill.: Thomas, 1972. Pp. 28–64. [416]

BENNETT, S., & KLEIN, H. Childhood schizophrenia: 30 years later. *American Journal of Psychiatry*, 1966, **122**, 1121–1124. [409]

BENSON, H., & WALLACE, R. K. Decreased drug abuse with transcendental meditation: A study of 1,862 subjects. In C. J. D. Zarafonetis (Ed.), *Drug abuse: Proceedings of the International Conference*. Philadelphia: Lea & Febiger, 1972. Pp. 369–376. [522, 532]

BENTLER, P. M. An infant's phobia treated with reciprocal inhibition therapy. *Journal of Child Psychology and Psychiatry*, 1962, **3**, 185–189. [377]

BENTON, J., MOSER, H. W., DODGE, P. R., & CARR, S. Modification of the schedule of myelinization in the rat by early nutritional deprivation. *Pediatrics*, 1966, **38**, 801–804. [142]

BERECZ, J. M. Phobias of childhood: Etiology and treatment. *Psychological Bulletin*, 1968, **70**, 694–720. [292, 377]

BEREITER, C., & ENGELMANN, S. *Teaching disadvantaged children in preschool*. Englewood Cliffs, N.J.: Prentice-Hall, 1967. [629]

BERG, I. Economic factors in delinquency. In U. S. Task Force on Juvenile Delinquency, *Juvenile delinquency and youth crime*. Washington: U. S. Government Printing Office, 1967. Pp. 305–316. [484]

BERGIN, A. E. The evaluation of therapeutic outcomes. In A. E. Bergin & S. L. Garfield (Eds.), *Handbook of psychotherapy and behavior change: An empirical analysis*. New York: Wiley, 1971. Pp. 217–270. [642, 650]

BERKOWITZ, L. *Aggression: A social psychological analysis*. New York: McGraw-Hill, 1962. [465]

BERKUN, M., BIALEK, H., KERN, R., & YAGI, K. Experimental studies of psychological stress in man. *Psychological Monographs*, 1962, **76** (Whole No. 534). [157]

BERLYNE, D. E. *Conflict, arousal and curiosity*. New York: McGraw-Hill, 1960. [96]

BERNAL, M. E., DURYEE, J. S., PRUETT, H. L., & BURNS, B. J. Behavior modification and the brat syndrome. *Journal of Consulting and Clinical Psychology*, 1968, **32**, 447–456. [384]

BERNSTEIN, L., & PURCELL, K. Institutional treatment of asthmatic children. In H. I. Schneer (Ed.), *The asthmatic child: Psychosomatic approach to problems and treatment*. New York: Harper, 1963. Pp. 224–233. [179]

BERRY, H. K. Phenylketonuria: Diagnosis, treatment and long-term management. In G. Farrell (Ed.), *Congenital mental retardation*. Austin, Texas: University of Texas Press, 1969. Pp. 3–35. [216]

BETTELHEIM, B. *The empty fortress*. New York: Free Press, 1967. [413, 443, 454]

BIEBER, I. On behavior therapy: A critique. *Journal of the American Academy of Psychoanalysis*, 1973, **1**, 39–52. [402]

BIERMANN, G. The psychological development of children in a schizophrenic family environment. *Schweizer Archiv für Neurologie, Neurochirurgie, und Psychiatrie,* 1966, **97**, 329–360. [424]

BILLS, R. E. Nondirective play therapy with retarded readers. *Journal of Consulting Psychology,* 1950, **14**, 140–149. [609]

BINET, A., & SIMON, T. New methods for the diagnosis of the intellectual level of subnormals. *L'Annee Psychologique,* 1905 (a). Translated and reprinted in A. Binet & T. Simon, *The development of intelligence in children.* Baltimore: Williams & Wilkins, 1916. Pp. 37–90. [197]

BINET, A., & SIMON, T. Upon the necessity of establishing a scientific diagnosis of inferior states of intelligence. *L'Annee Psychologique,* 1905 (b). Translated and reprinted in A. Binet & T. Simon, *The development of intelligence in children.* Baltimore: Williams & Wilkins, 1916. Pp. 9–36. [196]

BINET, A., & SIMON, T. The development of intelligence in the child. *L'Annee Psychologique,* 1908. Translated and reprinted in A. Binet & T. Simon, *The development of intelligence in children.* Baltimore: Williams & Wilkins, 1916. Pp. 182–273. [199]

BIRCH, H. G. The problem of "brain damage" in children. In H. G. Birch (Ed.), *Brain damage in children: The biological and social aspects.* Baltimore: Williams & Wilkins, 1964. Pp. 3–12. [167, 189]

BIRCH, H. G., & GUSSOW, J. D. *Disadvantaged children: Health, nutrition, and school failure.* New York: Grune & Stratton, 1970. [143, 189, 219, 627–628, 650]

BIRCH, H. G., RICHARDSON, S. A., BAIRD, D., HOROBIN, G., & ILLSLEY, R. *Mental subnormality in the community: A clinical and epidemiologic study.* Baltimore: Williams & Wilkins, 1970. [208, 225–226, 257]

BLAKE, P., & MOSS, T. The development of socialization skills in an electively mute child. *Behavior Research and Therapy,* 1967, **5**, 349–356. [456]

BLATT, B. *Exodus from Pandemonium.* Boston: Allyn & Bacon, 1970. [249, 258]

BLATT, B., & KAPLAN, F. *Christmas in Purgatory: A photographic essay on mental retardation.* Boston: Allyn & Bacon, 1966. [249, 258]

BLEULER, E. *Dementia Praecox or the group of schizophrenias* (1911). New York: International Universities Press, 1950. [20–21, 408]

BLISS, E. L., & BRANCH, C. H. *Anorexia nervosa.* New York: Harper, 1960. [178]

BLITZER, J. R., ROLLINS, N., & BLACKWELL, A. Children who starve themselves. *Psychosomatic Medicine,* 1961, **23**, 369–383. [178]

BLOCH, J., JENNINGS, P. H., HARVEY, E., & SIMPSON. E. Interaction between allergic potential and psychopathology in childhood asthma. *Psychosomatic Medicine,* 1964, **26**, 308–320. [179]

BLOCK, J., & MARTIN, B. Predicting the behavior of children under frustration. *Journal of Abnormal and Social Psychology,* 1955, **51**, 281–285. [465]

BLOCK, J., PATTERSON, V., BLOCK, J., & JACKSON, D. D. A study of the parents of schizophrenic and neurotic children. *Psychiatry,* 1958, **21**, 387–397. [415]

BLUM, G. S. The Blacky Pictures with children. In A. I. Rabin & M. R. Haworth (Eds.), *Projective techniques with children.* New York: Grune & Stratton, 1960. Pp. 95–104. [588]

BOBROFF, A. Economic adjustment of 121 adults, formerly students in classes for mental retardates. *American Journal of Mental Deficiency,* 1956, **60**, 525–535. [252]

BOCKOVEN, J. S. *Moral treatment in American psychiatry.* New York: Springer, 1963; 2nd ed., 1972. [15, 37]

BOLTON, T. L. The growth of memory in school children. *American Journal of Psychology*, 1891, 4, 362–380. [195]

BOND, E. A. *Tenth grade abilities and achievements.* New York: Columbia University Press, 1940. [207]

BÖÖK, J. A., NICHTERN, S., & GRUENBERG, E. Cytogenetical investigations in childhood schizophrenia. *Acta Psychiatra Scandinavia*, 1963, 39, 309–323. [426]

BOOKBINDER, L. J. Simple conditioning vs. the dynamic approach to symptoms and symptom substitution: A reply to Yates. *Psychological Reports*, 1962, 10, 71–77. [399]

BORNSTEIN, B. Analysis of a phobic child. *Psychoanalytic Study of the Child*, 1949, Vol. III–IV, 181–226. [292–299, 377]

BOULLIN, D. J., COLEMAN, M., & O'BRIEN, R. A. Abnormalities in platelet 5-Hydroxytryptamine efflux in patients with infantile autism. *Nature*, 1970, 226, 371–372. [444]

BOULLIN, D. J., COLEMAN, M., O'BRIEN, R. A., & RIMLAND, B. Laboratory predictions of infantile autism based on 5-Hydroxtryptamine efflux from blood platelets and their correlation with the Rimland E-2 score. *Journal of Autism and Childhood Schizophrenia*, 1971, 1, 63–71. [444]

BOWER, E. M. Early identification of emotionally handicapped children in school. (2nd ed.) Springfield, Ill.: Thomas, 1969. [620]

BOWLBY, J. *Attachment.* New York: Basic Books, 1969. [99, 137, 161]

BOYD, P. R. Drug abuse and addiction in adolescents. In J. G. Howells (Ed.), *Modern perspectives in adolescent psychiatry.* New York: Brunner/Mazel, 1971. Pp. 290–328. [516, 518, 522, 528]

BRACKBILL, Y. The role of the cortex in orienting: Orienting reflex in an anencephalic human infant. *Developmental Psychology*, 1971, 5, 195–201. [153]

BRADLEY, C. The behavior of children receiving benzedrine. *American Journal of Psychiatry*, 1937, 94, 575–587. [183]

BRADWAY, K. P., & THOMPSON, C. W. Intelligence at adulthood: A twenty-five year follow-up. *Journal of Educational Psychology*, 1962, 53, 1–14. [211–212]

BRADWAY, K. P., THOMPSON, C. W., & CRAVENS, R. B. Preschool IQs after twenty-five years. *Journal of Educational Psychology*, 1958, 49, 278–281. [213]

BRADY, J. P., & LIND, D. L. Experimental analysis of hysterical blindness. *Archives of General Psychiatry*, 1961, 4, 331–339. [380]

BRAID, J. *Neurypnology or the rationale of nervous sleep, considered in relation with animal magnetism.* London: J. Churchill, 1843. [21]

BRAINE, M. D. S., HEIMER, C. B., WORTIS, H., & FREEDMAN, A. M. Factors associated with impairment of the early development of prematures. *Monographs of the Society for Research in Child Development*, 1966, 31 (Serial No. 196). [149]

BRAUCHT, G. N., BRAKARSH, D., FOLLINGSTAD, D., & BERRY, K. L. Deviant drug use in adolescence: A review of psychosocial correlates. *Psychological Bulletin*, 1973, 79, 92–106. [528–530, 541]

BRECHER, E. M. and the Editors of Consumer Reports. *Licit and illicit drugs.* Boston: Little, Brown, 1972. [541]

BREUER, J., & FREUD, S. Studies in hysteria (1893–1895). In *Standard edition of the complete psychological works of Sigmund Freud.* London: Hogarth, 1955. [22, 261, 286]

BREYER, L., & McGAUGH, J. L. Critique and reformulation of learning theory approaches to psychotherapy and neurosis. *Psychological Bulletin*, 1965, **63**, 338–358. [388]

BRIGHAM, J. C., RICKETTS, J. L., & JOHNSON, R. C. Reported maternal and paternal behaviors of solitary and social delinquents. *Journal of Consulting Psychology*, 1967, **31**, 420–422. [481]

BRITTON, R. S. Psychiatric disorders in the mothers of disturbed children. *Journal of Child Psychology and Psychiatry*, 1969, **10**, 245–258. [593]

BROADHURST, P. L. Studies in psychogenetics: The quantitative inheritance of behavior in rats investigated by selective and cross-breeding. *Bulletin of the British Psychological Society*, 1958, **34**, 2A. (Abstract) [114]

BROCKMAN, L. M., & RICCUITI, H. N. Severe protein-calorie malnutrition and cognitive development in early infancy and childhood. *Developmental Psychology*, 1971, **4**, 312–319. [162]

BRODY, M. W. Prognosis and results of psychoanalysis. In J. H. Nodine & J. H. Moyer (Eds.), *Psychosomatic medicine*. Philadelphia: Lea & Febiger, 1962. Pp. 729–733. [326, 328]

BRODY, S. Aims and methods in child psychotherapy. *Journal of the American Academy of Child Psychiatry*, 1964, **3**, 385–412. [290]

BROVERMAN, D. M., BROVERMAN, I. K., VOGEL, W., PALMER, R. D., & KLAIBER, E. L. The automatization cognitive style and physical development. *Child Development*, 1964, 1343–1359. [158–159]

BROVERMAN, D. M., CLARKSON, F. E., KLAIBER, E. L., & VOGEL, W. The ability to automatize: A function basic to learning and performance. Unpublished manuscript. Worcester State Hospital, Worcester, Mass., 1972. [158, 189]

BROVERMAN, D. M., KLAIBER, E. L., KOBAYASHI, Y., & VOGEL, W. Roles of activation and inhibition in sex differences in cognitive abilities. *Psychological Review*, 1968, **75**, 23–50. [189]

BROWN, C. *Manchild in the promised land*. New York: Signet, 1965. [483]

BROWN, J. L. Prognosis from presenting symptoms of preschool children with atypical development. *American Journal of Orthopsychiatry*, 1960, **30**, 382–390. [454–455]

BROWN, J. L. Follow-up of children with atypical development (infantile psychosis). *American Journal of Orthopsychiatry*, 1963, **33**, 855–861. [454]

BROWN, P., & ELLIOTT, R. Control of aggression in a nursery school class. *Journal of Experimental Child Psychology*, 1965, **2**, 103–107. [468, 515]

BROWN, R. *A first language: The early stages*. Cambridge: Harvard University Press, 1973. [4]

BROWNING, R. M., & STOVER, D. O. *Behavior modification in child treatment*. Chicago: Aldine-Atherton, 1971.' [451]

BRYSON, C. Q. Systematic identification of perceptual disabilities in autistic children. *Perceptual and Motor Skills*, 1970, **31**, 239–246. [449]

BRYT, A. Non-Freudian methods of psychoanalysis with children and adolescents. In B. B. Wolman (Ed.), *Manual of child psychopathology*. New York: McGraw-Hill, 1972. Pp. 865–899. [260]

BTESH, S. *Drug abuse: Nonmedical use of dependence producing drugs*. New York: Plenum, 1972. [520, 541]

BUCHER, B., & LOVAAS, O. I. Use of aversive stimulation in behavior modification. In M. R. Jones (Ed.), *Miami Symposium on the Prediction of Behavior, 1967:*

Aversive Stimulation. Coral Gables, Fla.: University of Miami Press, 1968. Pp. 77–145. [365]

BUCK, J. N. *The House-Tree-Person technique.* (Revised Manual) Beverly Hills, Cal.: Western Psychological Services, 1966. [587]

BURCHARD, J. D. Systematic socialization: A programmed environment for the habilitation of antisocial retardates. *Psychological Record,* 1967, **17**, 461–476. [509]

BURKE, B. S., BEAL, V. A., KIRKWOOD, S. R., & STUART, H. C. The influence of nutrition during pregnancy upon the conditions of the infant at birth. *Journal of Nutrition,* 1943, **26**, 569–583. [142]

BURKS, B. S. The relative influence of nature and nurture upon mental development: A comparative study of foster parent-foster child resemblance and true parent-true child resemblance. *Yearbook of the National Society for the Study of Education,* 1928, **27**, Part I, 219–316. [242]

BURNHAM, W. H. *The normal mind.* New York: Appleton, 1924. [337]

BURT, C. The inheritance of mental ability. *American Psychologist,* 1958, **13**, 1–15. [124, 234]

BURT, C. Intelligence and social mobility. *British Journal of Statistical Psychology,* 1961, **14**, Part I, 3–24. [235–238, 243]

BURT, C. The genetic determination of differences in intelligence: A study of monozygotic twins reared together and apart. *British Journal of Psychology,* 1966, **57**, 137–153. [235]

BURTON, R. V. The generality of honesty reconsidered. *Psychological Review,* 1963, **70**, 481–499. [471]

BURTON, R. V. Validity of retrospective reports assessed by the multitrait-multimethod analysis. *Developmental Psychology Monograph,* 1970, **3**, Part 2. [83]

BUSS, A. H. Instrumentality of aggression, feedback, and frustration as determinants of physical aggression. *Journal of Personality and Social Psychology,* 1966, **3**, 153–162. [467]

BUTCHER, J. N. MMPI characteristics of externalizing and internalizing boys and their parents. Paper presented at First Conference on Recent Developments in the Use of the MMPI, Minneapolis, March, 1966. [561, 592]

BUTCHER, J. N. (Ed.) *MMPI: Research developments and clinical applications.* New York: McGraw-Hill, 1969. [591]

BUTLER, E. W. Personality dimensions of delinquent girls. *Criminologica,* 1965, **3**, 7–10. [502]

CAHOON, D. D. Symptom substitution and the behavior therapies: A reappraisal. *Psychological Bulletin,* 1968, **69**, 149–156. [399]

CAMERON, N. A., & MAGARET, A. *Behavior pathology.* New York: Houghton, 1951. [340]

CAMPBELL, A. M. G., EVANS, M., THOMSON, J. L. G., & WILLIAMS, M. J. Cerebral atrophy in young cannabis smokers. *Lancet,* 1971, **2**, 1219–1225. [523]

CAPLAN, R. B. *Psychiatry and the community in nineteenth-century America.* New York: Basic Books, 1969. [37]

CAPUTE, A. J., NIEDERMEYER, E. F. L., & RICHARDSON, F. The electroencephalogram in children with minimal cerebral dysfunction. *Pediatrics,* 1968, 1104–1114. [168]

CAPUTO, D. V., & MANDELL, W. Consequences of low birth weight. *Developmental Psychology,* 1970, **3**, 363–383. [149]

REFERENCES

W., & REPUCCI, N. D. Juvenile correctional institutions. In D. Glaser
The handbook of criminology. Chicago: Rand McNally, 1973. [511–512]

H., K., JANSKY, J., & LANGFORD, W. S. *Predicting reading failure.* New
Harper, 1966. [170]

G., & MANDELL, W. A comparison of conditioning and psychotherapy in
eatment of functional enuresis. *Journal of Clinical Psychology,* 1966, **22,**
0. [382, 400]

G., & SACKS, S. Conditioning functional enuresis. *Journal of Consulting*
linical Psychology, 1972, **39,** 299–300. [382, 400]

M. K., CHURCHILL, D. W., PONTIUS, W., & GILKEY, K. M. A comparison
diagnostic systems for childhood schizophrenia and infantile autism.
l of Autism and Childhood Schizophrenia, 1971, **1,** 175–189. [438]

M. K., PONTIUS, W., NORTON, J. A., BARTON, S., ALLEN, J., & STEELE, R.
al practices and innate activity in normal, autistic, and brain-damaged in-
Journal of Autism and Childhood Schizophrenia, 1972, **2,** 49–66. [440]

R. Results of the treatment of psychoneuroses by the general practitioner.
ork State Journal of Medicine, 1946, **46,** 2164–2166. [327–329]

W., & NAJARIAN, P. Infant development under environmental handicap.
logical Monographs, 1957, **71,** (Whole No. 436). [161]

ent of Health, Education, and Welfare. *Mental Retardation Activities.*
ngton, D.C.: United States Government Printing Office, 1972. [627]

IERS, A. M., & CARLSON, C. F. *Your child is asleep.* Homewood, Ill.: Dor-
69. [447, 449, 459]

J. L. Schizophrenia in childhood. *Psychiatric Quarterly,* 1938, **12,** 366–
410]

J. L. Psychotherapy in childhood schizophrenia. *American Journal of*
try, 1947, **104,** 36–43. [413]

J. L. Some considerations relating to the genesis of autistic behavior in
n. *American Journal of Orthopsychiatry,* 1951, **21,** 335–350. [442]

J. L. Differential diagnosis between obsessive-compulsive neurosis and
hrenia in children. In P. H. Hoch & J. Zubin (Eds.), *Psychopathology of*
od. New York: Grune & Stratton, 1955. Pp. 240–253. [304–305]

A. *The mentally ill in America.* (2nd ed.) New York: Columbia Uni-
Press, 1949. [16, 19, 35]

L. M. Differential diagnosis of congenital aphasia. *Volta Review,* 1960,
364. [171]

A. O. *Comparative psychotherapy: An experimental analysis.* Chicago:
Atherton, 1971. [394]

C. Former educable retarded pupils. *Exceptional Children,* 1961, **27,**
. [237, 252]

H. F., & TARJAN, G. Mental retardation and the normal distribution
American Journal of Mental Deficiency, 1960, **64,** 991–994. [193, 227–228

SCARPITTI, F. R., & RECKLESS, W. C. Delinquency vulnerability: A cros
and longitudinal analysis. *American Sociological Review,* 1962, **27,** 515
91]

N. I., LOUGHMAN, W. D., MOGAR, R. E., & LIPSCOMB, W. R. LSD an
damage. *Science,* 1971, **172,** 431–440. [146]

27 of the American Psychological Association. *Issues in community p*

CARMICHAEL, H. T., & MASSERMAN, T. H. Results of treatment in a psychiatric outpatient department. *Journal of the American Medical Association,* 1939, **113,**
2292–2293. [328]

CARTER, C. H. *Handbook of mental retardation syndromes.* Springfield, Ill.:
Thomas, 1970. [215]

CARTER, H. D. Twin similarities in emotional traits. *Character and Personality,*
1935, **4,** 61–78. [128–129]

CASLER, L. Maternal deprivation: A critical review of the literature. *Monographs*
of the Society for Research in Child Development, 1961, **26** (Serial No. 80). [161]

CASLER, L. Perceptual deprivation in institutional settings. In G. Newton & S.
Levine (Eds.), *Early experience and behavior.* Springfield, Ill.: Thomas, 1968.
Pp. 573–626. [161]

CASS, L. Psychotherapy with the obsessive-compulsive child. In M. Hammer & A.
M. Kaplan (Eds.), *The practice of psychotherapy with children.* Homewood, Ill.:
Dorsey, 1967. Pp. 95–120. [302]

CASTANEDA, A., MCCANDLESS, B. R., & PALERMO, D. S. The children's form of the
Manifest Anxiety Scale. *Child Development,* 1956, **27,** 317–326. [589]

CATTELL, P. *The measurement of intelligence of infants and young children.* New
York: Psychological Corporation, 1960. [569]

CATTELL, R. B. *Personality.* New York: McGraw-Hill, 1950. [109]

CATTELL, R. B. *Personality and motivation: Structure and measurement.* Yonkers,
New York: World Book, 1957. [574]

CAVAN, R. S., & CAVAN, J. T. *Delinquency and crime: Cross-cultural perspectives.*
Philadelphia: J. B. Lippincott, 1968. [482]

CHALFANT, J. C., & SCHEFFELIN, M. A. *Central processing dysfunctions in children.*
Washington: U. S. Government Printing Office, 1969. [169]

CHAMOVE, A. S., WAISMAN, H. A., & HARLOW, H. F. Abnormal social behavior in
phenylketonuric monkeys. *Journal of Abnormal Psychology,* 1970, **76,** 62–68.
[215]

CHASSON, J. B. *Research design in clinical psychology and psychiatry.* New York:
Appleton-Century-Crofts, 1967. [92]

CHEIN, I., GERARD, D. L., LEE, R. S., & ROSENFELD, E. *The road to H: Narcotics,*
delinquency, and social policy. New York: Basic Books, 1964. [530, 532–533,
537–541]

CHESS, S. Autism in children with congenital rubella. *Journal of Autism and*
Childhood Schizophrenia, 1971, **1,** 33–37. [443]

CHESS, S., THOMAS, A., & BIRCH, H. G. Distortions in developmental reporting
made by parents of behaviorally disturbed children. *Journal of the American*
Academy of Child Psychiatry, 1966, **5,** 226–234. [54]

CHITTENDEN, G. An experimental study in measuring and modifying assertive behavior in young children. *Monographs of the Society for Research in Child*
Development, 1942, **7** (Serial No. 33). [468]

CHURCHILL, D. W. Psychotic children and behavior modification. *American Jour-*
nal of Psychiatry, 1969, **125,** 139–144. [456]

CHURCHILL, D. W. Effects of success and failure in psychotic children. *Archives*
of General Psychiatry, 1971, **25,** 208–214. [456]

CLECKLEY, H. *The mask of sanity.* (4th ed.) St. Louis: Mosby, 1964. [492, 502–503,
515]

CLEMENT, P. W., FAZZONE, R. A., & GOLDSTEIN, B. Tangible reinforcers and child group therapy. *Journal of the American Academy of Child Psychiatry*, 1970, **9**, 409–427. [398–399]

CLEMENT, P. W., & MILNE, D. C. Group play therapy and tangible reinforcers used to modify the behavior of 8-year-old boys. *Behavior Research and Therapy*, 1967, **5**, 301–312. [398, 609]

CLEMENT, P. W., ROBERTS, P. V., & LANTZ, C. E. Social models and token reinforcement in the treatment of shy, withdrawn boys. *Proceedings, 78th Annual Convention, American Psychological Association*, 1970, 515–216. [398]

CLOWARD, R., & OHLIN, L. *Delinquency and opportunity*. Glencoe, Ill.: Free Press, 1960. [485]

COCHRAN, M. L., & PEDRINI, D. T. The concurrent validity of the 1965 WRAT with adult retardates. *American Journal of Mental Deficiency*, 1969, **73**, 654–656. [208]

COHEN, H. L., & FILIPCZAK, J. *A new learning environment*. San Francisco: Jossey-Bass, 1971. [504, 509–510, 515, 574]

COLBY, K. M. *The skeptical psychoanalyst*. New York: Ronald Press, 1958. [310–311, 330]

COLE, J. K., & MAGNUSSEN, M. G. Family situation factors related to remainers and terminators of treatment. *Psychotherapy: Theory, Research, and Practice*, 1967, **4**, 107–109. [640]

COLLINS, L. F., MAXWELL, A. E., & CAMERON, K. A factor analysis of some child clinic data. *Journal of Mental Science*, 1962, **108**, 274–285. [552, 555]

Commission of Inquiry into the Non-Medical Use of Drugs. *Cannabis*. Ottawa: Information Canada, 1972. [521–523, 541]

COMREY, A. L. *A first course in factor analysis*. New York: Academic Press, 1973. [554]

CONNERS, C. K. Pharmacotherapy of psychopathology in children. In H. C. Quay & J. S. Werry (Eds.), *Psychopathological disorders of childhood*. New York: Wiley, 1972. Pp. 316–347. [186]

CONRAD, H. S., & JONES, H. E. A second study of familial resemblance in intelligence: Environmental and genetic implications of parent-child and sibling correlations in the total sample. In G. M. Whipple (Ed.), *Intelligence: Its nature and nurture. Part III. Thirty-ninth Yearbook of the National Society for the Study of Education*. Bloomington, Ill.: Public School Publishing, 1940. Pp. 97–141. [237]

CONWAY, J. The inheritance of intelligence and its social implications. *British Journal of Statistical Psychology*, 1958, **11**, Part II, 171–190. [243]

COOKE, G. Evaluation of the efficacy of the components of reciprocal inhibition psychotherapy. *Journal of Abnormal Psychology*, 1968, **73**, 464–467. [396]

COOPER, A. J. A case of bronchial asthma treated by behavior therapy. *Behavior Research and Therapy*, 1964, **1**, 351–356. [381]

COOPER, A., FURST, J. B., & BRIDGER, W. H. A brief commentary on the usefulness of studying fears of snakes. *Journal of Abnormal Psychology*, 1969, **74**, 413–414. [396]

CORAH, N. L., ANTHONY, E. J., PAINTER, P., STERN, J. A., & THURSTON, D. Effects of perinatal anoxia after 7 years. *Psychological Monographs*, 1965, **79**, 1–34 (Whole No. 596). [148]

CORBIN, H. P., & BICKFORD, R. F. Studies of the electroencephalogram of normal

children: Comparison of visual and automat... *cephalography and Clinical Neurophysiology*, 19...

CORNWELL, A. C., & BIRCH, H. G. Psychological ... reared children with Down's syndrome (mongoli... *Deficiency*, 1969, **74**, 341–350. [215]

CORTÉS, J. B., & GATTI, F. M. *Delinquency and c...* New York: Seminar Press, 1972. [467]

COX, B., & SARGENT, H. TAT responses of emot... stable children: Clinical judgment versus norm... *Techniques*, 1950, **14**, 61–74. [584]

COX, F. N. Sociometric status and individual ... therapy. *Journal of Abnormal and Social Psy...*

CRAFTS, M., STEPHENSON, G., & GRANGER, C. A co... self-governing regimes with adolescent psychop... *psychiatry*, 1964, **34**, 543–554. [506, 509]

CRAVIOTO, J., & ROBLES, B. Evolution of adapti... habilitation from kwashiorkor. *American Jou...* 449–464. [162]

CREAK, M. Schizophrenic syndrome in childho... party. *British Medical Journal*, 1961, **2**, 889–...

CRIGHTON, J., & JEHU, D. Treatment of examina... zation or psychotherapy in groups. *Behaviou...* 245–248. [394]

CRITCHLEY, M. *The dyslexic child*. Springfield, ...

DAHLSTROM, W. G., & WELSH, G. S. *An MMPI ...* of Minnesota Press, 1960. [314, 591]

DAIN, N. *Concepts of insanity in the United St...* University Press, 1964. [37]

DARWIN, C. *Origin of species*. London: J. Mu...

DARWIN, C. A biographical sketch of an infant...

DAVIDS, A., & DEVAULT, S. Maternal anxiety d... normalities. *Psychosomatic Medicine*, 1962, ...

DAVIDS, A., DEVAULT, S., & TALMADGE, M. ... abnormalities. *Journal of Consulting Psycho...*

DAVIS, K. Final note on a case of extreme iso... ogy, 1947, **52**, 432–437. [220]

DAVISON, G. C. Elimination of a sadistic fanta... A case study. *Journal of Abnormal Psycholo...*

DAVISON, G. C. Systematic desensitization as a ... nal of Abnormal Psychology, 1968, **73**, 91–99. ...

DAVISON, G. C., GOLDFRIED, M. R., & KRASNER ... havior modification: Theory and practice. ... 772. [332]

DAVITZ, J. The effects of previous training o... of Abnormal and Social Psychology, 1952, **4**...

DAWES, L. G. The psychoanalysis of a case of ... of fifteen. *Nervous Child*, 1953, **10**, 272–305...

DAWSON, J. L. M. Effects of sex hormones ... *Behavior Genetics*, 1972, **2**, 21–42. [159, 18...

DEAN, ... (Ed.), ...

DEHIRSC... York: ...

DELEON... the tr... 326–3...

DELEON... and C...

DEMYER... of fiv... Journ...

DEMYER... Parent... fants.

DENKER, ... New Y...

DENNIS, ... Psycho...

Departm... Washi...

DESLAUR... sey, 19...

DESPERT, ... 371. ...

DESPERT, ... Psychia...

DESPERT, ... childre...

DESPERT, ... schizop... childh...

DEUTSCH, ... versity ...

DICARLO... 62, 361...

DILORETO... Aldine...

DINGER, ... 353–36...

DINGMAN ... curve. ...

DINITZ, S... group ... 517. [...

DISHOTSK... genetic... Division

chology and preventive mental health. New York: Behavioral Publications, 1971. [650]

DOHRENWEND, B. P., & DOHRENWEND, B. S. The problem of validity in field studies of psychological disorders. *International Journal of Psychiatry,* 1965, **1**, 585–610. [631]

DOLL, E. A. *The measurement of social competence. A manual for the Vineland Social Maturity Scale.* Philadelphia: Educational Test Bureau, Educational Publishers, 1953. [148, 209]

DOLLARD, J., DOOB, L. W., MILLER, N. E., MOWRER, O. H., & SEARS, R. R. *Frustration and aggression.* New Haven: Yale University Press, 1939. [321, 464, 468]

DOLLARD, J., & MILLER, N. *Personality and psychotherapy.* New York: McGraw-Hill, 1950. [31, 259, 287, 340–341]

DONNELL, G. N., BERGREN, W. R., & KOCH, R. Abnormal galactose metabolism in man. In G. Farrell (Ed.), *Congenital mental retardation.* Austin: University of Texas Press, 1969. Pp. 87–105. [216]

DORFMAN, E. Personality outcomes of client-centered child therapy. *Psychological Monographs,* 1958, **72** (Whole No. 456). [608]

DOUGLAS, J. W. B. The age at which premature children walk. *Medical Officer,* 1956, **95**, 33–35. [150]

DRASS, S. D., & JONES, R. L. Learning disabled children as behavior modifiers. *Journal of Learning Disabilities,* 1971, **4**, 418–425. [387]

DREGER, R. M., LEWIS, P. M., RICH, T. A., MILLER, K. S., REID, M. P., OVERLADE, D. C., TAFFEL, C., & FLEMMING, E. L. Behavioral classification project. *Journal of Consulting Psychology,* 1964, **28**, 1–13. [63, 554]

DREIFUSS, S. E. Delayed development of hemispheric dominance. *Archives of Neurology,* 1963, **8**, 510–514. [155]

DRILLEN, C. M., & ELLIS, R. W. *The growth and development of the prematurely born infant.* Baltimore: Williams and Wilkins, 1964. [149]

DOUBROS, S. G., & DANIELS, G. J. An experimental approach to the reduction of overactive behavior. *Behavior Research and Therapy,* 1966, **4**, 251–258. [384]

DUBO, S., MCLEAN, J. A., CHING, A. Y. T., WRIGHT, H. L., KAUFFMAN, P. E., & SHELDON, J. M. A study of relationships between family situation, bronchial asthma, and personal adjustment in children. *Journal of Pediatrics,* 1961, **59**, 402–414. [180]

DUGDALE, R. L. *The Jukes* (1877). New York: Putnam, 1910. [19]

DUNLAP, K. *Habits: Their making and unmaking.* New York: Liveright, 1932. [338, 380]

DUNN, L. N. *Expanded manual for the Peabody Picture Vocabulary Test.* Minneapolis: American Guidance Service, Inc., 1965. [573]

EBBS, J. H., BROWN, A., TISDALL, F. F., MOYLE, W. J., & BELL, M. The influence of improved prenatal nutrition upon the infant. *Canadian Medical Association Journal,* 1942, **46**, 6–8. [142]

EDDY, N. B. Methadone maintenance for the management of persons with drug dependence of the morphine type. *Drug Dependence,* 1970, 3, 17–26. [536]

EDGERTON, R. B. *The cloak of competence: Stigma in the lives of the retarded.* Berkeley: University of California Press, 1967. [252]

EICHORN, D. Physiological development. In P. H. Mussen (Ed.), *Carmichael's manual of child psychology.* New York: Wiley, 1970. Vol. I. Pp. 157–283. [153, 189]

EISENBERG, L. The autistic child in adolescence. *American Journal of Psychiatry,* 1956, **112**, 607–612. [435]

EISENBERG, L. The classification of psychotic disorders in childhood. In L. D. Eron (Ed.), *The classification of behavior disorders.* Chicago: Aldine, 1967, 88–122. [451]

EISENBERG, L. Psychopharmacology in childhood: A critique. In E. Miller (Ed.), *Foundations of child psychiatry.* New York: Pergamon Press, 1968. Pp. 625–641. [184–187]

EISENBERG, L. Principles of drug therapy in child psychiatry with special reference to stimulant drugs. *American Journal of Orthopsychiatry,* 1971, **41**, 371–379. [190]

EISENBERG, L., BERLIN, C. I., DILL, A., & FRANK, S. Class and race effects on the intelligibility of monosyllables. *Child Development,* 1968, **39**, 1077–1089. [630]

EISENBERG, L., & KANNER, L. Early infantile autism, 1943–1955. *American Journal of Orthopsychiatry,* 1956, **26**, 556–566. [437]

EISENBERG, L., LACHMAN, R., MOLLING, P. A., LOCKNER, A., MIZELLE, J., & CONNERS, C. K. A psychopharmacologic experiment in a training school for delinquent boys: Methods, problems, findings. *American Journal of Orthopsychiatry,* 1963, **33**, 431–447. [505]

ELLIOT, C. D., & PUMFREY, P. D. The effects of non-directive play therapy on some maladjusted boys. *Educational Research,* 1972, **14**, 157–161. [609]

ELLIS, N. A behavioral research strategy in mental retardation: Defense and critique. *American Journal of Mental Deficiency,* 1969, **73**, 557–566. [258]

EMBREE, R. B. The status of college students in terms of IQs determined during childhood. *American Psychologist,* 1948, **3**, 259. [207]

EMMERICH, W. Personality development and concepts of structure. *Child Development,* 1968, **39**, 671–690. [92]

EMPEY, L. T., & LUBECK, S. G. *The Silverlake experiment: Testing delinquency theory and community intervention.* Chicago: Aldine, 1971. [508]

ENDLER, N. S., BOULTER, L. R., & OSSER, H. *Contemporary issues in developmental psychology.* New York: Holt, Rinehart, & Winston, 1968. [137]

ENGEL, E. Guest editorial: The making of an XYY. *American Journal of Mental Deficiency,* 1972, **77**, 123–127. [115]

ENGEL, G. L. Studies of ulcerative colitis. II. The nature of somatic processes and the adequacy of psychosomatic hypotheses. *American Journal of Medicine,* 1954, **16**, 416–433. [182]

ERIKSON, E. H. *Childhood and Society.* New York: Norton, 1950; 2nd ed., 1963. [24, 278–281, 288, 645]

ERIKSON, E. H. *Identity, Youth, and Crisis.* New York: Norton, 1968. [280, 288]

ERNHART, C. B., GRAHAM, F. K., EICHMAN, P. L., MARSHALL, J. M., & THURSTON, D. Brain injury in the preschool child: Some developmental considerations: II. Comparison of brain injured and normal children. *Psychological Monographs,* 1963, **77** (Whole No. 573). Pp. 17–33. [167]

ERNHART, C. B., GRAHAM, F. K., & THURSTON, D. Relationship of neonatal apnea to development at three years. *Archives of Neurology,* 1960, **2**, 504–510. [148]

ERON, L. D., HUESMANN, L. R., LEFKOWITZ, M. M., & WALDER, L. O. Does television violence cause aggression? *American Psychologist,* 1972, **27**, 253–263. [471]

ERON, L. D., WALDER, L. O., & LEFKOWITZ, M. M. *Learning of aggression in children.* Boston: Little, Brown, 1971. [470, 515]

ERRERA, P., & COLEMAN, J. V. A long-term follow-up study of neurotic phobic patients in a psychiatric clinic. *Journal of Nervous and Mental Disease*, 1963, 136, 267–271. [392]

EYMAN, R. K., O'CONNOR, G., TARJAN, G., & JUSTICE, R. S. Factors determining residential placement of mentally retarded children. *American Journal of Mental Deficiency*, 1972, 76, 692–698. [250]

EYSENCK, H. J. *The structure of human personality*. London: Methuen, 1953. [562]

EYSENCK, H. J. The inheritance of extroversion-introversion. *Acta Psychologica*, 1956, 12, 95–110. [126–128]

EYSENCK, H. J. *The dynamics of anxiety and hysteria*. New York: Praeger, 1957. [383, 574]

EYSENCK, H. J. Learning theory and behavior therapy. *Journal of Mental Science*, 1959, 195, 61–75. [332]

EYSENCK, H. J. (Ed.) *Behavior therapy and the neuroses*. New York: Pergamon Press, 1960. [336, 347]

EYSENCK, H. J. The effects of psychotherapy. *International Journal of Psychiatry*, 1965, 1, 97–178. [328, 639–642]

EYSENCK, H. J., & PRELL, D. B. The inheritance of neuroticism: An experimental study. *Journal of Mental Science*, 1951, 97, 441–465. [128]

EYSENCK, H. J., & RACHMAN, S. *The causes and cures of neurosis*. San Diego: R. R. Knapp, 1965. [376, 379–80, 562]

FARBER, B. *Mental retardation. Its social context and social consequences*. Boston: Houghton-Mifflin, 1968. [208]

FEINSTEIN, S. C., & WOLPERT, E. A. Juvenile manic depressive illness: Clinical and therapeutic considerations. *Journal of the American Academy of Child Psychiatry*, 1973, 12, 123–136. [411]

FELDMAN, F. Results of psychoanalysis in clinic case assignments. *Journal of the American Psychoanalytic Association*, 1968, 18, 274–300. [326]

FELDMAN, F., CANTOR, D., SOLL, S., & BACHRACH, W. Psychiatric study of a consecutive series of 34 patients with ulcerative colitis. *British Medical Journal*, 1967, 3, 14–17. [182]

FERBER, A., MENDELSOHN, M., & NAPIER, A. *The book of family therapy*. New York: Science House, 1972. [649]

FERREIRA, A. *Prenatal environment*. Springfield, Ill.: Thomas, 1970. [143]

FERSTER, C. B., & DeMYER, M. K. The development of performance in autistic children in an automatically controlled environment. *Journal of Chronic Diseases*, 1961, 13, 312–345. [455]

FERSTER, C. B., & PERROTT, M. C. *Behavior principles*. New York: Appleton-Century-Crofts, 1968. [356, 373]

FESHBACH, S. Aggression. In P. H. Mussen (Ed.), *Carmichael's manual of child psychology*. New York: Wiley, 1970. Vol. I. Pp. 159–260. [467, 515]

FINCH, S. M., & HESS, J. M. Ulcerative colitis in children. *American Journal of Psychiatry*, 1962, 118, 819–826. [182]

FISCHER, I., & GLANVILLE, B. Programmed teaching of autistic children. *Archives of General Psychiatry*, 1970, 23, 90–94. [456]

FISCHER, M., HARVALD, B., & HAUGE, M. A Danish twin study of schizophrenia. *British Journal of Psychiatry*, 1969, 115, 981–990. [428]

FISH, B. Drug therapy in children's psychiatric disorders. *Clinical Psychopharmacology. Modern Problems of Pharmacopsychiatry,* 1968, **1**, 60–72. [185]

FISH, B., SHAPIRO, T., & CAMPBELL, M. Long-term prognosis and the response of schizophrenic children to drug therapy. A controlled study of trifluoperazine. *American Journal of Psychiatry,* 1966, **123**, 32–39. [458, 570]

FISH, B., SHAPIRO, T., HALPERN, F., & WILE, R. The prediction of schizophrenia in infancy: III. A 10-year follow-up report of neurological and psychological development. *American Journal of Psychiatry,* 1965, **121**, 768–775. [417, 570]

FISH, B., WILE, R., SHAPIRO, T., & HALPERN, F. The prediction of schizophrenia in infancy: II. A 10-year follow-up report of predictions made at one month of age. In P. Hoch & J. Zubin (Eds.), *Psychopathology of schizophrenia.* New York: Grune & Stratton, 1966. Pp. 335–353. [417]

FITZELLE, G. T. Personality factors and certain attitudes toward childrearing among parents of asthmatic children. *Psychosomatic Medicine,* 1959, **21**, 208–217. [180]

FITZGIBBON, W. C. Public school programs for the mentally retarded. In A. A. Baumeister (Ed.), *Mental retardation: Appraisal, education, and rehabilitation.* Chicago: Aldine, 1967. Pp. 274–304. [253]

FOLKINS, C. H., LAWSON, K. D., OPTON, E. M., & LAZARUS, R. S. Desensitization and the experimental reduction of threat. *Journal of Abnormal Psychology,* 1968, **73**, 100–113. [396]

FORD, F. R. *Diseases of the nervous system in infancy, childhood, and adolescence.* (4th ed.) Springfield, Ill.: Thomas, 1960. [162–163]

FORER, B. R. The fallacy of personal validation: A classroom demonstration of gullibility. *Journal of Abnormal and Social Psychology,* 1949, **44**, 118–123. [576]

FORRESTER, R. M., STEIN, Z., & SUSSER, M. W. A trial of conditioning therapy in nocturnal enuresis. *Developmental Medicine and Child Neurology,* 1964, **6**, 158–166. [400]

FRAIBERG, S. *The magic years. Understanding and handling the problems of early childhood.* New York: Scribner, 1959. [330]

FRANK, G. H. The role of the family in the development of psychopathology. *Psychological Bulletin,* 1965, **64**, 191–205. [324]

FRANK, L. K. Projective methods for the study of personality. *Journal of Psychology,* 1939, **8**, 389–413. [579]

FRANKENBURG, W. K., & DODDS, J. B. *The Denver Developmental Screening Test Manual.* Denver: University of Colorado Press, 1968. [569]

FRANKS, C. M. *Behavior therapy: Appraisal and status.* New York: McGraw-Hill, 1969. [407]

FRASER, H. F. Patterns of abuse of narcotics: An historical review. In C. J. D. Zarafonetis (Ed.), *Drug abuse: Proceedings of the International Conference.* Philadelphia: Lea & Febiger, 1972. [520, 523]

FREEDMAN, A. M., EBIN, E. V., & WILSON, E. A. Autistic schizophrenic children: An experiment in the use of d-Lysergic Acid Diethylamide (LSD-25). *Archives of General Psychiatry,* 1962, **6**, 203–213. [459]

FREEDMAN, D. A. The role of early mother/child relations in the etiology of some cases of mental retardation. In G. Farrell (Ed.), *Congenital mental retardation.* Austin: University of Texas Press, 1969. Pp. 245–261. [218–219]

FREEDMAN, D. G. Smiling in blind infants and the issue of innate vs. acquired. *Journal of Child Psychology and Psychiatry,* 1964, **5**, 171–184. [131, 137]

FREEDMAN, D. G. An ethological approach to the genetical study of human behavior. In S. G. Vandenburg (Ed.), *Methods and goals in human behavior genetics.* New York: Academic Press, 1965. Pp. 141–161. [130–132, 137]

FREEDMAN, D. G. An evolutionary framework for behavior research. In S. G. Vandenburg (Ed.), *Progress in human behavior genetics.* Baltimore: Johns Hopkins Press, 1968. Pp. 1–5. [130, 137]

FREEDMAN, D. G. The impact of behavior genetics and ethology. In H. E. Rie (Ed.), *Perspectives in child psychopathology.* Chicago: Aldine-Atherton, 1971. Pp. 219–266. [130, 137]

FREEDMAN, D. G., & KELLER, B. Inheritance of behavior in infants. *Science,* 1963, **140,** 196–198. [130, 137]

FREEDMAN, D. G., LORING, C. B., & MARTIN, R. M. Personality development in infancy: A biological approach. In Y. Brackbill (Ed.), *Infancy and early childhood.* New York: Free Press, 1967. Pp. 427–502. [137]

FREEMAN, M. A reliability study of psychiatric diagnosis in childhood and adolescence. *Journal of Child Psychology and Psychiatry,* 1971, **12,** 43–54. [550]

FREIBERGS, V., DOUGLAS, V. I., & WEISS, G. The effect of chlorpromazine on concept learning in hyperactive children under 2 conditions of reinforcers. *Psychopharmacologia,* 1968, **13,** 299–310. [186]

FREUD, A. *The ego and the mechanisms of defense* (1936). Translated by Cecil Baines. New York: International Universities Press, 1946. [24, 273–275, 287, 468]

FREUD, A. *Normality and pathology in childhood.* New York: International Universities Press, 1965. [49, 285, 287, 290, 562]

FREUD, A. Indications and contraindications for child analysis. *Psychoanalytic Study of the Child,* 1968, **23,** 37–46. [289]

FREUD, A. *Difficulties in the path of psychoanalysis: A confrontation of past with present viewpoints.* New York: International Universities Press, 1969. [287]

FREUD, S. *New introductory lectures on psychoanalysis.* New York: Norton, 1933. [287]

FREUD, S. *An outline of psychoanalysis.* New York: Norton, 1940. [311]

FREUD, S. *A general introduction to psychoanalysis* (1916). New York: Permabooks, 1953. [287]

FREUD, S. The interpretation of dreams (1900). In *Standard edition of the complete psychological works of Sigmund Freud.* Vol. 4. London: Hogarth Press, 1953. [22, 286]

FREUD, S. Three essays on the theory of sexuality (1905). In *Standard edition of the complete psychological works of Sigmund Freud.* Vol. 7. London: Hogarth Press, 1953. Pp. 125–243. [22, 264, 286]

FREUD, S. Analysis of a phobia in a five-year-old boy (1909). In *Standard edition of the complete psychological works of Sigmund Freud.* Vol. 10. London: Hogarth Press, 1955. Pp. 3–149. [269–271, 315–316, 610]

FREUD, S. Beyond the pleasure principle (1922). In *Standard edition of the complete psychological works of Sigmund Freud.* Vol. 18. London: Hogarth Press, 1955. Pp. 3–64. [464]

FREUD, S. On the history of the psychoanalytical movement (1914). In *Standard edition of the complete psychological works of Sigmund Freud.* Vol. 14. London: Hogarth Press, 1957. Pp. 3–66. [23]

FREUD, S. Repression (1915). In *Standard edition of the complete psychological works of Sigmund Freud.* Vol. 14. London: Hogarth Press, 1957. Pp. 143–158. [266]

FREUD, S. Inhibition, symptoms, and anxiety (1926a). In *Standard edition of the complete psychological works of Sigmund Freud.* Vol. 20. London: Hogarth Press, 1959. Pp. 77–174. [267, 287, 374]

FREUD, S. The question of lay analysis (1926b). In *Standard edition of the complete psychological works of Sigmund Freud.* Vol. 20. London: Hogarth Press, 1959. Pp. 179–258. [24]

FREUD, S. The ego and the id (1923). In *Standard edition of the complete psychological works of Sigmund Freud.* Vol. 19. London: Hogarth, 1961. Pp. 3–66. [266]

FREUD, S. The neuro-psychoses of defence (1894). In *Standard edition of the complete psychological works of Sigmund Freud.* Vol. 3. London: Hogarth, 1962. Pp. 45–61. [263, 286]

FREUD, S. Introductory lectures on psychoanalysis. Part III. General theory of neuroses (1917). In *Standard edition of the complete psychological works of Sigmund Freud.* Vol. 16. London: Hogarth, 1963. Pp. 243–463. [265]

FRICK, W. B. School phobia: A critical review of the literature. *Merrill-Palmer Quarterly,* 1964, **10**, 361–373. [292, 377]

FRIEDHOFF, A. J. Biochemical aspects of schizophrenia. In A. R. Kaplan (Ed.), *Genetic factors in "schizophrenia."* Springfield, Ill.: Thomas, 1972. Pp. 339–350. [425]

FRIEDMAN, D. E., & SILVERSTONE, J. T. Treatment of phobic patients by systematic desensitization. *Lancet,* 1967, March 4, 470–472. [351]

FROMM, E. *Escape from freedom.* New York: Holt, 1941. [24]

FROMM, E. *Man for himself.* New York: Holt, 1947. [24]

FROMMER, E. A. Treatment of childhood depression with anti-depressant drugs. *British Medical Journal,* 1967, **1**, 729–732. [187]

FROSTIG, M., & ORPET, R. E. Cognitive theories and diagnostic procedures for children with learning difficulties. In B. B. Wolman (Ed.), *Manual of child psychopathology.* New York: McGraw-Hill, 1972. Pp. 820–843. [599]

FRUCHTER, B. *Introduction to factor analysis.* Princeton, N.J.: Van Nostrand, 1954. [554]

FULLER, J. L., & THOMPSON, W. R. *Behavior genetics.* New York: Wiley, 1960. [137]

FULLERTON, D. T., KOLLAR, E. J., & CALDWELL, A. B. A clinical study of ulcerative colitis. *Journal of the American Medical Association,* 1962, **181**, 463–471. [182]

FURMAN, S. S., SWEAT, L. G., & CROCETTI, G. M. Social class factors in the flow of children to outpatient psychiatric facilities. *American Journal of Public Health,* 1965, **55**, 385–392. [631]

FURTH, H. G. *Thinking without language.* New York: The Free Press, 1966. [629]

GALTON, F. *Hereditary genius.* London: Macmillan, 1869. [17, 200]

GARDNER, J. E. Behavior therapy treatment approach to a psychogenic seizure case. *Journal of Consulting Psychology,* 1967, **31**, 209–212. [381]

GARDNER, J. M. Behavior modification research in mental retardation: Search for an adequate paradigm. *American Journal of Mental Deficiency,* 1969, **73**, 844–851. [254]

GARDNER, J., & GARDNER, H. A note on selective imitation by a 6-week-old infant. *Child Development,* 1970, **41,** 1209–1213. [469]

GARDUK, E. L., & HAGGARD, E. A. Immediate effects on patients of psychoanalytic interpretations. *Psychological Issues,* 1972, **7,** Monograph 28. [316–318]

GARFIELD, S. L. Research on client variables in psychotherapy. In A. E. Bergin & S. L. Garfield (Eds.), *Handbook of psychotherapy and behavior change: An empirical analysis.* New York: Wiley, 1971. Pp. 271–298. [643]

GARMA, A. On the pathogenesis of peptic ulcer. *International Journal of Psychoanalysis,* 1950, **31,** 53–72. [175]

GARNER, A. M., & WENAR, C. *The mother-child interaction in psychosomatic disorders.* Urbana: University of Illinois Press, 1959. [175]

GASTAUT, H. Some considerations of the now-discredited notion of idiopathic, genuine, or essential epilepsy. In H. Gastaut, H. Jasper, J. Bancaud, & A. Waltregny (Eds.), *The physiopathogenesis of the epilepsies.* Springfield, Ill.: Thomas, 1969. Pp. 295–296. [174]

GAZZANIGA, M. S. The split brain in man. *Scientific American,* 1967, **217,** 24–29. [189]

GAZZANIGA, M. S. *The bisected brain.* New York: Appleton-Century-Crofts, 1970. [189]

GELDER, M. G., & MARKS, I. M. Severe agoraphobia: A controlled prospective trial of behavior therapy. *British Journal of Psychiatry,* 1966, **112,** 309–319. [391–392, 399]

GELDER, M. G., MARKS, I. M., & WOLFF, H. H. Desensitization and psychotherapy in the treatment of phobic states: A controlled inquiry. *British Journal of Psychiatry,* 1967, **113,** 53–73. [391–392, 399]

GELLIS, S. S., & HSIA, D. Y. The infant of the diabetic mother. *American Journal of the Diseases of Children,* 1959, **97,** 1–41. [144]

GENDREAU, P., & SUBOSKI, M. D. Classical discrimination eyelid conditioning in primary psychopaths. *Journal of Abnormal Psychology,* 1971, **77,** 242–246. [495]

GESCHWIND, N. The organization of language and the brain. *Science,* 1970, **170,** 940–944. [154]

GESCHWIND, N., & LEVITSKY, W. Human brain: Left-right asymmetries in temporal speech region. *Science,* 1968, **161,** 186–187. [154]

GESELL, A. A decade of progress in the mental hygiene of the preschool child. *Annals of the American Academy of Political and Social Science,* 1930, **151,** 143–148. [29]

GESELL, A. The stability of mental growth careers. In G. M. Whipple (Ed.), *Intelligence: Its nature and nurture. Thirty-Ninth Yearbook of the National Society for the Study of Education. Part III.* Bloomington, Ill.: Public School Publishing Co., 1940. Pp. 149–160. [157]

GESELL, A., & AMATRUDA, C. S. *Developmental diagnosis.* (2nd ed.) New York: Harper, 1947. [568–569]

GESELL, A., & ILG, F. L. *Infant and child in the culture of today.* New York: Harper, 1943. [33]

GIBBONS, D. C. *Delinquent behavior.* Englewood Cliffs, N.J.: Prentice-Hall, 1970. [476, 503–505]

GIBBS, F. A., & KNOTT, J. R. Growth of the electrical activity of the cortex. *Electroencephalography and Clinical Neurophysiology,* 1949, **1,** 223–229. [153]

GILBERT, J. G., & LOMBARDI, D. N. Personality characteristics of young male narcotic addicts. *Journal of Consulting Psychology,* 1967, **31**, 536–538. [530]

GINOTT, H. G. *Group psychotherapy with children.* New York: McGraw-Hill, 1961. [649]

GINSBURG, H., & OPPER, S. *Piaget's theory of intellectual development.* Englewood Cliffs, N.J.: Prentice-Hall, 1969. [37]

GITTLEMAN, M., & BIRCH, H. G. Childhood schizophrenia: Intellect, neurologic status, perinatal risk, prognosis, and family pathology. *Archives of General Psychiatry,* 1967, **17**, 16–25. [421]

GLASS, D. C. (Ed.). *Genetics.* New York: Rockefeller University Press, 1968. [137]

GLAVIN, J. P., QUAY, H. C., ANNESLEY, F. R., & WERRY, J. S. An experimental resource room for behavior problem children. *Exceptional Children,* 1971, **38**, 131–137. [618]

GLIDEWELL, J. C., DOMKE, H. R., & KANTOR, M. B. Screening in schools for behavior disorders: Use of mother's reports of symptoms. *Journal of Educational Research,* 1963, **56**, 508–515. [51]

GLUECK, S., & GLUECK, E. *Unraveling juvenile delinquency.* New York: Commonwealth Fund, 1950. [488]

GLUECK, S., & GLUECK, E. *Predicting delinquency and crime.* Cambridge: Harvard University Press, 1959. [88, 489]

GLUECK, S., & GLUECK, E. *Delinquents and nondelinquents in perspective.* Cambridge: Harvard University Press, 1968. [88]

GLUECK, S., & GLUECK, E. *Toward a typology of juvenile offenders. Implications for therapy and prevention.* New York: Grune & Stratton, 1970. [488]

GODDARD, H. H. *The Kallikak family: A study in the heredity of feeble-mindedness.* New York: Macmillan, 1912. [19, 200]

GODDARD, H. H. Introduction. In A. Binet & T. Simon, *The development of intelligence in children.* Baltimore: Williams & Wilkins, 1916. [200]

GOLD, S., & NEUFELD, I. A learning theory approach to the treatment of homosexuality. *Behavior Research and Therapy,* 1965, **2**, 201–204. [366]

GOLDBERG, L. Epidemiology of drug abuse in Sweden. In C. J. D. Zarafonetis (Ed.), *Drug abuse: Proceedings of the International Conference.* Philadelphia: Lea & Febiger, 1972. Pp. 27–66. [521]

GOLDENSOHN, E. S. Seizures and convulsive disorders. In B. B. Wolman (Ed.), *Handbook of clinical psychology.* New York: McGraw-Hill, 1965. Pp. 755–764. [174]

GOLDFARB, W. Receptor preferences in schizophrenic children. *AMA Archives of Neurology and Psychiatry,* 1956, **76**, 643–652. [410]

GOLDFARB, W. *Childhood schizophrenia.* Cambridge: Harvard University Press, 1961. [410, 418, 422, 453]

GOLDFARB, W. Childhood psychoses. In P. M. Mussen (Ed.), *Carmichael's manual of child psychology.* New York: Wiley, 1970. Vol. 2. Pp. 765–830. [411, 418, 462]

GOLDFARB, W., GOLDFARB, N., & POLLACK, R. A. Treatment of childhood schizophrenia: A three-year comparison of day and residential treatment. *Archives of General Psychiatry,* 1966, **14**, 119–128. [453]

GOLDFARB, W., GOLDFARB, N., & SCHOLL, H. The speech of mothers of schizophrenic children. *American Journal of Psychiatry,* 1966, **122**, 1220–1227. [414]

GOLDFRIED, M. R., & KENT, R. N. Traditional versus behavioral personality assessment: A comparison of methodological and theoretical assumptions. *Psychological Bulletin*, 1972, **77**, 409–420. [595, 605]

GOLDSCHMID, M. L., & DOMINO, G. Some para-diagnostic implications of the IQ among mentally retarded patients. *Training School Bulletin*, 1965, **61**, 178–183. [209]

GOLDSTEIN, H. Social and occupational adjustment. In H. A. Stevens & R. Heber (Eds.), *Mental retardation: A review of research*. Chicago: University of Chicago Press, 1964. Pp. 214–258. [252]

GOLDSTEIN, H. The efficacy of special classes and regular classes in the education of educable mentally retarded children. In J. Zubin & G. A. Jervis (Eds.) *Psychopathology of mental development*. New York: Grune & Stratton, 1967. Pp. 580–602. [253]

GOLDSTEIN, R., LANDAU, W. M., & KLEFFNER, F. R. Neurologic observations in a population of deaf and aphasic children. *Annals of Otology, Rinology, and Laryngology*, 1960, **69**, 756–767. [171]

GOODE, E. *The marijuana smokers*. New York: Basic Books, 1970. [541]

GOODENOUGH, F. L. *Measurement of intelligence by drawings*. Chicago: World Book, 1926. [572]

GOODENOUGH, F. L. Trends in modern psychology. *Psychological Bulletin*, 1934, **31**, 81–97. [33]

GOODMAN, H., GOTTLIEB, J., & HARRISON, R. H. Social acceptance of EMRs integrated into a nongraded elementary school. *American Journal of Mental Deficiency*, 1972, **76**, 412–417. [254]

GOODWIN, M. S., COWEN, M. A., & GOODWIN, T. C. Malabsorption and cerebral dysfunction: A multivariate and comparative study of autistic children. *Journal of Autism and Childhood Schizophrenia*, 1971, **1**, 48–62. [444]

GOTTESMAN, I. I. Genetic aspects of intelligent behavior. In N. Ellis (Ed.), *Handbook of mental deficiency: Psychological theory and research*. New York: McGraw-Hill, 1963. Pp. 253–296. (a) [230]

GOTTESMAN, I. I. Heritability of personality: A demonstration. *Psychological Monographs*, 1963, **77** (Whole No. 572). (b) [122–123, 127, 130, 137]

GOTTESMAN, I. I. Personality and natural selection. In S. G. Vandenberg (Ed.), *Methods and goals in human behavior genetics*. New York: Academic Press, 1965. Pp. 63–80. [123, 127, 130]

GOTTESMAN, I. I. Genetic variance in adaptive personality traits. *Journal of Child Psychology and Psychiatry*, 1966, **7**, 199–208. [122, 127]

GOTTESMAN, I. I. Beyond the fringe—Personality and psychopathology. In D. C. Glass (Ed.), *Genetics*. New York: Rockefeller University Press, 1968. Pp. 59–68. [110, 427]

GOTTESMAN, I. I., & SHIELDS, J. Schizophrenia in twins: 16 years consecutive admissions to a psychiatric clinic. *British Journal of Psychiatry*, 1966, **112**, 809–818. [428]

GOTTSCHALK, L. A. Effects of intensive psychotherapy on epileptic children. *Archives of Neurology and Psychiatry*, 1953, **70**, 361–384. [174]

GOTTSCHALK, L. A. The relationship of psychologic state and epileptic activity: Psychoanalytic observations on an epileptic child. *Psychoanalytic Study of the Child*, 1956, **11**, 352–380. [174]

GOTTSCHALK, L. A., TITCHENER, J. L., PIKER, H. N., & STEWART, S. S. Psychosocial factors associated with pregnancy in adolescent girls: A preliminary report. *Journal of Nervous and Mental Disease*, 1964, **138**, 524–534. [500]

GOUGH, H. G. Clinical versus statistical prediction in psychology. In L. Postman (Ed.), *Psychology in the making*. New York: Knopf, 1962. Pp. 526–584. [93]

GOUIN-DÉCARIE, T. A study of the mental and emotional development of the thalidomide child. In B. M. Foss (Ed.), *Determinants of infant behavior*. Vol. IV. London: Methuen, 1961. Pp. 167–187. [146]

GOUIN-DÉCARIE, T. *Intelligence and affectivity in early childhood*. New York: International Universities Press, 1965. [49]

GRACE, W. J., & GRAHAM, D. T. Relationship of specific attitudes and emotions to certain bodily diseases. *Psychosomatic Medicine*, 1952, **14**, 242–251. [176]

GRAFFAGNINO, P. N., BOELHOUWER, C., & REZNIKOFF, M. An organic factor in patients of a child psychiatric clinic. *Journal of the American Academy of Child Psychiatry*, 1968, **7**, 618–638. [168]

GRAHAM, D. T., LUNDY, R. M., BENJAMIN, L. S., KABLER, J. D., LEWIS, W. C., KUNISH, N. O., & GRAHAM, F. K. Specific attitudes in initial interviews with patients having different "psychosomatic" diseases. *Psychosomatic Medicine*, 1962, **24**, 257–266. [175]

GRAHAM, D. T., STERN, J. A., & WINOKUR, G. Experimental investigation of the specificity of attitude hypothesis in psychosomatic disease. *Psychosomatic Medicine*, 1958, **20**, 446–457. [177]

GRAHAM, F. K., & KENDALL, B. S. Performance of brain-damaged cases on a memory-for-designs test. *Journal of Abnormal and Social Psychology*, 1946, **41**, 303–314. [599]

GRAHAM, F. K., & KENDALL, B. S. Memory-for-designs test: Revised general manual. *Perceptual and Motor Skills*, 1960, **11**, (Part VII) 147–188. [599]

GRAHAM, G. G. Effect of infantile malnutrition on growth. *Federation Proceedings*, 1967, **26**, 139–143. [161–162]

GRAHAM, P., & RUTTER, M. The reliability and validity of the psychiatric assessment of the child. II. Interview with the parent. *British Journal of Psychiatry*, 1968, **114**, 581–592. [594]

GRAY, W. S. *Gray Oral Reading Tests*. Indianapolis: Bobbs-Merrill, 1963. [573]

GREEN, H. *I never promised you a rose garden*. New York: Signet, 1964. [462]

GRIESINGER, W. *Die pathologie und therapie der psychischen krankheiten* (1845). Translated as *Mental pathology and therapeutics* by C. L. Robertson & J. Rutherford. London: New Sydenham Society, 1867. [16, 20]

GRIFFITHS, R. *The abilities of babies: A study in mental measurement*. New York: McGraw-Hill, 1954. [569]

GRINDER, R. E. Relations between behavioral and cognitive dimensions of conscience in middle childhood. *Child Development*, 1964, **35**, 881–891. [473]

GROSSMAN, H. J. Manual on terminology and classification in mental retardation. (1973 Revision) *American Association on Mental Deficiency, Special Publication Series No. 2*, 1973. [218]

Group for the Advancement of Psychiatry. Psychopathological disorders in childhood: Theoretical considerations and a proposed classification. *GAP Report No. 62*, 1966. [68, 291, 307, 411–413, 452, 548–550, 565]

Group for the Advancement of Psychiatry. The field of family therapy. *GAP Report No. 78*, 1970. [612]

GRUEN, G. E., & VORE, D. A. Development of conservation in normal and retarded children. *Developmental Psychology*, 1972, **6**, 146–157. [246]

GUBBAY, S. S., LOBASCHER, M., & KINGERLEE, F. A neurological appraisal of autistic children: Results of a Western Australian survey. *Developmental Medicine and Child Neurology*, 1970, **12**, 422–429. [443]

GUERNEY, B. Filial therapy: Description and rationale. *Journal of Consulting Psychology*, 1964, **28**, 304–310. [608]

GUNZBURG, H. C. *Social competence and mental handicap*. Baltimore: Williams & Wilkins, 1968. [251]

GUSKIN, S. L., & SPICKER, H. H. Educational research in mental retardation. In N. R. Ellis (Ed.), *International review of research in mental retardation*. Vol. 3. New York: Academic Press, 1968. Pp. 217–278. [253]

GUTTMAN, E. S. Effects of short-term psychiatric treatment for boys in two California Youth Authority Institutions. Cited by D. C. Gibbons, *Delinquent behavior*. Englewood Cliffs, N.J.: Prentice-Hall, 1970. Pp. 255–256. [505]

HAFNER, A. J., BUTCHER, J. N., HALL, M. D., & QUAST, W. Parent personality and childhood disorders: A review of MMPI findings. In J. N. Butcher (Ed.), *MMPI: Research developments and clinical applications*. New York: McGraw-Hill, 1969. Pp. 181–190. [592]

HAFNER, A. J., QUAST, W., SPEER, D. C., & GRAMS, A. Children's anxiety scales in relation to self, parental, and psychiatric ratings of anxiety. *Journal of Consulting Psychology*, 1964, **28**, 255–558. [589–590]

HAGGARD, E. A., HIKEN, J. R., & ISAACS, K. S. Some effects of recording and filming on the psychotherapeutic process. *Psychiatry*, 1965, **28**, 169–191. [315–316]

HALEY, J. (Ed.) *Changing families: A family therapy reader*. New York: Grune & Stratton, 1971. [649]

HALL, C. S. The inheritance of emotionality. *Sigma Xi Quarterly*, 1938, **26**, 17–27. [114]

HALL, G. S. *Adolescence*. New York Appleton, 1904. [32]

HALLGREN, B. Specific dyslexia. *Acta Psychiatrica et Neurologica*, 1950. (Supplement 65). [170]

HALLSTEN, E. A., JR. Adolescent anorexia nervosa treated by desensitization. *Behavior Research and Therapy*, 1965, **3**, 87–91. [178, 381]

HALPERIN, S. L. Clinico-genetical study of mental defect. *American Journal of Mental Deficiency*, 1945, **50**, 8–26. [227]

HAMBLIN, R. L., BUCKHOLDT, D., FERRITOR, D., KOZLOFF, M., & BLACKWELL, L. *The humanization processes: A social, behavioral analysis of children's problems*. New York: Wiley-Interscience, 1971. [457, 509]

HAMBURG, D., BIBRING, G., FISHER, C., STANTON, A., WALLERSTEIN, R., WEINSTOCK, H., & HAGGARD, H. Report of ad hoc committee on central fact-gathering data of the American Psychoanalytic Association. *Journal of the American Psychoanalytic Association*, 1967, **15**, 841–861. [326–327]

HAMMER, E. F. The House-Tree-Person drawings as a projective technique with children. In A. I. Rabin & M. R. Haworth (Eds.), *Projective techniques with children*. New York: Grune & Stratton, 1960. Pp. 258–272. [587]

HANDLON, J. H. Hormonal activity and individual responses to stresses and easements in everyday living. In R. Roessler & N. S. Greenfield (Eds.), *Physiological Correlates of Psychological Disorder*. Madison: University of Wisconsin Press, 1962. Pp. 157–170. [157]

HARE, R. D. Detection threshold for electric shock in psychopaths. *Journal of Abnormal Psychology*, 1968, 73, 268–272. [495]

HARE, R. D. *Psychopathy: Theory and research.* New York: Wiley, 1970. [515]

HARE, R. D., & THORVALDSON, S. A. Psychopathy and response to electrical stimulation. *Journal of Abnormal Psychology*, 1970, 76, 370–374. [495]

HARING, N. G., & HAUCK, M. A. Improved learning conditions in the establishment of reading skills with disabled readers. *Exceptional Children*, 1969, 35, 341–352. [386, 574]

HARING, N. G., & PHILLIPS, E. L. *Educating emotionally disturbed children.* New York: McGraw-Hill, 1962. [616]

HARMAN, H. H. *Modern factor analysis.* Chicago: University of Chicago Press, 1967. [554]

HARMS, E. *Origins of modern psychiatry.* Springfield, Ill.: Thomas, 1967. [17]

HARPER, P. A., FISCHER, K., & RIDER, R. V. Neurological and intellectual status of prematures at three to five years of age. *Journal of Pediatrics,* 1959, 55, 679–690. [149, 570]

HARRIS, D. B. Children's drawings as measures of intellectual maturity. New York: Harcourt Brace Jovanovich, 1963. [572]

HARRIS, F. R., JOHNSTON, M. K., KELLEY, C. S., & WOLF, M. M. Effects of positive social reinforcement on regressed crawling of a nursery school child. *Journal of Educational Psychology,* 1964, 55, 34–41. [357]

HARRISON, S. I., McDERMOTT, J. F., WILSON, P. T.. & SCHRAGER, J. Social class and mental illness in children. *Archives of General Psychiatry,* 1965, 13, 411–417. [631]

HARTMANN, H. *Ego psychology and the problem of adaptation.* New York: International Universities Press, 1939. [24, 276, 646]

HARTMANN, H. Comments on the psychoanalytic theory of the ego. *Psychoanalytic Study of the Child,* 1950, 5, 74–96. (a) [276]

HARTMANN, H. Psychoanalysis and developmental psychology. *Psychoanalytic Study of the Child,* 1950, 5, 7–17. (b) [276–277]

HARTMANN, H. *Essays on ego psychology.* New York: International Universities Press, 1964. [276–277]

HARTMANN, H., KRIS, E., & LOWENSTEIN, R. M. Notes on the theory of aggression. *Psychoanalytic Study of the Child,* 1949, 3, 9–36. [277]

HARTSHORNE, H., & MAY, M. *Studies in the nature of character.* New York: Macmillan, 1928–1930. 3 vols. [471]

HATHAWAY, S. R., & McKINLEY, J. C. *The Minnesota Multiphasic Personality Inventory Manual.* (Rev. ed.) New York: Psychological Corporation, 1951. [590]

HAUGHTON, E., & ALLYON, T. Production and elimination of symptomatic behavior. In L. P. Ullmann & L. Krasner (Eds.), *Case studies in behavior modification.* New York: Holt, 1965. [355]

HAVELKOVA, M. Follow-up study of 71 children diagnosed as psychotic in preschool age. *American Journal of Orthopsychiatry,* 1968, 38, 846–857. [452]

HEBER, R. A manual on terminology and classification in mental retardation. (2nd ed.) *American Journal of Mental Deficiency, Monograph Supplement,* 1961. [193, 217–218, 221, 224, 551]

HECAEN, H., & DEAJURIAGUERRA, J. *Left-handedness, manual superiority, and cerebral dominance.* New York: Grune & Stratton, 1964. [154]

HEDBERG, E., HOLMDAHL, K., & PHERSON, S. On relationships between maternal health and congenital malformations. *Acta Obstetrica et Gynecologica Scandinavia,* 1967, **46**, 378–391. [143]

HEINICKE, C. M. Frequency of psychotherapeutic session as a factor affecting the child's developmental status. *Psychoanalytic Study of the Child,* 1965, **20**, 42–98. [284, 325]

HEINICKE, C. M. Frequency of psychotherapeutic session as a factor affecting outcome: Analysis of clinical ratings and test results. *Journal of Abnormal Psychology,* 1969, **74**, 553–560. [325, 329, 390]

HEINICKE, C. M., & GOLDMAN, A. Research on psychotherapy with children: A review and suggestions for further study. *American Journal of Orthopsychiatry,* 1960, **30**, 483–494. [640]

HENDRICK, I. Discussion of the "instinct to master." *Psychoanalytical Quarterly,* 1943, **12**, 561–565. [277]

HESS, E. H. Ethology and developmental psychology. In P. H. Mussen (Ed.), *Carmichael's manual of child psychology.* New York: Wiley, 1970. Vol. 1. Pp. 1–38. [98–99]

HESTON, L. L. Psychiatric disorders in foster home reared children of schizophrenic mothers. *British Journal of Psychiatry,* 1966, **112**, 819–825. [429–430]

HESTON, L. L., & DENNEY, D. Interactions between early life experience and biological factors in schizophrenia. In D. Rosenthal & S. Kety (Eds.), *The transmission of schizophrenia.* New York: Pergamon, 1968. Pp. 363–376. [430]

HETHERINGTON, E. M., & BRACKBILL, Y. Etiology and covariation of obstinacy, orderliness, and parsimony in young children. *Child Development,* 1963, **34**, 919–943. [320]

HETHERINGTON, E. M., STOUWIE, R. J., & RIDBERG, E. H. Patterns of family interaction and child-rearing attitudes related to three dimensions of juvenile delinquency. *Journal of Abnormal Psychology,* 1971, **78**, 160–176. [481–482, 501–502]

HEWETT, F. M. Teaching speech to an autistic child through operant conditioning. *American Journal of Orthopsychiatry,* 1965, **35**, 927–936. [456]

HEWETT, F. M. *The emotionally disturbed child in the classroom.* Boston: Allyn & Bacon, 1968. [387, 616]

HEWETT, F. M. Educational programs for children with behavior disorders. In H. C. Quay & J. S. Werry (Eds.), *Psychopathological disorders of childhood.* New York: Wiley, 1972. Pp. 388–413. [616]

HEWITT, L. E., & JENKINS, R. L. *Fundamental patterns of maladjustment: The dynamics of their origin.* Springfield, Ill.: State of Illinois, 1946. [481, 554]

HILL, H. E., HAERTZEN, C. A., & GLASER, R. Personality characteristics of narcotic addicts as indicated by the MMPI. *Journal of General Psychology,* 1960, **62**, 127–139. [530]

HINGTEN, J. N., COULTER, S. K., & CHURCHILL, D. W. Intensive reinforcement of imitative behavior in mute autistic children. *Archives of General Psychiatry,* 1967, **17**, 36–43. [456]

HIRSHOREN, A. A comparison of the predictive validity of the Revised Stanford-Binet Intelligence Scale and the Illinois Test of Psycholinguistic Abilities. *Exceptional Children,* 1969, **35**, 517–521. [573]

HOBBS, N. Helping disturbed children: Psychological and ecological strategies. *American Psychologist,* 1966, **21**, 1105–1115. [617]

HOCKMAN, C. H. Prenatal maternal stress in the rat: Its effect on emotional behavior in the offspring. *Journal of Comparative and Physiological Psychology,* 1961, **54,** 679–684. [144]

HOFFMAN, M. L. Moral development. In P. H. Mussen (Ed.), *Carmichael's manual of child psychology.* New York: Wiley, 1970. Vol. 2. Pp. 261–359. [472]

HOFFMAN, M. L. Father absence and conscience development. *Developmental Psychology,* 1971, **4,** 400–406. [472]

HOLLAND, C. J. Elimination by the parents of fire-setting in a 7-year-old boy. *Behavior Research and Therapy,* 1969, **7,** 135–137. [370]

HOLLINGSHEAD, A. B., & REDLICH, F. C. *Social class and mental illness.* New York: Wiley, 1958. [631]

HOLMES, F. B. An experimental investigation of a method of overcoming children's fears. *Child Development,* 1936, **7,** 6–30. [338, 351]

HOLT, L. E. *The care and feeding of children: A catechism for the use of mothers and children's nurse.* New York: Appleton, 1929. [33]

HOLT, R. R. Yet another look at clinical and statistical prediction: Or, is clinical psychology worthwhile? *American Psychologist,* 1970, **25,** 337–349. [93]

HOLTZMAN, W. H., THORPE, J. S., SWARTZ, J. D., & HERRON, E. W. *Inkblot perception and personality: Holtzman inkblot technique.* Austin: University of Texas Press, 1961. [582]

HOLZMAN, P. S. *Psychoanalysis and psychopathology.* New York: McGraw-Hill, 1970. [287]

HONZIK, M. P. Developmental studies of parent-child resemblance in intelligence. *Child Development,* 1957, **28,** 215–228. [242–243, 257]

HONZIK, M. P., MacFARLANE, J. W., & ALLEN, L. The stability of mental test performance between two and eighteen years. *Journal of Experimental Education,* 1948, **17,** 309–324. [212, 222–223]

HOOD-WILLIAMS, J. The results of psychotherapy with children: A reevaluation. *Journal of Consulting Psychology,* 1960, **24,** 83–87. [640]

HOOK, E. B. Behavioral implications of the human XYY genotype. *Science,* 1973, **179,** 139–150. [116, 498]

HOOK, E. B., & KIM, D. S. Height and antisocial behavior in XY and XYY boys. *Science,* 1971, **172,** 284–286. [498]

HORNEY, K. *New ways in psychoanalysis.* New York: Norton, 1939. [24]

HUGHES, J. G., EHEMANN, B., & BROWN, U. A. Electroencephalography of the newborn. *American Journal of Diseases of Children,* 1948, **76,** 626–633. [146]

HULL, C. L. *Principles of behavior.* New York: Appleton-Century-Crofts, 1943. [31, 340]

HULL, C. L. *Essentials of behavior.* New Haven: Yale University Press, 1951. [340]

HULL, C. L. *A behavior system: An introduction to behavior theory concerning the individual organism.* New Haven: Yale University Press, 1952. [31]

HUNT, G. H., & ODOROFF, M. E. Follow-up study of narcotic drug addicts after hospitalization. *Public Health Reports,* 1962, **77,** 41–54. [533]

HUNT, J. McV. *Intelligence and experience.* New York: Ronald Press, 1961. [257]

HUNT, R. G. Age, sex, and service patterns in a child guidance clinic. *Journal of Child Psychology and Psychiatry,* 1961, **2,** 185–192. [641]

HURLEY, J. R., & HOHN, R. L. Shifts in child-rearing attitudes linked with parenthood and occupation. *Developmental Psychology,* 1971, **4,** 324–328. [627]

HURST, L. A.   Hypothesis of a single-locus recessive genotype for schizophrenia.   In A. R. Kaplan (Ed.), *Genetic factors in schizophrenia*. Springfield, Ill.: Thomas, 1972. Pp. 219–245.   [426]

HUTCHINSON, R. R., ULRICH, R. E., & AZRIN, N. H.   Effects of age and related factors on the pain-aggression reaction. *Journal of Comparative and Physiological Psychology*, 1965, **59**, 365–369.   [466]

HUTT, C., & OUNSTED, C.   Gaze aversion and its significance in childhood autism. In Hutt, S. J., & Hutt, C. (Eds.) *Behavior Studies in Psychiatry*. New York: Pergamon Press, 1970. Pp. 103–120.   [99, 446–447]

HUTT, S J., & HUTT, C. (Eds.). *Behavior Studies in Psychiatry*. New York: Pergamon Press, 1970.   [447–448]

HUTT, S. J., HUTT, C., LEE, D., & OUNSTED, C.   A behavioral and electroencephalographic study of autistic children. *Journal of Psychiatric Research*, 1965, **3**, 181–197.   [446]

HYMAN, E. T., & GALE, E. N.   Galvanic skin response and reported anxiety during systematic desensitization. *Journal of Consulting and Clinical Psychology*, 1973, **40**, 108–114.   [396]

INOUYE, E.   Similarity and dissimilarity of schizophrenia in twins. *Proceedings of the 3rd World Congress of Psychiatry*, Montreal, 1961, **1**, 524–530.   [428]

ISBELL, H.   Pharmacological factors in drug dependence. In S. Btesh (Ed.), *Drug abuse: Nonmedical use of dependence-producing drugs*. New York: Plenum Press, 1972. Pp. 35–47.   [518]

JACOB, F., & MONOD, J.   On the regulation of gene activity. *Cold Spring Harbor Symposium on Quantitative Biology*, 1961, **26**, 193–209.   [109]

JACOBS, A., & WOLPIN, M. A.   A second look at systematic desensitization. In A. Jacobs & L. B. Sachs (Eds.), *Psychology of private events*. New York: Academic Press, 1971. Pp. 77–108.   [396]

JACOBS, P. A., BRUTON, M., MELVILLE, M. M., BRITTAIN, R. P., & McCLEMENT, W. F.   Aggressive behavior, mental subnormality, and the XYY male. *Nature*, 1965, **208**, 1351–1352.   [115]

JAFFE, J. H.   The maintenance approach to the management of opioid dependence. In C. J. D. Zarafonetis (Ed.), *Drug abuse: Proceedings of the International Conference*. Philadelphia: Lea & Febiger, 1972. Pp. 161–169.   [536]

JAMES, I. P.   Delinquency and heroin addiction in Britain. *British Journal of Criminology*, 1969, **9**, 108–124.   [520]

JARVIK, L. F., & ERLENMEYER-KIMLING, K. L.   Survey of familial correlations in measured intellectual functions. In J. Zubin & G. A. Jervis (Eds.), *Psychopathology of mental development*. New York: Grune & Stratton, 1967. Pp. 447–459. [243]

JASTAK, J. F., & JASTAK, S. R. *The Wide Range Achievement Test*. (Rev. ed.) Wilmington, Delaware: Guidance Associates, 1965.   [573]

JENKINS, R. L., & BOYER, A.   Types of delinquent behavior and background factors. *International Journal of Social Psychiatry*, 1968, **14**, 65–76.   [481]

JENSEN, A. R.   How much can we boost IQ and scholastic achievement? *Harvard Educational Review*, 1969, 39, 1–123.   [224]

JENSEN, A. R.   IQs of identical twins reared apart. *Behavior Genetics*, 1970, 1, 133–148.   [235]

JERSILD, A. T., & HOLMES, F. B.   Children's fears. *Child Development Monographs*, New York: Teachers' College, Columbia University, 1935, No. 20.   [563]

JOHNSTON, M. K., KELLEY, C. S., HARRIS, F. R., & WOLF, M. M. An application of reinforcement principles to development of motor skills of a young child. *Child Development,* 1966, 37, 379–387. [357]

Joint Commission on Mental Health of Children. *Crisis in child mental health: Challenge for the 1970s.* New York: Harper, 1968. [622, 625–627, 634, 649]

Joint Commission on Mental Health and Illness. *Action for mental health.* New York: Science Editions, 1961. [621]

JONES, E. *The life and work of Sigmund Freud.* New York: Basic Books. Vol. 1, 1953; Vol. 2, 1955; Vol. 3, 1957; abridged version: Anchor, 1963. [23, 37, 271, 287]

JONES, H. E. The environment and mental development. In L. Carmichael (Ed.), *Manual of child psychology.* New York: Wiley, 1954. Chapter 10. [213]

JONES, L. E. How 92% beat the dope habit. *Bulletin of the Los Angeles County Medical Association,* 1958, 19, 37. Cited by J. A. O'Donnell, The relapse rate in narcotic addiction: A critique of follow-up studies. In D. M. Wilner & G. G. Kassebaum (Eds.), *Narcotics.* New York: McGraw-Hill, 1965. Pp. 226–246. [533]

JONES, M. *The therapeutic community.* New York: Basic Books, 1953. [506]

JONES, M. C. A laboratory study of fear: The case of Peter. *Pedagogical Seminary,* 1924, 31, 308–315. (a) [335, 337, 344, 351]

JONES, M. C. The elimination of children's fears. *Journal of Experimental Psychology,* 1924, 7, 382–390. (b) [335, 337]

JONES, M. C. Personality antecedents and correlates of drinking patterns in women. *Journal of Consulting and Clinical Psychology,* 1971, 36, 61–69. [528]

Journal of the American College Health Association, 1970, 18, i. [183]

JUDD, L. L. Obsessive compulsive neurosis in children. *Archives of General Psychiatry,* 1965, 12, 136–143. [304, 378]

JUDD, L., & MANDELL, A. Chromosome studies in early infantile autism. *Archives of General Psychiatry,* 1968, 18, 450–457. [444–445]

JUEL-NIELSEN, N. Individual and environment. A psychiatric-psychological investigation of monozygotic twins reared apart. *Psychiatrica Scandanavia,* 1965, 40, 158–292 (Suppl. 183). [235]

JUNG, R., & HASSLER, R. The extrapyramidal motor system. In J. Field (Ed.) *Handbook of neurophysiology. Section I: Neurophysiology.* Vol. II. Washington, D.C.: American Physiological Society, 1960. Pp. 863–927. [152]

KAGAN, L., & MOSS, H. A. *Birth to maturity.* New York: Wiley, 1962. [33, 466]

KAHN, M. The physiology of catharsis. *Journal of Personality and Social Psychology,* 1966, 3, 278–286. [468]

KAHN, M., & BAKER, B. Desensitization with minimal therapist contact. *Journal of Abnormal Psychology,* 1968, 73, 198–200. [350]

KALLMANN, F. J. The genetic theory of schizophrenia. *American Journal of Psychiatry,* 1946, 103, 309–322. [428]

KALLMANN, F. J. *Heredity in health and mental disorder.* New York: W. W. Norton, 1953. [129]

KALLMANN, F. J. Genetic principles in manic depressive psychosis. In P. Hoch & J. Zubin (Eds), *Depression.* New York: Grune & Stratton, 1954. Pp. 1–24. [129]

KALLMANN, F. J., & ROTH, B. Genetic aspects of preadolescent schizophrenia. *American Journal of Psychiatry,* 1956, 112, 599–606. [121, 428–429]

KAMIL, L. J. Psychodynamic changes through systematic desensitization. *Journal of Abnormal Psychology,* 1970, 76, 199–205. [395]

KANFER, F. H., & PHILLIPS, J. S. *Learning foundations of behavior therapy.* New York: Wiley, 1970. [333, 363, 373, 389–390]

KANGAS, J., & BRADWAY, K. Intelligence at middle age: A thirty-eight year follow-up. *Developmental Psychology,* 1971, **5**, 333–337. [211, 252]

KANNER, L. Autistic disturbances of affective contact. *Nervous Child,* 1943, **2**, 217–250. [410, 433–436, 438, 442]

KANNER, L. To what extent is early infantile autism determined by constitutional inadequacies? *Association for Research on Nervous and Mental Diseases, Proceedings,* (1953), 1954, **33**, 378–385. [437, 439–440]

KANNER, L. *Child psychiatry.* (3rd ed.) Springfield, Ill.: Thomas, 1957. [62]

KANNER, L. *A history of the care and study of the mentally retarded.* Springfield, Ill.: Thomas, 1964. [194]

KANNER, L. Childhood psychosis: A historical overview. *Journal of Autism and Childhood Schizophrenia,* 1971, **1**, 14–19. [408, 436]

KANNER, L. Follow-up study of eleven autistic children originally reported in 1943. *Journal of Autism and Childhood Schizophrenia,* 1971, **1**, 119–145. [435]

KANNER, L., RODRIQUEZ, A., & ASHENDEN, B. How far can autistic children go in matters of social adaptation? *Journal of Autism and Childhood Schizophrenia,* 1972, **2**, 9–33. [435]

KAPLAN, A. R. *Genetic factors in "schizophrenia."* Springfield, Ill.: Thomas, 1972. [462]

KAPLAN, J. *Marijuana—the new prohibition.* New York: World Publishing, 1970. [541]

KARLSSON, J. L. A two-locus hypothesis for inheritance of schizophrenia. In A. R. Kaplan (Ed.), *Genetic factors in "schizophrenia."* Springfield, Ill.: Thomas, 1972. Pp. 246–255. [426, 445]

KASANIN, J., & KAUFMAN, M. R. A study of the functional psychoses in childhood. *American Journal of Psychiatry,* 1929, **9**, 307–384. [409]

KATZ, M. M., COLE, J. O., & BARTON, W. E. *The role and methodology of classification in psychiatry and psychopathology.* Washington, D.C.: U. S. Government Printing Office. Public Health Service Publication No. 1584, 1965. [566]

KAUFMAN, I., FRANK, T., FRIEND, J., HEIMS, L. W., & WEISS, R. Success and failure in the treatment of childhood schizophrenia. *American Journal of Psychiatry,* 1962, **118**, 909–913. [455]

KEHOE, M., & IRONSIDE, W. Studies on the experimental induction of depressive responses upon the secretion of gastric acid. *Psychosomatic Medicine,* 1962, **25**, 403–419. [182]

KELLER, O., & ALPER, B. *Halfway houses: Community-centered correction and treatment.* Lexington, Mass.: D. C. Heath, 1970. [508]

KENNEDY, R. J. R. *A Connecticut community revisited: A study of the social adjustment of a group of mentally deficient adults in 1948 and 1960.* Hartford: Connecticut State Department of Health, Office of Mental Retardation, 1966. [252]

KENNEDY, W. A. School phobia: Rapid treatment of fifty cases. *Journal of Abnormal Psychology,* 1965, **70**, 285–289. [378, 401]

KESSEN, W. Research design in the study of developmental problems. In P. H. Mussen (Ed.), *Handbook of research methods in child development.* New York: Wiley, 1960. [92]

KESSEN, W. *The child.* New York: Wiley, 1965. [37]

KESSEN, W., HAITH, M. M., & SALAPATEK, P. H. Human infancy: A bibliography and guide. In P. H. Mussen (Ed.), *Carmichael's manual of child psychology.* New York: Wiley, 1970. Vol. 1. Pp. 287–445. [95]

KESSLER, J. W. *Psychopathology of childhood.* Englewood Cliffs, N.J.: Prentice Hall, 1966. [477]

KESSLER, J. W. Neurosis in childhood. In B. B. Wolman (Ed.), *Manual of child psychopathology.* New York: McGraw-Hill, 1972. Pp. 387–435. [292]

KETY, S. S. Biochemical hypotheses and studies. In L. Bellak & L. Loeb (Eds.), *The schizophrenic syndrome.* New York: Grune & Stratton, 1969. Pp. 155–171. [425]

KIFNER, J. The drug scene: Many students now regard marijuana as a part of growing up. *The New York Times,* Jan. 11, 1968, p. 18. [525]

KIMBRELL, D. Comparison of PPVT, FRPVT, RS-B, and academic achievement scores among institutionalized educable mental retardates. *Perceptual and Motor Skills,* 1966, **23,** 1178. [208]

KIRK, S. A. Research in education. In H. A. Stevens & R. Heber (Eds.), *Mental retardation: A review of research.* Chicago: University of Chicago Press, 1964. Pp. 57–99. [250, 253]

KIRK, S. A., McCARTHY, J. J., & KIRK, W. D. *Illinois Test of Psycholinguistic Abilities.* Urbana: University of Illinois Press, 1968. [573]

KLAIBER, E. L., BROVERMAN, D. M., & KOBAYASHI, Y. The automatization cognitive style, androgens, and monamine oxidase. *Psychopharmacologia,* 1967, **11,** 320–336. [159]

KLAIBER, E. L., BROVERMAN, D. M., VOGEL, W., ABRAHAM, G. E., & CONE, F. L. Effects of infused testosterone on mental performance and serum LH. *Journal of Clinical Endocrinology and Metabolism,* 1971, **32,** 341–349. [159]

KLAPPER, Z. S., & BIRCH, H. G. A fourteen-year follow-up study of cerebral palsy: Intellectual change and stability. *American Journal of Orthopsychiatry,* 1967, **37,** 540–547. [218]

KLEBANOFF, L. B. Parental attitudes of mothers of schizophrenic, brain-injured and retarded, and normal children. *American Journal of Orthopsychiatry,* 1959, **29,** 445–454. [414]

KLEIN, M. *The psychoanalysis of children.* London: International Psychoanalytic Library, 1932. [273]

KLEIN, M. H., DITTMAN, A. T., PARLOFF, M. B., & GILL, M. M. Behavior therapy: Observations and reflections. *Journal of Consulting and Clinical Psychology,* 1969, **33,** 259–266. [388]

KLOPFER, B., AINSWORTH, M. D., KLOPFER, W. G., & HOLT, R. R. *Developments in the Rorschach technique. Vol. I. Technique and theory.* Yonkers, N.Y.: World Book Co., 1954. [581]

KNAPP, P. H., LEVIN, S., McCARTER, R. H., WERMER, H., & ZETZEL, E. Suitability for psychoanalysis: A review of one hundred supervised analytic cases. *Psychoanalytic Quarterly,* 1960, **29,** 459–477. [329]

KNIGHT, R. P. Evaluation of the results of psychoanalytic theory. *American Journal of Psychiatry,* 1941, **98,** 434–446. [326, 328–329, 347, 390]

KOHLBERG, L. Stage and sequence: The cognitive developmental approach to socialization. In D. A. Goslin (Ed.), *Handbook of socialization theory and research.* Chicago: Rand McNally, 1969. Pp. 347–480. [473]

KOHLBERG, L. From is to ought: How to commit the naturalistic fallacy and get away with it in the study of moral development. In T. Mischel (Ed.), *Cognitive development and epistemology.* New York: Academic Press, 1971. Pp. 151–235. [473]

KOHN, M., & ROSMAN, B. L. A social competence scale and symptom checklist for the preschool child. *Developmental Psychology,* 1972, **6**, 430–444. [555]

KOLVIN, I. Aversive imagery treatment in adolescents. *Behavior Research and Therapy,* 1967, **5**, 245–248. [366]

KONDAS, O. Reduction of examination anxiety and 'stage fright' by group desensitization and relaxation. *Behavior Research and Therapy,* 1967, **5**, 275–281. [353, 377, 396]

KOPPITZ, E. M. *The Bender Gestalt Test for young children.* New York: Grune & Stratton, 1964. [598]

KOUNIN, J. Experimental studies of rigidity: I. The measurement of rigidity in normal and feebleminded persons. *Character and Personality,* 1941, **9**, 251–272. (a) [246]

KOUNIN, J. Experimental studies of rigidity: II. The explanatory power of the concept of rigidity as applied to feeble mindedness. *Character and Personality,* 1941, **9**, 273–282. (b) [246]

KRAEPLIN, E. *Psychiatrie.* Leipzig: Barth, 1883; 1899; 1915. [20, 44]

KREBS, R. L. Some relationships between moral judgment, attention, and resistance to temptation. Unpublished doctoral dissertation, University of Chicago, 1968. [473]

KRINGLEN, E. An epidemiological-clinical twin study on schizophrenia. In D. Rosenthal & S. S. Kety (Eds.), *The transmission of schizophrenia.* New York: Pergamon Press, 1968. Pp. 49–63. [428]

KUBIE, L. S. Problems and techniques of psychoanalytic validation and progress. In E. Pumpian-Mindlin (Ed.), *Psychoanalysis as science.* Stanford, Cal.: Stanford University Press, 1952. Pp. 46–124. [322]

KUHLMANN, F. The Binet and Simon tests of intelligence in grading feebleminded children. *Journal of Psycho-asthenics,* 1912, **16**, 173–193. [200]

KUHN, T. S. *The structure of scientific revolutions.* Chicago: University of Chicago Press, 1st ed., 1962; 2nd ed., 1970. [76, 92]

KURLAND, H. D., YEAGER, C. T., & ARTHUR. R. J. Psychophysiologic aspects of severe behavior disorders. *Archives of General Psychiatry,* 1963, **8**, 599–604. [498]

KUSHLICK, A. Assessing the size of the problem of subnormality. In J. E. Meade & A. S. Parkes (Eds.), *Genetic and environmental factors in human ability.* Edinburgh: Oliver & Boyd, 1966. Pp. 121–147. [227]

KUSHNER, M. Faradic aversive controls in clinical practice. In C. Neuringer & J. L. Michael (Eds.), *Behavior modification in clinical psychology.* New York: Appleton-Century-Crofts, 1970. Pp. 26–51. [365, 380]

KYSAR, J. E. The two camps in child psychiatry: A report from a psychiatrist father of an autistic and retarded child. *American Journal of Psychiatry,* 1968, **125**, 103–109. [462]

LACEY, J. I., BATEMAN, D. E., & VANLEHN, R. Autonomic response specificity: An experimental study. *Psychosomatic Medicine,* 1953, **15**, 8–21. [175–176]

LANG, P. J. Behavior therapy with a case of nervous anorexia. In L. P. Ullmann & L. Krasner (Eds.), *Case studies in behavior modification.* New York: Holt, 1965. Pp. 217–221. [178]

LANG, P. J., LAZOVIK, A. D., & REYNOLDS, D. J. Desensitization, suggestibility, and pseudotherapy. *Journal of Abnormal Psychology,* 1965, **70**, 395–402. [395]

LANG, P. J., & MELAMED, B. G. Case report: Avoidance conditioning therapy of an infant with chronic ruminative vomiting. *Journal of Abnormal Psychology*, 1969, **74**, 1–8. [365]

LANG, P. J., SROUFE, L. A., & HASTINGS, J. E. Effects of feedback and instructional set on the control of cardiac-rate variability. *Journal of Experimental Psychology*, 1967, **75**, 425–431. [177]

LANGER, E. J., & ABELSON, R. P. A patient by any other name . . .: Clinician group difference in labeling bias. *Journal of Consulting and Clinical Psychology*, 1974, **41**, 4–9. [547–577]

LANGNER, T. S., HERSON, J. H., GREENE, E. L., JAMESON, J. D., & GOFF, J. A. Children of the city: Affluence, poverty, and mental health. In V. L. Allen (Ed.), *Psychological factors in poverty*. Chicago: Markham, 1970. Pp. 185–209. [631–632]

LAPOUSE, R. The epidemiology of behavior disorders in children. *American Journal of Diseases of Children*, 1966, **3**, 594–599. [51]

LAPOUSE, R., & MONK, M. A. Behavior deviations in a representative sample of children: Variation by sex, age, race, social class, and family size. *American Journal of Orthopsychiatry*, 1964, **34**, 436–446. [51]

LAUFER, M. Assessment of adolescent disturbances: The application of Anna Freud's Diagnostic Profile. *Psychoanalytic Study of the Child*, 1965, **20**, 99–123. [284]

LAZARUS, A. A. The elimination of children's phobias by deconditioning. In H. J. Eysenck (Ed.), *Behavior therapy and the neuroses*. New York: Pergamon Press, 1960. Pp. 114–122. [351, 377]

LAZARUS, A. A. Group therapy of phobic disorders by systematic desensitization. *Journal of Abnormal and Social Psychology*, 1961, **63**, 504–510. [347, 350]

LAZARUS, A. A. *Behavior therapy and beyond*. New York: McGraw-Hill, 1971. [388, 401, 407]

LAZARUS, A. A., & ABRAMOVITZ, A. The use of "emotive imagery" in the treatment of children's phobias. *Journal of Mental Science*, 1962, **108**, 191–195. [352–353, 377]

LAZARUS, A. A., DAVISON, G. C., & POLEFKA, D. A. Classical and operant factors in the treatment of a school phobia. *Journal of Abnormal Psychology*, 1965, **70**, 225–229. [378]

LAZARUS, A. A., & RACHMAN, S. The use of systematic desensitization in psychotherapy. *South African Medical Journal*, 1957, **31**, 934–937. [377]

LEAHY, A. M. Nature-nurture and intelligence. *Genetic Psychology Monographs*, 1935, **17**, 235–308. [242]

LEHRMAN, L. J., SIRLUCK, H., BLACK, B. J., & GLICK, S. J. Success and failure of treatment of children in the child guidance clinics of the Jewish Board of Guardians. New York: *Jewish Board of Guardians Research Monograph*, 1949, No. 1. [639]

LEITENBERG, H., AGRAS, W., BARLOW, D., & OLIVEAU, D. Contribution of selected positive reinforcement and therapeutic instructions to systematic desensitization therapy. *Journal of Abnormal Psychology*, 1969, **74**, 113–118. [396]

LEITER, R. G. *Leiter International Performance Scale*. Chicago: C. H. Stoelting, 1948. [572]

LEJEUNE, J., GAUTIER, M., & TURPIN, R. Study of the somatic chromosomes of nine mongoloid idiot children, 1959. In S. H. Boyer (Ed.), *Papers on human genetics.* Englewood Cliffs, N.J.: Prentice-Hall, 1963. [213]

LEMERE, F., & VOEGTLIN, W. An evaluation of the aversion treatment of alcoholism. *Quarterly Journal of Studies in Alcoholism,* 1950, **11,** 199–204. [364, 531]

LENNARD, H. L., BEAULIEU, M. R., & EMBREY, N. G. Interaction in families with a schizophrenic child. *Archives of General Psychiatry,* 1965, **12,** 166–183. [415]

LENNARD, H. L., EPSTEIN, L. J., BERNSTEIN, A., & RANSOM, D. C. Hazards implicit in prescribing psychoactive drugs. *Science,* 1970, **169,** 438–441. [183–184, 190]

LENNEBERG, E. H. Understanding language without the ability to speak: A case report. *Journal of Abnormal and Social Psychology,* 1962, **65,** 419–425. [154, 170]

LENNEBERG, E. H. *Biological foundations of language.* New York: Wiley, 1967. [150, 154, 189]

LENNEBERG, E. H. The effect of age on the outcome of central nervous system disease in children. In R. L. Isaacson (Ed.), *The neuropsychology of development.* New York: Wiley, 1968. Pp. 147–170. [143, 145, 147, 189, 219]

LERMAN, D. Evaluative studies of institutions for delinquents: Implications for research and social policy. *Social Work,* 1968, **13,** 55–64. [505]

LESSER, L., ASHENDEN, B. J., DEBUSKEY, M., & EISENBERG, L. Anorexia nervosa in children. *American Journal of Orthopsychiatry,* 1960, **30,** 572–580. [178]

LESSING, E. E., & SCHILLING, F. H. Relationship between treatment selection variables and treatment outcome in a child guidance clinic. *Journal of the American Academy of Child Psychiatry,* 1966, **5,** 313–348. [639]

LEVINE, S., & MULLINS, R. F. Hormones in infancy. In G. Newton & S. Levine (Eds.), *Early experience and behavior.* Springfield, Ill.: Thomas, 1968. Pp. 168–197. [158, 160]

LEVITT, E. E. The results of psychotherapy with children: An evaluation. *Journal of Consulting Psychology,* 1957, **21,** 189–196. [639]

LEVITT, E. E. Reply to Hood-Williams. *Journal of Consulting Psychology,* 1960, **24,** 89–91. [640]

LEVITT, E. E. Psychotherapy with children: A further evaluation. *Behavior Research and Therapy,* 1963, **1,** 45–51. [327–328, 639–640]

LEVITT, E. E. Research in psychotherapy with children. In A. E. Bergin & S. L. Garfield (Eds.), *Handbook of psychotherapy and behavior change: An empirical analysis.* New York: Wiley, 1971. Pp. 474–494. [639, 641–643]

LEVITT, E. E., BEISER, H. R., & ROBERTSON, R. E. A follow-up evaluation of cases treated at a community child guidance clinic. *American Journal of Orthopsychiatry,* 1959, **29,** 337–349. [639]

LEVY, H. Discussion. In G. Farrell (Ed.), *Congenital Mental Retardation.* Austin: University of Texas Press, 1969. Pp. 32–33. [216]

LEWIN, B. D., & ROSS, H. *Psychoanalytic education in the United States.* New York: Norton, 1960. [289]

LEZAK, M. D., & DIXON, H. The brain-injured child in a clinic population. A statistical description. *Exceptional Children,* 1964, **30,** 237–240. [166]

LIEBSON, I., & BIGELOW, G. A. A behavioral-pharmacological treatment of dually addicted patients. *Behavior Research and Therapy,* 1972, **10,** 403–405. [536]

LIEF, A. *The commonsense psychiatry of Dr. Adolf Meyer.* New York: McGraw-Hill, 1948. [24]

LINDNER, R. M., & SELIGER, R. V. Projective techniques and the medical psychologist. *Southern Medicine and Surgery*, 1945, 107, 355–356. [580]

LINDZEY, G. Seer versus sign. *Journal of Experimental Research in Personality*, 1965, 1, 17–26. [584, 605]

LINDZEY, G., & GOLDWYN, R. M. Validity of the Rosenzweig Picture-Frustration Study. *Journal of Personality*, 1954, 22, 519–547. [586]

LIVINGSTON, S. Epilepsy in infancy, childhood, and adolescence. In B. Wolman (Ed.), *Manual of child psychopathology*. New York: McGraw-Hill, 1972. Pp. 230–269. [190]

LOCKE, E. A. Is "behavior therapy" behavioristic? (An analysis of Wolpe's psychotherapeutic methods). *Psychological Bulletin*, 1971, 76, 318–327. [388]

LOMONT, J. F., & EDWARDS, J. E. The role of relaxation in systematic desensitization. *Behavior Research and Therapy*, 1967, 5, 11–25. [396]

LONDON, P. The end of ideology in behavior modification. *American Psychologist*. 1972, 27, 913–920. [388, 407]

LORENZ, K. *King Solomon's Ring*. London: Methuen, 1952. [136]

LORENZ, K. *Evolution and modification of behavior*. Chicago: University of Chicago Press, 1965. [98, 136]

LORENZ, K. *On aggression*. New York: Harcourt Brace Jovanovich, 1966. [136]

LOTTER, V. Epidemiology of autistic conditions in young children. *Social Psychiatry*, 1966, 1, 124–137. [438, 443]

LOTTER, V. Epidemiology of autistic conditions in young children. II. Some characteristics of the parents and children. *Social Psychology*, 1967, 1, 163–173. [439–440, 443]

LOVAAS, O. I. A behavior therapy approach to the treatment of childhood schizophrenia. In J. P. Hill (Ed.), *Minnesota Symposium on Child Psychology*, Vol. I. Minneapolis: University of Minnesota Press, 1967. Pp. 108–159. [354, 365, 369, 455–456]

LOVAAS, O. I. Some studies on the treatment of childhood schizophrenia. In J. M. Shlien (Ed.), *Research in psychotherapy*. Washington, D.C.: American Psychological Association, 1968. Pp. 103–121. [455–456]

LOVAAS, O. I., FREITAS, L., NELSON, K., & WHALEN, C. The establishment of imitation and its use for the development of complex behavior in schizophrenic children. *Behavior Research and Therapy*, 1967, 5, 171–181. [369, 456]

LOVAAS, O. I., SCHAEFFER, B., & SIMMONS, J. O. Building social behavior in autistic children by use of electric shock. *Journal of Experimental Research in Personality*, 1965, 1, 99–109. [455]

LOVAAS, O. I., SCHREIBMAN, L., KOEGEL, R., & REHM, R. Selective responding by autistic children to multiple sensory input. *Journal of Abnormal Psychology*, 1971, 77, 211–222. [449]

LOVE, L. R., KASWAN, J., & BUGENTAL, D. E. Differential effectiveness of three clinical interventions for different socioeconomic groupings. *Journal of Consulting and Clinical Psychology*, 1972, 39, 347–360. [637–638]

LOVIBOND, S. H. *Conditioning and enuresis*. Oxford: Pergamon Press, 1964. [382, 399, 407]

LOVIBOND, S. H., & COOTE, M. A. Enuresis. In C. G. Costello (Ed.), *Symptoms of psychopathology*. New York: Wiley, 1970. Pp. 373–396. [382, 399, 407]

LOWE, L. H. Families of children with early childhood schizophrenia. *Archives of General Psychiatry*, 1966, 14, 26–30. [414, 439–440, 451]

LOWELL, F. E. A study of the variability of IQs in retest. *Journal of Applied Psychology,* 1941, **25**, 341–356. [221–222]

LUBORSKY, L. New directions in research on neurotic and psychosomatic symptoms. *American Scientist,* 1970, **58**, 661–668. [318]

LUBORSKY, L., CHANDLER, M., AUERBACH, A. H., COHEN, J., & BACHRACH, H. M. Factors influencing the outcome of psychotherapy: A review of quantitative research. *Psychological Bulletin,* 1971, **75**, 145–185. [643]

LUBS, H. A., & RUDDLE, F. H. Chromosomal abnormalities in the human population: Estimation of rates based on New Haven newborn study. *Science,* 1970, **169**, 495–497. [116]

LUFF, M. C., & GARROD, M. The after-results of psychotherapy in five hundred adult cases. *British Medical Journal,* 1935, **2**, 54–59. [328]

LUXEMBURGER, H. Vorläufiger Bericht über psychiatrische Serienuntersuchungen an Zwillingen. *Zeitschrift für die gesamte Neurologie und Psychiatrie,* 1928, **116**, 397–347. [428]

LYKKEN, D. T. A study of anxiety in the sociopathic personality. *Journal of Abnormal and Social Psychology,* 1957, **55**, 6–10. [494]

MACFARLANE, J. W., ALLEN, L., & HONZIK, M. P. *A developmental study of the behavior problems of normal children between twenty-one months and fourteen years.* Berkeley & Los Angeles: University of California Press, 1954. [51–52]

MACHOVER, K. *Personality projection in the drawing of the human figure.* Springfield, Ill.: Thomas, 1949. [587]

MACHOVER, K. Sex differences in the developmental pattern of children as seen in human figure drawings. In A. I. Rabin & M. R. Haworth (Eds.), *Projective techniques with children.* New York: Grune & Stratton, 1960. Pp. 238–257. [587]

MACKIE, R. P. Spotlighting advances in special education. *Exceptional Children,* 1965, **32**, 77–81. [250]

MACMILLAN, D. L. Motivational differences: Cultural-familial retardates vs. normal subjects on expectancy for failure. *American Journal of Mental Deficiency,* 1969, **74**, 254–258. [247]

MAHARISHI MAHESH YOGI. *The science of being and art of living.* London: International S. R. M., 1966. [531]

MAHER, B. *Principles of psychopathology.* New York: McGraw-Hill, 1966. [156]

MAHER, B. *Introduction to research in psychopathology.* New York: McGraw-Hill, 1970. [92]

MAHL, G. *Psychological conflict and defense.* New York: Harcourt Brace Jovanovich, 1971. [287, 342]

MAHL, G. F., & KARPE, R. Emotions and hydrochloric acid secretion during psychoanalytic hours. *Psychosomatic Medicine,* 1953, **15**, 312–327. [182]

MAHLER, M. On child psychosis and schizophrenia: Autistic and symbiotic infantile psychosis. *Psychoanalytic Study of the Child,* 1952, **7**, 286–305. [410, 451]

MAHLER, M. On early infantile psychosis. The symbiotic and autistic syndromes. *Journal of the American Academy of Child Psychiatry,* 1965, **4**, 554–568. [451]

MAHLER, M. S., & FURER, M. Child psychosis: A theoretical statement and its implications. *Journal of Autism and Childhood Schizophrenia,* 1972, **2**, 213–218. [451]

MALLICK, S. K., & McCANDLESS, B. R. A study of catharsis of aggression. *Journal of Personality and Social Psychology,* 1966, **4**, 591–596. [465, 468]

MALMO, R. B., & SHAGASS, C. Physiologic study of symptom mechanisms in psychiatric patients under stress. *Psychosomatic Medicine*, 1949, **11**, 25–29. [176]

MALPASS, L. F. Programmed instruction for retarded children. In A. A. Baumeister (Ed.), *Mental Retardation: Appraisal, education, and rehabilitation*. Chicago: Aldine, 1967. Pp. 213–231. [254]

MANOSEVITZ, M., LINDZEY, G., & THIESSEN, D. O. *Behavioral genetics: Method and research*. New York: Appleton-Century-Crofts, 1969. [137]

MARGOLIS, M. The mother-child relationship in bronchial asthma. *Journal of Abnormal and Social Psychology*, 1961, **63**, 360–367. [180]

MARKS, I. M. *Fears and phobias*. New York: Academic Press, 1969. [407]

MARKS, I. M., & GELDER, M. G. Common ground between behavior therapy and psychodynamic methods. *British Journal of Medical Psychology*, 1966, **39**, 11–23. [259]

MARKS, I. M., GELDER, M. G., & EDWARDS, G. Hypnosis and desensitization for phobias: A controlled prospective trial. *British Journal of Psychiatry*, 1968, **114**, 1263–1274. [391–392]

MARKS, P. A. An assessment of the diagnostic process in a child guidance setting. *Psychological Monographs*, 1961, **75** (Whole No. 507). [592]

MARTIN, G. L., ENGLAND, G., KAPROWY, E., KILGOUR, K., & PILEK, V. Operant conditioning of kindergarten-class behavior in autistic children. *Behavior Research and Therapy*, 1968, **6**, 281–294. [456]

MARTIN, M., BURKHOLDER, R., ROSENTHAL, T. L., THARP, R. G., & THORNE, G. L. Programming behavior change and reintegration into school milieux of extreme adolescent deviates. *Behavior Research and Therapy*, 1968, **6**, 371–384. [362]

MASLOW, P., FROSTIG, M., LEFEVER, D. W., & WHITTLESEY, J. R. B. The Marianne Frostig developmental test of visual perception 1963 standardization. *Perceptual and Motor Skills*, 1964, **19**, 463–499. [599]

MASON, M. K. Learning to speak after six and one-half years of silence. *Journal of Speech Disorders*, 1942, **7**, 295–304. [220–221]

MASSERMAN, J. H. *Behavior and neurosis*. Chicago: University of Chicago Press, 1943. [323]

MASSERMAN, J. H. Experimental neuroses. *Scientific American*, 1950, **182**, 38–43. [323]

MASSERMAN, J. H. Ethology, comparative biodynamics, and psychoanalytic research. In J. Scher (Ed.), *Theories of the mind*. New York: Free Press, 1963. [323, 326, 390]

MAUGH, T. H. LSD and the drug culture: New evidence of hazard. *Science*, 1973, **179**, 1221–1222. [146, 525]

MCADOO, W. G., & ROESKE, N. A. A comparison of defectors and continuers in a child guidance clinic. *Journal of Consulting and Clinical Psychology*, 1973, **40**, 328–334. [640]

MCCALL, R. B., HOGARTY, P. S., & HURLBURT, N. Transitions in infant sensorimotor development and the prediction of childhood IQ. *American Psychologist*, 1972, **27**, 728–748. [206]

MCCLEARN, G. E. Genetic influences on behavior and development. In P. H. Mussen (Ed.), *Carmichael's Manual of Child Psychology*. New York: Wiley, 1970. Vol. I. Pp. 39–76. [105, 109, 137]

MCCLELLAND, D. C. (Ed.). *Studies in motivation*. New York: Appleton, 1955. [583]

McCLELLAND, D. C. *The achieving society.* Princeton, N. J.: Van Nostrand, 1961. [583]

McCLELLAND, D. C. Longitudinal trends in the relation of thought to action. *Journal of Consulting Psychology,* 1966, **30**, 479–483. [583]

McCLELLAND, D. C., ATKINSON, J. W., CLARK, R. A., & LOWELL, E. L. *The achievement motive.* New York: Appleton-Century-Crofts, 1953. [45]

McCORD, W., McCORD, J., & HOWARD, A. Familial correlates of aggression in non-delinquent male children. *Journal of Abnormal and Social Psychology,* 1961, **62**, 79–83. [470]

McCORD, W., McCORD, J., & ZOLA, I. K. *Origins of crime.* New York: Columbia University Press, 1959. [490, 513]

McCORKLE, L., ELIAS, A., & BIXBY, F. *The Highfields Story: A unique experiment in the treatment of juvenile delinquency.* New York: Holt, 1958. [507, 515]

McDERMOTT, J. F., HARRISON, S. I., SCHRAGER, J., LINDY, J., & KILLINS, E. W. Social class and mental illness in children: The question of childhood psychosis. *American Journal of Orthopsychiatry,* 1967, **37**, 548–57. [451]

McDONALD, L. *Social class and delinquency.* London: Faber & Faber, 1969. [484]

McFIE, J. The effects of hemispherectomy on intellectual functioning in cases of infantile hemiplegia. *Journal of Neurology, Neurosurgery, and Psychiatry,* 1961, **24**, 240–249. [155]

McGREW, W. C. *An ethological study of children's behavior.* New York: Academic Press, 1972. [99]

McKAY, H. D. Report on the careers of male delinquents in Chicago. In U. S. Task Force on Juvenile Delinquency, *Juvenile delinquency and youth crime,* Washington, D.C.: U. S. Government Printing Office, 1967. Pp. 107–113. [504]

McNEMAR, Q. *The revision of the Stanford-Binet Scale.* Boston: Houghton-Mifflin, 1942. [203]

McNEMAR, Q. *Psychiological statistics.* New York: Wiley, 1962; 4th ed., 1969. [81, 122]

MEDNICK, S. A. Breakdown in individuals at high risk for schizophrenia: Possible predispositional perinatal factors. *Mental Hygiene,* 1970, **54**, 50–63. [84, 423–427]

MEDNICK, S. A., & McNEIL, T. F. Current methodology in research on the etiology of schizophrenia: Serious difficulties which suggest the use of the high-risk-group method. *Psychological Bulletin,* 1968, **70**, 681–693. [423]

MEDNICK, S. A., MURA, E., SCHULSINGER, F., & MEDNICK, B. Perinatal conditions and infant development in children with schizophrenic parents. *Social Biology,* 1971, **18**, 103–113. [423]

MEDNICK, S. A., & SCHULSINGER, F. A longitudinal study of children with a high risk for schizophrenia: A preliminary report. In S. G. Vandenberg (Ed.), *Methods and goals in human behavior genetics.* New York: Academic Press, 1965. Pp. 255–295. [422]

MEDNICK, S. A., & SCHULSINGER, F. Some premorbid characteristics related to breakdown in children with schizophrenic mothers. In D. Rosenthal and S. Kety (Eds.), *The transmission of schizophrenia.* Oxford: Pergamon Press, 1968. [560]

MEDNICK, S. A., & SCHULSINGER, F. Studies of children at high risk for schizophrenia. Unpublished manuscript, New School for Social Research, 1972. [423]

MEEHL, P. E. *Clinical versus statistical prediction.* Minneapolis: University of Minnesota Press, 1954. [88–89, 93, 605]

MEEHL, P. E. Psychotherapy. In C. P. Stone and Q. McNemar (Eds.), *Annual review of psychology*. Vol. 6. Stanford, Cal.: Annual Reviews, 1955. Pp. 357–378. [342]

MEEHL, P. E. Schizotaxia, schizotypy, schizophrenia. *American Psychologist*, 1962, **17**, 827–838. [77]

MEEHL, P. E. Seer over sign: The first good example. *Journal of Experimental Research in Personality*, 1965, **1**, 27–32. [605]

MEICHENBAUM, D. H., BOWERS, K. S., & ROSS, R. R. Modification of classroom behavior of institutionalized female adolescent offenders. *Behavior Research and Therapy*, 1968, **6**, 343–353. [509]

MELTZOFF, J., & KORNREICH, M. *Research in psychotherapy*. New York: Atherton, 1970. [329, 650]

MENOLASCINO, F. Psychoses of childhood: Experiences of a mental retardation pilot project. *American Journal of Mental Deficiency*, 1965, **70**, 83–92. [422]

MENSH, I. N. Drug addiction. In C. G. Costello (Ed.), *Symptoms of psychopathology: A handbook*. New York, Wiley, 1970. Pp. 511–534. [541]

MERTON, R. K. Social structure and anomie. In R. K. Merton (Ed.), *Social theory and social structure*. (Rev. ed.) New York: Free Press, 1957. Pp. 161–194. [484]

METRAKOS, J. D., & METRAKOS, K. Genetic factors in epilepsy. In E. Niedermeyer (Ed.), *Epilepsy. Modern problems of pharmopsychiatry*. Vol. 4. New York: Karger, 1970. Pp. 71–86. [174]

METZ, J. R. Stimulation preferences of autistic children. *Journal of Abnormal Psychology*, 1967, **72**, 529–535. [447]

MEYER, V. Modification of expectations in cases with obsessional rituals. *Behavior Research and Therapy*, 1966, **4**, 273–280. [379]

MEYERS, D. I., & GOLDFARB. W. Studies of perlexity in mothers of schizophrenic children. *American Journal of Orthopsychiatry*, 1961, **31**, 551–564. [418–420]

MEYERS, D. I., & GOLDFARB, W. Psychiatric appraisal of parents and siblings of schizophrenic children. *American Journal of Psychiatry*, 1962, **118**, 902–908. [419, 421, 424]

MEYERSON, L., KERR, N., & MICHAEL, J. L. Behavior modification in rehabilitation. In S. W. Bijou & D. M. Baer (Eds.), *Child development: Readings in experimental analysis*. New York: Appleton-Century-Crofts, 1967. Pp. 214–239. [254]

MICHAELS, J. J., & STIVER, I. P. The impulsive psychopathic character according to the diagnostic profile. *Psychoanalytic Study of the Child*, 1965, **20**, 124–141. [284]

MIGLER, B., & WOLPE, J. Automated self de-sensitization: A case report. *Behavior Research and Therapy*, 1967, **5**, 133–135. [350]

MILGRAM, N. The rationale and irrational in Zigler's motivational approach to mental retardation. *American Journal of Mental Deficiency*, 1969, **73**, 527–532. [258]

MILLER, L. C. Dimensions of psychopathology in middle childhood. *Psychological Reports*, 1967, **21**, 897–903. [555]

MILLER, L. C., BARRETT, C. L., HAMPE, E., & NOBLE, H. Comparison of reciprocal inhibition, psychotherapy, and waiting list control for phobic children. *Journal of Abnormal Psychology*, 1972, **79**, 269–279. [391–393, 637]

MILLER, N. E., & BUGELSKI, R. Minor studies in aggression: The influence of frustrations imposed by the in-group on attitudes expressed toward out-groups. *Journal of Psychology*, 1948, **25**, 437–442. [465]

MILLER, N. E., & DOLLARD, J. *Social learning and imitation.* New Haven: Yale University Press, 1941. [468]

MILLER, W. B. Lower-class culture as a generating milieu of gang delinquency. *Journal of Social Issues,* 1958, **14,** 5–19. [484]

MILLER, W. B. The impact of a "total-community" delinquency control project. *Social Problems,* 1962, **10,** 168–191. [513]

MILLON, T. *Modern psychopathology: A biosocial approach to maladaptive learning and functioning.* Philadelphia: Saunders, 1969. [210]

MINDE, K. K., & WEISS, G. C. The assessment of drug effects in children as compared to adults. *Journal of the American Academy of Child Psychiatry,* 1970, **9,** 124–133. [185]

MIRSKY, I. A. Physiologic, psychologic, and social determinants in the etiology of duodenal ulcer. *American Journal of Digestive Diseases,* 1958, **3,** 285–314. [180–181]

MISCHEL, W. *Personality and assessment.* New York: Wiley, 1968. [605]

MITTELMANN, B. Motility in infants, children, and adults. *Psychoanalytic Study of the Child,* 1954, **9,** 142–177. [277]

MONACHESI, E. D., & HATHAWAY, S. R. The personality of delinquents. In J. N. Butcher (Ed.), *MMPI: Research developments and clinical applications.* New York: McGraw-Hill, 1969. Pp. 207–220. [481, 591]

MÖNCKEBERG, F. Effect of early marasmic malnutrition on subsequent physical and psychological development. In N. S. Scrimshaw & J. E. Gordon (Eds.), *Malnutrition, learning, and behavior.* Cambridge: M.I.T. Press, 1968. Pp. 269–278. [161–162]

MONEY, J. Behavior genetics: Principles, methods, and examples from XO, XXY, and XYY syndromes. *Seminars in Psychiatry,* 1970, **2,** 11–29. [115]

MONEY, J., & EHRHARDT, A. A. *Man and woman. Boy and girl. The differentiation and dimorphism of gender identity from conception to maturity.* Baltimore: Johns Hopkins, 1972. [141, 189]

MONEY, J., & MITTENTHAL, S. Lack of personality pathology in Turner's syndrome: Relation to cytogenetics, hormones, and physique. *Behavior Genetics,* 1970, **1,** 43–56. [115]

MONEY, J., WOLFF, G., & ANNECILLO, C. Pain agnosia and self-injury in the syndrome of reversible somatotropin deficiency (Psychosocial dwarfism). *Journal of Autism and Childhood Schizophrenia,* 1972, **2,** 127–139. [157]

MONTAGU, M. F. A. *Prenatal influences.* Springfield, Ill.: Thomas, 1962. [143–146]

MOORE, B. E., & FINE, B. D. *A glossary of psychoanalytic terms.* (2nd ed.) New York: American Psychoanalytic Association, 1968. [94, 287, 291, 302, 306]

MOORE, N. Behavior therapy in bronchial asthma: A controlled study. *Journal of Psychosomatic Research,* 1965, **9,** 257–276. [391]

MORGAN, C. D., & MURRAY, H. A. A method for investigating fantasies: The Thematic Apperception Test. *Archives of Neurology and Psychiatry,* 1935, **34,** 289–306. [583]

MORGANSTERN, K. P. Implosive and flooding procedures: A critical review. *Psychological Bulletin,* 1973, **79,** 318–334. [367]

MORRIS, D. *The naked ape.* New York: McGraw-Hill, 1967. Dell paperback, 1969. [98, 136]

MOWRER, O. H. *Learning theory and personality dynamics.* New York: Ronald Press, 1950. [340]

MOWRER, O. H., & MOWRER, W. M. Enuresis: A method for its study and treatment. *American Journal of Orthopsychiatry*, 1938, 8, 436–459. [338, 351, 382, 399]

MUELLER, K. H. Programs for deviant girls. In W. W. Wattenberg (Ed.), *Social deviancy among youth. Sixty-fifth Yearbook of the National Society for the Study of Education.* Chicago: National Society for the Study of Education, 1966. Pp. 344–372. [500]

MUELLER, M. W. Prediction of achievement of educable mentally retarded children. *American Journal of Mental Deficiency*, 1969, 73, 590–596. [208]

MULAIK, S. A. *The foundations of factor analysis.* New York: McGraw-Hill, 1972. [554]

MURPHY, D. P. *Congenital malformation.* (2nd ed.) Philadelphia: University of Pennsylvania Press, 1947. [146]

MURPHY, F. J., SHIRLEY, M. M., & WITMER, H. L. The incidence of hidden delinquency. *American Journal of Orthopsychiatry*, 1946, 16, 686–695. [478]

MURRAY, H. A. *Thematic Apperception Test.* Cambridge: Harvard University Press, 1943. [583]

MURRAY, H. A. Foreword. In H. Anderson & G. Anderson (Eds.), *An introduction to projective techniques.* Englewood Cliffs, N.J.: Prentice-Hall, 1951. Pp. xi–xiv. [580]

MURRAY, H. A. Preparations for the scaffold of a comprehensive system. In S. Koch (Ed.), *Psychology: A study of science.* Vol. 3. New York: McGraw-Hill, 1959. Pp. 7–54. [580]

MURRAY, J. P. Television and violence: Implications of the Surgeon General's research program. *American Psychologist*, 1973, 28, 472–478. [471]

MUSSEN, P. H. (Ed.) *Handbook of research methods in child development.* New York: Wiley, 1960. [92]

MUSSEN, P. H. (Ed.) *Carmichael's handbook of child psychology.* New York: Wiley 1970. Vols. 1 & 2. [136]

MUSSEN, P. H., CONGER, J. J., & KAGAN, J. *Child development and personality.* New York: Harper, 1969. [189]

NATIONAL INSTITUTE OF MENTAL HEALTH. *Outpatient Psychiatric Clinics Annual Statistical Report.* Washington: Public Health Service Publication 1854, 1966. [641]

NELSON, E. A., GRINDER, R. E., & CHALLAS, J. H. Resistance to temptation and moral judgment: Behavioral correlates of Kohlberg's measure of moral development. Mimeographed paper, University of Wisconsin, 1968. [473]

NELSON, E. A., GRINDER, R. E., & MUTTERER, M. L. Sources of variance in behavioral measures of honesty in temptation situations: Methodological analyses. *Developmental Psychology*, 1969, 1, 265–279. [471]

NEUSTATTER, W. L. The results of fifty cases treated by psychotherapy. *Lancet*, 1935, 1, 796–799. [328]

NEWMAN, H. H., FREEMAN, F. N., & HOLZINGER, K. J. *Twins, a study of heredity and environment.* Chicago: University of Chicago Press, 1937. [124, 234]

NEWTON, M. R., & BROWN, R. D. A preventive approach to developmental problems in school children. In E. M. Bower & W. G. Hollister (Eds.), *Behavioral science frontiers in education.* New York: Wiley, 1967. Pp. 499–527. [619]

NEW YORK STATE DEPARTMENT OF MENTAL HYGIENE. A special census of suspected and referred mental retardation, Onondaga County, New York. In *Technical Report of the Mental Health Research Unit*. Syracuse: Syracuse University Press, 1955. [226]

NEY, P. G., PALVESKY, A. E., & MARKELY, J. Relative effectiveness of operant conditioning and play therapy in childhood schizophrenia. *Journal of Autism and Childhood Schizophrenia*, 1971, 1, 337–349. [457]

NICHOLS, J. R. How opiates change behavior. *Scientific American*, 1965, 212, 80–88. [234, 527]

NOLAN, J. D., MATTIS, P. R., & HOLIDAY, W. C. Long-term effects of behavior therapy: A 12-month follow-up. *Journal of Abnormal Psychology*, 1970, 76, 88–92. [401]

NOVICK, J. Symptomatic treatment of acquired and persistent enuresis. *Journal of Abnormal Psychology*, 1966, 71, 363–368. [382, 401]

NOVICK, J. I. Comparison between short-term group and individual psychotherapy in effecting change in nondesirable behavior in children. *International Journal of Group Psychotherapy*, 1965, 15, 366–373. [609]

NYSWANDER, M. History of a nightmare. In D. Wakefield (Ed.), *The addict*. Greenwich, Conn.: Fawcett, 1963. Pp. 20–32. [517]

O'BRIEN, J. S., RAYNES, A. E., & PATCH, V. D. Treatment of heroin addiction with aversion therapy, relaxation training, and systematic desensitization. *Behavior Research and Therapy*, 1972, 10, 77–80. [537]

O'CONNOR, W. A., & STACHOWIAK, J. Patterns of interaction in families with low adjusted, high adjusted, and mentally retarded members. *Family Process*, 1971, 10, 229–241. [613]

O'DONNELL, J. A. The relapse rate in narcotic addiction: A critique of follow-up studies. In D. M. Wilner & G. G. Kassebaum (Eds.), *Narcotics*. New York: McGraw-Hill, 1965. Pp. 226–246. [532]

OGDON, D. P., BASS, C. L., THOMAS, E. R., & LORDI, W. Parents of autistic children. *American Journal of Orthopsychiatry*, 1968, 38, 653–658. [441]

O'LEARY, K. D., BECKER, W. C., EVANS, M. B., & SAUDARGAS, R. A. A token reinforcement program in a public school: A replication and systematic analysis. *Journal of Applied Behavior Analysis*, 1969, 2, 3–13. [360–361]

OLIVEAU, D. Systematic desensitization in an experimental setting: A follow-up study. *Behavior Research and Therapy*, 1967, 7, 377–380. [396]

OLIVEAU, D., AGRAS, W., LEITENBERG, H., MOORE, R., & WRIGHT, D. Systematic desensitization, therapeutically oriented instructions, and selective positive reinforcement. *Behavior Research and Therapy*, 1969, 7, 27–34. [396]

OLLENDICK, T., BALLA, D., & ZIGLER, E. Expectancy of success and the probability learning of retarded children. *Journal of Abnormal Psychology*, 1971, 77, 275–281. [248]

OLLENDICK, T., & GRUEN, G. E. Treatment of a bodily injury phobia with implosive therapy. *Journal of Consulting and Clinical Psychology*, 1972, 38, 389–393. [367, 377]

OLTMAN, J. E., McGARRY, J. J., & FRIEDMAN, S. Parental deprivation and the "broken home" in dementia praecox and other mental disorders. *American Journal of Psychiatry*, 1952, 108, 685–694. [414]

ORNITZ, E. M., & RITVO, E. R. Perceptual inconstancy in early infantile autism. *Archives of General Psychiatry*, 1968, 18, 76–98. [439]

OTIS, N., & McCANDLESS, B. Responses to repeated frustrations of young children differentiated according to need area. *Journal of Abnormal and Social Psychology,* 1955, **50**, 349–353. [465]

OTTENBERG, P., STEIN, M., LEWIS, J., & HAMILTON, C. Learned asthma in the guinea pig. *Psychosomatic Medicine,* 1958, **20**, 395–400. [177]

OWEN, D. R. The 47, XYY male: A review. *Psychological Bulletin,* 1972, **78**, 209–233. [116]

OWEN, D. R., & SINES, J. O. Heritability of personality in children. *Behavior Genetics,* 1970, **1**, 235–247. [234]

OWEN, F. W., ADAMS, P. A., FORREST, T., STOLZ, L. M., & FISHER, S. Learning disorders in children: Sibling studies. *Society for Research in Child Development Monographs,* 1971, **36**, (Serial No. 144). [386]

PAINE, R. S., WERRY, J. S., & QUAY, H. C. A study of "minimal brain dysfunction." *Developmental Medicine and Child Neurology,* 1968, **10**, 505–520. [168]

PARLEE, M. B. Comments on "Roles of activation and inhibition in sex differences in cognitive abilities" by D. M. Broverman, E. L. Klaiber, Y. Kobayshi, & W. Vogel. *Psychological Review,* 1971, **79**, 180–184. [159]

PARRY-JONES, W. L., SANTER-WESTRATE, H. C., & CRAWLEY, R. C. Behavior therapy in a case of hysterical blindness. *Behavior Research and Therapy,* 1970, **8**, 79–85. [380]

PASAMANICK, B., & KNOBLOCH, H. Brain damage and reproductive causality. *American Journal of Orthopsychiatry,* 1960, **30**, 298–305. (a) [144–145]

PASAMANICK, B., & KNOBLOCH, H. Epidemiologic studies on the complications of pregnancy and the birth process. In G. Caplan (Ed.), *Prevention of mental disorders in children.* New York: Basic Books, 1960. Pp. 74–94. (b)

PASAMANICK, B., & LILIENFELD, A. M. Association of maternal and fetal factors with development of mental deficiency. *Journal of the American Medical Association,* 1955, **159**, 155–160. (a) [145]

PASAMANICK, B., & LILIENFELD, A. M. Maternal and fetal factors in the development of epilepsy. Relationship to some clinical features of epilepsy. *Neurology,* 1955, **5**, 77–83. (b) [174]

PATTERSON, G. R. A learning theory approach to the treatment of the school phobic child. In L. P. Ullmann & L. Krasner (Eds.), *Case studies in behavior modification.* New York: Holt, Rinehart, & Winston, 1965. [377–378]

PATTERSON, G. R., & BRODSKY, G. A behavior modification programme for a child with multiple problem behaviors. *Journal of Child Psychology and Psychiatry,* 1966, **7**, 277–295. [385]

PATTERSON, G. R., & COBB, J. A. A dyadic analysis of "aggressive" behaviors. In J. P. Hill (Ed.), *Minnesota Symposia on Child Psychology,* Vol. 5. Minneapolis: University of Minnesota Press, 1971. Pp. 72–129. [385, 468, 515]

PATTERSON, G. R., JONES, R., WHITTIER, J., & WRIGHT, M. A. A behavior modification technique for the hyperactive child. *Behavior Research and Therapy,* 1965, **2**, 217–226. [383–384]

PATTERSON, G. R., LITTMAN, R. A., & BRICKER, W. Assertive behavior in children: A step toward a theory of aggression. *Monographs of the Society for Research in Child Development,* 1967, **32**, (Serial No. 113). [467]

PATTERSON, G. R., & REID, J. B. Reciprocity and coercion: Two facets of social systems. In C. Neuringer & J. L. Michael (Eds.), *Behavior modification in clinical psychology.* New York: Appleton-Century-Crofts, 1970. Pp. 133–177. [371]

PAUL, G. L. *Insight vs. desensitization in psychotherapy.* Stanford, Cal.: Stanford University Press, 1966. [395]

PAUL, G. L. Insight vs. desensitization in psychotherapy two years after termination. *Journal of Consulting Psychology,* 1967, 31, 333–348. [395, 401]

PAUL, G. L. Two-year follow-up of systematic desensitization in therapy groups. *Journal of Abnormal Psychology,* 1967, 73, 119–130. [395]

PAUL, G. L., & SHANNON, D. T. Treatment of anxiety through systematic desensitization in therapy groups. *Journal of Abnormal Psychology,* 1966, 71, 124–135. [395]

PAWLICK, R. Behavior-therapy research with children: A critical review. *Canadian Journal of Behavioral Science,* 1970, 2, 163–173. [390]

PEARSON, G. H. J. (Ed.) *A handbook of child psychoanalysis.* New York: Basic Books, 1968. [330]

PECKHAM, R. Problems in job adjustment of the mentally retarded. *American Journal of Mental Deficiency,* 1951, 56, 448–453. [252]

PEIPER, A. *Cerebral function in infancy and childhood.* New York: Consultants Bureau, 1963. [154]

PENFIELD, W., & ROBERTS, L. *Speech and brain mechanisms.* Princeton: Princeton University Press, 1959. [151, 154, 171, 189]

PENROSE, L. S. *Recent advances in human genetics.* London: Churchill, 1961. [101]

PENROSE, L. S. *The biology of mental defect.* (3rd ed.) London: Sidgwick and Jackson, 1963. [108, 143–147, 227–228]

PERKINS, M. J. *Effects of play therapy and behavior modification approaches with conduct problem boys.* (Doctoral dissertation, University of Illinois, 1967) *Dissertation Abstracts,* 1968, 28 (8-B), 3478–3479. [608]

PETERSON, D. R. Behavior problems of middle childhood. *Journal of Consulting Psychology,* 1961, 25, 205–209. [554–555, 561]

PETERSON, D. R. *The clinical study of social behavior.* New York: Appleton-Century-Crofts, 1968. [92, 605]

PETERSON, D. R. Attitudes concerning the Doctor of Psychology program. *Professional Psychology,* Nov., 1969, 44–47. [43]

PETERSON, D. R., & BECKER, W. C. Family interaction and delinquency. In H. C. Quay (Ed.), *Juvenile delinquency: Research and theory.* Princeton, N.J.: Van Nostrand, 1965. Pp. 63–99. [488]

PETERSON, D. R., BECKER, W. C., SHOEMAKER, D. J., LURIA, Z., & HELLMER, L. A. Child behavior problems and parental attitudes. *Child Development,* 1961, 32, 151–162. [593]

PETERSON, D. R., QUAY, H. C., & TIFFANY, T. L. Personality factors related to juvenile delinquency. *Child Development,* 1961, 32, 355–372. [480]

PETERSON, L., & SMITH, L. A comparison of the post-school adjustment of educable mentally retarded adults with that of adults of normal intelligence. *Exceptional Children,* 1960, 26, 404–408. [252]

PIAGET, J. *The moral judgment of the child.* New York: Harcourt, 1932. [472]

PIAGET, J. *Play, dreams, and imitation in childhood.* New York: Norton, 1951. [97, 248]

PIAGET, J., & INHELDER, B. *The psychology of the child.* New York: Basic Books, 1969. [59]

PIERCE, C. M. Enuresis. In A. M. Freedman & H. I. Kaplan (Eds.), *Comprehensive textbook of psychiatry.* Baltimore: Williams & Wilkins, 1967. Pp. 1380–1383. [313]

PIERREL, R., & SHERMAN, J. G. Train your pet the Barnabus way. *Brown Alumni Monthly,* 1963, Feb., 8–14. [356]

PINNEAU, S. R. *Changes in intelligence quotient: Infancy to maturity.* Boston: Houghton-Mifflin, 1961. [204]

PIOTROWSKI, Z. A. Rorschach method in review. In D. Bower & L. E. Abt (Eds.), *Progress in clinical psychology II.* New York: Grune & Stratton, 1956. Pp. 16–31. [581]

PITFIELD, M., & OPPENHEIM, A. Child-rearing attitudes of mothers of psychotic children. *Journal of Child Psychology and Psychiatry,* 1964, **5**, 51–57. [414]

PLUMMER, G. Anomalies occurring in children exposed in utero to the atomic bomb in Hiroshima. *Pediatrics,* 1952, **10**, 687–693. [146]

POLAN, C. C., & SPENCER, B. L. Checklist of symptoms of autism in early life. *West Virginia Medical Journal,* 1959, **55**, 198–204. [438]

POLLACK, M. Mental subnormality and "childhood schizophrenia." In J. Zubin & G. A. Jervis (Eds.), *Psychopathology of mental development.* New York: Grune & Stratton, 1967. Pp. 460–471. [421]

POLLACK, M., GITTELMAN, M., MILLER, R., BERMAN, P., & BAKWIN, R. A developmental, pediatric, neurological, psychological, and psychiatric comparison of psychotic children and their sibs. *American Journal of Orthopsychiatry,* 1970, **40**, 329–330. [421]

POLLACK, M., & WOERNER, M. G. Pre- and perinatal complications and "childhood schizophrenia." *Journal of Child Psychology and Psychiatry,* 1966, **7**, 235–242. [421]

POLLIN, W. A possible genetic factor related to psychosis. *American Journal of Psychiatry,* 1971, **128**, 311–317. [432]

POLLIN, W. A new approach to the use of twin study data in studies of the pathogenesis of schizophrenia and neurosis. In A. R. Kaplan (Ed.), *Genetic factors in "schizophrenia."* Springfield, Ill.: Thomas, 1972. Pp. 374–379. [429]

POLLIN, W., STABENAU, J. R., MOSHER, L., & TUPIN, J. Life history differences in identical twins discordant for schizophrenia. *American Journal of Orthopsychiatry,* 1966, **36**, 492–509. [431]

POPPER, K. R. *The logic of scientific discovery.* New York: Science Editions, 1961. [69]

PORTER, R. W., BRADY, J. V., CONRAD, D., MASON, J. W., GALAMBOS, R., & RIOCH, D. McK. Some experimental observations on gastrointestinal lesions in behaviorally conditioned monkeys. *Psychosomatic Medicine,* 1958, **20**, 379–394. [182]

PORTEUS, S. D. *Porteus Maze Test: Fifty years' application.* Palo Alto, Cal.: Pacific Books, 1965. [572]

PORTNOY, S. M. Power of child care worker and therapist figures and their effectiveness as models for emotionally disturbed children in residential treatment. *Journal of Consulting and Clinical Psychology,* 1973, **40**, 15–19. [454]

POTTER, H. W. Schizophrenia in children. *American Journal of Psychiatry,* 1933, **12**, 1253–1270. [409]

POWELL, G. F., BRASEL, J. A., RAITI, S., & BLIZZARD, R. M. Emotional deprivation and growth retardation simulating idiopathic hypopituitarism. II. Endocrinologic evaluation of the syndrome. *New England Journal of Medicine*, 1967, **276**, 1279–1283. [157, 160, 219]

POWERS, E., & WITMER, H. *An experiment in the prevention of delinquency*. New York: Columbia University Press, 1951. [489, 513]

President's Commission on Law Enforcement and Administration of Justice. *Task Force Report: Juvenile Delinquency and Youth Crime*. Washington, D.C.: U. S. Government Printing Office, 1967. [476]

PRITCHARD, J. A. *A treatise on insanity*. Philadelphia: Haswell, Barrington, & Haswell, 1835. [492]

PROCTOR, J. T. Hysteria in childhood. *American Journal of Orthopsychiatry*, 1958, **28**, 394–407. [307]

PROCTOR, J. T. The treatment of hysteria in childhood. In M. Hammer & A. M. Kaplan (Eds.), *The practice of psychotherapy with children*. Homewood, Ill.: Dorsey, 1967. Pp. 121–150. [307–308]

PROVENCE, S., & LIPTON, R. C. *Infants in institutions*. New York: International Universities Press, 1962. [160]

PURCELL, K. Distinctions between subgroups of asthmatic children: Children's perceptions of events associated with asthma. *Pediatrics*, 1963, **31**, 486–494. [179]

PURTELL, J. J., ROBINS, E., & COHEN, M. E. Observations on clinical aspects of hysteria: A quantitative study of 50 hysteric patients and 156 control subjects. *Journal of the American Medical Association*, 1951, **146**, 902–909. [307–308]

PYLES, M. K., STOLZ, H. R., & MACFARLANE, J. W. The accuracy of mothers' reports on birth and developmental data. *Child Development*, 1935, **6**, 165–176. [83]

QUAY, H. C. Dimensions of personality in delinquent boys as inferred from the factor analysis of case history data. *Child Development*, 1965, **35**, 479–484. [480, 512]

QUAY, H. C., & QUAY, L. C. Behavior problems in early adolescence. *Child Development*, 1965, **36**, 215–220. [481, 555]

QUAY, L. C. Academic skills. In N. R. Ellis (Ed.), *Handbook of mental deficiency*. New York: McGraw-Hill, 1963. Pp. 664–690. [253]

QUAY, L. C. Language dialect, reinforcement, and the intelligence test performance of Negro children. *Child Development*, 1971, **42**, 5–15. [630]

RACHMAN, S. Studies in desensitization. 1. The separate effects of relaxation and desensitization. *Behavior Research and Therapy*, 1965, **3**, 245–251. [396]

RACHMAN, S. *Phobias: Their nature and control*. Springfield, Ill.: Thomas, 1968. [407]

RACHMAN, S., & EYSENCK, H. J. Reply to a "critique and reformulation" of behavior therapy. *Psychological Bulletin*, 1966, **65**, 165–169. [388]

RACHMAN, S., & TEASDALE, J. *Aversion therapy and behavior disorders: An analysis*. London: Routledge and Kegan Paul, 1969. [364–365]

RANDOLPH, M. H., RICHARDSON, H., & JOHNSON, R. C. A comparison of social and solitary male delinquents. *Journal of Consulting Psychology*, 1961, **25**, 293–295. [481]

RANK, B. Adaptation of the psychoanalytic technique for the treatment of young children with atypical development. *American Journal of Orthopsychiatry*, 1949, **19**, 130–139. [410, 413, 442, 454]

RAPAPORT, D. *Organization and pathology of thought*. New York: Columbia University Press, 1951. [24]

RAPAPORT, D. The structure of psychoanalytic theory: A systematizing attempt. In J. S. Koch (Ed.), *Psychology: A study of science.* New York: McGraw-Hill, 1959. Pp. 55–183. [314]

RAPAPORT, D. *Collected papers of David Rapaport.* Merton Gill (Ed.). New York: Basic Books, 1967. [277]

RASOR, R. W. Narcotic addiction in young people in the United States. In C. W. M. Wilson (Ed.), *The pharmacological and epidemiological aspects of adolescent drug dependence.* Oxford: Pergamon Press, 1968. Pp. 11–26. [528]

RAVEN, J. C. *Progressive matrices* New York: Psychological Corporation, 1960. [572]

RAWLS, D. J., RAWLS, J. R., & HARRISON, C. W. An investigation of six- to eleven-year-old children with allergic disorders. *Journal of Consulting and Clinical Psychology,* 1971, **36**, 260–264. [180]

RAWSON, M. B. *Developmental language disability.* Baltimore: Johns Hopkins Press, 1968. [170]

RAYMOND, M. Case of fetishism treated by aversion therapy. *British Medical Journal,* 1956, **83**, 854–857. [364]

RAZIN, A. M. A-B variable in psychotherapy: A critical review. *Psychological Bulletin,* 1971, **75**, 1–21. [643]

REDL, F., & WINEMAN, D. *The aggressive child.* New York: Free Press, 1957. [506, 515]

REED, E. W., & REED, S. C. *Mental retardation. A family study.* Philadelphia: Saunders, 1965. [238–239]

REES, L. The importance of psychological, allergic, and infective factors in childhood asthma. *Journal of Psychosomatic Research,* 1964, **7**, 253–262. [179]

REICH, T., CLAYTON, P. J., & WINOKUR, G. Family history studies: V. The genetics of mania. *American Journal of Psychiatry,* 1969, **125**, 1358–1369. [129]

REICHENBACH, H. *Experience and prediction.* Chicago: University of Chicago Press, 1938. [69]

RENAUD, H., & ESTESS, F. Life history interviews with one hundred normal American males: "Pathogenicity" of childhood. *American Journal of Orthopsychiatry,* 1961, **31**, 786–802. [324]

REYNOLDS, G. S. *A primer of operant conditioning.* Glenview, Ill.: Scott, Foresman, 1968. [373]

REZNIKOFF, M., & HONEYMAN, M. S. MMPI profiles of monozygotic and dizygotic twin pairs. *Journal of Consulting Psychology,* 1967, **31**, 100. [122–123, 127, 130]

RICE, E. P., EKDAHL, M. C., & MILLER, L. *Children of mentally-ill parents.* New York: Behavioral Publications, 1971. [633]

RICE, G., KEPECS, J. G., & YAHALOM, I. Differences in communicative impact between mothers of psychotic and nonpsychotic children. *American Journal of Orthopsychiatry,* 1966, **36**, 528–543. [414]

RICHARDS, T. W., & SIMONS, M. P. The Fels Child Behavior Scales. *Genetic Psychology Monographs,* 1941, **24**, 259–309. [128]

RICKS, D. F., & BERRY, J. C. Family and symptom patterns that precede schizophrenia. In M. Roff & D. F. Ricks (Eds.), *Life history research in psychopathology.* Minneapolis: University of Minnesota Press, 1970. Pp. 31–50. [413]

RIESS, B. F. Psychoanalytic theory and related approaches. In B. B. Wollman (Ed.), *Manual of child psychopathology.* New York: McGraw-Hill, 1972. Pp. 1178–1195. [312]

RIESSMAN, F. A neighborhood-based mental health approach. In E. L. Cowen, E. A. Gardner, & M. Zax (Eds.), *Emergent approaches to mental health problems*. New York: Appleton-Century-Crofts, 1967. Pp. 162–184. [626]

RIMLAND, B. *Infantile autism*. New York: Appleton-Century-Crofts, 1964. [438, 445]

RIMLAND, B. On the objective diagnosis of infantile autism. *Acta Paedopsychiatrica*, 1968, **35**, 146–161. [439]

RIMLAND, B. The differentiation of childhood psychoses: An analysis of checklists for 2218 psychotic children. *Journal of Autism and Childhood Schizophrenia*, 1971, **1**, 161–174. [438]

RING, F. O. Testing the validity of personality profiles in psychosomatic illnesses. *American Journal of Psychiatry*, 1957, **113**, 1075–1080. [175]

RISLEY, T. R. The effects and side effects of punishing the autistic behaviors of a deviant child. *Journal of Applied Behavior Analysis*, 1968, **1**, 21–34. [455]

RISLEY, T. R., & WOLF, M. M. Experimental manipulation of autistic behavior and generalization into the home. Paper presented at the American Psychological Association Convention, Los Angeles, 1964. [456]

RISLEY, T. R., & WOLF, M. Establishing functional speech in echolalic children. *Behavior Research and Therapy*, 1967, **5**, 73–88. [456]

RITTER, B. The group desensitization of children's snake phobias using vicarious and contact desensitization procedures. *Behavior Research and Therapy*, 1968, **6**, 1–6. [369, 397–398, 609]

RITVO, E. R., CANTWELL, D., JOHNSON, E., CLEMENTS, M., BENBROOK, F., SLAGLE, S., KELLY, P., & RITZ, M. Social class factors in autism. *Journal of Autism and Childhood Schizophrenia*, 1971, **1**, 297–310. [439]

RITVO, S. Correlation of a childhood and adult neurosis: Based on the adult analysis of a reported childhood case. *International Journal of Psychoanalysis*, 1966, **47**, 130–131. [299]

ROBINS, E., & O'NEAL, P. Clinical features of hysteria in children. *Nervous Child*, 1953, **10**, 246–271. [307–308]

ROBINS, L. The accuracy of parental recall of aspects of child development and of child rearing practices. *Journal of Abnormal and Social Psychology*, 1963, **66**, 261–270. [83]

ROBINS, L. N. *Deviant children grown up*. Baltimore: Williams & Wilkins, 1966. [66, 68, 493]

ROBINS, L. N. The adult development of the anti-social child. *Seminars in Psychiatry*, 1970, **2**, 420–434. [494]

ROBINS, L. N., DARVISH, H. S., & MURPHY, G. E. The long-term outcome for adolescent drug users: A follow-up study of 76 users and 146 nonusers. In J. Zubin & A. M. Freedman (Eds.), *The psychopathology of adolescence*. New York: Grune & Stratton, 1970. Pp. 159–178. [523]

ROBINSON, R., DeMARCHE, D. F., & WAGLE, M. *Community resources in mental health*. New York: Basic Books, 1960. [621]

ROEN, S. R. Evaluative research and community mental health. In A. E. Bergin & S. L. Garfield (Eds.), *Handbook of psychotherapy and behavior change: An empirical analysis*. New York: Wiley, 1971. Pp. 776–811. [635, 650]

ROGERS, C. R. *Client-centered therapy. Its current practice, implications, and theory*. Boston: Houghton-Mifflin, 1951. [46, 607]

ROGERS, C. R. Persons or science? A philosophical question. *American Psychologist*, 1955, **10**, 267–278. [62, 68]

ROGERS, C. R. (Ed.) *The therapeutic relationship and its impact: A study of psychotherapy with schizophrenics*. Madison: University of Wisconsin Press, 1967. [390]

ROGERS, C. R., & DYMOND, R. F. (Eds.) *Psychotherapy and personality change*. Chicago: University of Chicago Press, 1954. [68, 390, 608]

ROHRS, C. C., MURPHY, J. P., & DENSEN-GERBER, J. The therapeutic community: The Odyssey House concept. In C. J. D. Zarefonetis (Ed.), *Drug abuse: Proceedings of the International Conference*. Philadelphia: Lea & Febiger, 1972. Pp. 571–575. [535–536]

ROLF, J. E. The social and academic competence of children vulnerable to schizophrenia and other behavior pathologies. *Journal of Abnormal Psychology*, 1972, **80**, 225–243. [561]

ROLO, A., KRIMSKY, L., ABRAMSON, H., & GOLDFARB, L. Preliminary method study of LSD with children. *International Journal of Neuropsychiatry*, 1965, **1**, 552–555. [459]

ROSANOFF, A. J., HANDY, L. M., PLESSET, I. R., & BRUSH, S. The etiology of so-called schizophrenic psychoses with special reference to their occurrence in twins. *American Journal of Psychiatry*, 1934, **91**, 247–286. [428]

ROSE, S. D. *Treating children in groups. A behavioral approach*. San Francisco: Jossey-Bass, 1972. [609, 649]

ROSEN, B. M., BAHN, A. K., & KRAMER, M. Demographic and diagnostic characteristics of psychiatric clinic patients in the U. S. A., 1961. *American Journal of Orthopsychiatry*, 1964, **34**, 455–468. [63, 544]

ROSEN, B. M., WIENER, J., HENCH, C. L., WILLNER, S. G., & BAHN, A. K. A nationwide survey of outpatient psychiatric clinic functions, intake policies, and practices. *American Journal of Psychiatry*, 1966, **122**, 908–915. [622, 641]

ROSEN, C. An experimental study of visual perceptual training and reading achievements in first grade. *Perceptual and Motor Skills*, 1966, **22**, 979–986. [600]

ROSEN, M., DIGGORY, J. C., & WERLINSKY, B. E. Goal-setting expectancy of success in institutionalized and noninstitutionalized mental sub-normals. *American Journal of Mental Deficiency*, 1966, **71**, 249–255. [248]

ROSENBERG, B., & SILVERSTEIN, H. *The varieties of delinquent experience*. Waltham, Mass.: Blaisdell, 1969. [486, 515]

ROSENHAN, D. L. On being sane in insane places. *Science*, 1973, **179**, 250–258. [546, 566, 578]

ROSENTHAL, D. *Genetic theory and abnormal behavior*. New York: McGraw-Hill, 1970. (a) [137, 426–427, 462, 499]

ROSENTHAL, D. The design of studies to evaluate hereditary and environmental contributions to the etiology of behavioral disorders. Paper presented at the American Psychological Association Convention, Miami Beach, Sept. 5, 1970. (b) [125, 126]

ROSENTHAL, D. *Genetics of psychopathology*. New York: McGraw-Hill, 1971. [137]

ROSENTHAL, D. Three adoption studies of heredity in the schizophrenic disorders. *International Journal of Mental Health*, 1972, **1**, 63–75. [431]

ROSENTHAL, D., WENDER, P. H., KETY, S. S., WELNER, J., & SCHULSINGER, F. The adopted-away offspring of schizophrenics. *American Journal of Psychiatry*, 1971, **128**, 307–311. [431]

ROSENZWEIG, M. R., KRECH, D., BENNETT, E. L., & DIAMOND, M. C. Modifying brain chemistry and anatomy by enrichment or impoverishment of experience. In G. Newton & S. Levine (Eds.), *Early experience and behavior.* Springfield, Ill.: Thomas, 1968. Pp. 258–298. [160]

ROSENZWEIG, S. The Rosenzweig Picture-Frustration Study. In A. I. Rabin & M. R. Haworth (Eds.), *Projective techniques with children.* New York: Grune & Stratton, 1960. Pp. 149–176. [586]

ROSENZWEIG, S. Validity of the Rosenzweig Picture-Frustration Study with felons and delinquents. *Journal of Consulting Psychology*, 1963, **27**, 535–536. [586]

ROSENZWEIG, S. Sex differences in reaction to frustration among adolescents. In J. Zubin & A. M. Freedman (Eds.), *The psychopathology of adolescence.* New York: Grune & Stratton, 1970. Pp. 90–102. [501]

ROSS, A. O. Behavior therapy. In H. C. Quay & J. S. Werry (Eds.), *Psychopathological disorders of childhood.* New York: Wiley, 1972. Pp. 273–315. [332]

ROSS, A. O., & LACEY, H. M. Characteristics of terminators and remainers in child guidance treatment. *Journal of Consulting Psychology*, 1961, **25**, 420–424. [640]

ROSS, R. T. The mental growth of mongoloid defectives. *American Journal of Mental Deficiency*, 1962, **66**, 736–738. [215]

ROTTER, J. B. *Clinical psychology.* (2nd ed.) Englewood Cliffs, N.J.: Prentice-Hall, 1971. [194]

ROTTER, J., & RAFFERTY, J. *Manual for the Rotter Incomplete Sentence Blank.* New York: Psychological Corporation, 1958. [588]

ROUTTENBERG, A. The two arousal hypothesis: Reticular formation and limbic system. *Psychological Review*, 1968, **75**, 51–80. [447]

RUBIN, E. Z., SIMSON, C. B., & BETWEE, M. C. *Emotionally handicapped children and the elementary school.* Detroit: Wayne State University Press, 1966. [616]

RUBIN, R., & BALOW, B. Learning and behavior disorders: A longitudinal study. *Exceptional Children*, 1971, **38**, 293–299. [618]

RUBIN, T. I. *Jordi/Lisa and David.* New York: Ballantine, 1968. [413, 461]

RUSH, B. *Medical inquiries and observations upon the diseases of the mind.* Philadelphia: Kimber & Richardson, 1812. Reprinted by: New York: Hafner Publishing Co., 1962. [15]

RUTTER, M., & BARTAK, L. Causes of infantile autism: Some considerations from recent research. *Journal of Autism and Childhood Schizophrenia*, 1971, **1**, 20–32. [443]

RUTTER, M., & GRAHAM, P. The reliability and validity of the psychiatric assessment of the child: I. Interview with the child. *British Journal of Psychiatry*, 1968, **114**, 563–579. [578]

RUTTER, M., KORN, S., & BIRCH, H. G. Genetic and environmental factors in the development of primary reaction patterns. *British Journal of Social and Clinical Psychology*, 1963, **2**, 161–173. [131, 133]

SAGER, R. Genes outside the chromosomes. *Scientific American*, 1965, **212** 70–81. [102]

SANDBERG, A. A., KOEPF, G. F., ISHIHARA, T., & HAUSCHKA, T. S. XYY human male. *Lancet*, 1961, **2**, 488–489. [115]

SANDERS, B., ZIGLER, E., & BUTTERFIELD, E. Outer-directedness in the discrimination learning of normal and mentally retarded children. *Journal of Abnormal Psychology*, 1968, **73**, 368–375. [249]

SANDIFER, M. G., PETTUS, C., & QUADE, D. A study of psychiatric diagnosis. *Journal of Nervous and Mental Disease*, 1964, **139**, 350–356. [544, 550]

SANDLER, J., & JOFFE, W. G. Notes on obsessional manifestations in children. *Psychoanalytic Study of the Child*, 1965, **20**, 425–438. [302]

SARASON, S. B., DAVIDSON, K. S., LIGHTHALL, F. F., WAITE, P. R., & RUEBUSH, B. K. *Anxiety in elementary school children: A report of research.* New York: Wiley, 1960. [589]

SARASON, S. B., & DORIS, J. *Psychological problems in mental deficiency.* New York: Harper, 1969. [257]

SARASON, S. B., LEVINE, M., GOLDENBERG, I. I., CHERLIN, D. L., & BENNETT, E. M. *Psychology in community settings: Clinical, educational, vocational, social aspects.* New York: Wiley, 1966. [619]

SARNOFF, I. *Testing Freudian concepts.* New York: Springer, 1971. [322]

SARNOFF, I., & CORWIN, S. M. Castration anxiety and the fear of death. *Journal of Personality*, 1959, **27**, 374–385. [323]

SASLOW, H. L. The comparability of the Peabody Picture Vocabulary Test and the Revised Stanford-Binet, Form L-M, with cerebral palsied children. *American Psychologist*, 1961, **16**, 377. [209]

SATIR, V. M. *Conjoint family therapy.* (Rev. ed.) Palo Alto: Science and Behavior Books, 1967. [612, 649]

SATZ, P., RARDIN, D., & ROSS, J. An evaluation of a theory of specific developmental dyslexia. *Child Development*, 1971, **42**, 2009–2021. [170]

SAWYER, J. Measurement *and* prediction, clinical *and* statistical. *Psychological Bulletin*, 1966, **66**, 178–200. [89–90, 93, 605]

SAYEGH, Y., & DENNIS, W. The effect of supplementary experiences upon the development of infants in institutions. *Child Development*, 1965, **36**, 81–90. [161]

SCARPITTI, F. R., MURRAY, E., DINITZ, S., & RECKLESS, W. C. The "good" boy in a high delinquency area: Four years later. *American Sociological Review*, 1960, **25**, 555–558. [491]

SCARR, S. Environmental bias in twin studies. In S. G. Vandenberg (Ed.), *Progress in human behavior genetics.* Baltimore: Johns Hopkins University Press, 1968. Pp. 205–213. [123]

SCARR, S. Social introversion-extroversion as a heritable response. *Child Development*, 1969, **40**, 823–832. [127]

SCARR-SALAPATEK, S. Race, social class, and IQ. *Science*, 1971, **174**, 1285–1295. [119]

SCHACHTER, S. The interaction of cognitive and physiological determinants of emotional state. *Advances in Experimental Social Psychology*, 1966, **2**, 227–236. [186]

SCHACHTER, S., & LATANÉ, B. Crime, cognition, and the autonomic nervous system. In D. Levine (Ed.), *Nebraska Symposium on Motivation.* Lincoln: University of Nebraska Press, 1964. Pp. 221–273. [495]

SCHAIN, R. J., & YANNET, H. Infantile autism: An analysis of 50 cases and a consideration of certain neurophysiologic concepts. *Journal of Pediatrics*, 1960, **57**, 560–567. [440, 443]

SCHIFFER, M. *The therapeutic play group.* New York: Grune & Stratton, 1969. [649]

SCHMAUK, F. J. Punishment, arousal, and avoidance learning in sociopaths. *Journal of Abnormal Psychology*, 1970, **76**, 325–335. [496, 597]

SCHMECK, H. U.S. sets diet drug recall in drive on amphetamines. *New York Times*, April 2, 1973, p. 1. [525]

SCHMIDT, H. O., & FONDA, C. P. The reliability of psychiatric diagnosis: A new look. *Journal of Abnormal and Social Psychology*, 1956, **52**, 262–267. [544, 550]

SCHOFIELD, W., & BALIAN, L. A comparative study of the personal histories of schizophrenics and nonpsychiatric patients. *Journal of Abnormal and Social Psychology*, 1959, **59**, 216–225. [324, 414]

SCHONELL, F. E. *Educating spastic children.* Edinburgh: Oliver & Boyd, 1956. [218]

SCHOPLER, E. Early infantile autism and receptor processes. *Archives of General Psychiatry*, 1965, **13**, 327–335. [447]

SCHOPLER, E., & LOFTIN, J. Thinking disorders in parents of young psychotic children. *Journal of Abnormal Psychology*, 1969, **74**, 281–287. (a) [415]

SCHOPLER, E., & LOFTIN, J. Thought disorders in parents of psychotic children: A function of test anxiety. *Archives of General Psychiatry*, 1969, **20**, 174–181. (b) [415]

SCHULMAN, J. L., KASPAR, J. C., & THRONE, F. M. *Brain damage and behavior. A clinical-experimental study.* Springfield, Ill.: Thomas, 1965. [168]

SCHWADE, E. D., & GEIGER, S. G. Severe behavior disorders with abnormal electroencephalograms. *Diseases of the Nervous System.* 1960, **11**, 616–620. [498]

SCHWARZ, R. H., & JENS, K. G. The expectation of success as it modifies the achievement of mentally retarded adolescents. *American Journal of Mental Deficiency*, 1969, **73**, 946–949. [248]

SCHWITZGEBEL, R. *Streetcorner research: An experimental approach to the juvenile delinquent.* Cambridge: Harvard University Press, 1964. [513]

SCOTT, D. P. *About epilepsy.* London: G. Duckworth, 1969. [152, 172–174, 190]

SCOTT, R. W., PETERS, R. D., GILLESPIE, W. J., BLANCHARD, E., EDMUNDSON, E. D., & YOUNG, L. D. The use of shaping and reinforcement in the operant acceleration and deceleration of heartrate. *Behavior Research and Therapy*, 1973, **11**, 179–185. [381]

SCOTT, W. A., & JOHNSON, R. C. Comparative validities of direct and indirect personality tests. *Journal of Consulting and Clinical Psychology*, 1972, **38**, 301–318. [596]

SEARLE, L. V. The organization of hereditary maze-brightness and maze-dullness. *Genetic Psychology Monographs*, 1949, **39**, 279–325. [114]

SEARS, R. R. Experimental studies of projection: I. Attribution of traits. *Journal of Social Psychology*, 1936, **7**, 151–163. [321]

SEARS, R. R. Experimental analysis of psychoanalytic phenomena. In J. McV. Hunt (Ed.), *Personality and the behavior disorders.* New York: Ronald Press, 1944. Pp. 306–332. [321]

SEARS, R. R. Relation of early socialization experiences to aggression in middle childhood. *Journal of Abnormal and Social Psychology*, 1961, **63**, 466–492. [466]

SEARS, R. R., MACCOBY, E. E., & LEVIN, H. *Patterns of child rearing.* New York: Harper, 1957. [466]

SEARS, R. R., RAU, L., & ALPERT, R. *Identification and child rearing.* Stanford, Cal.: Stanford University Press, 1965. [471]

Sears, R. R., Whiting, J. W. M., Nowlis, V., & Sears, P. S. Some child-rearing antecedents of aggression and dependency in young children. *Genetic Psychology Monographs,* 1953, 47, 135–234. [466]

Seay, B., & Harlow, H. F. Maternal separation in the rhesus monkey. *Journal of Nervous and Mental Disease,* 1965, 140, 434–441. [466]

Sechzer, J. A., Faro, M. D., Barker, J. N., Barsky, D., Gutierrez, S., & Windle, W. F. Developmental behaviors: Delayed appearance in monkeys asphyxiated at birth. *Science,* 1971, 171, 1173–1175. [148]

Seitz, P. F. D. The consensus problem in psychoanalytic research. In L. Gottschalk & A. Auerbach (Eds.), *Methods of research in psychotherapy.* New York: Appleton-Century-Crofts, 1966. Pp. 209–225. [316]

Severson, R. A. The case for the classroom management consultant. *American Psychological Association Experimental Publication System,* 1971, 11, Ms. 397–36. [596]

Sewell, W. H., & Mussen, P. H. The effects of feeding, weaning, and scheduling procedures on childhood adjustment and the formation of oral symptoms. *Child Development,* 1952, 23, 185–191. [319]

Shaffer, L. The problem of psychotherapy. *American Psychologist,* 1947, 2, 459–467. [340]

Shapiro, J., MacHattie, L., Eron, L., Ihler, G., Ippen, K., & Beckwith, J. Isolation of pure *lac* operon DNA. *Nature,* 1969, 224, 768–774. [76, 100]

Sharan, S. Family interaction with schizophrenics and their siblings. *Journal of Abnormal Psychology,* 1966, 71, 345–353. [416]

Share, J., Koch, R., Webb, A., & Graliker, B. The longitudinal development of infants and young children with Down's syndrome (mongolism). *American Journal of Mental Deficiency,* 1964, 68, 685–692. [215]

Sharp, S. E. Individual psychology: A study in psychological method. *American Journal of Psychology,* 1898, 10, 329–391. [195]

Shaw, C. R. *The Jack Roller.* Chicago: University of Chicago Press, 1930. [483, 504]

Shaw, C. R., & McKay, H. D. *Juvenile delinquency and urban areas.* (Rev. ed.) Chicago: University of Chicago Press, 1969. [477]

Shaw, F. J. A stimulus-response analysis of repression and insight in psychotherapy. *Psychological Review,* 1946, 53, 36–42. [340]

Shaw, F. J. Some postulates concerning psychotherapy. *Journal of Consulting Psychology,* 1948, 12, 426–431. [340]

Shechtman, A. Age patterns in children's psychiatric symptoms. *Child Development,* 1970, 4, 683–693. (a) [560]

Shechtman, A. Psychiatric symptoms in normal and disturbed children. *Journal of Clinical Psychology,* 1970, 26, 38–41. (b) [562]

Shechtman, A. Psychiatric symptoms observed in normal and disturbed black children. *Journal of Clinical Psychology,* 1971, 27, 445–447. [562]

Shepherd, M., Oppenheim, B., & Mitchell, S. *Childhood behavior and mental health.* New York: Grune & Stratton, 1971. [641]

Sherman, A. R. Real-life exposure as a primary therapeutic factor in the desensitization treatment of fear. *Journal of Abnormal Psychology,* 1972, 79, 19–28. [398]

Sherwin, A. C., Schoelly, M. L., Klein, B. L., Schwartz, M. C., & Khan, M. G. Determination of psychiatric impairment in children, *Journal of Nervous and Mental Disease,* 1965, 141, 333–341. [579]

SHIELDS, J. Personality differences and neurotic traits in normal twin school children. A study in psychiatric genetics. *Eugenics Review,* 1954, **45,** 213–246. [128]

SHIELDS, J. *Monozygotic twins.* London: Oxford University Press, 1962. [124, 127, 129]

SHINOHARA, M., & JENKINS, R. L. MMPI study of three types of delinquents. *Journal of Clinical Psychology,* 1967, **23,** 156–163. [481]

SHNEIDMAN, E. S. The MAPS Test with children. In A. I. Rubin & M. R. Haworth (Eds.), *Projective techniques with children.* New York: Grune & Stratton, 1960. Pp. 130–148. [585]

SHOBEN, E. J., JR. Psychotherapy as a problem in learning theory. *Psychological Bulletin,* 1949, **46,** 366–392. [340]

SHOOR, M., SPEED, M. H., & BARTELT, C. Syndrome of the adolescent child molester. *American Journal of Psychiatry,* 1966, **122,** 783–789. [499]

SHORT, J. F., JR., & NYE, F. I. Extent of unrecorded juvenile delinquency: Tentative conclusions. *Journal of Criminal Law and Criminology,* 1958, **49** (4). [479, 500, 519]

SHORT, J. F., TENNYSON, R. A., & HOWARD, K. I. Behavior dimensions of gang delinquency. *American Sociological Review,* 1963, **28,** 411–428. [485]

SILVERSTEIN, A. B. Psychological testing practices in state institutions for the mentally retarded. *American Journal of Mental Deficiency,* 1963, **68,** 440–445. [205]

SILVERSTEIN, A. B. Note on prevalence. *American Journal of Mental Deficiency,* 1973, **77,** 380–382. [193]

SILVERSTEIN, A., & ROBINSON, H. The representation of orthopedic difficulties in children's figure drawings. *Journal of Consulting Psychology,* 1956, **20,** 333. [587]

SIMMONS, J., LEIKEN, S., LOVAAS, O., SCHAEFFER, B., & PERLOFF, B. Modification of autistic behavior with LSD-25. *American Journal of Psychiatry,* 1966, **122,** 1201–1211. [458]

SINCLAIR-DE-ZWART, H. Developmental psycholinguistics. In D. Elkind & J. Flavell (Eds.) *Studies in cognitive development.* New York: Oxford University Press, 1969. Pp. 315–336. [4]

SINGER, M., & WYNNE, L. C. Differentiating characteristics of parents of childhood schizophrenics, childhood neurotics, and young adult schizophrenics. *American Journal of Psychiatry,* 1963, **120,** 234–243. [441]

SKAARBREVIK, K. J. A follow-up study of educable mentally retarded in Norway. *American Journal of Mental Deficiency,* 1971, **75,** 560–565. [252]

SKEELS, H. M. Some Iowa studies of the mental growth of children in relation to differentials of the environment: A summary. In G. M. Whipple (Ed.), *Intelligence: Its nature and nurture. Thirty-ninth Yearbook of the National Society for the Study of Education.* Bloomington, Ill.: Public School Publishing Co., 1940. Pp. 281–308. [243]

SKEELS, H. M. Adult status of children with contrasting early life experiences. *Monographs of the Society for Research in Child Development,* 1966, **31** (Serial No. 105). [240, 244, 257]

SKINNER, B. F. *The behavior of organisms.* New York: Appleton, 1938. [31]

SKINNER, B. F. Baby in a box. *Ladies Home Journal,* October, 1945. [31, 343]

SKINNER, B. F. *Walden two.* New York: Macmillan, 1948. [31, 343]

SKINNER, B. F. *Science and human behavior.* New York: Macmillan, 1953. [343, 354, 362]

SKINNER, B. F. *Beyond freedom and dignity.* New York: Knopf, 1971. [343]

SKODAK, M., & SKEELS, H. M. A final follow-up study of one hundred adopted children. *Journal of Genetic Psychology,* 1949, **75**, 85–125. [241–244, 257]

SLATER, E. *Psychotic and neurotic illnesses in twins.* London: Her Majesty's Stationery Office, 1953. [428]

SLATER, E. The case for a major partially dominant gene. In A. R. Kaplan (Ed.), *Genetic factors in "schizophrenia."* Springfield, Ill.: Thomas, 1972. Pp. 173–180. [426]

SLAVSON, S. R. *Child psychotherapy.* New York: Columbia University Press, 1952. [609]

SMALL, J. G., DeMYER, M. K., & MILSTEIN, V. CNV responses of autistic and normal children. *Journal of Autism and Childhood Schizophrenia,* 1971, **1**, 215–231. [449]

SMART, R. G., & FEJER, D. Illicit drug users: Their social backgrounds, drug use, and psychopathology. *Journal of Health and Social Behavior,* 1969, **10**, 297–308. [529]

SMART, R. G., & FEJER, D. Drug use among adolescents and their parents: Closing the generation gap in mood modification. *Journal of Abnormal Psychology,* 1972, **79**, 153–160. [529]

SMITH, R. C. Speed and violence: Compulsive methamphetamine abuse and criminality in the Haight-Ashbury district. In C. J. D. Zarafonetis (Ed.), *Drug abuse: Proceedings of the International Conference.* Philadelphia: Lea & Febiger, 1972. Pp. 435–448. [526]

SMITH, R. E., & SHARPE, T. M. Treatment of a school phobia with implosive therapy. *Journal of Consulting and Clinical Psychology,* 1970, **35**, 239–243. [368, 377]

SMITH, R. T. A comparison of socio-environmental factors in monozygotic and dizygotic twins, testing an assumption. In S. G. Vandenberg (Ed.), *Methods and goals in human behavior genetics.* New York: Academic Press, 1965. Pp. 45–61. [123]

SOLOMON, P., KUBZANSKY, P. E., LEIDERMAN, P. H., MENDELSON, J. H., TRUMBULL, R., & WEXLER, D. (Eds.) *Sensory deprivation.* Cambridge: Harvard University Press, 1961. [159]

SOLYOM, L., ZAMANZADEH, D., LEDWIDGE, B., & KENNY, F. Aversion relief treatment of obsessive neurosis. In R. D. Rubin, H. Fensterheim, A. A. Lazarus, & C. M. Franks (Eds.), *Advances in behavior therapy.* New York: Academic Press, 1971. Pp. 93–109. [378–379]

SONTAG, L. W., BAKER, C. T., & NELSON, V. L. Mental growth and personality development: A longitudinal study. *Monographs of the Society for Research in Child Development,* 1958, **23** (Serial No. 68). [211–214]

SONTAG, L. W., & WALLACE, R. F. The effect of cigarette smoking during pregnancy upon the fetal heart rate. *American Journal of Obstetrics and Gynecology,* 1935, **29**, 77–82. [146]

SPEER, D. C., FOSSUM, M., LIPPMAN, H. S., SCHWARTZ, R., & SLOCUM, B. A comparison of middle- and lower-class families in treatment at a child guidance clinic. *American Journal of Orthopsychiatry,* 1968, **38**, 814–822. [632]

SPERLING, M. School phobias: Classification, dynamics, and treatment. *Psychoanalytic Study of the Child,* 1967, **22**, 375–401. [292]

SPIEGEL, H. Is symptom removal dangerous? *American Journal of Psychiatry,* 1967, **10**, 1279–1282. [399]

SPOCK, B. *Baby and child care.* (2nd ed.) New York: Pocket Books, 1968. [33, 34, 37]

SQUIER, R., & DUNBAR, F. Emotional factors in the course of pregnancy. *Psychosomatic Medicine,* 1946, **8**, 161–175. [144]

STAATS, A. W., MINKE, K. A., GOODWIN, W., & LANDEEN, J. Cognitive behavior modification: "Motivated learning" reading treatment with subprofessional therapy technicians. *Behavior Research and Therapy,* 1967, **5**, 283–299. [387]

STAMPFL, T. G., & LEVIS, D. J. Essentials of implosive therapy: A learning theory-based psychodynamic behavioral therapy. *Journal of Abnormal Psychology,* 1967, **72**, 496–503. [366]

STARR, P. H. Some observations on the diagnostic aspects of childhood hysteria. *Nervous Child,* 1953, **10**, 214–231. [307, 309]

STECHLER, G. A longitudinal follow-up of neonatal apnea. *Child Development,* 1964, **35**, 333–348. (a) [570]

STECHLER, G. Newborn attention as affected by medication during labor. *Science,* 1964, **144**, 315–317. (b) [146]

STEIN, K. B., SARBIN, T. R., & KULIK, J. A. Further validation of antisocial personality types. *Journal of Consulting and Clinical Psychology,* 1971, **36**, 177–182. [482]

STEIN, Z., & SUSSER, M. W. The families of dull children: Part II. Identifying family types and subcultures. *Journal of Mental Science,* 1960, **106**, 1296–1303. (a) [227]

STEIN, Z., & SUSSER, M. Families of dull children: Part III. Social selection by family type. *Journal of Mental Science,* 1960, **106**, 1304–1310. (b) [218, 227]

STEIN, Z., & SUSSER, M. The social distribution of mental retardation. *American Journal of Mental Deficiency,* 1963, **67**, 811–821. [227]

STEIN, Z., SUSSER, M., SAENGER, G., & MAROLLA, F. Nutrition and mental performance. *Science,* 1972, **178**, 708–712. [143]

STENN, P. G., KLAIBER, E. L., VOGEL, W., & BROVERMAN, D. Testosterone effects upon photic stimulation of the electroencephalogram (EEG) and mental performance of humans. *Perceptual and Motor Skills,* 1972, **34**, 372–378. [159]

STENNETT, R. G. Emotional handicap in the elementary years: Phase or disease? *American Journal of Orthopsychiatry,* 1966, **36**, 444. [620]

STEPHENSON, R., & SCARPITTI, F. Essexfields: A nonresidential experiment in group-centered rehabilitation of delinquents. *American Journal of Corrections,* 1969, **31**, 12–18. [508]

STEVENS, J. R., & MILSTEIN, V. Severe psychiatric disorders of childhood. Electroencephalogram and clinical correlates. *American Journal of Diseases in Childhood,* 1970, **120**, 182–192. [168]

STEVENS, J. R., SACHDEV, K., & MILSTEIN, V. Behavior disorders of childhood and the electroencephalogram. *Archives of Neurology,* 1968, **18**, 160–177. [168]

STEVENSON, H. W. (Ed.) Concept of development. *Society for Research in Child Development Monographs,* 1966, **31** (Serial No. 107). [37]

STEVENSON, H. W., HALE, G. A., KLEIN, R. E., & MILLER, L. K. Interrelations and correlates in children's learning and problem solving. *Monographs of the Society for Research in Child Development,* 1968, **33** (Serial No. 123). [207]

STEWART, L. H. Social and emotional adjustment during adolescence as related to the development of psychosomatic illness in adulthood. *Genetic Psychology Monographs,* 1962, **65,** 175–215. [177]

STOCH, M. B., & SMYTH, P. M. Does undernutrition during infancy inhibit brain growth and subsequent intellectual development? *Archives of Diseases of Childhood,* 1963, **38,** 546–552. [162]

STOCH, M. B., & SMYTHE, P. M. Undernutrition during infancy, and subsequent brain growth and intellectual development. In N. S. Scrimshaw and J. E. Gordon (Eds.), *Malnutrition, learning, and behavior.* Cambridge: M.I.T. Press, 1968. Pp. 278–288. [162]

STOLLER, R. J., & GEERSTMA, R. H. The consistency of psychiatrists' clinical judgments. *Journal of Nervous and Mental Disease,* 1963, **137,** 58–68. [577]

STOVER, L., GUERNEY, B. G., & O'CONNELL, M. Measurements of acceptance following self-direction, involvement, and empathy in adult-child interaction. *Journal of Psychology,* 1971, **77,** 261–269. [608]

STRAUSS, A. A., & LEHTINEN, L. E. *Psychopathology and education of the brain-injured child.* New York: Grune & Stratton, 1947. [165–166]

STREAN, H. S. A family therapist looks at "Little Hans." *Family Process,* 1967, **6,** 227–234. [612]

STREET, D., VINTER, R., & PERROW, C. *Organization for treatment: A comparative study of institutions for delinquents.* New York: Free Press, 1966. [504, 515]

STROH, G., & BUICK, D. The effect of relative sensory isolation on the behavior of two autistic children. In S. J. Hutt & C. Hutt (Eds.), *Behavior studies in psychiatry.* New York: Pergamon Press, 1970. Pp. 161–174. [459]

STRONG, E. K. *Vocational interests of men and women.* Stanford: Stanford University Press, 1943. [590]

SUINN, R. M., & OSKAMP, S. *The predictive validity of projective measures.* Springfield, Ill.: Thomas, 1969.   [581, 584, 587–588, 605]

SULLIVAN, H. S. *The interpersonal theory of psychiatry.* New York: Norton, 1953. [24]

SUPER, D. E., & CRITES, J. O. *Appraising vocational fitness.* (2nd ed.) New York: Harper, 1962. [209]

SWEETSTER, W. *Mental hygiene.* New York: Putnam, 1843. [29]

SYMONDS, A., & HERMAN, M. The patterns of schizophrenia in adolescence: A report on 50 cases of adolescent girls. *Psychiatric Quarterly,* 1957, **31,** 521–530. [410]

TAFT, L. T., & GOLDFARB, W. Prenatal and perinatal factors in childhood schizophrenia. *Developmental Medicine and Child Neurology,* 1963, **6,** 32–43. [418]

TANNER, J. M. Physical growth. In P. H. Mussen (Ed.), *Carmichael's manual of child psychology.* (3rd ed.) New York: Wiley, 1970. Vol. 1. Pp. 77–155. [140–141, 147–153, 156–157, 189]

TARJAN, G., WRIGHT, S. W., EYMAN, R. K., & KEERAN, C. V. Natural history of mental retardation: Some aspects of epidemiology. *American Journal of Mental Deficiency,* 1973, **77,** 369–379. [193]

TAYLOR, E. M. *Psychological appraisal of children with cerebral defects.* Cambridge: Harvard University Press, 1959. [218]

TAYLOR, J. A. A personality scale of manifest anxiety. *Journal of Abnormal and Social Psychology,* 1953, **48,** 285–290. [589]

TAYLOR, W. S. A critique of sublimation in males: A study of forty superior single men. *Genetic Psychology Monographs*, 1933, **13**, 1–115. [321]

TEMERLIN, M. K. Suggestion effects in psychiatric diagnosis. *Journal of Nervous and Mental Disease*, 1968, **147**, 349–353. [547, 577]

TERMAN, L. M. *The measurement of intelligence*. Boston: Houghton-Mifflin, 1916. [32–33, 201]

TERMAN, L., LYMAN, G., ORDAHL, G., ORDAHL, L. E., GALBREATH, N., & TALBERT, W. *The Stanford revision and extension of the Binet-Simon Measuring Scale of Intelligence*. Baltimore: Warwick and York, 1917. [202, 203]

TERMAN, L. M., & MERRILL, M. A. *Measuring intelligence*. Boston: Houghton-Mifflin, 1937. [202]

TERMAN, L. M., & MERRILL, M. A. *Stanford-Binet Intelligence Scale. Manual for the third revision, Form L-M*. Boston: Houghton-Mifflin, 1960; 1973. [198, 202–205]

TERMAN, L. M., & ODEN, M. H. *Genetic studies of genius, V: The gifted group at mid-life*. Stanford, Calif.: Sanford University Press, 1959. [33, 202, 235–238]

TEUBER, H. L., & RUDEL, R. G. Behavior after cerebral lesions in children and adults. *Developmental Medicine and Child Neurology*, 1962, **4**, 3–20. [163–164]

THARP, R. G., & WETZEL, R. J. *Behavior modification in the natural environment*. New York: Academic Press, 1970. [407]

THOMAS, A., BIRCH, H. G., CHESS, S., HERTZIG, M., & KORN S. *Individuality in early childhood*. New York: New York University Press, 1963. [133, 137]

THOMAS, A., CHESS, S., & BIRCH, H. G. *Temperament and behavior disorders in children*. New York: New York University Press, 1968. [51, 133–134, 137, 192, 324–325, 593]

THOMAS, A., CHESS, S., & BIRCH, H. The origins of personality. *Scientific American*, 1970, **223**, 102–109. [137]

THOMPSON, W. R. Influence of prenatal maternal anxiety on emotionality in young rats. *Science*, 1957, **125**, 698–699. [143–144]

THOMPSON, T., & GRABOWSKI, J. *Behavior modification of the mentally retarded*. New York: Oxford University Press, 1972. [254, 258, 407]

THOMPSON, T., PICKENS, R., & MEISCH, R. A. *Readings in behavioral pharmacology*. New York: Appleton-Century-Crofts, 1970. [183]

THORNDIKE, E. L. *Educational psychology, Vol. II: The psychology of learning*. New York: Teacher's College, Columbia University, 1913. [334, 354]

TIENARI, P. Schizophrenia in monozygotic male twins. In D. Rosenthal & S. S. Kety (Eds.), *The transmission of schizophrenia*. New York: Pergamon Press, 1968. Pp. 27–36. [428]

TINBERGEN, N. *Social behavior in animals*. London: Methuen, 1964; Science Paperback (2nd ed.), 1965. [98, 136]

TOMPKINS, W. T. The clinical significance of nutritional deficiencies in pregnancy. *Bulletin of the New York Academy of Medicine*, 1948, **24**, 376–388. [142]

TOWNE, R. C., JOINER, L. M., & SCHURR, T. The effects of special classes on the self-concepts of academic ability of the educable mentally retarded: A time series experiment. Paper read at the 45th Annual Council for Exceptional Children Convention, St. Louis, 1967. [253]

TREFFERT, D. A. Epidemiology of infantile autism. *Archives of General Psychiatry*, 1970, **22**, 431–438. [439–440, 443]

TRYON, R. C. Individual differences. In F. A. Moss (Ed.), *Comparative Psychology*. New York: Prentice-Hall, 1934. [113]

TRYON, R. C. Genetic differences in maze-learning ability in rats. *Yearbook of the National Society for the Study of Education,* 1940, **39**, Part 1, 111–119. (a) [112–114]

TRYON, R. C. Studies in individual differences in maze ability, VII. The specific components of maze ability and a general theory of psychological components. *Journal of Comparative and Physiological Psychology,* 1940, **30**, 283–355. (b) [112–114]

TULKIN, S. R. Race, class, family and school achievement. *Journal of Personality and Social Psychology,* 1968, **9**, 31–37. [207]

TULKIN, S. R., & NEWBROUGH, J. R. Social class, race, and sex differences on the Raven (1956) Standard Progressive Matrices. *Journal of Consulting and Clinical Psychology,* 1968, **32**, 400–406. [207]

TUNLEY, R. *Kids, crimes, and chaos.* New York: Harper, 1962. [476–477]

TURNURE, J. E., & ZIGLER, E. Outer-directedness in the problem-solving of normal and retarded children. *Journal of Abnormal and Social Psychology,* 1964, **69**, 427–436. [249]

TWITCHELL, T. E. Review of *Minimal brain dysfunction in children* by P. H. Wender. *Science,* 1971, **174**, 135–136. [190]

ULLMANN, L. P. The major concepts taught to behavior therapy trainees. In A. M. Graziano (Ed.), *Behavior therapy with children.* Chicago: Aldine-Atherton, 1971, **11**, 367–375. [402]

ULLMANN, L. P., & KRASNER, L. *A psychological approach to abnormal behavior.* Englewood Cliffs, N.J.: Prentice-Hall, 1969. [37, 67, 254, 343, 373, 380–381]

ULRICH, R. E., STACHNIK, T. J., & STAINTON, N. R. Student acceptance of generalized personality interpretations. *Psychological Reports,* 1963, **13**, 831–834. [575–576]

UPDEGRAFF, R., & KEISTER, M. A study of children's reactions to failure and an experimental attempt to modify them. *Child Development,* 1937, **8**, 241–248. [468]

U. S. CHILDREN'S BUREAU. *Infant care.* Washington: U. S. Government Printing Office, 1914; 1929; 1963. [34]

U. S. CHILDREN'S BUREAU. *Statistics on public institutions for delinquent children,* 1970. Washington: U. S. Government Printing Office, 1971. [503]

U. S. CHILDREN'S BUREAU. *Juvenile court statistics.* Washington: U. S. Department of Health, Education, and Welfare, Children's Bureau, 1972. [476–477, 499]

U. S. DEPARTMENT OF JUSTICE. *Uniform crime reports for the United States.* Washington, D.C.: U. S. Government Printing Office, 1972. [474–475]

UNITED STATES HOUSE COMMITTEE ON ARMED SERVICES. Inquiry into alleged drug abuse in the armed services: Report of a special subcommittee. 92nd Congress, second session, 1971. HASC. 92–94. [522]

U. S. PUBLIC HEALTH SERVICE. *Marijuana and health.* Second Annual Report to Congress from the Secretary of Health, Education, and Welfare. Washington: Government Printing Office, 1972. [522]

VACC, N. A. A study of emotionally disturbed children in regular and special classes. *Exceptional Children,* 1968, **35**, 197–204. [615]

VALINS, S. The perception and labeling of bodily changes as determinants of emotional behavior. In P. Black (Ed.), *Physiological correlates of emotion*. New York: Academic Press, 1970. Pp. 229–243. [186]

VANDENBERG, S. G. (Ed.). *Methods and goals in human behavior genetics*. New York: Academic Press, 1965. [137]

VANDENBERG, S. G. Hereditary factors in normal personality traits as measured by inventories. In J. Wortis (Ed.), *Recent advances in biological psychiatry*. New York: Plenum Press, 1967, Vol. 9. Pp. 65–104. [122–123, 127]

VANDENBERG, S. G. (Ed.). *Progress in human behavior genetics*. Baltimore: Johns Hopkins University Press, 1968. [137]

VANDENBERG, S. G. What do we know about the inheritance of intelligence and how do we know it? In R. Cancro (Ed.), *Intelligence: Genetic and environmental influences*. New York: Grune & Stratton, 1971. Pp. 182–218. [234]

VANDENBERG, S. G., STAFFORD, R. E., & BROWN, A. M. The Louisville Twin Study. In S. G. Vandenberg (Ed.), *Progress in human behavior genetics*. Baltimore: Johns Hopkins Press, 1968. Pp. 153–204. [127]

VOGEL, W., BROVERMAN, D. M., & KLAIBER, E. L. EEG responses in regularly menstruating women and in amenorrheic women treated with ovarian hormones. *Science,* 1971, **172**, 388–391. [158]

VORSTER, D. An investigation into the part played by organic factors in childhood schizophrenia. *Journal of Mental Science*, 1960, **106**, 494–522.

VOSS, H. L. The predictive efficiency of the Glueck Social Prediction Table. *Journal of Criminal Law, Crime, and Police Science*, 1963, **54**, 421–430. [489]

WAELDER, R. Review of *psychoanalysis, scientific method, and philosophy,* by S. Hook. *Journal of the American Psychoanalytic Association*, 1962, **10**, 617–637. [313]

WAHLER, R. G. Oppositional children: A quest for parental reinforcement control. *Journal of Applied Behavioral Analysis*, 1969, **2**, 159–170. [363, 369]

WALDER, L. O., COHEN, S. I., BREITER, D. E., DASTON, P. G., HIRSCH, I. S., & LEIBOWITZ, J. M. Teaching behavioral principles to parents of disturbed children. In A. M. Graziano (Ed.), *Behavior therapy with children*. Chicago: Aldine-Atherton, 1971. Pp. 382–387. [371]

WALLACE, H. E. R., & WHYTE, M. B. H. Natural history of the psychoneuroses. *British Medical Journal*, 1959, **1**, 144–149. [328]

WALTER, R. D., COLBERT, E. G., KOEGLER, R. R., PALMER, J. O., & BOND, P. M. A controlled study of the 14 and 6 per-second EEG pattern. *American Medical Association Archives of General Psychiatry*, 1960, **2**, 559–566. [498]

WALTERS, R. H., & BROWN, M. Studies of reinforcement of aggression: III. Transfer of responses to an interpersonal situation. *Child Development*, 1963, **34**, 563–571. [467]

WALTON, D. The application of learning theory to the treatment of a case of bronchial asthma. In H. J. Eysenck (Ed.), *Behavior therapy and the neuroses*. New York: Pergamon Press, 1960. Pp. 188–189. (a) [381]

WALTON, D. The application of learning theory to the treatment of neurodermatitis. In H. J. Eysenck (Ed.), *Behavior therapy and the neuroses*. New York: Pergamon Press, 1960. Pp. 272–274. (b) [381]

WARREN, M. Q. The case for differential treatment of delinquents. *Annals of the American Academy of Political and Social Science*, 1969, **381**, 47–59. [511, 515]

WARREN, M. Q. Classification for treatment. Presented at National Institute of

Law Enforcement and Criminal Justice Seminar on the classification of criminal behavior: Uses and the state of research. Washington, D. C.: May 4, 1972. [511]

WATSON, J. B. Psychology as the behaviorist views it. *Psychological Review,* 1913, **20,** 158–177. [29]

WATSON, J. B. *Psychology from the standpoint of a behaviorist.* Philadelphia: J. B. Lippincott, 1919. [30]

WATSON, J. B. *Behaviorism.* New York: Peoples Publishing Co., 1924. [30, 95]

WATSON, J. B., & RAYNER, R. Conditioned emotional reactions. *Journal of Experimental Psychology,* 1920, **3,** 1–14. [334]

WATSON, J. D., & CRICK, F. H. C. Molecular structure of nucleic acids—a structure for deoxyribose nucleic acid. *Nature,* 1953, **171,** 737–738. [102]

WATTENBERG, W. W., & SAUNDERS, F. Sex differences among juvenile offenders. *Sociology and Social Research,* 1954, **39,** 24–31. [500–501]

WAWRZASZEK, F., JOHNSON, O. G., & SCIERA, J. L. A comparison of H-T-P responses of handicapped and non-handicapped children. *Journal of Clinical Psychology,* 1958, **14,** 160–162. [588]

WAXLER, N. E., & MISHLER, E. G. Parental interaction with schizophrenic children and well siblings. *Archives of General Psychiatry,* 1971, **25,** 223–231. [416]

WEBER, D. *Der frühkindliche Autismus unter dem Aspekt der Entwicklung.* Bern: Verlag Hans Huber, 1970. [440, 443–445, 450]

WECHSLER, D. *The measurement of adult intelligence.* Baltimore: Williams & Wilkins, 1939. [205]

WECHSLER, D. *Wechsler Intelligence Scale for Children.* New York: Psychological Corp., 1949. [205]

WECHSLER, D. *Manual for the Wechsler Adult Intelligence Scale.* New York: Psychological Corp., 1955. [205]

WECHSLER, D. *Wechsler Preschool and Primary Scale of Intelligence.* New York: Psychological Corp., 1967. [205]

WEEKS, H. *Youthful offenders at Highfields.* Ann Arbor: University of Michigan Press, 1958. [507, 515]

WEIL-MALHERBE, H., & SZARA, S. I. *The biochemistry of functional and experimental psychoses.* Springfield, Ill.: Thomas, 1971. [425]

WEINER, H., THALER, M., REISER, M. F., & MIRSKY, I. A. Etiology of duodenal ulcer. I. Relation of specific psychological characteristics to rate of gastric secretion (Serum pepsinogen). *Psychosomatic Medicine,* 1957, **19,** 1–10. [58, 180]

WEINSTEIN, L. The Project Re-ED Schools for emotionally disturbed children: Effectiveness as viewed by referring agencies, parents, and teachers. *Exceptional Children,* 1969, **35,** 703–711. [617]

WEINTRAUB, S. A. Self-control as a correlate of an Internalizing–Externalizing symptom dimension. *Journal of Abnormal Child Psychology,* 1973, **1,** 292–307. [561]

WEISS, G., WERRY, J., MINDE, K., DOUGLAS, V., & SYKES, D. Studies of the hyperactive child. V. The effects of dextroamphetamine and chlorpromazine on behavior and intellectual functioning. *Journal of Child Psychology and Psychiatry,* 1968, **9,** 145–156. [186]

WEISS, L., & MASLING, J. Further validation of a Rorschach measure of oral imagery: A study of six clinical groups. *Journal of Abnormal Psychology,* 1970, **76,** 83–87. [320]

WEISS, R. L. Operant conditioning techniques in psychological assessment. In

P. W. McReynolds (Ed.), *Advances in psychological assessment*. Vol. 1. Palo Alto, Calif.: Science and Behavior Books, 1968. Pp. 169–190. [596]

WEITZMAN, B. Behavior therapy and psychotherapy. *Psychological Review*, 1967, **74**, 300–317. [388]

WELSH, G. S., & DAHLSTROM, W. G. *Basic readings on the MMPI in psychology and medicine*. Minneapolis: University of Minnesota Press, 1956. [591]

WENAR, C., RUTTENBERG, B. A., DRATMAN, M. L., & WOLF, E. G. Changing autistic behavior: The effectiveness of three milieus. *Archives of General Psychiatry*, 1967, **17**, 26–35. [453]

WENDER, P. *Minimal brain dysfunction in children*. New York: Wiley-Interscience, 1971. [168, 186, 190]

WENRICH, W. W. *A primer of behavior modification*. Belmont, Calif.: Brooks/Cole, 1970. [373]

WERRY, J. S. The conditioning treatment of enuresis. *American Journal of Psychiatry*, 1966, **123**, 226–229. [383]

WERRY, J. S. Childhood psychosis. In H. C. Quay and J. S. Werry (Eds.), *Psychopathological disorders of childhood*. New York: Wiley, 1972. Pp. 173–233. (a) [412, 458]

WERRY, J. S. Organic factors in child psychopathology. In H. C. Quay & J. S. Werry (Eds.), *Psychopathological disorders of childhood*. New York: Wiley, 1972. Pp. 83–121. (b) [168]

WERRY, J. S., & COHRSSEN, J. Enuresis: An etiological and therapeutic study. *Journal of Pediatrics*, 1965, **67**, 423–431. [400–401]

WERRY, J. S., WEISS, G., DOUGLAS, V., & MARTIN, J. Studies on the hyperactive child: The effect of chlorpromazine upon behavior and learning ability. *Journal of the American Academy of Child Psychiatry*, 1966, **5**, 292–312. [186]

WERTHEIMER, M. Studies in the theory of Gestalt Psychology. *Psychologische Forschungen*, 1923, **4**. [598]

WETZEL, R. J., BAKER, J., RONEY, M., & MARTIN, M. Outpatient treatment of autistic behavior. *Behavior Research and Therapy*, 1966, **4**, 167–177. [371, 456]

WHALEN, C. K., & HENKER, B. A. Creating therapeutic pyramids using mentally retarded patients. *American Journal of Mental Deficiency*, 1969, **74**, 331–337. [254]

WHALEN, C. K., & HENKER, B. A. Pyramid therapy in a hospital for the retarded: Methods, program evaluation, and long term effects. *American Journal of Mental Deficiency*, 1971, **75**, 414–434. [254]

WHITE, P. T., DeMYER, W., & DeMYER, M. EEG abnormalities in early childhood schizophrenia: A double-blind study of psychiatrically disturbed and normal children during Promazine sedation. *American Journal of Psychiatry*, 1964, **120**, 250–258. [422]

WHITE, R. W. Motivation reconsidered: The concept of competence. *Psychological Review*, 1959, **66**, 297–333. [96]

WHITE, R. W. Ego and reality in psychoanalytic theory. *Psychological Issues*, 1963, 3 (Monogr. 11). [277]

WIESEL, T. N., & HUBEL, D. H. Effects of visual deprivation on morphology and physiology of cells in the cat's lateral geniculate body. *Journal of Neurophysiology*, 1963, **26**, 978–993. [159]

WIEST, W. M. Some recent criticisms of behaviorism and learning theory. *Psychological Bulletin*, 1967, **67**, 214–225. [388]

WIKLER, A., DIXON, J. F., & PARKER, J. B. Brain function in problem children and controls: Psychometric, neurological, and electroencephalographic comparisons. *American Journal of Psychiatry*, 1970, **127**, 634–645. [168]

WILDE, G. J. S. Inheritance of personality traits. *Acta Psychologica*, 1964, **22**, 37–51. [128]

WILNER, D. M., & KASSEBAUM, G. G. (Eds.). *Narcotics*. New York: McGraw-Hill, 1965. [541]

WILSON, C. W. M. Drug dependence or drug abuse? In C. W. M. Wilson (Ed.) *The pharmacological and epidemiological aspects of adolescent drug dependence*. Oxford: Pergamon Press, 1968. Pp. 141–158. [516]

WIMBERGER, H. C., & GREGORY, R. J. A behavior checklist for use in child psychiatry clinics. *Journal of the American Academy of Child Psychiatry*, 1968, **7**, 677–688. [594]

WIMBERGER, H. C., & MILLAR, G. The therapeutic effect of the initial clinic contact in child psychiatry patients. In C. Lesse (Ed.), *An evaluation of the results of the psychotherapies*. Springfield, Ill.: Thomas, 1968. Pp. 179–189. [595]

WINICK, M. Food, time, and cellular growth of the brain. *New York State, Journal of Medicine*, 1969, **69**, 302–304. [142]

WINICK, M. Fetal malnutrition and growth processes. *Hospital Practice*, 1970. (a) [142]

WINICK, M. Nutrition and nerve cell growth. *Proceedings of the Federation of American Societies for Experimental Biology*, 1970, **29**, 1510–1515. (b) [142]

WINICK, M., & ROSSO, P. Head circumference and cellular growth of the brain in normal and marasmic children. *Journal of Pediatrics*, 1969, **74**, 774–778. [162]

WINICK, M., ROSSO, P., & WATERLOW, J. Cellular growth of cerebrum, cerebellum, and brain stem in normal and marasmic children. *Experimental Neurology*, 1970, **26**, 393–400. [162]

WING, L. *Autistic children: A guide for parents*. New York: Brunner/Mazel, 1972. [462]

WINOKUR, G., CLAYTON, P., & REICH, T. *Manic-depressive illness*. St. Louis: C. V. Mosby, 1969. [129]

WIRT, R. D., & BROEN, W. E. The relation of the Children's Manifest Anxiety Scale to the concept of anxiety as used in the clinic. *Journal of Consulting Psychology*, 1956, **20**, 482. [590]

WISE, N. B. Juvenile delinquency among middle-class girls. In E. W. Vaz (Ed.), *Middle-class juvenile delinquency*. New York: Harper, 1967. Pp. 179–188. [500, 519]

WISSLER, C. The correlation of mental and physical tests. *Psychological Monographs*, 1901, **3**, No. 6. [195]

WITMER, H. L., & KELLER, J. Outgrowing childhood problems: A study in the value of child guidance treatment. *Smith College Studies in Social Work*, 1942, **13**, 74–90. [639]

WOLF, M. G. Effects of emotional disturbance in childhood on intelligence. *American Journal of Orthopsychiatry*, 1965, **35**, 906–908. [223]

WOLF, M. M., GILES, D. K., & HALL, R. V. Experiments with token reinforcement in a remedial classroom. *Behavior Research and Therapy*, 1968, **6**, 51–64. [387, 399]

WOLF, M. M., RISLEY, T. R., & MEES, H. L. Application of operant conditioning procedures to the behavior problems of an autistic child. *Behavior Research and Therapy,* 1964, **1**, 305–312. [456]

WOLF, S., & WOLFF, H. G. *Human gastric function.* New York: Oxford University Press, 1947. [181]

WOLFENSTEIN, M. Trends in infant care. *American Journal of Orthopsychiatry,* 1953, **23**, 120–130. [37]

WOLFF, P. The developmental psychologies of Jean Piaget and psychoanalysis. *Psychological Issues,* 1960, **2** (Monogr. 5). [49]

WOLMAN, B. B. *Children without childhood.* New York: Grune & Stratton, 1970. [413]

WOLOWITZ, H. Food preferences as an index of orality. *Journal of Abnormal and Social Psychology,* 1964, **69**, 650–654. [320]

WOLPE, J. *Psychotherapy by reciprocal inhibition.* Stanford, Calif.: Stanford University Press, 1958. [343, 345, 373, 378–379, 381]

WOLPE, J. Behavior therapy in complex neurotic states. *British Journal of Psychiatry,* 1964, **110**, 28–34. [379]

WOLPE, J. *The practice of behavior therapy.* New York: Pergamon Press, 1969. [332, 348–349, 373]

WOLPE, J., & RACHMAN, S. Psychoanalytic "evidence": A critique based on Freud's case of little Hans. *Journal of Nervous and Mental Disease,* 1960, **131**, 135–148. [287, 315, 610]

WOODS, W. A., & COOK, W. E. Proficiency in drawing and placement of hands in drawings of the human figure. *Journal of Consulting Psychology,* 1954, **18**, 119–121. [587]

WRIGHT, B. P. Selfishness, guilt feelings, and social distance. Iowa City: Master's Thesis, State University of Iowa, 1940. Cited by R. R. Sears, Experimental analysis of psychoanalytic phenomena. In J. McV. Hunt (Ed.), *Personality and the behavior disorders.* New York: Ronald, 1944. Pp. 306–332. [321]

WYATT, R. J., MURPHY, D. L., BELMAKER, R., COHEN, S., DONNELLY, C. H., & POLLIN, W. Reduced monoamine oxidase activity in platelets: A possible genetic marker for vulnerability to schizophrenia. *Science,* 1973, **179**, 916–918. [432]

YABLONSKY, L. *The tunnel back: Synanon.* New York: Macmillan, 1965. [533, 541]

YABLONSKY, L., & DEDERICH, C. E. Synanon: An analysis of some dimensions of the social structure of an antiaddiction society. In D. M. Wilner & G. G. Kassebaum (Eds.), *Narcotics.* New York: McGraw-Hill, 1965. Pp. 193–216. [534–535]

YAKOLEV, P. I., & LECOURS, A. R. The myelogenetic cycles of regional maturation of the brain. In A. Minkowski (Ed.), *Regional development of the brain in early life.* Philadelphia: F. A. Davis, 1967. Pp. 3–70. [152]

YAMAZAKI, J. N., WRIGHT, S. W., & WRIGHT, P. M. Outcome of pregnancies in women exposed to the atomic bomb in Nagasaki. *American Journal of the Diseases of Children,* 1954, **87**, 448. [146]

YARROW, M. R., CAMPBELL, J. D., & BURTON, R. V. Recollections of childhood: A study of the retrospective method. *Monographs of the Society for Research in Child Development,* 1970, **35** (Serial No. 138). [83]

YASKIN, J. C. The psychoneuroses and neuroses. A review of a hundred cases with special reference to treatment and results. *American Journal of Psychiatry,* 1936, **93**, 107–125. [328]

YATES, A. J. A comment on Bookbinder's critique of "symptoms and symptom substitution." *Psychological Reports,* 1962, **11**, 102. [399]

YATES, A. J. Symptoms and symptom substitution. *Psychological Review,* 1958, **65**, 371–374. [399]

YOAKUM, C. S., & YERKES, R. M. *Army mental tests.* New York: Holt, 1920. [202]

YOLLES, S. F., & KRAMER, M. Vital statistics. In L. Bellak & L. Loeb (Eds.), *The schizophrenic syndrome.* New York: Grune & Stratton, 1969. Pp. 66–113. [412]

YOUNG, G. C. Conditioning treatment of enuresis. *Developmental Medicine and Child Neurology,* 1965, **7**, 557–562. [400]

YOUNG, G. C., & MORGAN, R. T. T. Overlearning in the conditioning treatment of enuresis. *Behavior Research and Therapy,* 1972, **10**, 147–151. [383]

YOUNG, L. *Wednesday's children: A study of child neglect and abuse.* New York: McGraw-Hill, 1964. [627, 633]

YOUNG, W. C., GOY, R. W., & PHOENIX, C. H. Hormones and sexual behavior. *Science,* 1964, **143**, 212–218. [141, 650]

ZAMENHOF, S., vanMARTHENS, E., & GRAUEL, L. DNA (cell number) in neonatal brain: Second generation (F_2) alteration by maternal (F_0) dietary protein restriction. *Science,* 1971, **172**, 850–851. [142]

ZANGWILL, O. L. *Cerebral dominance and its relation to psychological function.* Springfield, Ill.: Thomas, 1960. [154]

ZARAFONETIS, C. J. D. *Drug abuse: Proceedings of the International Conference.* Philadelphia: Lea & Febiger, 1972. [541]

ZEAMAN, D. T., & HOUSE, B. J. Mongoloid MA is proportional to log CA. *Child Development,* 1962, **33**, 481–488. [215]

ZEISSET, R. M. Desensitization and relaxation in the modification of psychiatric patients' interview behavior. *Journal of Abnormal Psychology,* 1968, **73**, 18–24. [391–392]

ZETZEL, E. R. Discussion of Eysenck's "The effects of psychotherapy." *International Journal of Psychiatry,* 1965, **1**, 144–150. [329]

ZIGLER, E. Familial mental retardation: A continuing dilemma. *Science,* 1967, **155**, 292–298. [218, 228, 258]

ZIGLER, E. Developmental versus difference theories of mental retardation and the problem of motivation. *American Journal of Mental Deficiency,* 1969, **73**, 536–556. [258]

ZIGLER, E. The retarded child as a whole person. In H. E. Adams & W. K. Boardman (Eds.), *Advances in experimental clinical psychology.* New York: Pergamon Press, 1971. Pp. 47–121. [246, 249, 258]

ZIGLER, E., & PHILLIPS, L. Psychiatric diagnosis: A critique. *Journal of Abnormal and Social Psychology,* 1961, **63**, 607–618. [565]

ZUBIN, J., ERON, L., & SCHUMER, F. *An experimental approach to projective techniques.* New York: Wiley, 1965. [580–582, 585–586, 605]

ZUCKERMAN, M., OLTEAN, M., & MONASHKIN, I. The parental attitudes of mothers of schizophrenics. *Journal of Consulting Psychology,* 1958, **22**, 307–310. [414]

ZUK, G. *Family therapy.* New York: Behavioral Science Publications, 1971. [649]

Index

Page numbers for citations of historically important persons are included in this index. Page numbers for citations of specific published works are given with each work in the References, pp. 651–716.